Interaction:

Readings in Human Psychology

Edited and with an introduction by

Kenneth O. Doyle, Jr.

UNIVERSITY OF MINNESOTA

Interaction:

READINGS IN HUMAN PSYCHOLOGY

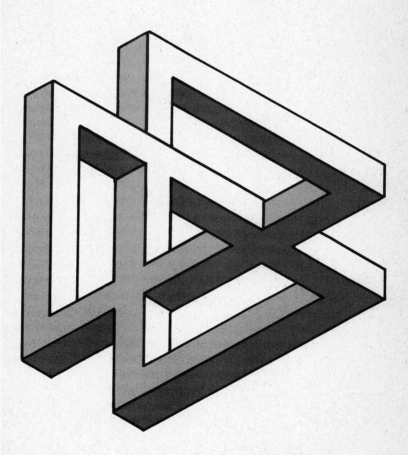

D. C. HEATH AND COMPANY
Lexington, Massachusetts   Toronto   London

The "impossible triangle," symbol of the interaction of physiological, psychological, and sociocultural forces, is reproduced by permission of Cambridge University Press from Penrose and Penrose, "Impossible Objects: A Special Type of Visual Illusion," *British Journal of Psychology*, vol. 49, pp. 31–33.

*To those men and women
whose work has contributed to
this book*

Contents

PERSPECTIVE   xi

part **1**

GROWTH AND DEVELOPMENT   1

    The Changing American Child—A Speculative Analysis   3
        URIE BRONFENBRENNER

    Psychosexual Development   15
        WILLIAM SIMON AND JOHN GAGNON

    The Case History of a Construct: Ego Identity Status   28
        JAMES E. MARCIA

    Environmental Determinants of Human Life   39
        RENÉ DUBOS

    Dreams and Human Potential   52
        STANLEY KRIPPNER AND WILLIAM HUGHES

part **2**

MOTIVATION   71

    From *Physical Control of the Mind*   73
        JOSÉ M. R. DELGADO

    Bystander Intervention in Emergencies: Diffusion of Responsibility   90
        JOHN M. DARLEY AND BIBB LATANÉ

    The Experience of Living in Cities   101
        STANLEY MILGRAM

Humanistic Theory: The Third Revolution in Psychology   120
FLOYD W. MATSON

Physiological and Cultural Determinants of Behavior   130
NEAL E. MILLER

part 3

SENSATION AND PERCEPTION   147

A Russian Report on the Postoperative Newly Seeing   149
IVAN D. LONDON

The Physical Environment: A Problem for a Psychology of
Stimulation   154
JOACHIM F. WOHLWILL

Cognitive Effects on Bodily Functioning   164
STANLEY SCHACHTER

Influence of a Female Model on Perceived Characteristics
of an Automobile   172
GEORGE H. SMITH AND RAYME ENGEL

Subliminal Stimulation: An Overview   176
JAMES V. MCCONNELL, RICHARD L. CUTLER, ELTON B. MCNEIL

part 4

LEARNING AND THINKING   199

Educational Applications of Mnemonic Devices   201
GORDON H. BOWER

Memory Transfer Through Cannibalism in Planarians   211
JAMES V. MCCONNELL

Reaction Patterns to Severe, Chronic Stress in American Army
Prisoners of War of the Chinese   221
EDGAR H. SCHEIN

Teaching Machines: An Application of Principles from the
Laboratory   231
JAMES G. HOLLAND

Learning and Thinking   246
JEROME S. BRUNER

part **5**

INTELLIGENCE AND ABILITIES 255

Measuring Differences Between People 257
MARVIN D. DUNNETTE

Woman's Intellect 280
ELEANOR E. MACCOBY

Environmental Components of Measured Intelligence 293
JANE W. KESSLER

Unknowns in the IQ Equation 308
SANDRA SCARR-SALAPATEK

The Nature and Nurture of Creative Talent 324
DONALD W. MACKINNON

part **6**

PERSONALITY AND ADJUSTMENT 343

Toward a Concept of the Normal Personality 345
EDWARD JOSEPH SHOBEN, JR.

The Sources of Student Dissent 357
KENNETH KENISTON

Interpersonal Relationships—Crux of the Sexual Renaissance 385
LESTER A. KIRKENDALL AND ROGER W. LIBBY

Is Love an Art? 399
ERICH FROMM

On Hanging Loose and Loving: The Dilemma of Present Youth 403
HENRY MILLER

part **7**

PSYCHOTHERAPY AND INTERVENTION 415

The Nature of the Process: General Factors 417
WILLIAM SCHOFIELD

Perspectives on Drug Use   426
HELEN H. NOWLIS

Behavioral Approaches to Family and Couple Therapy   440
ROBERT LIBERMAN

Understanding Laboratory Education: An Overview   456
CLAYTON P. ALDERFER

Yoga and Psychoanalysis   472
J. S. NEKI

part **8**

SOCIAL ISSUES   481

The Prejudiced Society   483
EARL RAAB AND SEYMOUR MARTIN LIPSET

Poverty, Social Disintegration and Personality   501
MORTON BEISER

Violence and Human Behavior   523
MARVIN E. WOLFGANG

Behavior Instrumentation and Social Technology   544
ROBERT L. SCHWITZGEBEL

The Future of Drugs and Drugs of the Future   557
NATHAN S. KLINE

Interpersonal Relationships: USA 2000   571
CARL R. ROGERS

INDEX   583

Perspective

I

Psychology can be deadly. It can be disjointed, hypertechnical, irrelevant, and dull. At the other extreme, it can be sensational. Like a Sunday supplement, it can tease us and leave us with nothing.

What psychology ought to be is something in between. First, it should be sound pedagogy. What we ask students to learn and teachers to teach ought to be educationally valuable and worth the time and effort to pursue it. There is no need to sacrifice scholarship for popularity, to trade rigor for large audiences. At the same time, what we learn and what we teach ought to be interesting, especially in the beginning courses. There is no requirement that rigor and scholarship be dry and dusty.

The trick is to find this middle ground where pedagogy is not dull, where interest is not vain. One possibility might be general human psychology. This is certainly an area of natural human interest—there is nothing more fascinating to you and me than me and you. And even more important, general human psychology furnishes a literature that can illustrate sound psychological principles, precise methodology, and fine exposition. We have chosen general human psychology as the scope of this collection.

II

How can we choose articles for a collection of readings in general human psychology? We can search the literature for those that meet selected criteria. As we have already stressed, each selection must be substantive, competently describing or illustrating at least one important principle, point, or concept. Each must also be stimulating, both in the sense of general appeal and in the sense of being just different enough, just difficult enough, to pique the reader's interest. At the same time, each article must be readable and intelligible and sufficiently pertinent and current to describe psychology today and its growing responsiveness to present-day questions. Finally, the collection as a whole must be broad and balanced enough to impart the flavor of the field and to show the styles and predilections of its many adherents.

III

Although this collection could be organized under any of several plans, we have selected two as exceptionally meaningful. The first entails sectioning psychology into the eight or so subdivisions that make up the traditional introductory course: Growth and Development, Motivation, Sensation and Perception, Learning and Thinking, Intelligence and Abilities, Personality and Adjustment, Psychotherapy and Intervention, and Social Issues. These represent the fields with which most psychologists identify.

The second arrangement is perhaps more exciting, and is certainly less traditional. Within each of those eight fields, we have juxtaposed articles germane to the three main arenas of human behavior: the personal, the physical, and the social. To give an example, for human motivation not only have we gathered together selections that describe or illustrate why people do what they do, but we have chosen articles that emphasize the influence of physiological conditions, personal characteristics, and social factors on how people behave. This twofold framework—arenas of behavior within traditional topics—preserves the expository ease and clarity of the routine topical approach and yet adds a new dimension, the interaction of personal, physiological, and social psychology.

IV

Within this organization, what route will the book travel? For a basic introduction to the individual, it will begin with human growth and development.

GROWTH AND DEVELOPMENT.   The thrust of the initial articles is that people, constantly influenced by physical, personal, and social factors, are continually growing, developing, and evolving through a series of identities, and that throughout this process there exists a certain oneness, a certain stability of personality.

MOTIVATION.   But we wonder why people behave and grow as they do. The second part, then, concentrates on human motivation. Personal, physical, and social variables are especially evident here; behavior is motivated by the constitution of the physical organism, by the tendency toward fulfilment of the personal being, and by the effects of social and cultural milieus. In a sense, both development and motivation can be considered general psychologies, since each permeates all behavior. But behavior can be examined specifically too, as the next few sections will show.

SENSATION AND PERCEPTION.   Behavior begins with something sensed, so we consider aspects of the reception and the processing of sensory information. The main point of these articles is that the interpretation or "perception" of information is not so mechanical and objective as we might like to believe; rather it is substantially influenced by physical, personal, and social factors.

LEARNING AND THINKING.   Once the person has sensed something, once he is "in touch" with the environment, he can begin to act. Actions that the person initiates to deal with his environment are called "adaptive behaviors," and two of the most intriguing of these are learning and thinking. Learning in psychology, however, is not always the same as learning in the classroom. The psychological study of learning dissects behavior into its components to see how the isolated behaviors occur and develop and to deduce principles of simple behavior that might apply to more complex endeavors. But psychology's simple learning can overlap education's more complex learning, and that overlap—particularly where personal, physical, and social factors meet— is the subject of this section.

INTELLIGENCE AND ABILITIES.   Out of sensory experience and cognitive activity develop additional adaptive powers, intelligence and abilities. There have traditionally been two foci in the investigation of these qualities: first, the study of their nature, number, and variety; and, second, the study of the differences among people that these qualities portray. The articles under this heading trace the history of attempts to define and measure intelligence and the "specific" abilities; also they show how the psychological testing movement grew out of these pursuits, and they examine the source and meaning of the concept of Individual Differences in intelligence, creativity, and other human traits.

PERSONALITY AND ADJUSTMENT.   Once we have partitioned the person in order to examine certain behaviors in detail, we must put him or her back together to see the total personality. Every article thus far has dealt with some aspect of human personality; now we shall have an opportunity to look at the whole picture. In contrast to psychology's usual emphasis on pathology, these articles underscore the positive, healthful aspects of personal adjustment. Some of the most common forums of adjustment are considered: acceptance and alienation, sex and love, freedom and commitment. Again we note the influence of body, mind, and society.

PSYCHOTHERAPY AND INTERVENTION.   What can psychology do to help when adjustment falters? This section offers examples of the principal forms of help that psychology can provide—individual psychotherapy, drug therapy, behavior therapy, and group therapy. At the same time, it notes that maladjustment, in both its origin and amelioration, can be approached from the perspectives of physiology, psychology, and sociology.

SOCIAL ISSUES. Finally, just as general human psychology can provide the knowledge that therapists use to help individual patients, it can also offer some insights that society might use to deal with its problems. The last few readings explore some of our most urgent social problems from a psychological point of view. These problems and their proposed solutions involve the body, the mind, society, and—most important of all—the interplay of all three.

V

One task remains. The entire purpose of this introduction is to provide some perspective for this collection, to say why it came to be, how it was developed and arranged, and where it will proceed. To study human behavior, we must take it apart, concentrate on its components, and *analyze* it; otherwise it would be too vast, too complex for us to manage. But dissection is only a convenient fiction; we know that the person is a whole and that when we analyze we run the risk of destroying what we are trying to understand. So let us *synthesize*. As we look at human growth, motivation, learning, and all other topics, we should remember that they are all at work in every single person. When we explore the personal, physical, and social aspects of human behavior, we should examine how they all contribute to the total picture. It is in that totality that real understanding lies—in the *Interaction*.

PART **1**

Growth and Development

All of psychology could be included under the rubric Growth and Development, *since all behavior is subject to continuous growth and development. But a broader view would suggest that developmental psychology is one of the many vantage points from which to observe the human panorama. Because of the logical and chronological primacy of developmental psychology as well as because of its generality, we begin this collection with some contributions to the study of human growth.*

Underlying developmental psychology are two apparent paradoxes, each reflecting an ancient philosophical conflict. The first is that we experience personal stability in the midst of enduring change. Conception, birth, infancy, childhood, adolescence, adulthood, old age, and death—each of these is a phase, or stage, in human development, each more complex, each unfolding from the one before. The normal person has no difficulty recognizing this continuity; from past to present to future, I recognize that I am still I. But even the very healthy person does not always realize the interplay of these stages, the extent to which past influences present and future, what the present tells of the past. To know me, really, is to know who I was and who I will be; to know how I think, feel, and behave now, is to understand how I thought, felt, and behaved in the past, and will behave in the future.

The other paradox of developmental psychology is that we experience a peculiar oneness in diversity. Personal, physical, social—each of us recognizes these three diverse areas of life; but not everyone realizes the interplay, the extent to which each influences the other.

The Changing American Child— A Speculative Analysis

URIE BRONFENBRENNER

Neither of the paradoxes of developmental psychology is lost on the author of the first selection. Urie Bronfenbrenner is a psychologist with special interests in human development, socialization, and interpersonal perception. In "The Changing American Child" he presents his synthesis of these areas. This article is of special interest not only for its discussion of the relationship between child-rearing practices and the evolution of civilization, but also for its particular emphasis on the effects that the values of one generation can have on the values and, indeed, on the whole personality of the next. When you study this selection, pay special attention to the way parents' changing attitudes and behaviors—with respect to affection and discipline, for example—seem to have influenced their childrens' personalities. Could these data describe a dilemma in which values that we cherish in parents, like equality and free expression of affection, lead to values that may be maladaptive in their children, like overdependence and irresponsibility? Watch for Bronfenbrenner's interpretation.

A Question of Moment

It is now a matter of scientific record that patterns of child rearing in the United States have changed appreciably over the past twenty-five years [Bronfenbrenner, 1958]. Middle class parents especially have moved away from the more rigid and strict styles of care and discipline advocated in the early Twenties and Thirties toward modes of response involving greater

SOURCE: From *Journal of Social Issues* 17, no. 1:6–17. Copyright © 1961 by the Society for the Psychological Study of Social Issues, a division of the American Psychological Association. Reprinted by permission.

Note: This paper draws heavily on results from a program of research being conducted by the author in collaboration with Edward C. Devereux and George J. Suci. The contribution of these colleagues to facts and ideas presented in this paper is gratefully acknowledged. The research program is supported in part with grants from the National Science Foundation and the National Institutes of Health.

tolerance of the child's impulses and desires, freer expression of affection, and increased reliance on "psychological" methods of discipline, such as reasoning and appeals to guilt, as distinguished from more direct techniques like physical punishment. At the same time, the gap between the social classes in their goals and methods of child rearing appears to be narrowing, with working class parents beginning to adopt both the values and techniques of the middle class. Finally, there is dramatic correspondence between these observed shifts in parental values and behavior and the changing character of the attitudes and practices advocated in successive editions of such widely read manuals as the Children's Bureau bulletin on *Infant Care* and Spock's *Baby and Child Care*. Such correspondence should not be taken to mean that the expert has now become the principal instigator and instrument of social change, since the ideas of scientists and professional workers themselves reflect in part the operation of deep-rooted cultural processes. Nevertheless, the fact remains that changes in values and practices advocated by prestigeful professional figures can be substantially accelerated by rapid and widespread dissemination through the press, mass media of communication, and public discussion.

Given these facts, it becomes especially important to gauge the effect of the changes that are advocated and adopted. Nowhere is this issue more significant, both scientifically and socially, than in the sphere of familial values and behavior. It is certainly no trivial matter to ask whether the changes that have occurred in the attitudes and actions of parents over the past twenty-five years have been such as to affect the personality development of their children, so that the boys and girls of today are somewhat different in character structure from those of a decade or more ago. Or, to put the question more succinctly: has the changing American parent produced a changing American child?

A Strategy of Inference

Do we have any basis for answering this intriguing question? To begin with, do we have any evidence of changes in the behavior of children in successive decades analogous to those we have already been able to find for parents? If so, we could take an important first step toward a solution of the problem. Unfortunately, in contrast to his gratifying experience in seeking and finding appropriate data on parents, the present writer has, to date, been unable to locate enough instances in which comparable methods of behavioral assessment have been employed with different groups of children of similar ages over an extended period of time. Although the absence of such material precludes any direct and unequivocal approach to the question at hand, it is nevertheless possible, through a series of inferences from facts already known, to arrive at some estimate of what the answer might be. Specifically, although as yet we have no comparable data on the relation between parental and child behavior for different families at successive points in time, we do have facts on the influence of parental treatment on child behavior at a given point in time; that is, we know that certain variations in parental behavior tend to be accompanied by systematic differences in the personality characteristics of children. If we are willing to assume that these same relationships obtained not only at a given moment but across different points in time, we are in a position to infer the possible effects on children of changing patterns of child rearing over the years. It is this strategy that we propose to follow.

The Changing American Parent

We have already noted the major changes in parental behavior discerned in a recent analysis of data reported over a twenty-five year period. These secular trends may be summarized as follows:

1. Greater permissiveness toward the child's spontaneous desires
2. Freer expression of affection
3. Increased reliance on indirect "psychological" techniques of discipline (such as reasoning or appeals to guilt) vs. direct methods (like physical punishment, scolding, or threats)
4. In consequence of the above shifts in the direction of what are predominantly middle class values and techniques, a narrowing of the gap between social classes in their patterns of child rearing.

Since the above analysis was published, a new study has documented an additional trend. Bronson, Katten, and Livson [1959] have compared patterns of paternal and maternal authority and affection in two generations of families from the California Guidance Study. Unfortunately, the time span surveyed overlaps only partially with the twenty-five year period covered in our own analysis, the first California generation having been raised in the early 1900's and the second in the late '20's and early '30's. Accordingly, if we are to consider the California results along with the others cited above, we must make the somewhat risky assumption that a trend discerned in the first three decades of the century has continued in the same direction through the early 1950's. With this important qualification, an examination of the data cited by Bronson et al. [1959] points to still another, secular trend—a shift over the years in the pattern of parental role differentiation within the family. Specifically:

5. In succeeding generations the relative position of the father vis-à-vis the mother is shifting with the former becoming increasingly more affectionate and less authoritarian, and the latter becoming relatively more important as the agent of discipline, especially for boys.

"Psychological" Techniques of Discipline and Their Effects

In pursuing our analytic strategy, we next seek evidence of the effects on the behavior of children of variations in parental treatment of the type noted in our inventory. We may begin by noting that the variables involved in the first three secular trends constitute a complex that has received considerable attention in recent research in parent-child relationships. Within the last three years, two sets of investigators, working independently, have called attention to the greater efficacy of "love-oriented" or "psychological" techniques in bringing about desired behavior in the child [Sears, Maccoby, and Levin, 1957; Miller and Swanson, 1958; 1960]. The present writer, noting that such methods are especially favored by middle class parents, offered the following analysis of the nature of these techniques and the reasons for their effectiveness.

Such parents are, in the first place, more likely to overlook offenses, and when they do punish, they are less likely to ridicule or inflict physical pain. Instead, they reason with the youngster, isolate him, appeal to guilt, show disappointment—in short, convey in a variety of ways, on the one hand, the kind of behavior that is expected of the child; on the other, the realization that transgression means the interruption of a mutually valued relationship. . . .

These findings [of greater efficacy] mean that middle class parents, though in one sense more lenient in their discipline techniques, are using methods that are actually more compelling. Moreover, the compelling power of these practices is probably enhanced by the more permissive treatment accorded to middle class children in the early years of life. The successful use of withdrawal of love as a discipline technique implies the prior existence of a gratifying relationship; the more love present in the first instance, the greater the threat implied in its withdrawal [Bronfenbrenner, 1958].

It is now a well established fact that children from middle class families tend to excel those from lower class in many characteristics ordinarily regarded as desirable, such as self-control, achievement, responsibility, leadership, popularity, and adjustment in general.[1] If, as seems plausible, such differences in behavior are attributable at least in part to class-linked variations in parental treatment, the strategy of inference we have adopted would appear on first blush to lead to a rather optimistic conclusion. Since, over the years, increasing numbers of parents have been adopting the more effective socialization techniques typically employed by the middle class, does it not follow that successive generations of children should show gains in the development of effective behavior and desirable personality characteristics?

Unfortunately, this welcome conclusion, however logical, is premature, for it fails to take into account all of the available facts.

Sex, Socialization, and Social Class

To begin with, the parental behaviors we have been discussing are differentially distributed not only by socio-economic status but also by sex. As we

---

[1] For a summary of findings on social class differences in children's behavior and personality characteristics, see Mussen, P. H., and Conger, J. J., *Child Development and Personality*. New York: Harper, 1956.

have pointed out elsewhere [Bronfenbrenner, 1961], girls are exposed to more affection and less punishment than boys, but at the same time are more likely to be subjected to "love-oriented" discipline of the type which encourages the development of internalized controls. And, consistent with our line of reasoning, girls are found repeatedly to be "more obedient, cooperative, and in general better socialized than boys at comparable age levels." But this is not the whole story.

. . . At the same time, the research results indicate that girls tend to be more anxious, timid, dependent, and sensitive to rejection. If these differences are a function of differential treatment by parents, then it would seem that the more "efficient" methods of child rearing employed with girls involve some risk of what might be called "oversocialization" [Bronfenbrenner, 1961].

One could argue, of course, that the contrasting behaviors of boys and girls have less to do with differential parental treatment than with genetically-based maturational influences. Nevertheless, two independent lines of evidence suggest that socialization techniques do contribute to individual differences, *within the same sex*, precisely in the types of personality characteristics noted above. In the first place, variations in child behavior and parental treatment strikingly similar to those we have cited for the two sexes are reported in a recent comprehensive study of differences between first and later born children [Schachter, 1959]. Like girls, first children receive more attention, are more likely to be exposed to "psychological" discipline, and end up more anxious and dependent, whereas later children, like boys, are more aggressive and self-confident.

A second line of evidence comes from our own current research. We have been concerned with the role of parents in the development of such "constructive" personality characteristics as responsibility and leadership among adolescent boys and girls. Our findings reveal not only the usual differences in adolescents' and parents' behaviors associated with the sex of the child, but also a striking contrast in the relationship between parental and child behaviors for the two sexes. To start on firm and familiar ground, girls are rated by their teachers as more responsible than boys, whereas the latter obtain higher scores on leadership. Expected differences similarly appear in the realm of parental behavior: girls receive more affection, praise, and companionship; boys are subjected to more physical punishment and achievement demands. Quite unanticipated, however, at least by us, was the finding that both parental affection and discipline appeared to facilitate effective psychological functioning in boys, but to impede the development of such constructive behavior in girls. Closer examination of our data indicated that both extremes of either affection or discipline were deleterious for all children, but that the process of socialization entailed somewhat different risks for the two sexes. Girls were especially susceptible to the detrimental influence of overprotection; boys to the ill effects of insufficient parental discipline and support. Or, to put it in more colloquial terms: boys suffered more often from too little taming, girls from too much.

In an attempt to account for this contrasting pattern of relationships, we proposed the notion of differential optimal levels of affection and authority for the two sexes.

The qualities of independence, initiative, and self-sufficiency, which are especially valued for boys in our culture, apparently require for their development a somewhat different balance of authority and affection than is found in the "love-oriented" strategy characteristically applied with girls. While an affectional context is important for the socialization of boys, it must evidently be accompanied by and be compatible with a strong component of parental discipline. Otherwise, the boy finds himself in the same situation as the girl, who, having received greater affection, is more sensitive to its withdrawal, with the result that a little discipline goes a long way and strong authority is constricting rather than constructive [Bronfenbrenner, 1961].

What is more, available data suggest that this very process may already be operating for boys from upper middle class homes. To begin with, differential treatment of the sexes is at a minimum for these families. Contrasting parental attitudes and behaviors toward boys and girls are pronounced only at lower class levels, and decrease as one moves up the socio-economic scale [Kohn, 1959; Bronfenbrenner, 1961]. Thus our own results show that it is primarily at lower middle class levels that boys get more punishment than girls, and the latter receive greater warmth and attention. With an increase in the family's social position, direct discipline drops off, especially for boys, and indulgence and protectiveness decrease for girls. As a result, patterns of parental treatment for the two sexes begin to converge. In like manner, we find that the differential effects of parental behavior on the two sexes are marked only in the lower middle class. It is here that girls especially risk being over-protected and boys not receiving sufficient discipline and support. In upper middle class the picture changes. Girls are not as readily debilitated by parental affection and power; nor is parental discipline as effective in fostering the development of responsibility and leadership in boys.

All these trends point to the conclusion that the "risks" experienced by each sex during the process of socialization tend to be somewhat different at different social class levels. Thus the danger of overprotection for girls is especially great in lower class families, but lower in upper middle class because of the decreased likelihood of overprotection. Analogously, boys are in greater danger of suffering from inadequate discipline and support in lower middle than in upper middle class. But the upper middle class boy, unlike the girl, exchanges one hazard for another. Since at this upper level the more potent "psychological" techniques of discipline are likely to be employed with both sexes, the boy presumably now too runs the risk of being "oversocialized," of losing some of his capacity for independent aggressive accomplishment.

Accordingly, if our line of reasoning is correct, we should expect a changing pattern of sex differences at successive socio-economic levels. Specifically, aspects of effective psychological functioning favoring girls should be most pronounced in the upper middle class; those favoring boys in the lower middle. A recent analysis of some of our data bears out this expectation. Girls excel boys on such variables as *responsibility* and *social acceptance* primarily at the higher socio-economic levels. In contrast, boys surpass girls on such traits as *leadership, level of aspiration,* and *competitiveness* almost exclusively in lower middle class. Indeed, with a rise in a family's social position, the differences tend to reverse themselves with girls now excelling boys.[2]

Trends in Personality Development: A First Approximation

The implications for our original line of inquiry are clear. We are suggesting that the "love-oriented" socialization techniques, which over the past twenty-five years have been employed in increasing degree by American middle class families, may have negative as well as constructive aspects. While fostering the internalization of adult standards and the development of socialized behavior, they may also have the effect of undermining capacities for initiative and independence, particularly in boys. Males exposed to this "modern" pattern of child rearing might be expected to differ from their counterparts of a quarter century ago in being somewhat more conforming and anxious, less enterprising and self-sufficient, and, in general, possessing more of the virtues and liabilities commonly associated with feminine character structure.[3]

At long last, then, our strategy of inference has led us to a first major conclusion. The term "major" is appropriate since the conclusion takes as its points of departure and return four of the secular trends which served as the impetus for our inquiry. Specifically, through a series of empirical links and theoretical extrapolations, we have arrived at an estimate of the effects on children of the tendency of successive generations of parents to become progressively more permissive, to express affection more freely, to utilize "psychological" techniques of discipline, and, by moving in these directions to narrow the gap between the social classes in their patterns of child rearing.

Family Structure and Personality Development

But one other secular trend remains to be considered: what of the changing pattern of parental role differentiation during the first three decades of the century? If our extrapolation is correct, the balance of power within the family has continued to shift with fathers yielding parental authority to mothers and taking on some of the nurturant and affectional functions tradi-

---

[2] These shifts in sex difference with a rise in class status are significant at the 5% level of confidence (one-tailed test).

[3] Strikingly similar conclusions were reached almost fifteen years ago in a provocative essay by Arnold Green ("The Middle Class Male Child and Neurosis," *American Sociological Review* 11 (1946):31–41). With little to go on beyond scattered clinical observations and impressions, Green was able to detect many of the same trends which we have begun to discern in more recent systematic empirical data.

tionally associated with the maternal role. Again we have no direct evidence of the effects of such secular changes on successive generations of children, and must look for leads to analogous data on contemporaneous relationships.

We may begin by considering the contribution of each parent to the socialization processes we have examined thus far. Our data indicate that it is primarily mothers who tend to employ "love-oriented" techniques of discipline and fathers who rely on more direct methods like physical punishment. The above statement must be qualified, however, by reference to the sex of the child, for it is only in relation to boys that fathers use direct punishment more than mothers. More generally, . . . the results reveal a tendency for each parent to be somewhat more active, firm, and demanding with a child of the same sex, more lenient and indulgent with a child of the opposite sex. . . . The reversal is most complete with respect to discipline, with fathers being stricter with boys, mothers with girls. In the spheres of affection and protectiveness, there is no actual shift in preference, but the tendency to be especially warm and solicitous with girls is much more pronounced among fathers than among mothers. In fact, generally speaking, it is the father who is more likely to treat children of the two sexes differently [Bronfenbrenner, 1961].

Consistent with this pattern of results, it is primarily the behavior of fathers that accounts for the differential effects of parental behavior on the two sexes and for the individual differences within each sex. In other words, it is paternal authority and affection that tend especially to be salutary for sons but detrimental for daughters. But as might be anticipated from what we already know, these trends are pronounced only in the lower middle class; with a rise in the family's social status, both parents tend to have similar effects on their children, both within and across sexes. Such a trend is entirely to be expected since parental role differentiation tends to decrease markedly as one ascends the socio-economic ladder. It is almost exclusively in lower middle class homes that fathers are more strict with boys and mothers with girls. To the extent that direct discipline is employed in upper middle class families, it tends to be exercised by both parents equally. Here again we see a parallelism between shifts in parental behavior across time and social class in the direction of forms (in this instance of family structure) favored by the upper middle class group.

What kinds of children, then, can we expect to develop in families in which the father plays a predominantly affectionate role, and a relatively low level of discipline is exercised equally by both parents? A tentative answer to this question is supplied by a preliminary analysis of our data in which the relation between parental role structure and adolescent behavior was examined with controls for the family's social class position. The results of this analysis are summarized as follows: . . . Both responsibility and leadership are fostered by the relatively greater salience of the parent of the same sex. . . . Boys tend to be more responsible when the father rather than the mother is the principal disciplinarian; girls are more dependable when the mother is the major authority figure. . . . In short, boys thrive in a patriarchal context, girls in a matriarchal. . . . The most dependent and least dependable adolescents describe family arrangements that are neither patriarchal nor matriarchal, but equalitarian. To state the issue in more provocative form, our data suggest that the democratic family, which for so many years has been held up and aspired to as a model by professionals and enlightened laymen, tends to produce young people who "do not take initiative," "look to others for direction and decision," and "cannot be counted on to fulfill obligations" [Bronfenbrenner, 1961].

In the wake of so sweeping a conclusion, it is important to call attention to the tentative, if not tenuous character of our findings. The results were based on a single study employing crude questionnaire methods and rating scales. Also, our interpretation is limited by the somewhat "attenuated" character of most of the families classified as patriarchal or matriarchal in our sample. Extreme concentrations of power in one or another parent were comparatively rare. Had they been more frequent, we suspect the data would have shown that such extreme asymmetrical patterns of authority were detrimental rather than salutary for effective psychological development, perhaps even more disorganizing than equalitarian forms.

Nevertheless, our findings do find some peripheral support in the work of others. A number of investigations, for example, point to the special importance of the father in the socialization of boys [Bandura and Walters, 1959; Mussen and Distler, 1959]. Further corroborative evidence appears in the growing series of studies of effects of paternal absence [Bach, 1946; Sears, Pintler and Sears, 1946; Lynn and Sawrey, 1959; Tiller, 1958]. The absence of the father apparently not only affects the behavior of the child directly but also influences the mother in the direction of greater over-protectiveness. The effect of both these tendencies is especially critical for male children; boys from father-absent homes tend to be markedly more submissive and dependent. Studies dealing explicitly with the influence of parental role structure in intact families are few and far between. Papanek [1957], in an unpublished doctoral dissertation, reports greater sex-role differentiation among children from homes in which the parental roles were differentiated. And in a carefully controlled study, Kohn and Clausen [1956] find that "schizophrenic patients more frequently than normal persons report that their mothers played a very strong authority role and the father a very weak authority role." Finally, what might best be called complementary evidence for our inferences regarding trends in family structure and their effects comes from the work of Miller, Swanson, and their associates [1958; 1960] on the differing patterns of behavior exhibited by families from *bureaucratic* and *entrepreneurial* work settings. These investigators argue that the entrepreneurial-bureaucratic dichotomy represents a new cleavage in American social structure that cuts across and overrides social class influences and carries with it its own characteristic patterns of family structure and socialization. Thus one investigation [Gold and Slater, 1958] contrasts the exercise of power in families of husbands employed in two kinds of job situations: (a) those working in large organizations with three or more levels of supervision; (b) those self-employed or working in small organizations with few levels of supervision. With appropriate controls for social class, equalitarian families were found more frequently in the bureaucratic groups; patriarchal and, to a lesser extent, matriarchal in the entrepreneurial setting. Another study [Miller and Swanson, 1958] shows that, in line with Miller and Swanson's hypotheses, parents from these same two groups tend to favor rather different ends and means of socialization, with entrepreneurial families putting considerably more emphasis on the development of independence and mastery and on the use of "psychological" techniques of discipline. These differences appear at both upper and lower middle class levels but are less pronounced in higher socio-economic strata. It is Miller and Swanson's belief, however, that the trend is toward the bureaucratic way of life, with its less structured patterns of family organization and child rearing. The evidence we have cited on secular changes in family structure and the inferences we have drawn regarding their possible effects on personality development are on the whole consistent with their views.

Looking Forward

If Miller and Swanson are correct in the prediction that America is moving toward a bureaucratic society that emphasizes, to put it colloquially, "getting along" rather than "getting ahead," then presumably we can look forward to ever increasing numbers of equalitarian families who, in turn, will produce successive generations of ever more adaptable but unaggressive "organization men." But recent signs do not all point in this direction. In our review of secular trends in child rearing practices we detected in the data from the more recent studies a slowing up in the headlong rush toward greater permissiveness and toward reliance on indirect methods of discipline. We pointed out also that if the most recent editions of well-thumbed guidebooks on child care are as reliable harbingers of the future as they have been in the past, we can anticipate something of a return to the more explicit discipline techniques of an earlier era. Perhaps the most important forces, however, acting to redirect both the aims and methods of child rearing in America emanate from behind the Iron Curtain. With the firing of the first Sputnik, Achievement began to replace Adjustment as the highest goal of the American way of life. We have become concerned—perhaps even obsessed—with "education for excellence" and the maximal utilization of our intellectual resources. Already, ability grouping, and the guidance counsellor who is its prophet, have moved down from the junior high to the elementary school, and parents can be counted on to do their part in preparing their youngsters for survival in the new competitive world of applications and achievement tests.

But if a new trend in parental behavior is to develop, it must do so in the context of changes already under way. And if the focus of parental authority is shifting from husband to wife, then perhaps we should anticipate that pressures for achievement will be imposed primarily by mothers rather than fathers. Moreover, the mother's continuing strong emotional investment in the child should provide her with a powerful lever for evoking desired performance. It is noteworthy in this connection that recent studies of the familial origins of need-achievement point to the matriarchy as the optimal context for development of the motive to excel [Strodtbeck, 1958; Rosen and D'Andrade, 1959].

The prospect of a society in which socialization techniques are directed toward maximizing achievement drive is not altogether a pleasant one. As a number of investigators have shown [Baldwin, Kalhorn and Breese, 1945; Baldwin, 1948; Haggard, 1957; Winterbottom, 1958; Rosen and D'Andrade, 1959], high achievement motivation appears to flourish in a family atmosphere of "cold democracy" in which initial high levels of maternal involvement are followed by pressures for independence and accomplishment.[4] Nor does the product of this process give ground for reassurance. True, children from achievement-oriented homes excel in planfulness and performance, but they are also more aggressive, tense, domineering, and cruel [Baldwin, Kalhorn and Breese, 1945; Baldwin, 1948; Haggard, 1957]. It would appear that education for excellence if pursued single-mindedly may entail some sobering social costs.

But by now we are in danger of having stretched our chain of inference beyond the strength of its weakest link. Our speculative analysis has become far more speculative than analytic and to pursue it further would bring us past the bounds of science into the realms of science fiction. In concluding our discussion, we would re-emphasize that speculations should, by their very nature, be held suspect. It is for good reason that, like "damn Yankees" they too carry their almost inseparable sobriquets: speculations are either "idle" or "wild." Given the scientific and social importance of the issues we have raised, we would dismiss the first of these labels out of hand, but the second cannot be disposed of so easily. Like the impetuous child, the "wild" speculation responds best to the sobering influence of friendly but firm discipline, in this instance from the hand of the behavioral scientist. As we look ahead to the next twenty-five years of human socialization, let us hope that the "optimal levels" of involvement and discipline can be achieved not only by the parent who is unavoidably engaged in the process, but also by the scientist who attempts to understand its working, and who—also unavoidably—contributes to shaping its course.

References

1. BACH, G. R. Father-fantasies and father-typing in father-separated children. *Child Development* 17 (1946):63–79.

[4] Cold democracy under female administration appears to foster the development of achievement not only in the home but in the classroom as well. In a review of research on teaching effectiveness, Ackerman reports that teachers most successful in bringing about gains in achievement score for their pupils were judged "least considerate," while those thought friendly and congenial were least effective. (Ackerman, W. I., "Teacher Competence and Pupil Change," *Harvard Educational Review* 24 (1954):273–89.)

2. BALDWIN, A. L., KALHORN, J., AND BREESE, F. H. The appraisal of parent behavior. *Psychological Monographs* 58, no. 3 (1945) (Whole No. 268).

3. BALDWIN, A. L. Socialization and the parent-child relationship. *Child Development* 19 (1948):127–36.

4. BANDURA, A., AND WALTERS, R. H. *Adolescent Aggression*. New York: Ronald Press, 1959.

5. BRONFENBRENNER, U. Socialization and social class through time and space. In E. Maccoby, T. M. Newcomb, and E. L. Hartley, *Readings in Social Psychology*. New York: Holt, 1958, pp. 400–25.

6. BRONFENBRENNER, U. Some familial antecedents of responsibility and leadership in adolescents. In L. Petrullo and B. M. Bass, *Leadership and Interpersonal Behavior*. New York: Holt, Rinehart and Winston, 1961.

7. BRONSON, W. C., KATTEN, E. S., AND LIVSON, N. Patterns of authority and affection in two generations. *Journal of Abnormal and Social Psychology* 58 (1959):143–52.

8. GOLD, M., AND SLATER, C. Office, factory, store—and family: A study of integration setting. *American Sociological Review* 23 (1958):64–74.

9. HAGGARD, E. A. Socialization, personality, and academic achievement in gifted children. *School Review* 65 (1957):388–414.

10. KOHN, M. L., AND CLAUSEN, J. A. Parental authority behavior and schizophrenia. *American Journal of Orthopsychiatry* 26 (1956):297–313.

11. KOHN, M. L. Social class and parental values. *American Journal of Sociology* 44 (1959):337–51.

12. LYNN, D. B., AND SAWREY, W. L. The effects of father-absence on Norwegian boys and girls. *Journal of Abnormal and Social Psychology* 59 (1959):258–62.

13. MILLER, D. R., AND SWANSON, G. E. *The Changing American Parent*. New York: John Wiley & Sons, 1958.

14. MILLER, D. R., AND SWANSON, G. E. *Inner Conflict and Defense*. New York: Holt, 1960.

15. MUSSEN, P., AND DISTLER, L. Masculinity, identification, and father-son relationships. *Journal of Abnormal and Social Psychology* 59 (1959):350–56.

16. PAPANEK, M. Authority and Interpersonal Relations in the Family. Unpublished doctoral dissertation on file at Radcliffe College Library, 1957.

17. ROSEN, B. L., AND D'ANDRADE, R. The psychosocial origins of achievement motivation. *Sociometry* 22 (1959):185–217.

18. SCHACHTER, S. *The Psychology of Affiliation*. Stanford, Cal.: Stanford University Press, 1959.

19. SEARS, R. R., PINTLER, M. H., AND SEARS, P. S. Effects of father-separation on pre-school children's doll play aggression. *Child Development* 17 (1946):219–43.

20. SEARS, R. R., MACCOBY, ELEANOR, AND LEVIN, M. *Patterns of Child Rearing*. Evanston, Ill.: Row Peterson, 1957.

21. STRODTBECK, F. L. Family interaction, values, and achievement. In D. C. McClelland, A. L. Baldwin, U. Bronfenbrenner, and F. L. Strodtbeck, *Talent and Society*. Princeton, N. J.: Van Nostrand, 1958, pp. 135–94.

22. TILLER, P. O. Father-absence and personality development of children in sailor families. *Nordisk Psykologis Monograph Series* 9 (1958).

23. WINTERBOTTOM, M. R. The relation of need achievement to learning experiences in independence and mastery. In J. W. Atkinson, *Motives in Fantasy, Action, and Society*. Princeton, N. J.: Van Nostrand, 1958, pp. 453–94.

Psychosexual Development

WILLIAM SIMON AND JOHN GAGNON

Like Bronfenbrenner, the authors of this article underscore society's role in personal growth, more specifically, personal sexual growth. The traditional view of sexual development—at least to those of Freudian persuasion—has been that the person is born with a sexuality that he or she continually struggles to keep under control. A more recent view is that the child must learn, from society, to be sexual. Simon and Gagnon's special contribution here is the suggestion that sexual orientation derives not so much from primitive biology, or the physical, as from the individual's response to the promptings and pressures of other people, the social. Note how even among young children society uses guilt to manipulate its members into reading and also following the approved sexual "script."

Erik Erikson has observed that, prior to Sigmund Freud, "sexologists" tended to believe that sexual capacities appeared suddenly with the onset of adolescence. Sexuality followed those external evidences of physiological change that occurred concurrent with or just after puberty. Psychoanalysis changed all that. In Freud's view, libido—the generation of psychosexual energies—should be viewed as a fundamental element of human experience at least beginning with birth, and possibly before that. Libido, therefore, is essential, a biological constant to be coped with at all levels of individual, social, and cultural development. The truth of this received wisdom, that is, that sexual development is a continuous contest between biological drive and cultural restraint should be seriously questioned. Obviously sexuality has roots in biological processes, but so do many other capacities including many that involve physical and mental competence and vigor. There is, however, abundant evidence that the final states which these capacities attain escape the rigid impress of biology. This independence of biological constraint is rarely claimed for the area of sexuality, but we would like to argue that the sexual

SOURCE: From William Simon and John H. Gagnon, "On Psychosexual Development," in David A. Goslin, ed., *Handbook of Socialization Theory and Research*. Copyright © 1969 by Rand McNally and Company, Chicago, pp. 733–51. Reprinted by permission.

is precisely that realm where the sociocultural forms most completely dominate biological influences.

It is difficult to get data that might shed much light on the earliest aspects of these questions: Adults are hardly equipped with total recall and the preverbal or primitively verbal child does not have ability to report accurately on his own internal state. But it seems obvious—and it is a basic assumption of this paper—that with the beginnings of adolescence many new factors come into play, and to emphasize a straight-line developmental continuity with infant and childhood experiences may be seriously misleading. In particular, it is dangerous to assume that because some childhood behavior appears sexual to adults, it must be sexual. An infant or a child engaged in genital play (even if orgasm is observed) can in no sense be seen as experiencing the complex set of feelings that accompanies adult or even adolescent masturbation.

Therefore, the authors reject the unproven assumption that "powerful" psychosexual drives are fixed biological attributes. More importantly, we reject the even more dubious assumption that sexual capacities or experiences tend to translate immediately into a kind of universal "knowing" or innate wisdom—that sexuality has a magical ability, possessed by no other capacity, that allows biological drives to be expressed directly in psychosocial and social behaviors.

The prevailing image of sexuality—particularly that of the Freudian tradition—is that of an intense, high-pressure drive that forces a person to seek physical sexual gratification, a drive that expresses itself indirectly if it cannot be expressed directly. The available data suggest to us a different picture—one that shows either lower levels of intensity, or, at least, greater variability. We find that there are many social situations or life-roles in which reduced sex activity or even deliberate celibacy is undertaken with little evidence that the libido has shifted in compensation to some other sphere.

A part of the legacy of Freud is that we have all become remarkably adept at discovering "sexual" elements in nonsexual behavior and symbolism. What we suggest instead (following Kenneth Burke's three-decade-old insight) is the reverse—that sexual behavior can often express and serve nonsexual motives.

No Play Without a Script

We see sexual behavior therefore as *scripted* behavior, not the masked expression of a primordial drive. The individual can learn sexual behavior as he or she learns other behavior—through scripts that in this case give the self, other persons, and situations erotic abilities or content. Desire, privacy, opportunity, and propinquity with an attractive member of the opposite sex are not, in themselves, enough; in ordinary circumstances, nothing sexual will occur unless one or both actors organize these elements into an appropriate script. The very concern with foreplay in sex suggests this. From one point of view, foreplay may be defined as merely progressive physical excitement generated by touching naturally erogenous zones. The authors have referred to this conception elsewhere as the "rubbing of two sticks together to make a fire" model. It would seem to be more valuable to see this activity as symbolically invested behavior through which the body is eroticized and through which mute, inarticulate motions and gestures are translated into a sociosexual drama.

A belief in the sociocultural dominance of sexual behavior finds support in cross-cultural research as well as in data restricted to the United States. Psychosexual development is universal—but it takes many forms and tempos. People in different cultures construct their scripts differently; and in our own society, different segments of the population act out different psychosexual dramas—something much less likely to occur if they were all reacting more or less blindly to the same superordinate urge. The most marked differences occur, of course, between male and female patterns of sexual behavior. Obviously, some of this is due to biological differences, including differences in hormonal functions at different ages. But the significance of social scripts predominate; the recent work of Masters and Johnson, for example, clearly points to far greater orgasmic capacities on the part of females than our culture would lead us to suspect. And within each sex—especially among men—different social and economic groups have different patterns.

Let us examine some of these variations, and see if we can decipher the scripts.

Childhood

Whether one agrees with Freud or not, it is obvious that we do not become sexual all at once. There is continuity with the past. Even infant experiences can strongly influence later sexual development.

But continuity is not causality. Childhood experiences (even those that appear sexual) will in all likelihood be influential not because they are intrinsically sexual, but because they can affect a number of developmental trends, *including* the sexual. What situations in infancy—or even early childhood—can be called psychosexual in any sense other than that of creating potentials?

The key term, therefore, must remain potentiation. In infancy, we can locate some of the experiences (or sensations) that will bring about a sense of the body and its capacities for pleasure and discomfort and those that will influence the child's ability to relate to others. It is possible, of course, that through these primitive experiences, ranges are being established—but they are very broad and overlapping. Moreover, if these are profound experiences to the child—and they may well be that—they are not expressions of biological necessity, but of the earliest forms of social learning.

In childhood, after infancy there is what appears to be some real sex play. About half of all adults report that they did engage in some form of sex play as children; and the total who actually did may be half again as many. But, however the adult interprets it later, what did it mean to the child at the time? One suspects that, as in much of childhood role-playing, their sense of the adult meanings attributed to the behavior is fragmentary and ill-formed. Many of the adults recall that, at the time, they were concerned with being found out. But here, too, were they concerned because of the real content of sex play, or because of the mystery and the lure of the forbidden that so often enchant the child? The child may be assimilating outside information about sex for which, at the time, he has no real internal correlate or understanding.

A small number of persons do have sociosexual activity during preadoles-cence—most of it initiated by adults. But for the majority of these, little apparently follows from it. Without appropriate sexual scripts, the experience remains unassimilated—at least in adult terms. For some, it is clear, a severe reaction may follow from falling "victim" to the sexuality of an adult—but, again, does this reaction come from the sexual act itself or from the social response, the strong reactions of others? (There is some evidence that early sexual activity of this sort is associated with deviant adjustments in later life. But this, too, may not be the result of sexual experiences in themselves so much as the consequence of having fallen out of the social main stream and, therefore, of running greater risks of isolation and alienation.)

In short, relatively few become truly active sexually before adolescence. And when they do (for girls more often than boys), it is seldom immediately related to sexual feelings or gratifications but is a use of sex for nonsexual goals and purposes. The "seductive" Lolita is rare; but she is significant: She illustrates a more general pattern of psychosexual development—a commit-ment to the social relationships linked to sex before one can really grasp the social meaning of the physical relationships.

Of great importance are the values (or feelings, or images) that children pick up as being related to sex. Although we talk a lot about sexuality, as though trying to exorcise the demon of shame, learning about sex in our society is in large part learning about guilt; and learning how to manage sexuality commonly involves learning how to manage guilt. An important source of guilt in children comes from the imputation to them by adults of sexual appetites or abilities that they may not have, but that they learn, how-ever imperfectly, to pretend they have. The gestural concomitants of sexual modesty are learned early. For instance, when do girls learn to sit or pick up objects with their knees together? When do they learn that the bust must be covered? However, since this behavior is learned unlinked to later adult sexual performances, what children must make of all this is very mysterious.

The learning of sex roles, or sex identities, involves many things that are remote from actual sexual experience, or that become involved with sexuality only after puberty. Masculinity or femininity, their meaning and postures, are rehearsed before adolescence in many nonsexual ways.

A number of scholars have pointed, for instance, to the importance of aggressive, deference, dependency, and dominance behavior in childhood.

Jerome Kagan and Howard Moss have found that aggressive behavior in males and dependency in females are relatively stable aspects of development. But what is social role, and what is biology? They found that when aggressive behavior occurred among girls, it tended to appear most often among those from well-educated families that were more tolerant of deviation. Curiously, they also reported that "it was impossible to predict the character of adult sexuality in women from their preadolescent and early adolescent behavior," and that "erotic activity is more anxiety-arousing for females than for males," because "the traditional ego ideal for women dictates inhibition of sexual impulses."

The belief in the importance of early sex-role learning for boys can be viewed in two ways. First, it may directly indicate an early sexual capacity in male children. Or second, early masculine identification may merely be an appropriate framework within which the sexual impulse (salient with puberty) and the socially available sexual scripts (or accepted patterns of sexual behavior) can most conveniently find expression. Our bias, of course, is toward the second.

But, as Kagan and Moss also noted, the sex role learned by the child does not reliably predict how he will act sexually as an adult. This finding also can be interpreted in the same two alternative ways. Where sexuality is viewed as a biological constant which struggles to express itself, the female sex role learning can be interpreted as the successful repression of sexual impulses. The other interpretation suggests that the difference lies not in learning how to handle a preexistent sexuality, but in learning how to *be* sexual. Differences between men and women, therefore, will have consequences both for *what* is done sexually, as well as *when*.

Once again we prefer the latter interpretation, and some recent work that we have done with lesbians supports it. We observed that many of the major elements of their sex lives—the start of actual genital sexual behavior, the onset and frequency of masturbation, the time of entry in sociosexual patterns, the number of partners, and the reports of feelings of sexual deprivation—were for these homosexual women almost identical with those of ordinary women. Since sexuality would seem to be more important for lesbians—after all, they sacrifice much in order to follow their own sexual pathways—this is surprising. We concluded that the primary factor was something both categories of women share—the sex-role learning that occurs before sexuality itself becomes significant.

Social class also appears significant, more for boys than girls. Sex-role learning may vary by class; lower-class boys are supposed to be more aggressive and put much greater emphasis on early heterosexuality. The middle and upper classes tend to tolerate more deviance from traditional attitudes regarding appropriate male sex-role performances.

Given all these circumstances, it seems rather naive to think of sexuality as a constant pressure, with a peculiar necessity all its own. For us, the crucial period of childhood has significance not because of sexual occurrences, but because of nonsexual developments that will provide the names and judgments for later encounters with sexuality.

Adolescence

The actual beginnings and endings of adolescence are vague. Generally, the beginning marks the first time society, as such, acknowledges that the individual has sexual capacity. Training in the postures and rhetoric of the sexual experience is now accelerated. Most important, the adolescent begins to regard those about him (particularly his peers, but also adults) as sexual actors and finds confirmation from others for this view.

For some, as noted, adolescent sexual experience begins before they are considered adolescents. Kinsey reports that a tenth of his female sample and a fifth of his male sample had experienced orgasm through masturbation by age 12. But still, for the vast majority, despite some casual play and exploration that post-Freudians might view as masked sexuality, sexual experience begins with adolescence. Even those who have had prior experience find that it acquires new meanings with adolescence. They now relate such meanings to both larger spheres of social life and greater senses of self. For example, it is not uncommon during the transition between childhood and adolescence for boys and, more rarely, girls to report arousal and orgasm while doing things not manifestly sexual—climbing trees, sliding down bannisters, or other activities that involve genital contact—without defining them as sexual. Often they do not even take it seriously enough to try to explore or repeat what was, in all likelihood, a pleasurable experience.

Adolescent sexual development, therefore, really represents the beginning of adult sexuality. It marks a definite break with what went on before. Not only will future experiences occur in new and more complex contexts, but they will be conceived of as explicitly sexual and thereby begin to complicate social relationships. The need to manage sexuality will rise not only from physical needs and desires, but also from the new implications of personal relationships. Playing, or associating, with members of the opposite sex now acquires different meanings.

At adolescence, changes in the developments of boys and girls diverge and must be considered separately. The one thing both share at this point is a reinforcement of their new status by a dramatic biological event—for girls, menstruation, and for boys, the discovery of the ability to ejaculate. But here they part. For boys, the beginning of a commitment to sexuality is primarily genital; within two years of puberty all but a relatively few have had the experience of orgasm, almost universally brought about by masturbation. The corresponding organizing event for girls is not genitally sexual but social: they have arrived at an age where they will learn role performances linked with proximity to marriage. In contrast to boys, only two-thirds of girls will report ever having masturbated (and, characteristically, the frequency is much less). For women, it is not until the late twenties that the incidence of orgasm from any source reaches that of boys at age 16. In fact, significantly, about half of the females who masturbate do so only after having experienced orgasm in some situation involving others. This contrast points to a basic distinction between the developmental processes for males and females: males move from privatized personal sexuality to sociosexuality; females do the reverse and at a later stage in the life cycle.

The Turned-On Boys

We have worked hard to demonstrate the dominance of social, psychological, and cultural influences over the biological; now, dealing with adolescent boys, we must briefly reverse course. There is much evidence that the early male sexual impulses—again, initially through masturbation—are linked to physiological changes, to high hormonal inputs during puberty. This produces an organism that, to put it simply, is more easily turned on. Male adolescents report frequent erections, often without apparent stimulation of any kind. Even so, though there is greater biological sensitization and hence masturbation is more likely, the meaning, organization, and continuance of this activity still tends to be subordinate to social and psychological factors.

Masturbation provokes guilt and anxiety among most adolescent boys. This is not likely to change in spite of more "enlightened" rhetoric and discourse on the subject (generally, we have shifted from stark warnings of mental, moral, and physical damage to vague counsels against nonsocial or "inappropriate" behavior). However, it may be that this very guilt and anxiety gives the sexual experience an intensity of feeling that is often attributed to sex itself.

Such guilt and anxiety do not follow simply from social disapproval. Rather, they seem to come from several sources, including the difficulty the boy has in presenting himself as a sexual being to his immediate family, particularly his parents. Another source is the fantasies or plans associated with masturbation—fantasies about doing sexual "things" to others or having others do sexual "things" to oneself; or having to learn and rehearse available but proscribed sexual scripts or patterns of behavior. And, of course, some guilt and anxiety center around the general disapproval of masturbation. After the early period of adolescence, in fact, most youths will not admit to their peers that they did or do it.

Nevertheless, masturbation is for most adolescent boys the major sexual activity, and they engage in it fairly frequently. It is an extremely positive and gratifying experience to them. Such an introduction to sexuality can lead to a capacity for detached sex activity—activity whose only sustaining motive is sexual. This may be the hallmark of male sexuality in our society.

Of the three sources of guilt and anxiety mentioned, the first—how to manage both sexuality and an attachment to family members—probably cuts across class lines. But the others should show remarkable class differences. The second one, how to manage a fairly elaborate and exotic fantasy life during masturbation, should be confined most typically to the higher classes, who are more experienced and adept at dealing with symbols. (It is possible, in fact, that this behavior, which girls rarely engage in, plays a role in the processes by which middle-class boys catch up with girls in measures of achievement and creativity and, by the end of adolescence, move out in front. However, this is only a hypothesis.)

The ability to fantasize during masturbation implies certain broad consequences. One is a tendency to see large parts of the environment in an erotic light, as well as the ability to respond, sexually and perhaps poetically, to many visual and auditory stimuli. We might also expect both a capacity and need for fairly elaborate forms of sexual activity. Further, since masturbatory fantasies generally deal with relationships and acts leading to coitus, they should also reinforce a developing capacity for heterosociality.

The third source of guilt and anxiety—the alleged "unmanliness" of masturbation—should more directly concern the lower-class male adolescent. ("Manliness" has always been an important value for lower-class males.) In these groups, social life is more often segregated by sex, and there are, generally, fewer rewarding social experiences from other sources. The adolescent therefore moves into heterosexual—if not heterosocial—relationships sooner than his middle-class counterparts. Sexual segregation makes it easier for him than for the middle-class boy to learn that he does not have to love everything he desires, and therefore to come more naturally to casual, if not exploitative, relationships. The second condition—fewer social rewards that his fellows would respect—should lead to an exaggerated concern for proving masculinity by direct displays of physical prowess, aggression, and visible sexual success. And these three, of course, may be mutually reinforcing.

In a sense, the lower-class male is the first to reach "sexual maturity" as defined by the Freudians. That is, he is generally the first to become aggressively heterosexual and exclusively genital. This characteristic, in fact, is a distinguishing difference between lower-class males and those above them socially.

But one consequence is that although their sex lives are almost exclusively heterosexual, they remain homosocial. They have intercourse with females, but the standards and the audience they refer to are those of their male fellows. Middle-class boys shift predominantly to coitus at a significantly later time. They, too, need and tend to have homosocial elements in their sexual lives. But their fantasies, their ability to symbolize, and their social training in a world in which distinctions between masculinity and femininity are less sharply drawn, allow them to withdraw more easily from an all-male world. This difference between social classes obviously has important consequences for stable adult relationships.

One thing common in male experience during adolescence is that while it provides much opportunity for sexual commitment, in one form or another, there is little training in how to handle emotional relations with girls. The imagery and rhetoric of romantic love is all around us; we are immersed in it.

But whereas much is undoubtedly absorbed by the adolescent, he is not likely to tie it closely to his sexuality. In fact, such a connection might be inhibiting, as indicated by the survival of the "bad-girl-who-does" and "good-girl-who-doesn't" distinction. This is important to keep in mind as we turn to the female side of the story.

With the Girls

In contrast to males, female sexual development during adolescence is so similar in all classes that it is easy to suspect that it is solely determined by biology. But, while girls do not have the same level of hormonal sensitization to sexuality at puberty as adolescent boys, there is little evidence of a biological or social inhibitor either. The "equipment" for sexual pleasure is clearly present by puberty, but tends not to be used by many females of any class. Masturbation rates are fairly low, and among those who do masturbate, fairly infrequent. Arousal from "sexual" materials or situations happens seldom, and exceedingly few girls report feeling sexually deprived during adolescence.

Basically, girls in our society are not encouraged to be sexual—and may be strongly discouraged from being so. Most of us accept the fact that while "bad boy" can mean many things, "bad girl" almost exclusively implies sexual delinquency. It is both difficult and dangerous for an adolescent girl to become too active sexually. As Joseph Rheingold puts it, where men need only fear sexual failure, women must fear both success and failure.

Does this long period of relative sexual inactivity among girls come from repression of an elemental drive, or merely from a failure to learn how to be sexual? The answers have important implications for their later sexual development. If it is repression, the path to a fuller sexuality must pass through processes of loss of inhibitions, during which the girl unlearns, in varying degrees, attitudes and values that block the expression of natural internal feelings. It also implies that the quest for ways to express directly sexual behavior and feelings that had been expressed nonsexually is secondary and of considerably less significance.

On the other hand, the "learning" answer suggests that women create or invent a capacity for sexual behavior, learning how and when to be aroused and how and when to respond. This approach implies greater flexibility; unlike the repression view, it makes sexuality both more and less than a basic force that may break loose at any time in strange or costly ways. The learning approach also lessens the power of sexuality altogether; all at once, particular kinds of sex activities need no longer be defined as either "healthy" or "sick." Lastly, subjectively, this approach appeals to the authors because it describes female sexuality in terms that seem less like a mere projection of male sexuality.

If sexual activity by adolescent girls assumes less specific forms than with boys, that does not mean that sexual learning and training do not occur. Curiously, though girls are, as a group, far less active sexually than boys, they receive far more training in self-consciously viewing themselves—and in viewing boys—as desirable mates. This is particularly true in recent years. Females begin early in adolescence to define attractiveness, at least partially, in sexual terms. We suspect that the use of sexual attractiveness for nonsexual purposes that marked our preadolescent "seductress" now begins to characterize many girls. Talcott Parsons' description of how the wife "uses" sex to bind the husband to the family, although harsh, may be quite accurate. More generally, in keeping with the childbearing and child-raising function of women, the development of a sexual role seems to involve a need to include in that role more than pleasure.

To round out the picture of the difference between the sexes, girls appear to be well-trained precisely in that area in which boys are poorly trained—that is, a belief in and a capacity for intense, emotionally-charged relationships and the language of romantic love. When girls during this period describe having been aroused sexually, they more often report it as a response to romantic, rather than erotic, words and actions.

In later adolescence, as dates, parties, and other sociosexual activities increase, boys—committed to sexuality and relatively untrained in the language and actions of romantic love—interact with girls, committed to romantic love and relatively untrained in sexuality. Dating and courtship may well be considered processes in which each sex trains the other in what each wants and expects. What data is available suggests that this exchange system does not always work very smoothly. Thus, ironically, it is not uncommon to find that the boy becomes emotionally involved with his partner and therefore lets up on trying to seduce her, at the same time that the girl comes to feel that the boy's affection is genuine and therefore that sexual intimacy is more permissible.

In our recent study of college students, we found that boys typically had intercourse with their first coital partners one to three times, while with girls it was ten or more. Clearly, for the majority of females first intercourse becomes possible only in stable relationships or in those with strong bonds.

"Woman, What Does She Want?"

The male experience does conform to the general Freudian expectation that there is a developmental movement from a predominantly genital sexual commitment to a loving relationship with another person. But this movement is, in effect, reversed for females, with love or affection often a necessary precondition for intercourse. No wonder, therefore, that Freud had great difficulty understanding female sexuality—recall the concluding line in his great essay on women: "Woman, what does she want?" This "error"—the assumption that female sexuality is similar to or a mirror image of that of the male —may come from the fact that so many of those who constructed the theory were men. With Freud, in addition, we must remember the very concept of sexuality essential to most of nineteenth century Europe—it was an elemental beast that had to be curbed.

It has been noted that there are very few class differences in sexuality among females, far fewer than among males. One difference, however, is very relevant to this discussion—the age of first intercourse. This varies inversely with social class—that is, the higher the class, the later the age of first intercourse—a relationship that is also true of first marriage. The correlation between these two ages suggest the necessary social and emotional linkage between courtship and the entrance into sexual activity on the part of women. A second difference, perhaps only indirectly related to social class, has to do with educational achievement: here, a sharp border line seems to separate from all other women those who have or have had graduate or professional work. If sexual success may be measured by the percentage of sex acts that culminate in orgasm, graduate and professional women are the most sexually successful women in the nation.

Why? One possible interpretation derives from the work of Abraham Maslow: Women who get so far in higher education are more likely to be more aggressive, perhaps to have strong needs to dominate; both these characteristics are associated with heightened sexuality. Another, more general interpretation would be that in a society in which girls are expected primarily to become wives and mothers, going on to graduate school represents a kind of deviancy—a failure of, or alienation from, normal female social adjustment. In effect, then, it would be this flawed socialization—not biology—that produced both commitment toward advanced training and toward heightened sexuality.

For both males and females, increasingly greater involvement in the social aspects of sexuality—"socializing" with the opposite sex—may be one factor that marks the end of adolescence. We know little about this transition, especially among noncollege boys and girls; but our present feeling is that sexuality plays an important role in it. First, sociosexuality is important in family formation and also in learning the roles and obligations involved in being an adult. Second, and more fundamental, late adolescence is when a youth is seeking, and experimenting toward finding, his identity—who and what he is and will be; and sociosexual activity is the one aspect of this exploration that we associate particularly with late adolescence.

Young people are particularly vulnerable at this time. This may be partly due to the fact that society has difficulty protecting the adolescent from the consequences of sexual behavior that it pretends he is not engaged in. But, more importantly, it may be because, at all ages, we all have great problems in discussing our sexual feelings and experiences in personal terms. These, in turn, make it extremely difficult to get support from others for an adolescent's experiments toward trying to invent his sexual self. We suspect that success or failure in the discovery or management of sexual identity may have consequences in personal development far beyond merely the sexual sphere—

perhaps in confidence and feelings of self-worth, belonging, competence, guilt, force of personality, and so on.

Adulthood

In our society, all but a few ultimately marry. Handling sexual commitments inside marriage makes up the larger part of adult experience. Again, we have too little data for firm findings. The data we do have come largely from studies of broken and troubled marriages, and we do not know to what extent sexual problems in such marriages exceed those of intact marriages. It is possible that, because we have assumed that sex is important in most people's lives, we have exaggerated its importance in holding marriages together. Also, it is quite possible that, once people are married, sexuality declines relatively, becoming less important than other gratifications (such as domesticity or parenthood); or it may be that these other gratifications can minimize the effect of sexual dissatisfaction. Further, it may be possible that individuals learn to get sexual gratification, or an equivalent, from activities that are non-sexual, or only partially sexual.

The sexual desires and commitments of males are the main determinants of the rate of sexual activity in our society. Men are most interested in inter-course in the early years of marriage—woman's interest peaks much later; nonetheless, coital rates decline steadily throughout marriage. This decline derives from many things, only one of which is decline in biological capacity. With many men, it is more difficult to relate sexually to a wife who is preg-nant or a mother. Lower-class adult men receive less support and plaudits from their male friends for married sexual performance than they did as single adolescents; and we might also add the lower-class disadvantage of less train-ing in the use of auxiliary or symbolic sexually stimulating materials. For middle-class men, the decline is not as steep, owing perhaps to their greater ability to find stimulation from auxiliary sources, such as literature, movies, music, and romantic or erotic conversation. It should be further noted that for about 30 percent of college-educated men, masturbation continues regu-larly during marriage, even when the wife is available. An additional (if unknown) proportion do not physically masturbate, but derive additional excitement from the fantasies that accompany intercourse.

But even middle-class sexual activity declines more rapidly than bodily changes can account for. Perhaps the ways males learn to be sexual in our society make it very difficult to keep it up at a high level with the same woman for a long time. However, this may not be vital in maintaining the family, or even in the man's personal sense of well-being, because, as previously sug-gested, sexual dissatisfaction may become less important as other satisfactions increase. Therefore, it need seldom result in crisis.

About half of all married men and a quarter of all married women will have intercourse outside of marriage at one time or another. For women, infidelity seems to have been on the increase since the turn of the century—at the same time that their rates of orgasm have been increasing. It is possible that the very nature of female sexuality is changing. Work being done now may give us new light on this. For men, there are strong social-class differences—the lower class accounts for most extramarital activity, especially during the early years of marriage. We have observed that it is difficult for a lower-class man to acquire the appreciation of his fellows for married intercourse; extramarital sex, of course, is another matter.

In general, we feel that far from sexual needs affecting other adult concerns, the reverse may be true: adult sexual activity may become that aspect of a person's life most often used to act out other needs. There are some data that suggest this. Men who have trouble handling authority relationships at work more often have dreams about homosexuality; some others, under heavy stress on the job, have been shown to have more frequent episodic homosexual experiences. Such phenomena as the rise of sadomasochistic practices and experiments in groups sex may also be tied to nonsexual tensions, the use of sex for nonsexual purposes.

It is only fairly recently in the history of man that he has been able to begin to understand that his own time and place do not embody some eternal principle or necessity, but are only dots on a continuum. It is difficult for many to believe that man can change, and is changing, in important ways. This conservative view is evident even in contemporary behavioral science; and a conception of man as having relatively constant sexual needs has become part of it. In an ever-changing world, it is perhaps comforting to think that man's sexuality does not change very much, and therefore is relatively easily explained. We cannot accept this. Instead, we have attempted to offer a description of sexual development as a variable social invention—an invention that in itself explains little, and requires much continuing explanation.

The Case History of a Construct: Ego Identity Status

JAMES E. MARCIA

This selection speaks on a more personal level. Erik Erikson's formulation of the eight stages of identity development has been one of the principal contributions to modern personality psychology. His view is that each person passes through a series of critical periods, and that at the core of each phase is a specific personal crisis. The fifth of these critical periods is adolescence; according to Erikson, the healthy individual emerges from adolescence with a sense of "ego identity." In this article, Marcia notes that the term *ego identity* is wanting in the specific behavioral definition that would make it scientifically meaningful, so he undertakes a specification of ego identity in terms of the behaviors that would be exhibited by people who have (and have not) achieved it. Note how this orientation toward behavioral terminology leads Marcia to propose four different "ego identity statuses," and how he goes about submitting this expanded version of Erikson's theory to empirical test.

Few psychologists experience the science vs. service conflict more than the clinical psychologist. While he espouses the scientific method as the most effective route to knowledge about human behavior he finds that he must sometimes use methods best described as artistic in his search for the wisdom necessary to deal with the human heart. In the latter task, many clinicians find psychoanalytic theory a valuable source of ideas. However, this theory pays a high price, scientifically speaking, for its attempts to deal with the broader and deeper aspects of personality. Just as individual behavior can appear both confusing and contradictory to us, so does psychoanalytic theory involve many vague concepts and ill-defined terms. Perhaps this is because it attempts to account for so much so inclusively. Be that as it may, the clinical psychologist is frequently caught in the bind of using a scientifically non-

SOURCE: From *Readings in General Psychology* by W. Edgar Vinacke. Copyright © 1968 by Litton Educational Publishing, Inc. Reprinted by permission of Van Nostrand Reinhold Company.

proven theory when he wears his "clinical hat" and then having to dissociate himself from that theory when wearing his "scientific hat."

One promising way out of this dilemma may be in the ego psychoanalytic theory of Erik Erikson. A major difficulty, from the psychologists' point of view, with the id-oriented approach of traditional psychoanalysts has been their failure to predict specific behaviors from alleged unconscious motives. Frequently, this has been because of a lack of consideration of the ways in which an individual's environment may nurture, use, abuse, and mold the expression of basic drives. Erikson, while accepting the biological emphasis inherent in the Freudian *psychosexual* approach to human development, goes on to outline a *psychosocial* scheme based on hypothesized stages of ego growth. These stages of ego growth parallel and then extend beyond the psychosexual stages—each psychosocial stage is marked by a specific crisis in ego growth. The content of these crises involves the development of particular attitudes toward oneself, one's world, and one's relationship to his world. For example, at the oral psychosexual stage, the basic psychosocial crisis involves the infant's development of a sense of basic trust vs. mistrust. The rapprochement that was suggested earlier between Erikson's ego psychoanalytic theory and the scientific commitment of the clinical psychologist may be intitiated by asking the simple question: "If a particular crisis is resolved, what behaviors should one observe?"

Erikson suggests that the human life cycle involves eight crises in ego growth. These crises, their chronological sequence, and parallel psychosexual stages are presented in the following chart.

Age	Psychosexual Stages	Psychosocial Crises
Infancy	Oral	Basic trust vs. mistrust
Early childhood	Anal	Autonomy vs. shame, doubt
Play age	Phallic	Initiative vs. guilt
School age	Latency	Industry vs. inferiority
Adolescence	Genital	Ego identity vs. identity diffusion (or role confusion)
Young adult		Intimacy vs. isolation
Adulthood		Generativity vs. stagnation
Maturity		Ego integrity vs. despair

Presenting the psychosocial stages in this way suggests a certain independence among them as well as the possibility of a permanent solution.

Neither is the case. The solution of each crisis has ramifications for the solution of the next and is prefigured by the solution of the preceding one. For example, the development of predominant mistrust at infancy may lead to a distrust of time (and consequent difficulty in delaying gratification) at adolescence, contributing to a sense of identity diffusion. Similarly, failure to make the occupational and ideological commitments at adolescence necessary to achieve a sense of ego identity may lead to difficulty in interpersonal commitments at young adulthood and, hence, contribute to a feeling of isolation.

Not only are crises interdependent, they may also recur. A fairly common example of this is the "adolescent" identity crisis experienced at maturity when the individual contemplates retirement.

While the question may be simple, the means of answering it are not. The work discussed in this paper has been with that stage of ego growth occurring in late adolescence: the identity crisis. At every stage, there is, hopefully, a "cogwheeling" or mutuality between an individual's needs and capabilities and his society's rewards and demands. The individual's conflicting needs at this stage of late adolescence are both for a feeling of belongingness and independence, for sexual expression and control, for responsibility and freedom. His capabilities are loyalty, skill in the society's technology (e.g., reading and writing), procreation, and realistic decision-making. Society's rewards include citizenship, certain adult privileges (e.g., drinking, driving), greater latitude for sexual expression, increased earning power, and recognition by other adults. Society's demands involve occupational selection, choice of a marriage partner, "responsible" behavior, and the beginning of contribution to the life cycles of others.

According to Erikson, one emerges from the identity crisis with some sense of ego identity or of identity diffusion. Stated simply, ego identity refers to the individual's feeling of knowing who he is and where he is going. Identity diffusion (or role confusion) refers to an individual's sense of uncertainty about both his place and his direction in the scheme of things. The best literary description of ego identity and identity diffusion is to be found in Erikson's highly readable works. The problem here was to answer, empirically, the following questions: Can "ego identity" be defined so as to be measured? Can it then be measured? Having measured it, can behavioral predictions be made? Until these questions were answered, the concepts, while appealing and valuable from a therapeutic and philosophical point of view, were scientifically meaningless.

The initial problem was to get ego identity out into the open, which, to a psychologist, usually means into the laboratory. What behaviors should be observed if some degree of ego identity has been achieved? To look solely at an individual's feelings about himself would miss an essential contribution of Erikson's approach: the psychosocial aspect. Hence, elements of both the individual's needs and capabilities together with his society's rewards and demands had to be taken into account. The two social components or areas chosen were *occupation* and *ideology*. The societal demand that the late adolescent "get a job" has been celebrated both in song and countless stories, many of the latter emanating from vocational counseling centers on college campuses across the country. The demand to develop an ideology (or philosophy of life or *weltanschauung*) while not so obvious, is equally pressing. As the adolescent changes his role from that of a "taker" to a "giver," from one who was cared for to one who is on the threshold of caring for others, he must adopt a way of viewing the world that facilitates and makes meaningful this transition. This revision in world outlook usually takes the form of some sort of personal religious-political-economic theory. Hence, expressed *commitment* to an occupation and an ideology was chosen as one criterion for the presence of ego identity.

However, commitment alone was not enough. Not all occupations are "chosen," nor are all ideologies "developed." The son of a Methodist, Republican physician who becomes a Methodist, Republican physician with little or no thought in the matter cannot be said to have *achieved* an identity. It appears more that he finds himself at the identity crisis accepting the labels pasted on him since childhood, and cheerfully committing himself to being his parents' alter ego. Another variable, then, in addition to mere commitment was needed. "Crisis" was chosen to refer to a period of decision-making when previous choices, beliefs, and identifications were brought up for questioning by the individual. With the establishment of *crisis* as a variable, half of the first task—an operational definition of ego identity—was completed. Two variables, crisis and commitment, in two areas, occupation and ideology, were to define the extent of ego identity or identity diffusion.

At this point, a new outlook on the problem emerged. The various combinations of the criteria yielded something like separate kinds of "ego identities" rather than just "how much" ego identity. It was decided to approach the identity crisis in terms of *ego identity statuses*; that is, a number of ways in which the identity crisis could be dealt with, only one of which was the achievement of ego identity. Four ego identity statuses were defined: identity achievement, moratorium, foreclosure, and identity diffusion. Identity achievement individuals had experienced a crisis and were committed to an occupation and ideology. Moratorium individuals were currently *in* the crisis or decision-making period with only vague commitments to occupation and ideology. Foreclosure subjects, while committed to an occupation and ideology, seemed to have experienced no crisis period, their commitments being largely parentally determined. Identity diffusion individuals might or might not have come to crisis period; regardless, they were strikingly uncommitted to occupation and ideology.

We now had definitions of ego identity status that would permit at least a rudimentary form of measurement: categorization. The next problem was to decide upon which technique to use to assess an individual's particular status. It was decided that a moderately structured interview with a scoring manual would provide both the degree of accuracy and flexibility demanded by the nature of the statuses. Constructing the interview was a fairly straight-forward procedure; questions were devised to tap crisis and commitment in the two areas of occupation and ideology, the latter divided into religion and politics. The building of a scoring manual was a considerably more arduous task. First, theoretical criteria for each variable (crisis and commitment) in each area (occupation, religion, and politics) for each of the four identity statuses were spelled out. Then, by means of actual interviews, examples were gathered. The manual was compiled and taped interviews together with the manual were given to other psychologists not connected with the research to see if they could agree on the placing of individuals in statuses. Areas where they disagreed in their judgments, or where the manual was unclear, were revised. A new sample of interviews was then taped and the new tapes were rated again. Finally, the manual was sufficiently clear that judges could agree on an individual's identity status about 70–75% of the time. While far from ideal, this was thought to be adequate for such complex, global judg-ments. At this point, a more complete description of each of the identity statuses based on their interviews seems in order.

Identity Achievement

OCCUPATION

He has seriously considered several occupational choices or deviated from what his parents had planned for him. He is reluctant to switch fields and seems to think of himself as *a* teacher, engineer, etc. (Being *a* something means the difference between "taking courses in education" and seeing one-self as a "teacher.") Although his ultimate choice may be only a variation of the parental wishes, he seems to have experienced a crisis period and made a resolution on his own terms. *An example:* His father was a farmer and wanted him to be one; his mother and the townspeople wanted him to be a minister; he decided to be a veterinarian. He says: "I would rather have my DVM than a Ph.D. in anything."

RELIGION

He appears to have gone through a period of doubting either his past belief or unbelief. This has resulted in a re-evaluation of faith and a commitment to some action (church going, religious discussions, etc.). He may end up as religious or not, in the conventional sense; regardless, he seems to have rethought childhood concepts and achieved a resolution that leaves him free to act. *An example:* He went through a period of rejecting his father's religion. A period of atheism followed disillusionment with a God who would permit an evil world. He resolved the dilemma by deciding that the amount of good balanced evil. He is fairly active in church and plans to raise his children in it.

POLITICS

The presence of a crisis period is more difficult to ascertain here than in the other two areas. He shows some differences from his parents' political opinions; for example, he may see himself as more liberal than they are. Evidence of commitment is usually seen in the vigor of his pronouncements, his tendency to dispute political questions with others, and any political action-taking. *An example:* A period in the Army angered him at being reacted to according to group membership rather than as an individual. He was attracted to the individualism of conservativism and is against social welfare. He sees a relationship between principles of human nature learned in college classes and his political beliefs.

GENERAL COMMENT

The identity achievement seems generally able to "make it." Particularly, he does not appear as if he would be overwhelmed by sudden shifts in environment or by unexpected burdens of responsibility. He also seems to be making some solid interpersonal commitments—e.g., engagement, marriage, etc.

Moratorium

OCCUPATION

He is dealing with issues often described as "adolescent." He is concerned less with preparing for a specific career than with choosing that career. His parents' plans are still important to him, and he seems to be working to achieve a compromise among them, society's demands, and his own capabilities. It is not that he feels totally bewildered and all at sea, but that he is vitally concerned and rather internally preoccupied with resolving what at times seem to be unresolvable questions. *An example:* He says: "Other people think I'm an easygoing clown. Inside, I'm a big knot. I'd just like some peace and quiet. The future does seem better than the past, though: I'm not so concerned now about what people think." He's majoring in speech, wants to work for a degree in either psychology or sociology while in the Army. In general, wants to do something to help people.

RELIGION

He seems to be dealing with fundamental religious-philosophical questions, not just a mere "shopping around" among denominations. *An example:* He has doubts about the existence of God and wonders whether there is any kind of Supreme Being. It scares him when he thinks about it, but he still does. He has tentatively decided that there is some kind of God.

POLITICS

Although he is in doubt about political and religious commitment, he seems dissatisfied with the doubt and is trying to effect a resolution. *An example*: He is confused about politics. He is a Democrat, but has heard about conservatism and is questioning it. On the other hand, the current governor is an inept conservative and this disenchants him. He doesn't really know.

GENERAL COMMENT

At his best, a moratorium is enthusiastic, questioning, idealistic, and usually rather verbal. At his worst, he is paralyzed, unable to act decisively in one way or another—not because of a lack of commitment, but more often because of equal and opposite commitments.

Foreclosure

OCCUPATION

It is difficult to distinguish where his parents' goals for him leave off and where his begin. He seems to have experienced either no choice period, or only a brief and inconsequential one. He is becoming what others have influenced him or intended him to become since childhood. In addition, all of this seems acceptable to him. *An example*: His father was a farmer and he'll be a farmer. He says: "I plan to go back and help dad farm." He took agriculture at college because "that's all I know." Although he gave cursory consideration to other fields, "farming was always at the top of the list." "I was brought up like my family was; I was with them so long I just stayed that way."

RELIGION

His faith (or lack of it) is virtually "the faith of his fathers (or mothers, as the case may be) living still." College experiences serve only as confirmation of childhood beliefs. Dissent seems absent. *An example*: His religion is the same as his parents'. He says: "Maybe it's just a habit with me, I don't know. I've thought a lot and you meet all kinds of people here, but I really haven't changed any of my beliefs. I just have more understanding than I did before. I plan to bring up my children in the church, just the way my dad did with me."

POLITICS

Again, he is what his parents are with little or no personal stamp of his own. *An example:* Referring to him and parents both being Republican: "You still pull that way, Republican, if your parents are that way. You feel like it's where you should be."

GENERAL COMMENT

Because of his commitment and apparent self-assuredness, a foreclosure appears in everyday life like an identity achievement, although he is characterized by a certain rigidity. However, one feels that if he were placed in a situation where parental values were nonfunctional he would soon be greatly at a loss. It may be that only situations of severe stress would differentiate him from identity achievement.

Identity Diffusion

There appear to be several varieties of identity diffusion. One is a *pre*crisis lack of commitment. This individual might have been a foreclosure if strong enough parental values had been established. However, it is likely that the parental attitude was one of "it's up to you; we don't care what you do." Under the guise of democratic child-rearing, the parents may have provided no consistent structure which could be a guide for the growing individual, and, later on, an image against which to compare himself. Because he never really *was* anything, it is almost impossible for him to conceive of himself as *being* anything. The problems that are so immediate and self-consuming for the moratorium never really occur to this precrisis diffuse person.

There are probably two kinds of *post*crisis diffuse individuals. The first is the "playboy" who seems committed only to a lack of commitment. This individual actively seeks to avoid entangling alliances; his motto: "Play the field." No areas of potential gratification are really relinquished; all things must be kept within the realm of possibility. A second type of postcrisis diffuse is the "loner" for whom any investment of himself in either ideas or people is so frightening that he shies away from any deep involvement. His isolation from others may lead to the development of disorganized thought processes. The main element in all these identity diffuse persons remains a lack of commitment.

OCCUPATION

No one occupational choice is decided upon, nor is there much real concern about it, as contrasted with moratoriums. There is frequently little conception of what a person in the stated preferred occupation does in a day-to-day routine. Any occupational choice would be readily disposed of should opportunities arise elsewhere. There is sometimes an "external" orientation, so that what happens to the individual is seen as a result of luck or fate. An example: His major is engineering. In response to a question about his willingness to change he says: "Oh, I can change. I want to travel, want to try a lot of things. I don't want to get stuck behind a drawing board. I want a degree mainly as an 'in' to production or something else. I just don't want to get tied down."

RELIGION

He is either uninterested in religious matters or takes a smorgasbord approach in which one religious faith is as good as any other and he is not averse to sampling from all. He will sometimes state his beliefs as being the same as his parents', yet show little commitment to them. *An example:* He says: "I haven't picked one religion. I'm not interested in any, although I guess it's all right for some people. I just don't care a whole lot about it."

POLITICS

Both political and social interest are low. He has little idea or concern about where he stands vis-à-vis society. It is as if the world went its way and he went his with little intercourse between the two. *An example:* He has no interest in politics. He never discusses it with his parents. When given an opportunity in the interview to make a choice between Kennedy and Goldwater, he was unable to.

GENERAL COMMENT

A striking feature of the identity diffusions, aside from their defining characteristic of lack of commitment, is the wide range of adjustment within the group. It varies from the playboy who appears fairly carefree to the loner who is pretty miserable much of the time. There may be some value to future investigations in distinguishing among these varieties of identity diffusion.

Having developed and described the ego identity statuses, the final question of their predictive validity remained to be answered. In other words, all that had been done until this time was the invention of categories, based initially on Erikson's theory, but now extended beyond that theory. Their scientific value, aside from the techniques developed to reliably determine them, was no greater than Erikson's concepts. To establish their scientific worth it was necessary to demonstrate that individuals in different categories behave in predictably characteristic ways in an experimental setting. The experimental tasks to be chosen had to have certain features. They had to be fairly independent of the criteria used to establish the statuses, "meaningful" in the sense that they tapped behaviors having adaptive significance, and sufficiently varied to permit differential predictions for different statuses.

The two main tasks chosen were a concept attainment task administered under stressful conditions and a situation allowing for assessment of vulnerability to self-esteem manipulation. The rationale for the stressful concept attainment task went as follows. A main function of the ego, according to psychoanalytic theory, is the mediation between external (environmental) demands and internal (personal) needs. For example, the stronger the ego, the better able a person should be to think effectively even though he is anxious. According to Erikson's theory, the successful resolution of a psychosocial crisis should yield an increment to ego strength. Hence, the nearer an individual's identity status approaches identity achievement, the greater ego strength he should possess, and the better he should perform on a task requiring him to think under pressure.

The rationale for vulnerability to self-esteem manipulation went something like this. Some people fluctuate in their estimate of themselves with almost every comment that others make about them; other people seem relatively impervious to everyday give and take, and maintain a rather consistent view of themselves. Achieving an ego identity involves a process of deciding for oneself who and what one is to be. To the extent that this has been accomplished, one might be expected to have developed an *internal* locus for self-evaluation and, hence, be less likely to change his opinions of himself when given personality-relevant information by an external source.

As predicted, subjects in the identity achievement and moratorium statuses did a better job on the test of thinking under stress; they also changed less in their self-esteem when given either positive or negative feedback about their performance. Foreclosure and identity diffusion subjects did poorly on the stressful concept attainment task (even though they did not differ in intelligence from identity achievement and moratorium) and they also changed their opinions of themselves more when given the personality-relevant feedback. Some other interesting findings were that moratoriums (in crisis) were either much more anxious than the other statuses or more willing to admit to it; foreclosure subjects tended to agree with authoritarian views and also appeared to set unrealistically high goals for themselves.

The operational definition, fairly reliable measurement, and empirical validation of the ego identity statuses may appear to have closed the issue with respect to this particular segment of ego psychoanalytic theory. However, it seems to be in the nature of science that answers only beget more questions. For example: Why does one person appear in one identity status rather than another? Is it related to characteristics of his parents or their modes of child-rearing? Might the basic thought processes of subjects in one status differ from those in another—perhaps in the sense that one group (foreclosures) may view a stimulus situation as having rather few defining characteristics while another (moratorium) may see many possibilities in the same situation? Since movement from one status to another is not only possible but expected, to what status do, say, moratoriums or foreclosures tend to go? Under what conditions do they go there? All of the work has been done with college students. What about noncollege populations, or groups outside of Western culture? Do the statuses apply there? Most of the work thus far has been with men. What about ego identity in women? Why don't identity diffusions emerge experimentally as a more distinct group? Would subdividing them lead to more refined predictions? In short, there is much to be done.

Finally, one might still find himself asking the question: What is ego identity or identity status *really?* Actually, they are words—constructs put on behavior that allow future behaviors to be predicted. Both this work and the business of science, in general, may be seen as the invention and testing of such labels for phenomena in order to determine the labels' utility for prediction. It may be that the phenomena themselves have "underlying principles" waiting to be "discovered," but even if they have, we have no absolute way of apprehending these or knowing when we have found *the* answer. What we can do is to *impose* ordering principles (construct systems or theories) on events and thereby *give* them order. The identity statuses are such ordering devices; so long as they continue to yield predictions, they are useful and will be retained. When they cease to yield further predictions, which at some time they probably will, they will be discarded in favor of other constructs of labels that will do the job of predicting this area of human behavior more efficiently.

Environmental Determinants of Human Life

RENÉ DUBOS

The interplay between the physical and the social lies near the core of the old "nature-nurture" controversy. This enduring battle over the relative contributions of genetic endowment (nature) and environmental influence (nurture) has occupied psychologists for decades. The current resolution is something of a compromise: Genes determine a person's possible responses to the environment, while the environment governs the actual character of those responses. But how does the environment shape human behavior? At what stage or stages of personal growth are environmental influences the most potent? Is adaptation always a good thing? And how can we enhance the outcome of our accommodation to environmental forces? These are the questions to which this article is directed.

In *Genetics,* the second volume of this series, Professor Dobzhansky forcefully asserted that the genetic endowment does not determine the traits of a person; rather, the genes govern the responses of the body and the mind to environmental forces. My theme will be that the physical and mental personality is built out of these responses.

Because of the nature of his assignment and of his professional activities, Professor Dobzhansky emphasized in his essay the genetic determinants of personality and behavior. For the same reasons, I shall emphasize here the environmental determinants. This difference of approach is only for convenience, and does not originate from a difference in scientific convictions. Professor Dobzhansky and I represent the two complementary aspects of the nature-nurture interplay. I shall try to promote my own interests, however, by quoting a statement by Ralph Waldo Emerson that gives a slight edge to environment over heredity in the determinism of behavior.

SOURCE: From David C. Glass, ed., *Environmental Influences* (New York: Rockefeller University Press and Russell Sage Foundation, 1968). Copyright © 1968 by the Rockefeller University Press and Russell Sage Foundation. Reprinted by permission.

39

In his essay on "The Uses of Great Men," Emerson stated one century ago: "There are vices and follies incident to whole populations and ages. Men resemble their contemporaries *even more* than their progenitors." (Italics are mine.)

As a moralist, Emerson was primarily concerned with the intellectual and moral attributes of human beings, but his aphorism is just as valid for physical and physiological attributes. Men resemble their progenitors because they derive from them their genetic endowment. They resemble their contemporaries because, within a given country and social group, the members of a given generation develop under the influence of the same environmental factors. Since the human genetic pool remains essentially the same from one generation to the next, its phenotypic expression represents the responses to the total environment and the ways of life, which are continuously changing. In the following pages, I shall consider the consequences for human behavior of some of the environmental forces that are most characteristic of the modern world.

My presentation will be focused on three different aspects of man's response to the environment:

1. The effects of environmental factors are most profound and lasting—indeed often irreversible—when they take place early in life, during the developmental periods, prenatal as well as postnatal.

2. Although man is highly adaptable and can therefore achieve adjustments to extremely undesirable conditions, such adjustments often have long-range, indirect effects that are deleterious.

3. Because man is shaped by environmental forces, it is desirable that a wide range of experiences be made available to him so as to favor the phenotypic expression of various types of genetic potentialities. Diversity is an essential aspect of functionalism.

Barring nuclear warfare or some other global cataclysm, the world population will continue to increase for several decades, in affluent as well as in underdeveloped countries. With the low mortality rates that now prevail wherever modern policies of public health have been introduced, the population can be stabilized only if the number of children per couple is from 2.2 to 2.5. Even assuming a much more widespread and drastic family control than is practiced at present, it can be taken for granted that the world population will increase greatly in the immediate future and probably double within much less than a century. As a consequence, it can be assumed that the largest percentage of human beings will be born, will develop, and that their children will be born and develop within the confines of large urban agglomerations. Whatever individual tastes may be, mankind will thus be shaped by the urban environment.

Before considering the biological consequences of this fact, however, it must be pointed out that the phrase "urban environment" has a meaning somewhat different from the one conveyed by the word "city." The classical city of the

European tradition was compact and its inhabitants were apartment dwellers. Such is still the case in Rome, Florence, Paris, Hamburg, and other continental cities (although less so in English cities). In contrast, the typical American city is sprawling. Its inhabitants live in individual detached houses with a lawn that often exceeds in size the land available to the Chinese farmer. Its loose structure is influenced by the agrarian and nomadic tradition of American life. This is true even of huge Eastern cities like New York or Philadelphia, because a very large percentage of their inhabitants live in one-family houses that they own.

In many respects, life in the suburbias of megalopolis differs from life in the historical European city. By moving to suburbia, the modern urbanite tries to escape the constraints of city life and to recapture the pastoral and village atmosphere of the traditional past. The detached house with its garage and front lawn can be regarded as the equivalent of the farm, its dependencies, and its pastures. The huge urban area is divided into a multiplicity of water, sewage, and fire districts, zoning boards, and school systems, each subunit appearing to perpetuate the town-hall tradition of administrative autonomy.

The apartment house and the suburban house thus represent different formulas of life, and the differences have important consequences for the social and emotional aspects of behavior. But many other aspects of life are essentially the same in all Westernized areas of the world, whether the urban environment is of the compact European type or of the spreading American type.

The suburbanite may have a lawn in front of his house; but the air he breathes, the water he drinks, and the food he eats are as polluted chemically as that of the apartment dweller. He may have a tool shop in his basement; but he is increasingly dissociated from the rhythms of nature that have governed human life in the past and that have shaped its physiological functions. He may consider his home an inviolable castle, but, as much as the apartment dweller, he experiences crowding, traffic jams, aggressive competition, and social regimentation wherever he goes for work or for leisure. The very design and decoration of his living quarters is governed by the need to accommodate equipment that he does not understand, and his ways of life expose him to stimuli very different from those under which human evolution took place. To discuss the effects of the city or suburban environment is, in practice, tantamount to a discussion of the consequences of modern technology on human life.

The science of the effects that environmental factors exert on human characteristics has a long tradition, and reached a highly sophisticated level 2500 years ago in the Hippocratic writings. The treatise on "Airs, Waters, and Places," in particular, boldly suggested that climate, topography, soil, food, and water affect not only physical stature and health, but also behavioral patterns, military prowess, and political structures.

The evidence for environmental effects is even more striking in contemporary life than it was in Hippocratic times. Suffice it to mention the acceleration of physical and sexual maturation among all people who have adopted the ways of Western civilization; the change in the patterns of disease all over the world; the progressive disappearance of some of the neuroses, such as those based on sexual repression, that were most prevalent in Europe at the end of the nineteenth century.

The directive effects of environmental factors on phenotypic expression are particularly striking during the formative stages of prenatal and early postnatal development. Moreover, the effects of such early influences are long-lasting, often irreversible, and thus condition what the adult will become. (The word *irreversible* is used here to denote that no technique is, at the present time, available for reversing certain effects of early influences. Although such techniques may eventually be discovered, it is probable that many effects of early influences will be found to be truly irreversible, because, as stated on page 49, organization inhibits reorganization.) It seems justified, therefore, to deal first with the fact that practically all aspects of physiological and mental life reflect the biological remembrance of responses made by the organism to early environmental stimuli.

The profound and lasting effects of early environmental influences have been richly documented in a great variety of animal species. The following are but a few among the many environmental factors that have been manipulated experimentally: nutrition, infection, temperature, humidity, type of caging, extent and variety of stimuli, degree of crowding and of association with other animals of the same species. The effects observed have included initial rate of growth, ultimate size of the adult, resistance to various forms of stress, learning ability, behavioral patterns, emotional responses, and, indeed, most physiological as well as mental attributes.

The experiences of early life are of special importance in man because the human body, and especially the brain, are incompletely differentiated at the time of birth and develop as the infant responds to environmental stimuli. Anatomical structures, physiological attributes, and behavioral patterns can thus be shaped by the surroundings and the conditions of life during childhood.

Although information concerning the effects of early influences is, of course, difficult to document in human beings, it is nevertheless convincing. For example: Japanese teenagers are now much taller than their parents and differ in behavior from prewar teenagers, not as a result of genetic changes, but because the post-war environment in Japan is very different from that of the past. A similar phenomenon is observed in the settlements of Israeli kibbutzim. The kibbutz children are given a nutritious diet and live under sanitary conditions. Early in their teens, as a result, they tower over their parents, who originated in crowded and unsanitary ghettos in Central and Eastern Europe.

As mentioned earlier, the acceleration of growth in Japan and in the Israeli kibbutz constitutes but a particular case of a constant trend toward earlier maturation of children in Westernized countries. This is evidenced by greater weights and heights of children at each year of life, and by the earlier age of the first menstrual period. In Norway, for example, the mean age of menarche has fallen from 17 years in 1850 to 13 in 1960; similar findings have been reported from Sweden, Great Britain, the United States, and other affluent countries.

Growth is not only being accelerated; the final adult heights and weights are greater and are attained earlier. Some fifty years ago, maximum stature was not reached in general until the age of 29; now it is commonly reached at about 19 in boys and 17 in girls. Change in the age of puberty seems to consist of the restoration of the developmental timing that had prevailed in the past and that for some unknown reason became greatly retarded at the beginning of the nineteenth century.

The factors responsible for these dramatic changes in the rate of physical and sexual maturation are not completely understood. But there are good reasons to believe that improvements in nutrition and in the control of infections have played a large part in the acceleration of development during early childhood and that such changes, in turn, have been responsible for the larger size achieved by adults.

Although no systematic study has been made of the long-range consequences of the maturation rate, it can be assumed that being early or late in development exerts an influence upon self-confidence, social success, and, more generally, on the ease of finding one's place in the social order of things. In this regard, it is rather disturbing that our society increasingly tends to treat young men and women as children and to deny them the chance of engaging in responsible activities, even though all aspects of their development are accelerated.

As far as can be judged at present, early development does not mean a shorter adult life; in fact, menopause seems to be delayed as puberty is advanced. Whether the acceleration in physiological development increases the incidence of behavioral difficulties under the present social conditions is an important, but moot, question.

There is no doubt, on the other hand, that development is handicapped both quantitatively and qualitatively by certain toxic conditions, nutritional deficiencies, infectious processes, or sensory and emotional deprivations experienced during the prenatal and early postnatal phases of life. This well-established fact poses a number of grave social dilemmas, especially in the formulation of medical programs for the underprivileged countries.

Man is endowed with an extremely high level of adaptability to many different forms of stress, an attribute that enables him to survive, function, and multiply under a very wide range of conditions. Paradoxically, however, man's very adaptability may be his undoing in the long run. Tolerance to stressful conditions is achieved through histological, physiological, and mental responses that are usually homeostatic and therefore serve a useful purpose at the time they occur; but they may eventually become deleterious, especially if they are called into play early in life. The wisdom of the body is all too often a short-sighted wisdom. In practice, many types of chronic and degenerative disorders, both physical and mental, are the delayed and indirect effects of responses that first served a useful homeostatic purpose. Such chronic degenerative disorders are often referred to as "diseases of civilization," because they are most common in highly urbanized and technologized countries. But, in fact, a more accurate phrase would be "diseases of incomplete civilization," because they reflect mismanagement of our societies and ways of life. The factors involved in the genesis of chronic and degenerative disorders will not be discussed here. However, a few examples will be quoted to illustrate that in behavior, too, the development of tolerance can have consequences that are dangerous in the long run.

Studies with experimental animals have revealed that nutritional deprivations or imbalances occurring early in life (prenatal or postnatal) will interfere with the normal development of the brain and of learning ability. Furthermore, bad dietary habits acquired early in life tend to persist throughout the whole life span. For instance, rats that become used to low-protein diets tend to continue eating them even though a better diet is made available to them later. Such habituation is not only behavioral in origin; it has metabolic determinants. Epidemiological evidence indicates that similar phenomena occur in human beings.

Adjustment to malnutrition can have remote and indirect consequences of far-reaching importance. Recent physiological and behavioral studies have revealed that people born and raised in an environment where food intake is quantitatively or qualitatively inadequate achieve a certain form of physiological and behavioral adaptation to low food intake. They tend to restrict their physical and mental activity and thereby to reduce their nutritional needs; in other words, they become adjusted to undernutrition by living less intensely. Furthermore, throughout their whole life span they retain the physiological and mental imprinting caused by early nutritional deprivation. Physical and mental apathy and other forms of indolence have long been assumed to have a racial or climatic origin. In reality, these behavioral traits often constitute a form of physiological adjustment to malnutrition, especially when nutritional scarcity has occurred during very early life.

Adaptation to an inadequate food intake has obvious merits for survival under conditions of scarcity; indolence may even have some romantic appeal for the harried and tense observer from a competitive society. However, the dismal aspect of metabolic and mental adjustment to malnutrition is that it creates a vicious circle. It is responsible for much of the difficulty experienced in several parts of the world by those who attempt to stimulate national economies. Populations that have been deprived during early life remain healthy as long as little effort is required of them, but they commonly exhibit little resistance to stress. For this reason, probably, they find it difficult to make the efforts required to improve their economic status.

Undernutrition is now rare in affluent countries. However, malnutrition can take many other forms, including, perhaps, excessive artificial feeding of the infant. Unfortunately, little is known of the physical and mental effects that result from a nutritional regimen which differs qualitatively from that of the mother's milk and exceeds it quantitatively. Infants fed a rich and abundant diet tend to become large eaters as adults. There is much evidence that such acquired dietary habits are objectionable from the physiological point of view, and it would be surprising if they did not have behavioral manifestations. Rapid growth and large size may not be unmixed blessings, for, as already mentioned, earlier maturation may add to the behavioral problems of the teenagers in affluent societies.

Because many of the effects exerted by early influences persist throughout the entire life span, they affect the social and economic performance of adults and, therefore, of the whole society. Control of disease during childhood and guidance of early physical and mental development thus constitute a far-reaching aspect of medical action. Indeed, it can be unequivocally stated that the beneficial effects derived from building ultramodern hospitals with up-to-date equipment are trivial when compared with the results that could be achieved at much lower cost by providing infants and children with well-balanced food, sanitary conditions, and a stimulating environment. The aged obviously need help and sympathy; the adults naturally constitute the resources of the present; but the young represent the future. Much social wisdom will be needed to formulate medicosocial policies and research programs for a more rational appraisal of the comparative degrees of emphasis to be placed on the different age groups.

Many experiments with various animal species have revealed that crowding commonly results in disturbances of endocrine function and of behavior, but the precise effects differ profoundly, depending upon the conditions under which high population density is achieved. If adult animals (young or old), obtained from different sources, are brought together in the same area, they exhibit extremely aggressive behavior and a large percentage of them die. In contrast, if animals are born and allowed to multiply within a given enclosure, they can reach very high population densities without displaying destructive aggressiveness, because they commonly achieve a social organization that minimizes violent conflict. As the population pressure increases, however, more and more animals exhibit varieties of abnormal behavior. These deviants are not sick organically, but they act as if they were unaware of the presence of their cage-mates. Their behavior is asocial rather than antisocial.

The most unpleasant aspect of behavior among crowded rats is that it resembles so much the behavior in some crowded human communities. Man has developed a variety of social mechanisms that enable him to live in high population densities; Hong Kong and Holland, for example, prove that such densities are compatible with physical health and low crime rates. In other communities, however, extreme crowding leads to types of asocial behavior very similar to the social unawareness recognized in overcrowded animal populations.

The humanness of man is not innate; it is a product of socialization. Some of the peculiarly "human" traits disappear under conditions of extreme crowding, probably because man achieves his humanness only through contact with human beings under the proper conditions. Man needs the socializing effect of a truly human group in order to become and remain human.

History shows that sudden increases in population density can be as dangerous for man as they are for animals. The biological disturbances created during the Industrial Revolution by crowding in tenements and factories were probably most severe in groups that had immigrated from rural areas and were therefore unadapted to urban life. In contrast, the world is now becoming more and more urbanized. Constant and intimate contact with hordes of human beings has come to constitute the "normal" way of life, and men have adjusted to it. This change has certainly brought about all kinds of phenotypic adaptations that are making it easier for urban man to overcome biological and emotional threats. As already mentioned, the effects of progressive increase in population are less dramatic than those of sudden crowding, especially if the new members of the population are born and develop in the environment which is becoming crowded.

The readiness with which man adapts to potentially dangerous situations makes it unwise to apply directly to human life the results of experiments designed to test the acute effects of crowding on animals. Under normal circumstances, the consequences of human crowding are mollified by a multiplicity of social adaptations. In fact, crowding per se, i.e., population density, is probably far less important than the intensity of the social conflicts or the relative peace achieved after social adjustments have been made. Little is known concerning the density of population or the intensity of stimulation that is optimum in the long run for the body and the mind of man. Crowding is a relative term. The biological significance of population density must be evaluated in the light of the past experience of the group concerned, because this experience conditions the manner in which each of its members responds to the others as well as to environmental stimuli and trauma.

During its evolution, the human species probably became adapted to social life in small groups, where each member knew each of the others personally. Perhaps there was a need for larger social gatherings from time to time, but certainly not often. Now and then, furthermore, man needs to be by himself, or, at most, with a few intimate associates. Buddha, Lao Tzu, Moses, Christ, and all the great creators after them have searched in solitude to discover themselves and their mission. Man reacts to continued oversocialization with all sorts of frustrations, repressions, aggressions, and fears that soon develop into genuine neuroses.

Admittedly, it is possible to rear and train children in such a manner that they become habituated to oversocialized conditions—to such an extent, indeed, that they do not feel safe and happy outside a crowd of their own kind. This does not invalidate the view that there is danger even in our present level of overcrowding. For instance, children and even adults can be trained or habituated to avoid everything good and healthy, to search for happiness in overeating all sorts of unbalanced food, in perversions, of simply unsuitable amusements. Once habituated to these ways of life, the deprived individual feels dejected and miserable. Yet such habituations, as well as "adjustment" to crowded life, may in the long run do more harm than drug addiction or alcoholism.

The design of human settlements and homes may compensate to some extent for insufficient space, but there are limits to such compensation. Beyond these limits, overcrowding is likely to produce irreversible damage. It may even, eventually, change the prospect of nuclear warfare from a threat to a temptation—the salvage from an evil life. In the absence of a world holocaust, crowding will probably lead to the evolutionary selective survival of persons best adapted to regimented life. The two alternatives to population control are thus nuclear destruction and the social regimentation of the anthill.

Man, having evolved under the influence of cosmic forces, has been "imprinted" by the rhythms of nature—from those of the mother's heart beat to those associated with the daily and seasonal cycles. A process of adaptation is, of course, continuously going on between man and the new world he is creating. However, the traits that are built into the human fabric are not likely to be eliminated or significantly modified by social or technological changes in ways of life. Even when a man becomes an automated and urbane city dweller, his physiological processes remain geared to the daily rotation of the earth around the sun; the paleolithic bull that survives in his inner self still paws the earth whenever a threatening gesture is made on the social scene.

It is also questionable that man can really change his concepts of reality and accommodate them to those developed by theoretical and technological sciences. In many cases, the manifestations of nature revealed by complex instruments appear unrelated to what the untutored mind perceives. The reason is, of course, that much scientific research now depends on a complex technology, which converts natural phenomena into signs registered by instruments but meaningless to the senses. There is no convincing evidence that the phenomenology thus revealed is any more objective than the kind of reality perceived by direct experience. As repeatedly emphasized by Niels Bohr and other theoretical physicists, the aim of science is to order various fields of human experience rather than to provide an actual description of reality.

In any case, it is probable that man's ability to comprehend the world has limitations inherent in his mind. These limitations are determined by the genetic make-up of *Homo sapiens* that seems to have been almost stabilized some 100,000 years ago, when the human mind was being shaped by the sensual responses to the external world.

Admittedly, civilized man could survive and multiply in underground shelters, even though his regimented subterranean existence left him unaware of the robin's song in the spring, the whirl of dead leaves in the fall, and the moods of the wind. In the United States, schools are being built underground, with the justification that the rooms are easier to clean and the children's attention is not distracted by the outdoors!

Millions upon millions of human beings who have developed in the urban and industrial environment are no longer aware of the stench of automobile exhausts or of the ugliness generated by the urban sprawl; they hardly mind being trapped in automobile traffic, or spending much of a sunny afternoon on concrete highways among streams of motors cars. Life in the technologized environment seems to prove that man can become adapted to starless skies, treeless avenues, shapeless buildings, tasteless bread, joyless celebrations, spirit-less pleasures—to a life without reverence for the past, love for the present, or poetical anticipations of the future.

While there is no doubt that man can function and reproduce in a com-pletely artificial environment, it is probable that alienation from nature will eventually rob him of some of his important biological attributes and most desirable ethical and esthetic values. Until the present era, the population of all large cities has been constantly renewed by immigration from rural areas or from underdeveloped countries, but this biological transfusion will soon come to an end as the whole world becomes urbanized. Throughout history, furthermore, city dwellers had easy access to nature; but farmland, meadows, and woods are now progressively eliminated by the urban sprawl. Yet, the pathetic weekend exodus from urban areas and the wood-burning fireplaces in overheated city apartments bear witness that soil, water, sky, and even fire still represent values meaningful for human life. In fact, it is questionable that man can retain his physical and mental health if he loses contact with the natural forces that have shaped his biological and mental nature. Man is still of the earth, earthy, and like Anteus of the Greek legend, he loses his strength when both his feet are off the ground.

The most interesting effects of the environment for man's future are the ones that enable him to convert genetic potentialities into phenotypic realities. In this regard, it must be emphasized that mere exposure to a stimulus is not sufficient to affect the phenotype. Environmental information becomes for-mative only when it evokes a creative response from the organism.

The social importance of the formative effects exerted by the environment was expressed in a picturesque way by Winston Churchill in 1943 while dis-cussing the architecture best suited for the new Chambers of the House of Commons. The old building, which had been badly damaged by German bombardment, was uncomfortable and impractical. Yet Mr. Churchill urged that it be rebuilt exactly as it was before the war, instead of being replaced by one equipped for greater comfort and with better means of communication. He argued that the style of parliamentary debates in England had been conditioned by the physical characteristics of the old House, and that chang-ing its architecture would affect not only the manner of debates but also, as a result, the structure of English democracy. In his words, "We shape our buildings, and afterwards our buildings shape us."

Just as the physical environment can condition behavior, so does the social environment condition the way people perceive space in interpersonal encounters. Suffice it to quote here a few statements by Edward T. Hall, a social anthropologist who has repeatedly emphasized that people brought up in different cultures live in different perceptual worlds.

> Consider for a moment the difference between a Greek who garners information from the way people use their eyes and look at him, and the Navajo Indian whose eyes must never meet those of another person. Or consider the disparity between a German who must screen both sight and sound in order to have privacy, and the Italian who is involved with people visually or auditorially almost 24 hours a day. Compare the sensory world of the New England American, who must stay out of other people's olfactory range and who avoids breathing on anyone, and the Arab who has great difficulty interacting with others in any situation in which he is not warmly wrapped in the olfactory cloud of his companion. All the senses are involved in the perception of space; there is auditory, tactile, kinesthetic, and even thermal space. . . . The kind of private and public spaces that should be created for people in towns and cities depends upon their position on the involvement scale.

Needless to say, the national differences in perception of space during interpersonal encounters are not genetically determined; they are expressions of social influences rooted in history.

The preceding remarks give substance to the famous epigram by the Spanish philosopher Ortega y Gasset: "Man has no nature, what he has is history." But this does not deny that human history has biological determinants. Some of these determinants involve the early experiences of the individual person; others are the consequences of man's evolutionary past.

As mentioned earlier, the formative effects of the environment are especially pronounced and lasting when they occur during the early phases of life. The organism's structure—physical and mental—can be strongly affected only while the processes of organization are actively going on. Furthermore, as the biological system achieves its organization, it becomes increasingly resistant to change. Organization inhibits reorganization. These statements are valid not only for anatomical and physiological differentiation, but also for behavior patterns. A recent study of Boston slum children, for example, found that they continued to conform to the ways of life of their destitute parents despite intensive efforts by skilled nursery school workers to change their habits and tastes. As early as three or four years of age, the children were already victims of environmentally and culturally determined patterns; and there was much reason to fear that they would, in turn, imprint their own children with these patterns. They were not culturally deprived; they had a slum culture from which they could not escape.

The most crucial phases of physical and mental development occur very early in life. By age six, the brain is three times larger than it was at birth; its cytoarchitectonic structure has been essentially completed through an elaborate sprouting of dendrites and immense proliferation of synapses; language, thought, imagination, and the sense of self-identity have reached a high level of development. It is legitimate to assume, therefore, that the very structure of the brain and the fundamental patterns of behavior are conditioned by the early experiences of extrauterine existence, because their development occurs during the period when the infant is first subjected to the stimuli of the total environment.

The immense plasticity revealed by the development of the brain and of behavior patterns accounts for the fact that nurture affects so profoundly the phenotypic expression of human nature. Granted the genetic diversity of human beings, each individual genotype allows a very wide range within which experience can shape the phenotype.

Man's evolutionary past naturally imposes constraints on his life in the modern world. In fact, the frontiers of technology and sociology are determined by biological limitations built into man's fundamental genetic make-up, which has remained much the same since the late paleolithic times, and which will not change significantly in the foreseeable future.

There certainly exist in the human genetic pool, on the other hand, rich potentialities that have not yet been fully expressed and that will permit man to continue evolving socially. The diversity of civilizations originates from the multifarious responses made by human groups to environmental stimuli. This versatility of response, in turn, is a consequence of the wide range of potentialities in human beings. Of course, persons differ by reason of their genetic constitution. Except for identical twins, no two individuals are genetically alike. Equally important is that physical and mental traits are profoundly influenced by the accidents of experience, which are never exactly the same for two different persons. As a result, each person is unique, unprecedented, and unrepeatable.

Contrary to popular belief, genes do not determine the traits of a person; they merely govern his responses to the life experiences out of which the personality is built (as was pointed out by Dobzhansky in the second volume of this series). Through complex mechanisms that are only now being recognized, environmental stimuli determine which parts of the genetic endowment are repressed and which parts are activated. In other words, the life experiences determine the extent to which the genetic endowment is converted into functional attributes. From nutrition to education, from the topography of the land to religious background, countless are the influences that contribute to shaping the body and the mind of man. Each one of us lives, as it were, in a private world of our own.

Whether physical or mental, human potentialities can become expressed only to the extent that circumstances are favorable to their actualization. Society thus plays a large role in the unfolding and development of man's nature.

In practice, the latent potentialities of human beings have a better chance to become actualized when the social environment is sufficiently diversified to provide a variety of stimulating experiences, especially for the young. As more persons find the opportunity to express their biological endowment under diversified conditions, society becomes richer and civilizations continue to unfold. In contrast, if the surroundings and ways of life are highly stereotyped, the only components of man's nature that flourish are those adapted to the narrow range of prevailing conditions. Hence the dangers of many modern housing developments, which, although sanitary, are inimical to the development of human potentialities and are designed as if their only function was to provide disposable cubicles for dispensable people.

In his recent book, *The Myth of the Machine*, Lewis Mumford states that "If man had originally inhabited a world as blankly uniform as a 'high-rise' housing development, as featureless as a parking lot, as destitute of life as an automated factory, it is doubtful that he would have had a sufficiently varied experience to retain images, mold language, or acquire ideas." To this statement, Mr. Mumford would probably be willing to add that, irrespective of genetic constitution, most young people raised in a featureless environment and limited to a narrow range of life experiences will be crippled intellectually and emotionally.

We must shun uniformity of surroundings as much as absolute conformity to behavior, and make instead a deliberate effort to create as many diversified environments as possible. This may result in some loss of efficiency, but the more important goal is to provide the many kinds of soil that will permit the germination of the seeds now dormant in man's nature. In so far as possible, the duplication of uniformity must yield to the organization of diversity. Richness and variety of the physical and social environment constitute crucial aspects of functionalism, whether in the planning of cities, the design of dwellings, or the management of life.

Dreams and Human Potential

STANLEY KRIPPNER AND WILLIAM HUGHES

At first blush, the assertion that the everyday experience of dreaming is a process "geared toward self-actualization and the full development of the human potential" may seem somewhat exaggerated. However, the evidence amassed by the authors of this article—"hard" scientific studies as well as case histories and anecdotes—lends credence to the claim. Of particular interest with regard to personal development is their discussion of the creative aspects of dreaming.

Besides furnishing a comprehensive review of research on dreaming, this selection also offers an exceptional illustration of the interplay among physiological, psychological, and sociological factors. While most of the preceding authors have described this interplay in terms of mind *or* body and society, Krippner and Hughes blend all three. For example, while they point out that (physical) movements of the eyes indicate that a person is dreaming, they do not lose sight of the fact that our cultures influence the content of our dreams, nor do they overlook the utility of dream content in the diagnosis and treatment of psychopathology. Pay particular attention to these and the other examples of this interplay.

Once Chuang Chou dreamed that he was a butterfly. He fluttered about happily, quite pleased with the state he was in, and knew nothing about Chuang Chou. Presently he awoke and found that he was very much Chuang Chou again. Now, did Chou dream that he was a butterfly or was the butterfly now dreaming that he was Chou? (Chuang Tzu, Book II, c. 300 B.C.)

At the University of Chicago, in April, 1952, a graduate student noticed that periodically during the night the eyes of people who are asleep move rapidly

SOURCE: From *Journal of Humanistic Psychology* 10 (1):1–20. Copyright © 1970 by the Association for Humanistic Psychology, San Francisco. Reprinted by permission.

Note: The preparation of this paper was supported by grants from The Society for Comparative Philosophy, Sausalito, Calif., and The Foundation for the Study of Consciousness, Philadelphia, Pa. It was prepared by presentation at the annual meeting of the American Association for Humanistic Psychology, Silver Spring, Maryland, 1969.

for several minutes [Aserinsky and Kleitman, 1953]. This discovery represents one of the rare instances of a scientific breakthrough that opens up an entirely new field of research. As early as 1892 a psychologist had speculated that the eyeballs might move during dreaming [Ladd, cited by Trillin, 1965] but his speculation was soon forgotten and most physiologists held that the eyes were in a position of rest during sleep. The 1952 discovery led to other psycho-physiological findings that demonstrated that most of what had been believed about the dreaming process was not true.

Replacing the notion that dreams last only a few seconds was the finding that the EEG-monitored Rapid Eye Movement (REM) stages of sleep are rarely less than 10 minutes long and may last for an hour or more. In his doctoral dissertation, one investigator [Dement, 1958] demonstrated that the acting out, in waking life, of the content of the dream narrative takes about as long as the duration of the REM stages from which the dream was reported.

Replacing the idea that one dreams only before waking was the discovery that there is an average of four or five REM stages in the course of a typical night's sleep. The average young adult subject spends about 20 percent of his sleep time in the REM state. During infancy and childhood the proportion is much higher, while during old age it is somewhat lower.

Replacing the assumption that many people dream rarely or never was the finding that virtually everyone dreams every night. It is true that some people *remember* their dreams more frequently than others, but this fact is related to situational and personality variables rather than to the actual amount of dream time. Foulkes [1966] has concluded, "Those who generally deny or ignore their world of private and subjective experience during wakefulness seem to recall fewer dreams than do those who accept and exploit this dimension of experience (pp. 59–60)."

The psychophysiological data refute not only the folklore on dreams but also many of the theoretical stances held by Freudian and Adlerian psycho-analysts [Foulkes, 1964]. Both Freud and Adler felt that individuals dream in proportion to the number and intensity of their personal problems but the data demonstrate that the REM stages recur in a highly predictable cyclic pattern with few variations for each individual studied. Emotional problems often take advantage of the dreaming state and a skilled psychoanalyst can use dream content therapeutically. However, the recent research findings do not support the notion that one's emotional problems precipitate or "trigger" the REM state.

Evolutionary and Developmental Aspects of Dreaming

A clue as to the necessity of the dream state for human development may be found in studying the ontogenetic and phylogenetic data. The REM state has been observed in all higher mammalian species; considerable attention has been devoted to the cat, dog, monkey, and rat because of the similarity of

many of their EEG patterns to those of humans [Foulkes, 1966]. Some preliminary data suggest that the humanoid sleep-dream cycle does not occur
among the lower mammals [Allison and Goff, 1968], amphibians [Recht-
schaffen, Bassan, and Ledecky-Janecek, 1968], reptiles [Tauber, Roffwarg, and
Weitzman, 1966], or fish [Tauber, Weitzman, and Korey, 1969]. Nevertheless, enough similarities exist to point to an evolutionary development of the
REM state. For example, birds spend less than 1 percent of their total sleep
time in the REM state [Jouvet, 1967] in comparison with the higher mammals' 20 percent (e.g., sheep) to 60 percent (e.g., cats). Furthermore, one
species of fish has been identified which appears to engage in eye movement
activity during gross overall inactivity [Tauber, Weitzman, and Korey, 1969].

The evolutionary evidence shows that the hunting species (e.g., cat, dog,
man) enjoy more REM sleep than the hunted (e.g., rat, mouse, rabbit).
Furthermore, extensive REM sleep came as a rather late development in the
evolution of the vertebrates [Jouvet, 1967]. It may well be that the REM state
(which is characterized by less sensitivity to external stimuli than are other
sleep stages) was only able to develop to an appreciable extent among animals
that were not in danger of extermination if their predators came upon them
while they were dreaming—and while they were oblivious to external stimuli.

It is interesting to note that the larger animals with a longer life span and a
lower metabolic rate tend to have longer sleep-dream cycles. The average
length of time from the beginning of one REM stage to the next varies from
four minutes in the mouse to 90 minutes in adult man [Hartmann, 1966]. It
has even been suggested that cyclical dreaming evolved because this arrangement gave the organism an opportunity to come to a state of near waking
readiness and "sample" the environment for danger [Snyder, 1966]. For
example, when opossums are brought into a laboratory, they have a greater
number of spontaneous REM state awakenings, just as their prehistoric
brothers probably awoke more frequently when there were predators about.

Insofar as the proportion of the REM state is concerned, ontogeny does not
neatly recapitulate phylogeny. Dewan [1968] explains this paradox by noting
that REM sleep is basically a process for "programming" the brain; this programming system is homeostatic, organizing and storing memories (perceptual,
cognitive, and behavioral programs). Thus, lower or "fixed program" forms of
life do not need much or any REM time while newborn higher life forms
should have more REM time than adults to develop the central nervous
system. Among the higher mammals (e.g., cat, man), slow wave sleep does
not occur until the central nervous system has acquired a certain amount of
maturity. In addition, REM time increases with phylogenetic development—
although it decreases with ontogenetic development. The prematurely born
infant spends about 80 percent of his sleeping time in the REM state. The
full-term neonate spends about 50 percent of his sleep time dreaming, the
5-week-old infant about 40 percent, the 3-year-old child about 30 percent, the
young adult about 20 percent, and the aged individual about 15 percent
[Hartmann, 1966].

It is likely that the neonate—who sleeps three out of every four of his hours —spends more time in the REM state than in either the non-REM sleep state or the waking state. It is also possible that the fetus spends almost all of its time in the REM state.

An ancient Hindu tale describes man's three states of consciousness as *vaiswanara* (wakefulness), *prajna* (sleep in which dreams are absent), and *taijasa* (dreaming sleep). Why should *taijasa*, or at least its ontogenetic antecedent, assume such importance among the newly born as well as among developing fetuses?

Ullman [1969] has pointed out that the REM state is "a time when the sleeping brain most closely resembles the waking brain in its degree of electrical and physiological excitation" and notes the importance of the pons and the reticular activating system in REM sleep. Ephron and Carrington [1966] have suggested that the REM state serves the function of promoting cortical efficiency. Therefore, the REM state may be needed to process the novel internal and external perceptual data that impinge upon the fetus and the neonate. Improving the binocular coordination of the eyes is probably a corollary of REM sleep [Berger, 1969]. In addition, Roffwarg, Muzio, and Dement [1966] propose that the REM state itself is a source of stimulation:

> We have hypothesized that the REM mechanism serves as an endogenous source of stimulation, furnishing great quantities of functional excitation to higher centers. Such stimulation would be particularly crucial during the periods *in utero* and shortly after birth, before appreciable exogenous stimulation is available to the central nervous system. It might assist in structural maturation and differentiation of the sensory and motor areas within the central nervous system, partially preparing them to handle the enormous rush of stimulation provided by the postnatal milieu, as well as contributing to their further growth after birth.

If the REM state serves a developmental function, one might be able to detect a disturbed or atypical sleep-dream cycle among individuals with central nervous system dysfunction. If this dysfunction responds to therapy, one might expect to see a reflection of this change in the sleep-dream cycle.

Some data now exist to support both of these suppositions. Feinberg [1968] studied 27 mentally retarded adults diagnosed as mongolian, phenylketonuric, brain-damaged, etc. A significant positive relationship was found between their scores on an individually administered intelligence test and their amount of REM activity, with those subjects having the lowest test scores showing the least REM activity during their REM stages. Feinberg concluded, "These results further support the view that during sleep the brain carries out processes required for cognition" and that "the EEG of sleep is a more sensitive index of the integrity of brain function than any other physiological measure."

Greenberg and Dewan [1969] proposed that dreaming serves to integrate new information into existing past information stores and hypothesized that the improvement of speech production and comprehension (i.e., "reprogramming") would alter the sleep-dream cycle of aphasics. They studied six aphasic patients who were responding to speech therapy and compared them with nine aphasic patients who were not responding. The improving group had a greater proportion of REM stage sleep than the nonimproving group and it was concluded that the data were "evidence of a relationship between a clearly existing reprogramming situation (improvement in aphasia) and higher levels of REM sleep."

Thus, it appears that the REM state serves an evolutionary as well as a developmental function. Because the developmental function (i.e., stimulating the maturation and differentiation of the central nervous system) must exist within the evolutionary framework (i.e., assuring the organism's survival), ontogeny does not recapitulate phylogeny insofar as the proportion of sleep time spent in the REM state is concerned.

Nevertheless, the association between the REM state and cortical efficiency may make it a useful diagnostic tool in cases of central nervous system dysfunction as well as a prognostic instrument to predict and measure the effectiveness of therapeutic techniques in cases of cognitive disorder related to brain injury.

Psychological and Sociological Aspects of Dreaming

A nineteenth century writer stated that "a human being deprived of the possibility of dreaming would have to become mentally disturbed after some time . . ." [Robert, 1886]. By the simple device of awakening subjects for several concurrent nights as they entered the REM state, Dement [1960] deprived a number of subjects of dreaming. During the day, they seemed tense and irritable and when these subjects were finally allowed to sleep without interruption, their REM time was markedly increased. This study, and others like it, appear to demonstrate a definite need for REM sleep.

Because REM time is of such critical importance, it is essential that further research be done on the chemical agents which reduce or increase the proportion of time the sleeper spends in the REM state. Table 1 summarizes this work; it will be noted that barbiturates—often taken to induce sleep—decrease one's amount of REM time. The terrifying dreams that often occur when barbiturate use is suspended often motivate the individual to resume usage of the drug—an important factor in barbiturate addiction. Alcohol reduces the amount of time spent in the REM state and the vivid hallucinations experienced by the heavy drinker when he temporarily stops imbibing alcohol may represent an effort of his central nervous system to "catch up" on REM time [Hartmann, 1965].

The available data suggest that the basic necessity of the REM state is developmental in nature, and serves a programming function that promotes cortical efficiency. However, the individual superimposes a number of additional elements on the dream process—elements which reflect instinctoid

TABLE 1. *Effects of Selected Drugs on Rapid Eye Movement (REM) Sleep*

Drug (Partial List)	Effect on REM Sleep
Alcohol	Decrease
Amphetamines	Decrease
Barbiturates	Decrease
Caffeine	None
Chloral hydrate	None
Chlorpromazine	Decrease with small doses; increase with larger doses
LSD	Slight increase
Marijuana	Unknown
Resperine	Increase with small doses; decrease with larger doses
Typtophane	Increase

pressures (e.g., hunger, power, security, sex) as well as elements from one's unresolved traumatic experiences, current problems, and hopes for the future. It is this material which serves as the basis of dream interpretation, especially as undertaken by psychoanalysts.

Plato [1937] anticipated Freud's position on dreams when he spoke of man's ability, while dreaming, to commit any "conceivable folly or crime—not excepting incest or any other unnatural union, or parricide, or the eating of forbidden food. . . ." In addition, Freud's notion of "wish fulfillment" was foreshadowed by Lucretius [1924] in *De rerum natura*. The Freudian point of view [1955] holds that unconscious strivings, feelings, and wishes are expressed in dreams, often in a disguised fashion. Through free association and other psychoanalytic techniques, the Freudian analyst attempts to help the patient recall, interpret, and work through the dream material.

Artemidorous [1644], in the second century, A.D., produced the first systematic interpretation of dreams. He asserted that truth exists within dream symbols—as when Joseph interpreted Pharaoh's dream of the seven fat and seven lean cattle as seven years of plenty followed by seven years of famine. Rather than serving as evidence of communication with God, Artemidorous looked upon Pharaoh's dream as an indication of human intuition.

Contemporary writers have also utilized the concept of dream symbols, some of them departing from Freud's stress on psychosexual symbolism [1955]. Jung [1938] felt that dream symbols are often "archetypal"—reflecting the religious and mythic concerns of the patient as well as the sexual ones. Furthermore, Jung saw the life style of the dream as often different from the patient's waking style (or "typology"), thus pointing out ways in which the patient might grow and develop. Adler [1958] proposed that the dream was always consonant with one's waking life style and that the dream makes use of those images and incidents which best express the patient's present problem. This emphasis on the symbol that expresses rather than on the symbol that disguises is consistent with Adler's notion of a continuity between waking and dreaming style and is also the keystone of Fromm's [1951] and Hall's [1966] theories of dream symbolism.

Bonime [1962] has stressed the learning experience by which a psycho-analyst passes on the skill of dream interpretation to the patient. Feeling that dream content is basically a derivative of social experience, Bonime helps the patient relate dream symbols to his daily life. A similar point of view is taken by Ullman [1960] who states, "The elements in the dream are symbolic, not in the sense of disguising impulses, but because they represent the best approximation in personal terms that the individual can construct for himself of the real forces operating upon him and impinging upon the area of vulnerability with which the dream is concerned and which are not objectively known to the individual."

Ullman [1960] has also concerned himself with the roles that dreams play in a particular culture. He notes that dreams of preliterate people reflect the prevailing mythology and that dreams often act as a channel for a person's idiosyncratic modes of viewing the cultural myths. Ullman cites the case of a patient who dreamed that her sexual organs were separate from her functioning self and that they were bought and sold. He suggests that the patient may have been overly conditioned by those aspects of the American society which emphasize the buying and selling of various personal capacities which are divorced from the person and treated as objects. Ullman concludes:

> The view presented differs essentially from the classical Freudian position insofar as it considers the source of unconscious motivating influences as linked to specific experiences in a given social and cultural milieu and not as originating in the biological nature of man, or as due to man's inherent vulnerability because of his extreme dependence on symbolic processes. . . . When functional alterations in consciousness occur, as in states of dreaming, the key to their understanding lies not in such dualistic concepts as . . . wish-fulfillment and disguise, but in the basic notion that an individual in a state of partial arousal is striving to express in a very concrete way the totality of factors, some known, some unknown, governing his reactions to a specific life experience.

A provocative example of dream sociology involves the 12,000-member Senoi tribe of the Malay Peninsula who claim an absence from their society of violent crime or mental illness [Stewart, 1969]. Dreams play a major role in the cultural life pattern of the Senoi; at breakfast, the individual's dreams are discussed with members of the family who aid his interpretation of the content.

The Senoi assume that the dreamer creates mental images of the outside world as part of an adaptive process. As some of these images are negative, they will produce mental illness and/or hostility if allowed to become internalized. Therefore, the tribe assists in the individual's expression, neutralization, and utilization of dream imagery. Positive dreams are acted out socially while negative dreams are interpreted and discharged.

The social acceptance of the dream implies, to tribe members, a full acceptance of the individual. From an early age, the Senoi tribesman finds that the feelings and thoughts of his inner life are accepted by others. He also learns that by expressing his internal imagery, he can integrate his own personality at the same time that he is coordinating his behavior with the social pattern of the tribe. American culture, by emulating this aspect of personal development, may reduce the nation's growing rate of crime and violence. Stewart [1969] has noted that Westerners "do not respond to dreams as socially important" nor are dreams included in the educational process. He concludes, "This social neglect of the side of man's reflective thinking when the creative process is most free, seems poor education."

A few American institutions and groups (e.g., The Association for Research and Enlightenment, Virginia Beach, Va.) have sponsored ongoing seminars in dream interpretation for individuals interested in self-development. In addition, many individuals keep dream diaries and attempt to gain knowledge about the self in this manner.

In either instance, a number of specific suggestions are available to assist dream recall [Kettlekamp, 1968; Krippner, in Steiger, 1969; Progoff, 1963]:

1. When you first awaken in the morning, lie quietly before jumping out of bed. Let your mind dwell on the first thing that comes up. Do not allow day-time interests to interrupt. Your first waking thoughts may remind you of the contents of your last dream before awakening and allow you, with further practice, to remember more and more details of the dream. You may need to try this technique several mornings in a row in order to get results.

2. Keep a notebook of the dreams you do remember for a month. Look for important ideas or themes running through the dreams. You may discover that you have been working on a problem at night without being aware of it. You may even find instances in which your dreams suggested actions which you are actually able to carry out later.

3. Look for items in your dreams that might be symbolic of something. Avoid making hard and fast judgments. Get the opinion of your family and friends. Remember, however, that it is more important that you enjoy your dream than that you correctly analyze it. It is more important that you learn to appreciate your inner life than that you become an amateur psychoanalyst.

4. Look for puns in your dreams (e.g., a play on words, a play on numbers). These puns are common and can often be discovered. This may further aid you in finding the meaning in some of your dream images.

5. Before you go to sleep at night, review the work you have done on a problem or on a question that has frustrated you. Concentrate for several evenings in a row, if necessary. If you have given the problem enough pre-sleep attention, you may find upon awakening in the morning that you can remember a dream in which the possible solution appeared. This is one way of encouraging creative dreams.

6. Try directing your dream thoughts as you might direct your waking consciousness. If a negative image seems to be following a negative course, try to reverse it, either in that dream or in a continuation of the dream. If your dream is a positive one, extend it as long as you can and try to derive some use or valuable product from it.

7. Keep dream diaries. Record your dream for six months or a year. Try to get other members of your family or your circle of friends to do the same. Determine, as best as you can, which dreams reflected personal problems, which dreams involved national or international events, which dreams were creative, and which dreams were highly symbolic.

8. Avoid books which present non-scientific approaches to dreams—or read them with a skeptical attitude. Select books that present varied viewpoints on dreams but which lean heavily on scientific data and/or clinical experience [Bonime, 1962; Foulkes, 1966; Freud, 1955; Mac-Kenzie, 1965].

As an individual begins to remember his dreams, he will notice that there are qualitative differences among some of the nighttime memories. He may be recalling non-REM thoughts, hypnagogic images, and hypnopompic images as well as dreams.

Non-REM awakenings of sleeping subjects indicate that considerable mental activity occurs during non-REM sleep [Foulkes, 1966, pp. 99–120]. The non-REM reports differ qualitatively from REM reports in that they contain a greater proportion of conceptual thinking, less perceptual material, and content that is less vivid, emotional, or distorted. Non-REM sleep mentation seems to be populated by fewer people but the events bear a greater correspondence to the sleeper's daily life than during REM sleep. Basically, non-REM mentation seems to involve more direct and simplified thought processes that are less concerned with a manifestation of the inner life.

The hypnagogic state occurs between waking and going to sleep while the hypnopompic state occurs between sleep and awakening. Various images often occur in these borderline states but vary considerably from person to person [Bertini, Lewis, and Witkin, 1969]. For some people, however, there is no recollection of any experience during these times. For others, however, the hypnagogic and hypnopompic states may contain striking visualizations, majestic music, and/or personal insights.

The contents of the non-REM, hypnagogic, hypnopompic, and REM states are in large measure influenced by psychological and sociological factors. As more data are obtained on the sleep-dream cycle, researchers may find ways in which the integration of dream material and the utilization of its recall (both for therapeutic and self-development purposes) will assist in the actualization of human potential.

Creative Aspects of Dreaming

Many writers have seen little possibility that the dream in any way could perform a creative function. The Nobel Prize-winning zoologist, J. P. Medawar (in MacKenzie, 1965, p. 11) has stated that most dreams are totally devoid of meaning and "convey no information whatsoever." Mercutio, in Shakespeare's *Romeo and Juliet*, foreshadowed this assertion when he declaimed:

> I talk of dreams,
> Which are the children of an idle brain,
> Begot of nothing but vain fantasy,
> Which is as thin of substance as the air,
> And more inconstant than the wind.

An opposing point of view has been put forward by Ullman [1964] who noted four creative aspects of dreaming: the element of originality, the joining together of disparate elements into new patterns, the concern of the dreamer with essence, and the felt reaction of participating in an involuntary experience —a reaction that also characterizes other creative experiences. Ullman conceded that the end-product could be banal or ecstatic but noted "it is an act of creation to have the dream in the first place."

Adelson [1957] has reported that his less creative patients generally described simple and conventional dreams while his more creative patients reported dreams that were highly imaginative. One patient who was decidedly insensitive to artistic work "could not allow himself fancy, metaphor, or reverie"; he was "on guard against any mode of experience which was not logical, rational, and coherent." Another patient, highly creative, reported complex and fanciful dreams. Stimulated by these examples, Adelson made a formal study of 15 college girls who were students in a creative writing course. The eight "highly imaginative" subjects had more dreams in exotic settings—an African jungle, an Arabian mosque, a Parisian bistro—than the seven "uninventive" subjects whose dreams characteristically took place in their immediate environments. The imaginative subjects also had a greater proportion of dreams that were transformed in identity, in which humorous incidents occurred, and in which color played a significant part.

In a similar study [Schechter, Schmeidler, and Staal, 1965], creativity tests were administered to 105 college students who had kept dream diaries. It was found that art students remembered their dreams significantly more frequently than science and engineering students. In addition, there was a statistically significant relationship between dream imaginativeness and creativity test scores.

Several distinguished scientists and artists have utilized their dreams for creative purposes. Robert Louis Stevenson, early in his life, discovered that he could dream complete stories and even go back to them on succeeding nights if the end was unsatisfactory. He once described his dreaming consciousness as filled with "little people" who every evening provided him with "truncheons of tales upon their lighted theater." Perhaps his greatest dream achievement came one night when he pictured a criminal, pursued by the police, who imbibed a potion and changed his appearance. This dream eventually appeared as the classic story of Dr. Jekyll and Mr. Hyde. Goethe, Blake, Cowper,

Poe, Voltaire, Dante, Shelley, Heine, La Fontaine, Tolstoy, and Coleridge also found dream material useful for their poetry and prose.

A number of composers reportedly were inspired by melodies heard during the REM state. Tartini heard in a dream a sonata from which he drew inspiration for his famous "Devil's Trill." Mozart, Schumann, Saint-Saëns, and d'Indy claimed that some of their music was first heard by them in dreams [De Becker, 1968].

A number of instances exist in which dreams have served a problem-solving function. When he was a student, the physicist Niels Bohr had a vivid dream. He saw himself on a sun consisting of burning gas while planets seemed to whistle as they passed by. The planets appeared to be attached to the sun by thin filaments and revolved around it. Suddenly the burning gas cooled and solidified; the sun and planets crumbled away. Bohr awakened realizing he had conceptualized the model of an atom, the sun being the fixed center around which electrons revolved. Much of the basic theory upon which atomic physics is based came out of this dream.

Otto Loewi, a pharmacologist, won a Nobel Prize for the discovery that control of the heartbeat is not through direct nerve influence. When he accepted the Nobel Prize in 1936 he said, "The story of this discovery shows that an idea may sleep for decades in the unconscious mind and then suddenly return to the consciousness." Loewi had first disagreed with the prevailing theory in 1903, but it was not until 1920 that his ruminations on the problem congealed in the dream state. In fact, he wrote down this dream on paper and went back to sleep. The following morning, Loewi looked at his writing and was unable to decipher it. That night he had an identical dream, awakened, and went directly to his laboratory. He prepared two frogs for an experiment which demonstrated that nerves affect heart function through a mediating chemical rather than through a direct connection.

Louis Agassiz, the naturalist, once attempted to transfer the image of a fossil fish from a stone but found the image blurred. A few nights after he abandoned the project, he had a dream in which he saw the entire fossilized fish. The following morning, he hurried to his laboratory—but found the fossil to be as obscure as ever. The next night, the dream returned; he examined the slab the next morning but found the vague image unchanged. Hoping he might have the dream a third time, Agassiz placed pencil and paper by his bedside. When the dream returned, he took the paper and drew his image upon it with the pencil. On the following morning, he was surprised at the details he had produced in total darkness. Returning to his laboratory, he used the drawing as a guide and slowly began to chisel the slab. As a layer of stone fell loose, he found the fossil in excellent condition—the identical fossil which had occurred in his dreams. Other scientific discoveries emerged in dreams reported by Cannon (a neurologist) and Galen (a physician).

Elias Howe had been frustrated in his early attempts to perfect the sewing machine; for years, everything he tried had failed. One night, he dreamed he had been captured by savages who dragged him before their king. The king issued a royal ultimatum: if within 24 hours Howe had not produced a machine that would sew, he would die by the spear. Howe failed to meet the deadline and saw the savages approaching; he saw the spears slowly raise, then start to descend. Suddenly, Howe forgot his fear as he noticed that the spears all had eye-shaped holes in their tips. Howe awakened, realizing that, for his sewing machine, the eye of the needle should be near the point, not at the top or in the middle. Rushing to his laboratory, he filed a needle to the proper size, drilled a hole near its tip, and inserted it into the machine. It worked well and the problem was solved.

Another inventor, James Watt, had been working on lead shot for shotguns. The standard process involved cutting or chopping metal and was quite costly. About this time, Watt had a recurring dream. He seemed to be walking through a heavy storm; instead of rain, he was showered with tiny lead pellets. Awakening, he surmised that the dream might indicate that molten lead, falling through air, would harden into small spheres. Obtaining permission to experiment in a church which had a water-filled moat at its base, Watt melted several pounds of lead and flung it from the bell tower. Hastening down the stairs, he scooped from the bottom of the moat the tiny leaden pellets—inaugurating a process that revolutionized the lead shot industry.

While in the army, René Descartes spent a winter of inactive duty in a hotel room. Discontent with army life, ideas spun through his brain in a disconnected, contradictory fashion. One night he had a dream in which all his previous thoughts fell into harmony. That illumination was the beginning of the philosophical and mathematical formulations that were to change the course of Western thought.

Such philosophers as Al-Mamun and Synesius and the mathematicians Condorcet and Carden acknowledged their dependence on dream recall for some of their insights. Carden claimed that one of his books on mathematics was virtually composed in his dreams.

Fehr [in Wells, 1968] studied the working habits of his colleagues in mathematics. Of those who responded to his survey, the majority said that they had solved problems in their dreams or thought it was a likely possibility. Whether one solves his problems in the dream symbolically (e.g., Howe, Watt) or directly (e.g., Loewi, Agassiz), he has utilized an altered state of consciousness for creative, productive purposes.

Murphy [1958] has described the four phases in the creative process as immersion, consolidation, illumination, and evaluation. In the first phase, the sensitive mind is immersed in some medium which gives delight and fulfillment—color, tone, movement, space, time, words, images, social relationships, contemplation, etc. In the second phase this sensitivity leads to the acquisition of "storehouses full of experiences" and consolidation into ordered, structured patterns. From these storehouses, the illumination—whether it be sudden or gradual—emerges. This is followed up by the fourth phase in which the creative product is perfected, sifted, tested, and evaluated.

When the dream plays a role in an artistic development or a scientific breakthrough, it typically enters into the third stage of creative thinking. In the waking state, Archimedes leaped from the bathtub shouting, "I have it!" as he discovered the principle of displacement. In the daydreaming state, Kekulé saw the components of the benzene ring arrange themselves. In the dream state, Bohr conceptualized the structure of the atom and later worked out (in the fourth phase) the ramifications and implications of his insight.

It would make sense for creative people to pay close attention to their dreams and to use them for problem-solving whenever possible. Because the REM state plays an important role in storing perceptual, cognitive, and behavioral memories (thus helping to build up one's "storehouses full of experiences"), it is a natural arena in which a creative inspiration may occur.

Paranormal Aspects of Dreaming

In primitive and ancient societies, dreams were typically thought to be the work of supernatural entities, appearing to mortals with messages of hope or despair. Some peoples believed that the soul left the physical body in sleep and wandered in a spirit world. It was generally believed that dreams could provide a glimpse of the future, reveal events happening at a distance, or indicate the thoughts of another person [MacKenzie, 1965].

The development of psychoanalysis caused the observation of the paranormal dream to move from the anecdotal to the clinical level. Ever since the early conjectures of Freud [1933] regarding the possibility of telepathic influence on dream content, reports have appeared in the psychiatric literature describing presumptively paranormal dreams occurring in the context of the psychotherapeutic situation [e.g., Ehrenwald, 1948]. Tribbe [1969] speculates as to the connection between paranormal dream content and the dreamer's typical material:

> An individual's basic dream pattern runs continuously during REM periods much like a hyper-sensitive videotape that is being simultaneously produced and projected in the "closed circuit" of the mind. . . . This basic videotape, like photographic paper, is so very sensitive that it will pick up a wide variety of materials, some wholly extraneous. . . . The juxtaposition of images may frequently seem a meaningless hodge-podge—and some of the items have no meaning of value for the dreamer. . . . The discomfort of the sleeper, his biological pressures of the moment, his sex drive, all may force the creation of "added" dream material. Also there are the sensory and the extrasensory items that are seemingly forced, unwanted, upon the dreamer; then, there are extrasensory items which the "self" seemingly wants and has gone questing for. . . .

With the development of psychophysiological techniques for the monitoring of dreams, it became possible to move from a clinical level of discussion and observation to an experimental level involving the investigation of paranormal dreams. In 1962, a dream laboratory was established at the Maimonides Medical Center, Brooklyn, N.Y., for the study of telepathy and dreams. Eight experiments have been completed, five of which yielded statistically significant results. These studies can be briefly summarized:

Experimental Series I. For this study, a total of 12 volunteer subjects spent one night each at the Dream Laboratory. Two staff members, one male and one female, alternated as agents or senders, attempting to influence the subjects' dreams by means of telepathy. Target pictures were famous art prints, randomly selected from a large number of prints once the subjects had gone to bed.[1] On the following morning, the subjects were asked to match their dream recall against the entire collection of target pictures, selecting that art print which most closely resembled their dreams. These matchings by the 12 subjects proved to be statistically significant, indicating the success of the agents in transmitting information about the art prints via extrasensory means. Three outside judges did the same type of matching using copies of the art prints and typed transcripts of the subjects' dreams. The judges' matchings were not statistically significant for all 12 subjects. However, the judges were able to match dreams and targets from the male agent's subjects significantly more accurately than they were able to match dreams and targets from the female agent's subjects, indicating that the male agent was the better sender. A fourth judge used a slightly different matching procedure and was able to match dreams and target pictures from all twelve subjects at a statistically significant level of accuracy [Ullman, Krippner, and Feldstein, 1966].

Experimental Series II. The most successful of the 12 subjects and the better of the two agents in the first study were selected for Series II. Following a seven-night study, the subject matched his dreams against the collection of art prints at a statistically significant level of accuracy. Three outside judges matched the dream transcripts and the target pictures at a level of statistical significance even higher than that attained by the subject. A fourth judge utilized a slightly different matching procedure, again producing highly significant results [Ullman, Krippner, and Feldstein, 1966].

Experimental Series III. Twelve different subjects and two agents were utilized in a 12-night study. Similar judging procedures were utilized but the results were not statistically significant [Krippner, 1969].

Experimental Series IV. The most successful of the 12 subjects and the better of the two agents in the third study were paired for Series

[1] When the subject was in bed, the agent selected a number from a book which contained thousands of numerals. Usually the agent opened the book randomly, pointed to a line of numerals, added each digit in the line, and kept adding the digits until he obtained a one-digit number. Each art print was in an opaque envelope. The agent counted down the stack of envelopes until he reached the number arrived at through the random selection procedure. The envelope was taken to the agent's room (usually about 100 feet from the room in which the subject was sleeping) and opened it. The agent attempted, during the course of the night, to influence the subject's dreams by concentrating on the art print. The agent never knew what the art print for the night would be until the subject was in bed. Random procedures of this type were necessary to eliminate any possible sensory communication between the agent and the subject.

IV. Similar judging procedures were utilized for this eight-night study but the results were not statistically significant [Krippner, 1969].

Experimental Series V. For this study, two groups of subjects were created—a hypnosis group and a non-hypnosis, "relaxed" group. There were eight subjects in each group. All 16 subjects produced waking imagery in the Dream Laboratory, produced imagery from a rest period in the Dream Laboratory, and kept dream diaries for a week at home. The main statistical evaluation was accomplished by three outside judges who matched the transcripts against the art prints. Neither group produced significant results for the waking imagery material. For the hypnosis group, however, imagery produced during the rest period corresponded to the target pictures at statistically significant levels; nighttime dreams did not yield significant results. For the non-hypnosis group the results were reversed; imagery produced during the rest period produced nonsignificant results, but the dream diaries yielded a statistically significant degree of correspondence when matched with the target pictures. It may be that hypnosis speeded up the process of telepathic processing in the case of the hypnosis group; possibly, for the non-hypnosis group, telepathic effects took longer to emerge [Krippner, 1968].

Experimental Series VI. Another successful subject from Series I was selected for this 16-night experimental study. Without the knowledge of the subject, an agent concentrated on a target during only eight of the experimental nights; for the other eight nights there was neither an agent nor a target. Neither experimental condition produced statistically significant results [Krippner, 1969].

Experimental Series VII. The subject and agent who worked together for Series II were again paired. For each night of this eight-night study, a randomly selected target picture was accompanied by a box of "multisensory" materials. For example, a target picture depicting an artist was accompanied by a canvas and paints so that the agent could spend part of the night "acting out" the artist's role. Three judges evaluated the correspondences between each dream transcript and each art print; the results of this study were highly significant. These data suggest that human action and motility reinforce the sleeping subject's contact with the agent and the visual target [Ullman and Krippner, 1969].

Experimental Series VIII. For this study, a subject was allowed to select his agent for each of the experimental nights. Every morning, following the all-night session, he spent two hours discussing his dreams with a psychoanalyst. This procedure enabled the exploration of the psychodynamics of the paranormal dream. This was an eight-night study; both the subject's ratings and those of an outside judge were statistically significant [Krippner, 1969].

Two attempts to replicate the Maimonides studies [Hall, 1967; Globus, *et al.*, 1968] have been published. In addition, a successful attempt to influence the waking hours of sleeping subjects by extrasensory means has been reported [Bleksley, 1963].

Conclusion

The importance of altered states of consciousness and their relation to human potential was stressed by William James, America's first psychologist of eminence. James [1902] wrote that

> our normal waking consciousness . . . is but one special type of consciousness, whilst all about it, parted from it by the filmiest of screens, there lie potential forms of consciousness entirely different. We may go through life without suspecting their existence; but apply the requisite stimulus, and at a touch they are there in all their completeness. . . . No account of the universe in its totality can be final which leaves these other forms of consciousness quite disregarded.

The psychophysiological study of the sleep-dream cycle has confirmed James' speculations because the importance of the REM state (a profound alteration in "normal" consciousness) has been frequently demonstrated during the last decade.

Dreaming appears to be an active, creative, integrating process rather than a reactive or compensatory event [Weiss, 1964]. It is true that dreams may reflect instinctoid pressures as well as elements from a traumatic past, a disturbing present, or a wished-for future. In doing so, however, these elements lose their isolated nature and combine with the evolutionary, developmental, programming, data processing, problem-solving, and even paranormal aspects of an event which becomes an integrated whole. Dreaming, to use Maslow's terms [1962], is a "growth phenomenon" rather than a "deficiency phenomenon."

Contemporary interest in the dreaming process appears to be part of a larger movement affecting a growing proportion of the population. For most of its history, the American nation has been absorbed in externals. Americans have devoted their energies to the settling of the continent, the fight for independence, the winning of the West, the utilization of nature resources, the development of technology, the manufacture of consumer goods, the establishment of the country as a world power, and the exploration of outer space. In recent years, these external events have failed to stimulate many Americans— especially a sizable portion of the country's youth—whose attention has started to turn inward. Large numbers of college students, high school students, members of intentional communities, and adults in various professional fields have taken a keen interest in the altered states of consciousness which accompany sensory overload, sensory deprivation, hyponosis, meditation, spiritual discipline, feedback training, psychedelic chemical experience, reverie, and dreaming.

Most of the tradition-directed institutions of American society have little use for introspection, internal events, and the inner life. The pursuit of these interests is often regarded as "unproductive," "nonachieving," and "narcissistic." On the other hand, those individuals who make a persistent, conscientious, disciplined attempt to cope with internal events typically report that the quest has assisted their capacity to perceive and understand the various levels of reality, to accept and enjoy the self, to behave spontaneously, to appreciate art and nature, to develop close interpersonal relationships, to work creatively—in other words, to become a more fully realized human being [Maslow, 1962].

The current interest in dreams and other forms of altered consciousness is a promising development for humanistically oriented psychology, psychiatry, religion, education, and other fields of endeavor which seek to produce what Aldous Huxley [1962] has called "full-blown human beings." As a larger number of professionals and nonprofessionals become involved in the inner life, the possibility grows that there is a new consciousness emerging in our time—a consciousness geared toward self-actualization and the full development of the human potential.

References

1. ADELSON, J. Creativity and the dream. Paper read at the annual convention of the American Psychological Association, 1957.
2. ADLER, A. *What Life Should Mean to You.* New York: Capricorn, 1958.
3. ALLISON, T., AND GOFF, W. R. Sleep in a primitive mammal, the spiny anteater (Abstract). *Psychophysiology* 5 (1968):200.
4. ARTEMIDOROUS. *Oneiroctitica.* London: Wood, 1644.
5. ASERINSKY, E., AND KLEITMAN, N. Regularly occurring periods of eye motility and concomitant phenomena during sleep. *Science* 118 (1953):273–74.
6. BERGER, R. J. The sleep and dream cycle. In A. Kales, ed. *Sleep: Physiology and Pathology.* Philadelphia: Lippincott, 1969.
7. BERTINI, M., LEWIS, H. B., AND WITKIN, H. A. Some preliminary observations with an experimental procedure for the study of hypnagogic and related phenomena. In C. Tart, ed. *Altered States of Consciousness.* New York: John Wiley & Sons, 1969.
8. BLEKSLEY, A. An experiment on long-distance ESP during sleep. *Journal of Parapsychology* 27 (1963):1–15.
9. BONIME, W. *The Clinical Use of Dreams.* New York: Basic Books, 1962.
10. CAILLOIS, R., ed. *The Dream Adventure.* New York: Orion Press, 1963.
11. DE BECKER, R. *The Understanding of Dreams and Their Influence on the History of Man.* New York: Hawthorn Books, 1968.
12. DEMENT, W. "The Physiology of Dreaming." Unpublished doctoral dissertation, University of Chicago, 1958.
13. DEMENT, W. Effect of dream deprivation. *Science* 131 (1960):1705–07.
14. DEWAN, E. M. The P (programming) hypothesis for REMS (Abstract). *Psychophysiology* 4 (1968):365.
15. EHRENWALD, J. *Telepathy and Medical Psychology.* New York: Norton, 1948.
16. EPHRON, H. S., AND CARRINGTON, P. Rapid eye movement sleep and cortical homeostasis. *Psychological Review* 73 (1966):500–26.
17. FEINBERG, I. Eye movement activity during sleep and intellectual function in mental retardation. *Science* 159 (1968):1256.
18. FOULKES, D. Theories of dream formation and recent studies of sleep consciousness. *Psychological Bulletin* 62 (1964):236–47.

19. FOULKES, D. *The Psychology of Sleep*. New York: Charles Scribner's Sons, 1966.
20. FREUD, S. *The Interpretation of Dreams*. New York: Basic Books, 1955.
21. FREUD, S. *New Introductory Lectures on Psychoanalysis*. New York: W. W. Norton, 1933.
22. FROMM, E. *The Forgotten Language*. New York: Grove Press, 1951.
23. GLOBUS, G., et al. An appraisal of telepathic communication in dreams (Abstract). *Psychophysiology* 4 (1968):365.
24. GREENBERG, R., AND DEWAN, E. M. Aphasia and rapid eye movement sleep. *Nature* 223 (1969):183–84.
25. HALL, C. *The Meaning of Dreams*, 2nd ed. New York: McGraw-Hill, 1966.
26. HALL, C. Experimente zur telepathischen beeinflussung von träumen. *Zeitschrift für Parapsychologie und Grenzgebiete der Psychologie* 10 (1967):18–47.
27. HALL, C., AND VAN DE CASTLE, R. *The Content Analysis of Dreams*. New York: Appleton-Century-Crofts, 1966.
28. HARTMANN, E. L. The D-state: A review and discussion of studies on the physiologic state concomitant with dreaming. *New England Journal of Medicine* 273 (1965):30–35, 87–92.
29. HARTMANN, E. L. The D-state: A review and discussion of studies on the physiological state concomitant with dreaming. *International Journal of Psychiatry* 2 (1966):11–31.
30. HUXLEY, A. *Island*. New York: Harper & Row, 1962.
31. JAMES, W. *The Varieties of Religious Experience*. New York: Longmans, 1902.
32. JOUVET, M. The states of sleep. *Scientific American* 216 (1967):62–72.
33. JUNG, C. G. *Psychology and Religion*. New Haven: Yale University Press, 1938.
34. KETTELKAMP, L. *Dreams*. New York: William Morrow, 1968.
35. KRIPPNER, S. The paranormal dream and man's pliable future. *Psychoanalytic Review* 56 (1969):28–43.
36. KRIPPNER, S. An experimental study in hypnosis and telepathy. *American Journal of Clinical Hypnosis* 11 (1968):45–54.
37. LUCRETIUS. *De rerum natura*. Cambridge, Mass.: Harvard University Press, 1924.
38. MacKENZIE, N. *Dreams and Dreaming*. New York: Vanguard, 1965.
39. MASLOW, A. H. *Toward a Psychology of Being*. Princeton: Van Nostrand, 1962.
40. PLATO. *The Republic*. New York: Random House, 1937.
41. PROGOFF, I. *The Symbolic and the Real*. New York: Julian Press, 1963.
42. RECHTSCHAFFEN, A., BASSAN, M., AND LEDECKY-JANECEK, S. Activity patterns in *Caiman Sclerops (Crocodilia)* (Abstract). *Psychophysiology* 5 (1968):201.
43. RECHTSCHAFFEN, A., AND VERDONE, P. Amount of dreaming; effect of incentive, adaptation to laboratory, and individual differences. *Perceptual and Motor Skills* 19 (1964):947–58.
44. ROBERT, W. *Der traum als naturnotwendigkeit enklart*. Hamburg: H. Seippel, 1886.
45. ROFFWARG, H. P., MUZIO, J. N., AND DEMENT, W. C. Ontogenetic development of the human sleep-dream cycle. *Science* 152 (1966):604–19.
46. SCHECHTER, N., SCHMEIDLER, G. R., AND STAAL, M. Dream reports and creative tendencies in students of the arts, sciences, and engineering. *Journal of Consulting Psychology* 29 (1965):415–21.
47. SNYDER, F. Toward an evolutionary theory of dreaming. *American Journal of Psychiatry* 123 (1966):121–36.
48. STEIGER, B. New discoveries about dreaming. *Saga*, June 1969.
49. STEWART, K. Dream theory in Malaya. In C. Tart, ed. *Altered States of Consciousness*. New York: John Wiley & Sons, 1969.

50. TAUBER, E. S., ROFFWARG, H. P., AND WEITZMAN, E. D. Eye movements and electroencephalogram activity during sleep in diurnal lizards. *Nature* 212 (1966):1612–13.

51. TAUBER, E. S., WEITZMAN, E. D., AND KOREY, S. R. Eye movements during behavioral inactivity in certain Bermuda reef fish. *Communications in Behavioral Biology* 3 (1969):131–35.

52. TRIBBE, F. C. Personal communication, August 1969.

53. TRILLIN, C. A third state of existence. *New Yorker.* September 18, 1965.

54. ULLMAN, M. Discussion (of F. A. Weiss' Dreaming—a creative process). *American Journal of Psychoanalysis* 24 (1964):10–12.

55. ULLMAN, M. The social roots of the dream. *American Journal of Psychoanalysis* 20 (1960):180–96.

56. ULLMAN, M. The dream scene. *Journal of the American Society of Psychosomatic Dentistry and Medicine* 16 (1969):4–6.

57. ULLMAN, M., KRIPPNER, S., AND FELDSTEIN, S. Experimentally induced telepathic dreams: Two studies using EEG-REM monitoring technique. *International Journal of Neuropsychiatry* 2 (1966):420–37.

58. ULLMAN, M., AND KRIPPNER, S. A laboratory approach to the nocturnal dimension of paranormal experience: Report of a confirmatory study using the REM monitoring technique. *Biological Psychiatry* 1 (1969):259–70.

59. WEISS, F. A. Dreaming—a creative process. *American Journal of Psychoanalysis* 24 (1964):1–10.

60. WELLS, E. F. Your dreams: important—or nonsense? *Success Unlimited,* April 1968.

PART 2
Motivation

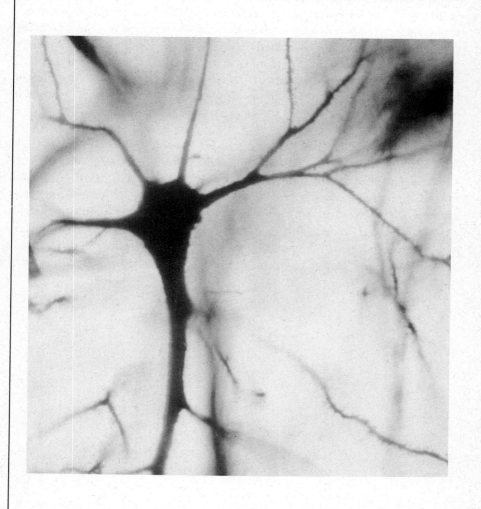

Why *a person behaves* is even more intriguing than what *he or she does.* *The why of human behavior is the stuff of motivational psychology.*

Two different themes run through the study of human motivation. The first relates to the disposition or orientation of the scholar. Whatever the reason—and this would be a fascinating study in itself—psychologists tend to align themselves with different schools of thought. The most prominent of these schools are Behaviorism, in which an objectively measurable "reinforcer" encourages an objectively observable response; Psychoanalysis, in which unconscious forces compel behavior; and Humanism, in which free choice guides behavior. No serious psychologist today would contend that any one of these schools has exclusive rights to truth, but different scholars for different reasons prefer different orientations. Some scholars even believe that each orientation has merit, and try to understand behavior from all three points of view!

The second theme relates to the kind of behavior studied. It is clear enough that we respond on a physical level to physical stimuli, on a personal level to psychological stimuli, and on a social level to social stimuli. But, again, the interesting fact is that each kind of behavior influences each other kind. For example, direct electrical stimulation of a certain area of the brain can control a person's level of anxiety; and, at the other end of the spectrum, the number of people around us can influence our responsiveness in emergency situations. The articles in this section will provide many more examples of this interplay.

Physical Control of the Mind

JOSÉ M. R. DELGADO

Particularly clear examples of one kind of physiological influence on human behavior come from J. M. R. Delgado's pioneering work in ESB, electrical stimulation of the brain. By means of tiny electrodes planted deep within the brain and activated by electrical impulses, Delgado—amid heated controversy—has demonstrated that direct physical stimulation occasions not only physical responses (reflex reactions), but psychological responses (anxiety, pleasure) and social responses (friendliness, talkativeness) as well. This excerpt from *Physical Control of the Mind* brings home the preeminent role of the brain in all arenas of human behavior.

HELL AND HEAVEN WITHIN THE BRAIN: THE SYSTEMS FOR PUNISHMENT AND REWARD

When man evolved above other powerful animals, the size and complexity of his brain increased, giving him superior intelligence along with more anguish, deeper sorrow, and greater sensitivity than any other living creature. Man also learned to enjoy beauty, to dream and to create, to love and to hate. In the education of children as well as in the training of animals, punishment and reward constitute the most powerful motivations for learning. In our hedonistic orientation of life to minimize pain and seek pleasure, we often attribute these qualities to the environment without realizing that sensations depend on a chain of events which culminates in the activation of determined intracerebral mechanisms. Physical damage, the loss of a beloved child, or apocalyptic disaster cannot make us suffer if some of our cerebral structures have been blocked by anesthesia. Pleasure is not in the skin being caressed or in a full stomach, but somewhere inside the cranial vault.

SOURCE: From pages 117–19 and 133–54 in *Physical Control of the Mind* by José M. R. Delgado. Copyright © 1969 by José M. R. Delgado. Reprinted by permission of Harper & Row, Publishers, Inc.

At the same time pain and pleasure have important psychic and cultural components related to individual history. Men inhibited by some extraordinary tribal or religious training to endure discomfort have been tortured to death without showing signs of suffering. It is also known that in the absence of physical injury, mental elaboration of information may produce the worst kind of suffering. Social rejection, guilt feelings, and other personal tragedies may produce greater autonomic, somatic, and psychological manifestations than actual physical pain.

There is strong reluctance to accept that such personal and refined interpretations of reality as being afraid and being in love are contingent on the membrane depolarization of determined clusters of neurons, but this is one aspect of emotional phenomena which should not be ignored. After frontal lobotomy, cancer patients have reported that the pain persisted undiminished, but that their subjective suffering was radically reduced, and they did not complain or request as much medication as before surgery. Lobotomized patients reacted to noxious stimuli as much, if not more, than before their operations, jumping at pinpricks and responding quickly to objective tests of excessive heat, but they showed decreased concern. It seems that in the frontal lobes there is a potentiating mechanism for the evaluation of personal suffering, and after lobotomy the initial sensation of pain is unmodified, while the reactive component to that feeling is greatly diminished. This mechanism is rather specific of the frontal lobes; bilateral destruction of the temporal lobes fails to modify personal suffering.

Important questions to resolve are: Do some cerebral structures have the specific role of analyzing determined types of sensations? Is the coding of information at the receptor level essential for the activation of these structures? Not too long ago, many scientists would have dismissed as naive the already demonstrated fact that punishment and reward can be induced at will by manipulating the controls of an electrical instrument connected to the brain.

Perception of Suffering

In textbooks and scientific papers, terms such as *pain receptors, pain fibers,* and *pain pathways* are frequently used, but it should be clarified that peripheral nerves do not carry sensations. Neuronal pathways transmit only patterns of electrical activity with a message that must be deciphered by the central nervous system, and in the absence of brain there is no pain, even if some reflex motor reactions may still be present. A decapitated frog cannot feel but will jump away with fairly good motor coordination when pinched in the hind legs. During competitive sports or on the battlefield, emotion and stress may temporarily block the feeling of pain in man, and often injuries are not immediately noticed. The cerebral interpretation of sensory signals is so decisive that the same stimulus may be considered pleasant or unpleasant depending on circumstances. A strong electrical shock on the feet scares a dog and inhibits its secretion of saliva. If, however, the same "painful" excitation is followed for several days by administration of food, the animal accepts the shock, wagging its tail happily and salivating in anticipation of the food reward. Some of these dogs have been trained to press a lever to trigger the electric shock which preceded food. During sexual relations in man, bites, scratches, and other potentially painful sensations are often interpreted as enjoyable, and some sexual deviates seek physical punishment as a source of pleasure.

The paradox is that while skin and viscera have plentiful nerve endings for sensory reception, the brain does not possess this type of innervation. In patients under local anesthesia, the cerebral tissue may be cut, burned, pulled apart, or frozen without causing any discomfort. This organ so insensitive to its own destruction is, however, the exquisite sensor of information received from the periphery. In higher animal species there is sensory differentiation involving specialized peripheral receptors which code external information into electrical impulses and internal analyzers which decode the circulating inputs in order to give rise to the perception of sensations. . . .

Anxiety, Fear, and Violence Evoked by ESB in Man

Anxiety has been considered the alpha and omega of psychiatry. It is one of the central themes of existential philosophy, and it shades the normal—and abnormal—life of most human beings. Several emotional states may be classified under the heading of anxiety, including fear, fright, panic, and terror, which are variations of the same basic experience. One of the most complex mental disturbances, unreasonable or excessive anxiety, including phobias and compulsive obsessions, often does not respond to standard therapies, and in some instances it has been improved by electrocoagulation of discrete areas of the frontal pole. Grey Walter [23] has claimed an 85 percent total social recovery in a group of sixty patients with anxiety and obsessions treated with carefully dosified coagulations made through electrodes implanted in the frontal lobes.

Without entering into semantic discussions, we may consider anxiety an emotional state of conscious or subconscious tension related to real or imaginary threats to psychological or physical individual integrity. A mild degree of anxiety may mobilize, while excessive degrees may paralyze somatic and mental activity. Beyond a certain limit, anxiety has unpleasant characteristics. In normal circumstances, it is produced, as is any other emotion, by sensory inputs from the environment and by recollections, both of which require mental elaboration of messages which may be influenced by humoral and neuronal factors. In addition, there is abundant evidence that anxiety and fear may be induced as either a primary or a secondary category of response by direct electrical stimulation of the brain. The perception or expectancy of pain can be frightening, and in some cases when ESB produced localized or generalized discomfort, patients have expressed concern about continuation of the exploratory procedures. In addition to the natural fear of possible further discomfort, there may have been a component of primary anxiety which would be difficult to evaluate.

Destruction of discrete parts of the thalamus produces relief from anxiety neurosis and obsessive-compulsive neurosis which is probably related to the interruption of tonic pathways to the frontal lobes. Stimulation of the thalamic nucleus, however, very seldom produces anxiety, and the reports of patients are limited to feelings of weakness, being different, dizziness, floating, and something like alcoholic intoxication [20].

Clearer demonstrations of direct induction of fear without any other accompanying sensations have been reported by several investigators. Lesions in the medial thalamus give effective pain relief with a minimal amount of sensory loss, and for this reason this area has often been explored electrically in cancer patients. In some cases it has produced acute anxiety attacks, which one patient vividly described as: "It's rather like the feeling of having just been missed by a car and leaped back to the curb and went B-r-r-r." Something in his guts felt very unpleasant, very unusual, and he certainly did not want to feel like that again [6]. The surprising fact is that the unpleasant sensation of fear was felt in one side of the body, contralateral to the brain stimulation. Sweet [21] has reported the case of a very intelligent patient, the dean of a graduate school, who after a unilateral sympathectomy to treat his upper limb hyperhydrosis, found that his previous and customary sensation of shivering while listening to a stirring passage of music occurred in only one side and he could not be thrilled in the sympathectomized half of his body. These cases were interesting because emotions are usually experienced in a rather diffuse and bilateral fashion unless innervation has been specifically interrupted.

The role of the thalamus in the integration of fear is also suggested by the study of a female patient whose spontaneous crippling attacks of anxiety of overwhelming intensity had led to several suicide attempts and a chronic state of depression and agitation quite refractory to drugs and psychotherapy. Stimulation of the dorsolateral nucleus of the thalamus evoked precisely the same type of attack at a level of symptomatology directly proportional to the applied intensity. It was possible to find the electrical threshold for a mild anxiety or to increase it to higher levels simply by turning the dial of the stimulator. "One could sit with one's hand on the knob and control the level of her anxiety" [6].

In one of our female patients, stimulation of a similar area in the thalamus induced a typical fearful expression and she turned to either side, visually exploring the room behind her. When asked what she was doing, she replied that she felt a threat and thought that something horrible was going to happen. This fearful sensation was perceived as real, and she had a premonition of imminent disaster of unknown cause. The effect was reliable on different days and was not altered by the use of lights and a movie camera to document the finding. Her motor activity and choice of words varied according to the environmental setting, but her facial expression and acute sensation of non-specific, unexplainable, but real fear were similar following different stimulations. The response started with a delay of less than one second, lasted for as long as the stimulation, and did not leave observable aftereffects. The patient remembered her fear but was not upset by the memory.

Some patients have displayed anxiety and restlessness when the pallidum was stimulated at frequencies above 8 cycles per second, and they also perceived a constriction or warmth in the chest [12]. A few reported a "vital anxiety in the left chest," and screamed anxiously if the stimulation was repeated. Intense emotional reactions have been evoked by stimulation of the amygdaloid nucleus, but responses varied in the same patient even with the same parameters of stimulation. The effect was sometimes rage, sometimes fear. One patient explained, "I don't know what came over me. I felt like an animal" [10].

The sensation of fear without any concomitant pain has also been observed as a result of ESB of the temporal lobe [22]. This effect may be classified as "illusion of fear" [18] because there was obviously no real reason to be afraid apart from the artificial electrical activation of some cerebral structures. In every case, however, fear is a cerebral interpretation of reality which depends on a variety of cultural and experiential factors with logical or illogical reasons. The fact that it can be aroused by stimulation of a few areas of the brain allows the exploration of the neuronal mechanisms of anxiety, and as a working hypothesis we may suppose that the emotional qualities of fear depend on the activation of determined structures located probably in the thalamus, amygdala, and a few other as yet unidentified nuclei. This activation usually depends on the symbolic evaluation of coded sensory inputs, but the threshold for this activation may be modified—and also reached—by direct application of ESB. Knowledge of intracerebral mechanisms of anxiety and fear will permit the establishment of a more rational pharmacological and psychiatric treatment of many suffering patients, and may also help us to understand and ameliorate the increasing level of anxiety in our civilization.

It is also known that in some tragic cases, abnormal neurological processes may be the causal factor for unreasonable and uncontrollable violence. Those afflicted may often hurt or even kill either strangers or close family members usually treated with affection. A typical example was J. P., a charming and attractive 20-year-old girl with a history of encephalitis at the age of eighteen months and many crises of temporal lobe seizures and grand mal attacks for the last ten years [4]. Her main social problem was the frequent and unpredictable occurrence of rage which on more than a dozen occasions resulted in an assault on another person such as inserting a knife into a stranger's myocardium or a pair of scissors into the pleural cavity of a nurse. The patient was committed to a ward for the criminally insane, and electrodes were implanted in her amygdala and hippocampus for exploration of possible neurological abnormalities. As she was rather impulsive, confinement in the EEG recording room was impractical, and she became one of the first clinical cases instrumented with a stimoceiver, which made it possible to study intracerebral activity without restraint. Depth recordings taken while the patient moved freely around the ward demonstrated marked electrical abnormalities in both amygdala and hippocampus. Spontaneous periods of aimless walking coincided with an increase in the number of high-voltage sharp waves. At other times, the patient's speech was spontaneously inhibited for several minutes during which she could not answer any questions although she retained partial comprehension and awareness. These periods coincided with bursts of spike activity localized to the optic radiation. Transitory emotional excitement was related with an increase in the number and duration of 16-cycles-per-second bursts; but the patient read papers, conversed with other people, and walked around without causing any noticeable alterations in the telemetered intracerebral electrical activity.

During depth explorations, it was demonstrated that crises of assaultive behavior similar to the patient's spontaneous bursts of anger could be elicited by radio stimulation of contact 3 in the right amygdala. A 1.2 milliampere excitation of this point was applied while she was playing the guitar and singing with enthusiasm and skill. At the seventh second of stimulation, she threw away the guitar and in a fit of rage launched an attack against the wall and then paced around the floor for several minutes, after which she gradually quieted down and resumed her usual cheerful behavior. This effect was repeated on two different days. The fact that only the contact located in the amygdala induced rage suggested that the neuronal field around contact 3 was involved in the patient's behavior problem, and this finding was of great clinical significance in the orientation of subsequent treatment by local coagulation.

The demonstration that amygdaloid stimulation may induce violent behavior has also been provided by other investigators. King [13] has described the case of a woman with feelings of depression and alienation, with an extremely flat tone of voice and a facial expression which was blank and unchanging during interviews, who upon stimulation of the amygdala with 5 milliamperes had greatly altered vocal inflections and an angry expression. During this time she said, "I feel like I want to get up from this chair! Please don't let me do it! Don't do this to me. I don't want to be mean!" When the interviewer asked if she would like to hit him, the patient answered, "Yeah, I want to hit something. I want to get something and just tear it up. Take it so I won't!" She then handed her scarf to the interviewer who gave her a stack of paper, and without any other verbal exchange, she tore it into shreds saying, "I don't like to feel like this." When the level of stimulation was reduced to 4 milliamperes, her attitude changed to a broad smile, and she explained, "I know it's silly, what I'm doing. I wanted to get up from this chair and run. I wanted to hit something, tear up something—anything. Not you, just anything. I just wanted to get up and tear. I had no control of myself." An increase in intensity up to 5 milliamperes again resulted in similar aggressive manifestations, and she raised her arm as if to strike.

It is notable that although the patients seemed to be out of control in these two instances of electrically induced aggression, they did not attack the interviewer, indicating that they were aware of their social situation. This finding is reminiscent of the behavior of stimulated monkeys who directed their aggressiveness according to previous experience and social rank and did not dare to challenge the authority of well-established bosses. Apparently ESB can induce a state of increased violent reactivity which is expressed in accordance with individual structure and environmental circumstances. We may conclude therefore that artificially evoked emotional change is only one more factor in the constellation of behavioral determinants.

Pleasurable Excitation of the Animal Brain

It is surprising that in science as well as in literature more attention has been paid to suffering than to happiness. The central theme of most novels is tragedy, while happy books are hard to find; excellent monographs have been published about pain, but similar studies of pleasure are nonexistent. Typically, in the monumental *Handbook of the American Physiological Society* [7], a full chapter is devoted to pain, and pleasure is not even listed in the general subject index. Evidently the pursuit of happiness has not aroused as much scientific interest as the fear of pain.

In psychological literature the study of reward is well represented, but even there it has been considered a second-rate sensation and perhaps an artifact of a diminuation of pain. It has been postulated that a truly "pleasant" sensation could not exist because organisms have a continuous tendency to minimize incoming stimuli. Pleasure was thus considered a subjective name for the diminution of drive, the withdrawal of a strong stimulation, or the reduction of pain. This "pain reduction" theory [15] has been fruitful as a basis for psychological investigations, but it is gloomy to think that we live in a world of punishment in which the only reality is suffering and that our brain can perceive different degrees of pain but no real pleasure.

Interest in the earlier ideas of hedonism has been renewed by recent experimental studies. According to this theory, pain and pleasure are relatively independent sensations and can be evoked by different types of stimuli which are recognized by separate cerebral mechanisms. Behavior is considered to be motivated by stimuli which the organism tries to minimize (pain) or by stimuli which the organism tries to maximize (pleasure). The brain is thought to have different systems for the reception of these two kinds of inputs, and the psychological state of pleasure or reward can be determined not only by the termination of pain but also by the onset of primary pleasure. The discovery of two anatomically distinct mechanisms in the brain, one for punishment, as mentioned earlier, and one for reward, provides a physiological basis for the dualistic motivation postulated in hedonism [5, 17].

The surprising fact is that animals of different species, including rats, cats, and monkeys, have voluntarily chosen to press a lever which provides electrical stimulation of specific cerebral areas. The demonstrations are highly convincing because animals which initially pressed a lever to obtain the reward of sugar pellets later pressed at similar or higher rates when electrical stimulation was substituted for food. These experiments showed conclusively that the animals enjoyed the electrical impulses which were delivered only at their own demand. Watching a rat or monkey stimulate its own brain is a fascinating spectacle. Usually each lever pressing triggers a brief 0.5- to 1.0-second brain stimulation which can be more rewarding than food. In a choice situation, hungry rats ran faster to reach the self-stimulation lever than to obtain pellets, and they persistently pressed this lever, ignoring food within easy reach. Rats have removed obstacles, run mazes, and even crossed electrified floors to reach the lever that provided cerebral stimulation.

Not all areas of the brain involved in pleasurable effects appear equally responsive. The highest lever-pressing rates (of up to a remarkable 5,000 times per hour) were recorded by animals self-stimulating in the posterior hypothalamus; excitation of rhinencephalic structures (of only about 200 times per hour) was considered moderately rewarding; and in sensory or motor areas, animals self-stimulated at merely a chance level (of 10 to 25 times per hour), and these areas were classified as neutral. As should be expected, when stimulation was shifted from rewarding areas to nuclei in the punishment system in the same animals, they pressed the lever once and never went back, showing that in the brain of the same animal there were two different groups of structures, one rewarding and the other aversive.

A systematic analysis of the neuroanatomical distribution of pleasurable areas in the rat [16] shows that 60 per cent of the brain is neutral, 35 per cent is rewarding, and only 5 per cent may elicit punishing effects. The idea that far more brain is involved in pleasure than in suffering is rather optimistic and gives hope that this predominance of the potential for pleasurable sensations can be developed into a more effective behavioral reality.

Because of the lack of verbal communication with animals, any ideas about what kind of pleasure, if any, may be experienced during ESB is a matter of speculation. There are some indications, however, that the perceived sensations could be related to anatomical differentiation of primary rewards of food and sex, because hungry animals self-stimulated at a higher rate in the middle hypothalamus, while administration of sexual hormones to castrated rats increased their lever pressing of more lateral hypothalamic points.

The controversial issue of how these findings in animals may relate to human behavior and the possible existence of areas involved in pleasure in the human brain has been resolved by the information obtained in patients with implanted electrodes.

Human Pleasure Evoked by ESB

On the basis of many studies during cerebral surgery, Penfield [18] has said of anger, joy, pleasure, and sexual excitement in the human brain that "so far as our experience goes, neither localized epileptic discharge nor electrical stimulation is capable of awakening any such emotion. One is tempted to believe that there are no specific cortical mechanisms associated with these emotions." This statement still holds true for the cerebral cortex, but studies in human subjects with implanted electrodes have demonstrated that electrical stimulation of the depth of the brain can induce pleasurable manifestations, as evidenced by the spontaneous verbal reports of patients, their facial expression and general behavior, and their desire to repeat the experience. In a group of twenty-three patients suffering from schizophrenia [8], electrical stimulation of the septal region, located deep in the frontal lobes, produced an enhancement of alertness sometimes accompanied by an increase in verbal output, euphoria, or pleasure. In a more systematic study in another group of patients, further evidence was presented of the rewarding effects of septal stimulation [1, 9]. One man suffering from narcolepsy was provided with a small stimulator and a built-in counter which recorded the number of times that he voluntarily stimulated each of several selected points in his brain during a period of seventeen weeks. The highest score was recorded from one point in the septal region, and the patient declared that pushing this particular button made him feel "good" as if he were building up to a sexual orgasm, although he was not able to reach the end point and often felt impatient and anxious. His narcolepsy was greatly relieved by pressing this "septal button." Another patient with psychomotor epilepsy also enjoyed septal self-stimulation, which again had the highest rate of button pressing and often induced sexual thoughts. Activation of the septal region by direct injection of acetylcholine produced local electrical changes in two epileptic patients and a shift in mood from disphoria to contentment and euphoria, usually with concomitant sexual motivation and some "orgastic sensations."

Further information was provided by another group of sixty-five patients suffering from schizophrenia or Parkinson's disease, in whom a total of 643 contacts were implanted, mainly in the anterior part of the brain [19]. Results of ESB were grouped as follows: 360 points were "Positive I," and with stimulation "the patients became relaxed, at ease, had a feeling of well-being, and/or were a little sleepy." Another 31 points were "Positive II," and "the patients were definitely changed . . . in a good mood, felt good. They were relaxed, at ease, and enjoyed themselves, frequently smiling. There was a slight euphoria, but the behavior was adequate." They sometimes wanted more stimulations. Excitation of another eight points evoked behavior classified as "Positive III," when "the euphoria was definitely beyond normal limits. The patients laughed out loud, enjoyed themselves, and positively liked the stimulation, and wanted more." ESB of another 38 points gave ambivalent results, and the patients expressed occasional pleasure or displeasure following excitation of the same area. From three other points, responses were termed "orgasm" because the patients initially expressed enjoyment and then suddenly were completely satisfied and did not want any more stimulation for a variable period of time. Finally, from about two hundred other points, ESB produced unpleasant reactions including anxiety, sadness, depression, fear, and emotional outbursts. One of the moving pictures taken in this study was very demonstrative, showing a patient with a sad expression and slightly depressed mood who smiled when a brief stimulation was applied to the rostral part of the brain, returning quickly to his usual depressed state, to smile again as soon as stimulation was reapplied. Then a ten-second stimulation completely changed his behavior and facial expression into a lasting pleasant and happy mood. Some mental patients have been provided with portable stimulators which they have used in a self-treatment of depressive states with apparent clinical success.

These results indicate the need for careful functional exploration during brain surgery in order to avoid excessive euphoria or depression when positive or negative reinforcing areas are damaged. Emotional instability, in which the subject bursts suddenly into tears or laughter without any apparent reason, has been observed following some neurosurgical interventions. These major behavior problems might have been avoided by sparing the region involved in emotional regulation.

In our own experience, pleasurable sensations were observed in three patients with psychomotor epilepsy [2, 3, 11]. The first case was V.P., a 36-year-old female with a long history of epileptic attacks which could not be controlled by medication. Electrodes were implanted in her right temporal lobe and upon stimulation of a contact located in the superior part about thirty millimeters below the surface, the patient reported a pleasant tingling sensation in the left side of her body "from my face down to the bottom of my legs." She started giggling and making funny comments, stating that she enjoyed the sensation "very much." Repetition of these stimulations made the patient more communicative and flirtatious, and she ended by openly expressing her desire to marry the therapist. Stimulation of other cerebral points failed to modify her mood and indicated the specificity of the evoked effect. During control interviews before and after ESB, her behavior was quite proper, without familiarity or excessive friendliness.

The second patient was J.M., an attractive, cooperative, and intelligent 30-year-old female who had suffered for eleven years from psychomotor and grand mal attacks which resisted medical therapy. Electrodes were implanted in her right temporal lobe, and stimulation of one of the points in the amygdala induced a pleasant sensation of relaxation and considerably increased her verbal output, which took on a more intimate character. This patient openly expressed her fondness for the therapist (who was new to her), kissed his hands, and talked about her immense gratitude for what was being done for her. A similar increase in verbal and emotional expression was repeated when the same point was stimulated on a different day, but it did not appear when other areas of the brain were explored. During control situations the patient was rather reserved and poised.

The third case was A.F., an 11-year-old boy with severe psychomotor epilepsy. Six days after electrode implantation in both temporal lobes, his fourth tape-recorded interview was carried out while electrical activity of the brain was continuously recorded and 5-second stimulations were applied in a prearranged sequence at intervals of about four minutes. The interviewer maintained an air of friendly interest throughout, usually without initiating conversation. After six other excitations, point LP located on the surface of the left temporal lobe was stimulated for the first time, and there was an open and precipitous declaration of pleasure. The patient had been silent for the previous five-minute interval, but immediately after this stimulation he exclaimed, "Hey! You can keep me here longer when you give me these; I like those." He went on to insist that the ongoing brain tests made him feel good. Similar statements with an emphatic expression of "feeling good" followed eight of a total sixteen stimulations of this point during the ninety-minute interview. Several of these manifestations were accompanied by a statement of fondness for the male interviewer, and the last one was accompanied by a voluptuous stretch. None of these manifestations appeared during the control prestimulation period of twenty-six minutes or during the twenty-two minutes when other points were excited. Statistical analysis of the difference between the frequency of pleasurable expressions before and after onset of stimulations proved that results were highly significant ($P < 0.001$).

The open expressions of pleasure in this interview and the general passivity of behavior could be linked, more or less intuitively, to feminine strivings. It was therefore remarkable that in the next interview, performed in a similar manner, the patient's expressions of confusion about his own sexual identity again appeared following stimulation of point LP. He suddenly began to discuss his desire to get married, but when asked, "To whom?" he did not immediately reply. Following stimulation of another point and a one-minute, twenty-second silence, the patient said, "I was thinking—there's—I was saying *this* to you. How to spell 'yes'—y-e-s. I mean y-o-s. No! 'You' ain't y-e-o. It's this. *Y-o-u.*" The topic was then completely dropped. The monitor who was listening from the next room interpreted this as a thinly veiled wish to marry the interviewer, and it was decided to stimulate the same site again after the prearranged schedule had been completed. During the following forty minutes, seven other points were stimulated, and the patient spoke about several topics of a completely different and unrelated content. Then LP was stimulated again, and the patient started making references to the facial hair of the interviewer and continued by mentioning pubic hair and his having been the object of genital sex play in the past. He then expressed doubt about his sexual identity, saying, "I was thinkin' if I was a boy or a girl—which one I'd like to be." Following another excitation he remarked with evident pleasure: "You're doin' it now," and then he said, "I'd like to be a girl."

In the interpretation of these results it is necessary to consider the psychological context in which electrical stimulation occurs, because the personality configuration of the subject, including both current psychodynamic and psychogenetic aspects, may be an essential determinant of the results of stimulation. Expression of feminine strivings in our patient probably was not the exclusive effect of ESB but the expression of already present personality factors which were activated by the stimulation. The balance between drive and defense may be modified by ESB, as suggested by the fact that after one stimulation the patient said without apparent anxiety, "I'd like to be a girl," but when this idea was presented to him by the therapist in a later interview without stimulation, the patient became markedly anxious and defensive. Minute-to-minute changes in personality function, influenced by the environment and by patient-interviewer relations, may modify the nature of specific responses, and these variables, which are difficult to assess, must be kept in mind.

Friendliness and Increased Conversation Under Electrical Control

Human relations evolve between the two opposite poles of love and hate which are determined by a highly complex and little understood combination of elements including basic drives, cultural imprinting, and refined emotional and intellectual characteristics. This subject has so many semantic and conceptual problems that few investigators have dared to approach it experimentally, and in spite of its essential importance, most textbooks of psychology evade its discussion. To define friendliness is difficult although its identification in typical cases is easy, and in our daily life we are continuously evaluating and classifying personal contacts as friendly or hostile. A smiling face, attentive eyes, a receptive hand, related body posture, intellectual interest, ideological agreement, kind words, sympathetic comments, and expressions of personal acceptance are among the common indicators of cordial interpersonal relations. The expression of friendship is a part of social behavior which obviously requires contact between two or more individuals. A mutually pleasurable relation creates a history and provides each individual with a variety of optic, acoustic, tactile, and other stimuli which are received and interpreted with a "friendly bias." The main characteristic of love and friendship is precisely that stimuli coming from a favored person are interpreted as more agreeable than similar stimuli originating from other sources, and this evaluation is necessarily related to neuronal activity.

Little is known about the cerebral mechanisms of friendliness, but as is the case for any behavorial manifestation, no emotional state is possible without a functioning brain, and it may be postulated that some cerebral structures are dispensable and others indispensable both for the interpretation of sensory inputs as amicable and for the expression of friendship. Strong support for this idea derives from the fact, repeatedly proved in neurosurgery, that destruction of some parts of the brain, such as the motor and sensory cortices, produces motor deficits without modifying affective behavior, while ablation of the frontal lobes may induce considerable alteration of emotional personality. Further support has been provided by electrical stimulation of the frontal lobes, which may induce friendly manifestations.

In patient A. F., mentioned earlier in connection with pleasurable manifestations, the third interview was characterized by changes in the character and degree of verbal output following stimulation of one point in the temporal cortex. Fourteen stimulations were applied, seven of them through point RP located in the inferolateral part of the right frontal lobe cortex, and the other seven through contacts located on the cortex of the right temporal lobe and depth of the left and right temporal lobes. The interview started with about five minutes of lively conversation, and during the next ten minutes the patient gradually quieted down until he spoke only about five seconds during every subsequent two-minute period. Throughout the interview the therapist encouraged spontaneous expression by reacting compassionately, by joking with, urging, and reassuring the patient, and by responding to any information offered. The attitude never produced more than a simple reply and often not even that.

In contrast to this basic situation, there were six instances of sharp increase in verbal communication and its friendly content. Each of these instances followed within forty seconds after stimulation of point RP. The only exception was the last excitation of this point when the voltage had been changed. The increases in verbal activity were rapid but brief and without any consistency in subject material, which was typical for the patient. Qualification and quantification of the patient's conversation was made by analyzing the recorded typescript which was divided into two-minute periods and judged independently by two investigators who had no knowledge of the timing or location of stimulations. Comparison of the two-minute periods before and after these stimulations revealed a verbal increase from seventeen to eighty-eight words and a greater number of friendly remarks, from six to fifty-three. These results were highly significant and their specificity was clear because no changes in verbalization were produced by stimulation of any of the other cerebral points. It was also evident that the evoked changes were not related to the interviewer's rather constant verbal activity. It was therefore concluded that the impressive increase in verbal expression and friendly remarks was the result of electrical stimulation of a specific point on the cortex of the temporal lobe.

HALLUCINATIONS, RECOLLECTIONS, AND ILLUSIONS IN MAN

Hallucinations may be defined as false perceptions in the absence of peripheral sensory stimulation, and they probably depend on two processes: (1) the recollection of stored information and (2) its false interpretation as an extrinsic experience entering through sensory inputs. Very little is known about the cerebral mechanisms responsible for these phenomena, but apparently the frontotemporal region of the brain is somehow involved because its electrical stimulation may evoke hallucinations.

In some patients electrical stimulation of the exposed temporal lobe has produced the perception of music. Occasionally it was a determined tune which could be recognized and hummed by the subject, and in some cases it was as if a radio or record were being played in the operating room. The sound did not seem to be a recollection but resembled an actual experience in which instruments of an orchestra or words of a song were heard [18]. These artificially induced hallucinations were not static but unfolded slowly while the electrode was held in place. A song was heard from beginning to end and not all at once; in a dream, familiar places were seen and well-known people spoke and acted.

Like spontaneous memories, the recollections induced by ESB could bring back the emotions felt at the time of the original experience, suggesting that neuronal mechanisms keep an integrated record of the past, including all the sensory inputs (visual, auditory, proprioceptive, etc.) and also the emotional significance of events. Electrical stimulation activated only one memory without reawakening any of the other records which must be stored in close proximity. This fact suggests the existence of cerebral mechanisms of reciprocal inhibition which allow the orderly recall of specific patterns of memory without a flood of unmanageable amounts of stored information. In no case has brain stimulation produced two psychical experiences at the same time, and the responses have been on an all-or-nothing basis.

In one of our patients, complex sensory hallucinations were evoked on different days when the depth of the tip of the left temporal lobe was electrically stimulated. The patient said, "You know, I just felt funny, just now. . . . Right then all of a sudden somethin' else came to me—these people—the way this person talked. This married couple—as though the fellow came into my mind—as though like he was saying somethin' like oh my mind drifted for a minute—to somethin' foolish. . . . It seemed like he was coming out with some word—sayin' some word silly."

The fact that stimulation of the temporal lobe can induce complex hallucinations may be considered well established, and this type of research represents a significant interaction between neurophysiology and psychoanalysis [14]. The mechanism of the evoked hallucinations, however, is far from clear, and it is difficult to know whether the experiences are new creations based on the recombination of items from memory storage and thus equivalent to psychotic hallucinations, or if the experiences are simply an exact playback of the past.

In either case, the applied electricity is not "creating" a new phenomenon but is triggering the orderly appearance at the conscious level of materials from the past, mixed in some cases with present perceptions. The order in the stream of perceived information is perhaps one of the most interesting qualities of this behavior because it indicates something about the mechanisms for storage of information in the brain. Memory does not seem to be preserved as single items but as interrelated collections of events, like the pearls on a string, and by pulling any pearl we have access to the whole series in perfect order. If memory were organized in this way, it would be similar to the strings of amino acids forming molecules of proteins and carrying genetic messages. Electrical stimulation may increase general neuronal excitability; and the memory traces which at this moment have a lower threshold may consequently be reactivated, reaching the perceptual level and forming the content of the hallucinatory experience while exerting a reciprocal inhibitory influence upon other traces. The excitability of individual traces may be modified by environmental factors and especially by the ideological content of the patient's thoughts prior to stimulation. Thus electrical excitation of the same point may produce a series of thematically related hallucinatory experiences with different specific details, as was the case in the patients that we have investigated.

All sensory inputs suffer distortion during the normal process of personal interpretation, which is determined to a great extent by past experience and depends heavily on cultural factors. A baby looking at the moon may extend his arms in an attempt to catch it without realizing the remoteness of celestial bodies. By comparing past and present experiences, we learn to evaluate distance, size, intensity, and other qualities of inputs. The mechanisms for these evaluations do not seem to be genetically determined and are related to neuronal activity which may be influenced by direct stimulation of the brain. We must remember that our only way to be in touch with external reality is by transducing physical and chemical events of the surroundings into electrical and chemical sequences at the sensory receptor level. The brain is not in touch with the environmental reality but with its symbolic code transmitted by neuronal pathways. Within this frame of personal distortion, our lives evolve within a range of "normality." Beyond this range, the distortion of perceptions qualifies as illusion. Illusions occur in a wide variety of regressed mental states, during moments of keen anticipation, and as a primary manifestation in some epileptic discharges. An hallucination is a false perception in the absence of sensory inputs, while an illusion requires an external sensory source which is misinterpreted by the individual. This distinction is convenient, and it will be observed in our discussion, although in practice the terms often overlap.

The following phenomena have been observed in patients:

1. Illusions (visual, auditory, labyrinthine, memory or déjà vu, sensation of remoteness or unreality).
2. Emotions (loneliness, fear, sadness).
3. Psychical hallucinations (vivid memory or a dream as complex as life experience itself).
4. Forced thinking (stereotyped thoughts crowding into the mind).

The first three groups of phenomena have been induced by different intracerebral stimulations. The most commonly reported effect has been the illusion of familiarity or déjà vu, which is characterized by surprise, interruption of conversation, and immediate spontaneous reporting that something unusual had just happened. For example, after a stimulation in the inferolateral part of the frontal lobe, one patient began to reply to the interviewer's question but suddenly stopped and said, "I was thinkin'—it felt like someone else was asking me that before." Occasionally a previously initiated statement would be completed, but there was always an overt desire to express the perceived experience. The effect was clearly felt as intrusive although not disturbing. After several of these experiences, the patient recognized the special quality of the phenomena and said, for example, "Hey—I had another strike. I have a feeling that someone once told me that before." The reliability of the response was remarkable, as was the consistency of its reporting, which was spontaneous and in most cases unsolicited. Each instance consisted usually of a reference to a remark made by the patient or the observer just before or during the moment of stimulation. The ideational content of the déjà vu was therefore dissimilar following each stimulation, but it always referred to the theme of the ongoing conversation. The common feature was the sensation, expressed by the patient, that the words, ideas, or situation were similar to a previous experience. There was no new perception, only the interpretation of a novel input as one already known and familiar. There was no anxiety or fear in the perception of these illusions, and the apparent effect was one of interested surprise with a rather pleasant, amusing quality which made the patient more alert and communicative. He was eager to report that something similar had happened before, and the word "before" was used in reporting most of these incidents. No lasting traces could be detected, and after the sensation of familiarity had been expressed, the patient's behavior continued in the same vein as before stimulation.

Knowledge of the cerebral mechanisms of psychic activities is so elemental that it would not be wise to speculate about the neuronal causality of illusions of familiarity. However, the fact that they may be elicited with reliability indicates the probable existence of interpretive functions in a determined area of the brain and opens the way for further experimental studies of how sensory inputs are processed by the individual. Penfield supposes that the cortex of the temporal lobe has a ganglionic mechanism which is utilized in the personal assessment of experiential reality regarding distance, sound, sight, intensity, strangeness, or familiarity of sensory inputs. This mechanism would be relatively independent from the mechanism utilized in the recording of contemporary experience and could be affected by epileptic abnormality or by direct brain stimulation. If we accept this hypothesis, we may assume that artificial influencing of electrical and chemical neuronal physiology could play a decisive role in the interpretation of reality with some independence from past experience and personal structure.

References

1. BISHOP, M. P., ELDER S. T., AND HEATH, R. G. Intracranial self-stimulation in man. *Science* 140 (1963):394–96.
2. DELGADO, J .M. R. Emotional behavior in animals and humans. *Psychiat. Res. Rep.* 12 (1960):259–71.
3. DELGADO, J. M. R., AND HAMLIN, H. Spontaneous and evoked electrical seizures in animals and in humans. In Estelle R. Ramey and Desmond S. O'Doherty, eds.

Electrical Studies on the Unanesthetized Brain. New York: Paul B. Hoeber, 1960, pp. 133–58.

4. DELGADO, J. M. R.; MARK, V.; SWEET, W.; ERVIN, F.; WEISS, G.; BACH-Y-RITA, G.; AND HAGIWARA, R. Intracerebral radio stimulation and recording in completely free patients. *J. Nerv. Ment. Dis.* 147 (1968):329–40.

5. DELGADO, J. M. R., ROBERTS, W. W., AND MILLER, N. E. Learning motivated by electrical stimulation of the brain. *Amer. J. Physiol.* 179 (1954):587–93.

6. ERVIN, F. Participant in "Brain Stimulation in Behaving Subjects." Neurosciences Research Program Workshop. December 1966.

7. FIELD, J., MAGOUN, H. W., AND HALL, W. E., eds. *Handbook of Physiology.* Section 1: *Neurophysiology.* Washington, D. C.: American Physiology Society, Vol. 1, 1959; Vols. 2 and 3, 1960.

8. HEATH, R. G. *Studies in Schizophrenia. A Multidisciplinary Approach to Mind-Brain Relationships.* Cambridge: Harvard University Press, 1954.

9. HEATH, R. G. Electrical self-stimulation of the brain in man. *Amer. J. Psychiat.* 120 (1963):571–77.

10. HEATH, R. G., MONROE, R. R., AND MICKLE, W. Stimulation of the amygdaloid nucleus in a schizophrenic patient. *Amer. J. Psychiat.* 111 (1955):862–63.

11. HIGGINS, J. W.; MAHL, G. F.; DELGADO, J. M. R.; AND HAMLIN, H. Behavioral changes during intracerebral electrical stimulation. *Arch. Neurol. Psychiat.* (Chicago) 76 (1956):399–419.

12. JUNG, R., AND HASSLER, R. The extrapyramidal motor system. In J. Field, H. W. Magoun, and V. E. Hall, eds. *Handbook of Physiology,* Section 1: *Neurophysiology,* Vol. 2. Baltimore, Md.: Williams & Wilkins Co., 1960, pp. 863–927.

13. KING, H. E. Psychological effects of excitation in the limbic system. In D. E. Sheer, ed. *Electrical Stimulation of the Brain.* Austin: University of Texas Press, 1961, pp. 477–86.

14. KUBIE, L. Some implications for psychoanalysis of modern concepts of the organization of the brain. *Psychoanalyt. Quart.* 22 (1953):21–68.

15. MILLER, N. E. *Learnable drives and rewards.* In S. S. Stevens, ed. *Handbook of Experimental Psychology.* New York: John Wiley & Sons, 1951, pp. 435–72.

16. OLDS, J. Hypothalamic substrates of reward. *Physiol. Rev.* 42 (1962):554–604.

17. OLDS, J., AND MILNER, P. Positive reinforcement produced by electrical stimulation of the septal area and other regions of the rat brain. *J. Comp. Physiol. Psychol.* 47 (1954):419–28.

18. PENFIELD, W., AND JASPER, H. *Epilepsy and the Functional Anatomy of the Human Brain.* Boston: Little, Brown, 1954.

19. SEM-JACOBSEN, C. W. *Depth-Electrographic Stimulation of the Human Brain and Behavior: From Fourteen Years of Studies and Treatment of Parkinson's Disease and Mental Disorders with Implanted Electrodes.* Springfield, Ill.: Charles C Thomas, 1968.

20. SPIEGEL, E. A., AND WYCIS, H. T. Stimulation of the brain stem and basal ganglia in man. In D. E. Sheer, ed. *Electrical Stimulation of the Brain.* Austin: University of Texas Press, 1961, pp. 487–97.

21. SWEET, W. H. Participant in "Brain Stimulation in Behaving Subjects." Neurosciences Research Program Workshop. December 1966.

22. VAN BUREN, J. M. Sensory, motor and autonomic effects of mesial temporal stimulation in man. *J. Neurosurg.* 18 (1961):273–88.

23. WALTER, W. G. Participant in "Brain Stimulation in Behaving Subjects." Neurosciences Research Program Workshop. December 1966.

Bystander Intervention in Emergencies: Diffusion of Responsibility

JOHN M. DARLEY and BIBB LATANÉ

The behavior Darley and Latané chose to study—social responsibility—illustrates another aspect of the interplay of behaviors, the way in which social conditions influence personal behavior. This article reports one of a series of experiments which suggest that it is the social context rather than personal apathy that leads to inaction in emergency situations. More specifically, Darley and Latané contend that people's refusal to help other people is neither the by-product of a "sick society"—a diagnosis advanced by some of our contemporaries—nor the manifestation of some deep-seated despair at the human condition; they provide experimental evidence that the explanation for bystander inaction lies more in one bystander's reactions to other bystanders, even to the simple number of other people witnessing the emergency.

Ss overheard an epileptic seizure. They believed either that they alone heard the emergency, or that 1 or 4 unseen others were also present. As predicted the presence of other bystanders reduced the individual's feelings of personal responsibility and lowered his speed of reporting ($p < .01$). In groups of size 3, males reported no faster than females, and females reported no slower when the 1 other bystander was a male rather than a female. In general, personality and background measures were not predictive of helping. Bystander inaction in real-life emergencies is often explained by "apathy," "alienation," and "anomie." This experiment suggests that the explanation may lie more in the bystander's response to other observers than in his indifference to the victim.

SOURCE: From John M. Darley and Bibb Latané, "Bystander Intervention in Emergencies: Diffusion of Responsibility," *Journal of Personality and Social Psychology* 8 (4) (1968): 377–83. Copyright © 1968 by the American Psychological Association and reproduced by permission.
Note: This research was supported in part by National Science Foundation Grants GS1238 and GS1239. Susan Darley contributed materially to the design of the experiment and ran the subjects, and she and Thomas Moriarty analyzed the data. Richard Nisbett, Susan Millman, Andrew Gordon, and Norma Neiman helped in preparing the tape recordings.

Several years ago, a young woman was stabbed to death in the middle of a street in a residential section of New York City. Although such murders are not entirely routine, the incident received little public attention until several weeks later when the New York Times disclosed another side to the case: at least 38 witnesses had observed the attack—and none had even attempted to intervene. Although the attacker took more than half an hour to kill Kitty Genovese, not one of the 38 people who watched from the safety of their own apartments came out to assist her. Not one even lifted the telephone to call the police [Rosenthal, 1964].

Preachers, professors, and news commentators sought the reasons for such apparently conscienceless and inhumane lack of intervention. Their conclusions ranged from "moral decay," to "dehumanization produced by the urban environment," to "alienation," "anomie," and "existential despair." An analysis of the situation, however, suggests that factors other than apathy and indifference were involved.

A person witnessing an emergency situation, particularly such a frightening and dangerous one as a stabbing, is in conflict. There are obvious humanitarian norms about helping the victim, but there are also rational and irrational fears about what might happen to a person who does intervene [Milgram and Hollander, 1964]. "I didn't want to get involved," is a familiar comment, and behind it lies fears of physical harm, public embarrassment, involvement with police procedures, lost work days and jobs, and other unknown dangers.

In certain circumstances, the norms favoring intervention may be weakened, leading bystanders to resolve the conflict in the direction of nonintervention. One of these circumstances may be the presence of other onlookers. For example, in the case above, each observer, by seeing lights and figures in other apartment house windows, knew that others were also watching. However, there was no way to tell how the other observers were reacting. These two facts provide several reasons why any individual may have delayed or failed to help. The responsibility for helping was diffused among the observers; there was also diffusion of any potential blame for not taking action; and finally, it was possible that somebody, unperceived, had already initiated helping action.

When only one bystander is present in an emergency, if help is to come, it must come from him. Although he may choose to ignore it (out of concern for his personal safety, or desires "not to get involved"), any pressure to intervene focuses uniquely on him. When there are several observers present, however, the pressures to intervene do not focus on any one of the observers; instead the responsibility for intervention is shared among all the onlookers and is not unique to any one. As a result, no one helps.

A second possibility is that potential blame may be diffused. However much we may wish to think that an individual's moral behavior is divorced from considerations of personal punishment or reward, there is both theory and evidence to the contrary [Aronfreed, 1964; Miller and Dollard, 1941, Whiting and Child, 1953]. It is perfectly reasonable to assume that, under circumstances of group responsibility for a punishable act, the punishment or blame that accrues to any one individual is often slight or nonexistent.

Finally, if others are known to be present, but their behavior cannot be closely observed, any one bystander can assume that one of the other observers is already taking action to end the emergency. Therefore, his own intervention would be only redundant—perhaps harmfully or confusingly so. Thus, given the presence of other onlookers whose behavior cannot be observed, any given bystander can rationalize his own inaction by convincing himself that "somebody else must be doing something."

These considerations lead to the hypothesis that the more bystanders to an emergency, the less likely, or the more slowly, any one bystander will intervene to provide aid. To test this proposition it would be necessary to create a situation in which a realistic "emergency" could plausibly occur. Each subject should also be blocked from communicating with others to prevent his getting information about their behavior during the emergency. Finally, the experimental situation should allow for the assessment of the speed and frequency of the subjects' reaction to the emergency. The experiment reported below attempted to fulfill these conditions.

Procedure

Overview. A college student arrived in the laboratory and was ushered into an individual room from which a communication system would enable him to talk to the other participants. It was explained to him that he was to take part in a discussion about personal problems associated with college life and that discussion would be held over the intercom system, rather than face-to-face, in order to avoid embarrassment by preserving the anonymity of the subjects. During the course of the discussion, one of the other subjects underwent what appeared to be a very serious nervous seizure similar to epilepsy. During the fit it was impossible for the subject to talk to the other discussants or to find out what, if anything, they were doing about the emergency. The dependent variable was the speed with which the subjects reported the emergency to the experimenter. The major independent variable was the number of people the subject thought to be in the discussion group.

Subjects. Fifty-nine female and thirteen male students in introductory psychology courses at New York University were contacted to take part in an unspecified experiment as part of a class requirement.

Method. Upon arriving for the experiment, the subject found himself in a long corridor with doors opening off it to several small rooms. An experimental assistant met him, took him to one of the rooms, and seated him at a table. After filling out a background information form, the subject was given a pair of headphones with an attached microphone and was told to listen for instructions.

Over the intercom, the experimenter explained that he was interested

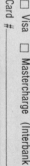

in learning about the kinds of personal problems faced by normal college students in a high pressure, urban environment. He said that to avoid possible embarrassment about discussing personal problems with strangers several precautions had been taken. First, subjects would remain anonymous, which was why they had been placed in individual rooms rather than face-to-face. (The actual reason for this was to allow tape recorder simulation of the other subjects and the emergency.) Second, since the discussion might be inhibited by the presence of outside listeners, the experimenter would not listen to the initial discussion, but would get the subject's reactions later, by questionnaire. (The real purpose of this was to remove the obviously responsible experimenter from the scene of the emergency.)

The subjects were told that since the experimenter was not present, it was necessary to impose some organization. Each person would talk in turn, presenting his problems to the group. Next, each person in turn would comment on what the others had said, and finally, there would be a free discussion. A mechanical switching device would regulate this discussion sequence and each subject's microphone would be on for about 2 minutes. While any microphone was on, all other microphones would be off. Only one subject, therefore, could be heard over the network at any given time. The subjects were thus led to realize when they later heard the seizure that only the victim's microphone was on and that there was no way of determining what any of the other witnesses were doing, nor of discussing the event and its possible solution with the others. When these instructions had been given, the discussion began.

In the discussion, the future victim spoke first, saying that he found it difficult to get adjusted to New York City and to his studies. Very hesitantly, and with obvious embarrassment, he mentioned that he was prone to seizures, particularly when studying hard or taking exams. The other people, including the real subject, took their turns and discussed similar problems (minus, of course, the proneness to seizures). The naive subject talked last in the series, after the last prerecorded voice was played.[1]

When it was again the victim's turn to talk, he made a few relatively calm comments, and then, growing increasingly louder and incoherent, he continued:

I-er-um-I think I-I need-er-if-if could-er-er-somebody er-er-er-er-er-er-er give me a little-er-give me a little help here because-er-I-er-I'm-er-er-h-h-having a-a-a real problem-er-right now and I-er-if somebody could help me out it would-it would-er-er s-s-sure be good . . . because-er-there-er-er-a cause I-er-I-uh-I've got a-a one of the-er-sei----er-er-things coming on and-and-and I could really-er-use some help so if somebody would er-give me a little h-help-uh-er-er-er-er-er c-could somebody-er-er-

<hr>

[1] To test whether the order in which the subjects spoke in the first discussion round significantly affected the subjects' speed of report, the order in which the subjects spoke was varied (in the six-person group). This had no significant or noticeable effect on the speed of the subjects' reports.

help-er-uh-uh-uh (choking sounds) . . . . I'm gonna die-er-er-I'm . . . gonna die-er-help-er-er-seizure-er-[chokes, then quiet].

The experimenter began timing the speed of the real subject's response at the beginning of the victim's speech. Informed judges listening to the tape have estimated that the victim's increasingly louder and more disconnected ramblings clearly represented a breakdown about 70 seconds after the signal for the victim's second speech. The victim's speech was abruptly cut off 125 seconds after this signal, which could be interpreted by the subject as indicating that the time allotted for that speaker had elapsed and the switching circuits had switched away from him. Times reported in the results are measured from the start of the fit.

Group size variable. The major independent variable of the study was the number of other people that the subject believed also heard the fit. By the assistant's comments before the experiment, and also by the number of voices heard to speak in the first round of the group discussion, the subject was led to believe that the discussion group was one of three sizes: either a two-person group (consisting of a person who would later have a fit and the real subject), a three-person group (consisting of the victim, the real subject, and one confederate voice), or a six-person group (consisting of the victim, the real subject, and four confederate voices). All the confederates' voices were tape-recorded.

Variations in group composition. Varying the kind as well as the number of bystanders present at an emergency should also vary the amount of responsibility felt by any single bystander. To test this, several variations of the three-person group were run. In one three-person condition, the taped bystander voice was that of a female, in another a male, and in the third a male who said that he was a premedical student who occasionally worked in the emergency wards at Bellevue hospital.

In the above conditions, the subjects were female college students. In a final condition males drawn from the same introductory psychology subject pool were tested in a three-person female-bystander condition.

Time to help. The major dependent variable was the time elapsed from the start of the victim's fit until the subject left her experimental cubicle. When the subject left her room, she saw the experimental assistant seated at the end of the hall, and invariably went to the assistant. If 6 minutes elapsed without the subject having emerged from her room, the experiment was terminated.

As soon as the subject reported the emergency, or after 6 minutes had elapsed, the experimental assistant disclosed the true nature of the experiment, and dealt with any emotions aroused in the subject. Finally the subject filled out a questionnaire concerning her thoughts and feelings during the emergency, and completed scales of Machiavellianism, anomie, and authoritarianism [Christie, 1964], a social desirability scale [Crowne & Marlowe, 1964], a social responsibility scale [Daniels & Berkowitz, 1964], and reported vital statistics and socioeconomic data.

Results

PLAUSIBILITY OF MANIPULATION

Judging by the subjects' nervousness when they reported the fit to the experimenter, by their surprise when they discovered that the fit was simulated, and by comments they made during the fit (when they thought their microphones were off), one can conclude that almost all of the subjects perceived the fit as real. There were two exceptions in different experimental conditions, and the data for these subjects were dropped from the analysis.

EFFECT OF GROUP SIZE ON HELPING

The number of bystanders that the subject perceived to be present had a major effect on the likelihood with which she would report the emergency (Table 1). Eighty-five percent of the subjects who thought they alone knew of the victim's plight reported the seizure before the victim was cut off, only 31% of those who thought four other bystanders were present did so.

TABLE 1. *Effects of Group's Size on Likelihood and Speed of Response*

Group Size	N	% Responding by End of Fit	Time in Sec.	Speed Score
2 (S & victim)	13	85	52	.87
3 (S, victim, & 1 other)	26	62	93	.72
6 (S, victim, & 4 others)	13	31	166	.51

Note. —p value of differences: $x^2 = 7.91$, $p < .02$; $F = 8.09$, $p < .01$, for speed scores.

* Editor's note: x^2 and F identify the statistics used to analyze these data. p is the probability of chance occurrence.

Every one of the subjects in the two-person groups, but only 62% of the subjects in the six-person groups, ever reported the emergency. The cumulative distributions of response times for groups of different perceived size (Figure 1) indicates that, by any point in time, more subjects from the two-person groups had responded than from the three-person groups, and more from the three-person groups than from the six-person groups.

Ninety-five percent of all the subjects who ever responded did so within the first half of the time available to them. No subject who had not reported within 3 minutes after the fit ever did so. The shape of these distributions suggest that had the experiment been allowed to run for a considerably longer time, few additional subjects would have responded.

SPEED OF RESPONSE

To achieve a more detailed analysis of the results, each subject's time score was transformed into a "speed" score by taking the reciprocal of the response time in seconds and multiplying by 100. The effect of this transformation was to deemphasize differences between longer time scores, thus reducing the contribution to the results of the arbitrary 6-minute limit on scores. A high speed score indicates a fast response.

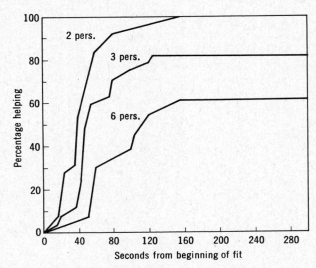

FIGURE 1.   *Cumulative distributions of helping responses.*

An analysis of variance indicates that the effect of group size is highly significant ($p < .01$). Duncan multiple-range tests indicate that all but the two- and three-person groups differ significantly from one another ($p < .05$).

VICTIM'S LIKELIHOOD OF BEING HELPED

An individual subject is less likely to respond if he thinks that others are present. But what of the victim? Is the inhibition of the response of each individual strong enough to counteract the fact that with five onlookers there are five times as many people available to help? From the data of this experiment, it is possible mathematically to create hypothetical groups with one, two, or five observers.[2] The calculations indicate that the victim is about equally likely to get help from one bystander as from two. The victim is considerably more likely to have gotten help from one or two observers than from five during the first minute of the fit. For instance, by 45 seconds after the start of the fit, the victim's chances of having been helped by the single bystanders were about 50%, compared to none in the five observer condition. After the first minute, the likelihood of getting help from at least one person is high in all three conditions.

[2] The formula for the probability that at least one person will help by a given time is $1 - (1 - P)^n$ where n is the number of observers and P is the probability of a single individual (who thinks he is one of n observers) helping by that time.

EFFECT OF GROUP COMPOSITION ON HELPING THE VICTIM

Several variations of the three-person group were run. In one pair of variations, the female subject thought the other bystander was either male or female; in another, she thought the other bystander was a premedical student who worked in an emergency ward at Bellevue Hospital. As Table 2 shows,

TABLE 2. *Effects of Group Composition on Likelihood and Speed of Response* [a]

Group Composition	N	% Responding by End of Fit	Time in Sec.	Speed Score
Female S, male other	13	62	94	74
Female S, female other	13	62	92	71
Female S, male medic other	5	100	60	77
Male S, female other	13	69	110	68

[a] Three-person group, male victim.

variations in sex and medical competence of the other bystander had no important or detectable affect on speed of response. Subjects responded equally frequently and fast whether the other bystander was female, male, or medically experienced.

SEX OF THE SUBJECT AND SPEED OF RESPONSE

Coping with emergencies is often thought to be the duty of males, especially when females are present, but there was no evidence that this was the case in this study. Male subjects responded to the emergency with almost exactly the same speed as did females (Table 2).

REASONS FOR INTERVENTION OR NONINTERVENTION

After the debriefing at the end of the experiment each subject was given a 15-item checklist and asked to check those thoughts which had "crossed your mind when you heard Subject 1 calling for help." Whatever the condition, each subject checked very few thoughts, and there were no significant differences in number or kind of thoughts in the different experimental groups. The only thoughts checked by more than a few subjects were "I didn't know what to do" (18 out of 65 subjects), "I thought it must be some sort of fake" (20 out of 65), and "I didn't know exactly what was happening" (26 out of 65).

It is possible that subjects were ashamed to report socially undesirable rationalizations, or, since the subjects checked the list *after* the true nature of the experiment had been explained to them, their memories might have been blurred. It is our impression, however, that most subjects checked few reasons because they had few coherent thoughts during the fit.

We asked all subjects whether the presence or absence of other bystanders had entered their minds during the time that they were hearing the fit. Subjects in the three- and six-person groups reported that they were aware that other people were present, but they felt that this made no difference to their own behavior.

INDIVIDUAL DIFFERENCE CORRELATES OF SPEED OF REPORT

The correlations between speed of report and various individual differences on the personality and background measures were obtained by normalizing the distribution of report speeds within each experimental condition and pooling these scores across all conditions ($n = 62-65$). Personality measures showed no important or significant correlations with speed of reporting the emergency. In fact, only one of the 16 individual difference measures, the size of the community in which the subject grew up, correlated ($r^* = -.26, p < .05$) with the speed of helping.

Discussion

Subjects, whether or not they intervened, believed the fit to be genuine and serious. "My God, he's having a fit," many subjects said to themselves (and were overheard via their microphones) at the onset of the fit. Others gasped or simply said "Oh." Several of the male subjects swore. One subject said to herself, "It's just my kind of luck, something has to happen to me!" Several subjects spoke aloud of their confusion about what course of action to take, "Oh God, what should I do?"

When those subjects who intervened stepped out of their rooms, they found the experimental assistant down the hall. With some uncertainty, but without panic, they reported the situation. "Hey, I think Number 1 is very sick. He's having a fit or something." After ostensibly checking on the situation, the experimenter returned to report that "everything is under control." The subjects accepted these assurances with obvious relief.

Subjects who failed to report the emergency showed few signs of the apathy and the indifference thought to characterize "unresponsive bystanders." When the experimenter entered her room to terminate the situation, the subject often asked if the victim was "all right." "Is he being taken care of?" "He's all right isn't he?" Many of these subjects showed physical signs of nervousness; they often had trembling hands and sweating palms. If anything, they seemed more emotionally aroused than did the subjects who reported the emergency.

Why, then, didn't they respond? It is our impression that nonintervening subjects had not decided *not* to respond. Rather they were still in a state of indecision and conflict concerning whether to respond or not. The emotional behavior of these nonresponding subjects was a sign of their continuing conflict, a conflict that other subjects resolved by responding.

The fit created a conflict situation of the avoidance-avoidance type. On the one hand, subjects worried about the guilt and shame they would feel if they did not help the person in distress. On the other hand, they were concerned not to make fools of themselves by overreacting, not to ruin the ongoing experiment by leaving their intercom, and not to destroy the anonymous nature of the situation which the experimenter had earlier stressed as im-

---

* Editor's note: r is the symbol for the "product-moment" correlation.

portant. For subjects in the two-person condition, the obvious distress of the victim and his need for help were so important that their conflict was easily resolved. For the subjects who knew there were other bystanders present, the cost of not helping was reduced and the conflict they were in more acute. Caught between the two negative alternatives of letting the victim continue to suffer or the costs of rushing in to help, the nonresponding bystanders vacillated between them rather than choosing not to respond. This distinction may be academic for the victim, since he got no help in either case, but it is an extremely important one for arriving at an understanding of the causes of bystanders' failures to help.

Although the subjects experienced stress and conflict during the experiment, their general reactions to it were highly positive. On a questionnaire administered after the experimenter had discussed the nature and purpose of the experiment, every single subject found the experiment either "interesting" or "very interesting" and was willing to participate in similar experiments in the future. All subjects felt they understood what the experiment was about and indicated that they thought the deceptions were necessary and justified. All but one felt they were better informed about the nature of psychological research in general.

Male subjects reported the emergency no faster than did females. These results (or lack of them) seem to conflict with the Berkowitz, Klanderman, and Harris [1964] finding that males tend to assume more responsibility and take more initiative than females in giving help to dependent others. Also, females reacted equally fast when the other bystander was another female, a male, or even a person practiced in dealing with medical emergencies. The ineffectiveness of these manipulations of group composition cannot be explained by general insensitivity of the speed measure, since the group-size variable had a marked effect on report speed.

It might be helpful in understanding this lack of difference to distinguish two general classes of intervention in emergency situations: direct and reportorial. Direct intervention (breaking up a fight, extinguishing a fire, swimming out to save a drowner) often requires skill, knowledge, or physical power. It may involve danger. American cultural norms and Berkowitz's results seem to suggest that males are more responsible than females for this kind of direct intervention.

A second way of dealing with an emergency is to report it to someone qualified to handle it, such as the police. For this kind of intervention, there seem to be no norms requiring male action. In the present study, subjects clearly intended to report the emergency rather than take direct action. For such indirect intervention, sex or medical competence does not appear to affect one's qualifications or responsibilities. Anybody, male or female, medically trained or not, can find the experimenter.

In this study, no subject was able to tell how the other subjects reacted to the fit. (Indeed, there were no other subjects actually present.) The effects of group size on speed of helping, therefore, are due simply to the perceived presence of others rather than to the influence of their actions. This means that the experimental situation is unlike emergencies, such as a fire, in which bystanders interact with each other. It is, however, similar to emergencies, such as the Genovese murder, in which spectators knew others were also watching but were prevented by walls between them from communication that might have counteracted the diffusion of responsibility.

The present results create serious difficulties for one class of commonly given explanations for the failure of bystanders to intervene in actual emergencies, those involving apathy or indifference. These explanations generally assert that people who fail to intervene are somehow different in kind from the rest of us, that they are "alienated by industrialization," "dehumanized by urbanization," "depersonalized by living in the cold society," or "psychopaths." These explanations serve a dual function for people who adopt them. First, they explain (if only in a nominal way) the puzzling and frightening problem of why people watch others die. Second, they give individuals reason to deny that they too might fail to help in a similar situation.

The results of this experiment seem to indicate that such personality variables may not be as important as these explanations suggest. Alienation, Machiavellianism, acceptance of social responsibility, need for approval, and authoritarianism are often cited in these explanations. Yet they did not predict the speed or likelihood of help. In sharp contrast, the perceived number of bystanders did. The explanation of bystander "apathy" may lie more in the bystander's response to other observers than in presumed personality deficiencies of "apathetic" individuals. Although this realization may force us to face the guilt-provoking possibility that we too might fail to intervene, it also suggests that individuals are not, of necessity, "noninterveners" because of their personalities. If people understand the situational forces that can make them hesitate to intervene, they may better overcome them.

References

1. Aronfreed, J. The origin of self-criticism. *Psychological Review* 71 (1964):193–219.
2. Berkowitz, L., Klanderman, S., and Harris, R. Effects of experimenter awareness and sex of subject on reactions to dependency relationships. *Sociometry* 27 (1964): 327–29.
3. Christie, R. The prevalence of Machiavellian orientations. Paper presented at the meeting of the American Psychological Association, Los Angeles, 1964.
4. Crowne, D., and Marlowe, D. *The Approval Motive.* New York: John Wiley & Sons, 1964.
5. Daniels, L., and Berkowitz, L. Liking and response to dependency relationships. *Human Relations* 16 (1963):141–48.
6. Milgram, S., and Hollander, P. Murder they heard. *Nation* 198 (1964):602–04.
7. Miller, N., and Dollard, J. *Social Learning and Imitation.* New Haven: Yale University Press, 1941.
8. Rosenthal, A. M. *Thirty-eight Witnesses.* New York: McGraw-Hill, 1964.
9. Whiting, J. W. M., and Child, I. *Child Training and Personality.* New Haven: Yale University Press, 1953.

The Experience of Living in Cities

STANLEY MILGRAM

Sometimes, not always without foundation, the charge is leveled that psychology is irrelevant to the pressing problems of modern life—problems associated with living in cities, for instance. One reason for this irrelevancy might be the tendency for too many psychologists to occupy themselves with the gathering of data and yet to evade the more demanding, and more meaningful, task of making sense of those data and of weaving them into theories. Without such systematic knowledge, attempts really to understand and to influence behavior can be difficult indeed.

In this article, Stanley Milgram begins to organize data about people's responses to urban life. Note how the single concept of "overload" seems to make sense out of many kinds of observed behavior. It sheds light on bystander inaction in emergencies (and is consistent with Darley and Latané's formulation in the preceding article) and on city dwellers' unwillingness to trust strangers; it helps to explain the social roles that people follow. The conceptual explanation of why people behave furnishes some rudimentary basis for influencing how they behave.

"When I first came to New York it seemed like a nightmare. As soon as I got off the train at Grand Central I was caught up in pushing, shoving crowds on 42nd Street. Sometimes people bumped into me without apology; what really frightened me was to see two people literally engaged in combat for possession of a cab. Why were they so rushed? Even drunks on the street were bypassed without a glance. People didn't seem to care about each other at all."

SOURCE: From S. Milgram, "The Experience of Living in Cities," *Science* 167, March 13, 1970, pp. 1461–68. Copyright © 1970 by the American Association for the Advancement of Science. Reproduced by permission.

Note: The author is professor of psychology at the Graduate Center of The City University of New York, New York 10036. This article is based on an address given on 2 September 1969 at the 77th annual meeting of the American Psychological Association in Washington, D. C.

Barbara Bengen worked closely with me in preparing the present version of this article. I thank Dr. Gary Winkel, editor of *Environment and Behavior*, for useful suggestions and advice.

This statement represents a common reaction to a great city, but it does not tell the whole story. Obviously cities have great appeal because of their variety, eventfulness, possibility of choice, and the stimulation of an intense atmosphere that many individuals find a desirable background to their lives. Where face-to-face contacts are important, the city offers unparalleled possibilities. It has been calculated by the Regional Plan Association [16] that in Nassau County, a suburb of New York City, an individual can meet 11,000 others within a 10-minute radius of his office by foot or car. In Newark, a moderate-sized city, he can meet more than 20,000 persons within this radius. But in midtown Manhattan he can meet fully 220,000. So there is an order-of-magnitude increment in the communication possibilities offered by a great city. That is one of the bases of its appeal and, indeed, of its functional necessity. The city provides options that no other social arrangement permits. But there is a negative side also, as we shall see.

Granted that cities are indispensable in complex society, we may still ask what contribution psychology can make to understanding the experience of living in them. What theories are relevant? How can we extend our knowledge of the psychological aspects of life in cities through empirical inquiry? If empirical inquiry is possible, along what lines should it proceed? In short, where do we start in constructing urban theory and in laying out lines of research?

Observation is the indispensable starting point. Any observer in the streets of midtown Manhattan will see (i) large numbers of people, (ii) a high population density, and (iii) heterogeneity of population. These three factors need to be at the root of any sociopsychological theory of city life, for they condition all aspects of our experience in the metropolis. Louis Wirth [21], if not the first to point to these factors, is nonetheless the sociologist who relied most heavily on them in his analysis of the city. Yet, for a psychologist, there is something unsatisfactory about Wirth's theoretical variables. Numbers, density, and heterogeneity are demographic facts but they are not yet psychological facts. They are external to the individual. Psychology needs an idea that links the individual's *experience* to the demographic circumstances of urban life.

One link is provided by the concept of overload. This term, drawn from systems analysis, refers to a system's inability to process inputs from the environment because there are too many inputs for the system to cope with, or because successive inputs come so fast that input A cannot be processed when input B is presented. When overload is present, adaptations occur. The system must set priorities and make choices. A may be processed first while B is kept in abeyance, or one input may be sacrificed altogether. City life, as we experience it, constitutes a continuous set of encounters with overload, and of resultant adaptations. Overload characteristically deforms daily life on several levels, impinging on role performance, the evolution of social norms, cognitive functioning, and the use of facilities.

The concept has been implicit in several theories of urban experience. In 1903 George Simmel [18] pointed out that, since urban dwellers come into contact with vast numbers of people each day, they conserve psychic energy by becoming acquainted with a far smaller proportion of people than their rural counterparts do, and by maintaining more superficial relationships even with these acquaintances. Wirth [21] points specifically to "the superficiality, the anonymity, and the transitory character of urban social relations."

One adaptive response to overload, therefore, is the allocation of less time to each input. A second adaptive mechanism is disregard of low-priority inputs. Principles of selectivity are formulated such that investment of time and energy are reserved for carefully defined inputs (the urbanite disregards the drunk sick on the street as he purposefully navigates through the crowd). Third, boundaries are redrawn in certain social transactions so that the overloaded system can shift the burden to the other party in the exchange; thus, harried New York bus drivers once made change for customers, but now this responsibility has been shifted to the client, who must have the exact fare ready. Fourth, reception is blocked off prior to entrance into a system; city dwellers increasingly use unlisted telephone numbers to prevent individuals from calling them, and a small but growing number resort to keeping the telephone off the hook to prevent incoming calls. More subtly, a city dweller blocks inputs by assuming an unfriendly countenance, which discourages others from initiating contact. Additionally, social screening devices are interposed between the individual and environmental inputs (in a town of 5000 anyone can drop in to chat with the mayor, but in the metropolis organizational screening devices deflect inputs to other destinations). Fifth, the intensity of inputs is diminished by filtering devices, so that only weak and relatively superficial forms of involvement with others are allowed. Sixth, specialized institutions are created to absorb inputs that would otherwise swamp the individual (welfare departments handle the financial needs of a million individuals in New York City, who would otherwise create an army of mendicants continuously importuning the pedestrian). The interposition of institutions between the individual and the social world, a characteristic of all modern society, and most notably of the large metropolis, has its negative side. It deprives the individual of a sense of direct contact and spontaneous integration in the life around him. It simultaneously protects and estranges the individual from his social environment.

Many of these adaptive mechanisms apply not only to individuals but to institutional systems as well, as Meier [14] has so brilliantly shown in connection with the library and the stock exchange.

In sum, the observed behavior of the urbanite in a wide range of situations appears to be determined largely by a variety of adaptations to overload. I now deal with several specific consequences of responses to overload, which make for differences in the tone of city and town.

Social Responsibility

The principal point of interest for a social psychology of the city is that moral and social involvement with individuals is necessarily restricted. This is a direct and necessary function of excess of input over capacity to process. Such restriction of involvement runs a broad spectrum from refusal to become involved in the needs of another person, even when the person desperately needs assistance, through refusal to do favors, to the simple withdrawal of courtesies (such as offering a lady a seat, or saying "sorry" when a pedestrian collision occurs). In any transaction more and more details need to be dropped as the total number of units to be processed increases and assaults an instrument of limited processing capacity.

The ultimate adaptation to an overloaded social environment is to totally disregard the needs, interests, and demands of those whom one does not define as relevant to the satisfaction of personal needs, and to develop highly efficient perceptual means of determining whether an individual falls into the category of friend or stranger. The disparity in the treatment of friends and strangers ought to be greater in cities than in towns; the time allotment and willingness to become involved with those who have no personal claim on one's time is likely to be less in cities than in towns.

BYSTANDER INTERVENTION IN CRISES

The most striking deficiencies in social responsibility in cities occur in crisis situations, such as the Genovese murder in Queens. In 1964, Catherine Genovese, coming home from a night job in the early hours of an April morning, was stabbed repeatedly, over an extended period of time. Thirty-eight residents of a respectable New York City neighborhood admit to having witnessed at least a part of the attack, but none went to her aid or called the police until after she was dead. Milgram and Hollander, writing in *The Nation* [15], analyzed the event in these terms:

> Urban friendships and associations are not primarily formed on the basis of physical proximity. A person with numerous close friends in different parts of the city may not know the occupant of an adjacent apartment. This does not mean that a city dweller has fewer friends than does a villager, or knows fewer persons who will come to his aid; however, it does mean that his allies are not constantly at hand. Miss Genovese required immediate aid from those physically present. There is no evidence that the city had deprived Miss Genovese of human associations, but the friends who might have rushed to her side were miles from the scene of her tragedy.
>
> Further, it is known that her cries for help were not directed to a specific person; they were general. But only individuals can act, and as the cries were not specifically directed, no particular person felt a special responsibility. The crime and the failure of community response seem absurd to us. At the time, it may well have seemed equally absurd to the Kew Gardens residents that not one of the neighbors would have called the police. A collective paralysis may have developed from the belief of each of the witnesses that someone else must surely have taken that obvious step.

Latané and Darley [11] have reported laboratory approaches to the study of bystander intervention and have established experimentally the following principle: the larger the number of bystanders, the less the likelihood that any one of them will intervene in an emergency.* Gaertner and Bickman [7] of The City University of New York have extended the bystander studies to an examination of help across ethnic lines. Blacks and whites, with clearly identifiable accents, called strangers (through what the caller represented as an error in telephone dialing), gave them a plausible story of being stranded on an outlying highway without more dimes, and asked the stranger to call a garage. The experimenters found that the white callers had a significantly better chance of obtaining assistance than the black callers. This suggests that ethnic allegiance may well be another means of coping with overload: the city dweller can reduce excessive demands and screen out urban hetero-geneity by responding along ethnic lines; overload is made more manageable by limiting the "span of sympathy."

In any quantitative characterization of the social texture of city life, a neces-sary first step is the application of such experimental methods as these to field situations in large cities and small towns. Theorists argue that the indifference shown in the Genovese case would not be found in a small town, but in the absence of solid experimental evidence the question remains an open one.

More than just callousness prevents bystanders from participating in alterca-tions between people. A rule of urban life is respect for other people's emo-tional and social privacy, perhaps because physical privacy is so hard to achieve. And in situations for which the standards are heterogeneous, it is much harder to know whether taking an active role is unwarranted meddling or an appropriate response to a critical situation. If a husband and wife are quarreling in public, at what point should a bystander step in? On the one hand, the heterogeneity of the city produces substantially greater tolerance about behavior, dress, and codes of ethics than is generally found in the small town, but this diversity also encourages people to withhold aid for fear of antagonizing the participants or crossing an inappropriate and difficult-to-define line.

Moreover, the frequency of demands present in the city gives rise to norms of noninvolvement. There are practical limitations to the Samaritan impulse in a major city. If a citizen attended to every needy person, if he were sensitive to and acted on every altruistic impulse that was evoked in the city, he could scarely keep his own affairs in order.

WILLINGNESS TO TRUST AND ASSIST STRANGERS

We now move away from crisis situations to less urgent examples of social responsibility. For it is not only in situations of dramatic need but in the

* Editor's note: The Darley and Latané article reprinted in this collection (page 91) reports one experiment in their series on bystander intervention.

TABLE 1. *Percentage of Entries Achieved by Investigators for City and Town Dwellings (See Text).*

	Entries Achieved (%)	
Experimenter	City *	Small Town †
Male		
No. 1	16	40
No. 2	12	60
Female		
No. 3	40	87
No. 4	40	100

* Number of requests for entry, 100.   † Number of requests for entry, 60.

ordinary, everyday willingness to lend a hand that the city dweller is said to be deficient relative to his small-town cousin. The comparative method must be used in any empirical examination of this question. A commonplace social situation is staged in an urban setting and in a small town—a situation to which a subject can respond by either extending help or withholding it. The responses in town and city are compared.

One factor in the purported unwillingness of urbanites to be helpful to strangers may well be their heightened sense of physical (and emotional) vulnerability—a feeling that is supported by urban crime statistics. A key test for distinguishing between city and town behavior, therefore, is determining how city dwellers compare with town dwellers in offering aid that increases their personal vulnerability and requires some trust of strangers. Altman, Levine, Nadien, and Villena [3] of The City University of New York devised a study to compare the behaviors of city and town dwellers in this respect. The criterion used in this study was the willingness of householders to allow strangers to enter their home to use the telephone. The student investigators individually rang doorbells, explained that they had misplaced the address of a friend nearby, and asked to use the phone. The investigators (two males and two females) made 100 requests for entry into homes in the city and 60 requests in the small towns. The results for middle-income housing developments in Manhattan were compared with data for several small towns (Stony Point, Spring Valley, Ramapo, Nyack, New City, and West Clarkstown) in Rockland County, outside of New York City. As Table 1 shows, in all cases there was a sharp increase in the proportion of entries achieved by an experimenter when he moved from the city to a small town. In the most extreme case the experimenter was five times as likely to gain admission to homes in a small town as to homes in Manhattan. Although the female experimenters had notably greater success both in cities and in towns than the male experimenters had, each of the four students did at least twice as well in towns as in cities. This suggests that the city-town distinction overrides even the predictably greater fear of male strangers than of female ones.

The lower level of helpfulness by city dwellers seems due in part to recognition of the dangers of living in Manhattan, rather than to mere indifference or coldness. It is significant that 75 percent of all the city respondents received and answered messages by shouting through closed doors and by peering out through peepholes; in the towns, by contrast, about 75 percent of the respondents opened the door.

Supporting the experimenters' quantitative results was their general observation that the town dwellers were noticeably more friendly and less suspicious than the city dwellers. In seeking to explain the reasons for the greater sense of psychological vulnerability city dwellers feel, above and beyond the differences in crime statistics, Villena [3] points out that, if a crime is committed in a village, a resident of a neighboring village may not perceive the crime as personally relevant, though the geographic distance may be small, whereas a criminal act committed anywhere in the city, though miles from the city-dweller's home is still verbally located within the city; thus, Villena says, "the inhabitant of the city possesses a larger vulnerable space."

CIVILITIES

Even at the most superficial level of involvement—the exercise of everyday civilities—urbanites are reputedly deficient. People bump into each other and often do not apologize. They knock over another person's packages and, as often as not, proceed on their way with a grumpy exclamation instead of an offer of assistance. Such behavior, which many visitors to great cities find distasteful, is less common, we are told, in smaller communities, where traditional courtesies are more likely to be observed.

In some instances it is not simply that, in the city, traditional courtesies are violated; rather, the cities develop new norms of noninvolvement. These are so well defined and so deeply a part of city life that *they* constitute the norms people are reluctant to violate. Men are actually embarrassed to give up a seat on the subway to an old woman; they mumble "I was getting off anyway," instead of making the gesture in a straightforward and gracious way. These norms develop because everyone realizes that, in situations of high population density, people cannot implicate themselves in each others' affairs, for to do so would create conditions of continual distraction which would frustrate purposeful action.

In discussing the effects of overload I do not imply that at every instant the city dweller is bombarded with an unmanageable number of inputs, and that his responses are determined by the excess of input at any given instant. Rather, adaptation occurs in the form of gradual evolution of norms of behavior. Norms are evolved in response to frequent discrete experiences of overload; they persist and become generalized modes of responding.

OVERLOAD ON COGNITIVE CAPACITIES: ANONYMITY

That we respond differently toward those whom we know and those who are strangers to us is a truism. An eager patron aggressively cuts in front of someone in a long movie line to save time only to confront a friend; he then behaves sheepishly. A man is involved in an automobile accident caused by another driver, emerges from his car shouting in rage, then moderates his behavior on discovering a friend driving the other car. The city dweller, when walking through the midtown streets, is in a state of continual anonymity vis-à-vis the other pedestrians.

Anonymity is part of a continuous spectrum ranging from total anonymity to full acquaintance, and it may well be that measurement of the precise degrees of anonymity in cities and towns would help to explain important distinctions between the quality of life in each. Conditions of full acquaintance, for example, offer security and familiarity, but they may also be stifling, because the individual is caught in a web of established relationships. Conditions of complete anonymity, by contrast, provide freedom from routinized social ties, but they may also create feelings of alienation and detachment.

Empirically one could investigate the proportion of activities in which the city dweller or the town dweller is known by others at given times in his daily life, and the proportion of activities in the course of which he interacts with individuals who know him. At his job, for instance, the city dweller may be known to as many people as his rural counterpart. However, when he is not fulfilling his occupational role—say, when merely traveling about the city— the urbanite is doubtless more anonymous than his rural counterpart.

Limited empirical work on anonymity has begun. Zimbardo [22] has tested whether the social anonymity and impersonality of the big city encourage greater vandalism than do small towns. Zimbardo arranged for one automobile to be left for 64 hours near the Bronx campus of New York University and for a counterpart to be left for the same number of hours near Stanford University in Palo Alto. The license plates on the two cars were removed and the hoods were opened, to provide "releaser cues" for potential vandals. The New York car was stripped of all movable parts within the first 24 hours, and by the end of 3 days was only a hunk of metal rubble. Unexpectedly, however, most of the destruction occurred during daylight hours, usually under the scrutiny of observers, and the leaders in the vandalism were well-dressed, white adults. The Palo Alto car was left untouched.

Zimbardo attributes the difference in the treatment accorded the two cars to the "acquired feelings of social anonymity provided by life in a city like New York," and he supports his conclusions with several other anecdotes illustrating casual, wanton vandalism in the city. In any comparative study of the effects of anonymity in city and town, however, there must be satisfactory control for other confounding factors: the large number of drug addicts in a city like New York; the higher proportion of slum-dwellers in the city; and so on.

Another direction for empirical study is investigation of the beneficial effects of anonymity. The impersonality of city life breeds its own tolerance for the private lives of the inhabitants. Individuality and even eccentricity, we may assume, can flourish more readily in the metropolis than in the small town.

Stigmatized persons may find it easier to lead comfortable lives in the city, free of the constant scrutiny of neighbors. To what degree can this assumed difference between city and town be shown empirically? Judith Waters [20], at The City University of New York, hypothesized that avowed homosexuals would be more likely to be accepted as tenants in a large city than in small towns, and she dispatched letters from homosexuals and from normal individuals to real estate agents in cities and towns across the country. The results of her study were inconclusive. But the general idea of examining the protective benefits of city life to the stigmatized ought to be pursued.

ROLE BEHAVIOR IN CITIES AND TOWNS

Another product of urban overload is the adjustment in roles made by urbanites in daily interactions. As Wirth has said [21]: "Urbanites meet one another in highly segmental roles. . . . They are less dependent upon particular persons, and their dependence upon others is confined to a highly fractionalized aspect of the other's round of activity." This tendency is particularly noticeable in transactions between customers and individuals offering professional or sales services. The owner of a country store has time to become well acquainted with his dozen-or-so daily customers, but the girl at the checkout counter of a busy A & P, serving hundreds of customers a day, barely has time to toss the green stamps into one customer's shopping bag before the next customer confronts her with his pile of groceries.

Meier, in his stimulating analysis of the city [14], discusses several adaptations a system may make when confronted by inputs that exceed its capacity to process them. Meier argues that, according to the principle of competition for scarce resources, the scope and time of the transaction shrink as customer volume and daily turnover rise. This, in fact, is what is meant by the "brusque" quality of city life. New standards have developed in cities concerning what levels of services are appropriate in business transactions (see Fig. 1).

McKenna and Morgenthau [13], in a seminar at The City University of New York, devised a study (i) to compare the willingness of city dwellers and small-town dwellers to do favors for strangers that entailed expenditure of a small amount of time and slight inconvenience but no personal vulnerability, and (ii) to determine whether the more compartmentalized, transitory relationships of the city would make urban salesgirls less likely than small-town salesgirls to carry out, for strangers, tasks not related to their customary roles.

To test for differences between city dwellers and small-town dwellers, a simple experiment was devised in which persons from both settings were asked (by telephone) to perform increasingly onerous favors for anonymous strangers.

Within the cities (Chicago, New York, and Philadelphia), half the calls were to housewives and the other half to salesgirls in women's apparel shops; the division was the same for the 37 small towns of the study, which were in

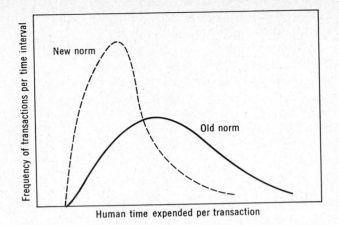

FIGURE 1. *Changes in the demand for time for a given task when the overall transaction frequency increases in a social system.* (*Reprinted with permission from R. L. Meier,* A Communications Theory of Urban Growth, *1962. Copyright by M.I.T. Press, 1962.*)

the same states as the cities. Each experimenter represented herself as a long-distance caller who had, through error, been connected with the respondent by the operator. The experimenter began by asking for simple information about the weather for purposes of travel. Next the experimenter excused herself on some pretext (asking the respondent to "please hold on"), put the phone down for almost a full minute, and then picked it up again and asked the respondent to provide the phone number of a hotel or motel in her vicinity at which the experimenter might stay during a forthcoming visit. Scores were assigned the subjects on the basis of how helpful they had been. McKenna summarizes her results in this matter:

> People in the city, whether they are engaged in a specific job or not, are less helpful and informative than people in small towns; . . . People at home, regardless of where they live, are less helpful and informative than people working in shops.

However, the absolute level of cooperativeness for urban subjects was found to be quite high, and does not accord with the stereotype of the urbanite as aloof, self-centered, and unwilling to help strangers. The quantitative differences obtained by McKenna and Morgenthau are less great than one might have expected. This again points up the need for extensive empirical research in rural-urban differences, research that goes far beyond that provided in the few illustrative pilot studies presented here. At this point we have very limited objective evidence on differences in the quality of social encounters in city and small town.

But the research needs to be guided by unifying theoretical concepts. As I have tried to demonstrate, the concept of overload helps to explain a wide

variety of contrasts between city behavior and town behavior: (i) the differences in role enactment (the tendency of urban dwellers to deal with one
another in highly segmented, functional terms, and of urban sales personnel
to devote limited time and attention to their customers); (ii) the evolution of
urban norms quite different from traditional town values (such as the acceptance of noninvolvement, impersonality, and aloofness in urban life); (iii) the
adaptation of the urban dweller's cognitive processes (his inability to identify
most of the people he sees daily, his screening of sensory stimuli, his development of blasé attitudes toward deviant or bizarre behavior, and his selectivity
in responding to human demands); and (iv) the competition for scarce
facilities in the city (the subway rush; the fight for taxis; traffic jams; standing
in line to await services). I suggest that contrasts between city and rural
behavior probably reflect the responses of similar people to very different
situations, rather than intrinsic differences in the personalities of rural and city
dwellers. The city is a situation to which individuals respond adaptively.

Further Aspects of Urban Experience

Some features of urban experience do not fit neatly into the system of analysis
presented thus far. They are no less important for that reason. The issues
raised next are difficult to treat in quantitative fashion. Yet I prefer discussing
them in a loose way to excluding them because appropriate language and data
have not yet been developed. My aim is to suggest how phenomena such as
"urban atmosphere" can be pinned down through techniques of measurement.

THE "ATMOSPHERE" OF GREAT CITIES

The contrast in the behavior of city and town dwellers has been a natural
starting point for urban social scientists. But even among great cities there are
marked differences in "atmosphere." The tone, pacing, and texture of social
encounters are different in London and New York, and many persons willingly
make financial sacrifices for the privilege of living within a specific urban
atmosphere which they find pleasing or stimulating. A second perspective in
the study of cities, therefore, is to define exactly what is meant by the atmosphere of a city and to pinpoint the factors that give rise to it. It may seem
that urban atmosphere is too evanescent a quality to be reduced to a set of
measurable variables, but I do not believe the matter can be judged before
substantial effort has been made in this direction. It is obvious that any
such approach must be comparative. It makes no sense at all to say that New
York is "vibrant" and "frenetic" unless one has some specific city in mind as
a basis of comparison.

In an undergraduate tutorial that I conducted at Harvard University some
years ago, New York, London, and Paris were selected as reference points for
attempts to measure urban atmosphere. We began with a simple question:
Does any consensus exist about the qualities that typify given cities? To

answer this question one could undertake a content analysis of travel-book, literary, and journalistic accounts of cities. A second approach, which we adopted, is to ask people to characterize (with descriptive terms and accounts of typical experiences) cities they have lived in or visited. In advertisements placed in *The New York Times* and the *Harvard Crimson* we asked people to give us accounts of specific incidents in London, Paris, or New York that best illuminated the character of that particular city. Questionnaires were then developed, and administered to persons who were familiar with at least two of the three cities.

Some distinctive patterns emerged [2]. The distinguishing themes concerning New York, for example, dealt with its diversity, its great size, its pace and level of activity, its cultural and entertainment opportunities, and the heterogeneity and segmentation ("ghettoization") of its population. New York elicited more descriptions in terms of physical qualities, pace, and emotional impact than Paris or London did, a fact which suggests that these are particularly important aspects of New York's ambiance.

A contrasting profile emerges for London; in this case respondents placed far greater emphasis on their interactions with the inhabitants than on physical surroundings. There was near unanimity on certain themes: those dealing with the tolerance and courtesy of London's inhabitants. One respondent said:

> When I was 12, my grandfather took me to the British Museum . . . one day by tube and recited the *Aeneid* in Latin for my benefit. . . .He is rather deaf, speaks very loudly and it embarrassed the hell out of me, until I realized that nobody was paying any attention. Londoners are extremely worldly and tolerant.

In contrast, respondents who described New Yorkers as aloof, cold, and rude referred to such incidents as the following:

> I saw a boy of 19 passing out anti-war leaflets to passersby. When he stopped at a corner, a man dressed in a business suit walked by him at a brisk pace, hit the boy's arm, and scattered the leaflets all over the street. The man kept walking at the same pace down the block.

We need to obtain many more such descriptions of incidents, using careful methods of sampling. By the application of factor-analytic techniques, relevant dimensions for each city can be discerned.

The responses for Paris were about equally divided between responses concerning its inhabitants and those regarding its physical and sensory attributes. Cafés and parks were often mentioned as contributing to the sense that Paris is a city of amenities, but many respondents complained that Parisians were inhospitable, nasty, and cold.

We cannot be certain, of course, to what degree these statements reflect actual characteristics of the cities in question and to what degree they simply tap the respondents' knowledge of widely held preconceptions. Indeed, one may point to three factors, apart from the actual atmospheres of the cities, that determine the subjects' responses.

1. A person's impression of a given city depends on his implicit standard of comparison. A New Yorker who visits Paris may well describe that city as "leisurely," whereas a compatriot from Richmond, Virginia, may consider Paris too "hectic." * Obtaining reciprocal judgment, in which New Yorkers judge Londoners, and Londoners judge New Yorkers, seems a useful way to take into account not only the city being judged but also the home city that serves as the visitor's base line.

2. Perceptions of a city are also affected by whether the observer is a tourist, a newcomer, or a longer-term resident. First, a tourist will be exposed to features of the city different from those familiar to a long-time resident. Second, a prerequisite for adapting to continuing life in a given city seems to be the filtering out of many observations about the city that the newcomer or tourist finds particularly arresting; this selective process seems to be part of the long-term resident's mechanisms for coping with overload. In the interest of psychic economy, the resident simply learns to tune out many aspects of daily life. One method for studying the specific impact of adaptation on perception of the city is to ask several pairs of newcomers and old-timers (one newcomer and one old-timer to a pair) to walk down certain city blocks and then report separately what each has observed.

Additionally, many persons have noted that when travelers return to New York from an extended sojourn abroad they often feel themselves confronted with "brutal ugliness" [1] and a distinctive, frenetic atmosphere whose contributing details are, for a few hours or days, remarkably sharp and clear. This period of fresh perception should receive special attention in the study of city atmosphere. For, in a few days, details which are initially arresting become less easy to specify. They are assimilated into an increasingly familiar background atmosphere which, though important in setting the tone of things, is difficult to analyze. There is no better point at which to begin the study of city atmosphere than at the moment when a traveler returns from abroad.

3. The popular myths and expectations each visitor brings to the city will also affect the way in which he perceives it [see 19]. Sometimes a person's preconceptions about a city are relatively accurate distillations of its character, but preconceptions may also reinforce myths of filtering the visitor's perceptions to conform with his expectations. Preconceptions affect not only a person's perceptions of a city but what he reports about it.

The influence of a person's urban base line on his perceptions of a given city, the differences between the observations of the long-time inhabitant and those of the newcomer, and the filtering effect of personal expectations and stereotypes raise serious questions about the validity of travelers' reports. Moreover,

---

* Editor's note: See Wohlwill's article (p. 154) for an elaboration of this idea in terms of "adaptation level."

no social psychologist wants to rely exclusively on verbal accounts if he is attempting to obtain an accurate and objective description of the cities' social texture, pace, and general atmosphere. What he needs to do is to devise means of embedding objective experimental measures in the daily flux of city life, measures that can accurately index the qualities of a given urban atmosphere.

Experimental Comparisons of Behavior

Roy Feldman [6] incorporated these principles in a comparative study of behavior toward compatriots and foreigners in Paris, Athens, and Boston. Feldman wanted to see

1. whether absolute levels and patterns of helpfulness varied significantly from city to city, and
2. whether inhabitants in each city tended to treat compatriots differently from foreigners.

He examined five concrete behavioral episodes, each carried out by a team of native experimenters and a team of American experimenters in the three cities. The episodes involved

1. asking natives of the city for street directions;
2. asking natives to mail a letter for the experimenter;
3. asking natives if they had just dropped a dollar bill (or the Greek or French equivalent) when the money actually belonged to the experimenter himself;
4. deliberately overpaying for goods in a store to see if the cashier would correct the mistake and return the excess money; and
5. determining whether taxicab drivers overcharged strangers and whether they took the most direct route available.

Feldman's results suggest some interesting contrasts in the profiles of the three cities. In Paris, for instance, certain stereotypes were borne out. Parisian cab drivers overcharged foreigners significantly more often than they overcharged compatriots. But other aspects of the Parisians' behavior were not in accord with American preconceptions: in mailing a letter for a stranger, Parisians treated foreigners significantly better than Athenians or Bostonians did, and, when asked to mail letters that were already stamped, Parisians actually treated foreigners better than they treated compatriots. Similarly, Parisians were significantly more honest than Athenians or Bostonians in resisting the temptation to claim money that was not theirs, and Parisians were the only citizens who were more honest with foreigners than with compatriots in this experiment.

Feldman's studies not only begin to quantify some of the variables that give a city its distinctive texture but they also provide a methodological model for other comparative research. His most important contribution is his successful application of objective, experimental measures to everyday situations, a mode of study which provides conclusions about urban life that are more pertinent than those achieved through laboratory experiments.

Tempo and Pace

Another important component of a city's atmosphere is its tempo or pace, an attribute frequently remarked on but less often studied. Does a city have a frenetic, hectic quality, or is it easygoing and leisurely? In any empirical treatment of this question, it is best to start in a very simple way. Walking speeds of pedestrians in different cities and in cities and towns should be measured and compared. William Berkowitz [4] of Lafayette College has undertaken an extensive series of studies of walking speeds in Philadelphia, New York, and Boston, as well as in small and moderate-sized towns. Berkowitz writes that "there does appear to be a significant linear relation between walking speed and size of municipality, but the absolute size of the difference varies by less than ten percent."

Perhaps the feeling of rapid tempo is due not so much to absolute pedestrian speeds as to the constant need to dodge others in a large city to avoid collisions with other pedestrians. (One basis for computing the adjustments needed to avoid collisions is to hypothesize a set of mechanical manikins sent walking along a city street and to calculate the number of collisions when no adjustments are made. Clearly, the higher the density of manikins the greater the number of collisions per unit of time, or, conversely, the greater the frequency of adjustments needed in higher population densities to avoid collisions.)

Patterns of automobile traffic contribute to a city's tempo. Driving an automobile provides a direct means of translating feelings about tempo into measurable acceleration, and a city's pace should be particularly evident in vehicular velocities, patterns of acceleration, and latency of response to traffic signals. The inexorable tempo of New York is expressed, further, in the manner in which pedestrians stand at busy intersections, impatiently awaiting a change in traffic light, making tentative excursions into the intersection, and frequently surging into the street even before the green light appears.

Visual Components

Hall has remarked [8] that the physical layout of the city also affects its atmosphere. A gridiron pattern of streets gives the visitor a feeling of rationality, orderliness, and predictability but is sometimes monotonous. Winding lanes or streets branching off at strange angles, with many forks (as in Paris or Greenwich Village), create feelings of surprise and esthetic pleasure, while forcing greater decision-making in plotting one's course. Some would argue that the visual component is all-important—that the "look" of Paris or New York can almost be equated with its atmosphere. To investigate this hypothesis, we might conduct studies in which only blind, or at least blindfolded, respondents were used. We would no doubt discover that each city has a distinctive texture even when the visual component is eliminated.

Sources of Ambiance

Thus far we have tried to pinpoint and measure some of the factors that contribute to the distinctive atmosphere of a great city. But we may also ask, Why do differences in urban atmosphere exist? How did they come about, and are they in any way related to the factors of density, large numbers, and heterogeneity discussed above?

First, there is the obvious factor that, even among great cities, populations and densities differ. The metropolitan areas of New York, London, and Paris, for example, contain 15 million, 12 million, and 8 million persons, respectively. London has average densities of 43 persons per acre, while Paris is more congested, with average densities of 114 persons per acre [9]. Whatever characteristics are specifically attributable to density are more likely to be pronounced in Paris than in London.

A second factor affecting the atmosphere of cities is the source from which the populations are drawn [17]. It is a characteristic of great cities that they do not reproduce their own populations, but that their numbers are constantly maintained and augmented by the influx of residents from other parts of the country. This can have a determining effect on the city's atmosphere. For example, Oslo is a city in which almost all of the residents are only one or two generations removed from a purely rural existence, and this contributes to its almost agricultural norms.

A third source of atmosphere is the general national culture. Paris combines adaptations to the demography of cities *and* certain values specific to French culture. New York is an admixture of American values and values that arise as a result of extraordinarily high density and large population.

Finally, one could speculate that the atmosphere of a great city is traceable to the specific historical conditions under which adaptations to urban overload occurred. For example, a city which acquired its mass and density during a period of commercial expansion will respond to new demographic conditions by adaptations designed to serve purely commercial needs. Thus, Chicago, which grew and became a great city under a purely commercial stimulus, adapted in a manner that emphasizes business needs. European capitals, on the other hand, incorporate many of the adaptations which were appropriate to the period of their increasing numbers and density. Because aristocratic values were prevalent at the time of the growth of these cities, the mechanisms developed for coping with overload were based on considerations other than pure efficiency. Thus, the manners, norms, and facilities of Paris and Vienna continue to reflect esthetic values and the idealization of leisure.

Cognitive Maps of Cities

When we speak of "behavioral comparisons" among cities, we must specify which parts of the city are most relevant for sampling purposes. In a sampling of "New Yorkers," should we include residents of Bay Ridge or Flatbush as well as inhabitants of Manhattan? And, if so, how should we weight our sample distribution? One approach to defining relevant boundaries in sampling is to determine which areas form the psychological or cognitive core of the city. We weight our samples most heavily in the areas considered by most people to represent the "essence" of the city.

The psychologist is less interested in the geographic layout of a city or in its political boundaries than in the cognitive representation of the city. Hans Blumenfeld [5] points out that the perceptual structure of a modern city can be expressed by the "silhouette" of the group of skyscrapers at its center and that of smaller groups of office buildings at its "subcenters" but that urban areas can no longer, because of their vast extent, be experienced as fully articulated sets of streets, squares, and space.

In *The Image of the City* [12], Kevin Lynch created a cognitive map of Boston by interviewing Bostonians. Perhaps his most significant finding was that, while certain landmarks, such as Paul Revere's house and the Boston Common, as well as the paths linking them, are known to almost all Bostonians, vast areas of the city are simply unknown to its inhabitants.

Using Lynch's technique, Donald Hooper [10] created a psychological map of New York from the answers to the study questionnaire on Paris, London, and New York. Hooper's results were similar to those of Lynch: New York appears to have a dense core of well-known landmarks in midtown Manhattan, surrounded by the vast unknown reaches of Queens, Brooklyn, and the Bronx. Times Square, Rockefeller Center, and the Fifth Avenue department stores alone comprise half the places specifically cited by respondents as the haunts in which they spent most of their time. However, outside the midtown area, only scattered landmarks were recognized. Another interesting pattern is evident: even the best-known symbols of New York are relatively self-contained, and the pathways joining them appear to be insignificant on the map.

The psychological map can be used for more than just sampling techniques. Lynch [12] argues, for instance, that a good city is highly "imageable," having many known symbols joined by widely known pathways, whereas dull cities are gray and nondescript. We might test the relative "imagibility" of several cities by determining the proportion of residents who recognize sampled geographic points and their accompanying pathways.

If we wanted to be even more precise we could construct a cognitive map that would not only show the symbols of the city but would measure the precise degree of cognitive significance of any given point in the city relative to any other. By applying a pattern of points to a map of New York City, for example, and taking photographs from each point, we could determine what proportion of a sample of the city's inhabitants could identify the locale specified by each point (see Fig. 2). We might even take the subjects blindfolded to a point represented on the map, then remove the blindfold and ask them to identify their location from the view around them.

One might also use psychological maps to gain insight into the differing perceptions of a given city that are held by members of its cultural subgroups,

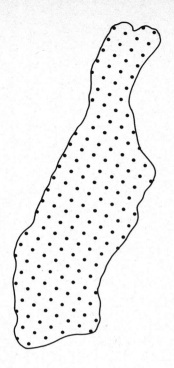

FIGURE 2.   *To create a psychological map of Manhattan, geographic points are sampled, and, from photographs, the subjects attempt to identify the location of each point. To each point a numerical index is assigned indicating the proportion of persons able to identify its location.*

and into the manner in which their perceptions may change. In the earlier stages of life, whites and Negroes alike probably have only a limited view of the city, centering on the immediate neighborhood in which they are raised. In adolescence, however, the field of knowledge of the white teen-ager probably undergoes rapid enlargement; he learns of opportunities in midtown and outlying sections and comes to see himself as functioning in a larger urban field. But the process of ghettoization, to which the black teen-ager is subjected, may well hamper the expansion of his sense of the city. These are speculative notions, but they are readily subject to precise test.

Conclusion

I have tried to indicate some organizing theory that starts with the basic facts of city life: large numbers, density, and heterogeneity. These are external to the individual. He experiences these factors as overloads at the level of roles, norms, cognitive functions, and facilities. These overloads lead to adaptive mechanisms which create the distinctive tone and behaviors of city life. These notions, of course, need to be examined by objective comparative studies of cities and towns.

A second perspective concerns the differing atmospheres of great cities, such as Paris, London, and New York. Each has a distinctive flavor, offering a differentiable quality of experience. More precise knowledge of urban atmosphere seems attainable through application of the tools of experimental inquiry.

References

1. ABELSON, P. *Science* 165 (1969):853.
2. ABUZA, N. "The Paris–London–New York Questionnaires." Harvard University, unpublished.
3. ALTMAN, D.; LEVINE, M.; NADIEN, M.; AND VILLENA, J. Graduate Center, The City University of New York. Unpublished research.
4. BERKOWITZ, W. Personal communication.
5. BLUMENFELD, H. In *The Quality of Urban Life.* Beverly Hills, Cal.: Sage, 1969.
6. FELDMAN, R. E. *J. Personality Soc. Psychol.* 10 (1968):202.
7. GAERTNER, S., AND BICKMAN, L. Graduate Center, The City University of New York. Unpublished research.
8. HALL, E. T. *The Hidden Dimension.* New York: Doubleday, 1966.
9. HALL, P. *The World Cities.* New York: McGraw-Hill, 1966.
10. HOOPER, D. Harvard University. Unpublished.
11. LATANÉ, B., AND DARLEY, J. *Amer. Sci.* 57 (1969):244.
12. LYNCH, K. *The Image of the City.* Cambridge, Mass.: M.I.T. Press and Harvard University Press, 1960.
13. McKENNA, W., AND MORGENTHAU, S. Graduate Center, The City University of New York. Unpublished research.
14. MEIER, R. L. *A Communications Theory of Urban Growth.* Cambridge, Mass.: M.I.T. Press, 1962.
15. MILGRAM, S., AND HOLLANDER, P. *Nation* 25 (1964):602.
16. *New York Times,* June 15, 1969.
17. PARK, R. E., BURGESS, E. W., AND McKENZIE, R. D. *The City.* Chicago: University of Chicago Press, 1967, pp. 1–45.
18. SIMMEL, G. *The Sociology of Georg Simmel.* K. H. Wolff, ed. New York: Macmillan, 1950. (Translated from *Die Grossstadte und das Geistesleben Die Grossstadt.* Dresden: Jansch, 1903.)
19. STRAUSS, A. L., ed. *The American City: A Sourcebook of Urban Imagery.* Chicago: Aldine, 1968.
20. WATERS, J. Graduate Center, The City University of New York. Unpublished research.
21. WIRTH, L. *Amer. J. Soc.* 44 (1938):1.
     Wirth's ideas have come under heavy criticism by contemporary city planners, who point out that the city is broken down into neighborhoods, which fulfill many of the functions of small towns. See, for example, H. J. Gans, *People and Plans: Essays on Urban Problems and Solutions,* New York: Basic Books, 1968; J. Jacobs, *The Death and Life of Great American Cities,* New York: Random House, 1961; G. D. Suttles, *The Social Order of the Slum,* Chicago: University of Chicago Press, 1968.
22. ZIMBARDO, P. G. Paper presented at the Nebraska Symposium on Motivation, 1969.

Humanistic Theory:
The Third Revolution in Psychology

FLOYD W. MATSON

Quite different in tone from the other articles in this section is this selection, in which Floyd Matson proclaims the humanists' concern with the wholeness and uniqueness of the person and strikes hard at psychologists of behavioral or psychoanalytic persuasion. Matson's impassioned prose and, more important, his almost elitist claim to concern for mankind seem to be characteristic of many "humanistic" psychologists.

In this article, Matson takes behaviorists and psychoanalysts to task mainly for their deterministic views of human motivation; this is a legitimate dispute, for the ancient dilemma of free will versus determinism has by no means been resolved. But to extend that dispute to an attack on the concepts and tools of the scientific method is a bit extreme. What benefits humankind is humanistic; and understanding of the person—whether couched in terms of *drives* or *instincts* or *identity* or *growth*—is the consummate humanism.

The oft-used term *humanistic psychology* has the appearance of what semanticists call a redundant tautology. After all, psychology is the science of mind, is it not? And is not mind the property of human beings? And is not all psychology then humanistic?

The answer to all of the questions is, in a word, no. Psychology is the study of more than mind, and of less than mind. It is the science of behavior, much of which is "mindless." Nor is the behavior studied by psychologists only that of humans; much of it, perhaps most, is that of animals. And where it is human behavior that is being studied, it is very often physiological rather than psychical. It would not be stretching the truth too far to observe that much of what goes on in psychology is not "psychological" at all. And that brings us to the reason for the third revolution—the renaissance of humanism in psychology.

SOURCE: This article first appeared in *The Humanist*, March/April 1971, and is reprinted by permission.

Humanistic psychology tries to tell it not like it is, but like it ought to be. It seeks to bring psychology back to its source, to the *psyche*, where it all began and where it finally culminates. But there is more to it than that. Humanistic psychology is not just the study of "human being"; it is a commitment to human becoming.

It was a humanistic philosopher, Kurt Riezler, who said that "science begins with respect for the subject matter." Unfortunately that is not the view of all scientists, whether in the hard sciences of nature or in the softer sciences of man and mind. It is almost, as it seems to me, a defining characteristic of behaviorist psychology that it begins with *dis*respect for the subject matter, and therefore leads straightaway to what Norbert Wiener (a pretty hard scientist himself) called the "inhuman use of human beings." At any rate, I know of no greater disrespect for the human subject than to treat him as an object—unless it is to demean that object further by fragmenting it into drives, traits, reflexes, and other mechanical hardware. But that is the procedure of behaviorism, if not of all experimental psychology; it is a procedure openly admitted, indeed triumphantly proclaimed, in the name of Science and Truth, of Objectivity and Rigor, and of all else that is holy in these precincts. And it leads in a straight line out of the ivory tower into the brave new world of Walden Two.

Everyone remembers, I am sure, that curious utopian novel, *Walden Two*, written more than 20 years ago by the preeminent behaviorist of our generation, B. F. Skinner. His book presented such a stark scenario of behavioral engineering and mind manipulation, such a "conditional" surrender of autonomy and freedom on the part of its docile characters, that many readers at the time mistakenly supposed it to be a clever put-on, a satirical prophecy of the nightmare shape of things to come if ever a free society should relax its vigilant defense of the values of liberty and responsibility—especially the liberty and responsibility of choice.

But that was what Skinner's novel openly defied and disparaged; the Elysian community it projected was a sort of crystal palace (or womb with a view) within which perfect peace and security might abide forever—tranquility without trauma, pleasure without pain, attainment without struggle—and all at the trivial price of the freedom to make choices, the right (as it were) to blunder. The key to the kingdom of Walden Two was operant conditioning; by this magical technique, applied to all residents from birth, the "Hamlet syndrome" (the anxiety of choice) was efficiently removed. Like that wonderful Mrs. Prothro in Dylan Thomas's Christmas story, who "said the right thing always," so the creatures of Skinner's novel were conditioned to make the right choices automatically. It was instant certitude, at the price of all volition. Like Pavlov's dogs, Skinner's people made only conditioned responses to the stimulus of their master's voice.

Let us recognize that such a homeostatic paradise, like the classless society and the heavenly city, has great seductive appeal for many, especially in an age of anxiety and a time of troubles. It appeals particularly to those with a low tolerance for ambiguity and a high rage for order. I believe it was Thomas Huxley who was so fearful of chance and choice as to declare that if he were offered a world of absolute security and certainty, at the price of surrendering his personal freedom, he would close instantly with the bargain. Unlike his grandson, Aldous, whose own futuristic novel made just the opposite point, the elder Huxley would surely have enjoyed the still life on Skinner's Walden Pond.

Let me recall now a different disposition, both existential and humanistic. It is Dostoevsky's underground man, struggling to be heard by the Establishment above. "After all," he says,

> I do not really insist on suffering or on prosperity either. I insist on my *caprice*, and its being guaranteed to me when necessary. Suffering would be out of place in vaudevilles, for instances; I know that. In the crystal palace it is even unthinkable; suffering means doubt, means negation, and what would be the good of a crystal palace if there could be any doubt about it? . . . You believe in a crystal edifice that can never be destroyed; that is, an edifice at which one would neither be able to stick out one's tongue nor thumb one's nose on the sly. And perhaps I am afraid of this edifice just because it is of crystal and can never be destroyed and that one could not even put one's tongue out at it even on the sly. (*The Short Novels of Dostoevsky*, Dial Press, New York, 1945, p. 152)

Now *there*, as Sartre might say, is an existentialism that is a humanism.

There have been, as I believe, three distinct conceptual revolutions in psychology during the course of the present century. The first, that of behaviorism, struck with the force of a revelation around 1913 and shook the foundations of academic psychology for a generation. Behaviorism arose in reaction to the excessive preoccupation of 19th-century psychology with consciousness, and with introspection as a way of getting at the data of conscious mental activity. The behaviorists reacted with a vengeance. They threw out not only consciousness, but all the resources of the mind. The mind, to them, was the ghost in the machine, and they did not believe in ghosts. The founding father of the movement, John B. Watson, declared in an early proclamation, a kind of behaviorist manifesto, that the behaviorist began "by sweeping aside all medieval conceptions. He dropped from his scientific vocabulary all subjective terms such as *sensation, perception, image, desire, purpose*, and even *thinking* and *emotion* as they were subjectively defined" (*Behaviorism* [1924], University of Chicago Press, Chicago, 1958, pp. 5–6).

Overt behavior, that which could be seen and measured, was all that counted. And all that was needed to explain it was the simple and classical formula of stimulus-response—with one added refinement, that of the conditioned reflex. It was this concept of conditioning, borrowed from the Russian laboratories of Pavlov and Bechterev, that gave the real revolutionary impetus to Watson's behaviorist movement. Conditioning was power; it was control. This was no merely objective psychology, for all its scientific claims; it was an applied psychology—and what it was applied to, or rather against, was man. "The interest of the behaviorist," said Watson, "is more than the interest of a spectator; he wants to control man's reactions as physical scientists want to control and manipulate other natural phenomena" (*Ibid.*, p. 11). Just as man was simply "an assembled organic machine ready to run," so the behaviorist was no pure scientist but an engineer unable to keep from tinkering with the machinery. Pointing out that such sciences as chemistry and biology were gaining control over their subject matter, Watson inquired, "Can psychology ever get control? Can I make someone who is not afraid of snakes, afraid of them, and how?" The answer was clear: And how!

"In short," said Watson, "the cry of the behaviorist is, 'Give me the baby and my world to bring it up in and I'll make it crawl and walk; I'll make it climb and use its hands in constructing buildings of stone or wood; I'll make it a thief, a gunman, or a dope fiend.' The possibility of shaping in any direction is almost endless" (*The Ways of Behaviorism*, Harper, New York, 1926, p. 35).

That should be enough to suggest the general character (and authoritarian personality) of behaviorist psychology, the first of the three psychological revolutions that have taken place in our century. The second revolution was, of course, that of Freud. It is noteworthy that psychoanalysis and behaviorism made their appearance at roughly the same time, give or take a decade, and that both of them emerged in reaction against the accent on consciousness in traditional psychology. Apart from these coincidences, however, there was little in common between these two movements, and there was a great deal that put them at opposite poles.

Whereas behaviorism placed all its stress upon the external environment (that is, upon stimuli from the outer world) as the controlling factor in behavior, psychoanalysis placed its emphasis upon the internal environment (upon stimuli from within, in the form of drives and instincts). For Freud, man was very much a creature of instinct—and in particular of two primary instincts, those of life and death (*Eros* and *Thanatos*). These two instincts were in conflict not only with each other but with the world, with culture. Society was based, said Freud, on renunciation of the instincts via the mechanism of repression. But the instincts did not give up without a struggle. In fact, they never gave up; they could not be vanquished, only temporarily blocked. Life, then, was a constant alternation between frustration and aggression. Neither for the individual person nor for the culture was there a permanent solution or "happy ending"; there were only compromises, expedients, working adjustments. The price of civilization, indeed, was mass neurosis— the result of the necessary suppression of the natural instincts of man. But if that seems bad, the alternative was worse; whenever the repressive forces are for a moment relaxed, declared Freud, "we see man as a savage beast to whom the thought of sparing his own kind is alien" (*Civilization and Its Discontents*, Hogarth, London, 1930, p. 86).

Perhaps the most interesting, not to say frightening, concept advanced by Freud was that of *Thanatos*, the aggression or death instinct, which he regarded as an innate and irresistible drive toward the destruction of oneself and others. What is especially significant about this bleak conception of man's aggressive nature is the "comeback" it has been making in recent years after a long period of almost total eclipse. The current revival of the shadow side of Freud, the pessimistic musings of his later years, does not tell us so much about Freud as it does about the temper of our own time. I shall return to this point.

The main point I want to make immediately about the psychoanalytic movement, in its Freudian form, is that it presents a picture of man as very much the "victim-spectator," as Gordon Allport has put it, of blind forces working through him. For all its differences with behaviorism, Freudian theory agrees in the fundamental image of man as a stimulus-response machine, although the stimuli that work their will upon the human being come from within rather than from without. Freud's determinism was not environmental, like Watson's, but psychogenetic; nevertheless, it was a determinism, and it left little room for spontaneity, creativity, rationality, or responsibility. The declared faith in conscious reason that underlay Freudian therapy (rather more than Freudian theory) did not prevent his insistently minimizing the role of reason as an actual or potential determinant of personality and conduct —nor, on the other hand, from maximizing the thrust of irrational forces that press their claims both from "below" (the id) and from "above" (the superego). In Freud's topographical map of the mind, the ego, itself only partially conscious, never achieves full autonomy but functions as a kind of buffer state between the rival powers of instinct and introjected culture, between animal nature and social nurture.

I have been deliberately hard on Freud in these remarks in order to emphasize those aspects of his theory and therapy that, by virtue of their pessimism and determinism, have called out over the years the critical and creative response that (for want of a better term) we may call "humanistic psychology." This new psychology, the third revolution, represents a reaction against *both* behaviorism and orthodox psychoanalysis; it is for that reason that humanistic psychology has been called the "third force." But perhaps the first thing to say about it is that, unlike the two movements of thought that precede and oppose it, humanistic psychology is not a single body of theory but a collection or convergence of a number of lines and schools of thought. If it owes nothing to behaviorism, it does owe much to psychoanalysis, although less perhaps to Freud himself than to the considerable number of Freudian heretics and deviationists, beginning with his own associates of the original Vienna Circle and culminating in the so-called neo-Freudians (anti-Freudians, really) of the second generation.

For despite the many differences among them, those who broke away one by one from the side of Freud shared a number of crucial insights and commitments. Adler, Jung, Rank, Stekel, Ferenczi—all these early associates found themselves unable to accept Freud's theory of instinctual determinism (specifically, his libido theory) and his tendency to find the source of all difficulty and motivation in the remote past. These deviationists began to place equal or greater emphasis upon the present (that is, upon the here and now, the "presence" of the patient) and also upon the future (that is, upon the pull of aspiration and purpose, the goal or life-plan of the individual). What this implied was a greater reliance upon the consciousness of the person in analysis or therapy: a new respect for his powers of will and of reason, his capacity to choose and to understand.

In Adler's work, this emphasis took the form of virtually converting the psychoanalytic therapy session into a dialogue or conversation on the conscious level—which of course enraged Freud, who thought that Adler had betrayed the basic postulate of unconscious motivation. In Jung's work, the new approach took the form of emphasizing what he called the "prospective factor," the pull of purpose as opposed to the push of instinct (and in particular the push of erotic instinct); it also took the form, in Jung's later years, of increasing stress upon understanding the other, whether neurotic patient or normal individual, in his unique identity. This involved a kind of intuitive and sympathetic understanding, which Jung distinguished from scientific knowledge and which led him finally to advocate abandoning the textbooks altogether in any venture into helping or healing. In the case of Otto Rank, another of the heretics of the original Freudian circle, the deviation took the form of an emphasis upon the existential will of the person, that is, upon his capacity for self-direction and self-control.

The common denominator in these various lines of theory and therapy was, I believe, *respect for the person*, recognition of the other not as a case, or an object, or a field of forces, or a bundle of instincts, but as himself. In terms of theory, it meant respect for his powers of creativity and responsibility; in terms of therapy, it meant respect for his values, his intentions, and, above all, his peculiar identity.

This recognition of *man-in-person*, as opposed to *man-in-general*, goes to the heart of the difference between humanistic psychology, in any of its forms or schools, and scientific psychologies such as behaviorism. Not only in psychoanalysis, but in other fields as well, increasing number of students have found themselves drawn to the unsettling conclusion that the definitive features of a human being cannot be made out at all from a "psychological distance," but can be brought into focus only by understanding (literally, by "standing under") the unique perspective of the individual himself.

This emphasis upon the human person, upon the individual in his wholeness and uniqueness, is a central feature of the "psychology of humanism." But there is an important corollary within which this personalistic emphasis would be inadequate and distorted. That corollary is the recognition, to use a phrase of Rank, that "the self needs the other." This recognition is variously expressed: For the neo-Freudians, it points to the importance of relationship in the growth of personality; for the existentialists, it leads to emphasis on the themes of dialogue, encounter, meeting, intersubjectivity, and so on.

While this recognition is broadly shared by humanistic psychotherapists, analysts, personality theorists, perceptual psychologists and others, perhaps the most impressive and systematic development of the idea has been provided by existential thinkers, both in psychology and philosophy. There is a striking similarity in the formulation of this self-other relationship by various existentialists. Martin Buber's philosophy of dialogue, centering around the I-Thou relation, is probably the most influential and possibly the most profound. Among other fruitful effects, it has given rise to a "psychology of meeting" that finds its paradigm in the therapeutic encounter. The significance of Buber's general concept has been well described by Will Herberg:

> The term I-Thou points to a relation of person to person, of subject to subject, a relation of reciprocity involving "meeting" or "encounter," while the term I-It points to a relation of person to thing, of subject to object, involving some form of utilization, domination, or control, even if it is only so-called "objective" knowing. The I-Thou relation, which Buber usually designated as "relation" par excellence, is one in which one can enter only with the whole of his being, as a genuine person. (*The Writings of Martin Buber*, Meridian Books, New York, 1956, p. 14)

It follows that the relationship of therapy in its ideal development represents an authentic encounter "on the sharp edge of existence" between two human beings, one seeking and the other helping. This mutual recognition, which is never immediate but only a possibility to be achieved, cuts through the conventional defenses and postures of both partners to permit each to reach out as a person to the other as a person. What is demanded of the doctor in particular, says Buber, is that he "himself step forth out of his protected professional superiority into the elementary situation between one who asks and one who is asked" (Maurice Friedman, *Martin Buber: The Life of Dialogue*, Harper Torchbooks, New York, 1960, p. 190).

Apart from its uses by existential psychologists and psychoanalysts—such as Ludwig Binswanger, Viktor Frankl, Rollo May, and others—Buber's immensely fertile concept of I-Thou "meeting" finds parallels and reverberations in the work of other existential philosophers, especially those commonly referred to as the religious existentialists or existential theologians. For Gabriel Marcel, who came independently to the formula of I-and-Thou, the sense of genuine encounter is conveyed by the term *intersubjectivity*, implying an authentic communication on the order of communion. "The fact is," writes Marcel, "that we can understand ourselves by starting from the other, or from others, and only by starting from them; . . . it is only in this perspective that a legitimate love of self can be conceived" (*The Mystery of Being*, Gateway, Chicago, 1960, volume 2, p. 9). This insight, quite similar to Fromm's concept of productive love and self-realization, implies a reciprocity of knowing in which what "I am" as well as what "Thou art" is made known only through the mutual experience of what "We are." Each communicant recognizes himself in the other.

In Paul Tillich's "therapeutic theology," this general appreciation of the enlightening role of engagement or meeting is applied directly to psychotherapy, which is regarded as the "community of healing." In common with other existentialists, Tillich believes that the personal troubles represented by neurosis stem fundamentally from failures in relationships with others, thereby resulting in self-alienation from any genuine contact with the world. The central therapeutic problem thus becomes one of "acceptance" or, more precisely, of successive stages of acceptance culminating in acceptance of oneself and of the world of others.

In this new kind of therapeutic encounter—and here is another humanistic tenet—there are no silent partners. The existential therapist (which is to say, the humanistic therapist) is no longer the blank screen or "mute catalyzer" that he was in Freud's day, but rather is a participant with the whole of his being. He participates not only for the purpose of helping, but even more basically for the purpose of knowing or understanding. "You must participate in a self," according to Tillich, "in order to know what it is. By participation you change it" (*The Courage to Be*, Yale University Press, New Haven, 1959, p. 124). The inference is that the kind of knowledge essential to psychology and psychotherapy is to be gained not by detached observation but by participant-observation (to use Harry Stack Sullivan's phrase). It may be possible, through detachment, to gain knowledge that is "useful"; but only through participation is it possible to gain the knowledge that is *helpful*.

In any adequate account of the sources and forces that have nourished the movement of humanistic psychology (which this brief sketch does not pretend to be), much more would have to be said in acknowledgment of the contributions of individual theorists and therapists. Fortunately, there are a number of comprehensive surveys available; among them, James Bugental's *Challenges of Humanistic Psychology*, Anthony Sutich and Miles Vich's *Readings in Humanistic Psychology*, and my own *The Broken Image* (especially Chapters 6 and 7). But even the present essay cannot avoid mention of at least a few of the movers and shakers behind the third revolution, notably: Abraham Maslow, who more than any other deserves to be recognized as the "spiritual father" of the humanistic movement in psychology; Gordon Allport, the great American personalist and heir to the mantle of William James; Rollo May, who introduced the existential approach to American psychology and has developed it creatively; Carl Rogers, whose therapeutic mandate of "unconditional regard" for the client resembles Tillich's philosophy of ultimate concern; Erich Fromm, the most influential of the neo-Freudians, who has long since moved from psychoanalysis to the higher ground of social philosophy and cultural criticism; Henry A. Murray, inspired teacher and exemplar of humanism; Charlotte Buhler, who has made us all aware of how important personal goal-values and the whole course of human life are to psychological understanding.

In conclusion—if I may be excused the puff of vanity—I wish to suggest something of the activist potential of humanistic psychology by repeating a few paragraphs from a talk I gave before the annual conference of the Association for Humanistic Psychology:

> I'd like to propose one line of commitment, and of protest, that we might well undertake as humanistic psychologists. That course is, following Jefferson, to swear undying opposition to all forms of tyranny over the mind of man. I propose that we commit ourselves to the defense of psychological liberty. For I believe that quite possibly the greatest threat of freedom in the world today (and tomorrow) is the threat to freedom of the mind—which is, at bottom, the power to choose.

> That freedom is threatened now on all sides. It is threatened by what Herbert Marcuse has called the "one-dimensional society," which seeks to reduce the categories of thought and discourse to a kind of consensual endorsement of the directives of an aggressive and acquisitive culture. It is threatened by the technology of mass society, mass culture and mass communication, which manufactures (*pace* Marshall McLuhan) a marshmallow world of plastic pleasures in which the bland lead the bland endlessly into the sea of tranquility.

> Freedom of the mind is also threatened by the biological revolution and its psychological corollaries—not only by the familiar cuckoo's nest of lobotomies and shock treatments, over which no one can fly, but by the imminent breakthroughs in "genetic surgery" and kindred interventions that promise to make feasible the rewiring and reprogramming of the brain mechanism.

> Perhaps most critically of all, our psychological liberty is threatened by failure of nerve: by our inability to live up to and live out the democratic dogma, which rests upon faith in the capacity of the ordinary human being to lead his own life, to go his own way and to grow his own way, to be himself and to know himself and to become more himself. This failure of nerve is rampant in the field of education; it is a kind of occupational disease of social work, where the aided person becomes a client who is treated as a patient who is diagnosed as incurable. And it is a pervasive feature of the landscape of academic psychology and behavioral science in so many saddening ways that it would take a book (which I have already written) to enumerate them all.

> But let me mention just one of the ways in which this failure of nerve manifests itself in the study of man. The old reactionary doctrine of Original Sin, of innate depravity, has lately been enjoying a very popular and large-scale revival. It takes the form of the hypothesis of aggression as a fixed instinctual endowment of man—a genetic taint in the blood, as it were, a dark stain in the double helix of each of us. The alleged discovery or rediscovery of this killer instinct is being hailed in the book clubs and popular journals as if it were the ultimate benediction, the final good news of man's redemption. How are we to account for the popu-

larity of this darkly pessimistic thesis? How account for the best-seller status of Lorenz's *On Aggression*, Ardrey's *Territorial Imperative* and *African Genesis*, and Desmond Morris's *Naked Ape?*

I believe the answer is clear: mass failure of nerve. Nothing could be better calculated to get us off the uncomfortable hook of personal responsibility, of self-control and self-determination, than this doctrine of our innate aggressive propensities. That's why we fight; that's why we hate; that's why we cannot love one another or ourselves. People are no damn good—and there's an end of it.

Well, I do not believe that humanistic psychologists will accept that cop-out. I propose therefore that we place the full weight of our movement, the whole third force of it, against this and all other threats to the freedom of the mind and the autonomy of the person. Let us become the active conscience of the psychological fraternity, searching out and exposing—and condemning—each and every dehumanizing, depersonalizing and demoralizing force that would move us further down the road to the Brave New World and the technocratic society—that social laboratory of the behaviorist's dreams and the humanist's nightmares.

For down that road lies not just the end of psychological freedom, but the death of humanity.

Physiological and Cultural Determinants of Behavior

NEAL E. MILLER

In this paper, presented during the centennial celebration of the National Academy of Sciences, Neal Miller surveys much of human motivation. He begins with the brain. How can the developing person organize the labyrinth of millions upon millions of neurons into something ordered enough to perceive a simple straight-line figure? What happens when we stimulate various patterns or clusters of these cells? Does the stimulus (temperature, chemicals, electricity) matter? It seems that some genetic formula arranges parts of the growing human embryo into a systematic array of brain cells, the stimulation of certain of which results in behavior. Depending on which cells are excited and the stimulus that excites them, the ultimate behavior may be perception of a figure, the experience of hunger, or an ulcer. This condition seems to be innate, and these behaviors rooted in the "wiring" of the organism. But what of learning? Surely the data of sociologists, anthropologists, and others who likewise interpret man and his relationships make it clear that behavior is to a great extent influenced by what we learn. Consider taboos, for example; no array of firing neurons exists that by itself is likely to prevent or encourage infanticide. "To understand man, we must study his culture as well as his physiology and psychology"—Miller's most important point in this exciting study is his distinction between the basic principles and the crucial conditions of human learning and behavior.

The preceding lectures have presented an exhilarating panorama of man's scientific discoveries ranging from the creation of the elements during cataclysmically violent explosions in the ancient vast galaxies of space to the more

SOURCE: From *Scientific Endeavor*, Rockefeller University Press, New York, 1965. Copyright © 1965 by the Rockefeller University Press. Reprinted by permission.
Note: The author wishes to thank Drs. W. Goodenough, G. P. Murdock, C. Pfaffman, and H. Riecken for making helpful comments on a rough draft of this paper, and Mrs. Emily Derow for overtime work in preparing the final copy in time for the meeting.
Some of the work on this paper was supported by grant MY 647 from NIMH of the United States Public Health Service.

recent evolution of living systems on our own tiny temperate earth. I have been given the task of making a transition from these topics to those for the next session. How is it that the organisms developing from certain complex helical molecules of DNA will be standing on this platform to talk to you about problems involved in the communication of scientific knowledge, its relationship to public policy, and the satisfaction of human aspirations?

I cannot answer this question, but I can sketch for you certain relevant steps toward an answer. These will also serve to illustrate a few of the many diverse recent advances in the broad area of behavioral science.

Behavioral scientists are beginning to learn something of how the brain works. The human brain has at least 10^{10} neurons, many of which have thousands of complex branches, resulting in a total of at least 10^{13} (a million times 10 million) synaptic connections. Many of these myriad connections appear to be innately determined. They provide an essential basis of aspects of everyday behavior which all of us casually take for granted. One of these is recognizing a horizontal line. This is not as simple as one might think, because as one's head and eyes move, the same horizontal line stimulates quite different arrays of points on the retina. We are beginning to learn something of how such perception is achieved.

Using microelectrodes to record the activity of individual neurons, Hubel and Wiesel [34] find in the visual cortex single nerve cells that fire whenever a specific horizontal line on the retina is illuminated. Presumably the many different receptors stimulated by the points on this specific line are each connected to this cell. Other cells fire when specific horizontal lines in other locations are illuminated. These cells do not respond to general changes in illumination or to small patches on the line. Yet other cells will fire whenever *any* horizontal line is illuminated. Presumably each of these neurons receives connections from many cells each responding to different horizontal lines. Because of the uniformity with which such cells are arranged in orderly columns, their connections presumably are largely innately pre-determined, although experience is necessary for certain other aspects of complex visual perception [24].

Similar arrangements are found for responding to lines oriented in other directions and to a considerable number of other salient features of the visual world. This work begins to give us an idea of how a multitude of specific connections in the brain abstract information from the stimulation of individual rods and cones and allow us to respond to more general attributes, such as a line running in a specific direction.

You have seen how one aspect of the innate organization of the brain provides a basis for everyday behavior. There are many other such examples. Even at the level of human social behavior, we may have many organized patterns, analogous to those which have been studied by the ethologists, which have not yet been recognized as instinctual because they are overlaid by social learning. I agree with previous speakers that innate behavior should continue to be vigorously investigated.

Our understanding of the mechanism of innate organization of the nervous system is being increased by recent research on lower animals. In one type of work Sperry and his associates cut the optic nerve, manipulate it in various unusual ways, and then observe the process of regeneration [4, 5]. When the eye of a frog is turned upside down, the fibers regenerating from the nerve cell in the retina do not grow along the nearest old path or remain in the same spatial relationship to each other. They are not guided by adaptive function. Instead, each of the 400,000 nerve fibers curves around to establish essentially the same connection that it had before, producing an orderly visual field which in this case is maladaptively inverted so that for the rest of its life the frog's tongue will snap downward when a fly buzzes by above. Recent experiments on the regeneration of cut optic nerves of fishes have shown that, even when the fibers are forced to detour and pass through abnormal routes in the brain, they will curve back to arrive at their preordained destination.

Such results make a number of older theories untenable and show that various parts of the embryo must differentiate into some fantastically specific coding system with appropriate matches between the more than a million receptors in the peripheral sense organs and the corresponding cells in the brain so that each of the connecting fibers will be guided to grow to the correct destination. Reflection on how a single fertilized egg cell can develop to produce these results gives one a deeper appreciation of the wonderful process of differentiation and orderly growth which has been discussed in Professor Sonneborn's illuminating lecture [66].

You have had a glimpse of one kind of research that is helping us to understand how the brain is organized and functions in the processing of information. Research on this and other functions is giving us a new picture of the brain. We know that the all-or-none conduction of the long nerve fibers called axones does not apply to the synapses which connect one nerve cell with another and are especially prevalent in the brain. Here the transmitting tip of an axone acts like a gland to secrete a chemical transmitting substance, such as acetylcholine, to achieve a finely graded response which may be either excitatory or inhibitory. These conclusions are founded on converging evidence from many techniques. Some of this work has been done by biophysicists who thrust micropipettes with several barrels into a single nerve cell, using a conductive solution in one pipette to record the electrical activity of the cell, while minute quantities of various chemicals are injected electrophoretically via the other barrels. Studies with the electron microscope have verified other details. Yet other studies have used a push-pull cannula to wash out and measure for a group of nerve cells the greater production of the transmitter, acetylcholine, when they are active than when they are not [18, 22].

The behavioral effects of stimulating considerable populations of cells in certain locations of the brain have been studied by Grossman in my laboratory [25]. He implanted a tiny cannula under anesthesia through which chemicals can later be introduced to specific sites in the brain of the normally behaving, unanesthetized animal. His studies have shown that after rat has been thoroughly satiated on both food and water, injecting a minute amount of acetylcholine or of carbachol directly into a certain part of the brain will cause it to drink, while epinephrine or norepinephrine injected into the same site will cause the same satiated rat to eat. A series of control studies support the most obvious interpretation of these results, namely, that the neuromechanisms involved in the motivations of hunger and thirst are chemically coded [26, 52].

Other fundamental changes in our ideas of the brain come from a study of the reticular formation, the central core of the brain which is characterized by a multitude of short interconnections in contrast with the longer fibers involved in the classical, more peripheral, sensory and motor systems which have long been understood. The study of this system and related nuclei has changed our concept of sleep. We now know that there is a wakefulness region of the brain. If this is damaged, the animal remains permanently somnolent. But there are also two different sleep centers. Instead of activating the animal, stimulation of these centers puts him to sleep. One center is responsible for a distinctive form of light sleep and the other for deep sleep. We no longer think of sleep as an overall decrease in the activity of the brain. We know that the rate of spontaneous firing of many cells is increased during sleep. The decreased responsiveness to external stimulation seems to be a change in the signal-to-noise ratio, which is produced more by increased noise than by decreased signal [43].

The brain used to be thought of as a passive switchboard, activated only when stimulated by the peripheral sense organs. Now we know that each signal impinges on a background of ongoing activity, is modified by this activity, and in turn modifies it. In addition to the pathways coming in from the sense organs are fibers carrying impulses from the brain to the sense organs. These impulses from the brain can either increase the rate of firing of a specific class of sense organs or decrease it. Impulses from the brain can also affect various relay points between the sense organs and the highest levels of the brain. In this way the brain can control its own input [41].

The mechanism I have just described gives us a physiological basis for some of the psychological phenomena of attention, an area in which there has been a great deal of recent research at the purely behavioral level. This purely behavioral research has discovered many lawful relationships for which the brain mechanisms have not yet been identified, although carefully controlled experiments have demonstrated that many of the phenomena, such as your capacity to listen selectively to either one of two equally loud conversations at a cocktail party, must occur centrally in the brain rather than peripherally in the sense organs [9].

In addition to its obvious relationship to the eyes, ears, nose, and taste buds that sense the external world, the brain is now known to contain within itself specialized receptors for sensing the internal state of the body. For example, by using a thermode to heat or cool a tiny specific region of the anterior hypothalamus, which is a primitive part of the brain, and by recording from there with microelectrodes, Nakayama, Hammel, Hardy, and Eisenman [57] have found that the majority of neurons are relatively unaffected by moderate changes in their temperature. However, there are some neurons here that increase their rate of firing when they are slightly heated, and others that increase their rate when they are slightly cooled. These cells seem to serve as, or be connected to, specialized "sense organs" for measuring small changes in the temperature of the surrounding blood.

Heating this region of an animal's brain causes panting and increased blood supply to the skin which serve to lower the body temperature. Cooling it causes the opposite effect of shivering and decreased blood supply to the skin [35]. It also stimulates the secretion of the thyroid, which in turn speeds up the body's burning of fuel [2]. In the experiments in which only this tiny region of the brain is cooled, these effects produce a fever, but when the whole body is cooled under normal conditions, they serve to restore the animal's temperature to normal. This is one example of a homeostatic mechanism that causes the internal environment to be held at an optimal level, in this case a constant level of temperature.

The regulative effects that I have just described are relatively direct. But the beautiful picture is extended still further by the fact that cooling this region of the brain will make a satiated animal hungry, so that it will eat, whereas heating this region elicits drinking [3]. Thus, this temperature-regulating mechanism is tied in with hunger and thirst which motivate behavior that helps the animal to anticipate its needs for the fuel it will burn to keep warm, or the water it will evaporate to cool off.

In short, a whole series of homeostatic mechanisms ranging from changes in metabolism to the motivation of the behavior of seeking food or water is touched off by the cells in the brain that respond to temperature.

A considerable number of other homeostatic mechanisms are known to be involved in the motivation of specific types of behavior. For example, certain receptors in the brain respond to osmotic pressure so that a minute injection into the proper place in the brain of a solution that is slightly more salty than body fluid will motivate animals that have just been satiated on water to drink and also to perform responses that they have learned to get water. Under normal circumstances such drinking reduces the salinity of the body fluids down to its proper level. Conversely, a minute injection of water will cause a dehydrated animal to stop drinking or working for water [46, 58].

Yet other cells of the brain respond to specific hormones so that activities such as nest-building in rats can be elicited by injecting a minute quantity of the proper hormone into the correct site in the brain [20]. Hormones can also exert an inhibitory effect on specific areas of the brain without affecting other areas. Thus the progestational steroids normally secreted by the ovary during pregnancy inhibit that part of the hypothalamus responsible for stimulating the pituitary to release the gonadotropic hormone which leads to ovulation. This hormone does not inhibit, however, other parts of the brain which are involved in sexual motivation, sexual performance, or sexual pleasure. A similar synthetic compound is used in oral contraception, a technique which would be considerably less attractive if this hormone's action on different parts of the brain were less specific [63].

Motivation has been mentioned a number of times. One of the exciting developments in recent years has been the rapid advance in our understanding of the brain mechanisms involved in certain basic motivations such as hunger and thirst. A combination of physiological and psychological techniques has been especially fruitful. In Figure 1 you will see a rat that has learned when hungry the habit of pushing back a little panel to get food. Since this rat has just been thoroughly satiated on food, it is not performing this habit. But as soon as the experimenter presses a key to stimulate a feeding center in the rat's brain with approximately 15-millionths of an ampere of current, hunger is elicited so that the rat promptly performs the learned habit of going directly to the right place and pushing open the panel to get the pellets of food hidden behind it. He does this repeatedly. As soon as the brain stimulation is turned off, the rat stops performing this habit. Stimulation of this part of the brain can also motivate a rat which has just been satiated on food to learn where to find food. Different tests of this kind prove that such stimulation elicits more than reflex eating; it functions just like hunger in motivating different types of learned food-seeking behavior [48].

Another advance has been the development of purely behavioral techniques for the laboratory study of non-homeostatic motivations, such as curiosity, the affection of the infant monkey for its mother, and the desire of a human child for social approval [6, 23, 29]. Progress in such research may be expected to continue; eventually a great deal more will be known about how to stimulate, instead of stultify, intellectual curiosity in the classroom and how to arrange the social situation so that the strong influence of the classmates will favor, instead of conflict with, the goals of the parents and teachers [10, 15].

I have sampled our scientific understanding of how the brain processes information, how it exerts a control over its own input, how it contains sense organs to help it to regulate the internal environment, and how it is involved in motivation. Let me turn now to certain recent knowledge about how we react to stress. Under stress, certain parts of the hypothalamus function as a gland to secrete substances which are carried by the blood stream and excite specific sites on the pituitary gland, causing it to secrete ACTH, which in turn causes the cortex of the adrenals to excrete ACH, which is one of the factors that causes the stomach to secrete hydrochloric acid. Under extreme circumstances, this acid and other effects of the complex reaction to stress are involved in producing ulcers in the stomach. Experimental studies have shown that direct electrical stimulation of appropriate areas of the hypothalamus can produce such ulcers [21].

Clinical observations suggest that chronic psychological stress can produce ulcers. These observations are confirmed by a variety of experiments in which various animals have been subjected to situations involving difficult decisions,

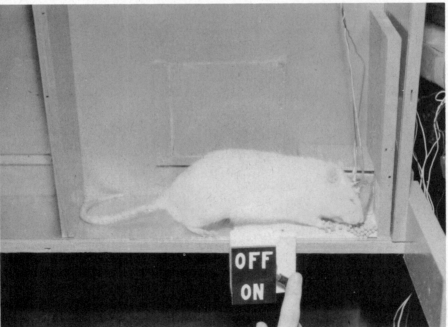

FIGURE 1. *Electrical stimulation in the "feeding area" of the lateral hypothalamus causes a rat, which was satiated and hence previously inactive, to go promptly to the right place and perform the learned habit of pushing back a hinged panel to get the pellets of food hidden behind it. (Photographed in author's laboratory. Photographs courtesy of Professor Miller.)*

136

or conflict between approaching a place to get food when hungry and staying away from it to avoid electric shocks. These experiments have shown that such psychological conditions, which presumably produce stress by activating the hypothalamus via the cortex, can elicit the pituitary-adrenal mechanism just described, increase the secretion of hydrochloric acid, and also produce ulcers [49, 59].

The same general stress mechanism seems to be involved also, along with many other factors such as the level of cholesterol and sodium chloride, in the development of arteriosclerosis, and in the production of high blood pressure. Such conditions have been produced by prolonged electrical stimulation of the hypothalamus and also by subjecting animals to psychological stresses which presumably initiate a similar chain of physiological reactions [27, 53]. Other studies are indicating that cultural conditions producing psychological stress can contribute to the physical symptoms of chronic high blood pressure. Scotch [64] has shown that members of the Zulu tribe, living in villages in which their culture is relatively unaltered, have a very low rate of hypertension. Those who have been moved to cities where their old culture patterns have been disrupted have an excessively high rate.* For both groups, the occurrence of hypertension is correlated with sociological variables presumably involved in stress, but these are different under the two sets of cultural conditions. Somewhat similar correlations between sociological conditions producing stress and hypertension have been suggested by studies of the Negroes in the Chicago area [69]. These are pioneering studies; their results must be accepted with some caution. More penetrating studies of the roles of sociological variables in psychosomatic symptoms are in progress.

As more work is being done on various aspects of stress, the convergence among the results of experimental studies by physiologists, clinical observations by psychiatrists, experimental studies by psychologists, and cultural studies by sociologists and anthropologists is becoming increasingly impressive. The results from different disciplines are beginning to fit together into a significant pattern. Additional parts of the puzzle lie within our reach, but we have just begun to grasp them.

Thus far, we have primarily sampled recent knowledge about innate physiological determinants of behavior. As Professors Hutchinson and Mayr have told you, one of the important innate capacities of higher animals is the ability to learn from experience [36, 45]. Recent advances in our knowledge of learning, memory, and reasoning merit an entire separate lecture, but there is not time [11, 14, 16, 19, 32, 37, 42, 47, 50, 51].

The great development of the human brain, which is disproportionately large in the areas representing the vocal apparatus, has been associated with a unique ability to learn and use language. Through language, the experience of one generation is passed on as a cultural heritage to the next. For long-lived

* Editor's note: Note the similarity between this and Wohlwill's analysis on p. 154 of this collection.

organisms, the process of natural selection is extraordinarily slow. Within the individual's lifetime, the process of learning directly from the environment is much faster, but still limited. When the cumulative effects of the lifetime learning of multitudes of different individuals in each generation can be passed on as part of the culture, however, developments proceed with an entirely different order of magnitude of ever accelerating speed.

Man's mode of adjustment to the environment is preeminently cultural. When a lower animal moves into a colder ecological niche, it slowly evolves the capacity to grow a thicker fur; when man moves into a much colder climate, he invents warmer clothes and a better house.

For the ancient men who had a much poorer cultural heritage, the process of innovation was vastly slower. Man has been in existence for approximately a million years. It is unlikely that his brain has evolved significantly in the last 50,000 years, and perhaps not for much longer. But man did not develop agriculture until 10,000 years ago. It took him about 5,000 more years to invent the wheel as a means of transportation, which as far as we know was invented only once and was never discovered by the Indians of North and South America, in spite of the fact that the Incas had paved roads [13]! The steam engine as a source of industrial power was invented two hundred years ago, the aeroplane within the lifetime of many of us in this room, and atomic energy and space vehicles still more recently. Compare the glacially slow initial progress with the torrent which you have seen during your own life. This is the effect of the cumulative heritage of culture.

Science is a recent product of this cultural development, one which is powerfuly accelerating the process. As President Seitz pointed out during the second session, science flourishes only under certain cultural conditions. Remember what happened to Galileo for advocating the heliocentric hypothesis, how the early anatomists were prevented from dissecting cadavers, and the present activities of antivivisectionists. Modern science would be impossible without an advanced educational system and a strong economic base. Without an enormous cultural heritage, members of the human species would never be giving the papers that are included in the next session on The Scientific Endeavor.

To understand man we must study his culture as well as his physiology and psychology. The basic *principles* of human learning and behavior depend on the innate physiological structure of man. But in many cases we have not yet been able to relate these principles to the innate physiology and have found it most useful to study them at the purely psychological, or in other words, behavioral level, and the discovery of the links to physiology will not eliminate psychology any more than the quantum mechanics of valences has eliminated the discipline of chemistry. On the other hand, the crucial *conditions* of human learning and behavior are being scientifically studied by anthropologists, sociologists, and other social scientists. In order to understand human behavior, one must know both the principles and the conditions [17]. That is why the scientific study of culture is important.

It is often said that human behavior is unpredictable. This is not true. Under appropriate cultural conditions there is a high degree of predictability. Without such predictability, civilization would be impossible. Look around you. It is safe to predict that no one will be sitting there naked. You might stop for a moment to think how much someone would have to pay you in order to make you undress at this meeting. This will give you some idea of the power of culture.

How bad a pest would some elderly relative of yours have to be before you would kill him? That is the strength of the cultural taboo in our society against murder. In India, cows, monkeys, parrots, insects, and other pests ravage the crops of an undernourished population making it extremely difficult to introduce efficient methods of modern agriculture which involve growing large fields of the same crop and hence invite multiplication of the pests that prey on that crop. Since the Hindu believes that any one of these animals might be the reincarnation of one of his relatives, he will not kill any of these pests. For him the sacredness of all animal life is more important than his own hunger for food. On the other hand, the Eskimo used to abandon his parents to certain death when they were too old to care for themselves, and the aged parents asked to be killed in this way [7]. These are but a few examples of the enormous power of the social conditions of culture.

The first emphasis of the social anthropologists was on the extreme diversity of cultures. They proved that an astonishing amount of human nature is the product of cultural conditions and hence is not the same everywhere. For example, there are some cultures in which different tribes have interacted for long periods without warfare, and in some cases even without military weapons. Peace is compatible with human nature [31, 54, 67, 71]!

Even within our own American society, we have various subcultures. In the different social classes, the ideas of what is right and what is wrong, the values placed on education, having an illegitimate child, aggression, saving money, and many other aspects of life are far more different than most of us realize [70]. There also are regional differences in culture, as illustrated by recent events in the deep South. Certain occupational groupings are minor subcultures. Everyone takes his own immediate culture for granted, and greatly underestimates the degree to which others react differently, because everyone tends to associate with people from a similar cultural background.

As they have advanced beyond their initial descriptions, anthropologists have found that the fact that many radically different ways of doing things in other cultures are quite possible does not mean that it is a matter of indifference how things are done in a given culture. They have learned much about how the different parts of a given culture dovetail in a lawful, functional way, so that changes of certain aspects may be strongly resisted, and if forced, may produce repercussions throughout the society. To give a simple example, in the Trobriand Islands, instead of a husband supporting his wife, a brother supports his sister, and if his sister has the status of being married to a chief, she must be well provided for. Each chief had many wives which were the source of his economic power, enabling him to supply food and drink for work parties which accomplished essential civil projects such as hollowing out great logs to produce ocean-going canoes. When pressure from colonial administrators caused abandonment of polygamy, the chiefs lost the extra income from having several brothers-in-law, they were too poor to throw work parties, their prestige and authority declined, and necessary civil tasks were neglected. A change in one aspect of the society had unexpected, far-reaching effects [44].

An additional example of the functional interdependence of various aspects of a culture comes from Murdock's [55] comparative study of 250 societies which also illustrates the modern trend toward quantitative work. In a statistical analysis he has found that different patterns of sexual taboos in these societies are highly correlated with the ways in which kinship terms, such as "Mother" or "Aunt," are applied to larger or smaller classes of maternal or paternal relatives. The various uses of kinship terms are related to family living arrangements—whether the bride moves in with the husband's relatives, the husband moves in with the bride's relatives, or both go off independently. These customs are in turn dependent upon economic behavior, for example, hunting *versus* agriculture. Murdock also has shown how those changes which are known to have occurred during the history of these societies progressed in a lawful sequence with the changes in economic behavior coming first, followed by changes in living arrangements, and then in kinship systems.

We have seen that cultural changes are occurring at an accelerated rate. There is less time now for different aspects of a society to adjust by the slow, blind processes of social trial-and-error which were sufficient in the past. Some of the later speakers may be dealing with problems of this kind in discussing new relationships between science, government, and the universities.

In the studies of the hypertension of the Zulus, we saw one symptom of the stress involved in changing from one culture pattern to another. Other effects of the disorganization produced by relatively milder changes are illustrated by the fact that in our own country problems of delinquency and crime have characteristically involved the children of the newest wave of immigrants. Yet other studies seem to show that certain sociological variables, especially social disorganization, are related to a higher rate of mental illness [33, 39, 56, 62, 68].

The functional relationships among the different parts of a society become especially important when attempts are made to introduce rapid technological changes in so-called "underdeveloped" countries. The changes occurring in such countries today create an urgent need for us to apply what we know, and at the same time present unparalleled opportunities for increasing our scientific understanding of the dynamics of rapid social change.

In recent years some political scientists and economists have greatly broadened their perspective by studying other societies and cultures, including some of the technologically underdeveloped ones. Instead of concentrating almost exclusively on official documents or government statistics, they have devised techniques for studying political and economic behavior in the field. Unfortunately, these developments, which are changing these subjects from what they were when most of us studied them in college, are beyond the scope of this paper [1, 12, 28, 60, 61].

I shall conclude with one more example illustrating the way in which different disciplines, ranging from the physiological to the cultural, have profitably converged on a behavioral problem. You will remember that culture must be learned by children and that such learning during childhood is a crucial link in passing it on from generation to generation. In addition to this general consideration, clinical observations have suggested that there may be certain critical periods in childhood during which experiences may have an especially profound and long-lasting effect.

These observations have been supported by recent experimental studies on animals. The imprinting, which Professor Mayr [45] has described, can occur only during a limited period of the newly hatched bird's life. Birds will not learn to follow an object if their first exposure is after the critical period. Female rats restrained from grooming themselves during a certain period of infancy do not show normal nest building in later life and will eat, instead of care for, their young. Similarly, monkeys reared with artificial mothers do not display normal maternal behavior in later life, and if isolated from other infant monkeys during a certain period of childhood will not acquire normal sexual behavior when adult. They also show other strikingly neurotic symptoms. Bottle-fed sheep do not develop gregariousness, but graze alone. That genetic factors are also involved, however, is shown by the fact that not all mammals become as gregarious as sheep [65].

The critical periods involve the interaction of developing innate patterns with learning. Their occurrence is firmly established in certain lower animals but we need to know much more about the detailed processes involved, and their occurrence in human infants.

Evidence that there are such critical periods in the development of the human infant has been secured by taking advantage of experiments of nature in which illness or other unusual circumstances have forced the child to be separated from its mother and mother-surrogate. In many, but not all, cases such separation seems to have had serious consequences for adult personality, shifting it toward chronic mistrust, hostility, and delinquency [8].

Experiments have recently shown that there are critical periods also for psychosomatic effects. It is well known that petting infant rats causes them to grow larger than control litter mates, and also to be superior as adults in certain avoidance-learning tasks. Similar petting at a slightly later age does not produce these effects. At first it was thought that the effects of handling were analogous to those of expressions of parental affection. This turned out to be a far too flattering misconception of the rat's reaction to being picked up by man. Electric shocks were found to produce similar effects. This and other studies showed that the effects were stressful, involving the links from the hypothalamus to the pituitary to the adrenal that we have already described [40].

Furthermore, biochemical studies of adult animals showed that the brief handling during an early critical period had a permanent effect on the adult animal's physiological reactivity to stress, for example, the production of corticosteroids.

Additional studies are showing that there are critical periods of development during which the injection of certain hormones in minute amounts, which would be ineffective if injected at other times, can have permanent effects upon the rat's physiological development, which in turn have profound effects on behavior [30]. Such studies may help us to understand some of the physiological mechanisms involved in critical periods in development.

To return to our previous theme, do the psychosomatic effects of infant stress upon subsequent growth and maturation apply to human as well as to rat infants? One cannot perform experiments on stress with human infants. There are, however, certain societies in which infants at different ages are subjected to certain stressful procedures, such as cutting or burning the skin to form a pattern of scars, piercing the lips or the ears, or molding certain soft bones by pressure. Landauer and Whiting [38] have recently made a cross-cultural study of the effects of such procedures on average adult height. They have found that there is a statistically reliable positive correlation between such procedures and mean height. The average superiority in height of the stressed group is more than two inches, and the data suggest that the first two years are the critical period for children.

Since this is a correlational study, they cannot be certain that there is a causal relationship. Nevertheless, the correlation remains when they analyze the data in such a way as to control for three factors likely to influence height: namely, genetic stock, diet as indicated by protein, and sunshine, which presumably is related to growth-inducing vitamin D.

In short, clinical observations, behavioral experiments on animals, the results of biochemical assays and interventions, and cross-cultural comparisons are converging to show that there are critical periods in infancy during which certain events may have an especially great effect on subsequent physical and behavioral development. The phenomena are real; they are significant; the next step is to discover more about the laws governing them.

In conclusion, current research emphasizes the extreme importance of both innate physiological and acquired cultural factors in human development. We are beginning to learn a few of the fascinating details of the ways in which physiological nature and cultural nurture interact to produce behavior. But the picture is not a simple one, and each new discovery discloses additional tantalizing problems, challenging us to advance scientific knowledge deeper into the vast unknown.

References

1. ALMOND, G. A., AND VERBA, S. *The Civic Culture.* Princeton, N. J.: Princeton University Press, 1963.
2. ANDERSSON, B.; EKMAN, L.; GALE, C. C.; AND SUNDSTEN, J. W. Activation of the thyroid gland by cooling of the preoptic region in the goat. *Acta Physiol. Scand.* 54 (1962):191–92.
3. ANDERSSON, B., AND LARSSON, B. Influence of local temperature changes in the preoptic area and rostral hypothalamus on the regulation of food and water intake. *Acta Physiol. Scand.* 52 (1961):75–89.
4. ARORA, H. L., AND SPERRY, R. W. Optic nerve regeneration after cross union of medial and lateral optic tracts. *Am. Zool.* 2 (1962):389.
5. ATTARDI, D. G., AND SPERRY, R. W. Preferential selection of central pathways by regenerating optic fibers. *Exp. Neurol.* 7 (1963):46–64.
6. BERLYNE, D. E. *Conflict Arousal and Curiosity.* New York: McGraw-Hill, 1960.
7. BOAS, F. *The Central Eskimo,* Bureau of American Ethnology, *Annual Report,* vol. 6 (1888).
8. BOWLBY, J. *Maternal Care and Mental Health.* Geneva: World Health Organization, 1952.
9. BROADBENT, D. E. *Perception and Communication.* New York: Pergamon Press, 1958.
10. BRONFENBRENNER, U. Soviet methods of character education; some implications for research. *Am. Psychol.* 17 (1962):550–64.
11. BUSH, R. R., GALANTER, E., AND LUCE, R. D. *Handbook of Mathematical Psychology.* New York: John Wiley & Sons, 1963.
12. CAMPBELL, A., MILLER, W., AND STOKES, E. *The American Voter.* New York: John Wiley & Sons, 1960.
13. CHILD, V. G. *What Happened in History.* Harmondsworth, England: Penguin Books, 1948.
14. COFER, C. N. *Verbal Learning and Verbal Behavior.* New York: McGraw-Hill, 1961.
15. COLEMAN, J. S. *The Adolescent Society.* Glencoe, Ill.: Free Press of Glencoe, 1961.
16. DELAFRESNAYE, J. F. *Brain Mechanisms and Learning.* Oxford: Blackwell Scientific Publications, 1961.
17. DOLLARD, J., AND MILLER, N. E. *Personality and Psychotherapy.* New York: McGraw-Hill, 1950.
18. ECCLES, J. C. *The Physiology of Synapses.* Heidelberg: Springer Verlag, and New York: Academic Press, 1964.
19. FIELDS, W. S., AND ABBOTT, W. *Information Storage and Neural Control.* Springfield, Ill.: Charles C Thomas, 1963.
20. FISHER, A. Maternal and sexual behavior induced by intracranial chemical stimulation. *Science* 124 (1956):228–29.
21. FRENCH, J. D.; PORTER, R. W.; CAVANAUGH, E. B.; AND LONGMIRE, R. L. Experimental observations on "psychosomatic" mechanisms. I. Gastrointestinal disturbances. *Arch. Neurol. and Psychiat.* 72 (1954):267–81.
22. GADDUM, J. H. Chemical transmission in the central nervous system. *Nature* 197 (1963):741–43.
23. GEWIRTZ, J. L., AND BAER, D. M. The effect of brief social deprivation on behavior for a social reinforcer. *J. Abnorm. Soc. Psychol.* 56 (1958):49–56.

24. GIBSON, E. J. Perceptual learning. In Farnsworth, A. R., ed., *Annual Review of Psychology*. Palo Alto, Cal.: Annual Reviews, Inc., vol. 14 (1963).

25. GROSSMAN, S. P. Direct adrenergic and cholinergic stimulation of hypothalamic mechanism. *Am. J. Physiol.* 202 (1962):872–82.

26. GROSSMAN, S. P. Effects of adrenergic and cholinergic blocking agents on hypothalamic mechanisms. *Am. J. Physiol.* 202 (1962):1230–36.

27. GUNN, C. G., FRIEDMAN, M., AND BYERS, S. O. Effects of chronic hypothalamus stimulation upon cholesterol-induced atherosclerosis in the rabbit. *J. Clin. Inv.* 39 (1960): 1963–72.

28. HAGEN, E. E. *On the Theory of Social Change*. Homewood, Ill.: Dorsey Press, 1962.

29. HARLOW, H. F., AND ZIMMERMAN, R. R. Affectional responses in the infant monkey. *Science* 130 (1959):421–32.

30. HARRIS, G. W., AND LEVINE, S. Sexual differentiation of the brain and its experimental control. *J. Physiol.* 163 (1962):42–43.

31. HENRY, J. *Jungle People*. New York: J. J. Augustin Press, 1941.

32. HOLLAND, J. G., AND SKINNER, B. F. *The Analysis of Behavior*. New York: McGraw-Hill, 1961.

33. HOLLINGSHEAD, A. B., AND REDLICH, F. *Social Class and Mental Illness*. New York: John Wiley & Sons, 1958.

34. HUBEL, D. H., AND WIESEL, T. N. Receptive fields, binocular interaction and functional architecture in the cat's visual cortex. *J. Physiol.* 160 (1963):106–54.

35. HUMMEL, H. T., HARDY, J. D., AND FUSCO, M. M. The thermoregulatory response to hypothalamic cooling in unanesthetized dogs. *Am. J. Physiol.* 198 (1960):481–86.

36. HUTCHINSON, G. E. The influence of the environment. In *Scientific Endeavor*. New York: Rockefeller University Press, 1965.

37. KIMBLE, G. A. *Hilgard and Marquis' Conditioning and Learning*, 2nd ed. New York: Appleton-Century-Crofts, 1961.

38. LANDAUER, T. K., AND WHITING, J. W. M. Infantile stimulation and adult stature of human males. *Am. Anthropol.* 66 (1964):1007.

39. LEIGHTON, A. H. *My Name Is Legion*. New York: Basic Books, Inc. (1959).

40. LEVINE, S. Psychological effects of infant stimulation. In Bliss, E. L., ed. *Roots of Behavior*. New York: Paul B. Hoeber, 1962, pp. 246–53.

41. LIVINGSTON, R. B. Central control of receptors and sensory transmission systems. In *Handbook of Physiology*, vol. 1, sect. 1, *Neurophysiology*. Edited by J. Field, H. W. Magoun, and V. E. Hull. Baltimore: Williams & Wilkins Co., 1959.

42. LOGAN, F. A. *Incentive: How the Conditions of Reinforcement Affect the Performance of Rats*. New Haven: Yale University Press, 1960.

43. MAGOUN, H. W. *The Waking Brain*, 2nd ed. Springfield, Ill.: Charles C Thomas, 1963.

44. MALINOWSKI, B. *Argonauts of the Western Pacific*. New York: E. P. Dutton & Co., 1922, pp. 63–64.

45. MAYR, E. The evolution of living systems. In *Scientific Endeavor*. New York: Rockefeller University Press, 1965.

46. MILLER, N. E. Learning and performance motivated by direct stimulation of the brain. In *Electrical Stimulation of the Brain*. Austin: University of Texas Press, 1961, pp. 387–96.

47. MILLER, N. E. Some reflections on the law of effect produce a new alternative to drive reduction. In *Nebraska Symposium on Motivation for 1963*. Lincoln: University of Nebraska Press, 1963, pp. 65–112.

48. MILLER, N. E. Some motivational effects of electrical and chemical stimulation of the brain. *EEG Journal*, suppl. 24. New York: Elsevier, 1963, pp. 247–59.

49. MILLER, N. E. Animal experiments on emotionally-induced ulcers. In *Proc. World Congress Psychiatry*, Montreal, Canada, June 4–10, 1961. Toronto: University of Toronto Press. Vol. 3:213–19, 1963.

50. MILLER, N. E. Some implications of modern behavior theory for personality and psychotherapy. In *Personality Change*. Edited by D. Byrne and P. Worchel. New York: John Wiley & Sons, 1964.

51. MILLER, N. E. Certain recent developments in experimental psychology. *Proc. Roy. Soc. London, Series B* 158 (1963):481–97.

52. MILLER, N. E., GOTTESMAN, K. S., AND EMERY, N. Dose-response to carbachol and norepinephrine in rat's hypothalamus. *Am. J. Physiol.* 206 (1964):1384–88.

53. MILLER, N. E., PFAFFMAN, C., AND SCHLOSBERG, H. Aspects of psychology and psychophysiology in the U.S.S.R. In R. A. Bauer, ed., *Some Views on Soviet Psychology*. New York: Timely Press, 1962, pp. 226–29.

54. MURDOCK, G. P. *Our Primitive Contemporaries*. New York: The Macmillan Co., 1934, p. 110.

55. MURDOCK, G. P. *Social Structure*. New York: Macmillan Co., 1949.

56. MYERS, J. K., AND ROBERTS, B. H. *Family and Class Dynamics in Mental Illness*. New York: John Wiley & Sons, 1959.

57. NAKAYAMA, T.; HAMMEL, T. T.; HARDY, J. D.; AND EISENMAN, J. S. Thermal stimulation of electrical activity of single units of the preoptic region. *Am J. Physiol.* 204 (1963):1122–26.

58. NOVIN, D. The relation between electrical conductivity of brain tissue and thirst in the rat. *J. Comp. Physiol. Psychol.* 55 (1962):145–154.

59. POLISH, E.; BRADY, J. V.; MASON, J. W.; THACH, J. S.; AND NIEMACK, W. Gastric contents and the occurrence of duodenal lesions in the rhesus monkey during avoidance behavior. *Gastroenterology* 43 (1962):193–201.

60. PYE, L. *Politics, Personality and Nation Building: Burma's Search for Identity*. New Haven: Yale University Press, 1962.

61. REYNOLDS, L. *Economics*. Homewood, Ill.: Richard D. Irwin, 1963.

62. SARASON, S. B., AND GLADWIN, T. *Psychological Problems in Mental Deficiency: Part II*. New York: Harper & Bros., 1959.

63. SAWYER, C. H., AND KAWAKAMI, M. Interaction between the central nervous system and hormones influencing ovulation. In C. A. Ville, ed., *The Control of Ovulation*. New York: Pergamon Press, 1961, pp. 79–97.

64. SCOTCH, N. A. Sociocultural factors in the epidemiology of Zulu hypertension. *Am. J. Pub. Health* 53 (1963):1205–13.

65. SCOTT, J. P. Critical periods in behavior development. *Science* 138 (1962):949–57.

66. SONNEBORN, T. M. "The Differentiation of Cells." In *Scientific Endeavor*. New York: Rockefeller University Press, 1965.

67. SPENCER, W., AND GILLEN, F. *The Arunta*. London: Macmillan & Co., 1927. Vol. 1:27–28.

68. SROLE, L. *Mental Health in the Metropolis: Midtown Manhattan Study*. New York: McGraw-Hill, 1962.

69. STAMLER, R. Acculturation and Negro blue-collar workers. In *The Blue Collar World*, A. B. Shostak and W. Gomberg, eds. Englewood Cliffs, N. J.: Prentice-Hall, 1964, pp. 282–98.

PART 3

Sensation and Perception

Development and Motivation can both be viewed as "general psychologies" in their own right, for all of behavior involves some developmental and motivational component. Whole texts have been written to underscore this point of view. But behavior can also be studied more specifically; having introduced general human psychology first in a developmental framework and then in a motivational one, we can now turn to the more discrete aspects of psychology. We begin with sensation and perception.

What we do, we do in conjunction with the world; and in order to interact with that world we need our senses. Different "sense receptors" take in information. We interpret; then we behave. Sensation studies the first of these steps; its topics are stimuli (light waves) and receptors (the eye). In contrast, Perception studies the more vital aspects of our interaction with the world, the psychological interpretations we impart to what we sense.

As in the rest of psychology, body, mind, and society interact in human perception. Whether we are observing (as Schachter will) that the social antics of people around us influence the labels we attach to our feelings, or noting (with Wohlwill) that the physical properties of the environment have a bearing on our state of mind and that state of mind affects the way we see the world, it becomes clear that physical, personal, and social experiences all govern our subjective interpretations of objective sensory material.

A Russian Report on the Postoperative Newly Seeing

IVAN D. LONDON

The first article in this section makes a clear distinction between the physical act of seeing and the psychological act of perceiving. Consider the children in the first case history, for example. They had been born blind, unable to see any more than you could if you were, say, looking at the world through waxed-paper goggles. After surgery had removed those cataracts, both children could *see* quite clearly, but they could not *perceive*. To put it in terms reminiscent of Miller's from the preceding article, once the cataracts had been removed, the stimuli from the physical world could excite rod and cone patterns in their eyes, and impulses could be transferred along neural pathways to the occipital lobes in the brain. There, where the appropriate neuronal pattern existed, was sight; the mechanics of vision had been satisfied. But the *conditions of perception* had not, for the children had not previously experienced these cortical patterns and had not had prior opportunity to compare those patterns to the world around them, and they still had to learn what those patterns represented. That is, they had to *learn* to *perceive*.

The work of the Russian physiologists, as London also points out, is often filled with exciting implications for psychology. We can share with him the disappointment reflected in the last sentence of this article, but we can also hope that through the accords of the 1972 Moscow Summit an era of Soviet-American scientific exchange may be at hand.

Surgical acquirement of vision by the congenitally blind has always excited great interest. Not only are the accounts of how these people "learn to see" provocative, but the theoretical implications of the process discerned are of considerable significance [1]. Authentic instances of cases where the congenitally or near-congenitally blind have been rendered seeing are not many [3], and those that have been reported have been the subject of dispute and

SOURCE: From *American Journal of Psychology* 73 (1960):478–82. Copyright © 1960 by the University of Illinois Press. Reprinted by permission.

interpretive disagreement [4]. For this reason, any addition to the literature reporting on restoration of vision to the congenitally blind supplements the meager stock of data extant and is, therefore, welcome.

In 1953 an article describing several cases of visual restoration appeared in *Vestnik Oftalmologii* [*Herald of Ophthalmology*], a Soviet journal [2]. While the account leaves much to be desired, it is unusual in some of its detail and also in that the writer of the article himself, A. I. Pokrovskiĭ, Director of the Eye Clinic of the Voronezh Medical Institute, performed the surgery and conducted the postoperative studies and observations. In other words, the account is not second-hand, but stems from direct personal encounter with the cases reported.

Pokrovskiĭ first reports on the cases of two children, born with mild cataracts which, while sight-depriving, permitted reaction to light. Pokrovskiĭ records the age of one of the children as 10 yr. at the time of operation, but fails to mention the age of the other. He reports the following of their progress toward visual perception:

1. After the operation both children were completely unable to recognize and name objects in their surroundings for some time, the dura-of which varied for each. Their usual reaction was that they saw "something," but what it was, they did not know.
2. Both quickly and easily recognized and named objects on running their fingers over them if these objects were of a kind frequently encountered in their home surroundings and, hence, familiar.
3. If they looked [at] and simultaneously touched objects not ordinarily encountered in their home environment, but possessing forms and certain properties, tactilely discriminable and reminiscent of some familiar object or other, the children, on the basis of tactile contact, applied to the former names appropriate to the latter.
4. For both children forms of objects were not visually discriminated, but were tactilely determined.
5. Size and bulk of objects were similarly determined.
6. The children were unable by vision alone to determine distance or, more exactly, the distance of the nearest objects. When walking, they collided with these objects and in the beginning employed the customary method of the blind to avoid them, putting their hands out in front and touching the objects in their way.
7. Both children were completely unable by vision alone to determine the number of objects presented to them, but could do so by touch.
8. Nor did they determine colors as such, distinguishing them only by brightness and naming one darker and another lighter.
9. They possessed no conception of perspective, and their conceptions of extent and space, developed through touch and movement, were very limited in comparison with the same conceptions in normal children of the same age.
10. In these newly seeing children, all the processes for discriminating objects, their form, size, etc., based in the beginning chiefly on the tactile-muscular analyzers [which include the receptors to the cortical

termini], were without question carried out more slowly than in normal children operating by vision alone.

Pokrovskiĭ then considers the cases of two children who became blind in their early years and who had sight restored to them after an interval of five years. After stating that their postoperative progress to full vision was similar to that of the two cases reported on above, Pokrovskiĭ notes the following differences.

1. Although the children did not recognize objects and reacted to them with "I see something," they did distinguish the size of this "something" in comparison with an object of different size.
2. They distinguished the colors of objects, though not too descriptively, and correctly named them.
3. The most noteworthy feature of progress to fuller vision in comparison with that of the 2 born blind was its duration, which was considerably shorter than in the case of the latter.

Pokrovskiĭ reports the following of the first case—a 9-yr. old girl, blinded at the age of five.

She said that she saw everything, but in the beginning—and of this one can be easily convinced—she did not perceive what she saw; without question she did not recognize by vision alone the familiar objects of her surroundings, though she could quickly recognize and name these objects on running her fingers over them. In other words, she had to compare the visual sensations, which after long blindness were new to her, with the tactile-motor perceptions customary for the blind in order immediately to recognize and, one may say, "see" the familiar object.

When she was shown a kitten, she said, "I see something gray; since I was a baby I have not seen anything like that." On touching it, she exclaimed joyfully—"A kitten!" She did not recognize a dog, but said, "I see something yellow." On stroking the dog's back with her hand, she immediately named it. On seeing a cow, she said, "I see something big, red and white." On seeing a horse, she said, "I see something big, gray and white." She looked long at this and the other animal, listened to the particular sound of their breathing, and after some prying questions about animals' tails, faces, and the like, said "Horse?" When she looked at a flower, she said, "I see something green." On touching the flower, she correctly named it as a flower.

She did not recognize buckets of various sizes and color, but on handling them she correctly named them and correctly judged their differences in size and color.

The girl could not judge the form of objects on the basis of merely sight, but on touching them did distinguish their forms. She distinguished the color and size of 2 little containers presented to her—one round, the other four-cornered—but she correctly determined their respective forms only by manipulating them.

In the beginning the girl could not determine the distances to objects closest to her. All objects in front of her appeared very near to her. When requested to grasp any particular object, she extended her hand in the proper direction, but as a rule failed when trying to grasp even objects very near to her.

The girl walked about her room during the first postoperative days very uncertainly, stumbling and knocking against objects standing in her way. But after several days she began to walk with steadily increasing confidence and after 2 weeks was already leading other patients around. Only when she found herself in unfamiliar surroundings, did she move around more circumspectly.

She began rather quickly to recognize the objects about her, and at the time of discharge from the hospital, after 3 weeks, had begun without tactile intercession to utilize her vision, not in full, but in sufficient measure.

Pokrovskiĭ also refers to a second case—a girl of 8 yr., who was blinded at the age of three. He reports that the progress toward visual perception was similar to that above, but very much slower. She was kept in the hospital for 2½ months and at the time of her discharge was not as advanced as the other girl although, as long as her surroundings were of the familiar kind, she was able to see and recognize things in her environment.

Pokrovskiĭ concludes by citing the cases of two patients who were blinded in their very early years and who were restored to sight much later in life—16 and 54 yr., respectively.

The 16 year old boy distinguished only light and grew up blind in a village as a member of a poor family living under very unfavorable conditions. Nobody had anything to do with him, and his mental development lagged greatly behind that of his seeing peers. His judgments of the surrounding world were elementary in the extreme. His behavior with respect to his surroundings before the operation reminded one of those born blind, and after a successful operation his development of visual perception also proceeded in accordance with that typical of the latter, but very slowly. While he recognized objects by fingering them, he was for a very long time unable to recognize them by sight alone. He did not have visual conceptions of size, form, bulk, color of objects, or their distance from him. He was unable to grasp an object in his visual field and erred many times in repeated attempts to accomplish this.

The patient was in the hospital for 2½ months after the operation and during this time learned to orient himself somewhat to his surroundings and to walk without stumbling against objects. He began to distinguish to some degree the form and size of objects and to distinguish their color not only by brightness but as more darkly or more brightly colored. However, even at the time of his discharge the visual perception of the patient was by no means as far advanced as in others with restored sight. From a letter, received from the patient 8 months after the operation, it was learned that he now goes about everywhere alone and distinguishes all colors of objects and that his vision has improved.

Concerning the patient who was blinded at the age of 2 or 3 yr. and who underwent surgery at the age of 54, Pokrovskiĭ then has this to report:

Before the operation he saw only light and did not distinguish color. He recognized his children and grandchildren by voice. Development of visual perception proceeded even more slowly than in the case just cited. Utilizing vision, he began to walk in the hospital with great difficulty and uncertainty. He was poor in recognizing people around him and, evidently, had frequent recourse to auditory cues in accordance with his previous wont. He would look for a long time at the face of his visiting son without recognizing him, but did so immediately at the sound of his voice. Unfortunately, it was not possible to keep track of this patient after discharge from the hospital.

Pokrovskiĭ discusses all of the above 6 cases in terms of Pavlovian theory and gives no indication of awareness of the differential importance of his observations and data for alternate theories. Pokrovskiĭ states that he and others have personally dealt with a number of other such cases, but restricts his account to the above six as representative. Direct communication with the author on his report, though attempted, has not yet been established.

References

1. HEBB, D. O. *The Organization of Behavior.* New York: John Wiley & Sons, 1949, pp. 1–335.
2. POKROVSKII, A. I. On the development of visual perceptions and judgments in the postoperative newly seeing in the light of the works of I. P. Pavlov. *Vestn. Oftal.* 32 (6) (1953):6–17.
3. VON SENDEN, M. *Raum- und Gestaltauffassung bei operierten Blindgeborenen vor und nach der Operation.* 1932, pp. 1–303.
4. WERTHEIMER, M. Hebb and Senden on the role of learning in perception. *American Journal of Psychology* 64 (1951):133–37.

The Physical Environment:
A Problem for a
Psychology of Stimulation

JOACHIM F. WOHLWILL

This article nicely complements London's by pointing out the important "dimensions of stimulation," those aspects of the environment that most readily capture the attention of our senses. But Wohlwill goes well beyond that basic review to incorporate his "psychology of stimulation" into a broader theoretical framework. His focus is the level of stimulation: How much stimulation is "best"? and for whom? In pursuit of these questions, he reminds us of two concepts from motivational psychology, "optimal level" and "adaptation level" of stimulation. To understand what he means by optimal level, consider the effects of anxiety on studying for final exams. Too little anxiety has little effect; why study? Too much anxiety is debilitating; you can't study if you're sick to your stomach. Somewhere in between is the optimal level of anxiety that is enough to propel you to your desk, but not so much that you sit there petrified. Adaptation level is quite similar. Through experience you "get used to" a particular level of stimulation, such as the activity that goes on around you. A bit more of this activity, or a bit less, might be a pleasant thing, but too much bustle or too much solitude could be unnerving. (One of the problems with the adaptation level concept— at least when it is applied to negative emotions like test anxiety—is that the concept seems to suggest that experiencing a bit more anxiety than you're used to would be pleasant, and feeling a lot less would be unpleasant. This criticism does not really apply to Wohlwill's work with positive emotion.)

When you study this article, watch how the author ties optimal level and adaptation level together as he discusses a possible way to predict why different people favor different places to vacation.

SOURCE: From *Journal of Social Issues* 22, no. 4:29–38. Copyright © 1966 by the Society for the Psychological Study of Social Issues, a division of the American Psychological Association. Reprinted by permission.

Introduction

As a psychologist this writer has been struck by a curious paradox. Psychologists never tire to point out the importance of stimulus factors as a determinant of behavior, and of the role of environmental influences in behavior. Yet, as a group they have had relatively little to say on the important problems relating to man's response to his physical environment to which this issue is devoted.* We may hope that the valuable contributions made to this area by Drs. Calhoun, Sommer, and Stea (to cite only the psychologists represented in this issue) portend a change in this state of affairs in the foreseeable future. Meanwhile it may be instructive to examine briefly, at the outset, some of the likely reasons for this seeming lack of attention given to these problems by psychologists; our primary aim, however, is to point more positively to some recent developments in the experimental psychology of motivation which appear to have interesting implications for the study of the impact of the physical environment on behavior and for approaches to environmental design.

That child psychologists, personality psychologists and social psychologists with an environmentalist bias should have neglected the role of the physical environment in behavior is readily understandable. For the most part they have been interested in the interpersonal, social and cultural aspects of the environment, in line with the prevalent drive theory of motivation, built on the concepts of appetitive and aversive reinforcement, which has featured much of their thinking. According to this conception, it is *people* who administer rewards and punishments; the natural and artificial surroundings in which people live thus have little power to influence behavior. Not surprisingly, this has been less true of those working outside of a stimulus-response reinforcement model, notably within a field-theoretical framework. Yet even here, where the vocabulary of boundaries, barriers and field forces might seem to favor attention to variables of the physical environment, primary interest has remained in the analysis of interpersonal interaction, social encounters, and the like.

Turning now to the side of experimental psychology, ever since the appearance in 1949 of Hebb's influential *The Organization of Behavior*, the role of sensory stimulation from the environment, not only for the normal development of perceptual and cognitive functions but for motivational processes as well, has become of increasing concern. Yet, starting from the premise that stimulation is good, indeed essential for the development and maintenance of normal behavior, most of the efforts of workers in this area have been devoted to demonstrating the deleterious effects of drastic reductions in level of stimulation, whether as a short-term condition with human adults (cf. the work on "sensory deprivation," [9]) or as a more prolonged condition of the early

---

* Editor's note: The *Journal of Social Issues*, from which this selection is reprinted, typically devotes an entire number to a single social issue. This exceptionally readable journal is noted for bringing together the viewpoints of many different disciplines.

experience of animals [e.g., 10, 1961]. Where attempts have been made to enhance the behavioral effectiveness of animals, e.g., their problem-solving ability, by providing for "enriched" stimulus environments, the research has typically started from a straightforward "the more, the better" assumption. The success of such efforts is not surprising, if one bears in mind the impoverished level of stimulation provided by the typical laboratory environment used as the base of comparison for most of these studies, but its relevance to the living conditions under which modern man operates is doubtful.

A recent extension of this stimulus-enrichment approach to the study of "imprinting" in newly hatched chicks, that is, the development of the following response to the mother, is particularly instructive in revealing the psychologists' conception of an optimal set of stimulus conditions. The authors describe the treatment to which the experimental animals were subjected immediately after hatching as follows:

> The complex environment . . . consisted of a black-walled enclosure with random stripes and blotches of white paint. Above was a bank of six 200-w light bulbs which flashed on and off at 1-sec. intervals. Two metronomes produced a constant ticking. A radio, tuned to a local AM station, played constantly at high volume. Every 30 min. E stroked each chick's back with a foam rubber brush and with a whisk broom for 15 sec., rang a bicycle bell for 2 min., and gave a gentle puff of air from an air compressor (5, p. 654).

Let it be recorded that this treatment apparently worked wonders on the imprinting response of these chicks, which developed both earlier and more strongly than for chicks who started life amidst more humdrum environmental conditions. Yet this positive result will not be altogether reassuring to some who may see in the treatment described above only a slight caricature of the frenetic bombardment from stimuli of all kinds encountered in certain urban environments. After all, newborn chicks, even of the Vantress Broiler variety used in this study, are not to be equated to human beings, and the imprinting response hardly constitutes a valid model of human behavior and adjustment. Such doubting Thomases could derive support for their skepticism, moreover, by pointing to the case of the typical "culturally deprived" child from the slums, who is apt to grow up under just such conditions of overstimulation, without great profit to his general intellectual development or emotional well being.

A whole host of questions arise at this point: Is there a particular level of stimulation conducive to optimal development? Does patterned stimulation differ in its effects on development from unpatterned (e.g., noise)? Above all, what is the role of meaning (as invested in language and in object stimuli) in modulating the effects of stimulation on development, and what conditions promote the sifting out of meaningful from meaningless stimuli by the child? Though some research with animals has been carried out relative to the first of these questions, the others have remained virtually untouched, so that in the aggregate the evidence available thus far is probably of limited significance for an understanding of the effects of the stimulus conditions characterizing our typical physical environments on the development of the individual.

Once we turn away from the study of the effects of stimulus experience on development, however, we find a considerable body of recent work that is of direct relevance for us, dealing with the stimulus correlates of the arousal of human attention and with human activity involving the seeking out of stimulation. Psychologists have come to recognize what persons in the amusement and recreation industries—to say nothing of observant parents—have known all along: that a large part of the everyday activity of the human (or of the animal, for that matter) has as its aim not to *reduce* unpleasant tensions, e.g., from the hunger or sex drives, but rather to heighten the level of incoming stimulation, by voluntary exposure to stimulus objects or situations that are novel, incongruous, surprising or complex. Man, it seems, is ever curious, ever eager to explore, and unlike the proverbial cat, appears generally to thrive on such activity.

This is not the place to review the extensive literature in this area, dealing with the motivational and arousal properties of stimulation, or to enter into a discussion of the complex theoretical issues raised by this work (cf. 1, 3, 4, 12). Let us rather examine its possible relevance to problems of man's response to his physical environment, and some of the questions raised by an attempt to apply such notions to this problem area. We will confine ourselves to a discussion, necessarily oversimplified, of three main questions.

Dimensions of Stimulation

What are the chief dimensions of stimulation that are of concern to the student of environmental psychology? Those most frequently discussed by psychologists include simple intensity, novelty, complexity, and temporal change or variation; to these we may add surprisingness and incongruity, which have been more specifically emphasized by Berlyne [1]. If only in an illustrative sense, all of these can be shown to touch on important aspects of our physical environment. To start with intensity, questions of level of noise and illumination have been of concern to industrial designers, architects and planners for some time, although outside of an industrial context there has been little systematic research on the effects of different levels of auditory or visual intensity on behavior. The importance of *novelty* is well known to observers of that favorite pastime, sightseeing, a facet of behavior which can play an important role in questions of urban design (e.g., the role of San Francisco's cable-cars), as well as in the administration of our natural recreation areas. *Complexity* of stimulation may well be a major factor in differential evaluation of urban, suburban and rural environments, as it is in the response to more particular features of our environment, e.g., samples of modern architecture or highway layouts. *Variation* in the stimulus imput enters into diverse problems in environmental design that in one way or another have concerned the need to reduce boredom or monotony, from the subtle variations in design introduced into the construction of housing à la Levittown to the layout of highways, e.g., the avoidance of long, straight stretches.[1]

Surprisingness and *incongruity* are likewise of interest to us, notably in architecture and landscape design. As an example, the pleasing effect of surprise in the exploration of a building complex is nicely brought out by Nairn [8, p. 33ff] in his perceptive analysis of the layout of the entrance to the Wellesley College campus. The same author lays a good deal of stress on the role of incongruity, though mainly in a negative sense, i.e., by bringing out the jarring effect of the juxtaposition of different structures lacking in any relationship to one another. Whether some degree of incongruity may nevertheless serve a positive function (in the sense of heightening our attention, if not necessarily our affective evaluation of a scene) must remain an unanswered question at this time. (We may note, in any event, that some degree of incongruity in our environment is inevitable, if only because architectural styles change—cf. the contemporary look of the area around Harvard Square.)

While it may thus be easy to illustrate the relevance of these "collative" variables (as Berlyne calls them) to our response to the physical environment, systematic research in this area will have to come to grips with the problems of operational definition and measurement of these variables, in situations not permitting their control or manipulation by the investigator. Even in the laboratory air-tight definitions allowing for consistent differentiation of the effects of novelty from surprise, on the one hand, or temporal variation on the other are difficult to formulate. Similarly the measurement of novelty (particularly in the long-term sense) and of complexity poses considerable problems. All of these are of course greatly magnified when dealing with ready-made stimuli taken from the actual physical environment, such as landscapes, or urban scenes. In such a situation it may be necessary to compromise to a certain extent with scientific rigor, but this is no reason to shy away from research in such real-life settings. If it is impossible to manipulate variables independently, their relative contributions can generally still be assessed through techniques of statistical control and multivariate analysis.

A more critical problem is that of the measurement of these variables, in the absence of systematic, controlled manipulation. Here we will have to resort to indirect methods based on ratings or other subjective scaling methods. It is worth noting in this connection, that a recent study [7] utilizing judges' ratings to assess complexity of landscapes, still showed consistent relationships be-

---

[1] Other ways in which the variable of temporal change, as well as of complexity of the stimulus input affect our perception of and locomotion within our geographical environment are brought out succinctly in the paper by A. E. Parr (*Journal of Social Issues* 22, no. 4 (1966). Many of the points made in that paper are quite apposite to the kind of analysis of the stimulus properties of our environment being presented here.

tween this variable and the relative interest (i.e., fixation times) of these stimuli. More recent developments in the area of stimulus scaling techniques [11], some of which allow for the construction of a metric scale even with purely subjective judgments, lessen the need for independent, objective measures of the physical stimulus.

The Concept of an Optimal Level of Stimulation

A number of psychologists working in this area have advanced an optimal-level hypothesis, postulating an inverted U-shaped relationship between magnitude of stimulation along the dimensions considered above and the arousal value of, interest in or preference for a given stimulus.* Except for variables representing continua of stimulus intensity, systematic evidence on this point is actually fairly meager.[2] Nevertheless the concept deserves our consideration, in view of its patent relevance to man's response to the wide range of stimulation encountered in the physical environment. It ties in directly, furthermore, with Helson's Adaptation-level theory, which represents a much more general framework for the study of the most diverse responses to any stimuli varying along some assumed dimension [cf. 6]. In a nutshell, this theory maintains that for any specified dimension of stimulus variation the individual establishes an AL (adaptation-level) which determines his judgmental or evaluative response to a given stimulus located on that dimension. In particular, with reference to an evaluative response, the principle is that deviations from the AL in either direction are evaluated positively within a certain range, while beyond these boundaries they are experienced as unpleasant. Thus we obtain a function such as the following:

Let us try to apply this hypothesis to a person's choice of a vacation spot. To this end, let us conceive of a hybrid dimension of "closeness to civilization," which probably represents a composite of such variables as intensity, complexity, temporal variation and novelty. Take a person living in a small eastern city, so that his AL may be assumed to be somewhere in the middle of our dimension. Where will he go for his vacation? He may either be drawn to the kaleidoscopic attractions of a big metropolis like New York, or, alternatively, to the restful vistas of Vermont or the Cape Cod seashore. However, in accordance with the notion that beyond a certain range marked discrepancies

---

* Editor's note: An "inverted-U-shaped relationship" simply means that moderate amounts of stimulation are more interesting or arousing than very low or very high amounts. Joined with the notion of adaptation level, this suggests that we "get used to" a certain level of stimulation, and that *moderate* changes in stimulation above or below that level are pleasant, while small changes are unnoticed and large changes are unpleasant.

[2] As Fiske and Maddi (3, p. 9) note, most of their book is concerned with understimulation, rather than overstimulation, which they identify with stress. But in view of the emphasis given in their own formulation to the concept of an optimal level of activation, their readiness to dismiss the problem of overstimulation as unimportant is difficult to understand.

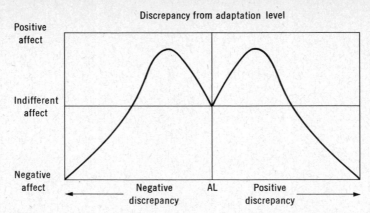

FIGURE 1.　*Changes in affective response to stimuli as a function of extent of deviation from adaptation level (after Helson, 1964).*

from the AL are no longer experienced as pleasant or desirable, we may hypothesize that, in the first case, our vacationer will tend to avoid or be repelled by places representing the more extreme levels of stimulation to be found in the big city (e.g., Times Square at New Years Eve; the subway during rush hour).[3] If, on the other hand, he chooses the open country, he is apt to want a motel room with TV, or to stick to the more populated resort areas.

This would seem to represent a plausible research hypothesis, though there are bound to be exceptions from this norm, e.g., hardy souls preferring a more nearly total isolation from civilization, or on the contrary a more intensive immersion in the stimulation offered by the big city. If so, this would show that not only the AL itself, but the degree of departure from it that would be experienced as pleasurable may vary considerably from one person to the next. This would admittedly make life more complex for the researcher investigating these problems, but would not pose any insuperable difficulties, provided independent measures of these parameters were available. It may also be noted that our model implies that such wilderness-fanciers would be least likely to come from a big metropolitan area; conversely, among those most

---

[3] Though this proposition might seem to lack surface plausibility, it derives some limited support from the results of a pilot study carried out by two Clark undergraduates, Kenneth Holm and Harlan Sherwin, who interviewed tourists at Penn. Station to obtain reactions to New York City. Of those who lived in suburban districts, one-third expressed some degree of positive reaction to the New York subways, whereas less than 10% of those residing in either small-town or country areas or in a metropolitan area gave any positive responses. It is also interesting to note that, in another sample of suburbanites, only 40% picked the crowds and noise as the aspects they disliked most about New York City, whereas 80% of the country-, small-town- or city-dwellers chose these aspects. (The suburbanites responded almost as frequently to the *dirt* of the city.)

strongly attracted to the excitement of the bustling metropolis, we should expect to find the visitor from a small town relatively underrepresented.

The Question of Long-Term Adaptation Effects

The concept of adaptation-level itself brings up a further question: What are the long-range effects of exposure to a given environment featured by a particular level of intensity, complexity, incongruity, etc., of stimulation? (In the very nature of the case, if the environment remains constant, novelty and surprisingness effectively cease to be relevant variables.) According to AL theory, the individual's AL will be shifted to a value corresponding more nearly to that environment.[4] This is of course no more than an expression of the fact of adaptation, whose pervasive action and potent effects are convincingly discussed in the papers of Lee and Sonnenfeld in this issue.[*] The question arises, however, whether in spite of the individual's capacity to adapt to an astonishingly wide range of environmental conditions, such prolonged exposure to stimulus environments falling near the extreme of the complexity or intensity dimension, for instance, may not leave its mark nevertheless. That is, it is possible that the arousal value or the subjective evaluation of the stimulus environment by the individual may become assimilated to some normal range, and his behavior become effectively adapted to it; yet more subtle long-term effects on behavior may nevertheless occur. For instance, a commuter subjected morning and evening to rush-hour traffic conditions on the New York subways may come to experience them as no more arousing than would his wife taking a quiet, uncrowded bus ride through suburban streets (though his evaluation of the experience is apt to remain rather more negative). He may even develop the knack of reading and assimilating "all the news that's fit to print," unaware of the din and shoving around him. Yet the cumulative effect of the exposure of these conditions may still leave a residue detectable in his behavior, which might take the form of heightened arousal thresholds, lessened frustration tolerance, or the like, representing the price being paid for this surface adaptation. Or take the child growing up among a steady backdrop of high-intensity TV signals, rattling subway trains and yells from neighbors: he may well adapt to these conditions of noise, but perhaps only by shutting out from awareness much of the input—notably speech—to which in fact he needs to become sensitized for his optimal development.

Admittedly we are operating largely on hunches in our estimates of such

---

[4] It should be noted that for environmental settings characterized by either very low or very high levels of stimulation, the AL should be expected to fall considerably short of this extreme value, since the effects of exposure to a given environment on the AL are superimposed on factors of a more intrinsic sort, relating to the individual's assumed needs for a certain modal level of stimulation lying within some intermediate range.

[*] Editor's note: *Journal of Social Issues* 22, no. 4 (1966).

long-term behavioral effects of exposure to particular levels of stimulation, but their possible reality can hardly be discounted, especially in view of the considerable evidence in this respect uncovered at the physiological level (cf. 2). There are, furthermore, undoubtedly large individual differences in tolerance of or adaptability to extreme levels of stimulation—as Wolpert argues forcefully in his paper in this issue, much migration behavior may be interpretable as an individual's response to his experienced level of stress emanating from the physical as well as the social environment.

Conclusion

In closing, we may express the hope that ultimately attention to questions such as these will lead to the creation of a science of environmental esthetics as a branch of psychology concerned with man's effective response to the qualitative and quantitative features of the world of natural and man-made stimuli surrounding him. Esthetics, to be sure, has not been a particularly flourishing branch of psychology in the past, no more than it has, until recently, represented an area of concern in our social, political and economic life. But it is perhaps not an entirely fortuitous coincidence that the attention which leaders in our public life have most recently been giving to the beautification of our artificial environment, as well as to the preservation of natural beauty, comes at the very time that the "new look" in the field of motivation is bringing psychologists ever closer to the realm of esthetics. (It is significant that the two books which are the primary sources with respect to this "new look," i.e., Berlyne [1]; Fiske and Maddi [3], both include a chapter on esthetics.) The time would thus seem most auspicious for experimental psychologists to take their place alongside their colleagues in social psychology, sociology, geography, architecture, planning, etc., in a broadside attack on the problems facing us in improving the quality of our environment.

References

1. BERLYNE, D. E. *Conflict, Arousal and Curiosity*. New York: McGraw-Hill, 1960.
2. DUBOS, R. *Man Adapting*. New Haven: Yale University Press, 1965.
3. FISKE, D. W., and MADDI, S. R., eds. *Functions of Varied Experience*. Homewood, Ill.: Dorsey Press, 1961.
4. FOWLER, H. *Curiosity and Exploratory Behavior*. New York: Macmillan, 1965.
5. HAYWOOD, H. C., AND ZIMMERMAN, D. W. Effects of early environmental complexity on the following response in chicks. *Percept. mot. Skills* 18 (1964):653–58.
6. HELSON, H. *Adaptation-Level Theory*. New York: Harper & Row, 1964.
7. LECKART, B. T., and BAKAN, P. Complexity judgments of photographs and looking time. *Percept. mot. Skills* 21 (1965):16–18.
8. NAIRN, I. *The American Landscape*. New York: Random House, 1965.
9. SOLOMON, P., et al., eds. *Sensory Deprivation*. Cambridge: Harvard University Press, 1961.

10. THOMPSON, R. W., and SCHAEFER, T., JR. "Early environmental stimulation." In D. W. Fiske, and S. R. Maddi, eds., *Functions of Varied Experience*. Homewood, Ill.: Dorsey Press, 1961, pp. 81–105.
11. TORGERSON, W. S. *Theory and Methods of Scaling*. New York: John Wiley & Sons, 1958.
12. WHITE, R. W. "Motivation reconsidered: the concept of competence." In D. W. Fiske and S. R. Maddi, eds., *Functions of Varied Experience*. Homewood, Ill.: Dorsey Press, 1961, pp. 278–325.

Cognitive Effects on Bodily Functioning

STANLEY SCHACHTER

Some of the most important research in recent years has centered on the relationship between psychological state and physiological state. In this article, Stanley Schachter discusses some of his research that indicates that the perception of physiological state is influenced by the social context in which the physical activation occurs and by the past or present personal experiences of the perceiver. There is perhaps no more forceful illustration of the interplay of body, mind, and society than the work reported here. The students in Schachter's experiment were physiologically aroused by adrenalin; they were asked to label their feelings. The labels they offered clearly reflected their social situations (euphoria engendered by the antics of another student) or their psychological states (anger induced by an infuriatingly personal questionnaire). Not only did the aroused students, whether angry or euphoric, label their emotions in terms of their social or psychological experiences, but they exhibited the behaviors that we associate with anger and euphoria. In short, their psychological and social states, combined with their physiological arousal, led these students to feel certain emotions and to act on them.

This selection is not a formal report of this experiment, but it furnishes the information we need to understand the design of the original study, and it gives us a glimpse of the line of thinking that resulted in this research.

Although we rarely bother to make the matter explicit, the assumption of an identity between a physiological state and a psychological or behavioral event is implicit in much contemporary work in such areas as psychopharmacology, psychophysiology, or any domain concerned with the relationship of bodily state to emotion or to behavior. Simply put, much of this work seems to proceed on the assumption that there is a simple, one-to-one relationship

SOURCE: From David C. Glass, ed., *Neurophysiology and Emotion* (New York: Rockefeller University Press and Russell Sage Foundation, 1967). Copyright © 1967 by the Rockefeller University Press and Russell Sage Foundation. Reprinted by permission.

Much of the research described in this paper was supported by Grant MH 05203 from the National Institute of Mental Health, United States Public Health Service, and by Grants G23758 and GS 732 from the National Science Foundation.

between a biochemical change or a physiological process and a specific behavior. It is as if we assumed that physiological state is an "unconditionally sufficient condition" to account for a psychological event.

Such an assumption has, of course, been enormously fruitful in many areas of purely biological and medical research. Spirochetes cause syphilis. Kill the spirochete and cure syphilis. An iodine-deficient diet leads to colloid goiters; repair the deficiency, repair the goiter. As one moves from the world of purely medical and physiological research, however, the assumption of such an "identity" seems to become more and more troublesome. It is this assumption, for example, which is the crux of the James-Cannon difficulties. James' view of emotion * rested squarely on the assumption of an identity between physiological and emotional state, and Cannon's brilliant critique of the James-Lange theory was, in essence, an attack on this assumption. It is this implicit assumption which is, I suspect, responsible for the impression of utter confusion in an area such as psychopharmacology, where it sometimes seems the rule rather than the exception to find a single drug proved in a variety of studies to have blatantly opposite behavioral effects. LSD, for example, has been proved to be a hallucinogenic and a non-hallucinogenic, to be a euphoriant, a depressant, and to have no effects on mood at all. This nightmarish pattern of conflicting and nonreplicable results is familiar to anyone who has delved into the literature on behavioral or "emotional" effects of many of the so-called psychotropic drugs. The pattern, however, is not limited only to the exotic drugs; even as familiar an agent as adrenalin has a similarly depressing history. Many years ago the endocrinologist Marañon [8] injected several hundred of his patients with adrenalin and then asked them to introspect. Some of his subjects simply described their physical symptoms and reported no emotional effects at all; others described their feelings in a fashion that Marañon labeled the "cold," or "as if," emotions; that is, they made statements such as "I feel *as if* I were afraid," or "*as if* I were awaiting a great happiness." Still other subjects described themselves as feeling genuine emotions. Of those who noted any emotional effects at all, some described themselves as feeling anxious, some as angry, some as euphoric. In short, adrenalin, producing almost identical and typical physiological effects in most of these subjects, produced a wide diversity of self-reports of feeling states. This situation is, I suspect, inevitable and will remain puzzling and discouraging as long as we persist in the assumption of an identity between the physiological and the psychological effects of a drug. If we do, my guess is that we will be just about as successful at deriving predictions about complex behavior from a knowledge of biochemical and physiological conditions as we would be at predicting the destination of a moving automobile from an exquisite

---

* Editor's note: In 1922, William James and C. G. Lange proposed an identity between physiological and emotional states. They suggested that bodily changes follow directly the *perception* of the exciting fact, and that the feeling of the same changes as they occur *is* the emotion. For example, we feel sad because we cry, not vice versa; the physiological state induced by crying is the state we identify as sadness.

knowledge of the workings of the internal combustion engine and of petroleum chemistry.

If we are eventually to make sense of this area, I believe we will be forced to adopt a set of concepts with which most physiologically inclined scientists feel somewhat uncomfortable and ill-at-ease, for they are concepts which are, at present, difficult to physiologize about or to reify. We will be forced to examine a subject's perception of his bodily state and his interpretation of it in terms of his immediate situation and his past experience. We will be forced to deal with concepts about perception, about cognition, about learning, and about the social situation.

In order to avoid any misunderstanding, let me make completely explicit that I am most certainly not suggesting that such notions as perception and cognition do not have physiological correlates. I am suggesting that at present we know virtually nothing about these physiological correlates, but that we can and must use nonphysiologically anchored concepts if we are to make headway in understanding the relations of complex behavioral patterns to physiological and biochemical processes.

To move from generalities, let us consider the effects of adrenalin or epinephrine. We know that an injection of ½ cc. of a 1:1000 solution of epinephrine causes an increase in heart rate, a marked increase in systolic blood pressure, a redistribution of blood with a cutaneous decrease, and a muscle and cerebral blood-flow increase. Blood sugar and lactic acid concentrations increase and respiration rate increases slightly. As far as the human subject is concerned, the major subjective symptoms are palpitation, slight tremor, and sometimes a feeling of flushing and accelerated breathing.

These are some of the measured physiological effects of an injection of epinephrine. In and of themselves are such bodily changes pleasant or unpleasant? Given these symptoms, should the subject describe himself as angry, or as anxious, or as manic or euphoric, or simply as sick? From the results of the Marañon study, any of these self-descriptions are possible. How can we make coherent sense of such findings?

Several years ago, bemused by such results, my colleagues and I undertook a program of research on the interaction of physiological and cognitive determinants of emotional state. This program was based on speculation about what was, at that time, a hypothetical event. Imagine a subject whom one somehow managed to inject covertly with adrenalin, or to feed a sympathomimetic agent, such as ephedrine. Such a subject would become aware of palpitations, tremor, etc., and at the same time be utterly unaware of why he felt this way. What would be the consequences of such a state?

In other contexts, [12] I have suggested that precisely this condition would lead to the arousal of evaluative needs; that is, pressures would operate on such an individual to understand and evaluate his bodily feelings. His bodily state roughly resembles the condition in which it has been at times of emotional excitement. How would he label his present feelings? I would suggest that such an individual would label his bodily feelings in terms of the situation in which he finds himself. Should he at the time be watching a horror film, he would probably decide that he was badly frightened. Should he be with a beautiful woman, he might decide that he was wildly in love or sexually excited. Should he be in an argument, he might explode in fury and hatred. Or, should the situation be completely inappropriate, he could decide that he was excited or upset by something that had recently happened. In any case, it is my basic assumption that the labels one attaches to a bodily state, how one describes his feelings, are a joint function of such cognitive factors and of a state of physiological arousal.

This line of thought, then, leads to the following propositions:

> Given a state of physiological arousal for which an individual has no immediate explanation, he will "label" this state and describe his feelings in terms of the cognitions available to him. To the extent that cognitive factors are potent determiners of emotional states, it could be anticipated that precisely the same state of physiological arousal could be called "joy" or "fury" or any of a great diversity of emotional labels, depending on the cognitive aspects of the situation.

> Given a state of physiological arousal for which an individual has a completely appropriate explanation (e.g., "I feel this way because I have just received an injection of adrenalin"), no evaluative needs will arise and the individual is unlikely to label his feelings in terms of the alternative cognitions available.

> Given the same cognitive circumstances, the individual will react emotionally or describe his feelings as emotions only to the extent that he experiences a state of physiological arousal.

The experimental test of these propositions requires, first, the experimental manipulation of a state of physiological arousal or sympathetic activation; second, the manipulation of the extent to which the subject has an appropriate or proper explanation of his bodily state; and third, the creation of situations from which explanatory cognitions may be derived.

In order to satisfy these requirements, Jerome Singer and I [17] constructed an experiment that was cast in the framework of a study of the effects of vitamin supplements on vision. As soon as a subject arrived, he was told: "In this experiment we would like to make various tests of your vision. We are particularly interested in how a vitamin compound called Suproxin affects the visual skills. If you agree to take part in the experiment we would like to give you an injection of Suproxin."

If a subject agreed (and all but one of the 185 subjects did), he received an injection of one of two forms of Suproxin—placebo or epinephrine. We have, then, two groups of subjects—placebo subjects on whom the injection can have no possible effects, and epinephrine subjects who, within a few minutes after injection, will become aware of the full battery of sympathomimetic symptoms.

In order to manipulate the extent to which subjects had a proper explanation of their bodily state, those who received epinephrine received one of two types of instructions.

> *Informed subjects.* Before receiving the injections, such subjects were told, "I should also tell you that some of our subjects have experienced side effects from the Suproxin. These side effects will only last for 15 or 20 minutes. Probably your hands will start to shake, your heart will start to pound, and your face may get warm and flushed."
>
> These subjects, then, are told precisely what they will feel and why they will feel it. For such subjects, the evaluative needs are low. They have an exact explanation for their bodily feelings, and cognitive or situational factors should have no effects on how the subject labels his feelings.
>
> *Uninformed subjects.* Such subjects are told that the injection will have no side effects at all. These subjects, then, will experience a state of sympathetic arousal, but the experimenter has given them no explanation for why they feel as they do. Evaluative needs then should be high, and cognitive-situational factors should have maximal effect on the way such a subject labels his bodily state.*

Finally, in order to expose subjects to situations from which they might derive explanatory cognitions relevant to their bodily state, they were placed in one of two situations immediately after injection:

> *Euphoria.* A subject was placed alone in a room with a stooge who had been introduced as a fellow subject and who, following a completely standardized routine, acted in a euphoric-manic fashion, doing such things as flying paper airplanes, hula-hooping, and the like, all the while keeping up a standard patter and occasionally attempting to induce the subject to join in.
>
> *Anger.* A subject was asked to fill out a long, infuriatingly personal questionnaire that asked such questions as:
> "With how many men (other than your father) has your mother had extramarital relationships?
> 4 and under————: 5–9————: 10 and over————."

Filling in the questionnaire alongside the subject was a stooge, again presumably a fellow subject, who openly grew more and more irritated at the questionnaire and who finally ripped the thing up in a rage, slammed it to the floor while biting out, "I'm not wasting any more time; I'm getting my books and leaving," and stamped out of the room.

In both situations, an observer, watching through a one-way mirror, systematically recorded the behavior of the subject in order to provide indexes of the extent to which the subject joined in the stooge's mood. Once these

* For purposes of brevity, the description of this experiment does not include details of all the conditions in this study. The chief omission is a description of a control condition introduced to evaluate alternative interpretations of the data. The interested reader is referred to the original paper by Schachter and Singer (1962) [17].

rigged situations had run their course, the experimenter returned and, with a plausible pretext, asked the subject to fill out a series of standardized scales to measure the intensity of anger or euphoria.

We have, then, a set of experimental conditions in which we are simultaneously manipulating the degree of sympathetic arousal and the extent to which subjects understand why they feel as they do, and measuring the impact of these variations on the extent to which the subject catches the mood of a situation rigged to induce euphoria in one set of conditions and to induce anger in another. From the line of thought that generated this study, it should be anticipated that subjects injected with epinephrine and told that there would be no side effects should catch the mood of the rigged situation to a greater extent than subjects who had been injected with a placebo or those who had been injected with epinephrine and given a completely appropriate explanation of what they would feel and why.

Examining first the results of the euphoria conditions, we find that this is exactly the case. The uninformed epinephrine subjects—those who had been told that there would be no side effects—tend to catch the stooge's mood with alacrity; they join the stooge's whirl of activity and invent new manic activities of their own. In marked contrast, the informed epinephrine subjects and the placebo subjects who give no indication of autonomic arousal tend simply to sit and stare at the stooge in mild disbelief. The relevant data are reported in detail elsewhere. For present purposes it should suffice to note that these differences between conditions are large and statistically significant on both observational and self-report measures of mood.

In the anger conditions, the pattern of results is precisely the same. Uninformed epinephrine subjects grow openly annoyed and irritated, while placebo and informed epinephrine subjects maintain their equanimity. The evidence is good, then, in support of our basic propositions. Given a state of physiological arousal for which a subject has no easy explanation, he proves readily manipulable into the disparate states of euphoria and anger. Given an identical physiological state for which the subject has an appropriate explanation, his mood is almost untouched by the rigged situation.

Such results are not limited to the states of anger and euphoria. In still other experiments in which similar techniques and comparisons were employed, we have been readily able to manipulate uninformed epinephrine subjects into amusement, as measured by laughter at a slapstick movie, [18] and into fearful or anxious states. [16]

In sum, precisely the same physiological state—an epinephrine-induced state of sympathetic arousal—can be manifested as anger, euphoria, amusement, fear, or, as in the informed subjects, as no mood or emotion at all. Such results are virtually incomprehensible if we persist in the assumption of an identity between physiological and psychological states, but they fall neatly into place if we specify the fashion in which cognitive and physiological factors interact. With the addition of cognitive propositions, we are able to specify and manipulate the conditions under which an injection of epinephrine will or will not lead to an emotional state and to predict what emotion will result. . . .

[At this point, Dr. Schachter begins to apply this interpretation to the problem of overeating. Obese people, he suggests, mislabel certain physiological states; they confuse inherent physiological stimuli relating to a need for food with learned social stimuli related, for example, to a need for consolation. This formulation, in essence that people eat for reasons other than true hunger, is consistent with psychoanalytic theory or common sense but more fully spelled out than either of these.

The rest of this engaging report is too lengthy to reproduce here.]

References

1. BEEBE, L. *The Big Spenders*. New York: Doubleday, 1966.
2. BLISS, E. L., and BRANCH, C. H. *Anorexia Nervosa*. New York: Paul B. Hoeber, 1960.
3. BRUCH, HILDE. Transformation of oral impulses in eating disorders: A conceptual approach. *Psychiat. Quart.* 35, no. 3 (1961):458–81.
4. CANNON, W. B. *Bodily Changes in Pain, Hunger, Fear and Rage*. New York: D. Appleton, 1915.
5. CARLSON, A. J. *The Control of Hunger in Health and Disease*. Chicago: University of Chicago Press, 1916.
6. GOLDMAN, R., JAFFA, M., and SCHACHTER, S. Yom Kippur, Air France, dormitory food and the eating behavior of obese and normal persons. Unpublished manuscript, 1967.
7. HASHIM, S. A., and VAN ITALLIE, T. B. Studies in normal and obese subjects with a monitored food dispensing device. *Ann. N. Y. Acad. Sci.* 131, art. 1 (1965):654–61.
8. MARAÑON, G. Contribution à l'étude de l'action émotive de l'adrénaline. *Revue Française D'Endocrinologia* 2, no. 5 (1924):301–25.
9. NISBETT, R. E., and SCHACHTER, S. The cognitive manipulation of pain. *J. Exp. Soc. Psychol.* 2, no. 3 (1966):227–36.
10. NISBETT, R. E. Taste, deprivation and weight determinants of eating behavior. Unpublished doctoral dissertation, Columbia University, 1966.
11. RAZRAN, G. The observable unconscious and the inferable conscious in current Soviet psychophysiology. *Psychol. Rev.* 68, no. 2 (1961):81–147.
12. SCHACHTER, S. *The Psychology of Affiliation*. Stanford: Stanford University Press, 1959.
13. SCHACHTER, S. The interaction of cognitive and physiological determinants of emotional state. In *Advances in Experimental Social Psychology*, vol. 1. L. Berkowitz, ed. New York: Academic Press, 1964. Pp. 49–80.
14. SCHACHTER, S., GOLDMAN, R., and GORDON, A. The effects of fear, food deprivation and obesity on eating. Unpublished manuscript, 1967.
15. SCHACHTER, S., and GROSS, L. Manipulated time and eating behavior. Unpublished manuscript, 1967.
16. SCHACHTER, S., and LATANÉ, B. Crime, cognition and the autonomic nervous system. In *Nebraska Symposium on Motivation*. D. Levine, ed. Lincoln: University of Nebraska Press, 1964. Pp. 221–73.

17. SCHACHTER, S., and SINGER, J. Cognitive, social, and physiological determinants of emotional state. *Psychol. Rev.* 69, no. 5 (1962):379–99.
18. SCHACHTER, S., and WHEELER, L. Epinephrine, chlorpromazine, and amusement. *J. Abn. and Soc. Psychol.* 65, no. 2 (1962):121–28.
19. STUNKARD, A. Obesity and the denial of hunger. *Psychosomat. Med.* 21, no. 4 (1959):281–89.
20. STUNKARD, A. Hunger and satiety. *Am. J. Psychiat.* 118, no. 3 (1961):212–17.
21. STUNKARD, A., and KOCH, C. The interpretation of gastric motility: I. Apparent bias in the reports of hunger by obese persons. *Arch. Gen. Psychiat.* 11 (1964):74–82.

Influence of a Female Model on Perceived Characteristics of an Automobile

GEORGE H. SMITH AND RAYME ENGEL

Personal judgment can also be influenced by our perceptions. In this short report, Smith and Engel test one of the cardinal assumptions of commercial advertising. This issue is, Does sex sell? It's rare to find a television commercial or magazine advertisement for a car—especially a sports car—that does not boast a picture of a scantily (or at least tightly) clad girl. Does this rather illogical use of the female form produce the intended effect? That is, does it sell cars? The data that Smith and Engel offer are by no means conclusive, but they do suggest that the movement to do away with such advertising faces at best an uphill battle.

This paper is reproduced from a collection of summaries, or abstracts, of technical papers. Its telegraphic style is intended to convey as much about the purpose, design, analysis, and results of the study as possible in as little space as possible. The authors have done an unusually good job in keeping this report readable as well as compact.

An experiment was conducted which shows that certain salient elements in a print advertisement, which are not intrinsic to the product, may nevertheless work at a more or less unconscious level to influence the way consumers feel about the product and the way they rate its objective characteristics. This is not a novel theory, but in practical advertising decisions it is often acted on as a matter of faith or hunch, and usually with unknown consequences, rather than on the basis of carefully controlled experimentation. The present study may suggest the feasibility of conducting inexpensive experiments in which selected stimuli are varied systematically and the effects assessed before spending large sums of money on a campaign in the mass media.

SOURCE: From George H. Smith and Rayme Engel, "Influence of a Female Model on the Perceived Characteristics of an Automobile," *Proceedings of the 76th Annual Convention of the American Psychological Association*, 1968. Copyright © 1968 by the American Psychological Association and reproduced by permission.

An automobile was selected as the product to be studied, and an attractive female model was the experimental variable. In today's advertising, a young woman is sometimes used to demonstrate features of a car, in which case she serves an explicit selling function; in other cases, she is included more or less decoratively but with, presumably, the implicit function of somehow making the car seem more attractive and worthwhile than if she were not present. This nonintrinsic (implicit) influence of the young female is the one which we chose to study.

The stimulus material consisted of two similar, plastic covered montages, each $13\frac{1}{2} \times 11$ in., with cardboard reinforcement. The experimental montage showed a medium priced two-door hard top automobile, beige color, with certain changes of detail to render it unidentifiable as to make. This montage included a female model standing in the right foreground with the car behind her. Clipped from *Playboy*, this young redhead clad in black lace panties and a simple sleeveless sweater was rated by 15 male observers as attractive in form and erotic in appeal. One hand rested on her hip while the other held a spear—on the theory that this phallic symbol (?) might make her seem more aggressively seductive! She had no obvious function of demonstrating or pointing out features of the car. The control montage contained the identical automobile, without the female. That part of the car concealed by her body in the experimental montage was blocked out by a neutral screen in the control montage.

After 2 waves of pretesting on 60 Ss,* the final phase of the research was done on 120 adult respondents obtained through personal interviews in a large upper middle-class housing development in East Brunswick, N. J. in the fall of 1966. Following an ABAB sequence, half the respondents received the experimental treatment and half received the control treatment.

No significant differences were found in the variance of the experimental and the control group on age, sex, income, and number of cars owned.† Each group of 60 Ss contained 35 males and 25 females; in each group more than 50% were between 35 and 44 years of age; they were comparable in economic status with the majority reporting between $10,000 and $15,000 annual income.

The 60 respondents in the experimental and the 60 in the control sample were asked to rate the design of the car on a 5-point scale from "Excellent" to "Poor"; to estimate list price with standard equipment; to estimate top speed of the car; and to rate it on seven bipolar concepts: appealing–not

Editor's notes:

* Ss is a technical abbreviation for *subjects* in an experiment. The pretesting the authors mention is often undertaken before the real experiment, a "dress rehearsal" to see if any unanticipated complications might arise and to help clarify the meaning of the experiment.

† That is, the two groups seemed about the same in terms of age, sex, income, and number of cars owned. A "significant" difference is a difference that does not occur by chance or accident.

appealing, lively–dull, youthful–not youthful, high horsepower–low horse-power, safe–unsafe, easy to handle–difficult to handle, wide wheelbase–narrow wheelbase (Osgood, 1957).

Mean scores for the 60 experimental Ss and the 60 control Ss were obtained for each test item; also, separately for the 35 males and 25 females in each group. The significance of the differences between means from independent samples were computed, using a two-tailed test.‡

Results strongly suggest that inclusion of the female model in the montage influences people's perception of the car in various ways. On items designed to tap the connotative or emotional features of the car, the 60 experimental and the 60 control Ss rated the vehicle very differently. The former saw it as more appealing ($p \leq .01$), more lively ($p \leq .01$), more youthful ($p \leq .01$), and as having a better or more excellent design ($p \leq .01$).**

But what about objective characteristics of the unidentified automobile, its assumed cost, and so on? Here too differences show up. The 60 experimental Ss, compared with the 60 controls, are more apt to rate the car as costing an average $340 more ($p \leq .01$), as able to move an average 7.3 mph faster ($p \leq .05$), as less safe ($p \leq .05$), and higher in horsepower ($p \leq .01$). The men but not the women judge the wheelbase to be larger ($p \leq .05$). The car is perhaps seen as harder to handle when the girl is added, but differences are not statistically significant.

In general, the 25 women in the experimental group respond in the same direction as the 35 males. The young female—the "love goddess" in the sociologists' lexicon—perhaps pervasively wields her influence on audiences of the mass media regardless of their own sex.

In supplementary interviews, 23 cooperative men in the experimental group were asked in an informal manner whether they thought the girl in the picture had any influence on their judgments. Twenty-two of these men not only denied this possibility but scarcely acknowledged being aware of the girl in the montage. One admitted that he had noticed the female model and may have been influenced by her presence. Comments from the others include: "I don't let anything but the thing itself influence my judgments. The other is just propaganda." "I never let myself be blinded by advertising; the car itself is what counts." "The car itself. The other is just dressing." "She could influence me, but not as far as the car is concerned." "Girls aren't that important!"

Findings are in line with a body of research which points to the way in which cues of one kind or another can restructure a person's perceptual field

‡ *Test* in this sense means a special kind of statistical analysis used to determine whether or not the observed differences between two groups are significant or not. This kind of test should be distinguished from the tests talked about in Part 5, Intelligence and Abilities.

** Statistical tests are never certain; they are always based on probability. The statements in parentheses are called probability statements and are read "*p* equal to or less than .01," that is, from the statistical analysis, the chances are equal to or less than 1 in 100 that the conclusion that there is a difference is in error.

without his conscious awareness of what is happening or perhaps with an unacknowledged need to deny what is happening [e.g., Berelson and Steiner, 1964; Smith, 1953].

The present investigation was limited in scope. Generalizations from it to a wide range of products, female types, and interactions of product and female are not justified. But this is just the point. When we undertook this study we frankly did not know how, if at all, the particular "love goddess" would influence imputed price, horsepower, and other attributes of the automobile. Only after extensive pretesting did we begin to formulate fairly firm hypotheses. Hindsight shows that we were generally right in our guesses about how things would turn out in the final phase of the study.

But in the absence of hindsight based on hard facts, we are left with the simple guess or assumption that the gratuitous inclusion of "attention getters" such as pretty girls, babies and dogs—or living creatures in general—probably does "something" for the advertised product, hopefully something good. Conducting research in advance to pin down what is actually happening in consumers' minds seems like a good idea.

The design we employed was adapted to the requirements of an unsponsored graduate thesis project. With relatively small investments of money and time, it could be modified for use by an advertiser or agency to gauge the effects of features in an advertisement which on hunch seem to have merit, but are not amenable to testing through the usual interviews. It seems perfectly clear from our limited data that we are overly optimistic if we expect rational creatures like consumers to know or admit that a girl or any other irrational feature of an ad influences them to see the product in a different light. This would be tantamount to admitting that they are being brainwashed, which not even politicians can afford to do!

References

1. BERELSON, B., and STEINER, G. A. *Human Behavior*. New York: Harcourt, Brace, 1964.
2. OSGOOD, C. *The Measurement of Meaning*. Urbana, Ill.: University of Illinois Press, 1957.
3. SMITH, G. H. Size-distance judgments of human faces. *Journal of General Psychology* 49 (1953):45–64.

Subliminal Stimulation: An Overview

JAMES V. MCCONNELL, RICHARD L. CUTLER, AND
ELTON B. MCNEIL

With an almost predictable regularity, widespread fear arises about the manipu-lation of people's minds by psychological techniques. Whether the topic is the selling of a president, hypnosis, or brain implantations, tremendous powers over other people are attributed to an Orwellian few. Subliminal stimulation is another of those topics. Subliminal stimulation means impinging stimuli on people with-out their being aware of it; the classical case is the allegation that people can be made to "Drink Coca-Cola" by the invisibly rapid flashing of that slogan on a movie screen. In this article, McConnell, Cutler, and McNeil examine the possi-bility of such control over human behavior. They review relevant research studies and raise pointed questions about the technology of subliminal stimulation. Per-haps the most important and reassuring point of their whole discussion is the suggestion of just how complicated such a program of mind control would be. But complexity is no assurance that a thing will not come to be; atom-smashing is a complicated process too. Therefore the authors devote the last part of their paper to a discussion of the ethical implications of what powers psychology has or might have eventually.

Seldom has anything in psychology caused such an immediate and widespread stir as the recent claim that the presentation of certain stimuli below the level of conscious awareness can influence people's behavior in a significant way. The controversy was precipitated primarily by a commercial firm which claimed that the subliminal presentation of the words "Eat Popcorn" and "Drink Coca-Cola" fantastically stimulated the respective sales of these products among the motion picture audiences who received the stimulation. Despite the fact that detailed reports of the experiment have not been made directly available in any published form, this technique was seized upon as the newest of the "new look" promises of the application of psychology to

SOURCE: From James V. McConnell, Richard L. Cutler, and Elton B. McNeil, "Subliminal Stimulation: An Overview," *American Psychologist* 13 (1958):229–42. Copyright © by the American Psychological Association and reproduced by permission.

advertising. While such claims and demonstrations will be considered in greater detail below, it is important to note here that they have given rise to a series of charges and countercharges, the effects of which have reached the United States Congress and the Federal Communications Commission [7, 117].

Rarely does a day pass without a statement in the public press relating to the Utopian promise or the 1984 threat of the technique [8, 17, 29, 37, 42, 45, 118, 132]. Since the process of choosing up sides promises to continue unabated, it appears wise to provide the potential combatants with a more factual basis for arriving at their positions than presently seems available. Meanwhile, the present writers have cautiously sought to avoid aligning themselves behind either of the barricades.

Obviously, the notion that one may influence the behavior of another individual without the individual's knowing about it is a fascinating one. It is of extreme interest, not only to psychologists and advertisers, but also to politicians, psychiatrists, passionate young men, and others, whose motives would be considered more or less sacred by the larger society. Equally obvious is the need for a clarification of the issues surrounding the application of subliminal perception. This clarification must involve the assessment of available scientific evidence, the answering of a series of technical questions, and the examination of what, if any, levels of behavior may indeed be influenced. Finally, a series of extremely complex ethical issues needs to be explored. It is the purpose of the present paper to undertake this task, in the hope of providing information upon which possible decisions involving its application may be based.

Recent History of the Technique

The custom of providing a chronological review of the literature will be violated in this paper, inasmuch as three separate threads of investigation seem worth tracing: (1) the recent demonstrations by advertisers which first aroused large-scale public interest in subliminal perception, (2) systematic research by psychologists relating directly to the influencing of behavior without the individual's awareness that he is being influenced, and (3) psychological research concerned primarily with the influence of inner states of the organism upon the threshold for conscious recognition of certain stimuli.

RECENT ADVERTISING DEMONSTRATIONS

While the advertising possibilities of subliminal stimulation were recognized by Hollingworth [59] as early as 1913, the intensive work in its application to this area has been carried out within the past two years. In 1956, BBC-TV, in conjunction with one of its regular broadcasts, transmitted the message "Pirie Breaks World Record" at a speed assumed to be subliminal [85]. At the conclusion of the regular program, viewers were asked to report whether they had noticed "anything unusual" about the program. While no reliable statistical data are available, it seems possible that those few viewers responding to the message possessed sufficiently low thresholds so that for them the message was supraliminal.

A demonstration by the commercial enterprise which has been most vocal in its claims for the advertising promise of the technique consisted of projecting, during alternate periods, the words "Eat Popcorn" and "Drink Coca-Cola" during the regular presentation of a motion picture program. As a result of this stimulation, reports contend,[1] popcorn sales rose more than 50% and Coca-Cola sales 18%, as compared to a "previous period." Despite the likelihood of serious methodological and technical defects (exposure time was reported as 1/3,000 sec, far faster than any previously reported stimulation), this demonstration has been the one which has caused the most stir in both the fields of advertising and psychology. There were no reports, however, of even the most rudimentary scientific precautions, such as adequate controls, provision for replication, etc., which leaves the skeptical scientist in a poor position to make any judgment about the validity of the study.

In a later demonstration for the press, technical difficulties permitted the viewers to become consciously aware of the fact that they were being stimulated. Although described as a purposeful and prearranged part of the demonstration, it left many of the reporters present unconvinced that the technical difficulties inherent in the technique have been surmounted.

The FCC, turning its attention to the problem, has reported that one TV station (WTWO, Bangor, Maine) has experimented with the transmission of public service announcements at subliminal levels, with "negative results" [117].

The uncontrolled and unsystematic nature of the demonstrations reported above makes very difficult the task of reaching a trustworthy conclusion about the effectiveness of subliminal stimulation in advertising. Whether the technique represents a promising means of communicating with the individual at a level of his unconsciousness or whether it reflects only the hyperenthusiasm of an entreprenurial group remain unanswered questions.

RESEARCH ON BEHAVIOR WITHOUT AWARENESS

In the hope of providing a more substantial foundation upon which to base judgments of the validity of advertising claims for subliminal stimulation, a systematic review of relevant scientific work was undertaken. While we believe that our review was comprehensive, we have decided not to provide an extensive critical discussion of the various studies, choosing instead to

[1] The essential facts of this study have not been reported in any journal. The discussion of this experiment and the findings reported by the commercial enterprise responsible for the study is based on reports in several general news accounts appearing in the popular press [7, 8, 16, 17, etc.].

present summative statements and conclusions based upon what seems to be sufficient evidence and consensus in the literature.[2]

The work of experimental psychologists in subliminal stimulation dates from Suslowa [119] in 1863, as reported by Baker [5]. Suslowa's experiments concerned the effect of electrical stimulation upon subjects' ability to make two-point threshold discriminations. He found that, even when the intensity of the electrical stimulation was so low that the subjects were not aware of its presence, their ability to discriminate one- from two-point stimulation was somewhat reduced.

In 1884, Peirce and Jastrow [94] were able to show that subjects could discriminate differences between weights significantly better than chance would allow, even though the differences were so small they had no confidence whatsoever in their judgments.

Numerous experimenters have relied upon this criterion of "zero confidence" to establish that discrimination of stimuli presented below the level of conscious awareness is possible. For example, Sidis [107] showed that subjects could reliably distinguish letters from numbers, even when the stimuli were presented at such a distance from them that the subjects thought they were relying on pure guesswork for their judgments.

In what was essentially a replication of Sidis' research, Stroh, Shaw, and Washburn [116] found evidence to support his conclusions. They found similar results when auditory stimuli (whispers) were presented at a distance such that the subjects were not consciously aware that they were hearing anything.

Several experiments have provided further support for Peirce and Jastrow's initial conclusions [44, 127]. Baker [5] found subjects able to discriminate diagonal from vertical crossed lines, and a dot-dash from a dash-dot auditory pattern. Miller [88] presented five geometric figures at four different levels of intensity below the threshold and found that, while subjects could discriminate which was being presented a significant proportion of the time, their ability to discriminate was reduced as the intensity of stimulation was further reduced. More recently, a series of studies by Blackwell [11] has shown that subjects can reliably identify during which of four time periods a subliminal spot of light is presented upon a homogeneous field. Blackwell, however, stresses that reliability of discrimination decreases as the intensity of the stimulus is further lowered. Several other supporting studies are available [28, 97, 130] which show essentially the same results, namely, that even when subjects have zero confidence in their judgments, they can discriminate reliably (though not perfectly) between stimuli.

In his review, Adams [1] points out certain general weaknesses inherent in studies of this type, but agrees with the present authors that discrimination

[2] The reader who wishes a more complete technical critique of studies in the field is referred to reviews by Adams [1], Collier [27], Coover [28], Lazarus and McCleary [76], and Miller [90].

can occur under certain circumstances. However, it is interesting to note that, in nearly all studies reporting relevant data, the reliability of the subjects' judgments increases directly with the intensity of the stimuli. If a valid extrapolation can be drawn from this finding, it would be that accuracy of perception increases as the stimulation approaches a supraliminal level.

A second series of studies has involved presenting subjects with variations of the Mueller-Lyer illusion, in which the angular lines have differed, subliminally, in hue or brightness from the background. The first of these studies, reported by Dunlap in 1900 [36], gave clear evidence that the subjects were influenced in their judgments of line length, even though they could not "see" the angular lines. Several replications of this study have been carried out, and while at least three have found partial support for Dunlap's conclusions [14, 59, 86], others have failed to find the phenomenon [123]. In another experiment conducted by Sidis in 1898 [107], subjects asked to fixate on a number series in the center of a card, and then asked to pick a number from this series, systematically chose that number which was written in the periphery of the card, even though they were not consciously aware of its presence. Coover [28] in 1917 showed essentially the same results by asking subjects to pick a number at random while they were fixating on a letter in the upper right portion of a card. He found that subjects tended to pick the number printed in the lower left of the card, even though they did not *usually* know it was there. In similar experiments, Collier [27] and Perky [95] showed that subjects could be made to produce drawings, even though they were not aware that they were being influenced in their actions. While these studies are not unequivocal in their findings, nor generally rigorous in their methodology, they too seem to support the contention that behavior of a sort can be influenced by subliminal means. However, they require cautious interpretation, since the degree of the subject's attention to the stimuli seems clearly to be a factor. Further, as contrasted to those studies where the subject is actually aware in advance of at least the general nature of the stimulation, these studies reveal a somewhat less pronounced effect of subliminal stimulation upon the subject's behavior.

While the studies reported above seem to indicate that discrimination without awareness may occur, it may reasonably be asked whether stimulation below the level of conscious awareness can produce any but the most simple modifications in behavior. A series of studies [24, 26, 73, 109], beginning with Newhall and Sears in 1933 [92], have attempted to show that it is possible to condition subjects to subliminal stimuli. Newhall and Sears found it possible to establish a weak and unstable conditioned response to light presented subliminally, when the light had been previously paired with shock. Baker [6] in 1938 reported the successful conditioning of the pupillary reflex to a subliminal auditory stimulus, but later experimenters have failed to replicate his results [57, 128]. In a now classic experiment, McCleary and Lazarus [79] found that nonsense syllables which had previously been associated with shock produced a greater psychogalvanic reflex when presented tachistoscopically at subliminal speeds than did nonshock syllables. Deiter [34] confirmed the McCleary and Lazarus findings and showed further that, when verbal instructions were substituted for the shock, no such differences were produced. Bach and Klein [4] have recently reported that they were able to influence subjects' judgments of whether the line drawing of a face (essentially neutral in its emotional expression) was "angry" or "happy" by projecting the appropriate words at subliminal speeds upon the drawing.

A series of related studies [58, 65, 89, 99, 105, 121, 122] have shown that, even when the subject is not aware that any cue is being given, certain responses can be learned or strengthened during the experimental process. For example, Cohen, Kalish, Thurston, and Cohen [25] showed that, when the experimenter said "right" to any sentence which the subject started with "I" or "We," the number of such sentences increased significantly. Klein [69] was able to produce both conditioning and extinction without awareness, using the Cohen et al. technique.

Several experimenters have used subliminal or "unnoticed" reward-punishment techniques to modify subjects' responses in a variety of situations, including free or chained association tasks, performance on personality tests, and interview elicited conversation [35, 41, 50, 56, 72, 78, 93, 120, 125, 126]. Typical is the work of Greenspoon [48], who reinforced the use of plural nouns by saying "mm-humm" after each plural mentioned by the subject. He found that, even though none of his subjects could verbalize the relationship between their response and his reinforcement, their use of plural nouns doubled. Sidowski [108] demonstrated essentially the same thing using a light, of which the subject was only peripherally aware, as a reinforcer for the use of plural words. Weiss [129], however, failed to find any increase in the frequency of "living things" responses, using a right-wrong reinforcement to free associations by the subjects.

This evidence suggests that subjects may either (1) "learn" certain subliminally presented stimuli or (2) make use of subliminal reinforcers either to learn or strengthen a previously learned response. Again, the critical observations of Adams [1] and the introduction of other possible explanations by Bricker and Chapanis [15] make necessary a cautious interpretation of these results.

EFFECTS OF INNER STATES UPON THRESHOLDS

Whatever the possibility that subliminal stimulation may significantly alter behavior, there is excellent evidence that certain inner states of the organism, as well as externally induced conditions, may significantly alter the recognition threshold of the individual. This, of course, has important implications for the susceptibility of the individual to the effects of subliminal stimulation. It is well known that physiological factors, such as fatigue, visual acuity, or satiation, may change the threshold of an individual for various kinds of stimuli.

Recent evidence has accumulated to show that, in addition to these physiological factors, certain "psychological states," such as psychological need, value, conflict, and defense, may also significantly influence thresholds, as well as other aspects of the perceptual process. Early work in this area is reported by Sanford [102, 103] who showed that subjects who had been deprived of food were more prone to produce "food-relevant" responses to a series of ambiguous stimuli. McClelland and Atkinson [80] showed that levels of the hunger drive were systematically related to the ease with which food responses were made when no words were presented on the screen.

While a complete review of the experimental work on "perceptual defense" and "selective vigilance" would take us too far afield, it seems wise to indicate, by example, some of the inner state factors which allegedly produce variations in recognition threshold. Bruner and Postman [19, 20, 21] and Bruner and Goodman [18] were able to show that such factors as symbolic value, need, tension and tension release, and emotional selectivity were important in the perceptual process. Ansbacher [3] had earlier demonstrated that the perception of numerosity was significantly affected by the monetary value of the stimuli. Rees and Israel [101] called attention to the fact that the mental set of the organism was an important factor in the perceptual process. Beams and Thompson [9] showed that emotional factors were important determiners of the perception of the magnitude of need-relevant objects. Other studies bearing upon the issue of inner state determiners of perception are reported by Carter and Schooler [23], Cowen and Beier [31, 32], and Levine, Chein, and Murphy [77].

More specifically related to the issue of altered recognition thresholds is a study by McGinnies [82] in which he demonstrated that emotionally toned words had generally higher thresholds than neutral words. Blum [13] has shown that subjects tend to be less likely to choose conflict-relevant stimuli from a group presented at subliminal speeds than to choose neutral stimuli. Lazarus, Ericksen, and Fonda [75] have shown that personality factors are at least in part determiners of the recognition threshold for classes of auditory stimuli. Reece [100] showed that the association of shock with certain stimuli had the effect of raising the recognition threshold for those stimuli.

While many writers have contended that the variations in threshold can be accounted for more parsimoniously than by introducing "motivational" factors such as need and value [60, 61, 111], and while the issue of the degree to which need states influence perception is still unresolved [22, 39, 40, 62, 74, 83], it is apparent that the recognition threshold is not a simple matter of intensity nor speed of presentation. Recent work by Postman and others [47, 96, 98], which has sought to illuminate the prerecognition processes operating to produce the apparent changes in threshold, does not alter the fact that individual differences in the perceptual process must be taken into account in any further work on the effects of subliminal stimulation.

Unanswered Methodological Questions

Having now concluded that, under certain conditions, the phenomenon of subliminal perception does occur, we turn our attention next to the many unanswered questions which this conclusion raises. For example, what kinds of behavior can be influenced by subliminal stimulation? What types of stimuli operate best at subthreshold intensities? Do all subliminal stimuli operate at the same "level of unconsciousness," or do different stimuli (or modes of stimulation) affect different levels of unconsciousness? What characteristics of the perceiver help determine the effectiveness of subliminal stimulation? All of these questions, as well as many others of a technological nature, will be discussed in the ensuing paragraphs.

A few words of caution concerning the word "subliminal" seem in order, however. It must be rememebered that the psychological limen is a statistical concept, a fact overlooked by far too many current textbook writers. The common definition of the limen is "that stimulus value which gives a response exactly half the time " [44, p. 111]. One of the difficulties involved in analyzing the many studies on subliminal perception is the fact that many experimenters have assumed that, because the stimuli which they employed were below the statistical limen for a given subject, the stimuli were therefore never consciously perceivable by the subject. This is, of course, not true. Stimuli slightly below the statistical limen might well be consciously perceivable as much as 49% of the time. Not only this, but thresholds vary from moment to moment, as well as from day to day. All this is not to deny that stimuli which are so weak that they are never consciously reportable under any circumstances may not indeed influence behavior. We simply wish to make the point that the range of stimulus intensities which are in fact "subliminal" may be smaller than many experimenters in the past have assumed. It has been commonly assumed that the several methods of producing subliminal stimuli, i.e., reducing intensity, duration, size, or clarity, are logically and methodologically equivalent. While this may be true, it remains to be demonstrated conclusively.

TYPES OF BEHAVIOR INFLUENCED BY SUBLIMINAL STIMULATION

One of the first questions that springs to mind concerns the types of response which can be elicited with subliminal stimulation. Let us assume for the moment that the below-threshold advertisements used in commercial demonstrations were the sole cause of increased popcorn buying among the movie audiences subjected to the ads. How did this come about? Did the stimulus "Eat Popcorn" elicit an already established response in some members of the audience? Or did the frequent repetitions of the stimulus message cause a shift in attitude towards popcorn eating which eventually resulted in the purchase of popcorn at the first opportunity the audience had? Did the ads merely raise an already existing, presumably learned, but weak need for popcorn to an above the action-threshold level, or did the ads actually create a need for popcorn where no need had existed beforehand? Did members of the audience rise like automatons during the course of the movie and thus miss part of the feature in order to satisfy a sudden craving for popcorn or in order to respond to a suddenly evoked stimulus-response connection? Or did they wait until a "rest period" to do their purchasing? How many patrons bought popcorn only after they had seen the film and were heading home? How many people purchased popcorn on their way *in* to see the next movie they attended? How many of those who purchased popcorn did so for the first time in their lives, or for the first time in recent memory? What if the message presented had been "Buy Christmas Seals," which are available only in one season? How many people failed to buy popcorn at the theater, but purchased it subsequently at the local supermarket?

Unfortunately, these pertinent questions have yet to be answered. Let us tentatively accept this demonstration that impulse buying of inexpensive items such as popcorn and Coca-Cola can be influenced by subliminal advertising, without yet knowing what the mechanism involved is. It remains to be demonstrated, however, that such ads could make a person of limited means wreck himself financially by purchasing a Cadillac merely because the ads told him to do so. Nor do we know if deep-seated, strongly emotional attitudes or long established behavior patterns can be shifted one way or another as a result of subliminal stimulation. The answers to these questions must come from further experimentation.

As we have already seen, people can make use of subthreshold stimuli in making difficult perceptual judgments in situations where they are required to call up images of various objects [95] and in situations where they are asked to "read the experimenter's mind" [88]. Kennedy [68] believes that some extrasensory-perception (ESP) experimenters may have obtained positive results because the "senders" unconsciously transmitted slight auditory and visual cues to their "receivers," and offers many experimental findings to back up his belief. Kennedy's studies also point up the difficult dilemma faced by people who object to subliminal stimulation as being an immoral or illegal attempt to influence other people. All of us, apparently, are constantly attempting to influence the people around us by means of sounds and movements we are unconscious of making. Correspondingly, all of us make some unconscious use of the cues presented to us by the people around us.

It also seems fairly clear that learning can take place when the stimuli to which the organism must respond are presented subliminally. Hankin [51] learned to predict changes in the flight of birds by utilizing wing-tip adjustments which were too slight to be consciously (reportably) noticeable. As we stated previously, Baker [6] obtained a conditioned pupillary response to subliminal auditory stimuli, although other investigators failed to replicate his findings. Miller [89] had subjects look at a mirror while trying to guess geometrical forms in an ESP-type experiment. Stimuli far below the statistical limen were projected on a mirror from behind. When the subjects were rewarded by praise for correct guesses and punished by electric shock for wrong guesses, learning took place. It is interesting to note that neither punishment alone nor reward alone was sufficient to produce learning.

Whether different types of learning than those reported above can take place using subliminal stimulation, and indeed how broad a range of human behavior can be influenced in any way whatsoever by subliminal stimulation, are questions which remain unanswered.

LEVELS OF UNCONSCIOUSNESS AFFECTED BY SUBLIMINAL STIMULATION [3]

We must now differentiate between stimuli which a subject cannot bring to awareness under any conditions (completely subliminal stimuli) and those stimuli of which he is merely not aware at the moment but could be made aware of should his set be changed. At any given moment, a vast conflux of stimuli impinges upon a subject's receptors. Few of the sensations arising from this stimulation ever enter the focus of attention. As Dallenbach was fond of reminding his Freshman classes: "Until I mentioned it, you were quite unaware that your shoes are full of feet." A great many experimenters have demonstrated that subjects could make use of stimuli well above the threshold of awareness but which could not be consciously reported on. Thus in one phase of her experiment, Perky [95] raised the intensity of the visual stimuli she was using to such a level that other psychologists who had not participated in the study apparently refused to believe that the subjects had not been aware of the stimuli. Perky's subjects, however, operating under a set to call up "images" of the stimuli presented, did not notice even relatively intense stimuli. Correspondingly, Newhall and Dodge [91] presented visual stimuli first at below-threshold intensities, then increased the intensities so slowly that the subjects were not aware of them even when the stimuli were well above threshold. When the stimuli were turned off suddenly, however, the subjects experienced afterimages. Thus certain stimuli may be well above threshold and yet be "subliminal" in the sense that they cannot be reported on under certain experimental conditions.

There are other levels of "unconsciousness" which are deserving of our attention, however. Much work has been done at the animal level in which conditioning has been attempted upon animals with various parts of the brain removed [33, 43]. The same is true of animals, under various types of anesthesia [106, 115]. Miller, in summarizing the experimental data dealing with conditioning and consciousness, concludes:

1. That conditioning can take place in other parts of the nervous system than the cortex—even in the spinal cord;

[3] For an excellent review of the many meanings of the word "unconsciousness," readers are referred to Miller's book of the same name [90].

2. That, if conditioned responses are evidences of consciousness, then consciousness is not mediated solely by the cortex;
3. That it may be possible to develop conditioning . . . at more than one level of the nervous system at the same time;
4. And that . . . animals are conditionable even when anesthetized [90, p. 100].

The nervous system has many levels of anatomical integration. Should we be surprised to discover that incoming stimuli may have an effect on a lower level and not on a higher and that under certain conditions this effect can later be demonstrated in terms of behavioral changes? We shall not be able to speak clearly of the effects of subliminal stimulation upon the various "levels of unconsciousness" until we have some better method of specifying exactly what these levels are and by what parts of the nervous system they are mediated. Experimentation is badly needed in this area.

TECHNOLOGICAL PROBLEMS INVOLVED IN STIMULATING SUBJECTS SUBLIMINALLY

The paucity of data presented by those dealing with subliminal perception on a commercial basis, as well as the equivocal nature of their results, suggests that there are many technological problems yet to be solved by these and other investigators. For example, during a two-hour movie (or a one-hour television show), how many times should the stimulus be repeated to make sure that the "message" gets across to the largest possible percentage of the audience? Should the stimulus be repeated every second, every five seconds, only once a minute? Is the effect cumulative, or is one presentation really enough? Is there a satiation effect, such that the audience becomes "unconsciously tired" of the stimulation, and "unconsciously blocks" the incoming subliminal sensations? Should the stimuli be presented "between frames" of the movie (that is, when the shutter of the film projector is closed and the screen momentarily blank as it is 24 times each second), or should the message be presented only when the screen already has a picture on it? How close to the threshold (statistical or otherwise) should the stimuli be? How many words long can the message be? If the message must be short, could successive stimulations present sequential parts of a longer advertisement? How much of the screen should the stimuli fill? Should the stimuli be presented only during "happier" moments in the film, in order to gain positive affect? Does any affect transfer at all from the film to the ad? Should one use pictures, or are words best? Must the words be familiar ones? And what about subliminal auditory, cutaneous, and olfactory stimulation?

As we have stated before, there has been so much talk and so little experimentation, and much of what experimentation has been done is so inadequately reported, that we can merely hazard guesses based on related but perhaps not always applicable studies.

To begin with, we can state with some assurance that, the closer to the threshold of awareness the stimuli are, the more effect they are likely to have. Study after study has reported increased effectiveness with increased intensity of stimulation [5, 14, 88, 97, 104]. The main difficulty seems to be that thresholds vary so much from subject to subject [112], and from day to day [114], that what is subliminal but effective for one person is likely to be subliminal but ineffective for a second, and supraliminal for a third. As is generally the case, anyone who wishes to use the technique of subliminal stimulation must first experiment upon the specific group of people whom he wishes to influence before he can decide what intensity levels will be most efficacious.

Somewhat the same conclusion holds for the question of how many times the stimuli should be presented. While under some conditions subliminal stimuli which did not influence behavior when presented only once seemed to "summate" when presented many times [10, 66], Bricker and Chapanis [15] found that one presentation of a stimulus slightly below the (statistical) limen was enough to increase the likelihood of its being recognized on subsequent trials. We interpret this to mean that too many presentations may well raise the "subliminal" stimuli above the limen of awareness if the stimuli themselves are not carefully chosen.

As for the physical properties of the message itself, we can but guess what the relevant issues are. Both verbal and pictorial presentations apparently are effective in the visual modality, but no one has tested the relative effectiveness of these two types of stimulation. Quite possibly subsequent experimentation will show that words are best for some situations (such as direct commands), while pictures are best for others.[4] It can be stated unequivocally, however, that advertisers should look to their basic English when writing their subliminal commercials. Several studies have shown that, the more familiar a subject is with the stimulus he is to perceive, the more readily he perceives it [22, 54, 63, 110]. We interpret these studies to mean that unfamiliar stimuli may be ineffective when presented subliminally, even though familiar messages may "get through."

The exact length the message should be, its composition, and the background in which it should be presented are variables upon which no work has been done and about which no conclusions can presently be drawn. Suffice it to say, however, that a message which would be short enough to be perceived by one person might be too long for another person to perceive under any conditions.

Which modalities are most useful for subliminal stimulation? While most of the work has been done on the visual modality, Vanderplas and Blake [124] and Kurland [71] have found subthreshold auditory stimuli to be effective, and earlier in this paper we have reported similar studies with cutaneous stimulation. Advertisers who wish to "sneak up on" their patrons by pre-

---

[4] Perhaps much of the work on sensory preconditioning is applicable here. When Ellson [38] presented his subjects with both a light and a buzzer for many trials, then presented the light alone, subjects "heard" the buzzer too

senting subliminal stimuli in one modality while the patrons are attending to supraliminal stimuli from another modality are probably doomed to failure, however. Collier [27] presented subliminal geometric forms simultaneously to both the visual and the cutaneous modalities and found little, if any, lowering of thresholds. Correspondingly, it should be remembered that Hernandez-Peon et al. [55] found that some part of the nervous system acts as a kind of gating mechanism, and when an organism is attending strongly to one modality, the other modalities are probably "shut off" to most incoming stimuli.

Even if experimenters succeed in finding answers to many of the questions raised above concerning the physical characteristics of the stimuli to be employed, it is quite probable that they will have succeeded in discovering the source of only a small part of the variance operant in subliminal perception. For, as always, the major source of variance will come from the perceiver himself.

CHARACTERISTICS OF THE PERCEIVER WHICH AFFECT SUBLIMINAL PERCEPTION

The following section of this paper might well be considered a plea for the recognition that individual differences exist and that they must be taken into account by anyone who wishes to deal with individuals. We know next to nothing about the relationships between such factors as age, sex, social class, etc. and subliminal perception. Perhaps only one study is relevant: Perky [95] found that children were as much influenced by subthreshold visual stimulation as were naive adults. It is quite likely that many differences in the perception of subliminal stimuli do exist between individuals of differing classes, ages, and sexes. As always, only experimentation can determine what these differences are.

We do have some idea, however, of how what might be called "personality factors" influence subliminal perception. First and foremost, there seems little doubt but that a high need state affects perception. Gilchrist and Nesberg [46] found that, the greater the need state, the more their subjects tended to overestimate the brightness of objects relevant to that need. It should be noted that they were dealing with difference limens, not absolute limens, but other studies to be quoted later show the same effect for absolute limens. It should be noted also that Gilchrist and Nesberg apparently overlooked evidence in their own data that a strong need affects judgments of non-need-related objects in the same direction (but not as much) as it does need-related objects. Wispe and Drambarean, dealing with visual duration thresholds, concluded that "need-related words were recognized more rapidly as need increased" [131, p. 31]. McClelland and Lieberman [81] found that subjects with high need achievement scores had lower visual thresholds for "success" words than did subjects not scoring as high on need achievement. Do all of these findings mean that subliminal ads will work only when some fairly strong need (of any kind) is present in the viewers? Only experimentation can answer this question.

What about abnormalities of personality? What effect do they have? Kurland [71] tested auditory recognition thresholds using emotional and neutral words. He found that hospitalized neurotics perceived the emotional words at significantly lower thresholds than did a group of normal subjects. Does this mean that neurotics are more likely to respond to low-intensity subliminal commands than normals? Should advertisers take a "neurotic inventory" of their audiences?

A more pertinent problem is posed by the findings of Krech and Calvin [70]. Using a Wechsler Vocabulary Score of 30.5 as their cutting point, they found that almost all college students above this score showed better visual discriminations of patterns presented at close to liminal values than did almost all students scoring below the cutting point. Does this mean that the higher the IQ, the better the subliminal perception? What is the relationship between the value of the absolute limen and intelligence? Will advertisers have to present their messages at such high intensities (in order that the "average man" might perceive the message) that the more intelligent members of the audience will be consciously aware of the advertising?

One further fascinating problem is posed by Huntley's work [64]. He surreptitiously obtained photographs of the hands and profiles of his subjects, as well as handwriting samples and recordings of their voices. Six months later each subject was presented with the whole series of samples, among which were his own. Each subject was asked to make preference ratings of the samples. Huntley reports evidence of a significant tendency for subjects to prefer their own forms of expression above all others, even though in most cases they were totally unaware that the samples were their own and even though many subjects were unable to identify their own samples when told they were included in the series. If an advertiser is making a direct appeal to one specific individual, it would seem then that he should make use of the photographs and recordings of that individual's behavior as the subliminal stimuli. If an advertiser is making an appeal to a more general audience, however, it might be that he would find the use of pictures and recordings of Hollywood stars, etc., more efficacious than mere line drawings, printed messages, and unknown voices.

Nor can the advertiser afford to overlook the effects of set and attention. Miller [88], Perky [95], and Blake and Vanderplas [12], among others, discovered that giving the subject the proper set lowered the recognition threshold greatly. In fact, in many cases the stimulus intensity which was subliminal but effective for sophisticated subjects was far too subliminal to have much, if any, effect upon naive subjects. Thus advertisers might do well to tell their audiences that subliminal messages were being presented to them, in order to bring all members of that audience closer to a uniform threshold. Does this not, however, vitiate some of the effect of subliminal advertising?

As for attentional effects, we have presented evidence earlier [46] that strong needs seem to have an "alerting" effect upon the organism, lowering recognition thresholds for *all* stimuli, not just need-related stimuli. In addition to this, two studies by Hartmann [52, 53], as well as two by Spencer [113, 114], lead us to the belief that subliminal stimuli might best be presented when either the television or movie screen was blank of other pictures. Perhaps, then, subliminal commercials in movie houses should be shown between features; while on television the commercials should consist of an appropriate period of apparent "visual silence," during which the audience would not be aware of the subliminal stimulation presented, but might react to it later.

One fact emerges from all the above. Anyone who wishes to utilize subliminal stimulation for commercial or other purposes can be likened to a stranger entering into a misty, confused countryside where there are but a few landmarks. Before this technique is used in the market place, if it is to be used at all, a tremendous amount of research should be done, and by competent experimenters.

The Ethics of Subliminal Influence

From its beginnings as a purely academic offshoot of philosophy, psychology has, with ever increasing momentum, grown in the public perception as a practical and applied discipline. As psychologists were called upon to communicate and interpret their insights and research findings to lay persons, it was necessary to make decisions about what constituted proper professional behavior, since it was evident that the misuse of such information would reflect directly on the community of psychologists. As a growing number of our research efforts are viewed as useful to society, the problem of effective and honest communication becomes magnified, although its essential nature does not change. Recently, to our dismay, the announcement of a commercial application of long established psychological principles has assumed nightmarish qualities, and we find ourselves unwillingly cast in the role of invaders of personal privacy and enemies of society. A kind of guilt by association seems to be occurring, and, as future incidents of this kind will, it threatens to undermine the public relations we have built with years of caution and concern for the public welfare. The highly emotional public reaction to the "discovery" of subliminal perception should serve as an object lesson to our profession, for in the bright glare of publicity we can see urgent ethical issues as well as an omen of things to come. When the theoretical notion $E = mc^2$ became the applied reality of an atom bomb, the community of physicists became deeply concerned with social as well as scientific responsibility. Judging from the intensity of the public alarm when confronted with a bare minimum of fact about this subliminal social atom, there exists a clear need for psychologists to examine the ethical problems that are a part of this era of the application of their findings.

The vehemence of the reaction to the proposed use of a device to project subliminal, or from the public's point of view "hidden," messages to viewers indicates that the proposal touches a sensitive area. One of the basic contributors to this reaction seems to be the feeling that a technique which avowedly tampers with the psychological status of the individual ought to be under the regulation or control of a trusted scientific group. As a professional group, psychologists would fit this description, for in the *Ethical Standards of Psychologists* [2] there is a clear statement of their motives and relationship to society:

> Principle 1.12-1 The psychologist's ultimate allegiance is to society, and his professional behavior should demonstrate an awareness of his social responsibilities. The welfare of the profession and the individual psychologist are clearly subordinate to the welfare of the public. . . .

Both this statement and the long record of responsible behavior of the members of the profession would certainly seem to be sufficient to reduce any anxiety the public might have over the possible unscrupulous use of this or any other device. It is precisely the fact that the public *is* aware that decisions about the use of subliminal perception devices rest not with psychologists but with commercial agencies that may be distressing to the public. The aura of open-for-business flamboyance and the sketchily presented percentages in the first public announcement tended to reinforce existing apprehensions rather than allay them.

Although subliminal perception happens now to be the focus of a great deal of reaction, it is merely the most recent in a succession of perturbing events to which the public has been exposed. It has become the focus of, and is likely to become the whipping boy for, a host of techniques which now occupy the twilight zone of infringement of personal psychological freedom. It must be remembered that to the lay person the notion of an unconscious part of the "mind" is eerie, vague, and more than a little mysterious. Unable fully to comprehend the systematic and theoretical aspects of such a concept, he must be content with overly popularized and dramatic versions of it. In every form of mass media the American public has been exposed to convincing images of the bearded hypnotist (with piercing eye) who achieves his nefarious ends by controlling the unconscious of his victim. It has been treated to the spectacle of the seeming reincarnation of Bridey Murphy out of the unconscious of an American housewife and, in *Three Faces of Eve*, to complex multiple personalities hidden in the psychic recesses of a single individual. With such uncanny and disturbing images as an emotional backdrop, the appearance of *The Hidden Persuaders* on the best seller lists formed the indelible impression of the exploitation of the unconscious for purposes of profit and personal gain. In combination, this growth of emotionally charged attitudes toward the unconscious and the suspicions about commercial morality came to be a potentially explosive set of tensions which was triggered off by the first commercial use of subliminal techniques.

What is to be the psychologist's position in regard to future developments with subliminal perception? The apparent discrepancy between the claims being made for the technique and the available research evidence suggests a need for considerable scientific caution as well as extensive investigation. The responsibility of psychologists in this instance is clearly indicated in the code of ethics:

> Principle 2.12-1 The psychologist should refuse to suggest, support, or condone unwarranted assumptions, invalid applications, or unjustified conclusions in the use of psychological instruments or techniques.

The flurry of claim and opinion about the effectiveness of subliminal methods seems to be based more on enthusiasm than controlled scientific experimentation, and it is here that psychology can be of service. Until acceptable scientific answers are forthcoming, we believe psychologists should guard against a premature commitment which might jeopardize public respect for them. The course of scientific history is strewn with the desiccated remains of projects pursued with more vigor than wisdom.

Scientific caution is essential, but it falls short of meeting the ethical issue raised by the nature of subliminal perception itself. The most strident public objections have been directed toward the possibility that suggestions or attempts to influence or persuade may be administered without the knowledge or consent of the audience. Assurances that widespread adoption of this technique would provide increased enjoyment through the elimination of commercial intrusions, or that the users will establish an ethical control over the content of the messages presented, can only fail to be convincing in light of past experience. The suggestion that the public can be taught means of detecting when it is being exposed to a planned subliminal stimulation is far from reassuring since such a suggestion implies that the ability to defend oneself warrants being attacked. A captive audience is not a happy audience, and even the plan to inform the viewers in advance concerning the details of what is to be presented subliminally may not prevent the public from reacting to this technique as a demand that it surrender an additional degree of personal freedom. Fresh from similar encounters, the public may not allow this freedom to be wrested from it.

Finally, the argument that a great deal of our normal perception occurs on the fringe of conscious awareness and that subliminal events are no more effective than weak conscious stimuli rests on opinion and not fact. This seems particularly dangerous clinical ground on which to tread since the effect, on behavior, of stimuli which may possibly be inserted directly into the unconscious has yet to be explored. Assurances that this technique can only "remind" a person of something he already knows or "support" a set of urges already in existence but cannot establish a completely new set of urges or needs are reckless assertions having no evidence to support them. So it seems that the aspect of subliminal projection which is marked by the greatest potential risk to the individual's emotional equilibrium is the aspect about which the least is scientifically known.

The psychologist's ethical quandary, then, stems directly from the inescapable implication of deviousness in the use of such a technique. The appropriate guidelines for conduct are provided in this ethical statement:

> Principle 2.62-2   It is unethical to employ psychological techniques for devious purposes, for entertainment, or for other reasons not consonant with the best interests of a client or with the development of psychology as a science.

It is obvious that "devious purposes" and "the best interests . . . of psychology as a science" are not self-defining terms and must be interpreted by the individual psychologist in light of the circumstances of each situation. It is a trying and complex decision to make. If in his mature judgment the intended uses of the principles of subliminal perception do not meet acceptable ethical standards, the psychologist is obligated to dissociate himself from the endeavor and to labor in behalf of the public welfare to which he owes his first allegiance. In this respect, the responsibility of the social scientist must always be that of watchdog over his own actions as well as the actions of those to whom he lends his professional support.

The furor which promises to accompany the further application of a variety of devices involving subliminal perception is certain to embroil psychology in a dispute not of its own choosing. The indiscriminate and uncontrolled application of psychological principles is increasing at a fearsome rate in the form of motivation research, propaganda, public relations, and a host of other "useful" practices based on the work of psychologists. In a very real sense this era of applied psychology will be a test of the workability of the psychologist's code of ethics and promises to stimulate the profession to give further consideration to its responsibility for assisting society to use its findings wisely.

References

1. ADAMS, J. K. Laboratory studies of behavior without awareness. *Psychol. Bull.* 54 (1957):383–405.
2. AMERICAN PSYCHOLOGICAL ASSOCIATION, Committee on Ethical Standards for Psychology. *Ethical standards of psychologists.* Washington: APA, 1953.
3. ANSBACHER, H. Perception of number as affected by the monetary value of the objects. *Arch. Psychol.* 30, no. 215 (1937).
4. BACH, S., and KLEIN, G. S. Conscious effects of prolonged subliminal exposures of words. *Amer. Psychologist* 12 (1957):397. (Abstract)
5. BAKER, L. E. The influence of subliminal stimuli upon verbal behavior. *J. Exp. Psychol.* 20 (1937):84–100.
6. BAKER, L. E. The pupillary response conditioned to subliminal auditory stimuli. *Psychol. Monogr.* 50, no. 3 (1938) (Whole No. 223).
7. Ban on subliminal ads, pending FCC probe, is urged. *Adv. Age* 28, no. 45 (1957).
8. BATTELLE, PHYLLIS. The lady objects to id tampering. *Publishers Auxiliary* 92, no. 40 (1957).
9. BEAMS, H. L., and THOMPSON, G. G. Affectivity as a factor in the perception of the magnitude of food objects. *Amer. Psychologist* 7 (1952):323. (Abstract)

10. BEITEL, R. J., JR. Spatial summation of subliminal stimuli in the retina of the human eye. *J. Gen. Psychol.* 10 (1934):311–27.

11. BLACKWELL, H. R. Personal Communication, 1958.

12. BLAKE, R. R., and VANDERPLAS, J. M. The effects of prerecognition hypotheses on veridical recognition thresholds in auditory perception. *J. Pers.* 19 (1950–1951):95–115.

13. BLUM, G. S. Perceptual defense revisited. *J. Abnorm. Soc. Psychol.* 56 (1955):24–29.

14. BRESSLER, J. Illusion in the case of subliminal visual stimulation. *J. Gen. Psychol.* 5 (1931):244–50.

15. BRICKER, P. D., and CHAPANIS, A. Do incorrectly perceived tachistoscopic stimuli convey some information? *Psychol. Rev.* 60 (1953):181–88.

16. BRITT, S. H. Subliminal advertising—fact or fantasy? *Adv. Age* 28 (1957):103.

17. BROOKS, J. The little ad that isn't there. *Consumer Rep.* 23, no. 1 (1957).

18. BRUNER, J. S., and GOODMAN, C. C. Value and need as organizing factors in perception. *J. Abnorm. Soc. Psychol.* 42 (1947):33–44.

19. BRUNER, J. S., and POSTMAN, L. Emotional selectivity in perception and action. *J. Pers.* 16 (1947):69–77.

20. BRUNER, J. S., and POSTMAN, L. Tension and tension-release as organizing factors in perception. *J. Pers.* 16 (1947):300–08.

21. BRUNER, J. S., and POSTMAN, L. Symbolic value as an organizing factor in perception. *J. Soc. Psychol.* 27 (1948):203–08.

22. BRUNER, J. S., and POSTMAN, L. Perception, cognition, and behavior. *J. Pers.* 18 (1949):14–31.

23. CARTER, L. F., and SCHOOLER, K. Value, need, and other factors in perception. *Psychol. Rev.* 56 (1949):200–07.

24. CASON, H., and KATCHER, NAOMI. An attempt to condition breathing and eyelid responses to a subliminal electric stimulus. *J. Exp. Psychol.* 16 (1934):831–42.

25. COHEN, B .D.; KALISH, H. I.; THURSTON, J. R.; and COHEN, E. Experimental manipulation of verbal behavior. *J. Exp. Psychol.* 47 (1954):106–10.

26. COHEN, L. H., HILGARD, E. R., and WENDT, G. R. Sensitivity to light in a case of hysterical blindness studied by reinforcement-inhibition and conditioning methods. *Yale J. Biol. Med.* 6 (1933):61–67.

27. COLLIER, R. M. An experimental study of the effects of subliminal stimuli. *Psychol. Monogr.* 52, no. 5 (1940) (Whole No. 236).

28. COOVER, J. E. Experiments in psychical research. *Psychical Res. Monogr.* no. 1 (1917).

29. COUSINS, N. Smudging the subconscious. *Saturday Rev.* 40, no. 40 (1957).

30. COWEN, E. L., and BEIER, E. G. The influence of "threat-expectancy" on perception. *J. Pers.* 19 (1950–1951):85–94.

31. COWEN, E. L., and BEIER, E. G. A further study of the "threat-expectancy" variable in perception. *Amer. Psychologist* 7 (1952):320–21. (Abstract)

32. COWEN, E. L., and BEIER, E. G. Threat-expectancy, word frequencies, and perceptual prerecognition hypotheses. *J. Abnorm. Soc. Psychol.* 49 (1954):178–82.

33. CULLER, E., and METTLER, F. A. Conditioned behavior in a decorticate dog. *J. Comp. Psychol.* 18 (1934):291–303.

34. DEITER, J. The Nature of Subception. Unpublished doctoral dissertation, University of Kansas, 1953.

35. DIVEN, K. Certain determinants in the conditioning of anxiety reactions. *J. Psychol.* 3 (1937):291–308.

36. DUNLAP, K. Effect of imperceptible shadows on the judgments of distance. *Psychol. Rev.* 7 (1900):435–53.

37. DuSHANE, G. The invisible word, or no thresholds barred. *Science* 126 (1957):681.

38. ELLSON, D. G. Hallucinations produced by sensory conditioning. *J. Exp. Psychol.* 28 (1941):1–20.

39. ERIKSEN, C. W. The case for perceptual defense. *Psychol. Rev.* 61 (1954):175–82.

40. ERIKSEN, C. W. Subception: Fact or artifact? *Psychol. Rev.* 63 (1956):74–80.

41. ERIKSEN, C. W., and KUETHE, J. L. Avoidance conditioning of verbal behavior without awareness: A paradigm of repression. *J. Abnorm. Soc. Psychol.*, 53 (1956):203–09.

42. FINK, A. A. *Questions about Subliminal Advertising.* New York: Author, 1957.

43. FOLEY, J. P., JR. The cortical interpretion of conditioning. *J. Gen. Psychol.* 9 (1933):228–34.

44. FULLERTON, G. S., and CATTELL, J. McK. On the perception of small differences. *Univers. Penn. Publ., Philos. Ser.*, no. 2 (1892).

45. "Ghost" ads overrated. *Sci. Newsltr.* 72, no. 17 (1957).

46. GILCHRIST, J. C., and NESBERG, L. S. Need and perceptual change in need-related objects. *J. Exp. Psychol.* 44 (1952):369–76.

47. GOODNOW, JACQUELINE J., and POSTMAN, L. Probability learning in a problem-solving situation. *J. Exp. Psychol.* 49 (1955):16–22.

48. GREENSPOON, J. The reinforcing effect of two spoken sounds on the frequency of two responses. *Amer. J. Psychol.* 68 (1955):409–16.

49. GUILFORD, J. P. *Psychometric Methods.* New York: McGraw-Hill, 1936.

50. HAGGARD, E. A. Experimental studies in affective processes: I. Some effects of cognitive structure and active participation on certain autonomic reactions during and following experimentally induced stress. *J. Exp. Psychol.* 33 (1943):257–84.

51. HANKIN, H. *Common Sense.* New York: Dutton, 1926.

52. HARTMANN, G. W. I. The increase of visual acuity in one eye through the illumination of the other. *J. Exp. Psychol.* 16 (1933):383–92.

53. HARTMANN, G. W. II. Changes in visual acuity through simultaneous stimulation of other sense organs. *J. Exp. Psychol.* 16 (1933):393–407.

54. HENLE, MARY. An experimental investigation of past experience as a determinant of visual form perception. *J. Exp. Psychol.* 30 (1942):1–21.

55. HERNANDEZ-PEON, R., SCHERRER, H., and MICHEL, J. Modification of electrical activity of cochlear nucleus during "attention" in unanesthetized cats. *Science* 123 (1955):331–32.

56. HILDUM, D. C., and BROWN, R. W. Verbal reinforcement and interviewer bias. *J. Abnorm. Soc. Psychol.*, 53 (1956):108–11.

57. HILGARD, E. R., MILLER, J., and OHLSON, J. A. Three attempts to secure pupillary conditioning to auditory stimuli near the absolute threshold. *J. Exp. Psychol.* 29 (1941):89–103.

58. HILGARD, E. R., and WENDT, G. R. The problem of reflex sensitivity to light studied in a case of hemianopsia. *Yale J. Biol. Med.* 5 (1933):373–85.

59. HOLLINGWORTH, H. L. *Advertising and Selling.* New York: Appleton, 1913.

60. HOWES, D. A statistical theory of the phenonmenon of subception. *Psychol. Rev.* 61 (1954):98–110.

61. HOWES, D. On the interpretation of word frequency as a variable affecting speed of recognition. *J. Exp. Psychol.* 48 (1954):106–12.

62. Howes, D., and Solomon, R. L. A note on McGinnies' "Emotionality and perceptual defense." *Psychol. Rev.* 57 (1950):235–40.

63. Howes, D., and Solomon, R. L. Visual duration threshold as a function of word probability. *J. Exp. Psychol.* 41 (1951):401–10.

64. Huntley, C. W. Judgments of self based upon records of expressive behavior. *J. Abnorm. Soc. Psychol.* 48 (1953), 398–427.

65. Irwin, F. W.; Kaufman, K.; Prior, G.; and Weaver, H. B. On "Learning without awareness of what is being learned." *J. Exp. Psychol.* 17 (1934):823–27.

66. Karn, H. W. The function of intensity in the spatial summation of subliminal stimuli in the retina. *J. Gen. Psychol.* 12 (1935):95–107.

67. Kennedy, J. L. Experiments on "unconscious whispering." *Psychol. Bull.* 35 (1938):526. (Abstract)

68. Kennedy, J. L. A methodological review of extrasensory perception. *Psychol. Bull.* 36 (1939):59–103.

69. Klein, G. S., Meister, D., and Schlesinger, H. J. The effect of personal values on perception: An experimental critique. *Amer. Psychologist* 4 (1949):252–53. (Abstract)

70. Krech, D., and Calvin, A. Levels of perceptual organization and cognition. *J. Obnorm. Soc. Psychol.* 48 (1953):394–400.

71. Kurland, S. H. The lack of generality in defense mechanisms as indicated in auditory perception. *J. Abnorm. Soc. Psychol.* 49 (1954):173–77.

72. Lacey, J. I., and Smith, R. L. Conditioning and generalization of unconscious anxiety. *Science* 120 (1954):1045–52.

73. Lacey, J. I., Smith, R. L., and Green, A. Use of conditional autonomic responses in the study of anxiety. *Psychosom. Med.* 17 (1955):208–17.

74. Lazarus, R. S. Subception: Fact or artifact? A reply to Eriksen. *Psychol. Rev.* 63 (1956):343–47.

75. Lazarus, R. S., Eriksen, C. W., and Fonda, C. P. Personality dynamics and auditory perceptual recognition. *J. Pers.* 19 (1950–1951):471–82.

76. Lazarus, R. S., and McCleary, R. A. Automatic discrimination without awareness: A study of subception. *Psychol. Rev.* 58 (1951):113–22.

77. Levine, R., Chein, I., and Murphy, G. The relation of the intensity of a need to the amount of perceptual distortion. *J. Psychol.* 13 (1942):283–93.

78. Lysak, W. The effects of punishment upon syllable recognition thresholds. *J. Exp. Psychol.* 47 (1954):343–50.

79. McCleary, R. A., and Lazarus, R. S. Autonomic discrimination without awareness: An interim report. *J. Pers.* 18 (1949):171–79.

80. McClelland, D. C., and Atkinson, J. W. The projective expression of needs: I. The effect of different intensities of the hunger drive on perception. *J. Psychol.* 25 (1948):205–22.

81. McClelland, D. C., and Lieberman, A. M. The effect of need for achievement on recognition of need-related words. *J. Pers.* 18 (1949):236–51.

82. McGinnies, E. Emotionality and perceptual defense. *Psychol. Rev.* 56 (1949):244–51.

83. McGinnies, E. Discussion of Howes' and Solomon's note on "Emotionality and perceptual defense." *Psychol. Rev.* 57 (1950):229–34.

84. Mandler, G., and Kaplan, W. K. Subjective evaluation and reinforcing effect of a verbal stimulus. *Science* 124 (1956):582–83.

85. Mannes, Marya. Ain't nobody here but us commercials. *Reporter* 17, no. 6 (1957).

86. MANRO, H. M., and WASHBURN, M. F. Effect of imperceptible lines on judgment of distance. *Amer. J. Psychol.* 19 (1908):242–43.

87. Michigan State prof. tells weaknesses of invisible commercials. *Publishers Auxiliary* 92, no. 40 (1957).

88. MILLER, J. G. Discrimination without awareness. *Amer. J. Psychol.* 52 (1939):562–78.

89. MILLER, J. G. The role of motivation in learning without awareness. *Amer. J. Psychol.* 53 (1940):229–39.

90. MILLER, J. G. *Unconsciousness.* New York: John Wiley & Sons, 1942.

91. NEWHALL, S. M., and DODGE, R. Colored after images from unperceived weak chromatic stimulation. *J. Exp. Psychol.* 10 (1927):1–17.

92. NEWHALL, S .M., and SEARS, R. R. Conditioning finger retraction to visual stimuli near the absolute threshold. *Comp. Psychol. Monogr.* 9, no. 43 (1933).

93. NUTHMANN, ANN M. Conditioning of a response class on a personality test. *J. Abnorm. Soc. Psychol.* 54 (1957):19–23.

94. PEIRCE, C. S., and JASTROW, J. On small differences of sensation. *Mem. Nat. Acad. Sci.* 3 (1884):73–83.

95. PERKY, C. W. An experimental study of imagination. *Amer. J. Psychol* 21 (1910):422–52.

96. PHILBRICK, E. B., and POSTMAN, L. A further analysis of "learning without awareness." *Amer. J. Psychol.* 68 (1955):417–24.

97. PILLAI, R. P. B. K. A study of the threshold in relation to the investigations on subliminal impressions and allied phenomena. *Brit. J. Educ. Psychol.* 9 (1939):97–98.

98. POSTMAN, L., and JARRETT, R. F. An experimental analysis of "learning without awareness." *Amer. J. Psychol.* 65 (1952):244–55.

99. RAZRAN, G. Stimulus generalization of conditioned responses. *Psychol. Bull.* 46 (1949):337–65.

100. REECE, M. M. The effect of shock on recognition thresholds. *J. Abnorm. Soc. Psychol.* 49 (1954):165–72.

101. REES, H. J., and ISRAEL, H. E. An investigation of the establishment and operation of mental sets. *Psychol. Monogr.* 46, no. 6 (1935) (Whole No. 210).

102. SANFORD, R. N. The effects of abstinence from food upon imaginal processes: A preliminary experiment. *J. Psychol.* 2 (1936):129–36.

103. SANFORD, R. N. The effects of abstinence from food upon imaginal processes: A further experiment. *J. Psychol.* 3 (1937):145–59.

104. SCHAFER, T. H. Influence of the preceding item on units of the noise masked threshold by a modified constant method. *J. Exp. Psychol.* 40 (1950):365–71.

105. SEARS, R. R., and COHEN, L. H. Hysterical anesthesia, analgesia, and asterognosis. *Arch. Neurol. Psychiat.* 29 (1933):260–71.

106. SETTLAGE, T. The effect of sodium amytal on the formation and elicitation of conditioned reflexes. *J. Comp. Psychol.* 22 (1936):339–43.

107. SIDIS, B. *The Psychology of Suggestion.* New York: Appleton, 1898.

108. SIDOWSKI, J. B. Influence of awareness of reinforcement on verbal conditioning. *J. Exp. Psychol.* 48 (1954):355–60.

109. SILVERMAN, A., and BAKER, L. E. An attempt to condition various responses to subliminal electrical stimulation. *J. Exp. Psychol.* 18 (1935):246–54.

110. SMOKE, K. L. An objective study of concept formation. *Psychol. Monogr.* 42, no. 4 (1932) (Whole No. 191).

111. SOLOMON, R. L., and HOWES, D. H. Word frequency, personal values, and visual duration thresholds. *Psychol. Rev.* 58 (1951):256–70.

112. SOLOMON, R. L., and POSTMAN, L. Frequency of usage as a determinant of recognition thresholds for words. *J. Exp. Psychol.* 43 (1952):195–201.

113. SPENCER, L. T. The concept of the threshold and Heymans' law of inhibition: I. Correlation between the visual threshold and Heymans' coefficient of inhibition of binocular vision. *J. Exp. Psychol.* 11 (1928):88–97.

114. SPENCER, L. T., and COHEN, L. H. The concept of the threshold and Heymans' law of the inhibition. II. *J. Exp. Psychol.* 11 (1928):194–201.

115. STERLING, K., and MILLER, J. G. Conditioning under anesthesia. *Amer. J. Psychol.* 54 (1941):92–101.

116. STROH, M., SHAW, A. M., and WASHBURN, M. F. A study in guessing. *Amer. J. Psychol.* 19 (1908):243–45.

117. Subliminal ad okay if it sells: Lessler; FCC peers into subliminal picture on TV. *Adv. Age* 28, no. 48 (1957).

118. Subliminal ads wash no brains, declare Moore, Becker, developers of precon device. *Adv. Age* 28, no. 48 (1957).

119. SUSLOWA, M. Veranderungen der Hautgefule unter dem Einflusse electrischer Reizung. *Z. Rationelle Med.* 18 (1863):155–60.

120. TAFFEL, C. Anxiety and the conditioning of verbal behavior. *J. Abnorm. Soc. Psychol.* 51 (1955):496–501.

121. THORNDIKE, E. L. *The Fundamentals of Learning.* New York: Teachers College, Columbia University, 1932.

122. THORNDIKE, E. L., and ROCK, R. T. Learning without awareness of what is being learned or intent to learn it. *J. Exp. Psychol.* 17 (1934):1–19.

123. TITCHENER, E. B., and PYLE, W. H. Effect of imperceptible shadows on the judgment of distance. *Proc. Amer. Phil. Soc.*, 46 (1907):94–109.

124. VANDERPLAS, J. M., and BLAKE, R. R. Selective sensitization in auditory perception. *J. Pers.* 18 (1949):252–66.

125. VERPLANCK, W. S. The control of the content of conversation: Reinforcement of statements of opinion. *J. Abnorm. Soc. Psychol.* 51 (1955):668–76.

126. VERPLANCK, W. S. The operant conditioning of human motor behavior. *Psychol. Bull.* 53 (1956):70–83.

127. VINACKE, W. E. The discrimination of color and form at levels of illumination below conscious awareness. *Arch. Psychol.* 38, no. 267 (1942).

128. WEDELL, C. H., TAYLOR, F. V., and SKOLNICK, A. An attempt to condition the pupillary response. *J. Exp. Psychol.* 27 (1940):517–31.

129. WEISS, R. L. The influence of "set for speed" on "learning without awareness." *Amer. J. Psychol.* 68 (1955):425–31.

130. WILLIAMS, A. C. Perception of subliminal visual stimuli. *J. Psychol.* 6 (1938):187–99.

131. WISPE, L. G., and DRAMBAREAN, N. C. Physiological need, word frequency, and visual duration thresholds. *J. Exp. Psychol.* 46 (1953):25–31.

132. WOOLF, J. D. Subliminal perception is nothing new. *Adv. Age* 28, no. 43 (1957).

PART 4

Learning and Thinking

Once sensation and perception have helped us to become aware of the world and to recognize it, then we can begin to behave meaningfully in it. The behaviors that we use in our efforts to operate on the world and cope with it are called adaptive behaviors. Prominent among these are learning and thinking.

All animals learn, but people are especially adept learners. We learn many specific habits and skills, like riding bicycles, using cutlery, and typing; but we also acquire, process, and retain a wealth of information from a variety of sources. We manipulate this information. We think.

Learning in psychology was for many years the almost exclusive province of the rat. It was not really until the 1950s that principles from "rat psychology" were applied to human beings and that educators began to take note of practices like conditioning, reinforcement, shaping, and extinction (see Holland's article in this section). These principles, however, seemed to be most potent for learning factual materials and for improving the quality of specific behaviors like style of penmanship and speed of reading. But learning means more than that to most of us. It means the acquisition and retention of higher forms of knowledge; it means the organization and manipulation of that knowledge, and also abstraction, insight, and problem solving. It involves thinking. The attention of psychology turned also to these matters: What is this "higher form" of learning? What is thinking? What do these entail? Why do we—and don't we—remember? What influences do physical, personal, and social factors exert on learning and thinking? The articles in this section represent the answers of different psychologists to these questions.

Educational Applications of Mnemonic Devices

GORDON H. BOWER

Whether it's "thirty days hath September . . ." for remembering the number of days in each month, or a lengthy French exclamation for recalling the value of pi to thirty decimal places, the intriguing thing about mnemonic devices is their ability to guide the easy recall of great amounts of complicated material. They work by grouping and systematizing the disjointed terms of what is to be learned into compact units that can be assimilated with ease. In this article, Gordon Bower describes and evaluates several classes of these techniques, those based on coding schemata, associations, and "pegwords."

Mnemonic devices have been known and used since the time of ancient Greece (Mnemosyne, mythology's mother of the Muses, was the personification of memory), but it is only very recently that they have come to be considered "reputable" learning aids.

I will talk about mnemonic devices and their educational applications. Let me tell you how the talk will be organized. First, I will claim that mnemonics are very effective learning aids—I will not review much evidence there, but will give one result to illustrate the power of such methods. Second, I will claim that rote learning is where mnemonics are most applicable, and I will argue that education inevitably requires the learning of some rote materials. Third, I will discuss a few mnemonic devices and the general class of tasks to which they are applicable. Fourth, I will indicate how particular educational applications will require a good behavioral analysis of the learning task itself before one can construct viable mnemonics for it. Fifth and last, I will mention some of the problems of applying mnemonics in practical educational settings.

To begin at my first point, let me say that there can now be no doubt that deliberate use of mnemonics helps children and adults to learn faster. To doubt that is to doubt God, country, and the value of motherhood. Many

SOURCE: Paper read by Professor Bower, American Educational Research Association convention, Minneapolis, Minnesota, February 1970. Reprinted by permission.

controlled laboratory studies have now shown impressive gains produced by mnemonics methods in various learning tasks—in paired associates, serial ordering, free recall—with both meaningful and meaningless or nonsense material.

The gains in learning can be spectacular in many instances, with quite large effects. I will give just one example from our research, a study showing how memory is improved by having the person impose a unifying thematic organization upon the material. The experimental subject, a college student, was handed a list of ten unrelated nouns and asked to learn them in serial order. He was told to do this by making up and weaving a narrative story around these nouns using them in the correct order with these nouns serving as the main actors or actions in the narrative. This story construction usually took him about one to two minutes. The time he took was recorded and the same amount of time was given to a yoked control subject who was handed the same list of words and told to memorize them for serial recall, but he was not told to make up a story around the words. Both students were tested for recall immediately after the list was studied; this immediate recall was about perfect for both students, so there was no difficulty there. The difficulty stemmed from the fact that twelve different lists of words were studied successively by the subject one after another, all this within an interval of thirty to forty minutes. At the end of that time, the subjects were tested for recall of each list by probing with the first word for recall of the remaining words in the list.

The results for the two conditions are shown in Figure 1 giving the percentage words recalled in the 12 lists by the Narrative-story subjects and by the Control subjects. You can see that there was a tremendous effect due to the narrative-story construction. Recall averaged 94 per cent for Narrative subjects versus 14 per cent for Control subjects. With that kind of effect, one does not bother doing statistical tests. So in this specific instance, the mnemonic device increased recall by a factor of about 7, and those are the kinds of effects I will be talking about.

Figure 1 illustrates the magnitude of effects that can be produced by particular mnemonics. The illustration was for the learning of serial lists of unrelated words but the value of mnemonics has been demonstrated in other laboratory tasks. It is a fascinating job for the psychologist to try to figure out why specific mnemonics are so effective—for example, why mental imagery is remembered so well. I do a lot of that kind of research, but it isn't of much relevance to the educational applications that concern us today. Most of the mnemonics demonstrations I know about have been with small amounts of artificial laboratory material, using compliant college students as subjects, observed over an hour or so of learning or retention. For obvious practical and economic reasons, there is no research that uses mnemonics with massive amounts of highly structured content material distributed over months—say, material like that presented in a high school history or physics course. But I see no reason to doubt that mnemonics will be helpful in such situations for learning the more arbitrary or isolated components of structured materials.

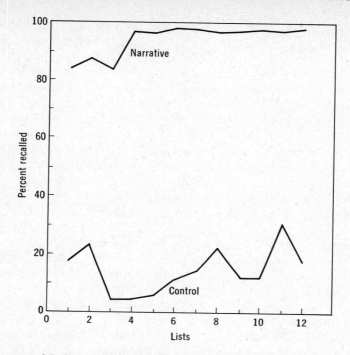

FIGURE 1. *Median percentages of words recalled in correct serial order for the 12 successive lists (from Bower and Clark, 1969).*

You probably want to ask, "In what situations can mnemonic devices be helpful?" and the answer to this is the second main point of this talk. The general answer is that mnemonics are useful for improving memory of arbitrary associations or lists of arbitrary facts; they can also be useful for organizing familiar facts so as to make the whole set more accessible for perfect recall. These are, roughly speaking, rote learning situations. Despite protests to the contrary by teachers, I am impressed that rote learning constitutes a large percentage of what gets taught and learned in schools, particularly after basic reading, writing, and math are learned. We teachers are fond of denying that our students must rote memorize huge amounts of material in order to be certified as competent in our subject. Rather we state educational goals in terms of developing the student's greater love for and appreciation of the subject matter, or developing his ability to make insightful criticisms, theoretical comparisons, arguments, and the like. By and large, that is a lot of high-sounding bunk—at the very least, these are only extra requirements beyond the rote memorization of basic facts that we demand of our students. Any geography student who thinks Minneapolis is in France, or any art history student who thinks Salvador Dali painted the Sistine Chapel, is going to flunk his exams if he pulls such boners often enough. So we do demand a lot of memorization from our students.

We try to ease that burden by organizing or structuring the course content so that the student can comprehend new concepts and relationships between concepts, so he'll be able to subsume new facts or ideas under previously learned hierarchies, and the like. Such teaching efforts towards organizing material into comprehensible form are much to be desired, and most of our workaday school learning is of this kind that proceeds almost incidentally without conscious intent to memorize. But comprehension of structural relationships among highly organized concepts, as in some physical theories, still does not relieve the student from having to learn many arbitrary lists of facts, many unfamiliar words or concepts, lists of applications and how they are derived, and so on, all these arbitrary facts to be associated to the tightly knit conceptual structure of the theory. At the least, mnemonics can serve as retrieval aids for lists of arbitrary facts, making them readily accessible to recall.

So I have now claimed that mnemonics are effective, that they work with and seem especially appropriate for materials usually learned by rote methods, and that such materials exist in most educational curricula. My third topic is to briefly characterize a few mnemonic techniques and indicate what they are good for, giving a relatively abstract characterization. Any good paperback book on "How to improve your memory" will give a representative list of techniques. The word *mnemonics* refers to a grab-bag assortment of different procedures or methods for cognitive or imaginative elaboration of the materials to be learned with the purpose of helping the person to remember better. Different mnemonic methods are appropriate for different kinds of learning tasks, and some tasks require a combination of methods. The particular assortment of methods one finds in mnemonics books is a historical accident the character of which has been influenced by two specific factors: first, some mnemonics are purely for show business, for the stage performer: they make a spectacular performance, like rapidly memorizing a deck of playing cards, but one would be hard pressed to see the practical usefulness of the method; second, most mnemonics have been devised for solving the common memory problems which most of us encounter in everyday life—how to remember names and faces, telephone numbers, addresses, appointments, errands, shopping lists, speeches, and the plot of stories we have read or heard, and so forth. These are the sorts of problems brought to mnemonics teachers by their lay audiences; and their solutions to how to remember such materials are what get taught and written up in most books on "How to Develop a Super-powered Memory."

I will touch briefly on just a few of the techniques. First are coding techniques; these are for learning numerical information by converting a meaningless number into a familiar and meaningful word. This system is useful for remembering numerical information like historical dates, economic data, population figures, ages of people, telephone numbers, street addresses, and so on. A part of the system is illustrated in Table 1. The idea is for the person to first learn a list of digit-to-consonant sound substitutions, and then he uses

TABLE 1. *Illustrations of the Digit-letter Conversion Code and Its Use*

$1 = t$	
$2 = n$	$14 = $ TourR
$3 = m$	$342 = $ MoRoN
$4 = r$	$3214 = $ MeNToR
.	
.	
.	

Note: Vowels and certain consonants
are not assigned a digit value, so they
can be inserted freely between the
critical consonants to spell a familiar
word.

this list to substitute a string of consonants for a string of digits. The consonants are then to be augmented by inserting vowels to make a meaningful word, and then the person is to remember the word by some technique or other. For example, one can remember that World War I began in 1914 because when the war started, all tours to Europe stopped. The key word here is tours; it has the critical consonants *t*, which stands for the digit *1*, and *r*, which stands for *4*, so that *tours* converts into 14, so one recovers the fact that the war started in 1914. That is the sort of thing one can do with the procedure. Of course, to be efficient, the person has to practice the code until he becomes reasonably skilled, much like a Morse code telegrapher, but it pays off when one considers that we are constantly inundated with numerical information which we would like to remember like the date of this meeting or what hotel room we're staying in.

A second set of mnemonics is useful for doing associative learning, where several units are to be associated with one another. This includes arbitrary listings that have to be learned—for example, the color code for electrical resistors, the periodic table of chemistry, the principal products of Brazil, or English equivalents of foreign language vocabulary items. It also includes less rote appearing things like learning definitions of new concepts, extending the list of semantic features we know about a familiar concept, relating concepts, and associating subjects to predicates in sentences. Generally speaking, the prescription is to search for a familiar relation between the several items that are to be associated, trying to assimilate the new connection to things known before.

Figure 2 tries to simplify and summarize a vast number of things that can be done here depending on the materials A and B that are to be associated and the relations possible between A and B. These associating strategies include things like construction of mental imagery of some interaction between A and B, or viewing A and B as parts of a perceptual or conceptual unity, or finding a relation between A and B, or finding an intermediator term that is easily related to and suggested by item A and which readily suggests

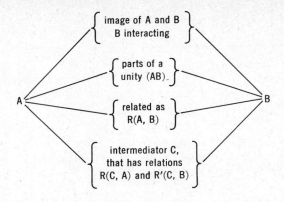

FIGURE 2. *Schematic classification of different kinds of mediators for linking or associating item A to item B. The functor notation, R(A,B), designates a relation such as predication, set inclusion, actor-action-object sentences of the form "The A verbs (R) the B." An example intermediator shown at bottom would be use of a mediator which sounds like the German word (A) but has a meaning similar to the English translation (B).*

item B. Each of these possible mediation routes has been studied by psychologists in very many experiments, so a lot is known here. The appropriate elaboration strategy here depends on the type of materials but I will spare you all the messy details.

Another mnemonic is the pegword system, which is a scheme for cuing recall of arbitrary lists of facts regardless of how unrelated they may be. The problem in freely recalling a large set of items is to provide oneself with cues or reminders of all the items. Pegword schemes solve this problem by having the learner use a well-known list of cues as the conceptual pegs upon which he hooks the successive items that are to be recalled. The scheme is illustrated in Table 2, showing the first few pegs, 1-is-a-gun, 2-is-a-shoe, etc. The first item is hooked to the first peg by the person constructing an imaginary scene of interaction between gun and the first item, and he does likewise with the later

TABLE 2. *Illustration of the First Four Pegwords or Key Images, and How They Are to Be Associated to the Successive Words of Any New List Which Is to Be Remembered*

No.	Key Image (Stimulus)	Response
one	gun	1st word
two	shoe	2nd word
three	tree	3rd word
four	door	4th word
·	·	·
·	·	·
·	·	·

items. When recall is requested, the person can run through his well-known peg list, call to mind the imaginary scene he constructed around each peg, recognize and then recall the other item represented in that imaginal scene. This system works quite well in boosting free recall, and it has been validated in several instances with actual school-learning materials, like geographic facts about a country. The scheme also provides serial order information. Such pegword systems are useful for learning arbitrary lists of things—for example, the order of presidents of the United States, the 50 states and their capital cities, sequences of significant historical events, a listing of the various laws of visual perception, the list of defining criteria of mammals, and so on. It is good for practically any arbitrary list where the items are in some sense already familiar and meaningful to the person and his main problem is one of getting ready and reliable access to what he knows.

Other ordering schemes exist, such as the narrative chaining method we used in that experiment I talked about before or the use of especially coined words or coined sentences to remember the serial order of familiar items—like the "On Old Olympus' Towering Tops" limerick for cuing recall of the twelve cranial nerves. But I have given enough of a sketch so you can get the idea of what mnemonics are about.

One can combine several devices to perform ingenious tricks, of course. An acquaintance of mine, a 96-year old gent, can memorize perfectly a new list of 50 three-digit numbers given to him at the rate of one every 5 or 10 seconds; he will recall them perfectly and also be able to say which number was the twenty-third, and that 749 was the twelfth item you gave him. How does he achieve such astounding feats? By a combination of the pegword system and the number-to-word coding system, he has concrete images associated as pegs to each of the first 50 integers; he also has a coded conversion word for each of the first 1000 numbers; so he simply forms mental images between the nth pegword and the word code corresponding to the nth 3-digit number you have given him. Thus, if the third number in the list is 342, his peg number is TREE, his code for 342 is MORON, so he images a moron sitting up in the branches of a tree.

You may say, well fine, that stuff is all well and good for stage freaks or exhibitionists, but what good will it do in an educational setting? I am convinced mnemonics can do a lot of good in increasing learning and retention of educational materials with children or adults. That doesn't amount to much of a claim because I suspect that current methods for teaching rote materials in the schools are haphazard and stress simple repetition and drill, and I know we can beat that in many instances.

Let us consider how mnemonics might be implemented in educational settings. There are basically two approaches, as I see it. The cheap way is just to give each child or student one or more methods courses on how to memorize, tailoring it to his level and showing applications to materials of current relevance to his education and to his life situation. This is in effect the Dale Carnegie sort of course that is currently given to lay audiences by commercial memory experts, and they are undeniably effective in many instances. There could be recurrent instruction and training in mnemonics techniques throughout a child's school career. However, this approach is likely to lead to mediocre results in many instances, because the program does not ensure that the appropriate cognitive behaviors occur in the natural classroom setting away from the mnemonics-methods course. Much like speed-reading techniques, a mnemonic technique is of no use unless it is applied, and it is likely that many students would have to be shown repeatedly how to apply mnemonics to each of their lessons.

The second plan would be to attack on two fronts at once—teach students the general methods as before but also have the texts and the teachers programmed to provide content material with a liberal infusion of mnemonics to help the student remember the content. That involves several things, like convincing teachers that they should attend to such matters, and developing texts and supplementary materials written not only with the aim of presenting the content material but with due attention to presenting mnemonics to help the student remember the material. Developing a mnemonics-infused content text would involve several sorts of issues.

First, one would need a clear conception of exactly what is worth remembering in the course, so one can decide what the student has to remember. For example, does each subdivision or unit of information have to be ordered, can it be grouped and hierarchically organized in some special way, need it be remembered verbatim or is just the gist of the proposition sufficient, can the ideas or relations be represented pictorially, and so on.

Second, one would need a fairly good knowledge of what the student already knows, since most mnemonics relate the unknown new material to the known old material. To use a currently popular term, what the mnemonics-oriented textbook writer needs is a pretty thorough "task analysis."

Third, and finally, he needs a large amount of creative imagination to make up mnemonics that fit the material at issue. Making up a mnemonic is like solving a problem, namely, finding and displaying comprehensible relationships between the familiar things someone knows and the new material he is to learn. For this reason, making up a good mnemonic has many of the features of theorem proving, namely, to construct a path relating one set of known or given statements to another set of unknown statements. That takes some imagination and it would be time-consuming to do that for a whole course or textbook, but it would be no more so than the development of most programmed textbooks.

In any event, if one were to go this route, he might first mount a mnemonics attack on a particular course content, writing a sort of textbook for how to remember that specific material. A lesser goal would be to seek more substantial experimental validation of teaching by mnemonics; this could be done with a smaller amount of content material, say a chapter of a biology or history text, or a couple of brief 1–2 page texts. These lesser materials, that can be made up in a matter of days, are much preferred by researchers, as opposed to testing with materials that may take months or years to develop.

Let me mention just a few more of the problems of applying mnemonics in educational settings. First, for some materials it is simply difficult to think up mnemonics to ease their learning, and we should just learn to live with that, until an appropriately ingenious person shows us how to do it.

Second, we do not know the long-term effect of massive use of mnemonics by a student: for example, mnemonics may appear effective in laboratory experiments because they are rather distinctive and interesting curiosities for our educationally jaded subjects, but such techniques might begin to lose their unique effectiveness when they are being used over and over for learning most things. I mention this as a possibility, though I consider it very improbable, judging from the daily performance of memory experts I know who have been using the systems for years.

Third, it is possible that whether mnemonic method A or B is better for remembering some given material depends on individual characteristics of the learner. I think this is doubtless true for certain obvious variables like mental age; an intelligent college student may show differential success with methods A vs. B whereas a retarded 4-year-old child may not have the basic cognitive skills or equipment needed in order to implement the methods effectively. In this respect, it is helpful for the educational mnemonist to have comparisons of mnemonic techniques across mental ages of the sort provided by Joan Bean's study cited by Rohwer. What I definitely wish to prevent, however, is the public's common interpretation, that since the methods' effectiveness varies with the person, then there is nothing to be done short of very expensive tailoring of an educational program for each student. That is surely the counsel of despair, is just as surely false, and it must be rejected if educational innovation is to proceed.

Fourth, in introducing mnemonics into an on-going curriculum, one is likely to meet some initial social resistance from teachers or from students—either because they do not want to admit that one should ever memorize anything, or because they are not convinced that mnemonics will work, so they will not use them. Like many things, mnemonic techniques are easy to parody and poke fun at. But that makes them none the less effective when they are used, and there is nothing like success to reinforce someone in a new method of learning. Critics rarely make explicit what is the alternative to conscious attempts to cognitively elaborate the material so as to memorize it: the unspoken alternatives are usually dumb, blind repetition, or simply outright failure, and no one seems to want to champion those alternatives.

I have mentioned some general difficulties in applying mnemonics in educational settings, but I do not intend to dash cold water on attempts at such applications. Quite the contrary, I think these applications should proceed with all deliberate speed. In my opinion, the educational potential of applying mnemonics is about as great today as was the potential of programmed instruction 15 years ago. In other words, I am convinced there is much educational gold in these hills.

Reference

1. BOWER, G. H., and CLARK, M. C. Narrative stories as mediators for serial learning. *Psychonomic Science* (1969):181–82.

Memory Transfer Through Cannibalism in Planarians

JAMES V. MCCONNELL

Very different from the mnemonics approach is the following reminder of the physiological basis of cognitive behavior. James McConnell scandalized the psychological establishment when he first published his research on memory transfer through cannabilism in planarians. Although his work is now generally accepted, it is still too early to understand the ramifications of that work. The implication is that someday it may be possible to bypass the tedium of years of technical study and gain mastery over, say, mathematics by receiving an injection of chemicals extracted from the body of a math instructor! As exciting and appealing a possibility as this may be, many complicated questions are still unanswered. For instance, if what McConnell suggests is the case, that some "deliberately modified" form of RNA is responsible for learning, then how do we go about making the necessary modifications? Do we have to make a different modification for each topic we want to "teach"? What other effects—physiological, psychological, and social—might these injections have on the person who receives them? Difficult as these questions are, we should remember that they might never have been asked if it were not for research like that reported here.

The research that I am going to outline today had its start several years ago, and I trust you will allow me to give you a few of the pertinent background details, if only to convince you that our work is more serious than it sometimes sounds, and of sufficient scope at least to approach respectability.† It was in 1953, when I was a graduate student at the University of Texas, that

SOURCE: From *International Journal of Neuropsychiatry* 3 (1962):S42–S48. Copyright © 1962 by the International Journal of Neuropsychiatry. Reprinted by permission of *Journal of Behavioral Neuropsychiatry*.

* Note: Much of the research reported in this paper was supported by grants from the National Institutes of Mental Health and from the Atomic Energy Commission.

† For an excellent survey of the history of worm running, see the forthcoming paper by Allan L. Jacobson [8].

a fellow student, Robert Thompson, suggested to me that we attempt to condition a planarian, or common flatworm. Having avoided the rigors of introductory Zoology up to that point, my only prior experience with worms had been at the business end of a fishing pole. I soon discovered, however, that fishing worms are round, while planarians are flat. Planarians are also usually less than an inch in length, and rather interesting in their own right.

Flatworms occupy a unique niche on the phylogenetic scale, being the lowest organism to possess bilateral symmetry, a rude form of encephalization, and a human, synaptic-type nervous system. According to some psychological theories—the ones that postulate that learning is a matter of reshuffling connections among neurons—the planarian should be the lowest organism to be able to demonstrate "true" learning. As far as we knew in 1953, no one had ever demonstrated unequivocally that these organisms could indeed be trained. Since then, of course, we have discovered the usual obscure reference that antedates our work by 30 years—it appears in Dutch and was published in a little-read European journal [15]—but I am not at all sure that even this knowledge would have deterred us. At any rate, Thompson and I set out in 1953 to attempt classical conditioning in planarians.

Imagine a trough gouged out of plastic, 12 inches in length, semi-circular in cross-section, and filled with pond water. At either end are brass electrodes attached to a power source. Above the trough are two electric light bulbs. Back and forth in the trough crawls a single flatworm, and in front of the apparatus sits the experimenter, his eye on the worm, his hands on two switches. When the worm is gliding smoothly in a straight line on the bottom of the trough, the experimenter turns on the lights for 3 seconds. After a light has been on for two of the three seconds, the experimenter adds one second of electric shock, which passes through the water and causes the worm to contract. The experimenter records the behavior of the worm during the two-second period after the light has come on but before the shock has started. If the animal gives a noticeable turning movement or a contraction prior to the onset of the shock, this is scored as a "correct" or "conditioned" response [10].

From this brief description of the experimental paradigm, many of you will recognize that Thompson and I were attempting to establish a form of Pavlovian conditioning in our experimental animals (Group E), and according to our data, we were successful. Planarians occasionally give a mild and presumably innate response to the onset of the light even when it has not been previously paired with shock, so we ran a control group that received just trials of photic (light) stimulation (Group LC); we also ran a control group that received just shock, occasionally interspersing a test trial of light alone (Group SC). All animals were given 150 trials. Over that period of time, as Tables 1 and 2 show, the experimental animals, which received light paired with shock, showed a significant increase in responsivity, while the control groups showed either no change at all or a significant decline.

Hence Thompson and I concluded that we had accomplished what we set out to accomplish—namely, we had proven that worms could be conditioned [14].

TABLE 1. *Mean Turns, Contractions, and Combined Responses on the First 50 and Last 50 Trials for Groups E (Experimental) and LC (Light Control)*

Group	Response	First 50 Trials	Last 50 Trials	Diff.	P
E	Turns	12.6	16.6	4.0	.01
	Contractions	1.2	5.0	3.8	.01
	Combined	13.8	21.6	7.8	.01
LC	Turns	11.7	7.6	−4.1	.01
	Contractions	0.6	2.1	1.5	
	Combined	12.3	9.7	−2.6	

TABLE 2. *Mean Turns, Contractions, and Combined Responses on the First 15 and Last 15 Test Trials for Group SC (Shock Control)*

Response	First 15 Test Trials	Last 15 Test Trials	Diff.*
Turns	5.4	4.2	−1.2
Contractions	0.2	0.4	0.2
Combined	5.6	4.6	−1.0

* None of the differences is significant at the .05 level of confidence.

Those of you who have ever chopped up a planarian in a Zoology course will know that these animals have enormous powers of regeneration. A large specimen may be cut into perhaps 50 pieces, each of which will eventually regenerate into a complete organism. It was while we were running that first experiment that Thompson and I wondered aloud, feeling rather foolish as we did so, what would happen if we conditioned a flatworm, then cut it in two and let both halves regenerate. Which half would retain the memory? As it happened, we never got around to performing that experiment at Texas, for Thompson received his doctorate soon after we finished our first study and went on to Louisiana State University and bigger and better things— namely, rats. When I went to the University of Michigan in 1956, however, I was faced with the difficult problem that in the academic world, one must publish or perish. The only thing I knew much about was flatworms, so I talked two bright young students, Allan Jacobson and Daniel Kimble, into performing the obvious experiment on learning and regeneration.

Kimble, Jacobson and I did the following. We took our experimental animals and trained them to a criterion of 23 responses out of any block of 25 trials. When they had reached this criterion, we assumed that they were properly conditioned and immediately cut them in half across the middle. Head and tail sections were then put in individual bowls and allowed about 4 weeks to regenerate. At the end of this period, these experimental animals (Group E) were re-trained to the same criterion and savings scores calculated. We also ran a group of worms which were cut, allowed to regenerate, and then were conditioned for the first time—this to tell us if cutting and subsequent regeneration in any way sensitized the animals to conditioning (Group RC). Another control group was conditioned, then allowed to rest uncut for a month before being retested (Group TC)—this to tell us how much forgetting we could expect in our experimental animals had we not cut them in half.

In all honesty I must admit that we did not obtain the results we had expected. We had assumed that the regenerated heads would show fairly complete retention of the response for, after all, the head section retained the primitive brain and "everybody knows" that the brain is where memories are located. And, as Tables 3, 4, and 5 indicate, the heads did show just as much retention as did the uncut control animals. We had also hoped, in

TABLE 3. *Number of Trials to Criterion for Group E (Experimental)*

S	Original Training	Retest Head	Retest Tail
E1	99	50	51
E2	191	37	24
E3	97	48	72
E4	83	35	44
E5	200	30	25
Mean	134	40	43.2

TABLE 4. *Number of Trials to Criterion for Group RC (Regeneration Control)*

S	Head	Tail
RC1	134	150
RC2	188	179
RC3	276	85
RC4	395	300
RC5	250	325
Mean	248.6	207.8

TABLE 5. *Number of Trials for Group TC (Time Control)*

S	Original Training	Retest
TC1	123	24
TC2	153	25
TC3	195	62
TC4	131	43
TC5	325	45
Mean	185.4	39.8

our heart of hearts, that perhaps the tails would show a slight but perhaps significant retention of some kind, merely because we thought this would be an interesting finding. We were astounded, then, to discover that the tails not only showed as much retention as did the heads, but in many cases did much better than the heads and showed absolutely no forgetting whatsoever. Obviously memory, in the flatworm, was being stored throughout the animal's body, and as additional proof of this we found that if we cut the worm into three or even more pieces, each section typically showed clear-cut retention of the conditioned response [12].

It was at this time that we first postulated our theory that conditioning caused some chemical change throughout the worm's body, and it was also about then that Reeva Jacobson came along to help us test what seemed at the time to be rather an odd hypothesis. She took planarians, cut off their tails, and conditioned the heads before any regeneration could take place. Then she let her animals grow new tails. She next removed these new tails and let them grow new heads, ending up with apparently completely reformed organisms. These total regenerates, as we called them, were then tested for any "savings" of the original conditioning. By now we knew what to expect from planarians, and so we weren't too surprised when Reeva's regenerated flatworms showed a significant retention of what the original organism had learned. True, as Table 6 suggests, these total regenerates did not demonstrate the complete retention that our original animals had shown, but they did remember enough so that our hypothesis seemed vindicated [13].

TABLE 6. *Number of Trials to Criterion for Totally Regenerated Animals*

S	Original Training	Retest After Total Regeneration
1	200	166
2	325	143
3	300	220
4	327	51
5	75	62
6	381	94
Mean	268	122.7
SD	102	60

By now, worms were in the *Zeitgeist*. Edward Ernhart, working with Carl Sherrick at Washington University, demonstrated not only that flatworms could learn a two-unit T-maze, but also that this maze habit was retained by their animals following cutting and regeneration. Again, the tails remembered at least as much as did the head [4]. Ernhart is perhaps most famous, however, for a more recent study of his. If one takes a a flatworm, and splits the head straight down the middle, time and time again, the two halves will not heal together but will each regenerate into a complete head. One ends up, then, with a two-headed worm. Ernhart compared the length of time it took two-headed animals to be conditioned with the length of time it took one-headed (or normal) animals to reach the same criterion and found that he had validated an old aphorism—two heads are indeed better than one [3].

Roy John and William Corning, working at the University of Rochester, became quite interested in the chemical theory of learning about this time, and undertook one of the most spectacular pieces of research yet to come from any worm laboratory. John reasoned that learning in flatworms had to be mediated, at least in part, by some molecular change within the organism's cells. Since Hydén had found changes in RNA in nerve cells as a result of experience [7], John believed that RNA might be implicated in learning and retention in planarians. So he and Corning conditioned a number of flatworms, cut them in half, and let them regenerate in a weak solution of ribonuclease, which breaks up RNA. When they compared their experimental animals with a number of controls, they found evidence that the experimental heads were relatively unaffected by the ribonuclease, while the tails showed complete forgetting. The tails could be retrained, but it took approximately as long the second time as it had the first [1].

Ralph Gerard, the noted neurophysiologist, interprets the data as follows: There are probably two distinct but related physiological mechanisms for learning in planarians. The first such mechanism is the familiar one of neural interconnections which are reshuffled in the brain due to the animal's experiences—the so-called circuit-diagram model, if I may be permitted the analogy. Structural changes in the neural pathways in the brain would presumably not be altered by ribonuclease, which accounts for the fact that the Rochester head-regenerates showed no real forgetting. The second type of memory mechanism, however, involves a change in the coding of the RNA molecules in the cells throughout the worm's body. Presumably whenever the animal learns, the RNA is altered appropriately so that when regeneration takes place, the altered RNA builds the memory into the regenerated animal right from the start. If the RNA were destroyed by the ribonuclease, it is likely that the DNA in the cells would replace the RNA, but this replacement RNA would not carry the changed code since the DNA was presumably unaffected by the learning [5].

If all of this sounds rather complex, you must forgive me. I am not at all sure that at this early date we have more than the vaguest notion just how learning could affect RNA nor how, much less why, this altered RNA might build the memory into the regenerating tissue. The important thing to remember is that John's hunch that RNA might be involved in memory seems to have been substantiated.

Before further discussing RNA and memory, I should like to detail, briefly, some other research that Roy John and Bill Corning, at Rochester, and my own group of worm runners at the University of Michigan and at the Britannica Center in Palo Alto, have been pursuing jointly. In 1957, when we got our first results on retention of learning following regeneration, and came up with our chemical hypothesis, it seemed to us that we might be able to transfer a memory from a trained animal to an untrained animal if we could somehow get the right chemicals out of the first worm and into the second. We spent several years trying to test this admittedly wild notion without much success. First we tried grafting the head of a trained animal onto the tail of an untrained planarian, but this never worked very well. If one reads introductory zoology texts, one often gets the notion that this little operation is most easy to perform. Sadly enough, the best average on record is three successes out of 150 attempts [9] and we simply did not have 150 trained heads to waste. We tried grinding the trained worms up and injecting the pieces into untrained animals, but we never could master the injection techniques. It was only some time after we began this work that it occurred to us that we could let the animals do the transferring for us. For, under the proper conditions, one worm will eat another. And since planarians have but the most rudimentary of digestive tracts, there seemed an excellent chance that the tissue from the food worm would pass into the body of the cannibal relatively unchanged.

So, with Barbara Humphries as our chief experimenter, we conditioned a number of worms, chopped them into small pieces and hand-fed the pieces to untrained cannibals. We also took the precaution of feeding a number of untrained worms to untrained cannibals for a control or comparison group. Our first pilot study gave us such unbelievable results that we immediately instituted several changes in our procedure and repeated the study not once, but four times. And each time the results were quite significant—and still rather unbelievable. I should mention before going any further that the chief procedural change we made was the institution of a "blind" running technique which helped guard against experimenter bias. Under this blind procedure, the person actually training the worms never knows anything about the animals he runs—we follow an elaborate coding system in which each animal's code letter is changed daily. The experimenter then doesn't know which animal is in which group, nor even which animal is which from day to day. Thus, as far as we could tell, we could not have unconsciously tampered with the data.

The results of this work, as Table 7 shows, were somewhat startling. In all five studies, it was clear that the cannibals which had fed on trained worms gave approximately half again as many conditioned responses during the first days of training as did the cannibals which had fed on untrained worms. In our studies, the differences between the two groups tended to disappear after the first few days as the control animals approached criterion. The experimental animals were presumably so close to criterion right from the start that the slope of their learning curve was much less than that of the controls [6, 11].

I would also like to mention a couple of fortunate mistakes we made which

TABLE 7. *Number of Responses in First 25 Training Trials for Cannibals Fed Conditioned Planarians (Experimentals) and for Cannibals Fed Unconditioned Planarians (Controls)*

Number of Responses in First 25 Trials

Experimentals	Controls
4	1
6	1
7	3
8	4
8	4
8	4
9	5
10	5
10	5
10	6
11	6
12	6
13	6
14	7
14	7
15	10
15	10
15	11
15	11
17	16
18	22
19	
mean 11.73	7.14

do not prove anything but which are interesting evidence in their own right. One time our elaborate coding system broke down and a control animal was fed a piece of conditioned worm. For several days prior to this feeding, the control animal had been responding at an average of 2 or 3 times out of any 25 trials. Immediately following this inadvertent meal of conditioned tissue, the animal performed at criterion level, giving 23 responses out of the next 25 trials. Then there was one group of cannibals which we accidentally fed animals that had been given a number of conditioning trials, but which were not even close to criterion when we cut them up. The cannibals which ate these trained but not-yet-conditioned worms showed absolutely no transfer effect at all.

Now, if we had been the only ones to have obtained such results, our findings might be dismissed as the achievement of crackpots. Luckily for us, Corning, Karpick, and John instituted their own program of cannibalism shortly after we did and so far have run two large and very well controlled studies, both using the blind technique, and have obtained results which are essentially identical to ours [2].

And, as if this were not enough, our work has just been replicated by a high school student. Let me quote briefly from the Washington *Post* of 25 March, 1962.

A 17-year-old girl's rather startling answer to a rather startling question—"Is Knowledge Edible?"—brought her one of the two top prizes in a Northern Virginia Science Fair yesterday. Tentatively, Ruth Ann Ziegler's answer is "yes."

What Miss Ziegler found was that a worm who eats an educated worm learns things twice as fast as his brother who eats an uneducated worm. Hence her title, "Is Knowledge Edible?"

By electrical shocks she taught flatworms to respond to light. An ordinary flatworm needs about 260 shocks before he responds without one. He is then "conditioned."

Experiments taught Miss Ziegler that a worm fed the head of an unconditioned worm needs an average of 264 shocks. A worm fed an unconditioned tail needs 269.

But a worm fed a conditioned tail takes only 168 shocks and a worm fed a conditioned head a mere 140 shocks.

This experiment was part of Miss Ziegler's effort to see if conditioned learning is affected by chemicals and, if it is, if it can be passed on through regeneration and ingestion. It's apparently "yes" all the way.

Frankly, we are not quite sure where all of this work leaves us—except that we are most definitely out on a limb of some kind. At the moment, a number of laboratories around the country are starting investigations into the biochemistry of learning, using planarians as their tools. Specifically, several of us are attempting to extract RNA, DNA and other biochemicals from conditioned worms to feed to untrained cannibals. If we can show, for example, that RNA and only RNA causes the memory transfer, we can surely hope to determine the subtle molecular differences between "trained" and "untrained" RNA. If this could be done, we would be one step closer to cracking the problem of the molecular properties of memory—perhaps a giant step closer at that, particularly if it turns out that teaching the animals different sorts of habits causes different sorts of changes in the RNA molecules. But perhaps that is too much to hope for at the present.

Now, in conclusion, let me attempt to tie all of this research together. We have shown that planarians are capable of learning, that this learning survives cutting and regeneration, that the memory storage mechanism has a biochemical component (probably RNA) which is widely distributed throughout the animal's body, and that learning seems to be transferrable from one animal to another via cannibalistic ingestion. If memory in higher organisms is also mediated via biochemical changes, and if these changes are specific to the habits learned, we might eventually discover a substance (probably RNA with a deliberately modified structure) which would facilitate learning if it were incorporated into animal or human bodies. If so, the research we have been doing with our lowly flatworms may have practical consequences we never dreamed of when we began our work some nine years ago.

References

1. Corning, W. C., and John, E. R. *Science* 134 (1961):1363–65.
2. Corning, W. C., Karpick, R., and John, E. R. Personal communication from E. R. John, 1961.
3. Ernhart, E. N. *Worm Runner's Digest* 2 (1960):92–94.
4. Ernhart, E. N., and Sherrick, C., Jr. "Retention of a maze habit following regeneration in planaria (*D. maculata*)." Paper read at Midwestern Psychological Association, St. Louis, May 1959.
5. Gerard, Ralph. Personal communication, 1961.
6. Humphries, Barbara M., and Jacobson, Reeva. *Worm Runner's Digest* 3 (1961): 41–47.
7. Hydén, Holgar. In Farber, Seymour M., and Wilson, Roger H. L., eds. *Control of the Mind.* New York: McGraw-Hill, 1961.
8. Jacobson, Allan L. "Learning in Flatworms and Annelids," *Psychol. Bull.*, in press.
9. Kenk, Roman. *J. Exp. Zool.* 87 (1941):55–69.
10. McConnell, James V., Cornwell, P. R., and Clay, Margaret L. *Amer J. Psychol.* 73 (1960):618–22.
11. McConnell, James V., Jacobson, Reeva and Humphries, Barbara M. *Worm Runner's Digest,* 3 (1961):41–47.
12. McConnell, James V., Jacobson, A. L., and Kimble, D. P. *J. Comp. Physiol. Psychol.* 52 (1959):1–5.
13. McConnell, James V., Jacobson, Reeva, and Maynard, D. M. *Amer. Psychologist* 14 (1959):410. (Abstract.)
14. Thompson, Robert, and McConnell, James V. *J. Comp. Physiol. Psychol.* 48 (1955):65–68.
15. Van Oye, P. *Natuurwetenschappelijk Tijdschrift* 2 (1920):1–9.

Reaction Patterns to Severe, Chronic Stress in American Army Prisoners of War of the Chinese

EDGAR H. SCHEIN

This article rounds out the psychological, physiological, and sociological influences on learning and thinking. This study of "brainwashing" during the Korean war describes and assesses the effects of carefully planned social manipulations on prisoners of war. In arguing for the primacy of social factors, rather than physical or psychological, for producing collaboration with the captors, Schein suggests that the most important element in brainwashing is the disintegration of prisoners' personalities through the destruction of their formal and informal group identifications. We take our strength from other people, testing our beliefs against their beliefs, drawing support from them when our own strength is waning. Watch how the captors here systematically eliminated these social sources of strength. The point of this article is that persuasion depends on the social conditions that make people ready to accept new ideas, while resistance to persuasion depends on the social conditions that sustain people when their usual supports are stripped away.

In this paper I will outline some of the constellations of stress which prisoners of war faced during the Korean conflict, and describe some of the reaction patterns to these stresses. Rather than presenting a complete catalogue of their experiences [3], I have selected those aspects which seem to me to throw some light on the problem of collaboration with the enemy. I will

SOURCE: From *Journal of Social Issues* 13, no. 3:21–30. Copyright © 1957 by the Society for the Psychological Study of Social Issues, a division of the American Psychological Association. Reprinted by permission.

Note: This work was completed while the author was a captain, U. S. Army Medical Service Corps, assigned to the Walter Reed Army Institute of Research. I would like to acknowledge the invaluable help and guidance of Dr. David McK. Rioch and Capt. Harold Williams as well as the staff of the Neuropsychiatric Division of the Walter Reed Army Institute of Research. Portions of this paper were read at the meetings of the Group for the Advancement of Psychiatry, Asbury Park, New Jersey, November, 1956.

221

give particular emphasis to the *social* psychological factors, because the Chinese approach to treatment of prisoners seemed to emphasize control over groups, rather than individuals.

My material is based on a variety of sources. I was in Korea during the repatriation, and had the opportunity to interview extensively 20 unselected repatriates. This basic material was supplemented by the information gathered by three psychiatrists, Drs. Harvey Strassman, Patrick Israel, and Clinton Tempereau, who together had seen some 300 men. On board ship returning to the United States, I also had the opportunity to sit in on bull sessions among repatriates in which many of the prison experiences were discussed. Additional details were obtained from the Army dossiers on the men.

The typical experience of the prisoner of war must be divided into two broad phases. The first phase lasted anywhere from one to six months beginning with capture, followed by exhausting marches to the north of Korea and severe privation in inadequately equipped temporary camps, terminating in assignment to a permanent prisoner of war camp.

The second phase, lasting two or more years, was marked by chronic pressures to collaborate and to give up existing group loyalties in favor of new ones. Thus, while physical stresses had been outstanding in the first six months, psychological stresses were outstanding in this second period.

The reactions of the men toward capture were influenced by their overall attitude toward the Korean situation. Many of them felt inadequately prepared, both physically and psychologically. The physical training, equipment, and rotation system all came in for retrospective criticism, though this response might have been merely a rationalization for being captured. When the Chinese entered the war they penetrated into rear areas, where they captured many men who were taken completely by surprise. The men felt that when positions were over-run, their leadership was often less than adequate. Thus, many men were disposed to blame the UN command for the unfortunate event of being captured.

On the psychological side, the men were not clearly aware of what they were fighting for or what kind of enemy they were opposing. In addition, the reports of the atrocities committed by the North Koreans led most men to expect death, torture, or non-repatriation if captured.

It was in such a context that the soldier found his Chinese captor extending his hand in a friendly gesture and saying "Welcome" or "Congratulations, you've been *liberated*." This Chinese tactic was part of their "lenient policy" which was explained to groups of prisoners shortly after capture in these terms: because the UN had entered the war illegally and was an aggressor, all UN military personnel were in fact war criminals, and *could* be shot summarily. But the average soldier was, after all, only carrying out orders for his leaders who were the real criminals. Therefore, the Chinese soldier would consider the POW a "student," and would teach him the "truth" about the war. Anyone who did not cooperate by going to school and by learning voluntarily could be reverted to his "war criminal" status and shot, particularly if a confession of "criminal" deeds could be obtained from him.

In the weeks following capture, the men were collected in large groups and marched north. From a physical point of view, the stresses during these marches were very severe: there was no medicine for the wounded, the food was unpalatable and insufficient, especially by our standards, clothing was scarce in the face of severe winter weather, and shelter was inadequate and overcrowded. The Chinese set a severe pace and showed little consideration for weariness that was the product of wounds, diarrhea, and frostbite. Men who were not able to keep up were abandoned unless they were helped by their fellows. The men marched only at night, and were kept under cover during the day, ostensibly as protection against strafing by our own planes.

From a psychological point of view this situation is best described as a recurring cycle of fear, relief, and new fear. The men were afraid that they might die, that they might never be repatriated, that they might never again have a chance to communicate with the outside, and that no one even knew they were alive. The Chinese, on the other hand, were reassuring and promised that the men would be repatriated soon, that conditions would improve, and that they would soon be permitted to communicate with the outside.

One of the chief problems for the men was the disorganization within the group itself. It was difficult to maintain close group ties if one was competing with others for the essentials of life, and if one spent one's resting time in overcrowded huts among others who had severe diarrhea and were occasionally incontinent. Lines of authority often broke down, and with this, group cohesion and morale suffered. A few men attempted to escape, but they were usually recaptured in a short time and returned to the group. The Chinese also fostered low morale and the feeling of being abandoned by systematically reporting false news about United Nation defeats and losses.

In this situation goals became increasingly short-run. As long as the men were marching, they had something to do and could look forward to relief from the harsh conditions of the march. However, arrival at a temporary camp was usually a severe disappointment. Not only were physical conditions as bad as ever, but the sedentary life in overcrowded quarters produced more disease and still lower morale.

What happened to the men under these conditions? During the one- to two-week marches they became increasingly apathetic.[1] They developed a slow, plodding gait, called by one man a "prisoners' shuffle." Uppermost in their minds were fantasies of food: men remembered all the good meals they had ever had, or planned detailed menus for years into the future. To a lesser extent they thought of loved ones at home, and about cars which seemed to them to symbolize freedom and the return home.

[1] A more detailed discussion of the apathy reaction may be found in Strassman, Thaler, and Schein [4].

In the temporary camps disease and exposure took a heavy toll in lives. But it was the feeling of many men, including some of the doctors who survived the experience, that some of these deaths were not warranted by a man's physical condition. Instead, what appeared to happen was that some men became so apathetic that they ceased to care about their bodily needs. They retreated further into themselves, refused to eat even what little food was available, refused to get any exercise, and eventually lay down as if waiting to die. The reports were emphatic concerning the lucidity and sanity of these men. They seemed willing to accept the prospect of death rather than to continue fighting a severely frustrating and depriving environment.

Two things seemed to save a man who was close to such "apathy" death: getting him on his feet and doing something, no matter how trivial, or getting him angry or concerned about some present or future problem. Usually it was the effort of a friend who maternally and insistently motivated the individual toward realistic goals which snapped him out of such a state of resignation. In one case such "therapy" consisted of kicking the man until he was mad enough to get up and fight.

Throughout this time, the Chinese played the role of the benevolent but handicapped captor. Prisoners were always reminded that it was their *own* Air Force bombing which was responsible for the inadequate supplies. Furthermore, they were reminded that they were getting treatment which was just as good as that which the average Chinese was getting. One important effect of this was that a man could never give *full* vent to his hostility toward the Chinese, even in fantasy. In their *manner* and *words* they were usually solicitous and sympathetic. These Chinese also implied that conditions could be better for a prisoner if he would take a more "cooperative" attitude, if he would support their propaganda for peace. Thus a man was made to feel that he was himself responsible for his traumatic circumstances.

Arrival at a permanent camp usually brought relief from many of these physical hardships. Food, shelter, and medicine, while not plentiful, appeared to be sufficient for the maintenance of life and some degree of health. However, the Chinese now increased sharply their efforts to involve prisoners in their own propaganda program, and to undermine loyalties to their country. This marks the beginning of the second phase of the imprisonment experience.

The Chinese program of subversion and indoctrination was thoroughly integrated into the entire camp routine and involved the manipulation of the entire social milieu of the prison camp. Its aims appeared to be to manage a large group of prisoners with a minimum staff of guards, to indoctrinate them with the Communist political ideology, to interrogate them to obtain intelligence information and confessions for propaganda purposes, and to develop a corps of collaborators within the prisoner group. What success the Chinese had stemmed from their *total* control of the environment, not from the application of any one technique.

The most significant feature of Chinese prisoner camp control was the systematic destruction of the prisoners' formal and informal group structure. Soon after arrival at a camp, the men were segregated by race, nationality, and rank. The Chinese put their own men in charge of the platoons and companies, and made arbitrary selections of POW squad leaders to remind the prisoners that their old rank system no longer had any validity. In addition, the Chinese attempted to undermine *informal* group structure by prohibiting any kind of group meeting, and by systematically fomenting mutual distrust by playing men off against one another. The most effective device to this end was the practice of obtaining from informers or Chinese spies detailed information about someone's activities, no matter how trivial, then calling him in to interrogate him about it. Such detailed surveillance of the men's activities made them feel that their own ranks were so infiltrated by spies and informers that it was not safe to trust anyone.

A similar device was used to obtain information during interrogation. After a man had resisted giving information for hours or days, he would be shown a signed statement by one of his fellow prisoners giving that same information. Still another device was to make prisoners who had not collaborated look like collaborators, by bestowing special favors upon them.

A particularly successful Chinese technique was their use of testimonials from other prisoners, such as the false germ-warfare confessions, and appeals based on familiar contexts, such as peace appeals. Confessions by prisoners or propaganda lectures given by collaborators had a particularly demoralizing effect, because only if resistance had been *unanimous* could a man solidly believe that his values were correct, even if he could not defend them logically.

If the men, in spite of their state of social disorganization, did manage to organize any kind of group activity, the Chinese would quickly break up the group by removing its leaders or key members and assigning them to another camp.

Loyalties to home and country were undermined by the systematic manipulation of mail. Usually only mail which carried bad news was delivered. If a man received no mail at all, the Chinese suggested that his loved ones had abandoned him.

Feelings of social isolation were increased by the complete information control maintained in the camps. Only the Communist press, radio, magazines, and movies were allowed.

The weakening of the prisoner group's social structure is particularly significant because we depend to such an extent on consensual validation in judging ourselves and others. The prisoners lost their most important sources of information and support concerning standards of behavior and beliefs. Often men who attempted to resist the Chinese by means other than *outright* obstruction or aggression failed to obtain the active support of others, often earning their suspicion instead.

At the same time, the Chinese did create a situation in which meaningful social relationships could be had through common political activity, such as the "peace" committees which served as propaganda organs. The Chinese interrogators or instructors sometimes lived with prisoners for long periods of time in order to establish close personal relationships with them.

The Communist doctrines were presented through compulsory lectures followed by compulsory group discussions, for the purpose of justifying the conclusions given at the end of the lectures. On the whole, this phase of indoctrination was ineffective because of the crudeness of the propaganda material used in the lectures. However, its constant repetition seemed eventually to influence those men who did not have well formed political opinions to start with, particularly because no counter-arguments could be heard. The group discussions were effective only if their monitor was someone who could keep control over the group and keep it on the topic of discussion. Attempts by the Chinese to use "progressive" POWs in the role of monitors were seldom successful because they aroused too much hostility in the men.

The Chinese also attempted to get prisoners to use mutual criticism and self-criticism in the fashion in which it is used within China.[2] Whenever a POW was caught breaking one of the innumerable camp rules, he was required to give an elaborate confession and self-criticism, no matter how trivial the offense. In general, the POWs were able to use this opportunity to ridicule the Chinese by taking advantage of their lack of understanding of slang and American idiom. They would emphasize the wrong parts of sentences or insert words and phrases which made it apparent to other prisoners that the joke was on the Chinese. Often men were required to make these confessions in front of large groups of other prisoners. If the man could successfully communicate by a linguistic device his lack of sincerity, this ritual could backfire on the Chinese by giving the men an opportunity to express their solidarity (by sharing a communication which could not be understood by the Chinese). However, in other instances, prisoners who viewed such public confessions felt contempt for the confessor and felt their own group was being undermined still further by such public humiliation.

Various tales of how prisoners resisted the pressures put on them have been widely circulated in the press. For example, a number of prisoners ridiculed the Chinese by playing baseball with a basketball, yet telling the Chinese this was the correct way to play the game. Such stories suggest that morale and group solidarity was actually quite high in the camps. Our interviews with the men suggest that morale climbed sharply during the *last six to nine months* of imprisonment when the armistice talks were under way, when the compulsory indoctrination program had been put on a voluntary basis, and when the Chinese were improving camp conditions in anticipation of the repatriation. However, we heard practically no stories of successful group resistance or high morale from the first year or so in the camps when the indoctrination program was seriously pursued by the Chinese. (At that time the men had neither the time nor the opportunity to play any kind of games,

[2] See the paper by Robert J. Lifton in *Journal of Social Issues* 13 (1957) no. 3.

because all their time was spent on indoctrination activities or exhausting labor.)

Throughout, the Chinese created an environment in which rewards such as extra food, medicine, special privileges, and status were given for cooperation and collaboration, while threats of death, non-repatriation, reprisal against family, torture, decreases in food and medicine, and imprisonment served to keep men from offering much resistance. Only imprisonment was consistently used as an actual punishment. *Chronic* resistance was usually handled by transferring the prisoner to a so-called "reactionary" camp.

Whatever behavior the Chinese attempted to elicit, they always *paced* their demands very carefully, they always required some level of *participation* from the prisoner, no matter how trivial, and they *repeated* endlessly.

To what extent did these pressures produce either changes in beliefs and attitudes, or collaboration? Close observation of the repatriates and the reports of the men themselves suggest that the Chinese did not have much success in changing beliefs and attitudes. Doubt and confusion were created in many prisoners as a result of having to examine so closely their own way of thinking, but very few changes, if any, occurred that resembled actual *conversion* to Communism. The type of prisoner who was most likely to become *sympathetic* toward Communism was the one who had chronically occupied a low status position in this society, and for whom the democratic principles were not very salient or meaningful.

In producing collaboration, however, the Chinese were far more effective. By collaboration I mean such activities as giving lectures for the Communists, writing and broadcasting propaganda, giving false confessions, writing and signing petitions, informing on fellow POWs, and so on; none of these activities required a personal change of belief. Some 10 to 15 per cent of the men chronically collaborated, but the dynamics of this response are very complex. By far the greatest determinant was the amount of pressure the Chinese put on a particular prisoner. Beyond this, the reports of the men permit one to isolate several sets of motives that operated, though it is impossible to tell how many cases of each type there may have been.

1. Some men collaborated for outright opportunistic reasons; these men lacked any kind of stable group identification, and exploited the situation for its material benefits without any regard for the consequences to themselves, their fellow prisoners, or their country.

2. Some men collaborated because their egos were too weak to withstand the physical and psychological rigors; these men were primarily motivated by fear, though they often rationalized their behavior; they were unable to resist any kind of authority figure, and could be blackmailed by the Chinese once they had begun to collaborate.

3. Some men collaborated with the firm conviction that they were infiltrating the Chinese ranks and obtaining intelligence information which

would be useful to the UN forces. This was a convenient rationalization for anyone who could not withstand the pressures. Many of these men were initially tricked into collaboration or were motivated by a desire to communicate with the outside world. None of these men became ideologically confused; what Communist beliefs they might have professed were for the benefit of the Chinese only.

4. The prisoner who was vulnerable to the ideological appeal because of his low status in this society often collaborated with the conviction that he was doing the right thing in supporting the Communist peace movement. This group included the younger and less intelligent men from backward or rural areas, the malcontents, and members of various minority groups. These men often viewed themselves as failures in our society, and felt that society had never given them a chance. They were positively attracted by the immediate status and privileges which went with being a "progressive," and by the promise of important roles which they could presumably play in the peace movement of the future.

Perhaps the most important thing to note about collaboration is the manner in which the social disorganization contributed to it. A man might make a slanted radio broadcast in order to communicate with the outside, he might start reading Communist literature out of sheer boredom, he might give information which he knew the Chinese already had, and so on. Once this happened, however, the Chinese rewarded him, increased pressure on him to collaborate, and blackmailed him by threatening exposure. At the same time, in most cases, his fellow prisoners forced him into further collaboration by mistrusting him and ostracising him. Thus a man had to stand entirely on his own judgment and strength, and both of these often failed. One of the most common failures was a man's lack of awareness concerning the effects of his own actions on the other prisoners, and the value of these actions for the Chinese propaganda effort. The man who confessed to germ warfare, thinking he could repudiate such a confession later, did not realize its immediate propaganda value to the Communists.

A certain percentage of men, though the exact number is difficult to estimate, exhibited chronic resistance and obstructionism toward Chinese indoctrination efforts. Many of these men were well integrated with secure, stable group identifications who could withstand the social isolation and still exercise good judgment. Others were chronic obstructionists whose histories showed recurring resistance to any form of authority. Still others were idealists or martyrs to religious and ethical principles, and still others were anxious, guilt-ridden individuals who could only cope with their own strong impulses to collaborate by denying them and over-reacting in the other direction.

By far the largest group of prisoners, however, established a complex compromise between the demands of the Chinese, and their own value system. This adjustment, called by the men "playing it cool," consisted primarily of a physical and emotional withdrawal from the whole environment. These men learned to suspend their feelings and to adopt an attitude of watching and waiting, rather than hoping and planning. This reaction, though passive, was not as severe as the apathy described earlier. It was a difficult adjustment to maintain because some concessions had to be made to the Chinese in the form of trivial or well-timed collaborative acts, and in the form of a feigned interest in the indoctrination program. At the same time, each man had to be prepared to deal with the hostility of his buddies if he made an error in judgment.

Discussion

This paper has placed particular emphasis on the social psychological factors involved in "brainwashing" because it is my opinion that the process is primarily concerned with social forces, not with the strengths and weaknesses of individual minds. It has often been asserted that drugs, hypnotic techniques, refined "mental tortures" and, more recently, implanted electrodes can make the task of the "brainwasher" much easier by rendering the human mind submissive with a minimum of effort.[3] There is little question that such techniques can be used to elicit confessions or signatures on documents prepared by the captor; but so can withdrawal of food, water, or air produce the same results. The point is that the Chinese Communists do not appear to be interested in obtaining merely a confession or *transient* submission. Instead, they appear to be interested in producing changes in men which will be lasting and self-sustaining. A germ-warfare confession alone was not enough—the POW had to "testify" before an international commission explaining in detail how the bombs had been dropped, and had to tell his story in other prison camps to his fellow POWs.

There is little evidence that drugs, post-hypnotic suggestion, or implanted electrodes can now or ever will be able to produce the kind of behavior exhibited by many prisoners who collaborated and made false confessions. On the other hand, there is increasing evidence [1, 2] that Russian and Chinese interrogation and indoctrination techniques involve the destruction of the person's social ties and identifications, and the partial destruction of his ego. If this is successfully accomplished, the person is offered a new identity for himself and given the opportunity to identify with new groups. What physical torture and deprivation are involved in this process may be either a calculated attempt to degrade and humiliate a man or destroy his image of himself as a dignified human being, or the product of fortuitous circumstances, i.e., failure of supply lines to the prison, loss of temper on the part of the interrogator, an attempt to inspire fear in other prisoners by torturing

[3] For example, see the paper by James G. Miller in *Journal of Social Issues* 13 (1957) no. 3.

one of them, and so on. We do not have sufficient evidence to determine which of these alternatives represents Communist intentions; possibly all of them are involved in the actual prison situation.

Ultimately that which sustains humans is their personality integration born out of secure and stable group identifications. One may be able to produce temporary submission by direct intervention in cortical processes, but only by destroying a man's self-image and his group supports can one produce any lasting changes in his beliefs and attitudes. By concerning ourselves with the problem of artificially creating submission in man, we run the real risk of overlooking the fact that we are in a genuine struggle of ideas with other portions of the world and that man often submits himself directly to ideas and principles.

To understand and combat "brainwashing" we must look at those social conditions which make people ready to accept new ideas from anyone who states them clearly and forcefully, and those social conditions which give people the sense of integrity which will sustain them when their immediate social and emotional supports are stripped away.

References

1. HINKLE, LAWRENCE E., and WOLFF, HAROLD G. Communist interrogation and indoctrination of "Enemies of the State." *Archives of Neurology and Psychiatry* 76 (1956): 115–74.
2. LIFTON, ROBERT L. "Thought reform" of Western civilians in Chinese Communist prisons. *Psychiatry* 19 (1956):173–98.
3. SCHEIN, EDGAR H. The Chinese indoctrination program for prisoners of war. *Psychiatry* 19 (1956):149–72.
4. STRASSMAN, HARVEY D., THALER, MARGARET, and SCHEIN, EDGAR H. A prisoner of war syndrome: Apathy as a reaction to severe stress. *American Journal of Psychiatry* 112 (1956):998–1003.

Teaching Machines:
An Application of Principles
from the Laboratory

JAMES G. HOLLAND

Psychologists before the 1950s were reluctant to bring laboratory learning (rats) into the classroom, perhaps because laboratory learning appeared to deal exclusively with very simple forms of behavior (bar pressing), which seemed qualitatively different from what we pursue in school. Some psychologists, however, have argued that this apparent difference is not a real one, that learning an abstract concept is the same kind of a process as learning to press a bar. This point of view gave rise to what came to be called "behavioral engineering," a technology that (in its educational application) divorces learning from such concepts as "mind" and "knowledge" and emphasizes instead the analysis of behavior into chains of discrete but related units. According to this framework we do not eat, but we emit a series of responses, the final one of which is swallowing. We approach the table; we sit; we reach for and grasp the fork; and so forth. Once a complex act has been analyzed into its behavioral elements, we are in a position to control each element, or the whole chain, by the application of certain principles of learning. We can make eating happen more slowly or quickly, at one place or another, standing, sitting, or lying down; we can substitute one food "preference" for another or change almost any aspect of the entire process. The classroom-learning case is essentially the same; analyze the behavior into its elements and apply the principles of learning. In this article, James Holland details six of these principles as teaching machines apply them.

SOURCE: From *Proceedings of the 1959 Invitational Conference on Testing Problems.* Copyright © 1960 by Educational Testing Service. All rights reserved. Reprinted in *Testing Problems in Perspective.* Copyright © 1966 by American Council on Education. Reprinted by permission.

Note: This article was invited by the editorial board. It was previously presented before the 1959 Invitational Conference on Testing Problems sponsored by the Educational Testing Service, and will appear in the *Proceedings of the Invitational Conference on Testing Problems* in 1960. The work discussed in this paper has been supported by grants from the Carnegie Corporation and the Ford Foundation.

231

Much has been said of teaching machines recently—but the emphasis has tended to be on the gadgets rather than on the much more significant development of a new technology of education initiated by B. F. Skinner [1954, 1958]. The technology does use a device called a teaching machine, which presents a finely graded series of problems and provides immediate "reward" or reinforcement for the student's correct answers. But emphasis on machines has tended to obscure the more important facets of the new technology based on application of principles from the laboratory. The machines of today are not necessarily better than those of yesterday. Indeed, adequate machines could have been built hundreds of years ago. The movement today is not simply the mechanization of teaching, but instead the development of a new technology—a behavioral engineering of teaching procedures.

The history of unsuccessful teaching machines illustrates the relatively greater importance of the technique as opposed to the gadgets. The first teaching machine was patented 93 years ago. There have since been a series of patents and a promising burst of activity initiated by Sidney Pressey [1926] in the 1920's. None of these early efforts really caught hold. But during this period in which the idea of mechanized teaching has been latent, the science of behavior has developed principles which permit extremely precise control of behavior. This new technology is not only the so-called automation of teaching, but is an attempt to obtain the kind of behavioral control shown possible in the laboratory.

We have, of course, seen other practical applications of scientific psychology. We are all familiar with the development of a technology of testing, which permits placing an individual in situations suited to his abilities. We are also familiar with another technology called human engineering, which fits machines and jobs to the capacities of man. One places a man in a job that suits him; the other alters the job to suit the man; *neither* attempts to alter or control man's behavior.

For years in the laboratory we have controlled the behavior of experimental subjects—both animal and human—by a widening array of principles and techniques. The new technology of education is the application of behavioral laws in modifying or controlling behavior. Such a technology became possible with the realization that we are actually referring to a verbal repertoire [Skinner, 1957] controlled by the same laws as other behavior. The old, defunct explanatory concepts of knowledge, meaning, mind, or symbolic processes have never offered the possibility of manipulation or control; but behavior, verbal or otherwise, can be controlled with ease and precision.

While machines are not the essential or defining aspect of this technology, they do play an important role in providing some of this fine control the technology requires. We will now examine several machines and notice the advantages they offer.

At Harvard there is a self-instruction room with ten booths, each containing a machine such as the one shown in Fig. 1. The student gets one set of ma-

FIGURE 1. *Student working at a write-in teaching machine.*

terial from the attendant and places it in the machine. He closes the machine and begins his studies.

This machine presents one item of material at a time. The subject reads the statement, which has one or more words missing, and he completes it by writing in the answer space. He then raises the lever and a small shutter opens, revealing the correct answer. Simultaneously, his answer is moved under glass, where it can be read and compared with the now-exposed correct answer. After comparing his answer with the correct answer, the student indicates to the machine, with an appropriate movement of the lever, whether his answer was correct or incorrect, and the next item appears in the window. He repeats all items answered wrong after he completes the set of items. He does not repeat correctly answered items.

A critical feature of the machine is that it provides immediate reinforcement for correct answers. Being correct is known to be a reinforcer for humans. In machine teaching, reinforcement is immediate. We know from laboratory work [Perin, 1943] that a delay between a response and its reinforcement of a few seconds will greatly reduce the effectiveness of the reinforcement. Adult human subjects can sustain at least small delays; nevertheless, any delay makes reinforcement less effective.

Although other techniques such as programmed workbooks [Homme and Glaser, 1959] and flashcards are sometimes used in this new behavioral technology, they offer less control. Teaching machines eliminate undesirable forms of responses which would also be successful in obtaining the right answer. For example, the teaching machine insures that the student answers before peeking at the indicated answer. There is a strong temptation to glance ahead with only a poorly formulated, unwritten answer when programmed workbooks or flashcards are used.

This write-in machine is a prototype of the most common machine. There is another machine used for teaching young children material which consistently has a single possible answer. In the machine the constructed answer is automatically compared with the true answer. The child is presented a problem, perhaps a statement such as $2 + 2 =$ ___, and he must provide the 4. By moving a slider appropriately, he can insert the 4 into the answer space. He then turns the crank, and the next item appears immediately, so that immediate reinforcement is provided.

Both of the machines we have seen thus far require the student to compose the answer. Figure 2 shows a machine for a less mature organism who cannot

FIGURE 2.   *Child working on the preverbal machine. In the upper rectangular window is a sample which is to be matched with a figure in one of the three lower windows. If the child presses the correct lower window, the material advances to the next frame. In this case, the match is in terms of form, with size and color irrelevant.*

yet compose an answer. This machine can be used for teaching preschool children.[1] There is a large top window and three small windows. In the large window, there is some sort of problem; and in the three smaller windows, there are three alternative choices. For example, in the machine as seen in the picture, the subject chooses one of the three alternatives which has the same form as the sample, independent, in this case, of color or size. When the correct choice is made, the next frame is presented.

A teaching machine for a still lower organism is shown in Fig. 3.

FIGURE 3. *A pigeon "naming colors." The pigeon pecks the color name corresponding to the color of the light projected above him.*

This pigeon, with the aid of a teaching machine, has learned to hit the name plaque appropriate for a color projected above him. The principal difference between this and the other machines is that food reinforcement is used. With humans, simply being correct is sufficient reinforcement— pigeons will not work for such meager gains.

[1] Hively, W. An exploratory investigation of an apparatus for studying and teaching visual discrimination using preschool children [Hively, 1960–65].

Enough of machines. They should not be allowed to obscure the truly important feature of the new technology, namely, the application of methods for behavioral control in developing programs for teaching. We need to say no more about the well-known principle of immediate reinforcement. Our second principle is also well known. Behavior is learned only when it is *emitted* and reinforced. But in the classroom, the student performs very little, verbally. However, while working with a machine, the student necessarily emits appropriate behavior, and this behavior is usually reinforced because the material is so designed that the student is usually correct. Not only is reinforcement needed for learning, but a high density of correct items is necessary because material which generates errors is punishing. Laboratory experiments [Azrin, 1956] have shown that punishment lowers the rate of the punished behavior. In our experience with teaching machines, we have also observed that students stop work when the material is so difficult that they make many errors. Furthermore, they become irritated, almost aggressive, when errors are made.

The third important principle is that of gradual progression to establish complex repertoires. A visitor once asked if Skinner had realized that pigeons were so smart before he began using them as subjects. The answer given by a helpful graduate student was that they weren't so smart before Skinner began using them. And indeed they weren't. The behavior developed in many experiments is like that developed in the classroom. Both are complex operants. Both require a careful program of gradual progression. We cannot wait for a student to describe the content of a psychology course before reinforcing the performance; nor can we wait for a pigeon to emit such an improbable bit of behavior as turning a circle, facing a disk on the wall, pecking it if lit, and then bending down to a now-exposed food tray and eating. When developing a complex performance in a pigeon, we may first reinforce simply the behavior of approaching the food tray when it is presented with a loud click. Later, the pigeon learns to peck a key which produces the click and the food tray. Still later, he may learn to peck this key only when it is lit, the peck being followed by the loud click and approach to the food tray. In the next step, he may learn to raise his head or hop from one foot to another, or walk a figure eight, in order to produce the lighted key which he then pecks; the click follows, and he approaches the food tray. This principle of gradual progression runs through many of the teaching-machine techniques. Both human and avian scholars deserve the same careful tutorage. The teaching-machine program moves in very finely graded steps, working from simple to an ever-higher level of complexity. Such a gradual development is illustrated in Table 1 by a few items taken from a psychology program.[2]

2 This program, prepared by J. G. Holland and B. F. Skinner, is entitled A *self-tutoring introduction to a science of behavior.*

TABLE 1. *Items from the Psychology Program (11). These Items Illustrate the Gradual Development of a New Concept.*

Item	Correct Answer	Percentage of Students Giving the Answer
1. Performing animals are sometimes trained with "rewards." The behavior of a hungry animal can be "rewarded" with _____.	Food	96
2. A technical term for "reward" is reinforcment. To "reward" an organism with food is to _____ it with food.	Reinforce	100
3. *Technically* speaking, a thirsty organism can be _____ with water.	Reinforced	100
50. A school teacher is likely, whenever possible, to dismiss a class when her students are rowdy because she has been _____ by elimination of the stimuli arising from a rowdy class.	Reinforced	92
51. The teacher who dismisses a class when it is rowdy causes the frequency of future rowdy behavior to (1) _____, since dismissal from class is probably a(n) (2) _____ for rowdy children.	(1) Increase (2) Reinforcement	86
54. If an airplane spotter never sees the kind of plane he is to spot, his frequency of scanning the sky (1) _____. In other words his "looking" behavior is (2) _____.	(1) Decreases (2) Extinguished (or: Not Reinforced)	94

The principle of gradual progression serves not simply to make the student correct as often as possible, but it is also the fastest way to develop a complex repertoire. In fact, a new complex operant may never appear except through separately reinforcing members of a graded series [Keller and Schoenfeld, 1950]. Only this way can we quickly create a *new pattern* of behavior. The pigeon would not have learned the complex sequence necessary to receive the food if it had not learned each step in its proper order. Obviously, a child can't begin with advanced mathematics, but neither can he begin with $2 + 2 = 4$—even this is too complex and requires a gradual progression.

Our fourth principle is, in a sense, another form of gradual progression— one which involves the gradual withdrawal of stimulus support. This we shall call fading. This method will be illustrated with some neuroanatomy material.[3] Figure 4A is a fully labelled cross section of the medulla oblongata. This is placed before the student while he works with a large set of items pertaining to the spatial arrangement of the various structures. For example, "posterior to the cuneate nuclei are the _____." The answer is: "the cuneate fasciculi." After many such items, he begins another set and has another picture (Fig. 4B), but now the structures before him are labelled only with initials. A new set of items again asks a long series of questions pertaining to the spatial position of the various structures. For example, "between the gracile and the trigeminal nuclei are _____." The answer is the "cuneate nuclei." After many more items, he proceeds to a new set and the next picture. This time (Fig. 4C), the picture is unlabelled. Again, he goes through a series of new items, not simple repetitions of the previous ones, but items pertaining to the same problem of the spatial location of the different structures. This set is followed by still another but with no picture at all. He is now able to discuss the spatial position of the structures without any visual representations of the structures before him. In a sense, he has his own private map of the medulla. He may further demonstrate his newly acquired ability by accurately drawing the medulla. The neuroanatomy example is an elaborate example of fading. Fading is also applied in a more simple form in constructing verbal programs without pictorial displays. A single item may in one sentence give a definition or a general law and in a second sentence in that same item, an example in which a key word is omitted. This would be followed by a new example in the next frame, but with the definition or law lacking.

This brings us to our fifth principle: control of the student's observing and echoic behavior. In the classroom the student is often treated as though he were some kind of passive receiver of information, who can sop up information spoken by the teacher, written on the blackboard, or presented by films. But all of these are effective only insofar as the student has some behavior with respect to the material. He must listen carefully, or read carefully, thus engaging in usually covert echoic behavior. Ineffectiveness of classroom techniques is often credited to "inattention" or poor "concentration." It has been shown [Reid, 1953; Wyckoff, 1952] that if a discrimination is to be learned, adequate observing behavior must first be established. We have further found that observing behavior, or speaking loosely, "attention," is subject to the same forms of control as other behavior [Holland, 1958]. This control of observing behavior is of prime importance. When the student becomes very "inattentive" in the classroom, the teaching material flows on; but with a machine, he moves ahead only as he finishes an item. Lapses in active participation result in nothing more than the machine sitting idle until the student continues. There is, however, a more subtle aspect to the control of observing behavior

___

[3] This material has been prepared by D. M. Brethower in collaboration with the present author, and it is being used at Harvard for research purposes.

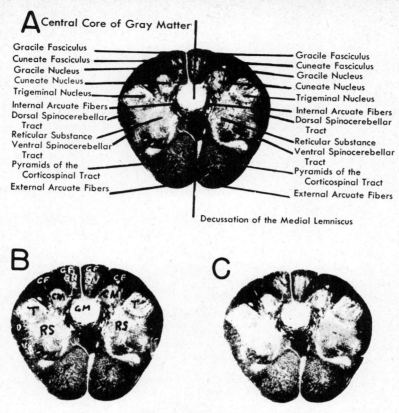

FIGURE 4.   *An illustration of the technique of fading. Section A is in front of the student while he is working on the earliest items of a neuroanatomy program; Section B is in front of the student for later items; and Section C, for still later items.*

than this obvious mechanical one. In many of the examples we have seen, success in answering the problem depends only on the student's careful observation of the material in front of him at the moment. This may be illustrated by more material from the psychology program. A graph showing stimulus-generalization data is in front of the student while he works on the machine. In the program he may complete a statement: "As the wavelength changes in either direction from the wavelength present during reinforcement, the number of responses _____." The answer is "decreases." The item serves only to control the behavior of observing the data. Of course, many more such items are used to discuss the same data.

This principle of controlled observation extends to the details of writing a single item. For example, "Two events may have a common effect. An operant reinforced with two reinforcers appropriate to different deprivations will vary with _____ deprivations." The answer is "two" or "both." Here, the programmer's choice of the omission serves to insure a careful reading of the item. *Only* those parts of an item which must be read to correctly complete a blank can safely be assumed to be learned.

Our sixth principle deals with discrimination training. In learning spoken languages, for example, it is necessary to be able to identify the speech sounds. A student may listen to a pair of words on a special phonograph which repeats the passage as many times as he desires. The visual write-in machine instructs him to listen to a specific passage. For example, the student may hear two words such as: "sit, set." He listens as many times as he needs and then writes the phonetic symbols in the write-in machine. He then operates the machine, thereby exposing the true answer and providing immediate reinforcement for his correct discrimination.

However, little academic education is *simple* discrimination. More often, it is abstraction or concept formation. An abstraction is a response to a single isolated property of a stimulus. Such a property cannot exist alone. Redness is an abstraction. Anything that is red has other properties as well—size, shape, position in space, to name a few. There are red balls, red cars, red walls. The term red applies to all of them, but not to green balls, blue cars, or yellow walls. To establish an abstraction [Hovland, 1952, 1953], we must provide many examples. Each must have the common property, but among the various examples there must be a wide range of other properties. This is best illustrated by examples from the preverbal machine shown in Fig. 5.

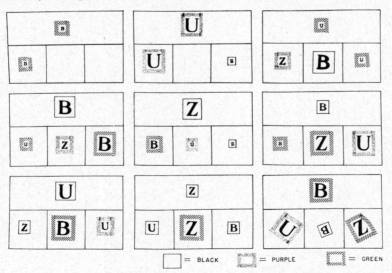

FIGURE 5. *Selected items from a program which teaches young children to respond in terms of the abstract property of form. The upper rectangle in each of the frames is the sample. The child must pick the alternative which corresponds to the sample in form. The color of each letter, as it appeared in the program, is indicated by the various shaded areas.*

These are from a program [4] which teaches a child to respond to the abstract property of form. In each item, the upper figure is the sample and the lower three are the alternatives. While developing a program for establishing an abstraction, we remember our earlier principles and move through a gradual progression. The first several items would be like the first one; here, there is a sample and a single match, the other two being blank. The sample and its match are exactly alike at this stage. After many such items, we would begin to have others like the next one, in which the sample and its match again correspond in size, color, and form—but an additional incorrect alternative has been added which differs from the sample in all these aspects. Later, we move on to frames with three choices; again, the sample and its match correspond exactly. Next, the sample and the match may differ in some property such as color, in the case of the next item shown, or size in the next. It is essential that the program contain many items among which the sample and correct match differ in all properties except the one providing the basis for the abstraction. Otherwise, the abstraction will be incomplete because the extraneous property will share some of the control over the abstract response. As we move on with additional examples, the sample and the correct match differ both in color and in size, and the incorrect alternatives are beginning to share some of the extraneous properties with the sample. The student continues with many such problems in which the only common property between the sample and the correct match is the shape, regardless of size and color. Even now our abstraction may be incomplete. We have kept the figures in only one orientation. Therefore, we also have a series in which the samples are rotated as in the next item. A great deal of academic education consists of trying to teach abstractions. Concepts such as force, reinforcement, supply and demand, freedom, and many, many other possible examples are all abstractions. Furthermore, in the academic setting, the student seldom adequately forms abstractions. The trigonometry student commonly uses triangles with the right angle as one of the two lower angles. If the triangle is rotated 90°, so that the right angle is upward, the student often does not recognize it as a right triangle. Neither is an abstraction developed simply by learning a definition. The psychology student who learns the definition of reinforcement in formal terms and is acquainted with a laboratory example of food reinforcement may not realize the horrible consequences of sending his girl friend flowers to end an argument. Thus, in the psychology program, we follow the pattern in the preverbal example to develop a new concept. Wide ranges of examples are analyzed which differ in as many aspects as possible, each still having the common property which characterizes the concept.

The last principle I shall discuss is really a question of a methodology which has served so well in the laboratory. This principle is to let the student write the program. A few years ago, the cartoon shown in Fig. 6 was published in the *Columbia Jester*.

[4] This program was prepared by B. F. Skinner.

FIGURE 6. "Boy, do we have this guy conditioned. Every time I press the bar down he drops a pellet in."

The rat leaning on the bar is saying to the other rat: "Boy, do we have this guy conditioned. Every time I press the bar down, he drops a pellet in." Although said in jest, it is true that the rat controls the experimenter's behavior. When interesting things are observed about the rat's behavior, the control circuits are rewired to investigate the interesting new facet of behavior. In a sense, the rat is wiring the control circuit. Similarly, the behavioral engineer who prepares good teaching-machine material must be under the control of the student's responses. When the student has trouble with part of a program, the programmer must correct this. The student's answers reveal ambiguities in items; they reveal gaps in the program and erroneous assumptions as to the student's background. The answers will show when the program is progressing too rapidly, when additional prompts are necessary, or when the programmer should try new techniques. When unexpected errors are made, they indicate deficiencies *not* in the student but in the program.

The most extensive experience with this principle of modifying the program to fit the student has been at Harvard with the psychology program. In 1958, we had a program consisting of 48 disks or lessons of 29 frames each. After using the program and making a detailed, item-by-item analysis of the students' answers, we diagnosed the particular deficiencies in the program and revised it accordingly. The program was also extended to cover a larger

TABLE 2. *A Comparison of the Students' Errors in Using the Revised (1959) and Unrevised (1958) Program in Psychology*

	Percent Errors	Percent Items Improperly Scored by Students
1958	20.1	3.6
1959	11.0	1.4

amount of subject matter; and in 1959, it consisted of 60 disks. You have already seen a few items from the course. After using the revised material in 1959, we evaluated the extent of its improvement. The next figure shows the percentage of errors on the first 20 disks for each of the 2 years.

The revision eliminated about half the errors. The last column of the table gives percentage of improper self-scoring by the students. Revision also cut these scoring errors approximately in half. Furthermore, the revision decreased the time required to complete the material. Although the second year's material had more disks—60 as opposed to 48—it actually required the average student about 1 hour less to complete the work than the shorter, first version had done. Frequency distributions on the median times in minutes for completion of the various disks are shown in Fig. 7. These are the times required

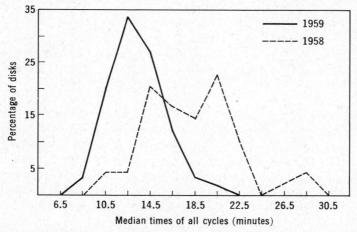

FIGURE 7. *Frequency distributions for the median times to complete the disks or "lessons" for the revised (1959) and unrevised (1958) psychology program. Raw frequencies were converted to percentages to equate the area under the curves.*

for the median student to move through each set of material answering every item once and to repeat items answered incorrectly. Notice the considerable time required for many disks in the first year's material. Primarily, this was because students repeated the larger number of items missed in the first cycle.

But the improved material provided faster performance, even when the delay due to repetition of incorrectly answered items is not considered. The frequency distributions for the first cycle only are provided in Fig. 8.

These data exclude the time used in repeating items. Here, too, the revision produced slightly more rapid progress.

Such careful tailoring of material to fit the student is impossible with most teaching techniques. With teaching machines, as in no other teaching technique, the programmer is able to revise his material in view of the students' particular difficulties. The student can write the program; he cannot write the textbook.

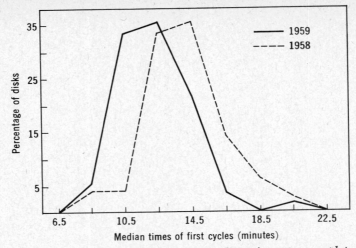

FIGURE 8. *Frequency distributions for the median times to complete only the first cycles for the revised (1959) and unrevised (1958) psychology program. Raw frequencies were converted to percentages to equate the area under the curves.*

We have seen that the principles evolved from the laboratory study of behavior have provided the possibility for the behavioral engineering of teaching. This new technology is thoroughly grounded in some of the better-established facts of behavioral control. The future of education is bright if persons who prepare teaching-machine programs appreciate this, and appropriately educate themselves in a special, but truly *not* esoteric, discipline. But it is vital that we continue to apply these techniques in preparing programs. The ill-advised efforts of some of our friends, who automatize their courses without adopting the new technology, have an extremely good chance of burying the whole movement in an avalanche of teaching-machine tapes.

References

1. AZRIN, H. H. Some effects of two intermittent schedules of immediate and nonimmediate punishment. *J. Psychol.* 42 (1956):3–21.
2. HIVELY, W. An exploratory investigation of an apparatus for studying and teaching visual discrimination using preschool children. In A. A. Lumsdaine and R. Glaser, eds. *Teaching Machines and Programmed Learning.* Washington, D.C.: National Education Association, Dept. of Audio-Visual Instruction, 1960–65.
3. HOLLAND, J. G. Human vigilance. *Science* 128 (1958):61–67.
4. HOMME, L. E., and GLASER, R. Relationships between programmed textbooks and teaching machines. In E. Galanter, ed. *Automatic Teaching.* New York: John Wiley & Sons, 1959. Pp. 103–7.
5. HOVLAND, C. I. A set of flower designs for experiments in concept formation. *Amer. J. Psychol.* 66 (1953):140–42.
6. HOVLAND, C. I. A "communication analysis" of concept learning. *Psychol. Rev.* 59 (1952):461–72.

7. KELLER, F. S., and SCHOENFELD, W. N. *Principles of Psychology.* New York: Appleton-Century-Crofts, 1950.

8. PERIN, C. T. The effect of delayed reinforcement upon the differentiation of bar responses in white rats. *J. Exp. Psychol.* 32 (1943):95–109.

9. PRESSEY, S. L. Simple apparatus which gives tests and scores and teaches. *Sch. and Soc.* 23 (1926):373–76.

10. REID, L. S. The development of noncontinuity behavior through continuity learning. *J. Exp. Psychol.* 46 (1953):107–12.

11. SKINNER, B. F. The science of learning and the art of teaching. *Harvard Educ. Rev.* 29 (1954):86–97.

12. SKINNER, B. F. *Verbal Behavior.* New York: Appleton-Century-Crofts, 1957.

13. SKINNER, B. F. Teaching machines. *Science* 128 (1958):969–77.

14. WYCKOFF, L. B. The role of observing responses in discrimination learning. *Psychol. Rev.* 59 (1952):431–42.

Learning and Thinking

JEROME S. BRUNER

Once we have learned something, we want to be able to take advantage of what we have learned; we want to apply that learning to the mastery of new problems. In other words, we want to think. Jerome Bruner, drawing on his experience as director of the Cognition Project at Harvard, here describes his conception of the relationship between learning and thinking. His focus is "generic learning," the learning of knowledge-organizing principles (or abstractions, in Holland's sense from the preceding article) in such a fashion that these principles can be readily applied to new problems. He makes several suggestions for the pursuit and application of generic learning. First, he says, we need activity. We need to search into the unknown by organizing and manipulating existing knowledge; we need to test our thinking against our learning in much the same way as Schein suggested we test our opinions against the opinions of others. Second, we need to recognize the continuity of knowledge and organize our learning in such a way that we can perceive the interrelatedness of all elements of knowledge, for it is from understanding these relationships that the principles arise. Finally, we need to preserve the force and the passion of reality. We should not emasculate reality for the sake of a picture that is sweet and neat and clean.

Bruner's conception is a simple one, but his two primary concepts—the organization and the manipulation of knowledge—have considerable practical significance.

I

I have been engaged, these last few years, in research on what makes it possible for organisms—human and subhuman alike—to take advantage of past learning in attempting to deal with and master new problems before them now. It is a problem with a deceptively simple ring to it. In pursuit of it, my colleagues

SOURCE: From Jerome S. Bruner, "Learning and Thinking," *Harvard Educational Review* 29, Summer 1959, 184–92. Copyright © 1959 by President and Fellows of Harvard College. Reprinted by permission.
Note: Paper presented to Massachusetts Council on Teacher Education, February 13, 1958.

and I have found ourselves observing children in schoolrooms, watching them learning. It has been a revealing experience.

We have come to recognize in this work that one of the principal objectives of learning is to save us from subsequent learning. This seems a paradox, but it is not. Another way of putting the matter is to say that when we learn something, the objective is to learn it in such a way that we get a maximum of travel out of what we have learned. A homely example is provided by the relationship in arithmetic between addition and multiplication. If the principle of addition has been grasped in its deeper sense, in its generic sense, then it is unnecessary to learn multiplication. For, in principle, multiplication is only repeated addition. It is not, as we would say in our curricula, another "unit."

Learning something in a generic way is like leaping over a barrier. On the other side of the barrier is thinking. When the generic has been grasped, it is then that we are able to recognize the new problems we encounter as exemplars of old principles we have mastered. Once over the barrier, we are able to benefit from what William James long ago called "the electric sense of analogy."

There are two interesting features in generic learning—in the kind of learning that permits us to cross the barrier into thinking. One of them is *organization;* the other is *manipulation.* If we are to use our past learning, we must organize it in such a way that it is no longer bound to the specific situation in which the learning occurred. Let me give an example from the history of science. It would have been possible for Galileo to have published a handbook of the distances traversed per unit time by falling bodies. School boys for centuries thereafter could easily have been tortured by the task of having to remember the Galilean tables. Such tables, cumbersome though they might have been, would have contained all the necessary information for dealing with free-falling bodies. Instead, Galileo had the inspiration to reorganize this welter of information into a highly simplified form. You recall the compact expression $S = \frac{1}{2} gt^2$: it not only summarizes all possible handbooks but organizes their knowledge in a way that makes manipulation possible. Not only do we know the distances fallen, but we can use the knowledge for bodies that fall anywhere, in any gravitational field—not just our own.

One of the most notable things about the human mind is its limited capacity for dealing at any one moment with diverse arrays of information. It has been known for a long time that we can deal only with about seven independent items of information at once; beyond that point we exceed our "channel capacity," to use our current jargon. We simply cannot manipulate large masses of information. Because of these limits, we must condense and recode. The seven things we deal with must be worth their weight. A simple formula that can regenerate the distance fallen by any free body, past or future, is under these conditions highly nutritious for its weight. Good organization achieves the kind of economical representation of facts that makes it possible to use the facts in the future. Sheer brute learning, noble though it may be, is not enough. Facts simply learned without a generic organization are the naked and useless untruth. The proper reward of learning is not that it pleases the teacher or the parents, nor is it that we become "quiz kids." The proper reward is that we can now use what we have learned, can cross the barrier from learning into thinking. Are we mindful of these matters in our conduct of teaching?

What has been said thus far must seem singularly lacking in relevance to magic, to art, and to poetry. It appears to relate principally to the learning of mathematics, science, and the social studies. But there is an analogous point to be made about the learning of the arts and literature. If one has read literature and beheld works of art in such a way as to be able to think with their aid, then one has also grasped a deeper, simplifying principle. The underlying principle that gives one the power to use literature and the arts in one's thinking is not of the order of a generic condensation of knowledge. Rather it is metaphoric in nature, and perhaps the best way of describing this class of principles is to call them guiding myths.

Let me take an example from mythology. Recall when you read for the first time the story of Perseus slaying the hateful Medusa. You recall that to look directly upon the Medusa was to be turned to stone. The secret of Perseus was to direct the killing thrust of his sword by the reflection of Medusa on his polished shield. It is an exciting story, full of the ingenuity that Hercules had taught us to expect. Beneath the story, beneath all great stories, there is a deeper metaphoric meaning. I did not understand this meaning for many years, indeed, not until my son asked me what the myth of Perseus "meant." It occurred to me that the polished shield might symbolize all of the devices by which we are able to take action against evil without becoming contaminated by it. The law suggested itself as one such device, enabling us to act against those who trespassed against morality without ourselves having to trespass in our action. I do not wish to hold a brief for my interpretation of the Perseus myth. But I would like to make one point about it.

Man must cope with a relatively limited number of plights—birth, growth, loneliness, the passions, death, and not very many more. They are plights that are neither solved nor by-passed by being "adjusted." An adjusted man must face his passions just as surely as he faces death. I would urge that a grasp of the basic plights through the basic myths of art and literature provides the organizing principle by which knowledge of the human condition is rendered into a form that makes thinking possible, by which we go beyond learning to the use of knowledge. I am not suggesting that the Greek myths are better than other forms of literature. I urge simply that there be exposure to, and interpretation of, literature that deals deeply with the human condition. I have learned as much from Charlie Brown of *Peanuts* as I have learned from Perseus. The pablum school readers, stripped of rich imagery in the interest of "readability," stripped of passion in the erroneous belief that the deeper human condition will not interest the child—these are no more the vehicles for getting over the barrier to thinking than are the methods of teaching mathematics by a rote parroting at the blackboard.

II

I should like to consider now some conditions in our schools today that promote and inhibit progress across the barrier from learning to thinking. I should point out in advance that I am not very cheerful on this subject.

THE PASSIVITY OF KNOWLEDGE-GETTING

I have been struck during the past year or so, sitting in classrooms as an observer, by the passivity of the process we call education. The emphasis is upon gaining and storing information, gaining it and storing it in the form in which it is presented. We carry the remainder in long division so, peaches are grown in Georgia, transportation is vital to cities, New York is our largest port, and so on. Can the facts or the methods presented be mimicked? If so, the unit is at an end. There is little effort indeed which goes into the process of putting the information together, finding out what is generic about it. Long division is a skill, like threading a needle. The excitement of it as a method of partitioning things that relates it to such matters as subtraction is rarely stressed. One of the great inventions of man—elementary number theory—is presented as a cookbook. I have yet to see a teacher present one way of doing division and then put it squarely to the class to suggest six other ways of doing it—for there are at least six other ways of doing it than any one that might be taught in a school. So too with algebra. Algebra is not a set of rules for manipulating numbers and letters except in a trivial sense. It is a way of thinking, a way of coping with the drama of the unknown. Lincoln Steffens, in his *Autobiography*, complains upon his graduation from the University of California that his teachers had taught him only of the known, how to commit it to mind, and had done little to instruct him in the art of approaching the unknown, the art of posing questions. How does one ask questions about the unknown? Well, algebra is one technique, the technique for arranging the known in such a way that one is enabled to discern the value of an unknown quantity. It is an enriching strategy, algebra, but only if it is grasped as an extended instance of common sense.

Once I did see a teacher specifically encourage a class to organize and use minimal information to draw a maximum number of inferences. The teacher modeled his technique, I suppose, on the tried method of the storyteller. He presented the beginnings of the Whiskey Rebellion and said to his pupils, much in the manner of Ellery Queen speaking to his readers, "You now have enough to reconstruct the rest of the story. Let's see if we can do it." He was urging them to cross the barrier from learning into thinking. It is unhappily true that this is a rare exception in our schools.

So knowledge-getting becomes passive. Thinking is the reward for learning, and we may be systematically depriving our students of this reward as far as school learning is concerned.

One experiment which I can report provides encouragement. It was devised and carried out by the research group with which I am associated at Harvard in collaboration with teachers in the fifth grade of a good public school. It is on the unpromising topic of the geography of the North Central States and is currently in progress so that I cannot give all of the results. We hit upon the happy idea of presenting this chunk of geography not as a set of knowns, but as a set of unknowns. One class was presented blank maps, containing only tracings of the rivers and lakes of the area as well as the natural resources. They were asked as a first exercise to indicate where the principal cities would be located, where the railroads, and where the main highways. Books and maps were not permitted and "looking up the facts" was cast in a sinful light. Upon completing this exercise, a class discussion was begun in which the children attempted to justify why the major city would be here, a large city there, a railroad on this line, etc.

The discussion was a hot one. After an hour, and much pleading, permission was given to consult the rolled up wall map. I will never forget one young student, as he pointed his finger at the foot of Lake Michigan, shouting, "Yipee, *Chicago* is at the end of the pointing-down lake." And another replying, "Well, OK: but Chicago's no good for the rivers and it should be here where there is a big city (St. Louis)." These children were thinking, and learning was an instrument for checking and improving the process. To at least a half dozen children in the class it is not a matter of indifference that no big city is to be found at the junction of Lake Huron, Lake Michigan, and Lake Ontario. They were slightly shaken up transportation theorists when the facts were in.

The children in another class taught conventionally, got their facts all right, sitting down, benchbound. And that was that. We will see in six months which group remembers more. But whichever does, one thing I will predict. One group learned geography as a set of rational acts of induction—that cities spring up where there is water, where there are natural resources, where there are things to be processed and shipped. The other group learned passively that there were arbitrary cities at arbitrary places by arbitrary bodies of water and arbitrary sources of supply. One learned geography as a form of activity. The other stored some names and positions as a passive form of registration.

THE EPISODIC CURRICULUM

In a social studies class of an elementary school in a well-to-do suburb of one of our great eastern cities, I saw groups of twelve-year-old children doing a "project" on the southeastern states. Each team was gathering facts that might eventually end up on a map or a chart or some other graphic device. The fact-gathering was atomized and episodic. Here were the industrial products of North Carolina. There was the list of the five principal cities of Georgia. I asked the children of one team what life would be like and what people would worry about in a place where the principal products were peanuts, cotton, and peaches. The question was greeted as "unfair." They were gathering facts.

It is not just the schools. The informational environment of America seems increasingly to be going through such an atomization. Entertainment is in fifteen-minute episodes on TV, to be taken while sitting down. The school curriculum is built of episodic units, each a task to itself: "We have now finished addition. Let us now move to multiplication." Even in our humor the "gag" threatens to replace the shrewd observer of the human comedy. I have seen an elementary school play fashioned entirely on a parody of radio commercials. It was a brave effort to tie the 10-second atoms together.

I do not wish to make it seem as if our present state of education is a decline from some previous Golden Age. For I do not think there has ever been a Golden Age in American public education. The difference now is that we can afford dross less well than ever before. The volume of positive knowledge increases at a rapid rate. Atomizing it into facts-to-be-filed is not likely to produce the kind of broad grasp that will be needed in the world of the next quarter century. And it is certainly no training for the higher education that more and more of our children will be getting.

I have not meant the above as a plea for the "central subject" or the "project" method of teaching. It is, rather, a plea for the recognition of the continuity of knowledge. One hears professional educators speak of "coverage," that certain topics must be covered. There are indeed many things that must be covered, but they are not unconnected things. The object of learning is to gain facts in a context of connectivity that permits the facts to be used generatively. The larger the number of isolated facts, the more staggering the number of connections between them—unless one can reduce them to some deeper order. Not all of them can [be so reduced]. Yet it is an ideal worth striving for, be it in the fifth grade or in graduate school. As Robert Oppenheimer put it in a recent address before the American Academy, "Everything cannot be connected with everything in the world we live in. Everything can be connected with anything."

THE EMBARRASSMENT OF PASSION

I should like to consider now the guiding myth. Let me begin with a summary of the young Christopher Columbus as he is presented in a popular social studies textbook. Young Chris is walking along the waterfront in his home town and gets to wondering where all those ships go. Eventually he comes back to his brother's cobbler shop and exclaims, "Gee, Bart, I wonder where all those ships go, whether maybe if they just kept going they wouldn't come back because the world is round." Bart replies with pleasant brotherly encouragement. Chris is a well-adjusted kid. Bart is a nice big brother. And where is the passion that drove this obsessed man across uncharted oceans? What impelled this Columbus with such force that he finally enlisted the aid of Ferdinand and Isabella over the protest of their advisors? Everything is there in the story except the essential truth—the fanatical urge to explore in an age of exploration, the sense of an expanding world. Columbus did not have a schoolboy's whim, nor was he the well-adjusted grownup of this account. He was a man driven to explore, to control. The justification for the pablum that makes up such textbooks is that such accounts as these touch more directly on the life of the child.

What is this "life of the child" as seen by text writers and publishers? It is an image created out of an ideal of adjustment. The ideal of adjustment has little place for the driven man, the mythic hero, the idiosyncratic style. Its ideal is mediocentrism, reasonableness above all, being nice. Such an ideal does not touch closely the deeper life of the child. It does not appeal to the dark but energizing forces that lie close beneath the surface. The Old Testament, the Greek myths, the Norse legends—these are the embarrassing chronicles of men of passion. They were devised to catch and preserve the power and tragedy of the human condition—and its ambiguity, too. In their place, we have substituted the noncontroversial and the banal.

Here a special word is needed about the concept of "expressing yourself," which is our conception of how one may engage the deeper impulses of the child. I have seen a book review class in a public school in which the children had the choice of reporting on any book they wished to choose, in or out of the school library, and where the discussion by the other children had to do entirely with the manner in which the reciting child presented his material. Nothing was said about the book in the discussion. The emphasis was on nice presentation, and whether the book sounded interesting. I have no quarrel with rewarding self-expression. I wonder simply whether it is not perhaps desirable, too, to make known the canons of excellence. The children in this class were learning to be seductive in their recounting; they were not concerned with an honest accounting of the human condition. The books they had read were cute, there was no excitement in them, none to be extracted. Increasingly the children in American elementary schools grow out of touch with the guiding myths. Self-expression is not a substitute. Adjustment is a worthy ideal, if not an ennobling one. But when we strive to attain it by shutting our eyes to the turmoils of human life, we will not get adjustment, but a niggling fear of the unusual and the excellent.

THE QUALITY OF TEACHERS

I do not wish to mince words. The educational and cultural level of the majority of American teachers is not impressive. On the whole they do not have a good grasp of the subject matter that they are teaching; courses on method will not replace the absent subject matter. In time and with teaching experience this deficiency is often remedied. But in so many cases there is no time: the turnover in the teaching profession as we all know is enormous; the median number of years of teaching before departure for marriage or motherhood is around three.

This leaves us with a small core of experienced teachers. Do we use them to teach the new teachers on the job? No. The organization of the school with respect to utilization of talent is something short of imaginative. It consists of a principal on top and a group of discrete teachers beneath her, and that is all. In large metropolitan high schools this is sometimes supplemented by having departments at the head of which is an experienced teacher. The communication that goes on between teachers is usually at a highly informal level and can scarcely be called comprehensive. It is usually about problem children, not about social studies or mathematics or how to bring literature alive.

I would urge, and I believe that educators have taken steps in this direction, that we use our more experienced teachers for on-the-job training of less experienced, new teachers. I would also urge that there be established some means whereby the substantive topics taught in our elementary and high schools be included in some kind of special extension program provided by our eighteen hundred colleges and universities in the United States for the benefit of teachers. I am not speaking only of teachers colleges, but rather of all institutions of higher learning. Institutions of higher learning have a responsibility to the lower schools, and it can be exercised by arranging for continuous contact between those, for example, who teach history at the college level and those who are teaching history or social studies at the lower levels. And so, too, with literature or mathematics, or languages. To assume that somehow a teacher can be "prepared" simply by going through teacher training and then by taking courses on methods in summer school is, I think, fallacious. Often it is the case that the teacher, like her students, has not learned the material well enough to cross the barrier from learning to thinking.

III

It is quite plain, I think, that the task of improving the American schools is not simply one of technique—however comforting it would be to some professional educators to think so. What is at issue, rather, is a deeper problem, one that is more philosophical than psychological or technological in scope. Let me put it in all innocence. What do we conceive to be the end product of our educational effort? I cannot help but feel that this rather overly simplified question has become obscured in cant. There is such an official din in support of the view that we are "training well-rounded human beings to be responsible citizens" that one hesitates to raise the question whether such an objective is a meaningful guide to what one does in classroom teaching. Surely the objective is worthy, and it has influenced the techniques of education in America, not always happily. For much of what we have called the embarrassment of passion can, I think, be traced to this objective, and so too the blandness of the social studies curriculum. The ideal, sadly, has also led to the standardization of mediocrity by a failure of the schools to challenge the full capacity of the talented student.

Since the war, there has been a perceptible shift in the problems being faced by schools and parents alike. It is the New Competition. Will Johnny and Sally be able to get into the college of their first choice or, indeed, into any college at all? The origins of the concern are obvious enough—the "baby bulge" has made itself felt. The results are not all bad, I would urge, or need not be. There are, to be sure, severe problems of overcrowding that exacerbate the difficulties already inherent in public education. And it is true that parental pressures for grades and production are increasing the proportion of children with "learning blocks" being referred to child guidance clinics.

But the pressures and the competition are also rekindling our awareness of excellence and how it may be nurtured. The shake-up of our smugness by the evident technical thrust of the Soviet Union has added to this awareness. Let me urge that it is this new awareness that requires shaping of expression in the form of a new set of ideals. Grades, admission to college, followed by admission to graduate school—these are surely not the ideals but, rather, the external signs.

Perhaps the fitting ideal is precisely as we have described it earlier in these pages, the active pragmatic ideal of leaping the barrier from learning into thinking. It matters not *what* we have learned. What we can *do* with what we have learned: this is the issue. The pragmatic argument has long been elaborated on extrinsic grounds, that the higher one has gone in the educational system the greater the economic gain. Indeed, at least one eminent economist has proposed that parents finance college education for their children by long-term loans to be repaid by the children on the almost certain knowledge that higher earning results from such education. All of this is the case, and it is indeed admirable that educational progress and economic success are so intimately linked in our society. I would only suggest that the pragmatic ideal be applied also to the intrinsic aspects of education. Let us not judge our students simply on *what* they know. That is the philosophy of the quiz program. Rather, let them be judged on what they can generate from what they know—how well they can leap the barrier from learning to thinking.

PART 5

Intelligence and Abilities

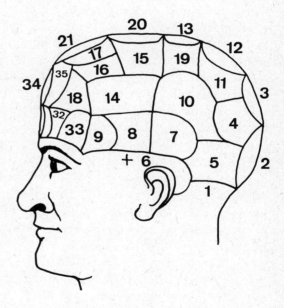

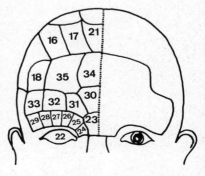

Intelligence and the more specific abilities (like manual dexterity) are adaptive powers, too. As with sensation and perception and learning and thinking, the nature and extent of these qualities determine how well a person can cope with his or her environment.

Like virtually everything else in psychology, the development of intellectual powers is governed by physiological, psychological, and sociological variables. The effects of brain damage on intellectual functioning furnish a gross kind of evidence that body influences mind, but subtler evidence is also available. For example, Kessler's article in this section cites research that indicates that a mother's nutrition during pregnancy may affect her child's tested intelligence later in life. Sociological forces, too, have their effect. Both Kessler and Maccoby describe the influences of different social milieus: living in an orphanage versus living at home, growing up with emotionally disturbed parents, leading an overprotected childhood, and so forth. Finally, some research points out that psychological factors also affect the intellect; Maccoby mentions studies that suggest that (when IQ scores do change over time) passive, shy, dependent children will show declining scores, competitive and dominant children, rising ones.

The mental testing movement for which psychology is so well known is intimately connected with studies of intelligence and abilities. The history of this movement is fascinating. Three thousand years ago, the Chinese, who were very much concerned with the nature and extent of human abilities, developed a series of tests in writing, arithmetic, law, agriculture, fiscal administration, and other subjects so that government jobs could be awarded on the basis of personal talent. This same polygamy of intelligence and abilities, testing, and personnel decisions was prominent in ancient Greece and continues to thrive in contemporary America. The process common to each of these societies has been observing that individual differences do exist, defining and measuring these differences, and putting those measurements to some practical use.

When you study the articles in this section, pay special attention to the different factors that govern the growth of intelligence and to the more recent trends in the mental testing movement.

Measuring Differences Between People

MARVIN D. DUNNETTE

In the first selection, Marvin Dunnette discusses diverse and competing attempts
to define and measure intelligence and abilities. Although he writes from the
perspective of an industrial psychologist interested in choosing among different
applicants for a job, much of what he says applies to other kinds of personnel
selection (for example, college admissions testing) and also to testing in general.
His bent is strongly empirical; that is, he is interested in facts and observations
rather than speculations and offhand theorizing.

Much of his present discussion revolves around a distinction (borrowed from
Cronbach) between "maximum performance measures" and "typical behavior
measures." Maximum performance measures are attempts to find out how much
or how well a person can do at a particular task, like a college examination. Typical behavior measures deal not with what a person can do when he or she is
really trying but with what a person usually does, thinks, or feels. Perhaps the
clearest way to distinguish the two is to point out that typical behavior measures
never involve right or wrong answers, while maximum performance measures, or
"tests," always do.

With this distinction in mind, Dunnette traces the modern history of the
mental testing movement and distinguishes different trends in the construction
of both kinds of measuring instruments. Pay particular attention to his arguments for the empirical approach, but note the cautions he offers about "blind"
empiricism.

The Recognition of Human Differences

For centuries, philosophers speculated about the nature of man. Kant argued
against a science of psychology because he believed that human feelings,
sensations, images, and thoughts could never be accessible to observation and
measurement. But this does not rule out the observation of human *behavior*
and of the external conditions or stimuli under which the behavior occurs.

The early Greeks were strongly aware of human differences in the ability to learn. Socrates developed and refined tests of how much his students learned, and he used the tests to assess and to enrich their learning. The Greeks also graded boys on an elaborate series of physical tests to keep tab on them as they matured and acquired the skills of manhood. Plato clearly recognized the differing abilities of men and saw the need for accurate assignment of individuals to the particular occupations (soldier, statesman, teacher, etc.) for which they were best suited so that they would make maximum contributions to society.

MEASUREMENT OF HUMAN DIFFERENCES

However, true measurement of individual differences (that is, the assignment of quantitative values to observable differences in human behavior) had to await someone with a desire to understand differences between people and who had the wherewithal for developing mathematical methods for measuring such differences. Both the desire and the means were provided by the genius of Sir Francis Galton, who founded the study of individual differences. In his book *Hereditary Genius*, published in 1869, he presented the elements of a system for classifying men according to their eminence (abilities). He stated that true eminence was extremely rare, characterizing only one person out of every 4,000, that *all* human abilities were distributed according to the normal probability curve, and that persons could therefore be classified according to the known frequencies of the normal distribution.

Galton's first efforts (illustrated in Figure 1) simply ordered people in a number of broad categories. However, he also recognized the desirability of

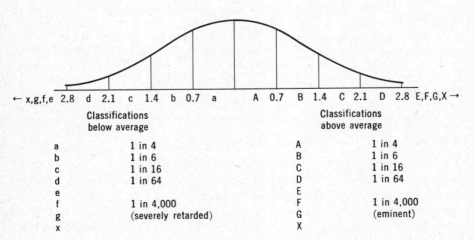

FIGURE 1. *Galton's classification of persons according to their abilities and the proportion of persons in each class.*

expressing each person's relative standing in the form of a single score or index, and, to do this, he invented the standard score.

The Development of Psychological Measures

Galton's concern with eminence and the relative contributions made by men to society led him and others to seek ways of measuring human differences in learning ability. At first, it was expected that learning ability should be reflected in such things as sensory sensitivity, quickness of response, and various physical proficiencies. As a consequence, the "mental tests" of the late 1800s consisted of reaction times and measures of tactual sensitivity, keenness of vision and hearing, strength of grip, tapping speed, and the like. However, differences on these measures showed no relation to differences in the ability to learn as reflected by school grades or teachers' ratings of pupil performance.

TOWARD COMPLEX PROCESSES

In 1895, the French psychologist Alfred Binet published an article severely criticizing the practices of sensory and motor testing. With his colleague Henri, Binet argued that more complex mental processes should be studied; he emphasized the importance of studying and *measuring* the higher faculties such as memory, imagery, imagination, attention, and comprehension—an argument that probably would have been "laughed out of court" had it not been for the groundwork laid by Galton's earlier emphasis on the meaningfulness and importance of measuring individual differences and the classification of persons "according to their natural abilities."

During the next decade, Binet tried a number of short tasks designed to tap the complex mental processes of school children. He reasoned that as children grow they are exposed to similar things, and they have opportunities to learn and to develop skills in dealing with the world they live in. He thought mental ability might be estimated by simply observing how a child copes with tasks similar to the ones he has faced in his day-to-day activities. Binet asked youngsters to identify familiar objects, name the months in order, name coins, arrange scrambled words into meaningful sentences, and define abstract words. These tasks obviously were far more complex and closer to the kind of functioning demanded in the real world than the reaction-time, sensory, and motor tests being espoused by most of the laboratory psychologists of the time.

Binet was an *empiricist* who did not completely trust his own judgment for choosing test items. He demanded that children's responses to each of his test tasks be compared with other aspects of their behavior. He reasoned that, to be useful, a test item should yield different responses from children identified by their teachers as quick learners and those identified as slow learners. Thus, Binet was probably the first psychologist to use methods of *item analysis* to decide whether responses to any given item were or were not related to important behaviors outside the test. As we shall see, this *empirical* approach to test development has much to recommend it and is, in fact, the method used by the authors of nearly all our more widely used and most effective psychological tests today.

In Binet's approach, children of the same age were rated by their teacher as "quick" and "slow" learners, and these ratings were compared with the children's performance on several simple tasks. (See hypothetical data in Table 1.)

TABLE 1.

	Percentage of Children Performing Task Correctly		Difference
	Quick Learners (N = 10)	Slow Learners (N = 10)	(Quick—Slow)
Task 1: Count to five without error.	60%	20%	+40%
Task 2: Follow a lighted match with the eyes.	90	100	−10
Task 3: Use the word *home* correctly in a sentence.	80	60	+20
Task 4: Define the meaning of the word *sorry*.	20	0	+20
Task 5: Point to objects of different colors, red, yellow, and blue.	70	20	+50

Tasks 1 and 5 discriminate sharply between quick and slow learners. Many more quick learners perform the two tasks correctly. Tasks 1 and 5 can be said, therefore, to be good indicators of whatever behaviors are involved in this particular teacher's rating of learning ability; tasks 2, 3, and 4 are poor indicators. Tasks 1 and 5 are worthy of further study as possible measures of learning ability or "intelligence." However, knowledge about these tasks would need to be extended in a number of ways. Since the numbers of children used for this comparison were so small, it would be well to repeat the study on other children to see whether the same two tasks prove to be best. This would provide other sets of teacher observations against which to compare the results. Moreover, it would be well to obtain information on other kinds of estimates of learning ability. Another one Binet used was a simple age comparison; he assumed that older children, because of their greater exposure to learning situations and because of their greater growth, should develop more ability to learn than younger children.

THE EMPIRICAL METHOD OF TEST DEVELOPMENT

We have gone into detail in describing Binet's approach because it so aptly illustrates the crucial steps in the empirical development of psychological measures.

First, people are observed to differ in a particular behavior—a behavior sufficiently important to society that it seems worthwhile to seek to understand it better. For Binet, the important behavior was *learning ability*.

Second, behavioral observations are made of a number of individuals; they are rated, labeled, or categorized according to the amount they show of the behavior being studied. For Binet, teacher's ratings, school attainment, and age comparisons served this purpose.

Third, a series of standardized tasks, questions, statements, or other stimuli are prepared which seem to be related to the behavior being studied. As we have seen, Binet rejected sensory and motor testing in favor of developing more complex tasks that seemed more accurate indicators of learning ability.

Fourth, the stimuli are presented to the individuals whose behavior has been observed; their responses are studied (item analysis) to discover which stimuli elicit behavior related to the behavior being studied. Most psychological measures *do not* measure the relevant behavior directly. As Chauncey and Dobbin [4] have pointed out, this method of empirically studying the responses to test items is very much like the methods used by physicists to detect the forces released by the atom. The cloud chamber does not measure the atom or its components directly, but the tracks of ionizing particles do permit deductions about the nature of the atom and the forces holding it together. In the same way, responses shown to be related to observations of the behavior we label *learning ability* enable the psychologist to deduce things about learning ability. Binet's greatest contribution was his application of empirical methods to the measurement of an important area of human behavior.

Measuring Intelligence

In 1905, the first Binet Test, consisting of thirty tasks ranging from very simple to rather difficult, was published and began to be used in the Paris schools. He called his series of tasks a *metrical scale of intelligence*, and with this contribution Binet set off an immediate worldwide response.

It was soon apparent to other investigators that the Binet Test yielded accurate estimates of children's mental status and good predictions of school accomplishment. In this country, Lewis Terman of Stanford University translated, revised, and greatly extended the Binet Test. In 1916, his Stanford-Binet Test was published; it consisted of ninety tasks arranged in order of increasing difficulty. Terman chose to express scores on the test as an Intelligence Quotient (IQ),[1] the ratio (multiplied by 100) between an individual's "mental age" (calculated from the tasks he successfully completed) and his chronological age. With this test, the measurement of individual differences came of age; an important aspect of human variation had been studied and a measure successfully developed. This development was met with a widespread response of research activity directed toward learning more about this new test and the nature of the underlying construct (intelligence) it was designed to measure.

THE GENERAL FACTOR, FACTOR ANALYSIS, AND MULTIPLE FACTORS

Charles Spearman, an English statistician and contemporary of Binet's, held [12] that humans possessed an underlying *general intelligence* or *g* factor accompanied by a myriad of *specific* abilities called *s* factors. He argued that a high correlation between grades in French and grades in the study of the classics was evidence of the common action of the underlying ability, *g*, but that the correlation was less than perfect because of the singular actions of abilities specific to the study of French and to the study of the classics.

The correlational procedures Spearman used to support his theoretical statements about intelligence marked the beginning of *factor analysis*. As we noted in the last chapter, factor analysis is a method for summarizing the correlations among a large number of measures in terms of a smaller number of clusters or factors. It is presumed that the factors constitute relatively more basic or fundamental dimensions underlying the many different measures on which the correlation matrix is based.

Subsequent factor analysts, notably L. L. Thurstone and J. P. Guilford, have argued that several factors are necessary to account for the range of observable differences among people. Intelligence appears to be many faceted, made up of a number of broad groupings of relatively independent aptitudes. For example, Thurstone concluded that the major cognitive abilities of man could be grouped into seven categories:

> *Verbal comprehension:* to understand the meaning of words and their relations to each other; to comprehend readily and accurately what is read; measured by test items such as:
>
> Which one of the following words means most nearly the same as *effusive?*
>
> 1. evasive
> 2. affluent
> 3. gushing

[1] The choice of IQ as a method of expressing scores was unfortunate, for it implied that "intelligence" was a global, all-encompassing, and unchanging human quality. The IQ came to be widely misinterpreted and misused. Finally, in 1960, it was decided to express scores on the third edition of the Stanford-Binet Test in terms of standard score units with a mean of 100 and a standard deviation of 16.

4. realistic
5. lethargic

Word fluency: to be fluent in naming or making words, such as making smaller words from the letters in a large one or playing anagrams; measured by test items such as:

> Using the letters in the word *Minneapolis,* write as many four letter words as you can in the next two minutes.
>
> ─────────
> ─────────
> ─────────
> ─────────

Number aptitude: to be speedy and accurate in making simple arithmetic calculations; measured by test items such as:

> Carry out the following calculations:
>
> $$346 \qquad 8732 \qquad 422 \times 32 = \text{─────}$$
> $$+722 \qquad -4843 \qquad 3630 \div 5 = \text{─────}$$

Inductive reasoning: to be able to discover a rule or principle and apply it to the solution of a problem, such as determining what is to come next in a series of numbers or words; measured by test items such as:

> What number should come next in the sequence of the following five numbers?
>
> $$\begin{matrix} 1 & & 2 & & \\ & 5 & & 4 & 3 \end{matrix}$$
>
> 1. 7
> 2. 1
> 3. 2
> 4. 4
> 5. 3

Memory: to have a good rote memory for paired words, lists of numbers, etc.; measured by test items such as:

> The examinee may be given a list of letters paired with symbols such as:
>
> | | | |
> |---|---|---|---|
> | A | * | E | ? |
> | B | , | F | ; |
> | C | ☆ | G | : |
> | D | ! | H | . |
>
> He is given a brief period to memorize the pairs. Then he is told to turn the page and write the appropriate symbols after each of the letters appearing there.

Spatial aptitude: to perceive fixed geometric relations among figures accurately and to be able to visualize their manipulation in space; measured by test items such as:

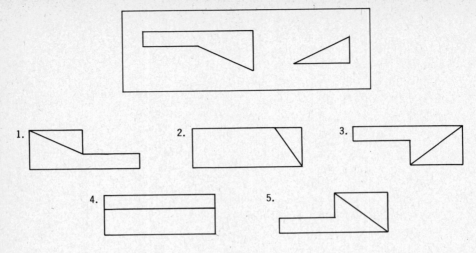

Which figure would result if the two pieces in the picture above were put together?

Perceptual speed: to perceive visual details quickly and accurately; measured by test items such as:

Make a check mark in front of each pair below in which the numbers are identical.

1. 367773————367713
2. 471352————471352
3. 581688————581688
4. 324579————334579
5. 875989————876898

EMPIRICISM AND FACTOR ANALYSIS

At this point, it is well to note some of the differences between Binet's approach to measuring intelligence and the factor-analytic approach. First, even though Binet did believe that human cognitive ability (intelligence) consisted of a number of faculties such as imagination, memory, attention, and comprehension, he made no pretense of separately identifying and measuring each one. Instead, he found it more useful to define intelligence as the sum total of a student's proficiency on all the problems or test items. This approach differs from that of factor analysis because factor analysis seeks to classify human abilities according to the patterns of their similarities and differences as expressed by correlation coefficients.

Second, as we have seen, Binet's justification for the selection of test items was an empirical relationship between success on an item and some observation of nontest behavior such as teachers' ratings or other estimates of school success or intellectual growth. In contrast, factor analysis is directed toward sampling and classifying adequately a large domain of *tested* abilities. The names or labels given to factors (such as Inductive Reasoning, Number

Ability, or Word Fluency) are based on the investigator's knowledge of or presumptions about the content of the tests making up a factor rather than on any effort to classify observed behavior outside the test. This characteristic of the factor-analytic approach is one reason why efforts to show relationships between scores on factorially developed tests and nontest behavior are often disappointing. As we shall see in Chapters 4 and 5, job behavior and behavioral observations of persons on jobs appear to be very complex factorially. We should not be surprised, therefore, to learn that any one factor of tested ability may be only a limited sampling and, therefore, a rather poor indicator of the complex behaviors demanded in most job situations. Because of this, it is often necessary to combine several of the factored tests of ability, and in many instances it is more efficient to use Binet's empirical approach.

Nevertheless, the classification of human tested abilities is important theoretically, and such a taxonomy may also take on added practical significance when more clearly defined and more complete classifications of nontest and job behaviors become available. Because of this, the work of factor analysts has continued unabated. By analyzing human tested abilities more and more thoroughly (for example, by factor analyzing sets of tests *within* each of the broad groupings defined by Thurstone), nearly 60 additional factors have been found.

THE THREE FACES OF INTELLECT

In 1956 Guilford [8, 9] summarized his own and others' factor-analytic results, systematizing for the first time the many factors observed. He viewed mental organization as lying along three dimensions. Along one dimension are the *operations* (the things a person can do); along a second are the *contents* (the kinds of material or content on which the operations may be performed); and along the third dimension are the *products* (the outcomes or results of the operations being performed on one or more of the contents). The classifications within each of the three areas are as follows:

Operations
1. Cognition—becoming aware of the existence of something.
2. Memory—remembering what was once known.
3. Convergent Thinking—organizing content in such a way as to produce a single correct solution to a problem.
4. Divergent Thinking—utilizing content to produce a wide range of variety of possible solutions to a problem.
5. Evaluation—making judgments or decisions.

Contents
1. Semantic—contents involving language.
2. Symbolic—contents involving numerical ideas and concepts.
3. Figural—contents involving various configurations, patterns, or shapes.
4. Behavioral—contents involving the way persons behave toward one another.

Products
1. Units—bits of information.
2. Classes—groupings of units.
3. Relations—similarities, differences, and contingencies among classes.
4. Systems—groupings of relations.
5. Transformations—concepts of how things change.
6. Implications—projections of concepts to deduce events that have not yet been observed.

According to Helmstadter [11], a person performing successfully all the operations containing semantic content would be said to have high verbal ability; a person performing all operations containing symbolic content would have high mathematical ability; one performing effectively the operations with figural content would have high spatial or artistic ability; and a person who could recognize, remember, solve, and evaluate contents involving interpersonal behavior would be said to possess high social ability.

Obviously, Guilford's suggested taxonomy of human abilities is a far cry from the intentions of Binet when he set out rather simply to develop indicators of school learning ability. Even so, it is interesting that Binet's early tests and certainly the 1960 revision of the Stanford-Binet Test include items sampling many of the factors suggested by Guilford's classification. The most notable lack, perhaps, is in the Operations area of Divergent Thinking. School performance, teachers' ratings, learning ability, etc., have typically emphasized convergent thinking—that is, finding a single correct answer to problems. It is no surprise that Binet "missed" this important aspect of human ability; he based his selection of items on ratings of nontest behaviors that failed to emphasize divergent thinking abilities. Only recently have psychologists and educators come to recognize the potential importance of the divergent thinking abilities in jobs placing a premium on creativeness and originality. The rationally derived tests of divergent thinking may fill the gap caused by Binet's early dependence on behavioral observations that were incomplete estimates of the ability to cope successfully with problems. Raw empiricism may succeed in developing good indicators of nontest behaviors, but it may miss important aspects of human variation if the criterion observations of the nontest behaviors are deficient or limited in some way. Ideally, both methods should be employed as we seek to measure individual differences and to understand human behavior more fully. The history of the development of our present knowledge of what constitutes human intelligence and the specification of the wide variety of human abilities is a clear illustration of the interactive and additive contributions of the two methods.

Measuring Other Human Differences

MOTOR SKILLS

So far, we have traced and discussed the development of measures of human cognitive abilities—those abilities crucial in developing an awareness and understanding of the elements of our environment. We have said nothing about the physical manipulation of objects in the environment. This involves the specification and measurement of *motor skills*, many of which have obvious relevance to the world of work. For example, the job of secretary involves not only a wide range of cognitive abilities such as verbal comprehension, perceptual speed, memory, and reasoning, but also, possibly, whatever motor skills may be necessary to handle a typewriter adequately. Scores of other jobs could be named (for example, bricklayer, auto mechanic, and watch repairman) that require relatively greater amounts of motor proficiency. Thus, the measurement of motor abilities is also important if an effective job of personnel selection and placement is to be done.

The major conclusion from a wealth of research on motor skills is that these abilities are highly specific. Tests designed to measure skills such as finger dexterity, steadiness, speed of response, and eye-hand coordination show only low intercorrelations. Summarizing over a decade of factor-analytic results with motor skills tests, Fleishman [6] concluded that there are eleven fairly independent groupings of motor skills. These are:

1. *Control precision*, involving tasks requiring finely controlled muscular adjustments, such as moving a lever to a precise setting.

2. *Multilimb coordination*, involving the ability to coordinate the movements of a number of limbs simultaneously, such as packing a box with both hands.

3. *Response orientation*, involving the ability to make correct and accurate movements in relation to a stimulus under highly speeded conditions, such as reaching out and flicking a switch when a warning horn sounds.

4. *Reaction time*, involving the speed of a person's response when a stimulus appears, such as pressing a key in response to a bell.

5. *Speed of arm movement*, involving the speed of gross arm movements where accuracy is not required, such as gathering trash or debris and throwing it into a large pile.

6. *Rate control*, involving the ability to make continuous motor adjustments relative to a moving target changing in speed and direction, such as holding a rod on a moving rotor.

7. *Manual dexterity*, involving skillful arm and hand movements in handling rather large objects under speeded conditions, such as placing blocks rapidly into a form board.

8. *Finger dexterity*, involving skillful manipulation of small objects (such as nuts and bolts) with the fingers.

9. *Arm-hand steadiness*, involving the ability to make precise arm-hand positioning movements that do not require strength or speed, such as threading a needle.

10. *Wrist-finger speed*, involving rapid tapping movements with the wrist and fingers, such as transmitting a continuous signal with a telegraphic key.

11. *Aiming,* involving an extremely narrow ability defined by a test in which the examinee places dots in circles as rapidly as possible.

Unfortunately, not much research has been done on the relative importance of each of these basic motor skills in successfully performing various industrial tasks. However, tests are available to measure each of the above abilities, either singly or in combination, and one or several of them may be added to a selection and placement test battery on the basis of job analysis results.

TYPICAL BEHAVIOR MEASURES

Cronbach [5] has chosen the term *maximum performance* measures to denote tests of cognition and motor abilities. Such tests are designed primarily to determine how much a person can do or how well he can perform on any given test. In contrast, a number of tests have been developed with no distinction between so-called right and wrong answers. Cronbach calls these tests *typical behavior* measures. These are the tests of attitudes, interests, personality, and the like; their prime purpose is to yield descriptions of an individual's typical behavior as he pursues his daily activities. There are no right or wrong answers except as they are descriptive of individual behavioral tendencies; instead of just one scoring key, such inventories tend to have several—each representing a mode or pattern of observed behavior relevant for describing differences between people. Information of this kind has obvious potential importance for making selection decisions because it indicates the pattern of behavior to be expected from a person after he has been placed on a job.

As a means of describing the kinds of typical behavior tests available, we can consider the methods used for developing such tests and some of the results obtained. The three major methods are *armchair theoretic, factor analytic,* and *empirical.*

THE ARMCHAIR THEORIST.   Based on his pet theory of human behavior, a test developer might simply sit at his desk (or in his armchair) and devise a set of stimulus materials (such as verbal statements, ambiguous pictures, ink-blots) to be used in eliciting responses from persons. He would then administer the test materials to a group of persons and decide, on the basis of his theory, what their responses might mean in terms of each person's major behavior tendencies. The final step would be to confirm or disconfirm the behavioral inferences by observing and measuring the actual subsequent behavior of the persons tested. However, this last step is very rarely undertaken by users of this method. Instead, evaluation of such tests usually occurs from the same place they were created—the armchair.

It should be obvious that the armchair approach has little to recommend it for developing tests useful in selection and placement programs. Most existing behavioral theories have at best doubtful validity, and it is unlikely that any test developer is so omniscient that he can accurately intuit what a person's responses to a set of stimuli may mean in terms of later observed behavior. Unfortunately, however, many tests and methods of this kind are still being used in industrial selection programs. Some examples of such methods are handwriting analysis, the Rorschach Test, and the Thematic Apperception Test.

THE FACTOR ANALYST. The factor-analytic approach should already be fairly familiar from our discussion of developing and defining cognitive and motor skill measures. Its use in developing typical behavior tests usually begins with a lengthy listing of terms (for example, all possible adjectives) or statements commonly used to describe human behavior. Observers then use the terms in rating or describing the actual behavior shown by persons who are well known to them. For example, sorority or fraternity members might describe each other, or clinical psychologists might describe their patients. The descriptions can then be correlated and factor-analyzed to yield the basic dimensions (taxonomy) of typically observed human behaviors. This approach has been used in many studies and as a basis for developing many inventories. Eight such studies have recently been summarized by Tupes and Christal [17]. The persons rated in the various studies ranged from airmen with only high school education to male and female college students and first-year graduate students. The observers carrying out the ratings ranged from psychologically unsophisticated persons (for example, the airmen) to clinical psychologists and psychiatrists with years of experience in observing human behavior. In spite of these wide differences among subjects and raters, the same five factors of typical behavior emerged from all studies.

1. *Surgency*—the tendency to be assertive, talkative, outgoing, and cheerful as opposed to being meek, mild, and reserved.
2. *Agreeableness*—the tendency to be good natured, cooperative, emotionally mature, and attentive to people.
3. *Dependability*—the tendency to be orderly, responsible, conscientious, and persevering.
4. *Emotional stability*—the tendency to be poised, calm and self-sufficient.
5. *Culture*—the tendency to be imaginative, cultured, socially polished, and independently minded.

The factor-analytic approach has a good deal to recommend it because it starts with observable behavioral tendencies and seeks to identify the minimum number of dimensions necessary for usefully describing the behavior shown by people in normal day-to-day intercourse. As suggested by the Tupes and Christal summary, factor-analytic studies have yielded a stable and useful classification of different modes of human interpersonal behavior. Tests designed to measure these behavioral tendencies are available and warrant inclusion in experimental selection and placement test batteries.

THE EMPIRICIST. The empiric approach follows much the same pattern of test development used by Binet and outlined in the early pages of this chapter. Whereas Binet was seeking a measure indicative of learning ability, the method has been employed to identify other patterns of behavior. The method has been used with notable success to identify the characteristic patterns of likes and dislikes of persons who have entered and persisted in a variety of professions (physician, lawyer, engineer, personnel director, etc.) and skilled trades (electrician, plumber, carpenter, etc.) In these instances, the behavior chosen for study has been occupational choice and occupational persistence, and the groups against which the statements of various kinds of likes and dislikes have been compared (item analyzed) are classified simply on the basis of occupational belonging. Two of the most widely used and successful measures of vocational interest were developed in this way—the *Strong Vocational Interest Blank* (SVIB) and the *Minnesota Vocational Interest Inventory* (MVII).

Other patterns of behavior, less easily defined and specified, have been used as a basis for test development. For example, the first scales of the widely used *Minnesota Multiphasic Personality Inventory* (MMPI) were chosen by comparing responses of groups of persons with different psychiatric disturbances (paranoia, schizophrenia, severe depression, etc.) with those given by emotionally undisturbed ("well") persons. Thus, the MMPI has come to play an important role in psychiatric diagnosis.

A similar test is the *California Psychological Inventory* (CPI). In this test the responses have been validated against "normal" patterns of observed behavior (such as dominance, sociability, social maturity, achievement motivation, etc.). Here, the behavioral criterion consisted of ratings of observed behavioral patterns occurring in everyday life. Item responses differentiating persons with different rated behaviors were chosen and scored to form the various scales; thus, the typical behaviors measured by the CPI are potentially more relevant to the world of work than the psychiatrically relevant behaviors tapped by the MMPI. Table 2 shows the test author's listing of the kinds of behaviors that research has shown are associated with high and low scores on each of the CPI scales.

Since the empirical method is so strongly behaviorally based, it is the most desirable method for developing typical behavior tests. Consider, for example, the relative degree of confidence that may be attached to behavioral inferences based respectively on armchair and on empirically developed tests. Experience shows the chances to be extremely slight that inferences derived from armchair inventories will prove valid. This is because so many *untested* assumptions necessarily lie between the enunciation of a behavior theory and the ultimate observation of behavior in the real world. Even if the major elements of a behavior theory undergirding a test were essentially correct (and this, unfortunately, is extremely unlikely for most of psychology's present "theories"), there would be no assurance that the stimuli (test items) chosen intuitively or the theorists' inferences about the behavioral meaning of an examinee's responses would have any semblance of reality or fact.

In contrast, the empirical method places no such burden on the shoulders of the test author. He simply accumulates experimental evidence that certain test item responses are or are not associated with certain defined patterns of behavior in the real world, and he chooses for his test those responses that are empirically related to the particular pattern of behavior he is interested in. There probably is no more clear example of the failure of the armchair method than of the failure of early sensory tests to reflect the real world of human behavior. Binet was successful because he broke with current theorizing and proceeded to select his test stimuli on empirical rather than on theoretical grounds.

POSSIBLE PROBLEMS WITH EMPIRICISM. It is imperative in the development of any test or specialized scoring key to determine the relative stability of the association between item responses and behavior patterns. It is possible, particularly if only a few persons have been used as experimental subjects, that apparent response differences may be the result of only random or chance fluctuations. The best way to check stability of any scoring key is *cross-validation*, as discussed in the last chapter. (A similar approach—the one used by Binet—is simply to carry out item analyses on several different groups and to select for the final test or scale only those items and responses showing consistent differences between persons with different observed behaviors—for example, high- versus low-rated learning ability.) The necessity for cross-validation is obvious; it is a safeguard for assuring that empirical results are based on real and not on chance differences. Even so, some tests on the market have *not* been properly cross-validated against the behavioral descriptions they are designed to measure. No confidence can be placed in a typical behavior test that has not been properly cross-validated.

A second problem with empirically developed tests grows out of the very strengths such tests possess. Such a test identifies certain specific behaviors used as the basis for item validation and selection, but little additional meaning can be attached initially to scores on the test. The lack of any cohesive theory during test development and the dependence of item selection on a rather narrowly specified behavior may result in interpretive sterility for scores. A critic of such a test might, for example, say, "Yes, I know that a high score means that a person has likes and dislikes similar to those of lawyers, but what does this *really* mean in terms of the behavior I might expect from such a person?" Such a critic is really asking for further definition of relationships between scores on the test and other observed behaviors. The initial empirical development of a test does not usually provide such additional information. Ordinarily, the test author should assume responsibility, along with other interested researchers, for seeking out and publicizing lawful relations between his measure and additional behavior observations and measures. The process is never ending, and a variety of research methods may be used.

Consider some of the research with the *Strong Vocational Interest Blank*. The first scales showed substantial differences between the likes and dislikes

TABLE 2. *Class I: Measures of Poise, Ascendancy, and Self-assurance*

High Scorers Tend to Be Seen as:	Scale and Purpose	Low Scorers Tend to Be Seen as:
Aggressive, confident, persistent, and planful; as being persuasive and verbally fluent; as self-reliant and independent; and as having leadership potential and initiative.	1. Do (dominance). To assess factors of leadership ability, dominance, persistence, and social initiative.	Retiring, inhibited, commonplace, indifferent, silent and unassuming; as being slow in thought and action; as avoiding of situations of tension and decision; and as lacking in self confidence.
Ambitious, active, forceful, insightful, resourceful, and versatile; as being ascendant and self-seeking; effective in communication; and as having personal scope and breadth of interests.	2. Cs (capacity for status). To serve as an index of an individual's capacity for status (not his actual or achieved status). The scale attempts to measure the personal qualities and attributes which underlie and lead to status.	Apathetic, shy, conventional, dull, mild, simple, and slow; as being stereotyped in thinking; restricted in outlook and interests; and as being uneasy and awkward in new or unfamiliar social situations.
Outgoing, enterprising, and ingenious; as being competitive and forward; and as original and fluent in thought.	3. Sy (sociability). To identify persons of outgoing, sociable, participative temperament.	Awkward, conventional, quiet, submissive, and unassuming; as being detached and passive in attitude; and as being suggestible and overly influenced by others' reactions and opinions.
Clever, enthusiastic, imaginative, quick, informal, spontaneous, and talkative; as being active and vigorous; and as having an expressive, ebullient nature.	4. Sp (social presence). To assess factors such as poise, spontaneity, and self-confidence in personal and social interaction.	Deliberate, moderate, patient, self-restrained, and simple; as vacillating and uncertain in decision; and as being literal and unoriginal in thinking and judging.
Intelligent, outspoken, sharp-witted, demanding, aggressive, and self-centered; as being persuasive and verbally fluent; and as possessing self-confidence and self-assurance.	5. Sa (self-acceptance). To assess factors such as sense of personal worth, self-acceptance, and capacity for independent thinking and action.	Methodical, conservative, dependable, conventional, easygoing, and quiet; as self-abasing and given to feelings of guilt and self-blame; and as being passive in action and narrow in interests.
Energetic, enterprising, alert, ambitious, and versatile; as being productive and active; and as valuing work and effort for its own sake.	6. Wb (sense of well-being). To identify persons who minimize their worries and complaints, and who are relatively free from self-doubt and disillusionment.	Unambitious, leisurely, awkward, cautious, apathetic, and conventional; as being self-defensive and apologetic; and as constricted in thought and action.

TABLE 2 (cont.). *Class II: Measures of Socialization, Maturity, and Responsibility*

High Scorers Tend to Be Seen as:	Scale and Purpose	Low Scorers Tend to Be Seen as:
Planful, responsible, thorough, progressive, capable, dignified, and independent; as being conscientious and dependable; resourceful and efficient; and as being alert to ethical and moral issues.	7. Re (responsibility). To identify persons of conscientious, responsible, and dependable disposition and temperament.	Immature, moody, lazy, awkward, changeable, and disbelieving; as being influenced by personal bias, spite, and dogmatism; and as under-controlled and impulsive in behavior.
Serious, honest, industrious, modest, obliging, sincere, and steady; as being conscientious and responsible; and as being self-denying and conforming.	8. So (socialization). To indicate the degree of social maturity, integrity and rectitude which the individual has attained.	Defensive, demanding, opinionated, resentful, stubborn, headstrong, rebellious, and undependable; as being guileful and deceitful in dealing with others; and as given to excess, exhibition, and ostentation in their behavior.
Calm, patient, practical, slow, self-denying, inhibited, thoughtful, and deliberate; as being strict and thorough in their own work and in their expectations for others; and as being honest and conscientious.	9. Sc (self-control). To assess the degree and adequacy of self-regulation and self-control and freedom from impulsivity and self-centeredness.	Impulsive, shrewd, excitable, irritable, self-centered, and uninhibited; as being aggressive and assertive; and as overemphasizing personal pleasure and self-gain.
Enterprising, informal, quick, tolerant, clear-thinking, and resourceful; as being intellectually able and verbally fluent; and as having broad and varied interests.	10. To (tolerance). To identify persons with permissive, accepting, and nonjudgmental social beliefs and attitude.	Suspicious, narrow, aloof, wary, and retiring; as being passive and overly judgmental in attitude; and as disbelieving and distrustful in personal and social outlook.
Co-operative, enterprising, outgoing, sociable, warm, and helpful; as being concerned with making a good impression; and as being diligent and persistent.	11. Gi (good impression). To identify persons capable of creating a favorable impression, and who are concerned about how others react to them.	Inhibited, cautious, shrewd, wary, aloof, and resentful; as being cool and distant in their relationships with others; and as being self-centered and too little concerned with the needs and wants of others.
Dependable, moderate, tactful, reliable, sincere, patient, steady, and realistic; as being honest and conscientious; and as having common sense and good judgment.	12. Cm (communality). To indicate the degree to which an individual's reactions and responses correspond to the modal ("common") pattern established for the inventory.	Impatient, changeable, complicated, imaginative, disorderly, nervous, restless, and confused; as being guileful and deceitful; inattentive and forgetful; and as having internal conflicts and problems.

TABLE 2 (cont.). *Class III: Measures of Achievement Potential and Intellectual Efficiency*

Scale and Purpose	High Scorers Tend to Be Seen as:	Low Scorers Tend to Be Seen as:
13. Ac (achievement via conformance). To identify those factors of interest and motivation which facilitate achievement in any setting where conformance is a positive behavior.	Capable, co-operative, efficient, organized, responsible, stable, and sincere; as being persistent and industrious; and as valuing intellectual activity and intellectual achievement.	Coarse, stubborn, aloof, awkward, insecure, and opinionated; as easily disorganized under stress or pressures to conform; and as pessimistic about their occupational futures.
14. Ai (achievement via independence). To identify those factors of interest and motivation which facilitate achievement in any setting where autonomy and independence are positive behaviors.	Mature, forceful, strong, dominant, demanding, and foresighted; as being independent and self-reliant; and as having superior intellectual ability and judgment.	Inhibited, anxious, cautious, dissatisfied, dull, and wary; as being submissive and compliant before authority; and as lacking in self-insight and self-understanding.
15. Ie (intellectual efficiency). To indicate the degree of personal and intellectual efficiency which the individual has attained.	Efficient, clear-thinking, capable, intelligent, progressive, planful, thorough, and resourceful; as being alert and well-informed; and as placing a high value on cognitive and intellectual matters.	Cautious, confused, easygoing, defensive, shallow, and unambitious; as being conventional and stereotyped in thinking; and as lacking in self-direction and self-discipline.

TABLE 2 (cont.). *Class IV: Measures of Intellectual and Interests Modes*

High Scorers *Tend to Be Seen as:*	Scale and Purpose	Low Scorers *Tend to Be Seen as:*
Observant, spontaneous, quick, perceptive, talkative, resourceful, and changeable; as being verbally fluent and socially ascendant; and as being rebellious toward rules, restrictions, and constraints.	16. *Py (psychological-mindedness). To measure the degree to which the individual is interested in, and responsive to, the inner needs, motives, and experiences of others.*	Apathetic, peaceable, serious, cautious, and unassuming; as being slow and deliberate in tempo; and as being overly conforming and conventional.
Insightful, informal, adventurous, confident, humorous, rebellious, idealistic, assertive, and egoistic; as being sarcastic and cynical; and as highly concerned with personal pleasure and diversion.	17. *Fx (flexibility). To indicate the degree of flexibility and adaptability of a person's thinking and social behavior.*	Deliberate, cautious, worrying, industrious, guarded, mannerly, methodical, and rigid; as being formal and pedantic in thought; and as being overly deferential to authority, custom, and tradition.
Appreciative, patient, helpful, gentle, moderate, persevering, and sincere; as being respectful and accepting of others; and as behaving in a conscientious and sympathetic way.	18. *Fe (femininity). To assess the masculinity or femininity of interests. (High scores indicate more feminine interests, low scores more masculine.)*	Outgoing, hard-headed, ambitious, masculine, active, robust, and restless; as being manipulative and opportunistic in dealing with others; blunt and direct in thinking and actions; and impatient with delay, indecision, and reflection.

Table 2 is reproduced by special permission from *The California Psychological Inventory* by Harrison G. Gough, Ph.D. Copyright 1956. Published by Consulting Psychologists Press, Inc.

of persons in different occupations, but many questions about the scales remained unanswered. How stable over time were different patterns of response on the SVIB? Which, if any, patterns of occupational interests tended to be relatively more and less similar to one another? Given early in persons' educational or work careers, did occupational interest scales on the SVIB predict tendencies to enter and remain in an occupation or were they useful only for identifying the occupation that a person had already entered? Over many years of research, Strong [14, 15] and others have managed to answer these questions. It is known now that after age 18 or 19, measured interests *are* highly stable individual qualities. It is also known that on the average, male college students scoring high on a specific occupational scale of the SVIB are about four times as likely to be in that occupation nearly twenty years later than college men scoring low on the same scale. Moreover, men most satisfied with their chosen professions at ages 40–45 tend to be those whose measured interests in college were most compatible with their actual career choices. Factor analyses have also aided in understanding the way in which measured vocational likes and dislikes group together—that is, the basic dimensions of vocational interests. Summarizing the results of many such studies, Super and Crites [16] suggest the following major factors of vocational interest:

Scientific activities
Social welfare activities (a helpful interest in people)
Literary, linguistic, and verbal activities (for example, journalism and law)
Materials manipulation (such as carpentry)
Systems interests (clerical and business detail jobs)
Persuasive personal contact activities (a manipulative interest in people)
Aesthetic expression
Aesthetic appreciation

These lines of evidence add greatly to what we know about scores on the SVIB. Similar research has been done on many other existing typical behavior inventories, such as the CPI and MMPI. The important point is, that the empirical method of item selection, *crucial* as it is as a first step in test development, still needs to be supplemented by further empirical studies designed to round out the meaning and interpretive significance of scores on the test.

USING TYPICAL BEHAVIOR MEASURES IN SELECTION. Finally, a word should be said about the potential usefulness of typical behavior tests in personnel selection and placement. Though widely used as aids in making selection decisions, the evidence regarding their accuracy for predicting job behavior is far from impressive. Among the major reasons are the following:

1. Only a few of these tests have been developed empirically. Unfortunately, the armchair method still characterizes most of the tests currently

being used. Since the initial development of many such tests was not behaviorally based, the odds are not highly in favor of their being related to important aspects of job behavior.

2. For the most part, job behavior has been inadequately studied in selection and test validation studies. At the worst, researchers have merely used global ratings or other crude measures to identify "successful" and "unsuccessful" employees with little or no attention to actual job behaviors making up so-called success or failure in any given setting. In such studies, the two groups have usually scored differently on tests of maximum performance (cognitive and motor tests), probably because the crude success classifications reflect, if anything, the *abilities* necessary for doing the job. On the other hand, the typical behavior measures have usually failed to show differences between the two groups—not an unexpected result in view of the failure to study and to specify carefully the kinds of job behaviors involved.

3. Typical behavior tests, as opposed to maximum performance tests, can be slanted or distorted by the examinee. An applicant for any given job probably has a fairly definite impression (though possibly erroneous) of the typical behavior characteristics shown by persons in such jobs. Assuming that he is probably eager to get the job, he may try to convince the examiner, through his replies to the test, that his own typical behavior is consonant with what he perceives to be the desired behavior patterns on the job. This tendency is called "faking the test."

There are no easy or sure answers to this problem. Probably the best answer —not widely employed—is to develop such tests directly on applicant samples and to base item selection on empirical relationships to later observed job behaviors. A myriad of other methods have been tried, such as special item formats ("forced choice") and special faking detection keys. Unfortunately, these methods are too technical and too numerous to warrant further discussion in this brief book.

BIOGRAPHICAL INFORMATION. One of the most promising reasons for developing typical behavior inventories is that one of the best predictors of future behavior is past behavior. Nearly all programs of personnel selection seek to tap elements of past behavior by interviewing, checking references, analyzing application blanks and personal data sheets, reviewing scholastic records, and the like. Unfortunately, it is difficult to know exactly how past behaviors relate to specific future behaviors that may be of interest. The methods mentioned above are usually poorly standardized. The nature and extent of the information attained differ from applicant to applicant; predictions must be based on varying knowledge with the usual result that they can be little more than vague impressions, subjective hunches, and intuitive feelings.

The most commonly used method in selection, the personal interview, is notoriously bad in this regard. It is handled differently by each interviewer, who in turn probably uses different methods with each applicant. At its worst, the personal interview may bog down into merely "passing the time of day," with little time devoted to learning about an applicant's typical past behavior patterns. Under the best conditions, a highly skilled interviewer may be able to gather a wide range of fairly accurate information from the past, but even then it is difficult to interpret the meaning of this data for predicting future behavior; and again reliance must be placed on intuitive hunches and guesses. Some interviewers' hunches turn out to be much better than those of others, but it is difficult to know ahead of time who the better and more accurate interviewers are.

In spite of all this, no one would suggest dispensing with the interview in personnel selection; it is the only way of seeing what the applicant looks like, of getting a feeling for how his personality "clicks" with yours, and of getting acquainted with him as a person. Moreover, it is still the best way for "selling" the company to a promising applicant and of creating in him a good impression of how he was dealt with during the selection process. Thus, as a public relations device, the interview is crucial; as a means of predicting expected future job behavior, it often is not much good.

The best way to capitalize on past behavior for predicting future behavior is to use the empirical method with a standardized biographical inventory to learn what job behaviors may be predicted from various elements of past behavior. In effect, elements of a person's past behavior—marital history, jobs held, activities in high school and college, amount of education, hobbies, past successes and failures, etc.—are treated as separate items to be compared against defined job behavior categories in much the same way that Binet compared performance on test items with learning ability ratings. In this way, items of a biographical inventory may be scored to yield predictions of typical behavior in the future. The resulting typical behavior inventory does not suffer from many of the usual difficulties encountered by personality and interest tests. For example, (1) the inventory is empirically developed; (2) it is linked directly to job behavior, thereby forcing a more careful study of job behavior than has been done for most typical behavior inventories; and, best of all, (3) it is much less likely to be "faked" because it includes information of actual past behavior which can, if necessary, be checked by independent means.

Since biographical inventories first came into wide use about twenty years ago, they have been used in a wide variety of studies and in many selection programs. Very often, a carefully developed typical behavior inventory based on biographical information has proved to be the single best predictor of future job behavior. Thus, biographical information constitutes one of the most fruitful sources of predictive data, to be considered along with measures of cognitive abilities, motor skills, and personality and interest measures.

Conclusions

In this chapter, we have presented a brief history and described the current status of the measurement of individual differences. It may seem that we have strayed far afield from our intended discourse on personnel selection and placement. This is not true, however, for psychology's concern with individual differences broadly summarizes the steps involved in any program of selection research or test validation. Analyzing jobs and job circumstances, and observing and measuring significant job behavior necessarily precedes the choice of tests in any selection program.

Now, sixty years after Binet's contributions, psychology has available a vast array of tests—some carefully developed and backed by years of research, others hastily thrown together and poorly researched. In this brief chapter, we have presented what we believe to be the major dimensions of human variation. We hope that the reader now possesses a framework for structuring his inferences concerning the cognitive abilities, motor skills, or patterns of typical behavior necessary for getting any particular job done. We urge him to turn to any of a number of standard reference works [1, 2, 3, 5, 7, 10, 11, 13] as aids for choosing the actual tests to be tried in a selection program.

References

1. ALBRIGHT, L. E., GLENNON, J. R., and SMITH, W. J. *The Use of Psychological Tests in Industry*. Cleveland: Howard Allen, 1963.
2. ANASTASI, ANNE. *Psychological Testing*. 2nd ed. New York: Macmillan, 1961.
3. BUROS, O. K., ed. *Sixth Mental Measurements Yearbook*. New Brunswick, N. J.: Gryphon Press, 1965.
4. CHAUNCEY, H., and DOBBIN, J. E. *Testing: Its Place in Education Today*. New York: Harper & Row, 1963.
5. CRONBACH, L. J. *Essentials of Psychological Testing*. 2nd ed. New York: Harper & Row, 1960.
6. FLEISHMAN, E. A. The Description and Prediction of Perceptual-Motor Skill Learning. In R. Glaser, ed. *Training Research and Education*. Pittsburgh: University of Pittsburgh Press, 1962.
7. FREEMAN, F. S. *Theory and Practice of Psychological Testing*. 3rd ed. New York: Holt, Rinehart and Winston, 1962.
8. GUILFORD, J. P. The structure of intellect. *Psychol. Bull.* 53 (1956):267–93.
9. GUILFORD, J. P. Three faces of intellect. *American Psychologist* 14 (1959):469–79.
10. GUION, R. M. *Personnel Testing*. New York: McGraw-Hill, 1965.
11. HELMSTADTER, G. C. *Principles of Psychological Measurement*. New York: Appleton-Century-Crofts, 1964.
12. SPEARMAN, C. *The Abilities of Man*. London: Macmillan, Ltd., 1927.
13. STONE, C. H., and KENDALL, W. E. *Effective Personnel Selection Procedures*. Englewood Cliffs, N. J.: Prentice-Hall, 1956.
14. STRONG, E. K., JR. *Vocational Interests of Men and Women*. Stanford: Stanford University Press, 1943.
15. STRONG, E. K., JR. *Vocational Interests 18 Years after College*. Minneapolis: University of Minn. Press, 1955.
16. SUPER, D. C., and CRITES, J. O. *Appraising Vocational Fitness*. New York: Harper & Row, 1962.
17. TUPES, E. C., and CHRISTAL, R. E. *Recurrent Personality Factors Based on Trait Ratings*. Technical Report ASD-TR-61-97. Personnel Laboratory, United States Air Force, Lackland Air Force Base, 1961.

Woman's Intellect

ELEANOR E. MACCOBY

Tests of the kind Dunnette describes can be very useful tools in the search for better understanding of people. In the next selection, Eleanor Maccoby compares men and women on a number of measures. The pattern of similarities and differences that she finds leads her to an analysis of the growth patterns of boy and girl children and a discussion of the difficult position of the intelligent girl in present-day society.

This article is an excellent example of thoughtful empiricism, as opposed to the blind empiricism that worries Dunnette. Maccoby reviews the literature on sex differences in intellectual functioning and becomes convinced that certain real differences do exist between men and women, particularly in the way members of the two sexes think. Men on the average are more analytic than women, and more comfortable with abstract thought. But Maccoby does not stop with just the facts. She begins to develop a theory, an explanation of how these differences came to be. She looks into the developmental years of the girl and offers some speculation (that will eventually require supporting data) about the effects of different childhood experiences on boys and girls. She pays special attention to social influences—how involved the mothers were in what their children were doing, how much freedom the children had, how much initiative they were allowed. Her theory creates a dilemma for the girl who wants to be an intellectual. The available data, interpreted as Maccoby interprets them, suggest that you can't have it both ways: the feminine girl is not likely to become a productive intellectual, and the intellectual girl is not likely to be considered feminine. But note Maccoby's solution. Although this article is a good ten years old, it clearly espouses some of the essential views of the "new" women's movement.

Not many years ago, families took it for granted that an intelligent son would be sent to college and an intelligent daughter would not. It is only during a brief span of thirty to forty years that large numbers of women have had

SOURCE: From *Man and Civilization: The Potential of Woman* by Farber and Wilson. Copyright © 1963 by McGraw-Hill, Inc. Used by permission of McGraw-Hill Book Company.

opportunities for higher education opened to them, but the period has been long enough so that we are in a position to begin to appraise the results. To those who had hoped that equal educational opportunities for women would yield equal intellectual achievements, an appraisal must be disappointing. A Madame Curie is conspicuous by her very rarity. Even in the field of letters, where many of women's special talents are presumed to lie, we have more men than women who are productive, creative writers. When it comes to achievement in science, the imbalance is much greater. Our colleges produce very few women who become intellectually excited by, and immersed in, a scientific research problem or who organize large bodies of diverse data into a new theoretical statement. And even though creative scientists must have moments of almost intuitive insight, woman's famous intuition does not appear to have helped her much in making a contribution to scientific thought.

Taking publication as an index of productivity (and although it is not an entirely satisfactory index, it is difficult to find a better one!) we find, from a study of 400 Radcliffe Ph.D.s [1956] that women published substantially less than men of comparable jobs and rank. Half of these women Ph.D.s had published little or nothing since earning their advanced degrees. So even with first-rate advanced graduate training, the difference between the sexes in intellectual achievement appears not to be erased.

It is evident that women have many other things they often choose to do with their lives, over and beyond pursuit of their intellectual interests. It is reasonable to believe that the other demands upon women are more incompatible with the life of an intellectual than would be the case for men. It is difficult to continue in the single-minded pursuit of a set of ideas while being a competent wife and mother—more difficult than for a man to do so while being a competent husband and father. These matters of conflicting interests and responsibilities will be discussed by others in this conference, and they are not our primary concern today. It is necessary to ask, however, whether they constitute the entire explanation for women's lack of signal accomplishment in the intellectual sphere. I am inclined to think they do not. One bit of evidence comes from the study of Radcliffe Ph.D.s already cited; the ones who had married had published as much as those who had not, and this would appear to indicate that even an unmarried professional woman (who presumably is more comparable to men with respect to the other demands on her time) is either under some special restraints affecting her intellectual productivity or lacks in some degree the positive motivation that would optimally affect her work.

If we examine woman's intellectual performance through a large range of her life cycle, we find other reasons for suspecting that it is not just the conflicting demands upon her time created by marriage and children that interfere with her achievement. There are not very good facts available on the subject, but I suspect careful studies would reveal that the educated woman does not behave as an intellectual during her college years, nor "go underground" during the period of life when she is raising young children and then emerge again as an intellectual when the children are grown and no longer require so much of her time. Rather, it appears that some of the restraints upon her intellectuality make themselves felt long before marriage and continue to be present during those long years from thirty-five to sixty-five when the most demanding phase of child rearing is over—the period when many men are at the peak of their productive careers. It seems possible that there may be some relevant early-formed personality traits, or even some early-established basic qualities of mind, that characterize women and that bear upon intellectual performance, and it is these factors that I would like to explore today.

Let us first review what is known concerning the development of intellectual abilities in girls. In attempting to determine what are the special intellectual qualities of females (if indeed such special qualities exist), we must stress the ways in which girls differ from boys in their performance. In doing so, we may give insufficient attention to the ways in which the two sexes are alike intellectually, or to the great variations among individuals of the same sex. But bearing this danger in mind, let us attempt to draw a quick picture of some of the reliably established sex differences in intellectual functioning.

The Stanford-Binet intelligence test, which was for many years the most widely used individual test, revealed few differences between boys and girls in total "intelligence" as this test measured it. From this fact it was widely assumed that the sexes might differ in interests and in temperament but not in underlying mental abilities. It was not widely known or understood that during the early phases of work on the Stanford-Binet test, when many items were being tried out for possible inclusion in the test, items which consistently revealed sex differences were discarded from the test whenever possible. The test builders hoped in this way to create a test on which the scores for boys and the scores for girls could be evaluated against the same norms. And for the most part they succeeded, although girls did come out slightly ahead in the early years and boys in the middle and later school years [McNemar, 1942]. But it is clearly not possible to use a test standardized in this way to investigate the magnitude of the sex differences that do exist or at what ages they make their appearance.

Relying now on test materials which were not standardized so as to eliminate a portion of existing sex differences, we find the following facts: Girls get off to a very good start. Insofar as it is possible to measure abilities which we would be willing to call intellectual abilities during the first three or four years of life, girls seem to be slightly ahead of boys. They articulate more clearly than boys; they say their first word at a slightly younger age on the average; they begin to combine words into sentences slightly sooner; they count accurately sooner [Oetzel, 1962]. In interpreting these facts we should remember that performance on the sorts of tests we have been able to devise for very young children does not predict very well what intellectual level the individual will ultimately reach. Furthermore, we know that girls are on a somewhat faster developmental timetable than boys from the standpoint of physical growth; this same slightly advanced timetable may apply to the maturation of certain motor and perceptual abilities that underlie intellectual performance, and again, this rate of maturation doesn't necessarily imply anything concerning the ultimate level to be reached.

But to continue with the description of sex differences in abilities. Upon entrance into school, girls learn to read a little more easily, and there are more boys who have reading problems severe enough to call for special remedial reading programs. But the differential between the sexes on some aspects of verbal skills soon begins to disappear. During the school years, there are no consistent differences to be found in vocabulary; and after about the fifth or sixth grade, most studies show the boys to be doing as well as the girls in reading comprehension. The girls do continue to excel in "language" skills such as spelling, punctuation, and diagraming sentences. They also excel in measures of verbal fluency"; for example, they write longer themes, they can think of more words with certain characteristics in a short time, and they can tell longer stories in response to stimulus pictures. So the stereotype that women talk more than men appears to have some basis in fact, but it does not imply a general superiority of the female in all aspects of verbal skill.

How about mathematical skills? It is commonly supposed that men have a consistent edge over women in this respect. It came as a surprise to us, therefore, when we recently reviewed the test results baring upon mathematical abilities [see Oetzel, 1962], to discover that the sexes do not differ consistently in the early and middle school years. Of course, during much of this time, it may be a misnomer to say that we are dealing with *mathematical* abilities. It would be more accurate to say that the skill usually measured between the ages of seven and eleven or twelve is skill at arithmetical computation. Children are also given some of the so-called arithmetical reasoning problems at these ages—questions about how long would it take three men to dig a basement if seven men can do it in 2½ days, or how long it would take a bullet to travel from one train to another if the speeds of the two trains and the time since starting are given—and girls appear to be able to handle these questions about as well as boys. It is not until high school that we begin to get quite consistent sex differences, with the boys forging ahead when they come to analytic geometry, trigonometry, and algebra and doing considerably better in tests involving quantitative reasoning. By the time the Scholastic Aptitude tests are administered for admission to college, we find that boys score on the average as much as 50 points higher on the mathematical portion of the test, while girls are scoring only 8 to 10 points higher on the verbal, or "language," segment. Of course, girls do not as frequently elect to take the more advanced math courses in high school, and it is difficult to know whether this is true because they lack the ability to handle the material or whether their interests lie elsewhere. The career fields which will require training in math—engineering, and the natural sciences—are primarily masculine fields, and girls may stop taking math simply because they are preparing themselves for more feminine occupations. But another possible explanation exists: that girls may indeed more often lack certain abstract or analytical qualities of mind that are not called into play during the learning of square root, decimals, etc., in the earlier grades, and that it is not until mathematics becomes more abstract (as it does in geometry and algebra) that this particular deficiency becomes a handicap to them.

At the moment, we lack definitive data that would make it possible to choose between these alternatives. But girls' characteristic difficulty with geometry does probably relate to a fairly consistent sex difference that may be detected at a considerably earlier age. Throughout the grade school years, boys do better than girls on tests of "spatial" ability. Some of you may have taken tests which include items for space ability: such tests require the subject, for example, to say how many surfaces there would be on the opposite side of a pile of cubes—the side the viewer cannot see—or to select from an array of jigsaw drawings those that would fit together to form a designated pattern. Another element in spatial ability involves finding a simple figure which is embedded in a more complex one. Newspapers sometimes carry drawings of landscapes in which one can find animals or human faces involving the same lines that are first perceived as parts of clouds, leaves, or tree trunks; the trick in finding these hidden figures is to be able to break away from the set that is established by the entire drawing of the landscape—to respond to only an isolated segment of the drawing and avoid being influenced by the momentarily irrelevant parts. There are formal tests of the ability to perceive parts of a visual field analytically, and the results very consistently show that boys can perceive more analytically, while the girls are more global, more influenced by all the elements of the field together.

The sex differences, to the extent of being bound by the field as a whole, are well illustrated by the performance of the two sexes on the so-called rod and frame test, a test used extensively by Witkin in his studies of individual differences in underlying modes of perceiving [Witkin, 1954]. In this test, the subject is seated in a darkened room. He looks at an illuminated frame that looks like a picture frame; and within this frame is an illuminated rod, which can be adjusted through various degrees of tilt to an upright position. The subject's task is to adjust the rod so that it looks straight up and down. Sometimes he is required to do this when the frame itself is tilted. Girls are consistently more influenced by the tilt of the frame; if it is tilted, they think the rod is upright when it is tilted to correspond to the tilt of the frame rather than when it is truly upright. Boys, on the other hand, are more able to ignore the frame and adjust the rod to the true upright. It is on the basis of tests of this kind, as well as the embedded-figures test, that girls have been labeled more "field dependent" [Witkin, 1954; Witkin, Dyk, Faterson, Goodenough, and Karp, 1962], and it is interesting to note that the greater field dependence of women and girls has been found in studies of people in a variety of cultures, from Western Europe to Hong Kong. It appears entirely possible that some of the difficulty many girls have with the kinds of analytical processes required in high school math could be traced to this earlier-established difference in their mode of dealing with a stimulus field.

Related to the greater field dependence of women is their greater difficulty in breaking an established set. Let me illustrate what is meant by set. Suppose you were asked to solve some number series—to say what would come next in a series of numbers. We would begin with some easy series. For example, we would ask what comes next after 2, 4, 6, 8—and you could easily say 10. Or what comes next after 2, 4, 8, 16, 32—and you would say 64. Now try this one: 14, 23, 34, 42, 50, 59, 72, 81—. Even if you knew New York very well, you would have difficulty recognizing these as the stops on the Eighth Avenue subway, because you were set for an entirely different kind of number series. If you had not had the other series first, you might recognize this series immediately and be able to continue it. There are special test problems which are designed to test an individual's ability to break away from an established set, to restructure a situation for a fresh attack on it, and men do better on such tests than women [Guetzkow, 1951; Sweeney, 1953].

Another kind of task that illustrates the difference between the sexes in their mode of dealing with problem materials is a task developed by Kagan et al. [1963]. Subjects are given an array of pictures or drawings showing a variety of objects and people with a variety of postures, modes of dress, and states of activity. The subjects are simply asked to group together the pictures that seem to belong together. Girls are more likely to form what Kagan calls "functional" groupings. For example, they will group together the picture of a doctor, a nurse, and a wheel chair, because they are all associated with the care of sick people. Boys, on the other hand, will be more likely to form groups by selecting out some detail they have in common—they will, for example, group together all the pictures of people who have their right arms raised. This kind of grouping Kagan calls "analytic" grouping, and the fact that boys do this kind of grouping more may be regarded as another instance of their tendency to break down a percept—to deal with detailed elements rather than the whole.

I would like to suggest, then, that the difficulty girls have with doing high-level work in math and science is only partly a result of the fact that these subjects are required for preparation for engineering and other distinctly masculine occupations; I suggest that girls on the average develop a somewhat different way of handling incoming information—that their thinking is less analytic, more global, and more perseverative—and that this kind of thinking may serve them very well for many kinds of functioning but that it is not the kind of thinking most conducive to high-level intellectual productivity, especially in science. Let me hasten to add that in trying to make this point I may have produced an exaggerated impression of the magnitude of the sex differences that exist. There are many women who think analytically, and many men who do not, but there are consistent differences in the average performance of the two sexes, and by concentrating on the differences we may be able to find some clues as to what underlies the development of intellectual processes in women.

Why do some people develop more analytic modes of thought than others?

So far, we are only beginning to make a research attack upon this question. But there do seem to be some consistent trends in the work that has been done so far. The key to the matter seems to lie in whether, and how soon, a child is encouraged to assume initiative, to take responsibility for himself, and to solve problems by himself, rather than rely upon others for the direction of his activities. An early study by David Levy [1943] was among the first to suggest the importance of independence training for certain intellectual functions. He studied a group of boys whom he labeled "overprotected." The behavior of the mothers of these boys was extreme in the direction of "babying" them at a late age—for example, some of the boys, at age ten or eleven, were still being led to school by the hand of their mothers, and their mothers were still dressing them each morning. These overprotected boys were quite good in their language work at school—they were good readers, for example. But they were notably poor at math.

Recently, Dr. Rau and I at Stanford studied a group of children who were good at verbal tasks but poor at math or space tasks and contrasted them with children who were good at math or space but relatively poor at verbal tasks. Dr. Elizabeth Bing observed these children in interaction with their mothers. She asked the mothers to give the children some problems to work on and noted how much the mother became involved as the child worked on the problems. To speak now only about the girls in the study, it was evident from Dr. Bing's reports [Bing, 1963] that the mothers of the highly verbal girls were intrusive: they offered suggestions, praised the child for performing well, and criticized her for performing poorly. The mothers of the girls who were best at math or spatial tasks, however, more often left their daughters alone to solve the problems by themselves.

Still another piece of evidence comes from some recent exploratory work of Witkin, Dyk, Faterson, Goodenough, and Karp [1962], who wished to discover what conditions of a child's life were associated with his being field-dependent versus field-independent on the rod-and-frame test and the embedded-figures test. Witkin interviewed mothers to ascertain their attitudes about child rearing and the methods they had used to raise the particular child whose modes of perceiving Witkin had measured. The mothers of the children who were analytic in their perceptions had given their children quite a bit of freedom to explore the environment at an early age and had tried to encourage them to do things on their own initiative; by contrast, the mothers of the children who were "field-dependent" in their perceptions had kept their children quite closely tied to the maternal apron strings, had talked to them a good deal about the dangerous aspects of the environment, and had been in general unwilling to tolerate self-assertiveness in their children. There were many other things that characterized these two groups of mothers, as well, and it is difficult to sort out the factors that were most crucial in the home lives of the children with different modes of perceiving. But the relationships that I have selected to report here are consistent with our own findings and those of Levy in suggesting that activities of parents which are designed to foster the independence of their children and encourage them to take initiative will be associated with analytic thinking in the children and good ability in the math-science area, while continued close control and restriction of the child will be associated with the more field-dependent, or global, modes of thinking in the child and *poor* ability in math.

If this is true, we must ask ourselves whether girls are allowed less independence, less self-assertiveness in early childhood than is allowed to boys. We have very little evidence indeed on this point. I know of no evidence that would show that boys are allowed to play outside alone or cross streets earlier than girls, for example, but it may very well be true that they are. At the moment we will simply have to consider it an unanswered question whether parents treat daughters differently from sons with respect to training for independence, and whether they do so to a sufficient degree to account for the differences between the sexes in their modes of perceiving and their differential skill at tasks, such as mathematics, which seem to require an especially high degree of analytical thinking.

I think we can begin to see, however, from what has been said so far, that when we begin to try to understand the intellectual performance of women and girls, we cannot understand them by studying these kinds of performance alone; we will find that intellectual development does not occur as a kind of isolated "unfolding" process obeying its own inner laws, but rather that it is responsive, in some degree, to the nature of the network of interpersonal relations in which the child is involved, and that certain modes of thought may depend on the development of certain aspects of the person that we have previously thought of as "personality" rather than as qualities of intellect.

Let me take another approach to illustrate this point. As you may know, the "intelligence" of an individual child as it is measured by standard intelligence tests is not constant over the period of his growth from birth to maturity. Some children show progressive increases in IQ as they grow older; others show a progressive decline. There are a few centers of child development research in this country which have studied groups of children longitudinally; that is, they have followed the same children from very early childhood into adulthood, and it is possible to determine from their data what some of the factors are which are associated with progressive changes in children's intelligence test scores. Sontag et al. at Fels Research Institute [1958] have selected from their files a group of cases of children whose intelligence test scores consistently improved from preschool years through age ten and contrasted them with a group whose scores consistently declined during this period. They asked these questions: What kinds of children show increases or decreases in IQ? Can one predict, from knowing something about the personality characteristics of young children, which ones will have rising, and which falling, IQs? The answer to the second question is clearly yes. Here is what a child is like at age six if he or she is among those whose IQs will increase during the next four years: he or she is competitive, self-assertive, independent, and dominant in interaction with other children. And the children who will show declining IQs during the next four years are children who are passive, shy, and dependent.

I'm sure it will already have struck you that the characteristics associated with a rising IQ are not very feminine characteristics. One of the people working on the Fels study I have just described was asked about what kind of developmental history was necessary to make a girl into an intellectual person; he replied, "The simplest way to put it is that she must be a tomboy at some point in her childhood."

Does this seem bizarre? Before we consider the implications for the raising of girls, let us see whether there is any other evidence, beyond the Fels study, for an association between the sorts of analytic thinking we have been discussing and the possession of nonfeminine traits by girls. First of all, if we may consider high ability in arithmetic and math as indicative of analytic skill [and it is known, for example, that skill in math is correlated with ability to find embedded figures while verbal skill is not (see Bieri, 1958)], then it is relevant to refer to a study of the autobiographies of a few famous women mathematicians, done by Plank and Plank [1954]. This study revealed that women mathematicians had one important element in common: they all described an unusually close relationship with their fathers, rather than their mothers, as they were growing up, and they attempted to pattern themselves on their fathers. Related to this is the finding of Bieri and his colleagues [1960], who devised measures to determine the degree to which a group of college women had identified with, or patterned themselves upon, each of their parents. They found that women who were especially good at finding the hidden figures in the embedded-figures test were more strongly identified with their fathers than their mothers, while the reverse was true of the women who were relatively poor at solving embedded figures. The women in this study were also given a test designed to measure their acceptance of authority, and the women who were good at solving the embedded-figures problems tended to be *low* in acceptance of authority—another indication of the importance of autonomy in the development of this particular kind of analytic thinking. In still another study [Milton, 1957], college students were given problems to solve, many of which required breaking of set, or "restructuring." For both sexes, the students who were most skillful at problem solving were those who scored at the more masculine end of personality tests designed to measure masculine versus feminine traits.

And finally, our own work at Stanford, in which we selected groups of fifth-grade girls who were especially good at arithmetical or spatial tasks, revealed the following characteristics of these girls: The girls who did better on spatial problems than other kinds of problems were somewhat more masculine and aggressive than other girls with similar total IQs and rather withdrawn from social contact with their age-mates. The girls whose area of greatest competence was numerical tasks were popular with their classmates, largely because they were seen as girls with high competence in planning and organizing. According to their own report, these girls were also less likely than others of similar IQ to ask their parents for help when they encountered difficulty in solving a problem. When the girls were observed in interaction with their mothers, it was the girls who were especially good at verbal tasks who most often asked their mothers for help; the girls who were best at either math or space tasks tended to work on their own. Thus we see that these girls not only were characterized by greater independence while working on problems but also possessed some traits we think of as being more characteristic of boys: aggression in the case of the high-space girls, dominance in the case of the high-number girls.

It would appear, then, that what evidence we have indicates that girls who do well at the various kinds of analytic thinking we have been discussing are not very feminine creatures, at least not according to the standards our present society sets for feminine behavior. It has been repeatedly shown, in studies of girls, that they early develop a greater interest in other people, and in what other people think of them, than do boys; they tend to be more influenced by the opinions of others, and they are more conforming to what they perceive to be the social demands of the situations they are in. It is probably these conformist tendencies that help them to excel at spelling and punctuation—the kinds of performance for which there is only one socially prescribed, right answer. But for higher-level intellectual productivity, it is independence of mind that is required—the ability to turn one's back on others at least for a time, while working alone on a problem—and it is this which girls, from an early age, appear to find so difficult to do.

But of course, not all girls find it difficult. And it is interesting to consider for a moment the situation of a little girl who at preschool age does have the qualities that could make her into an analytic thinker. She is full of curiosity, likes to explore things, is dominant and independent, probably likes to play with boys and wear blue jeans, and isn't especially interested in dolls. Assuming that her parents have been tolerant of her temperament, what happens when she enters school? One of the first blows is that the boys won't play with her any more—they form their own exclusive play groups, and she must fall back upon the company of girls. In many ways she begins to discover that she is not behaving as girls are expected to behave, and the disapproval she encounters generates a certain amount of anxiety. This may sound like pure speculation, but there is some evidence that this is the course that development does take in girls who start out as tomboys. Sears, in a recent study [1961], traced the development of aggression, and anxiety about aggression, between the ages of five and twelve. The boys who were most anxious about aggression at age twelve were the ones whose parents had not allowed fighting when they were younger, and at the age of five they had already become fairly unaggressive children. The girls who showed most anxiety about aggression at age twelve, however, were the ones who had been fairly aggressive at kindergarten age. But more importantly for our present discussion, the ones who showed most of this kind of anxiety in middle childhood were the ones who had been trained in ways inappropriate to their sex in preschool years. For example, in most American homes, there is a certain amount of division of labor between the parents such that mothers assume a larger role in the discipline and caretaking of daughters, fathers of sons. But the girls with high aggression anxiety levels in middle childhood had received an unusually high amount of both discipline and caretaking from their *fathers*. Furthermore, they had been encouraged to fight back when attacked by other children in the neighborhood—an encouragement which is more often reserved for boys in our culture. We see, then, that these girls were being to some degree masculinized in early childhood, and we can only assume that it was at least partly the social disapproval they encountered over their unfeminine behavior that produced the anxiety they manifested at a later time.

Let me make a leap from these findings to our present concerns with woman's intellect. Suppose a girl does succeed in maintaining, throughout her childhood years, the qualities of dominance, independence, and active striving that appear to be requisites for good analytic thinking. In so doing, she is defying the conventions concerning what is appropriate behavior for her sex. She may do this successfully, in many ways, but I suggest that it is a rare intellectual woman who will not have paid a price for it: a price in anxiety. And I hazard the guess that it is this anxiety which helps to account for the lack of productivity among those women who do make intellectual careers. We are beginning to know a good deal about the effects of anxiety on thinking: it is especially damaging to creative thinking, for it narrows the range of solution efforts, interferes with breaking set, and prevents scanning of the whole range of elements open to perception. When anxiety facilitates performance, as it sometimes does, it facilitates already well-learned tasks; it does not contribute to breaking new ground.

From the standpoint of those who want women to become intellectuals, this is something of a horror story. It would appear that even when a woman is suitably endowed intellectually and develops the right temperament and habits of thought to make use of her endowment, she must be fleet of foot indeed to scale the hurdles society has erected for her and to remain a whole and happy person while continuing to follow her intellectual bent.

From the standpoint of parents and educators who are charged with the responsibility of raising and training girls, the requisites for intellectual development in girls appear to pose something of a dilemma. Shall mothers encourage whatever tomboy tendencies they find in their young daughters? Shall teachers attempt to free girls from the emotional involvement with others that helps to make them so tractable in the classroom? I do not mean to imply that the concerted efforts of parents and teachers together would necessarily serve to make girls just like boys intellectually. I think it is quite possible that there are genetic factors that differentiate the two sexes and bear upon their intellectual performance other than what we have thought of as innate "intelligence." For example, there is good reason to believe that boys are innately more aggressive than girls—and I mean aggressive in the broader sense, not just as it implies fighting, but as it implies dominance and initiative as well—and if this quality is one which underlies the later growth of analytic thinking, then boys have an advantage which girls who are endowed with more passive qualities will find difficult to overcome. But it also appears likely that the way children are dealt with by the adults responsible for their care, and the social roles girls know they are preparing themselves for, have a bearing also on whether they will develop the characteristics that will be conducive to the growth of higher-level intellectual skills. And insofar as child training does have an influence, parents and educators have some difficult value judgments to make. What kinds of women do they want to produce? Do we want to encourage intellectuality in women if it must be done at the expense of femininity?

As always, when faced with this kind of devil-and-deep-blue-sea dilemma, it is wise to inquire whether there may not be some other alternative. I wonder whether our current social definition of the feminine woman and girl could not undergo some revisions without any damage to the essential functions of woman. Does a woman really need to be passive and dependent in order to be sexually attractive to men, or in order to be a good mother? Could we not accept and encourage the active, dominant, independent qualities of the intellectual girl without labeling her as masculine, and encourage in her whatever aspects of femininity *are* compatible with an analytic quality of mind? I recognize that I am raising some controversial and intricate issues here, for the social and economic role of woman is by very necessity a dependent one during her childbearing years. But these years have become a much smaller segment of her life span than they once were, and I ask whether our whole definition of femininity should be such as to prepare her for this segment of her life and no other. . . .

References

1. BIERI, J. Paternal identification, acceptance of authority, and within-sex differences in cognitive behavior. *J. Abnorm. Soc. Psychol.* 60 (1960):76–79.
2. BIERI, J., and GALINSKY, M. D. Sex differences in perceptual behavior. *J. Pers.* 26 (1958):1–12.
3. BING, ELIZABETH. The effect of child rearing practices on development of differential cognitive abilities. *Child Developm.*, 1963.
4. GUETZKOW, H. An analysis of the operation of set in problem-solving behavior. *J. Genet. Psychol.* 45 (1951):219–44.
5. KAGAN, JEROME, MOSS, HOWARD A., and SIEGEL, IRVING E. The psychological significance of styles of conceptualization. In J. C. Wright and J. Kagan, ed. Basic Cognitive Processes in Children, *Monogr. Soc. Res. Child Developm.* 23, no. 86 (1963).
6. LEVY, D. M. *Maternal Overprotection.* New York: Columbia University Press, 1943.
7. MACCOBY, ELEANOR E., and RAU, LUCY. *Differential Cognitive Abilities.* Final report, Cooperative Research Project No. 1040. Stanford, Cal.: Owen House, Stanford University, 1962.

8. McNemar, Quinn. *The Revision of the Stanford-Binet Scale: An Analysis of the Standardization Data.* Boston: Houghton Mifflin, 1942.

9. Milton, G. A. The effects of sex-role identification upon problem-solving skill. *J. Abnorm. Soc. Psychol.* 55 (1957):208–12.

10. Oetzel, Roberta. *Selected Bibliography on Sex Differences.* Mimeographed, prepared for Social Science Research Council. Stanford, Cal.: Owen House, Stanford University, 1962.

11. Plank, Emma H., and Plank, R. *Emotional components in arithmetic learning, as seen through autobiographies. The Psychoanalytic Study of the Child,* Vol. IX. New York: International Universities Press, 1954.

12. Radcliffe Committee on Graduate Education for Women. *Graduate Education for Women.* Cambridge, Mass.: Harvard University Press, 1956.

13. Sears, R. R. Relation of early socialization experiences to aggression in middle childhood. *J. Abnorm. Soc. Psychol.* 63 (1961):466–92.

14. Sontag, I. W., Baker, C. T., and Nelson, Virginia A. Mental growth and personality development: A longitudinal study. *Monogr. Soc. Res. Child Developm.* 23, no. 68 (1958).

15. Sweeney, E. J. "Sex Differences in Problem-solving." Dissertation submitted to Stanford University, 1953.

16. Witkin, H. A.; Lewis, Helen B.; Herzman, M.: Machover, Karen; Meissner, Pearl B.; and Wapner, S. *Personality through Perception.* New York: Harper & Row, 1954.

17. Witkin, H. A.; Dyk, R. B.; Faterson, H. E.; Goodenough, D. R.; and Karp, S. A. *Psychological Differentiation.* New York: John Wiley & Sons, 1962.

Environmental Components of
Measured Intelligence

JANE W. KESSLER

In the preceding article, Maccoby reminded us of social influences on intellectual development, and now Kessler reviews personal and physiological factors as well. Kessler's formulation is consistent with Dubos's point in the first section that, while genes govern the person's possible responses to the environment, it is *environmental* characteristics that shape the quality of those responses.

Her definition of the word *environment* is rightfully very broad. She uses it to include experiences before and during birth and in infancy and early childhood and to embrace sociocultural influences as well as personality characteristics. In short, she reviews personal, physical, and social influences at different stages of a person's life.

The picture she paints is one of a highly fluid intelligence, subject to substantial fluctuation over time, prey to environmental influences of all kinds. But it would be extreme to interpret all this as indicating that general intelligence is a totally empty concept, for it does provide reasonably good predictions of "scholastic potential," say, and of some of the other human abilities that are listed in Dunnette's article. On the other hand, it is difficult to understand why so many of us place so much stock in such a slippery concept, except when we observe that there is a tendency among psychologists and lay people alike to reify general intelligence, to make this hypothetical construct into something real in its own right, and to lose perspective about the importance of specific abilities. Kessler's review should help us guard against this tendency.

The fact that there are significant individual differences in intelligence is undisputed, and no one advances a single-cause explanation for this fact. It is customary to speak of intelligence as the product of the interaction of environment and genetic potentiality. A small minority of psychologists, for example, Burt and R. B. Cattell, prefer to restrict the term *intelligence* to

SOURCE: Reprinted from *The School Review* 73 (1965):339–353, by permission of the author and publisher. Copyright © 1965 by The University of Chicago Press.

inborn capacity. Objection to this view is taken on the basis that inborn capacity is of necessity a hypothetical construct, something which can be inferred but never directly measured. Even before birth, there are factors operating to influence the genetic potential, and it is several years *after* birth and exposure to environment before one can get reliable measures of intelligence. For these reasons, among others, it is impossible to measure inborn potential. Intelligence is better and more commonly used to describe mental functioning which can be observed in home life, at school, at work, and which is sampled by standardized psychological tests.

Since the genetic components of intellectual ability have been well covered in other articles, this paper attempts an analysis of four factors which can be subsumed under the broad heading of "environment": (1) prenatal and paranatal conditions; (2) early maternal care; (3) sociocultural influences; and (4) individual personality characteristics. The paper concludes with a discussion of the validity of IQ tests and the proper use of their results.

Environment

PRENATAL AND PARANATAL CONDITIONS

At birth babies are already different. Experimental studies of such behavior as spontaneous motor activity in the first week of life [4] and changes in skin temperature and cardiac rate in response to stimulation in three-day-old neonates [29] show differences falling into the normal distribution curve. Although heredity undoubtedly contributes a large share to these constitutional differences, the effects of the fetal environment and process of birth are perhaps equally important. Ashley-Montagu reviewed the many kinds of prenatal influences possible and concluded, contrary to the traditional view, that the placenta is apparently a highly permeable filter through which almost anything can be transferred to the fetus [1]. Abundant evidence has shown the effects of maternal nutrition upon the physical development of the fetus. There is also some evidence to show that the intelligence of the offspring, as measured by performance in later life, may be affected by the mother's nutrition during pregnancy. Harrell, Woodyard, and Gates reported the results of a study in Kentucky and Virginia concerning the influence of vitamin supplementation of the diets of pregnant and lactating women on the intelligence quotients obtained by their children at three to four years of age [14]. A statistically significant difference of 3.7 points was found between the Binet IQ's of the children whose mothers had had the vitamin supplements and those children whose mothers had received placebos during pregnancy and lactation. Since inadequate maternal nutrition is more prevalent in conditions of poverty, this provides a partial explanation for the lower mean IQ's in children from poor socioeconomic backgrounds.

Another possible influence on fetal reactions and development is the mother's emotional state. Sontag noted that bodily movements of fetuses increased several hundred per cent while their mothers were undergoing emotional stress [35]. When the mother's emotional upset lasted several weeks, fetal activity continued at an exaggerated level throughout the entire period. Other more recent studies have confirmed the general idea that the mother's emotional attitudes are reflected in the newborn [6]. It is hard to evaluate the long-range effects of prenatal influences because of the overlay of later events, but it was Sontag's contention that prolonged maternal emotional stress during pregnancy may have enduring consequences for the child.

Pasamanick and his co-workers have reported a number of retrospective investigations in which the pregnancy and birth histories of children with physical and mental problems are compared with the early case histories of "normal" children. They concluded that there is a continuum of reproductive casualty resulting from prematurity and complications of pregnancy. In the extreme, these complications resulted in death, but there were many survivors with lesser degrees of brain damage who subsequently developed a series of disorders extending from cerebral palsy, epilepsy, and mental retardation through all types of behavioral and learning disabilities [23]. An important part of the Pasamanick studies is the association of pregnancy abnormalities with certain life experiences related to socioeconomic status. It is not only possible, but highly probable, that the poor physical health and stressful emotional state of the pregnant mother in economically deprived circumstances put her baby at a significant disadvantage from the moment he is born.

EARLY MATERNAL CARE

The lasting importance of the maternal care provided the baby in the first years of life is highlighted by noting the serious consequences of deprivation. The publication which most forcefully draws attention to this is that of Bowlby [3]. Bowlby reviews direct studies of the development of children living in institutions and hospitals, retrospective studies investigating the early histories of adolescents or adults who developed psychological problems, and follow-up studies of children who had no consistent mother figure during the first year. The most frequently quoted follow-up study is that of Goldfarb [11] in which he compared fifteen adolescents, who had lived in an institution for the first three or four years of life, with fifteen adolescents, supposedly of similar genetic backgrounds, who had lived in foster homes since infancy. The mean Wechsler IQ of the institution children was 72.4 and of the group living in foster homes, 95.4. Along with the mental retardation of the "ex-institution" children, there were distinct emotional trends; chiefly, the absence of a normal capacity for inhibition. The institution group showed extremely difficult behavior with symptoms of hyperactivity, restlessness, inability to concentrate, and unmanageability. Furthermore, they seemed to have no genuine attachments to people although they were indiscriminately and insatiably demanding of affection.

A more recent study of infants in institutions was made by Provence and

Lipton [27]. They examined 75 children placed in an institution, 75 children with similar backgrounds placed in foster homes, and 75 children who remained with their own families. Although there were individual differences, the institutional children were significantly retarded in general development compared to both other groups. Language development was the first area revealing retardation, and it showed the greatest amount of retardation. It also took a longer period of family living for significant improvement to take place.

Studies with animal subjects also show that early experience influences adult problem-solving capacity. A classic experiment relating to this ability is that of Thompson and Heron who used dogs as subjects [39]. Some were reared under isolation in laboratory cages from the time of weaning to eight months of age. Their litter mates were reared for this same period in homes as pets. The cage-reared and pet-reared dogs were put together in a dog pasture for ten months; then, at eighteen months of age, their ability to solve mazes was tested. The pet-reared dogs were clearly superior to their cage-reared litter mates, indicating the permanent importance of the environmental differences in their early infancy.

In the face of such clear evidence concerning the effects of maternal care deprivation, the amount of misunderstanding has been surprising. First, some clinicians understood "maternal deprivation" to include *any* separation of the infant from the mother. This is not true; it is only prolonged separation with inadequate substitute mother care for which serious consequences may be expected. Second, many have thought that the dire consequences were inevitable and universal; that all children undergoing early institutionalization or other sorts of gross maternal deprivation develop an "affectionless character" or suffer retarded mental development. This is also untrue; but the fact that there are differences in vulnerability does not destroy the causal connections. In physical medicine not every individual exposed to a particular virus falls ill of the disease. Third, the inference has been made by some that every child of psychopathic disposition or with mental retardation has had this pathogenic experience in infancy. This also is not logical; many kinds of pathogenic factors can have the same end result. In this respect there is a difference between physical and mental illnesses. Physical illnesses are likely to be more specific in their symptomatology and be the result of more specific antecedent conditions. Psychological problems are less sharply delineated and may result from multiple rather than single causes.

Oversimplification of the maternal deprivation concept has had its effects on clinical opinion and practice. Concern about maternal care tends to exaggerate the role of the mother in the development of any and all psychological difficulties of her children. Prevention is conceived solely in terms of maternal love and attention, and the cause of psychological difficulties is automatically attributed to "maternal rejection." Another misinterpretation has arisen from the issue of the possible irreversibility of damage done by early deprivation. Somehow the evidence showing the lasting effects of early deprivation despite improved environmental opportunities has been taken by some to mean that the personality is fixed by the age of three years and that no further changes are possible. On the basis of common sense and ordinary observation, this stand is obviously untenable. In normal development, the child of three years is reasonably plastic, having a potential for a great deal of further learning and development. It is only in abnormal conditions that the capacity for change is lost. A child who has been exposed to pathogenic deprivation and reacted to it in a sensitive way is in some ways "scarred for life." Depending on circumstances and the endowment of the child, these scars may be barely noticeable or may be severely handicapping. But the results of the special conditions of maternal deprivation cannot be generalized to children under normal environmental conditions.

In terms of clinical practice, Prugh and Harlow object to the current tendency to believe that separation of the child from his mother is to be avoided at all costs [28]. They point out that there can be "masked deprivation" where the infant's needs are unfulfilled even though he remains at home. After clinical study of the parents of mentally retarded children who were in the IQ range from 50 to 80 and had no history of birth injury or demonstrable organic pathology, Goshen suggests that mental retardation can occur as the by-product of certain types of maternal attitudes [13]. Specifically, he suggests that neurotic maternal attitudes which are characterized by a failure to stimulate and evoke meaningful signals during critical periods of life can result in the child's failure to grasp the significance of language. This failure may proceed to a state recognizable as mental retardation. Goshen was concerned with mothers who were ordinarily capable and conscientious but temporarily unable to give more than perfunctory physical care to their infants. He concluded with the excellent recommendation that "when a mother develops a deep psychological depression during the first year of a child's life, it would seem to be an urgent necessity to place the child in the care of a healthy adult until the mother comes out of the depression" [13].

There is nothing mystical about the importance of "mother love" in the first year of life. Biological motherhood does not guarantee maternal devotion, and the baby will accept a substitute mother if one is provided. It is not the existence of the person that counts, but the part that she plays in the infant's daily life. The relationship with a single person is the key factor in the infant's development. The gratifications provided by the mother draw the baby's attention to the outside world and serve as a bridge to other objects external to himself. After the baby has come to know her and to attach some importance to her, he becomes aware of her absences, and this helps him in differentiating between self and not-self. Inevitably, the mother frustrates the baby at times, and this adds further impetus to the baby's drive to gain independence and control over the outside world. By virtue of the coincidence of neural maturational changes, the baby acquires at the same time new powers of perception, memory, discrimination, motor coordination, and imitation which create some new problems for him, but, at the same time, new ways of solving them. Thus, we see that during the first year the baby is normally in an ideal educational situation where ability, opportunity, and motivation combine in the service of a common goal—development.

SOCIOCULTURAL INFLUENCES

Although there is some connection between low socioeconomic status and (a) poor prenatal condition and (b) inadequate maternal care in the first year of life, the impact of these conditions on mental development is even greater at later ages. For many years there has been cogent evidence attesting to the effects of environment on measured intelligence. Skeels and Dye showed that the IQ's of retarded children in institutions could be raised by "differential stimulation" [33]; Skodak and Skeels studied the effects of adoptive homes in raising IQ's [34]; and Klineberg reported the effect of environment on Negro children who had moved from the South [20]. The lowest scores were obtained by the groups most recently arrived from the South, with a close correlation between the length of time lived in New York and intelligence test scores. The improvement seemed to take place almost entirely in the first five or six years; those children who had lived in New York for a longer period showed little further improvement, and those Negroes who had moved to the North were, as a group, approximately at the average of the whole Negro school population of their original home cities.

Other studies, conversely, show the deteriorating effect of cultural impoverishment. Gordon, for instance, studied a group of children who grew up on canal boats in England [12]. At young ages, the average IQ of these children was about 90 (low average) but when the children were older the IQ dropped consistently, so that in their teens it was well below the average for the general population. Sherman and Key studied some communities located in Appalachia and reported similar findings [32]. The lowering of IQ in the older children was related to the varying degrees of isolation and opportunities for schooling that were provided in the areas studied. This is similar to the "cumulative deficit phenomenon" recently described by Deutsch as taking place between the first- and fifth-grade years in lower-class children attending New York City schools [8].

Although the importance of environment on measured intelligence has been well substantiated for some period of time, very little was done with this knowledge. Attempts were made to construct "culture-free" tests of intelligence to get at the "underlying potential" but none was successful. For example, Rosenblum, Keller, and Papania tried the Davis-Eells ("Culture-Fair") test with a group of mentally handicapped school-aged boys of lower social-class standing and found that the mean score was not significantly higher than the mean IQ's obtained on the Binet, which is highly verbal in content [31]. The authors commented that, though the Davis-Eells test may not contain culturally biased items, the conditions under which the test was administered cannot be said to have been completely free of middle-class overtones. Although it was presented to the children as a series of games, the children were not fooled and revealed by their comments that they knew from the outset that they were taking a test. A "good" test-taking attitude is dependent on cultural factors insofar as the child has been schooled to think it is important and profitable to try to do one's best.

In the 1960's, many people began to take a new, hard look at the old knowledge. The new questions asked were, "In what ways does culture affect intelligence?" and "What can be done about it?" It was soon obvious that many children came to school ill-prepared for academic work, and attention was focused on the preschool years. The role of maturation in early child development was re-examined. The work of Gesell and his colleagues provided normative pictures of children at different ages and stressed the orderly sequence of behavioral changes with increasing age. The developmental principles that Gesell offered as explanations were couched in terms of embryology [9] and stressed *intrinsic* factors rather than external, environmental factors. His dictum that "training does not transcend maturation" [10] implied a passive approach to early child care. Not only was early training considered futile, it was viewed as dangerous to "pressure" a child before he reached the point of optimum "readiness." According to this philosophy the young child should be left alone as much as possible in order that intrinsic growth processes take their natural course of progression.

In some quarters there was question about this assumption of automatic growth in the young child. For one thing, the observations of the results of early maternal deprivation indicated the importance of the environment in stimulating and supporting the very beginnings of mental development. Animal experiments showed permanent loss of function without proper stimulation. By keeping chimpanzee babies in total darkness for varying lengths of time, Riesen and others found that certain anatomical structures of the retina were permanently damaged [30]. With a very different approach, namely, the study of mental development in young children in normal circumstances, Piaget came to the similar conclusion that nothing was so automatic that it did not require practice. Talking about the sucking reflex, Piaget stated that only practice leads to normal functioning [25].

> That is the first aspect of accommodation: contact with the object modified, in a way, the activity of the reflex, and, even if this activity were oriented hereditarily to such contact, the latter is no less necessary to the consolidation of the former. This is how certain instincts are lost or certain reflexes cease to function normally, due to the lack of a suitable environment [25].

The new thought that "readiness" is in part an acquisition of experience rather than solely a development of time prompted an analysis of the environmental conditions in which culturally disadvantaged children spent their first five years. Even more specifically, attention was drawn to the role of social class in language development [Deutsch, 7]. Children in the lower socioeconomic groups start to talk, on the average, at a later age than do children in higher socioeconomic groups. In the lower income groups, verbal productions from the child are likely to be ignored as of little value. It is regarded as more important that the child take care of himself and achieve independence from the mother as early as possible so she can turn her attention to other babies, earn extra money, or maintain the household. In contrast, parents of middle and high socioeconomic status are more likely to talk to their children and to listen with pride and pleasure to what their children have to say. Irwin demonstrated that talking *to* children from an early age (twelve months and up) increases the verbal productivity of the child [16]. He explained this in two ways. First, in classical learning terms, a certain behavior, that is, verbalization, is positively rewarded by the mother's attention. Second, in psychodynamic terms, the child normally identifies with his mother, and if she talks, so does he.

There have been efforts to pinpoint the language deficiencies prevailing in lower-class families. Errors in enunciation and grammatical syntax have been analyzed. Perhaps even more important than the quality of language is its use. John and Goldstein report that children from low-income homes have relatively little opportunity to engage in active dialogue when learning labels [19], and Bernstein points out that in poorer homes language is used in a restrictive fashion rather than in an explanatory one [2]. If the child asks for something, the parental response is an abbreviated acknowledgment rather than a complete sentence or thought which elaborates on the child's utterance. The feedback does not provide the child with more information than that with which he started. The parents, setting little store by words, are content with approximations and imprecise labels where "flower" covers "tree," "bush," "weed," and so on. As pointed out by John and Goldstein [19], it is only by corrective feedback that the child learns that a "dog" is not a horse or cat or some other four-legged object (discrimination). By the same process he learns that "dog" is not only the white Spitz but also the black police dog, the brown stuffed animal, and the picture of "Spot" in a book.

There are many theories regarding the intimate connections between language and thought. Piaget emphasizes the importance of language in the socialization process. Progression from primitive modes of thinking requires that the child become aware of himself as thinking, feeling, seeing, hearing, from a point of view unique to himself. He needs a dual perspective whereby he not only perceives reality but is aware of himself perceiving and is thus able, within limits, to discount and compensate for his own biases, blind spots, and restricted vision. He can only require his kind of awareness of self in contrast to something else, namely, the point of view of others. To see the world as it appears to someone else can only be done through the medium of language.

> Intelligence, just because it undergoes a gradual process of socialization,
> is enabled through the bond established by language between thoughts

and words to make an increasing use of concepts; whereas autism, just because it remains individual, is still tied to imagery, to organic activity, and even to organic movements. The mere fact, then, of telling one's thought, of telling it to others, or of keeping silence and telling it only to oneself must be of enormous importance to the fundamental structure and functioning of thought in general, and of child logic in particular [24].

Others have studied children's ability to solve complex problems as related to the use they make of language in verbal mediation. Jensen defines verbal mediation as "verbal behavior which facilitates further learning, which controls behavior and which permits the development of conceptual thinking" [18]. It appears that children who receive insufficient verbal stimulation in early childhood develop deficiencies not only in spoken language but also in verbal mediational behavior so that they are handicapped in the concept formation and problem-solving abilities required in the school learning situation.

The facts about early language development and later intellectual ability have given renewed impetus to preschool education. Hunt has proposed preschool enrichment as an antidote for cultural deprivation and social disadvantage [15]. In accordance with these new ideas, preschools in underprivileged, urban neighborhoods have been mushrooming in an effort to fill in the gaps, particularly in language, which are left by the parents. One hopes that the parents will not be forgotten in all the flurry. It is unlikely that the preschool teacher can equal the parent as an identification figure for the child. It would be profitable to give the parents the opportunity to identify with the teacher so that the parents in turn can serve as models for the child and support the educational efforts.

INDIVIDUAL PERSONALITY CHARACTERISTICS

The influence of sociocultural factors on intelligence development is usually considered in terms of group trends with little attention to the individual variations. The emphasis is on environmental conditions insofar as they provide the child with an opportunity to learn. There is less thought given to the role of motivation for learning; there is an assumption that if the proper opportunities are provided at the crucial times, the child will "naturally" seize upon these opportunities because of some intrinsic growth motivation. In Hunt's words,

> the problem for a teacher endeavoring to keep children interested in intellectual growth is one of providing circumstances so matched, or mismatched, to those with which her pupils are already familiar that an interesting and attractive challenge is continually provided [15].

Hunt feels that there is a "kind of intrinsic motivation which is inherent in information processing and action" and that "an opportunity to see and hear a variety of things is more important than the fate of instinctual needs and impulses" [15].

There is a tendency for exciting new ideas to be taken as a replacement for what went before. There is no fundamental conflict between the psychoanalytic ideas concerning the transformation of basic drives in the stimulation of intelligence and Hunt's suggestions regarding the importance of environmental stimulation for promoting intelligence. Early maternal deprivation has its devastating effect on intelligence not only because of lack of environmental stimulation but also because of the lack of emotional attachments. To put it simply, the child must care for a person before he really cares about things. Without an emotional attachment he tends to be either apathetic and disinterested in his environment, or he takes an obsessive interest in objects and things excluding those stimulations emanating from people. Such an exclusion has a disastrous effect on language development and eventually on the whole of mental development. This distortion is seen most clearly in autistic children, though other forms of childhood psychosis also block intellectual development as a by-product of the disturbed social relationships. Without help on the social score, these children are unable to take advantage of environmental opportunities for learning and remain fixed at primitive levels of thinking.

There are less pathological conditions where one also sees the interaction of personality factors and the development of intelligence. Learning requires activity, and if the parents keep the child dependent and in a state of enforced passivity, mental growth is often stunted as a consequence. An interesting study that corroborates this thesis was done by Sontag, Baker, and Nelson [36]. They compared the personalities of children who showed increases or decreases in measured intelligence over a period of years. According to their observations, the "passive, infantile dependent pattern" led to a decreasing level of Binet performance, whereas, "aggressive, self-reassuring mastery of tasks, competitive independent patterns" led to progressively advanced performance. Child therapists [for instance, Sperry, Ulrich, and Staver, 38] have noticed that therapy for learning problems is more effective with aggressive children than with passive, compliant children. Regardless of socioeconomic status, the drive for mastery is not the same in all children. This may in part by determined by inborn constitution, but it is also affected by parental attitudes toward the child's early strivings for independence and autonomy.

A second important connecting link between personality and intelligence is the fate of early childhood curiosity. During the age period of one to two years, curiosity finds expression primarily through physical acts. From the age of two years on, curiosity becomes increasingly intellectual. Although curiosity is generally thought of as a desirable characteristic, this holds true only for impersonal topics. Questions about God, death, sex differences, the origin of babies are often shunted aside by the nervous parent. Individual families may have special secrets which are constantly in evidence, but which at the same time are taboo for discussion. Forbidden secrets exist in families of all cultural descriptions but are perhaps more frequent in disorganized families of low socioeconomic level. For instance, a family forced to make repeated, surreptitious moves in order to "jump the rent" will not prepare the child in advance or explain it after the move. If the child cannot ask (and receive an answer) about such vital questions as to where he will sleep, where is Daddy, who is that man (or woman), he is not going to venture questions about the moon and the stars. Anxiety is one powerful incentive for wonderment. The child wants to know what is going to happen and why, in order to avoid surprises and prepare himself. If curiosity does not help to relieve anxiety, it has little value. Curiosity cannot be compartmentalized or restricted only to safe subjects.

A corollary to this problem of forbidden curiosity is the problem of forbidden knowledge. By independent observation the child may learn something about which he later feels guilty or anxious. Inner conflict may motivate the child to repress or hide his knowledge from others. This is one of the dynamic mechanisms involved in the oft-quoted case of "pseudo-imbecility" published by Mahler [21]. Many times the repressed or hidden knowledge is of a sexual nature because sexuality is commonly an emotionally charged topic, though any subject can be equally taboo in specific family circumstances. In these cases where the retardation is a defense against the anxiety of knowing, the child acts out the aphorism, "Where ignorance is bliss, it's folly to be wise."

There are many other possible points of connection between personality and mental development based on the mechanism of displacement. For example, conflicts in infantile feeding experiences do not inevitably result in symptoms of an oral nature only. Eating is a form of incorporation, a process of taking in from the outside world. Difficulties in taking in by mouth may spread to the perceptual processes of taking in through the eyes and ears. The possible connection is shown in everyday idioms such as "drinking in with the eyes," "devouring the sight," "digesting information," "a voracious reader," "hunger for knowledge," and so on. There is more than a similarity in process. The carry-over from eating to learning may stem from the repetition of a specific interpersonal relationship as well. A child who has been fed against his will, for instance, is likely to have residual feelings about superior, strong persons who force things on him. Learning requires the gracious acceptance of someone's superiority (at least on a pro tem basis) and can be blocked by unconscious feelings against someone who knows more than the learner. The neurotic children in whom eating conflicts have been displaced to the intellectual sphere, show poor absorption, appear not to understand what they are taught, and seem to forget from one time to the next [37].

Another kind of displacement is from genital conflicts. Here the child's major concern is with the genital differences between the sexes and his feelings about his own genital adequacy. Visual experience is important in learning about the sex difference. Jarvis, in an article on visual problems in reading disabilities, linked neurotic conflicts in looking with fantasies which deny the fact of castration in women [17]. A child warding off the anxiety caused by looking at one thing avoids looking at anything with close attention. For example, at the age levels of four and a half and five years, there are several items on the Stanford-Binet test which require comparison of visually presented objects in terms of their likenesses and differences. Occasionally a child will refuse to look at them, saying flatly, "They are all the same." If a child will not look for fear of seeing differences, he will have considerable difficulty in learning to read.

One could give other examples where the acquisition, retention, and/or demonstration of knowledge are blocked because of anxiety about one or another aspect of "knowing." When stupidity serves a defensive purpose to reduce anxiety, the child is immune to environmental stimulation no matter how well it is planned. Throughout a child's life there is constant interaction between mental and emotional development, and difficulties on the one side usually affect the other. Under normal conditions there is no incompatibility; affective and cognitive lines of development proceed together. In the absence of conflict there is indeed pleasure in "knowing" because it gives a sense of mastery and relieves the anxiety of helplessness.

Measurement of Intellectual Functioning

In talking about intelligence and the factors that influence its development, it is important to consider how intelligence is measured. Intelligence is judged by overt behavior. Some use diffuse standards of "adaptive" behavior, such as getting along well with people and meeting the demands of school and work. Quantitification of individual differences, however, demands the use of more limited, rigid criteria provided by intelligence-test performance. As measuring tools, IQ tests have much less reliability than tools of physical measurements. The probabilties of IQ changes over a period of time have been well researched. Pinneau prepared a series of tables which give the changes in Binet IQ's in individuals tested and retested at various ages [26]. One study showed that in a group of children first tested at six years and retested at twelve years, 50 per cent showed IQ changes of 8 points or more, with 25 per cent changing 13 points or more. The accumulation of such figures has completely destroyed the myth of IQ constancy. The changes are in part errors of measurement, and in part changes in the individual being tested.

The changes in the person can come about for many reasons. The opportunities the child has for experience is one possible causal factor. Psychologists do not hesitate to say that intelligence tests measure the results of learning and that no sharp distinction can be made between intelligence and attainment. In the words of Cureton:

It is obvious that every test of intelligence, as well as every test of school achievement, is a measure of a set of developed abilities. The difference lies in the choice of abilities to be measured and in the method of devising items to measure them. The general intelligence test, as its name implies, tries to measure general ability. To do this, it must include a variety of mental tasks, including samples of the more important types of mental operations and of symbolic content. The achievement test, on the contrary, limits the range of sampling to a relatively narrow and specific set of abilities. The symbolic content covered is fairly definite, and the range of mental operations called for is well-defined and not extremely extensive [5].

More recently, Vernon arrived at a similar conclusion. "There is no essential difference between the acquisition of, say, reading skills and the acquisition of reasoning or other capacities which would be conventionally regarded as part of intelligence" [40].

Environment is filtered through the individual's screen of perceptual styles, interests, ego ideals, and prejudices. Neurotic conflicts with their subsequent defenses, characterological traits, and specific anxieties all affect efficiency of intellectual functioning, sometimes serving to heighten it. It has been proposed that intelligence be regarded as a dynamic aspect of personality, and suggestions have been made regarding the analysis of intelligence-test behavior for such personality features as "coping styles" [22].

Considering errors of measurement and the effects of learning and personality on intelligence-test scores, one can appreciate that we are very far from measuring anything like "inborn potential." This does not render the intelligence test meaningless. The intelligence test is useful for short-range predictions of scholastic ability. The score is not an attribute of the child; by itself it does not explain why the child is the way he is. A good intelligence test gives important information about present functioning. When combined with an evaluation of the history and total situation of the child, it may provide the basis for remediation of deprivation and/or psychological conflict. The information from careful tests should not be brushed aside as irrelevant because it is environmentally produced. The term "pseudo-retardation" is a misnomer in that it implies retardation on a familial or organic basis. "Pseuo-retardation" may be less permanent but it is no less real at the moment. Intelligence tests (assuming that they have been carefully administered) are valid in describing present level, which is of necessity the starting point for therapists or teachers. Just as a child cannot jump from primer reading to Shakespeare, he cannot jump from magical thinking to an understanding of the principle of number equations. IQ results cannot be projected backward to evaluate genetic potentiality nor can they be projected into the future to determine the ceiling of achievement possibilities. It is quite sufficient that they be used for current planning.

References

1. ASHLEY-MONTAGU, M. F. *Prenatal Influences*. Springfield, Ill.: Charles C Thomas, 1962.
2. BERNSTEIN, BASIL. Language and social class. *British Journal of Sociology* (1960), pp. 271–76.
3. BOWLBY, JOHN. Maternal care and mental health. World Health Organization monograph, Series No. 2. 1951.
4. BROWNFIELD, E. D. "An Investigation of the Activity and Sensory Responses of Healthy, Newborn Infants." Ph.D. dissertation, Cornell University, 1956.
5. CURETON, E. E. The accomplishment quotient technique. *Journal of Experimental Education* 5 (1937):315–26.
6. DAVIDS, A. S., and TALMADGE, M. Anxiety, pregnancy and childbirth abnormalities. *Journal of Consulting Psychology* 25 (1961):74–77.
7. DEUTSCH, M. "The Role of Social Class in Language Development and Cognition." Mimeographed paper. Institute for Developmental Studies, Department of Psychiatry, New York Medical College. April 1964.
8. DEUTSCH, M. Facilitating development in the preschool child: Social and psychological perspectives. *Merrill-Palmer Quarterly* 10 (1964):249–63.
9. GESELL, A. *Infant Development: The Embryology of Early Human Behavior*. New York: Harper & Bros., 1932.
10. GESELL, A. The Developmental Psychology of Twins. In Carl Murchison, ed., *Handbook of Child Psychology*. Worcester, Mass.: Clark University Press, 1931, p. 189.
11. GOLDFARB, W. The effects of early institutional care on adolescent personality. *Journal of Experimental Education* 12 (1943):106–29.
12. GORDON, H. Mental and scholastic tests among retarded children: An enquiry into the effects of schooling on the various tests. *Education Pamphlets*, Board of Education, London, No. 44 (1923).
13. GOSHEN, CHARLES E. Mental retardation and neurotic maternal attitudes. *Archives of General Psychiatry* 9 (1963):168–75.
14. HARRELL, RUTH FLINN, WOODYARD, ELLA, and GATES, ARTHUR I. *The Effect of Mothers' Diets on the Intelligence of the Offspring*. New York: Teachers College Press, 1955. VII.
15. HUNT, J. McV. The psychological basis for using preschool enrichment as an antidote for cultural deprivation. *Merrill-Palmer Quarterly* 10 (1964):209–48.
16. IRWIN, O. C. In speech: The effect of systematic reading of stories. *Journal of Speech and Hearing Research* (1960), pp. 187–90.
17. JARVIS, VIVIAN. Clinical observations on the visual problem in reading disability. *Psychoanalytic study of the child*, vol. 13. New York: International Universities Press, 1958.
18. JENSEN, A. Learning in the preschool years. *Journal of Nursery Education* (January 1963), pp. 133–39.
19. JOHN, V. P., and GOLDSTEIN, L. S. The social context of language acquisition. *Merrill-Palmer Quarterly* 10 (1964):255–76.
20. KLINEBERG, O. *Negro Intelligence and Selective Migration*. New York: Columbia University Press, 1935.
21. MAHLER, MARGARET S. Pseudo-imbecility: A magic cap of indivisibility. *Psychoanalytic Quarterly* 11 (1942):149–64.

22. MORIARTY, A. E. Coping patterns of preschool children in response to intelligence test demands. *Genetic Psychology Monographs* 64, no. 1 (1961):3–127.

23. PASAMANICK, B., and KNOBLOCH, H. Epidemiologic studies on the complications of pregnancy and the birth process. In G. Caplan, *Prevention of Mental Disorders in Children*. New York: Basic Books, 1961.

24. PIAGET, J. *Language and Thought of the Child*. New York: Meridian Press, 1955, p. 64.

25. PIAGET, J. *The Origin of Intelligence in the Child*. Trans. Margaret Cook. New York: International Universities Press, 1952.

26. PINNEAU, SAMUEL. *Changes in Intelligence Quotient*. Boston: Houghton Mifflin, 1961.

27. PROVENCE, SALLY, and LIPTON, ROSE C. *Infants in Institutions*. New York: International Universities Press, 1962.

28. PRUGH, DANE G., and HARLOW, ROBERT G. Masked Deprivation in Infants and Young Children. In *Deprivation of Maternal Care: A Reassessment of Its Effects*. Geneva: World Health Organization, Public Health Papers, No. 14, 1962.

29. RICHMOND, JULIUS, and LUSTMAN, SEYMOUR. Autonomic function in the neonate: Implications for psychosomatic theory. *Psychosomatic Medicine* 17 (1955):269–75.

30. RIESEN, A. H. Plasticity of Behavior: Psychological Aspects. In H. F. Harlow and C. N. Woolsey, eds., *Biological and Biochemical Bases of Behavior*. Madison: University of Wisconsin Press, 1958, pp. 425–50.

31. ROSENBLUM, SIDNEY, KELLER, JAMES E., and PAPANIA, NED. Davis-Eells ("culture-fair") test performance of lower class retarded children. *Journal of Consulting Psychology* 19 (1955):51–54.

32. SHERMAN, M., and KEY, C. B. The intelligence of isolated mountain children. *Child Development* 3 (1932):279–90.

33. SKEELS, H. M., and DYE, H. B. A study of the effects of differential stimulation on mentally retarded children. *Proceedings of the American Association for Mental Deficiency* 44 (1939):114–36.

34. SKODAK, M., and SKEELS, H. M. A final follow-up study of one hundred adopted children. *Journal of Genetic Psychology* 75 (1949):85–125.

35. SONTAG, L. S. The significance of fetal environmental differences. *American Journal of Obstetrics and Gynecology* 42 (1941):996–1003.

36. SONTAG, L. S., BAKER, C. T., and NELSON, V. P. Personality as a determinant of performance. *American Journal of Orthopsychiatry* 25 (1955):555–62.

37. SPERRY, B., STAVER, NANCY, and MANN, HAROLD. Destructive fantasies in certain learning difficulties. *American Journal of Orthopsychiatry* 22 (1952):356–66.

38. SPERRY, B., ULRICH, D. N., and STAVER, NANCY. The relation of motility to boys' learning problems. *American Journal of Orthopsychiatry* 28 (1958):640–46.

39. THOMPSON, W. R., and HERON, W. The effects of restricting early experience on the problem-solving capacity of dogs. *Canadian Journal of Psychology* 8 (1954):17–31.

40. VERNON, P. E. *Intelligence and Attainment Tests*. New York: Philosophical Library, 1960, p. 39.

Unknowns in the IQ Equation

SANDRA SCARR-SALAPATEK

The late 1960s and early 70s witnessed a most explosive revival of the nature-nurture controversy in intelligence. Arthur Jensen's genetic differences hyothesis was met by picketing and bomb threats, Herrnstein's social formulation by accusations of racism and worse. Perhaps a great deal of the conflict could have been avoided if the public (and some professionals) had been able to distinguish fact from theory and if the protagonists had more effectively communicated the hypothetical nature of their remarks. Besides, as Kessler pointed out, there is altogether too much emphasis placed on the notion of general intelligence, which doesn't really seem to have so much to do with the way we live our lives. We may be experiencing another tempest in the academic teapot.

In the following review of the scientific merits of this brouhaha, Sandra Scarr-Salapatek focuses on research methodology. This is a difficult topic that makes for difficult reading—but that's the point: the complexity of the question and the current state of research make any public speculation about possible answers hazardous indeed.

Environment, Heredity, and Intelligence. Compiled from the *Harvard Educational Review*. Reprint Series No. 2. Harvard Educational Review, Cambridge, Mass., 1969. iv, 248 pp., illus. Paper, $4.95.

The IQ Argument. *Race, Intelligence and Education.* H. J. Eysenck. Library Press, New York, 1971. iv, 156 pp., illus. $5.95.

IQ. Richard Herrnstein, in the *Atlantic*, Vol. 228, No. 3, Sept. 1971, pp. 44–64.

IQ scores have been repeatedly estimated to have a large heritable component

SOURCE: From S. Scarr-Salapatek, "Unknowns in the IQ Equation," *Science* 174, December 17, 1971, pp. 1223–28. Copyright © 1971 by the American Association for the Advancement of Science. Reproduced by permission.

I thank Philip Salapatek, Richard Weinberg, I. I. Gottesman, and Leonard I. Heston for their critical reading of this paper. They are not in any way responsible for its content, however.

in United States and Northern European white populations.[1] Individual differences in IQ, many authors have concluded, arise far more from genetic than from environmental differences among people in these populations, at the present time, and under present environmental conditions. It has also been known for many years that white lower-class and black groups have lower IQ's, on the average, than white middle-class groups. Most behavioral scientists comfortably "explained" these group differences by appealing to obvious environmental differences between the groups in standards of living, educational opportunities, and the like. But recently an explosive controversy has developed over the heritability of between-group differences in IQ, the question at issue being: If individual differences within the white population as a whole can be attributed largely to heredity, is it not plausible that the average differences between social-class groups and between racial groups also reflect significant genetic differences? Can the former data be used to explain the latter?

To propose genetically based racial and social-class differences is anathema to most behavioral scientists, who fear any scientific confirmation of the pernicious racial and ethnic prejudices that abound in our society. But now that the issue has been openly raised, and has been projected into the public context of social and educational policies, a hard scientific look must be taken at what is known and at what inferences can be drawn from that knowledge.

The public controversy began when A. R. Jensen, in a long paper in the *Harvard Educational Review*, persuasively juxtaposed data on the heritability of IQ and the observed differences between groups. Jensen suggested that current large-scale educational attempts to raise the IQ's of lower-class children, white and black, were failing because of the high heritability of IQ. In a series of papers and rebuttals to criticism, in the same journal and elsewhere,[2] Jensen put forth the hypothesis that social-class and racial differences in mean IQ were due largely to differences in the gene distributions of these populations. At least, he said, the genetic-differences hypothesis was no less likely, and probably more likely, than a simple environmental hypothesis to explain the mean difference of 15 IQ points between blacks and whites [3]

---

[1] For a review of studies, see L. Erlenmeyer-Kimling and L. F. Jarvik, *Science* 142 (1963): 1477. Heritability is the ratio of genetic variance to total phenotypic variance. For human studies, heritability is used in its broad sense of total genetic variance/total phenotypic variance. In other words, "heritability" talks about how much of the observed differences among people depends on differences in their genetic make-up. See also Editor's note on p. 316.

[2] The *Harvard Educational Review* compilation includes Jensen's paper, "How much can we boost IQ and scholastic achievement?," comments on it by J. S. Kagan, J. McV. Hunt, J. F. Crow, C. Breiter, D. Elkind, L. J. Cronbach, and W. F. Brazziel, and a rejoinder by Jensen. See also A. R. Jensen, in J. Hellmuth, *Disadvantaged Child*, vol. 3 (Special Child Publ., Seattle, Wash., 1970).

[3] P. L. Nichols, thesis, University of Minnesota (1970). Nichols reports that in two large samples of black and white children, seven-year WISC [Wechsler Intelligence Scale for Children] IQ scores showed the same means and distributions for the two racial groups, once social-class variables were equated. These results are unlike those of several other studies, which found that matching socioeconomic status did not create equal means in

and the even larger average IQ differences between professionals and manual laborers within the white population.

Jensen's articles have been directed primarily at an academic audience. Herrnstein's article in the *Atlantic* and Eysenck's book (first published in England) have brought the argument to the attention of the wider lay audience. Both Herrnstein and Eysenck agree with Jensen's genetic-differences hypothesis as it pertains to individual differences and to social-class groups, but Eysenck centers his attention on the genetic explanation of racial-group differences, which Herrnstein only touches on. Needless to say, many other scientists will take issue with them.

Eysenck's Racial Thesis

Eysenck has written a popular account of the race, social-class, and IQ controversy in a generally inflammatory book. The provocative title and the disturbing cover picture of a forlorn black boy are clearly designed to tempt the lay reader into a pseudo-battle between Truth and Ignorance. In this case Truth is genetic-environmental interactionism [4] and Ignorance is naive environmentalism. For the careful reader, the battle fades out inconclusively as Eysenck admits that scientific evidence to date does not permit a clear choice of the genetic-differences interpretation of black inferiority on intelligence tests. A quick reading of the book, however, is sure to leave the reader believing that scientific evidence today strongly supports the conclusion that U.S. blacks are genetically inferior to whites in IQ.

The basic theses of the book are as follows:

1. IQ is a highly heritable characteristic in the U.S. white population and probably equally heritable in the U.S. black population.
2. On the average, blacks score considerably lower than whites on IQ tests.
3. U.S. blacks are probably a nonrandom, lower-IQ, sample of native African populations.
4. The average IQ difference between blacks and whites probably represents important genetic differences between the races.

---

the two racial groups (A. Shuey [15]; A. B. Wilson, *Racial Isolation in the Public Schools*, vol. 2 (Government Printing Office, Washington, D. C., 1967)). In Nichols's samples, prenatal and postnatal medical care was equally available to blacks and whites, which may have contributed to the relatively high IQ scores of the blacks in these samples.

[4] By interaction, Eysenck means simply $P = G + E$, or "heredity and environment acting together to produce the observed phenotype" (p. 111). He does not mean what most genticists and behavior geneticists mean by interaction; that is, the *differential* phenotypic effects produced by various combinations of genotypes and environments, as in the interaction term of analysis-of-variance statistics. Few thinking people are not interactionists in Eysenck's sense of the term, because that's the only way to get the organism and the environment into the same equation to account for variance in any phenotypic trait. How much of the phenotypic variance is accounted for by each of the terms in the equation is the real issue.

5. Drastic environmental changes will have to be made to improve the poor phenotypes* that U.S. blacks now achieve.

The evidence and nonevidence that Eysenck cites to support his genetic hypothesis of racial differences make a curious assortment. Audrey Shuey's review [15] of hundreds of studies showing mean phenotypic differences between black and white IQ's leads Eysenck to conclude:

All the evidence to date suggests the strong and indeed overwhelming importance of genetic factors in producing the great variety of intellectual differences which we observe in our culture, and much of the difference observed between certain racial groups. This evidence cannot be argued away by niggling and very minor criticisms of details which do not really throw doubts on the major points made in this book [p. 126].

To "explain" the genetic origins of these mean IQ differences he offers these suppositions:

White slavers wanted dull beasts of burden, ready to work themselves to death in the plantations, and under those conditions intelligence would have been counterselective. Thus there is every reason to expect that the particular sub-sample of the Negro race which is constituted of American Negroes is not an unselected sample of Negroes, but has been selected throughout history according to criteria which would put the highly intelligent at a disadvantage. The inevitable outcome of such selection would of course be a gene pool lacking some of the genes making for higher intelligence [p. 42].

Other ethnic minorities in the U.S. are also, in his view, genetically inferior, again because of the selective migration of lower IQ genotypes:

It is known [sic] that many other groups came to the U.S.A. due to pressures which made them very poor samples of the original populations. Italians, Spaniards, and Portuguese, as well as Greeks, are examples where the less able, less intelligent were forced through circumstances to emigrate, and where their American progeny showed significantly lower IQ's than would have been shown by a random sample of the original population [p. 43].

Although Eysenck is careful to say that these are not established facts (because no IQ tests were given to the immigrants or nonimmigrants in question?), the tone of his writing leaves no doubt about his judgment. There is something in this book to insult almost everyone except WASPs and Jews.

Despite his conviction that U.S. blacks are genetically inferior in IQ to whites, Eysenck is optimistic about the potential effects of radical environmental changes on the present array of Negro IQ phenotypes. He points to

---

* Editor's note: "Phenotype" refers to what we can observe in people, like hair color, sex, and IQ. "Genotype" refers to what we cannot observe, the genetic structure of the person. Phenotype depends on contributions from both environment and genes.

the very large IQ gains produced by intensive one-to-one tutoring of black urban children with low-IQ mothers, contrasting large environmental changes and large IQ gains in intensive programs of this sort with insignificant environmental improvements and small IQ changes obtained by Headstart and related programs. He correctly observes that, whatever the heritability of IQ (or, it should be added, of any characteristic), large phenotypic changes may be produced by creating appropriate, radically different environments never before encountered by those genotypes. On this basis, Eysenck calls for further research to determine the requisites of such environments.

Since Eysenck comes to this relatively benign position regarding potential improvement in IQ's, why, one may ask, is he at such pains to "prove" the genetic inferiority of blacks? Surprisingly, he expects that new environments, such as that provided by intensive educational tutoring, will not affect the black-white IQ differential, because black children and white will probably profit equally from such treatment. Since many middle-class white children already have learning environments similar to that provided by tutors for the urban black children, we must suppose that Eysenck expects great IQ gains from relatively small changes in white, middle-class environments.

This book is an uncritical popularization of Jensen's ideas without the nuances and qualifiers that make much of Jensen's writing credible or at least responsible. Both authors rely on Shuey's review [15], but Eysenck's way of doing it is to devote some 25 pages to quotes and paraphrases of her chapter summaries. For readers to whom the original Jensen article is accessible, Eysenck's book is a poor substitute; although he defends Jensen and Shuey, he does neither a service.

It is a maddeningly inconsistent book filled with contradictory caution and incaution; with hypotheses stated both as hypotheses and as conclusions; with both accurate and inaccurate statements on matters of fact. For example, Eysenck thinks evoked potentials* offer a better measure of "innate" intelligence than IQ tests. But on what basis? Recently F. B. Davis [2] has failed to find any relationship whatsoever between evoked potentials and either IQ scores or scholastic achievement, to which intelligence is supposed to be related. Another example is Eysenck's curious use of data to support a peculiar line of reasoning about the evolutionary inferiority of blacks: First, he reports that African and U.S. Negro babies have been shown to have precocious sensorimotor development by white norms (the difference, by several accounts, appears only in gross motor skills and even there is slight). Second, he notes that by three years of age U.S. white exceed U.S. black children in mean IQ scores. Finally he cites a (very slight) negative correlation, found in an early study, between sensorimotor intelligence in the first year of life and later IQ. From exaggerated statements of these various data, he concludes:

---

* Editor's note: "Evoked potentials" are electrical responses of the cortex of the brain to sensory stimulation. These are recorded by means of electrodes placed on the scalp.

These findings are important because of a very general view in biology according to which the more prolonged the infancy the greater in general are the cognitive or intellectual abilities of the species. This law appears to work even within a given species [p. 79].

Eysenck would apparently have us believe that Africans and their relatives in the U.S. are less highly evolved than Caucasians, whose longer infancy is related to later higher intelligence. I am aware of no evidence whatsoever to support a within-species relationship between longer infancy and higher adult capacities.

The book is carelessly put together, with no index; few references, and those not keyed to the text; and long, inadequately cited quotes that carry over several pages without clear beginnings and ends. Furthermore, considering the gravity of Eysenck's theses, the book has an occasional jocularity of tone that is offensive. A careful book on the genetic hypothesis, written for a lay audience, would have merited publication. This one, however, has been publicly disowned as irresponsible by the entire editorial staff of its London publisher, New Society. But never mind, the American publisher has used that and other condemnations to balance the accolades and make its advertisement [9] of the book more titillating.

Herrnstein's Social Thesis

Thanks to Jensen's provocative article, many academic psychologists who thought IQ tests belonged in the closet with the Rorschach inkblots have now explored the psychometric literature and found it to be a trove of scientific treasure. One of these is Richard Herrnstein, who from a Skinnerian background has become an admirer of intelligence tests—a considerable leap from shaping the behavior of pigeons and rats. In contrast to Eysenck's book, Herrnstein's popular account in the *Atlantic* of IQ testing and its values is generally responsible, if overly enthusiastic in parts.

Herrnstein unabashedly espouses IQ testing as "psychology's most telling accomplishment to date," despite the current controversy over the fairness of testing poor and minority-group children with IQ items devised by middle-class whites. His historical review of IQ test development, including tests of general intelligence and multiple abilities, is interesting and accurate. His account of the validity and usefulness of the tests centers on the fairly accurate prediction that can be made from IQ scores to academic and occupational achievement and income level. He clarifies the pattern of relationship between IQ and these criterion variables: High IQ is a necessary but not sufficient condition for high achievement, while low IQ virtually assures failure at high academic and occupational levels. About the usefulness of the tests, he concludes:

An IQ test can be given in an hour or two to a child, and from this infinitesimally small sample of his output, deeply important predictions follow —about schoolwork, occupation, income, satisfaction with life, and even life expectancy. The predictions are not perfect, for other factors always enter in, but no other single factor matters as much in as many spheres of life [p. 53].

One must assume that Herrnstein's enthusiasm for intelligence tests rests on population statistics, not on predictions for a particular child, because many children studied longitudinally have been shown to change IQ scores by 20 points or more from childhood to adulthood. It is likely that extremes of giftedness and retardation can be sorted out relatively early by IQ tests, but what about the 95 percent of the population in between? Their IQ scores may vary from dull to bright normal for many years. Important variations in IQ can occur up to late adolescence [7]. On a population basis Herrnstein is correct; the best early predictors of later achievement are ability measures taken from age five on. Predictions are based on correlations, however, which are not sensitive to absolute changes in value, only to rank orders. This is an important point to be discussed later.

After reviewing the evidence for average IQ differences by social class and race, Herrnstein poses the nature-nurture problem of "which is primary" in determining phenotypic differences in IQ. For racial groups, he explains, the origins of mean IQ differences are indeterminate at the present time because we have no information from heritability studies in the black population or from other, unspecified, lines of research which could favor primarily genetic or primarily environmental hypotheses. He is thoroughly convinced, however, that individual differences and social-class differences in IQ are highly heritable at the present time, and are destined, by environmental improvements, to become even more so:

If we make the relevant environment much more uniform (by making it as good as we can for everyone), then an even larger proportion of the variation in IQ will be attributable to the genes. The average person would be smarter, but intelligence would run in families even more obviously and with less regression toward the mean than we see today [p. 58].

For Herrnstein, society is, and will be even more strongly, a meritocracy based largely on inherited differences in IQ. He presents a "syllogism" (p. 58) to make his message clear:

1. If differences in mental abilities are inherited, and
2. If success requires those abilities, and
3. If earnings and prestige depend on success,
4. Then social standing (which reflects earnings and prestige) will be based to some extent on inherited differences among people.

Five "corollaries" for the future predict that the heritability of IQ will rise; that social mobility will become more strongly related to inherited IQ differences; that most bright people will be gathered in the top of the social structure, with the IQ dregs at the bottom; that many at the bottom will not have the intelligence needed for new jobs; and that the meritocracy will be built not just on inherited intelligence but on all inherited traits affecting success, which will presumably become correlated characters. Thus from the successful realization of our most precious, egalitarian, political and social goals there will arise a much more rigidly stratified society, a "virtual caste system" based on inborn ability.

To ameliorate this effect, society may have to move toward the socialist dictum, "From each according to his abilities, to each according to his needs," but Herrnstein sees complete equality of earnings and prestige as impossible because high-grade intelligence is scarce and must be recruited into those critical jobs that require it, by the promise of high earnings and high prestige. Although garbage collecting is critical to the health of the society, almost anyone can do it; to waste high-IQ persons on such jobs is to misallocate scarce resources at society's peril.

Herrnstein points to an ironic contrast between the effects of caste and class systems. Castes, which established artificial hereditary limits on social mobility guarantee the inequality of opportunity that preserves IQ heterogeneity at all levels of the system. Many bright people are arbitrarily kept down and many unintelligent people are artificially maintained at the top. When arbitrary bounds on mobility are removed, as in our class system, most of the bright rise to the top and most of the dull fall to the bottom of the social system, and IQ differences between top and bottom become increasingly hereditary. The greater the environmental equality, the greater the hereditary differences between levels in the social structure. The thesis of egalitarianism surely leads to its antithesis in a way that Karl Marx never anticipated.

Herrnstein proposes that our best strategy, in the face of increasing biological stratification, is publicly to recognize genetic human differences but to reallocate wealth to a considerable extent. The IQ have-nots need not be poor. Herrnstein does not delve into the psychological consequences of being publicly marked as genetically inferior.

Does the evidence support Herrnstein's view of hereditary social classes, now or in some future Utopia? Given his assumptions about the high heritability of IQ, the importance of IQ to social mobility, and the increasing environmental equality of rearing and opportunity, hereditary social classes are to some extent inevitable. But one can question the limits of genetic homogeneity in social-class groups and the evidence for his syllogism at present.

Is IQ as highly heritable throughout the social structure as Herrnstein assumes? Probably not. In a recent study of IQ heritability in various racial and social-class groups [14], I found much lower proportions of genetic variance* that would account for aptitude differences among lower-class than among middle-class children, in both black and white groups. Social disadvantage in prenatal and postnatal development can substantially lower phenotypic IQ and reduce the genotype-phenotype correlation. Thus, average phenotypic IQ differences between the social classes may be considerably larger than the genotypic differences.

Are social classes largely based on hereditary IQ differences now? Probably not as much as Herrnstein believes. Since opportunities for social mobility act at the phenotypic level, there still may be considerable genetic diversity for IQ at the bottom of the social structure. In earlier days arbitrary social barriers maintained genetic variability throughout the social structure. At present, individuals with high phenotypic IQ's are often upwardly mobile; but inherited wealth acts to maintain genetic diversity at the top, and nongenetic biological and social barriers to phenotypic development act to maintain a considerable genetic diversity of intelligence in the lower classes.

As P. E. Vernon has pointed out [19], we are inclined to forget that the majority of gifted children in recent generations have come from working-class, not middle-class, families. A larger percentage of middle-class children are gifted, but the working and lower classes produce gifted children in larger numbers. How many more disadvantaged children would have been bright if they had had middle-class gestation and rearing conditions?

I am inclined to think that intergenerational class mobility will always be with us, for three reasons. First, since normal IQ is a polygenic characteristic, various recombinations of parental genotypes will always produce more variable genotypes in the offspring than in the parents of all social-class groups, especially the extremes. Even if both parents, instead of primarily the male, achieved social-class status based on their IQ's, recombinations of their genes would always produce a range of offspring, who would be upwardly or downwardly mobile relative to their families of origin.

Second, since, as Herrnstein acknowledges, factors other than IQ—motivational, personality, and undetermined—also contribute to success or the lack of it, high IQ's will always be found among lower-class adults, in combination with schizophrenia, alcoholism, drug addiction, psychopathy, and other limiting factors. When recombined in offspring, high IQ can readily segregate with facilitating motivational and personality characteristics, thereby leading to upward mobility for many offspring. Similarly, middle-class parents will

* Editor's note: The "variance" is a statistic that describes the extent to which people differ among themselves with respect to some trait or quality; it refers to the total amount of variation in a group. "Analysis of variance" is a statistical procedure that allows one to separate the total variation of a group into portions of variance due to different factors. The h^2 statistic, the common estimate of "heritability," is an analysis of variance technique that separates total variation into that proportion due to genetic differences and that due to environmental differences; it is the ratio of variance due to genetic factors to the total variance. The actual value of h^2 is dependent upon the population of people to which the statistic is applied.

always produce some offspring with debilitating personal characteristics which lead to downward mobility.

Third, for all children to develop phenotypes that represent their best genotypic outcome (in current environments) would require enormous changes in the present social system. To improve and equalize all rearing environments would involve such massive intervention as to make Herrnstein's view of the future more problematic than he seems to believe.

Race as Caste

Races are castes between which there is very little mobility. Unlike the social-class system, where mobility based on IQ is sanctioned, the racial caste system, like the hereditary aristocracy of medieval Europe and the caste system of India, preserves within each group its full range of genetic diversity of intelligence. The Indian caste system was, according to Dobzhansky [4], a colossal genetic failure—or success, according to egalitarian values. After the abolition of castes at independence, Brahmins and untouchables were found to be equally educable despite—or because of—their many generations of segregated reproduction.

While we may tentatively conclude that there are some genetic IQ differences between social-class groups, we can make only wild speculations about racial groups. Average phenotypic IQ differences between races are not evidence for genetic differences (any more than they are evidence for environmental differences). Even if the heritabilities of IQ are extremely high in all races, there is still no warrant for equating within-group and between-group * heritabilities [18]. There are examples in agricultural experiments of within-group differences that are highly heritable but between-group differences that are entirely environmental. Draw two random samples of seeds from the same genetically heterogeneous population. Plant one sample in uniformly good conditions, the other in uniformly poor conditions. The average height difference between the populations of plants will be entirely environmental, although the individual differences in height within each sample will be entirely genetic. With known genotypes for seeds and known environments, genetic and environmental variances between groups can be studied. But racial groups are not random samples from the same population, nor are members reared in uniform conditions within each race. Racial groups are of unknown genetic equivalence for polygenic characteristics like IQ, and the differences in environments within and between the races may have as yet unquantified effects.

There is little to be gained from approaching the nature-nurture problem of race differences in IQ directly [1]. Direct comparisons of estimated within-

---

* Editor's note: The terms "within-group" and "between-group" come from analysis of variance. IQ differences that exist among a number of whites are an example of within-group differences; IQ differences between blacks and whites are between-group differences.

group heritabilities and the calculation of between-group heritabilities require assumptions that few investigators are willing to make, such as that all environmental differences are quantifiable, that differences in the environments of blacks and whites can be assumed to affect IQ in the same way in the two groups, and that differences in environments between groups can be "statistically controlled." A direct assault on race differences in IQ is vulnerable to many criticisms.

Indirect approaches may be less vulnerable. These include predictions of parent-child regression effects* and admixture studies.† Regression effects can be predicted to differ for blacks and whites if the two races indeed have genetically different population means. If the population mean for blacks is 15 IQ points lower than that of whites, then the offspring of high-IQ black parents should show greater regression (toward a lower population mean) than the offspring of whites of equally high IQ. Similarly, the offspring of low-IQ black parents should show less regression than those of white parents of equally low IQ. This hypothesis assumes that assortative mating for IQ is equal in the two races, which could be empirically determined but has not been studied as yet. Interpretable results from a parent-child regression study would also depend upon careful attention to intergenerational environmental changes, which could be greater in one race than the other.

Studies based on correlations between degree of white admixture and IQ scores *within* the black group would avoid many of the pitfalls of between-group comparisons. If serological genotypes can be used to identify persons with more and less white admixture, and if estimates of admixture based on blood groups are relatively independent of visible characteristics like skin color, then any positive correlation between degree of admixture and IQ would suggest genetic racial differences in IQ. Since blood groups have not been used directly as the basis of racial discrimination, positive findings would be relatively immune from environmentalist criticisms. The trick is to estimate individual admixture reliably. Several loci which have fairly different distributions of alleles in contemporary African and white populations have been proposed [12, 8]. No one has yet attempted a study of this sort.

Editor's notes:
  * "Parent-child regression effects" here means that a child's IQ will be closer to the population mean than the average of his parents' IQ's. This occurs for two reasons: first, because extreme IQ scores are less dependable than moderate scores (very high test scores are more likely to be erroneously high, and very low scores erroneously low than less extreme scores), and therefore the parents' true IQ's may not be so high or low as the test indicated; second, the more extreme the parents' IQ scores, the more likely they are to have resulted from unusually fortuitous (or unfortuitous) gene combinations which are unlikely to recur in their offspring. In either case, the child's IQ will be less extreme than the average of his parents' IQ's; that is, the child's IQ will have "regressed toward the population mean."
  † "Admixture studies" involve persons of mixed ancestry, whites with black ancestors, for instance, or blacks with white ancestors. The extent of this "admixture" can be roughly estimated by serological analysis, that is, by the study of the frequencies of various blood groups, which differ among populations.

h² and Phenotype*

Suppose that the heritabilities of IQ differences within all racial and social-class groups were .80, as Jensen estimates, and suppose that the children in all groups were reared under an equal range of conditions. Now, suppose that racial and social-class differences in mean IQ still remained. We would probably infer some degree of genetic difference between the groups. So what? The question now turns from a strictly scientific one to one of science and social policy.

As Eysenck, Jensen, and others [12, 8] have noted, eugenic and euthenic † strategies are both possible interventions to reduce the number of low-IQ individuals in all populations. Eugenic policies could be advanced to encourage or require reproductive abstinence by people who fall below a certain level of intelligence. The Reeds [11] have determined that one-fifth of the mental retardation among whites of the next generation could be prevented if no mentally retarded persons of this generation reproduced. There is no question that a eugenic program applied at the phenotypic level of parents' IQ would substantially reduce the number of low-IQ children in the future white population. I am aware of no studies in the black population to support a similar program, but some proportion of future retardation could surely be eliminated. It would be extremely important, however, to sort out genetic and environmental sources of low IQ both in racial and in social-class groups before advancing a eugenic program. The request or demand that some persons refrain from any reproduction should be a last resort, based on sure knowledge that their retardation is caused primarily by genetic factors and is not easily remedied by environmental intervention. Studies of the IQ levels of adopted children with mentally retarded natural parents would be most instructive, since some of the retardation observed among children of retarded parents may stem from the rearing environments provided by the parents.

In a pioneering study of adopted children and their adoptive and natural parents, Skodak [16] reported greater *correlations* † of children's IQ's with their natural than with their adoptive parents' IQ's. This statement has been often misunderstood to mean that the children's *levels* of intelligence more closely resembled their natural parents', which is completely false. Although

Editor's notes:
  * Remember that h² estimates the amount of observable variation in a population that is due to genetic differences.
  † Eugenics deals with improving what is inherited, while euthenics deals with improving the environment.
  ‡ "Correlation" is a statistic that relates two sets of scores. A positive correlation means that as a person's score on one measure goes up (or down), his score on the other measure goes up (or down); thus height and weight are positively correlated. A negative correlation means that as a person's score on one measure goes up, his score on the other measure goes down. But correlation does not take account of the *absolute* values of scores, just their pattern: whose scores were highest in both sets of scores, whose next highest, and so forth.

the rank order of the children's IQ's resembled that of their mothers' IQ's, the children's IQ's were higher, being distributed, like those of the adoptive parents, around a mean above 100, whereas their natural mothers' IQ's averaged only 85. The children, in fact, averaged 21 IQ points higher than their natural mothers. If the (unstudied) natural fathers' IQ's averaged around the population mean of 100, the mean of the children's would be expected to be 94, or 12 points lower than the mean obtained. The unexpected boost in IQ was presumably due to the better social environments provided by the adoptive families. Does this mean that phenotypic IQ can be substantially changed?

Even under existing conditions of child rearing, phenotypes of children reared by low-IQ parents could be markedly changed by giving them the same rearing environment as the top IQ group provide for their children. According to DeFries [3], if children whose parents average 20 IQ points below the population mean were reared in environments such as usually are provided only by parents in the top .01 percent of the population, these same children would average 5 points *above* the population mean instead of 15 points below, as they do when reared by their own families.

Euthenic policies depend upon the demonstration that different rearing conditions can change phenotypic IQ sufficiently to enable most people in a social class or racial group to function in future society. I think there is great promise in this line of research and practice, although its efficacy will depend ultimately on the cost and feasibility of implementing radical intervention programs. Regardless of the present heritability of IQ in any population, phenotypes can be changed by the introduction of new and different environments. (One merit of Eysenck's book is the attention he gives to this point.) Furthermore, it is impossible to predict phenotypic outcomes under very different conditions. For example, in the Milwaukee Project [6], in which the subjects are ghetto children whose mothers' IQ's are less than 70, intervention began soon after the children were born. Over a four-year period Heber has intensively tutored the children for several hours every day and has produced an enormous IQ difference between the experimental group (mean IQ 127) and a control group (mean IQ 90). If the tutored children continue to advance in environments which are radically different from their homes with retarded mothers, we shall have some measure of the present phenotypic range of reaction [5] of children whose average IQ's might have been in the 80 to 90 range. These data support Crow's comment on h^2 in his contribution to the *Harvard Educational Review* discussion (p. 158):

> It does not directly tell us how much improvement in IQ to expect from a given change in the environment. In particular, it offers no guidance as to the consequences of a new kind of environmental influence. For example, conventional heritability measures for height show a value of nearly 1. Yet, because of unidentified environmental influences, the mean height in the United States and in Japan has risen by a spectacular amount. An-

other kind of illustration is provided by the discovery of a cure for a hereditary disease. In such cases, any information on prior heritability may become irrelevant. Furthermore, heritability predictions are less dependable at the tails of the distribution.

To illustrate the phenotypic changes that can be produced by radically different environments for children with clear genetic anomalies, Rynders [13] has provided daily intensive tutoring for Down's syndrome infants. At the age of two, these children have average IQ's of 85 while control-group children, who are enrolled in a variety of other programs, average 68. Untreated children have even lower average IQ scores.

The efficacy of intervention programs for children whose expected IQ's are too low to permit full participation in society depends on their long-term effects on intelligence. Early childhood programs may be necessary but insufficient to produce functioning adults. There are critical research questions yet to be answered about euthenic programs, including what kinds, how much, how long, how soon, and toward what goals?

Does h^2 Matter?

There is growing disillusionment with the concept of heritability, as it is understood and misunderstood. Some who understand it very well would like to eliminate h^2 from human studies for at least two reasons. First, the usefulness of h^2 estimates in animal and plant genetics pertains to decisions about the efficacy of selective breeding to produce more desirable phenotypes. Selective breeding does not apply to the human case, at least so far. Second, if important phenotypic changes can be produced by radically different environments, then, it is asked, who cares about the heritability of IQ? Morton [9] has expressed these sentiments well:

> Considerable popular interest attaches to such questions as "is one class or ethnic group innately superior to another on a particular test?" The reasons are entirely emotional, since such a difference, if established, would serve as no better guide to provision of educational or other facilities than an unpretentious assessment of phenotypic differences.

I disagree. The simple assessment of phenotypic performance does not suggest any particular intervention strategy. Heritability estimates can have merit as indicators of the effects to be expected from various types of intervention programs. If, for example, IQ tests, which predict well to achievements in the larger society, show low heritabilities in a population, then it is probable that simply providing better environments which now exist will improve average performance in that population. If h^2 is high but environments sampled in that population are largely unfavorable, then (again) simple environmental improvement will probably change the mean phenotypic level. If h^2 is high and the environments sampled are largely favorable, then novel environmental manipulations are probably required to change phenotypes, and eugenic programs may be advocated.

The most common misunderstanding of the concept "heritability" relates to the myth of fixed intelligence: if h^2 is high, this reasoning goes, then intelligence is genetically fixed and unchangeable at the phenotypic level. This misconception ignores the fact that h^2 is a population statistic, bound to a given set of environmental conditions at a given point in time. Neither intelligence nor h^2 estimates are fixed.

It is absurd to deny that the frequencies of genes for behavior may vary between populations. For individual differences within populations, and for social-class differences, a genetic hypothesis is almost a necessity to explain some of the variance in IQ, especially among adults in contemporary white populations living in average or better environments. But what Jensen, Shuey, and Eysenck (and others) propose is that genetic racial differences are necessary to account for the current phenotypic differences in mean IQ between populations. That may be so, but it would be extremely difficult, given current methodological limitations, to gather evidence that would dislodge an environmental hypothesis to account for the same data. And to assert, despite the absence of evidence, and in the present social climate, that a particular race is genetically disfavored in intelligence is to scream "FIRE! . . . I think" in a crowded theater. Given that so little is known, further scientific study seems far more justifiable than public speculations.

References

1. CAVALLI-SFORZA, L. L., and BODMER, W. F. *The Genetics of Human Populations.* San Francisco: W. H. Freeman, 1971, pp. 753–804.

   They propose that the study of racial differences is useless and not scientifically supportable at the present time.

2. DAVIS, F. B. *The Measurement of Mental Capacity through Evoked-Potential Recordings.* Greenwich, Conn.: Educational Records Bureau, 1971.

   "As it turned out, no evidence was found that the latency periods obtained . . . displayed serviceable utility for predicting school performance or level of mental ability among pupils in preschool through grade 8" (p. v).

3. DeFRIES, J. C. Paper for the C.O.B.R.E. Research Workshop on Genetic Endowment and Environment in the Determination of Behavior, October 3–8, 1971, Rye, N. Y.

4. DOBZHANSKY, D. *Mankind Evolving.* New Haven: Yale University Press, 1962, pp. 234–38.

5. GOTTESMAN, I. I. In M. Deutsch, I. Katz, and A. R. Jensen, eds. *Social Class, Race, and Psychological Development.* New York: Holt, Rinehart and Winston, 1968, pp. 11–51.

6. HEBER, R. *Rehabilitation of Families at Risk for Mental Retardation.* Regional Rehabilitation Center, University of Wisconsin, 1969.

7. KAGAN, J., and Moss, H. A. *Birth to Maturity.* New York: John Wiley & Sons, 1962.

8. MACLEAN, C., and WORKMAN, P. L. Paper presented at meeting of the American Society of Human Genetics, Indianapolis, 1970.

9. Morton, N. E. Paper for the C.O.B.R.E. Research Workshop on Genetic Endowment and Environment in the Determination of Behavior, October 3–8, 1971, Rye, N. Y.

10. *New York Times*, October 8, 1971, p. 41.

11. Reed, E. W., and Redd, S. C. *Mental Retardation: A Family Study.* Philadelphia: W. B. Saunders, 1965. *Social Biology* 18, suppl., 42 (1971).

12. Reed, T. *Science* 165 (1969):762. *Am. J. Hum. Genet.* 21 (1969):1.

13. Rynders, J. Personal communication, November 1971.

14. Scarr-Salapatek, S. Race, Social Class, and IQ. *Science* 174 (1971), pp. 1289–95.

15. Shuey, A. *The Testing of Negro Intelligence.* New York: Social Science Press, 1966, pp. 499–519.

16. Skodak, M., and Skeels, H. M. *J. Genet. Psychol.* 75 (1949):85.

17. Strickland, S. P. *Am. Ed.* 7 (1971):3.

18. Thoday, J. J. *Biosocial Science* 1, suppl. 3 (1969):4.

19. Vernon, P. E. *Intelligence and Cultural Environment.* London: Methuen, 1969.

The Nature and Nurture
of Creative Talent

DONALD W. MACKINNON

Intelligence and creativity are distinct human characteristics. In this article, Donald MacKinnon recounts what his research has revealed about the creative process, what distinguishes highly creative people from less creative ones, and how educators might help develop the creative potential of their students.

This article is noteworthy not only for its readable and comprehensive discussion of the nature of creativity, but also because it provides the reader with an opportunity to observe the development of a good research design. Watch as the elements fall into place. First, the problem. What distinguishes creative from noncreative people? Second, the samples, an "experimental group" of exceptionally creative architects and "control groups" of less exceptional ones. Then, the research procedures, which include what Dunnette called tests of maximum performance and measures of typical behavior, as well as interviews and other opportunities for direct observation. Next a well organized presentation of results, and, finally, a discussion of the implications of the study. Notice how, like Maccoby, MacKinnon refuses simply to report the data but moves into an interpretation of what those data mean, particularly with respect to the nurture of creative talent.

Let me say first how deeply appreciative I am of the honor of having been chosen the Walter Van Dyke Bingham Lecturer for 1962. It has for me especial meaning to be provided this opportunity to honor the memory of a man I respected so much and whose work was such a pioneering contribution to that field of psychology to which I have given most of my energies as a psychologist. I am grateful, too, for this opportunity to express to Mrs. Bingham the gratitude of all psychologists for her generosity in establishing this

SOURCE: From Donald W. MacKinnon, "Nature and Nurture of Creative Talent," *American Psychologist* 17 (1962). Copyright © 1962 by the American Psychological Association and reproduced by permission.

Note: The Walter Van Dyke Bingham Lecture given at Yale University, New Haven, Connecticut, April 11, 1962.

series of annual lectures on the discovery and development of exceptional abilities and capacities. Our literature has been greatly enriched by the lectures which she has made possible.

I should like also to congratulate Yale University for having been chosen this year as the institution to be honored for its contributions to the study of talent, and to thank all those who have made such pleasant arrangements for this occasion.

There is a story, first told I believe by Mark Twain which, had Dr. Bingham known it, would have been, I am sure, one of his favorites. It is about a man who sought the greatest general who had ever lived. Upon inquiring as to where this individual might be found, he was told that the person he sought had died and gone to Heaven. At the Pearly Gates he informed St. Peter of the purpose of his quest, whereupon St. Peter pointed to a soul nearby. "But that," protested the inquirer, "isn't the greatest of all generals. I knew that person when he lived on earth, and he was only a cobbler." "I know that," replied St. Peter, "but if he had been a general he would have been the greatest of them all."

Dr. Bingham spent his life worrying about cobblers who might have been generals and indeed about all those who fail to become what they are capable of becoming because neither they nor others recognize their potentialities and nourish their realization. Dr. Bingham was one of the first to insist that it is not enough to recognize creative talent after it has come to expression. He reminded us that it is our task as psychologists and as educators either through our insights or through the use of validated predictors to discover talent when it is still potential and to provide that kind of social climate and intellectual environment which will facilitate its development and expression.

Whatever light I shall be able to shed on the nature and nurture of creative talent comes in the main from findings of researches carried on during the last six years in the Institute of Personality Assessment and Research on the Berkeley campus of the University of California, and supported in large part by the Carnegie Corporation of New York.

In undertaking such a study one of our first tasks was to decide what we would consider creativity to be. This was necessary, first, because creativity has been so variously described and defined, and second, because only when we had come to agreement as to how we would conceive creativity would we be in a position to know what kinds of persons we would want to study.

We came easily to agreement that true creativeness fulfills at least three conditions. It involves a response or an idea that is novel or at the very least statistically infrequent. But novelty or originality of thought or action, while a necessary aspect of creativity, is not sufficient. If a response is to lay claim to being a part of the creative process, it must to some extent be adaptive to, or of, reality. It must serve to solve a problem, fit a situation, or accomplish some recognizable goal. And, thirdly, true creativeness involves a sustaining of the original insight, an evaluation and elaboration of it, a developing of it to the full.

Creativity, from this point of view, is a process extended in time and characterized by originality, adaptiveness, and realization. It may be brief, as in a musical improvisation, or it may involve a considerable span of years as was required for Darwin's creation of the theory of evolution.

The acceptance of such a conception of creativity had two important consequences for our researchers. It meant that we would not seek to study creativity while it was still potential but only after it had been realized and had found expression in clearly identifiable creative products—buildings designed by architects, mathematical proofs developed by mathematicians, and the published writings of poets and novelists. Our conception of creativity forced us further to reject as indicators or criteria of creativeness the performance of individuals on so-called tests of creativity. While tests of this sort, that require that the subject think, for example, of unusual uses for common objects and the consequences of unusual events, may indeed measure the infrequency or originality of a subject's ideas in response to specific test items, they fail to reveal the extent to which the subject faced with real life problems is likely to come up with solutions that are novel and adaptive and which he will be motivated to apply in all of their ramifications.

Having thus determined that we would limit our researches to the study of persons who had already demonstrated a high level of creative work, we were still confronted with the problem of deciding from which fields of creative endeavor we would seek to recruit our subjects.

The fields which we finally sampled were those of creative writing, architecture, mathematics, industrial research, physical science, and engineering.

If one considers these activities in relation to the distinction often made between artistic and scientific creativity, it may be noted that we have sampled both of these domains as well as overlapping domains of creative striving which require that the practitioner be at one and the same time both artist and scientist.

Artistic creativity, represented in our studies by the work of poets, novelists, and essayists, results in products that are clearly expressions of the creator's inner states, his needs, perceptions, motivations, and the like. In this type of creativity, the creator externalizes something of himself into the public field.

In scientific creativity, the creative product is unrelated to the creator as a person, who in his creative work acts largely as a mediator between externally defined needs and goals. In this kind of creativeness, the creator, represented in our studies by industrial researchers, physical scientists, and engineers, simply operates on some aspect of his environment in such a manner as to produce a novel and appropriate product, but he adds little of himself or of his style as a person to the resultant.

Domains of creative striving in which the practitioner must be both artist and scientist were represented in our researches by mathematicians and architects. Mathematicians contribute to science, yet in a very real sense their important creative efforts are as much as anything else personal cosmologies in which they express themselves as does the artist in his creations. So, too, in architecture, creative products are both an expression of the architect and thus a very personal product, and at the same time an impersonal meeting of the demands of an external problem.

If in reporting the findings of our researches I draw most heavily upon data obtained from our study of architects [MacKinnon, 1962], it is for two reasons. First, it is the study for which, in collaboration with Wallace B. Hall, I have assumed primary responsibility. Second, it is in architects, of all our samples, that we can expect to find what is most generally characteristic of creative persons. Architecture, as a field of creative endeavor, requires that the successful practitioner be both artist and scientist—artist in that his designs must fulfill the demands of "Delight," and scientist in that they must meet the demands of "Firmnesse" and "Commodity," to use the words of Sir Henry Wotton [1624]. But surely, one can hardly think that the requirements of effective architecture are limited to these three demands. The succcessful and effective architect must, with the skill of a juggler, combine, reconcile, and exercise the diverse skills of businessman, lawyer, artist, engineer, and advertising man, as well as those of author and journalist, psychiatrist, educator, and psychologist. In what other profession can one expect better to observe the multifarious expressions of creativity?

It should be clear that any attempt to discover the distinguishing traits of creative persons can succeed only in so far as some group of qualified experts can agree upon who are the more and who are the less creative workers in a given field of endeavor. In our study of architects we began by asking a panel of experts—five professors of architecture, each working independently—to nominate the 40 most creative architects in the United States. All told they supplied us with 86 names instead of the 40 they would have mentioned had there been perfect agreement among them. While 13 of the 86 architects were nominated by all five panel members, and 9 nominated by four, 11 by three, and 13 by two, 40 were individual nominations each proposed by a single panel member.

The agreement among experts is not perfect, yet far greater than one might have expected. Later we asked 11 editors of the major American architectural journals, *Architectural Forum, Architectural Record,* the *Journal of the American Institute of Architects,* and *Progressive Architecture,* to rate the creativity of the 64 of the nominated architects whom we invited to participate in the study. Still later we asked the 40 nominated creative architects who actually accepted our invitation to be studied to rate the creativity of the invited 64 architects, themselves included. Since the editors' ratings of the creativity of the architects correlated $+ .88$ with the architects' own ratings, it is clear that under certain conditions and for certain groups it is possible to obtain remarkable agreement about the relative creativeness of individual members of a profession and thus meet the first requirement for an effective study of creative persons.

A second requirement for the successful establishment of the traits of creative individuals is their willingness to make themselves available for study. Our hope was to win the cooperation of each person whom we invited to participate in the research, but as I have already indicated in the case of the architects, to obtain 40 acceptances, 64 invitations had to be sent out.

The invitation to this group, as to all the creative groups which we have studied, was to come to Berkeley for a weekend of intensive study in the Institute of Personality Assessment and Research. There, in groups of ten, they have been studied by the variety of means which constitute the assessment method—by problem solving experiments; by tests designed to discover what a person does not know or is unable or unwilling to reveal about himself; by tests and questionnaires that permit a person to manifest various aspects of his personality and to express his attitudes, interests, and values; by searching interviews that cover the life history and reveal the present structure of the person; and by specially contrived social situations of a stressful character which call for the subject's best behavior in a socially defined role.

The response of creative persons to the invitation to reveal themselves under such trying circumstances has varied considerably. At the one extreme there have been those who replied in anger at what they perceive to be the audacity of psychologists in presuming to study so ineffable and mysterious a thing as the creative process and so sensitive a being as a creative person. At the other extreme were those who replied courteously and warmheartedly, welcoming the invitation to be studied, and manifesting even an eagerness to contribute to a better understanding of the creative person and the creative process.

Here we were face to face with a problem that plagues us in all our researches: Are those who are willing to be assessed different in important ways from those who refuse? With respect to psychological traits and characteristics we can never know. But with respect to differences in creativeness, if any, between the 40 who accepted and the 24 who declined our invitation, we know that the two groups are indistinguishable. When the nominating panel's ratings of creativity were converted to standard scores and the means for the 24 versus the 40 were compared, they were found to be identical. When the editors' ratings were similarly converted to standard scores, the mean for the nonassessed group was slightly higher (51.9) than for the assessed sample (48.7), but the difference is not statistically significant.

Certainly we cannot claim to have assessed the 40 most creative architects in the country, or the most creative of any of the groups we have studied; but it is clear that we have studied a highly creative group of architects indistinguishable in their creativity from the group of 24 who declined to be studied, and so with the other groups too.

A third requirement for the successful determination of the traits of highly creative persons in any field of endeavor is that the profession be widely sampled beyond those nominated as most creative, for the distinguishing characteristics of the restricted sample might well have nothing to do with their creativeness. Instead they might be traits characterizing all members of the profession whether creative or not, distinguishing the professional group as a whole but in no sense limited or peculiar to its highly creative members. In the case of the architects, to use them once again as an example, two additional samples were recruited for study, both of which matched the highly creative sample (whom I shall now call Architects I) with respect to age and geographic location of practice. The first supplementary sample (Architects II) had had at least two years of work experience and association with one of the originally nominated creative architects. The second additional sample (Architects III) was composed of architects who had never worked with any of the nominated creatives.

By selecting three samples in this manner, we hoped to tap a range of talent sufficiently wide to be fairly representative of the profession as a whole; and we appear to have succeeded. The mean rating of creativity for each of the three groups—the ratings having been made on a nine-point scale by six groups of architects and experts on architecture—was for Architects I, 5.46; for Architects II, 4.25; and for Architects III, 3.54, the differences in mean ratings between each group being statistically highly significant.

So much for method and research design. I turn now to a discussion of the nature of creative talent as it has been revealed to us in our researches.

Persons who are highly creative are inclined to have a good opinion of themselves, as evidenced by the large number of favorable adjectives which they use in self-description and by the relatively high scores they earn on a scale which measures basic acceptance of the self. Indeed, there is here a paradox, for in addition to their favorable self-perceptions the very basic self-acceptance of the more creative persons often permits them to speak more frankly and thus more critically and in unusual ways about themselves. It is clear, too, that the self-images of the more creative differ from the self-images of the less creative. For example, Architects I, in contrast to Architects II and III, more often describe themselves as inventive, determined, independent, individualistic, enthusiastic, and industrious. In striking contrast Architects II and III more often than Architects I describe themselves as responsible, sincere, reliable, dependable, clear thinking, tolerant, and understanding. In short, where creative architects more often stress their inventiveness, independence, and individuality, their enthusiasm, determination, and industry, less creative members of the profession are impressed by their virtue and good character and by their rationality and sympathetic concern for others.

The discrepancies between their descriptions of themselves as they are and as they would ideally be are remarkably alike for all architects regardless of their level of creativeness. All three groups reveal themselves as desiring more personal attractiveness, self-confidence, maturity, and intellectual competence, a higher level of energy, and better social relations. As for differences, however, Architects I would ideally be more sensitive, while both Architects II and III wish for opposites if not incompatibles; they would ideally be more original but at the same time more self-controlled and disciplined.

As for the relation between intelligence and creativity, save for the mathematicians where there is a low positive correlation between intelligence and the level of creativeness, we have found within our creative samples essentially zero relationship between the two variables, and this is not due to a narrow restriction in range of intelligence. Among creative architects who have a mean score of 113 on the Terman Concept Mastery Test [1956], individual scores range widely from 39 to 179, yet scores on this measure of intelligence correlate —.08 with rated creativity. Over the whole range of intelligence and creativity there is, of course, a positive relationship between the two variables. No feeble-minded subjects have shown up in any of our creative groups. It is clear, however, that above a certain required minimum level of intelligence which varies from field to field and in some instances may be surprisingly low, being more intelligent does not guarantee a corresponding increase in creativeness. It just is not true that the more intelligent person is necessarily the more creative one.

In view of the often asserted close association of genius with insanity it is also of some interest to inquire into the psychological health of our creative subjects. To this end we can look at their profiles on the Minnesota Multiphasic Personality Inventory (MMPI) [Hathaway and McKinley, 1945], a test originally developed to measure tendencies toward the major psychiatric disturbances that man is heir to: depression, hysteria, paranoia, schizophrenia, and the like. On the eight scales which measure the strength of these dispositions in the person, our creative subjects earn scores which, on the average, are some 5 to 10 points above the general population's average score of 50. It must be noted, however, that elevated scores of this degree on these scales do not have the same meaning for the personality functioning of persons who, like our subjects, are getting along well in their personal lives and professional careers, that they have for hospitalized patients. The manner in which creative subjects describe themselves on this test as well as in the life history psychiatric interview is less suggestive of psychopathology than it is of good intellect, complexity and richness of personality, general lack of defensiveness, and candor in self-description—in other words, an openness to experience and especially to experience of one's inner life. It must also be noted, however, that in the self-reports and in the MMPI profiles of many of our creative subjects, one can find rather clear evidence of psychopathology, but also evidence of adequate control mechanisms, as the success with which they live their productive and creative lives testifies.

However, the most striking aspect of the MMPI profiles of all our male creative groups is an extremely high peak on the Mf (femininity) scale. This tendency for creative males to score relatively high on femininity is also demonstrated on the Fe (femininity) scale of the California Psychological

Inventory (CPI) [Gough, 1957] and on the masculinity-femininity scale of the Strong Vocational Interest Blank [Strong, 1959]. Scores on the latter scale (where high score indicates more masculinity) correlate —.49 with rated creativity.

The evidence is clear: The more creative a person is the more he reveals an openness to his own feelings and emotions, a sensitive intellect and understanding self-awareness, and wide-ranging interests including many which in the American culture are thought of as feminine. In the realm of sexual identification and interests, our creative subjects appear to give more expression to the feminine side of their nature than do less creative persons. In the language of the Swiss psychologist, Carl G. Jung [1956], creative persons are not so completely identified with their masculine *persona* roles as to blind themselves to or to deny expression to the more feminine traits of the *anima*. For some, to be sure, the balance between masculine and feminine traits, interests, and identification, is a precarious one, and for several of our subjects it would appear that their presently achieved reconciliation of these opposites of their nature has been barely effected and only after considerable psychic stress and turmoil.

The perceptiveness of the creative and his openness to richness and complexity of experience is strikingly revealed on the Barron-Welsh Art Scale of the Welsh Figure Preference Test [Welsh, 1959], which presents to the subject a set of 62 abstract line drawings which range from simple and symmetrical figures to complex and asymmetrical ones. In the original study [Barron and Welsh, 1952] which standardized this scale, some 80 painters from New York, San Francisco, New Orleans, Chicago, and Minneapolis showed a marked preference for the complex and asymmetrical, or, as they often referred to them, the vital and dynamic figures. A contrasting sample of nonartists revealed a marked preference for the simple and symmetrical drawings.

All creative groups we have studied have shown a clear preference for the complex and asymmetrical, and in general the more creative a person is the stronger is this preference. Similarly, in our several samples, scores on an Institute scale which measures the preference for perceptual complexity are significantly correlated with creativity. In the sample of architects the correlation is +.48.

Presented with a large selection of one-inch squares of varicolored posterboard and asked to construct within a 30-minute period a pleasing, completely filled-in 8" × 10" mosaic [Hall, 1958], some subjects select the fewest colors possible (one used only one color, all white) while others seek to make order out of the largest possible number, using all of the 22 available colors. And, again citing results from the architects, there is a significant though low positive correlation of +.38 between the number of colors a subject chooses and his creativity as rated by the experts.

If one considers for a moment the meaning of these preferences on the art scale, on the mosaic test, and on the scale that measures preference for perceptual complexity, it is clear that creative persons are especially disposed to admit complexity and even disorder into their perceptions without being made anxious by the resulting chaos. It is not so much that they like disorder per se, but that they prefer the richness of the disordered to the stark barrenness of the simple. They appear to be challenged by disordered multiplicity which arouses in them a strong need which in them is serviced by a superior capacity to achieve the most difficult and far-reaching ordering of the richness they are willing to experience.

The creative person's openness to experience is further revealed on the Myers-Briggs Type Indicator [Myers, 1958], a test based largely upon Carl G. Jung's [1923] theory of psychological functions and types.

Employing the language of the test, though in doing so I oversimplify both it and the theory upon which it is based, one might say that whenever a person uses his mind for any purpose, he performs either an act of perception (he becomes aware of something) or an act of judgment (he comes to a conclusion about something). And most persons tend to show a rather consistent preference for and greater pleasure in one or the other of these, preferring either to perceive or to judge, though every one both perceives and judges.

An habitual preference for the judging attitude may lead to some prejudging and at the very least to the living of a life that is orderly, controlled, and carefully planned. A preference for the perceptive attitude results in a life that is more open to experience both from within and from without, and characterized by flexibility and spontaneity. A judging type places more emphasis upon the control and regulation of experience, while a perceptive type is inclined to be more open and receptive to all experience.

The majority of our creative writers, mathematicians, and architects are perceptive types. Only among research scientists do we find the majority to be judging types, and even in this group it is interesting to note that there is a positive correlation (+.25) between a scientist's preference for perception and his rated creativity as a scientific researcher. For architects, preference for perception correlates +.41 with rated creativity.

The second preference measured by the Type Indicator is for one of two types of perception: sense perception or sensation, which is a direct becoming aware of things by way of the senses versus intuitive perception or intuition, which is an indirect perception of the deeper meanings and possibilities inherent in things and situations. Again, everyone senses and intuits, but preliminary norms for the test suggest that in the United States three out of four persons show a preference for sense perception, concentrating upon immediate sensory experience and centering their attention upon existing facts. The one out of every four who shows a preference for intuitive perception, on the other hand, looks expectantly for a bridge or link between that which is given and present and that which is not yet thought of, focusing habitually upon possibilities.

One would expect creative persons not to be bound to the stimulus and the object but to be ever alert to the as-yet-not-realized. And that is precisely the way they show themselves to be on the Type Indicator. In contrast to an estimated 25% of the general population who are intuitive, 90% of the creative writers, 92% of the mathematicians, 93% of the research scientists, and 100% of the architects are intuitive as measured by this test.

In judging or evaluating experience, according to the underlying Jungian theory of the test, one makes use of thought or of feeling; thinking being a logical process aimed at an impersonal fact-weighing analysis, while feeling is a process of appreciation and evaluation of things that gives them a personal and subjective value. A preference for thinking or for feeling appears to be less related to one's creativity as such than to the type of materials or concepts with which one deals. Of our creative groups, writers prefer feeling, mathematicians, research scientists, and engineers prefer thinking, while architects split fifty-fifty in their preference for one or the other of the two functions.

The final preference in Jungian typology and on the test is the well-known one between introversion and extraversion. Approximately two-thirds of all our creative groups score as introverts, though there is no evidence that introverts as such are more creative than extraverts.

Turning to preferences among interests and values, one would expect the highly creative to be rather different from less creative people, and there is clear evidence that they are.

On the Strong Vocational Interest Blank, which measures the similarity of a person's expressed interests with the known interests of individuals successful in a number of occupations and professions, all of our creative subjects have shown, with only slight variation from group to group, interests similar to those of the psychologist, author-journalist, lawyer, architect, artist, and musician, and interests unlike those of the purchasing agent, office man, banker, farmer, carpenter, veterinarian, and interestingly enough, too, policeman and mortician. Leaving aside any consideration of the specific interests thus revealed we may focus our attention on the inferences that may be drawn from this pattern of scores which suggest that creative persons are relatively uninterested in small details, or in facts for their own sake, and more concerned with their meanings and implications, possessed of considerable cognitive flexibility, verbally skillful, interested in communicating with others and accurate in so doing, intellectually curious, and relatively disinterested in policing either their own impulses and images or those of others.

On the Allport-Vernon-Lindzey Study of Values [1951], a test designed to measure in the individual the relative strength of the six values of men as these values have been conceptualized and described by the German psychologist and educator, Eduard Spranger [1928], namely, the theoretical, economic, esthetic, social, political, and religious values, all of our creative groups have as their highest values the theoretical and the esthetic.

For creative research scientists the theoretical value is the highest, closely followed by the esthetic. For creative architects the highest value is the esthetic, with the theoretical value almost as high. For creative mathematicians, the two values are both high and approximately equally strong.

If, as the authors of the test believe, there is some incompatibility and conflict between the theoretical value with its cognitive and rational concern with truth and the esthetic value with its emotional concern with form and beauty, it would appear that the creative person has the capacity to tolerate the tension that strong opposing values create in him, and in his creative striving he effects some reconciliation of them. For the truly creative person it is not sufficient that problems be solved, there is the further demand that the solutions be elegant. He seeks both truth and beauty.

A summary description of the creative person—especially of the creative architect—as he reveals himself in his profile on the California Psychological Inventory [Gough, 1957] reads as follows:

> He is dominant (Do scale); possessed of those qualities and attributes which underlie and lead to the achievement of social status (Cs); poised, spontaneous, and self-confident in personal and social interaction (Sp); though not of an especially sociable or participative temperament (low Sy); intelligent, outspoken, sharp-witted, demanding, aggressive, and self-centered; persuasive and verbally fluent, self-confident and self-assured (Sa); and relatively uninhibited in expressing his worries and complaints (low Wb).
>
> He is relatively free from conventional restraints and inhibitions (low So and Sc), not preoccupied with the impression which he makes on others and thus perhaps capable of great independence and autonomy (low Gi), and relatively ready to recognize and admit self-views that are unusual and unconventional (low Cm).
>
> He is strongly motivated to achieve in situations in which independence in thought and action are called for (Ai). But, unlike his less creative colleagues, he is less inclined to strive for achievement in settings where conforming behavior is expected or required (Ac). In efficiency and steadiness of intellectual effort (Ie), however, he does not differ from his fellow workers.
>
> Finally, he is definitely more psychologically minded (Py), more flexible (Fx), and possessed of more femininity of interests (Fe) than architects in general.

There is one last finding that I wish to present, one that was foreshadowed by a discovery of Dr. Bingham in one of his attempts to study creativity. The subject of his study was Amy Lowell, a close friend of his and Mrs. Bingham's, with whom he discussed at length the birth and growth of her poems, seeking insight into the creative processes of her mind. He also administered to her a word association test and "found that she gave a higher proportion of unique responses than those of any one outside a mental institution" [Bingham, Millicent Todd, 1953, p. 11]. We, too, administered a word association test to our subjects and found the unusualness of mental associations one of the best predictors of creativity, and especially so when associations given by no more than 1% to 10% of the population, using the Minnesota norms [Russell and Jenkins, 1954], are weighted more heavily than those given by less than 1% of the population. Among architects, for example, this weighted score is for Architects I, 204; Architects II, 128; and Architects III, 114; while for the total sample this measure of unusualness of mental associations correlates +.50 with rated creativity.

And Dr. Bingham, like us, found that there are certain hazards in attempting to study a creative poet. His searchings were rewarded by a poem Amy Lowell later wrote which was first entitled "To the Impudent Psychologist" and published posthumously with the title "To a Gentleman who wanted to see the first drafts of my poems in the interest of psychological research into the workings of the creative mind." We, I must confess, were treated somewhat less kindly by one of our poets who, after assessment, published an article entitled "My Head Gets Tooken Apart" [Rexroth, 1959].

Having described the overall design of our studies, and having presented a selection of our findings which reveal at least some aspects of the nature of creative talent, I turn now, but with considerably less confidence, to the question as to how we can early identify and best encourage the development of creative potential. Our findings concerning the characteristics of highly creative persons are by now reasonably well established, but their implications for the nurture of creative talent are far from clear.

It is one thing to discover the distinguishing characteristics of mature, creative, productive individuals. It is quite another matter to conclude that the traits of creative persons observed several years after school and college characterized these same individuals when they were students. Nor can we be certain that finding these same traits in youngsters today will identify those with creative potential. Only empirical, longitudinal research, which we do not yet have, can settle such issues. Considering, however, the nature of the traits which discriminate creative adults from their noncreative peers, I would venture to guess that most students with creative potential have personality structures congruent with, though possibly less sharply delineated than, those of mature creatives.

Our problem is further complicated by the fact that though our creative subjects have told us about their experiences at home, in school, and in college, and about the forces and persons and situations which, as they see it, nurtured their creativeness, these are, after all, self-reports subject to the misperceptions and self-deceptions of all self-reports. Even if we were to assume that their testimony is essentially accurate we would still have no assurance that the conditions in the home, in school, and society, the qualities of interpersonal relations between instructor and student, and the aspects of the teaching-learning process which would appear to have contributed to creative development a generation ago would facilitate rather than inhibit creativity if these same factors were created in today's quite different world and far different educational climate.

In reporting upon events and situations in the life histories of our subjects which appear to have fostered their creative potential and independent spirit, I shall again restrict myself to architects. One finds in their histories a number of circumstances which, in the early years, could well have provided an opportunity as well as the necessity for developing the secure sense of personal autonomy and zestful commitment to their profession which so markedly characterize them.

What appears most often to have characterized the parents of these future creative architects was an extraordinary respect for the child and confidence in his ability to do what was appropriate. Thus they did not hesitate to grant him rather unusual freedom in exploring his universe and in making decisions for himself—and this early as well as late. The expectation of the parent that the child would act independently but reasonably and responsibly appears to have contributed immensely to the latter's sense of personal autonomy which was to develop to such a marked degree.

The obverse side of this was that there was often a lack of intense closeness with one or both of the parents. Most often this appeared in relation to the father rather than to the mother, but often it characterized the relationship with both parents. There were not strong emotional ties of either a positive or a negative sort between parent and child, but neither was there the type of relationship that fosters overdependency nor the type that results in severe rejection. Thus, if there was a certain distance in the relationship between child and parent, it had a liberating effect so far as the child was concerned. If he lacked something of the emotional closeness which some children experience with their parents, he was also spared that type of psychological exploitation that is so frequently seen in the life histories of clinical patients.

Closely related to this factor of some distance between parent and child were ambiguities in identification with the parents. In place of the more usual clear identification with one parent, there was a tendency for the architects to have identified either with both parents or with neither. It was not that the child's early milieu was a deprived one so far as models for identification and the promotion of ego ideals were concerned. It was rather that the larger familial sphere presented the child with a plentiful supply of diverse and effective models—in addition to the mother and father, grandfathers, uncles, and others who occupied prominent and responsible positions within their community—with whom important identifications could be made. Whatever the emotional interaction between father and son, whether distant, harmonious, or turbulent, the father presented a model of effective and resourceful behavior in an exceptionally demanding career. What is perhaps more significant, though, is the high incidence of distinctly autonomous mothers among families of the creative architects, who led active lives with interests and sometimes careers of their own apart from their husbands'.

Still other factors which would appear to have contributed to the development of the marked personal autonomy of our subjects were the types of discipline and religious training which they received, which suggest that within the family there existed clear standards of conduct and ideas as to what was right and wrong but at the same time an expectation if not requirement of active exploration and internalization of a framework of personal conduct. Discipline was almost always consistent and predictable. In most cases there were rules, family standards, and parental injunctions which were known explicitly by the children and seldom infringed. In nearly half the cases, corporal punishment was not employed and in only a few instances was the punishment harsh or cruel.

As for religious practices, the families of the creative architects showed considerable diversity, but what was most widely emphasized was the development of personal ethical codes rather than formal religious practices. For one-third of the families formal religion was important for one parent or for both, but in two-thirds of the families formal religion was either unimportant or practiced only perfunctorily. For the majority of the families, in which emphasis was placed upon the development of one's own ethical code, it is of interest to inquire into the values that were most stressed. They were most often values related to integrity (e.g., forthrightness, honesty, respect for others), quality (e.g., pride, diligence, joy in work, development of talent), intellectual and cultural endeavor, success and ambition, and being respectable and doing the right thing.

The families of the more creative architects tended to move more frequently, whether within a single community, or from community to community, or even from country to country. This, combined with the fact that the more creative architects as youngsters were given very much more freedom to roam and to explore widely, provided for them an enrichment of experience both cultural and personal which their less creative peers did not have.

But the frequent moving appears also to have resulted frequently in some estrangement of the family from its immediate neighborhood. And it is of interest that in almost every case in which the architect reported that his family differed in its behavior and values from those in the neighborhood, the family was different in showing greater cultural, artistic, and intellectual interests and pursuits.

To what extent this sort of cultural dislocation contributed to the frequently reported experiences of aloneness, shyness, isolation, and solitariness during childhood and adolescence, with little or no dating during adolescence, or to what extent these experiences stemmed from a natural introversion of interests and unusual sensitivity, we cannot say. They were doubtless mutually reinforcing factors in stimulating the young architect's awareness of his own inner life and his growing interest in his artistic skills and his ideational, imaginal, and symbolic processes.

Almost without exception, the creative architects manifested very early considerable interest and skill in drawing and painting. And also, with almost no exception, one or both of the parents were of artistic temperament and considerable skill. Often it was the mother who in the architect's early years fostered his artistic potentialities by her example as well as by her instruction. It is especially interesting to note, however, that while the visual and artistic abilities and interests of the child were encouraged and rewarded, these interests and abilities were, by and large, allowed to develop at their own speed, and this pace varied considerably among the architects. There was not an anxious concern on the part of the parents about the skills and abilities of the child. What is perhaps most significant was the wide-spread definite lack of strong pressures from the parents toward a particular career. And this was true both for pressures away from architecture as well as for pressures toward architecture by parents who were themselves architects.

The several aspects of the life history which I have described were first noted by Kenneth Craik in the protocols for the highly creative Architects I. Subsequently, in reading the protocols for Architects II and III as well as Architects I, a credit of one point for the presence of each of the factors was assigned and the total for each person taken as a score. The correlation of these life history scores with rated creativity of the architects is +.36, significant beyond the .005 level of confidence.

And now turn finally to a consideration of the implications of the nature of creative talent for the nurturing of it in school and college through the processes of education.

Our findings concerning the relations of intelligence to creativity suggest that we may have overestimated in our educational system the role of intelligence in creative achievement. If our expectation is that a child of a given intelligence will not respond creatively to a task which confronts him, and especially if we make this expectation known to the child, the probability that he will respond creatively is very much reduced. And later on, such a child, now grown older, may find doors closed to him so that he is definitely excluded from certain domains of learning. There is increasing reason to believe that in selecting students for special training of their talent we may have overweighted the role of intelligence either by setting the cutting point for selection on the intellective dimension too high or by assuming that regardless of other factors the student with the higher IQ is the more promising one and should consequently be chosen. Our data suggest, rather, that if a person has the minimum of intelligence required for mastery of a field of knowledge, whether he performs creatively or banally in that field will be crucially determined by nonintellective factors. We would do well then to pay more attention in the future than we have in the past to the nurturing of those nonintellective traits which in our studies have been shown to be intimately associated with creative talent.

There is the openness of the creative person to experience both from within and from without which suggests that whether we be parent or teacher we should use caution in setting limits upon what those whom we are nurturing experience and express.

Discipline and self-control are necessary. They must be learned if one is ever to be truly creative, but it is important that they not be overlearned. Furthermore, there is a time and place for their learning, and having been learned they should be used flexibly, not rigidly or compulsively.

If we consider this specifically with reference to the attitudes of perceiving and judging, everyone must judge as well as perceive. It is not a matter of using one to the exclusion of the other, but a question of how each is used and which is preferred. The danger for one's creative potential is not the judging or evaluating of one's experience but that one prejudges, thus excluding from perception large areas of experience. The danger in all parental instruction, as in all academic instruction, is that new ideas and new possibilities of action are criticized too soon and too often. Training in criticism is obviously important and so widely recognized that I need not plead its case. Rather I would urge that, if we wish to nurture creative potential, an equal emphasis be placed on perceptiveness, discussing with our students as well as with our children, at least upon occasion, the most fantastic of ideas and possibilities. It is the duty of parents to communicate and of professors to profess what they judge to be true, but it is no less their duty by example to encourage in their children and in their students an openness to all ideas and especially to those which most challenge and threaten their own judgments.

The creative person, as we have seen, is not only open to experience, but intuitive about it. We can train students to be accurate in their perceptions, and this, too, is a characteristic of the creative. But can we train them to be intuitive, and if so how?

I would suggest that rote learning, learning of facts for their own sake, repeated drill of material, too much emphasis upon facts unrelated to other facts, and excessive concern with memorizing, can all strengthen and reinforce sense perception. On the other hand, emphasis upon the transfer of training from one subject to another, the searching for common principles in terms of which facts from quite different domains of knowledge can be related, the stressing of analogies, and similes, and metaphors, a seeking for symbolic equivalents of experience in the widest possible number of sensory and imaginal modalities, exercises in imaginative play, training in retreating from the facts in order to see them in large perspective and in relation to more aspects of the larger context thus achieved—these and still other emphases in learning would, I believe, strengthen the disposition to intuitive perception as well as intuitive thinking.

If the widest possible relationships among facts are to be established, if the structure of knowledge [Bruner, 1960] is to be grasped, it is necessary that the student have a large body of facts which he has learned as well as a large array of reasoning skills which he has mastered. You will see, then, that what I am proposing is not that in teaching one disdain acute and accurate sense perception, but that one use it to build upon, leading the student always to an intuitive understanding of that which he experiences.

The independence of thought and action which our subjects reveal in the assessment setting appears to have long characterized them. It was already manifest in high school, though, according to their reports, tending to increase in college and thereafter.

In college our creative architects earned about a B average. In work and courses which caught their interest they could turn in an A performance, but in courses that failed to strike their imagination, they were quite willing to do no work at all. In general, their attitude in college appears to have been one of profound skepticism. They were unwilling to accept anything on the mere say-so of their instructors. Nothing was to be accepted on faith or because it had behind it the voice of authority. Such matters might be accepted, but only after the student on his own had demonstrated their validity to himself. In a sense, they were rebellious, but they did not run counter to the standards out of sheer rebelliousness. Rather, they were spirited in their disagreement and one gets the impression that they learned most from those who were not easy with them. But clearly many of them were not easy to take. One of the most rebellious, but as it turned out, one of the most creative, was advised by the Dean of his School to quit because he had no talent; and another, having been failed in his design dissertation which attacked the stylism of the faculty, took his degree in the art department.

These and other data should remind all of us who teach that creative students will not always be to our liking. This will be due not only to their independence in situations in which nonconformity may be seriously disruptive of the work of others, but because, as we have seen, more than most they will be experiencing large quantities of tension produced in them by the richness of their experience and the strong opposites of their nature. In struggling to reconcile these opposites and in striving to achieve creative solutions to the difficult problems which they have set themselves they will often show that psychic turbulence which is so characteristic of the creative person. If, however, we can only recognize the sources of their disturbance, which often enough will result in behavior disturbing to us, we may be in a better position to support and encourage them in their creative striving.

References

1. ALLPORT, G. W., VERNON, P. E., and LINDZEY, G. *Study of Values: Manual of Directions*. Rev. ed. Boston: Houghton Mifflin, 1951.
2. BARRON, F., and WELSH, G. S. Artistic perception as a possible factor in personality style: Its measurement by a figure preference test. *J. Psychol.* 33 (1952):199–203.
3. BINGHAM, MILLICENT TODD. Beyond Psychology. In *Homo sapiens auduboniensis: A tribute to Walter Van Dyke Bingham*. New York: National Audubon Society, 1953, pp. 5–29.
4. BRUNER, J. S. *The Process of Education*. Cambridge, Mass.: Harvard University Press, 1960.
5. GOUGH, H. G. *California Psychological Inventory Manual*. Palo Alto, Calif.: Consulting Psychologists Press, 1957.
6. HALL, W. B. "The development of a technique for assessing aesthetic predispositions

and its application to a sample of professional research scientists." Paper read at Western Psychological Association, Monterey, California,, April 1958.

7. HATHAWAY, S. R., and McKINLEY, J. C. *Minnesota Multiphasic Personality Inventory.* New York: Psychological Corporation, 1945.

8. JUNG, C. G. *Psychological Types.* New York: Harcourt, Brace, 1923.

9. JUNG, C. G. *Two Essays on Analytical Psychology.* New York: Meridian, 1956.

10. MACKINNON, D. W. The personality correlates of creativity: A study of American architects. In G. S. Nielsen, ed. *Proceedings of the XIV International Congress of Applied Psychology, Copenhagen 1961.* Vol. 2. Copenhagen: Munksgaard, 1962, pp. 11–39.

11. MYERS, ISABEL B. *Some Findings with Regard to Type and Manual for Myers-Briggs Type Indicator, Form E.* Swarthmore, Pa.: Author, 1958.

12. REXROTH, K. My head gets tooken apart. In *Bird in the Bush: Obvious Essays.* New York: New Directions Paperbook, 1959, pp. 65–74.

13. RUSSELL, W. A., and JENKINS, J. J. The complete Minnesota norms for responses to 100 words from the Kent-Rosanoff Word Association Test. Technical Report No. 11, 1954, University of Minnesota, Contact N8 onr-66216, Office of Naval Research.

14. SPRANGER, E. *Types of Men.* Trans. by Paul J. W. Pigors. Halle (Saale), Germany: Max Niemeyer, 1928.

15. STRONG, E. K., JR. *Manual for Strong Vocational Interest Blanks for Men and Women, Revised Blanks (Form M and W).* Palo Alto, Calif.: Consulting Psychologists Press, 1959.

16. TERMAN, L. M. *Concept Mastery Tests, Form T manual.* New York: Psychological Corporation, 1956.

17. WELSH, G. S. *Welsh Figure Preference Test: Preliminary manual.* Palo Alto, Calif.: Consulting Psychologists Press, 1959.

18. WOTTON, HENRY. *The Elements of Architecture.* London: John Bill, 1624.

PART 6

Personality and Adjustment

In the first two sections of this book, we looked at the whole person in terms of his or her development and motivation. Then we considered a number of more specific powers and attributes, like sensation and perception, learning and thinking, and intelligence and abilities. Now we return to the level of the whole and observe the adjustment of the person.

Adjustment is a twofold process that incorporates the person's efforts to change himself ("accommodation," to use Piaget's term) as well as his efforts to change the world ("assimilation"). In earlier sections we talked about testing our opinions against the opinions of others (Schein) and about testing our thinking against what we have learned (Bruner). Adjustment involves a similar process: We test ourselves—needs, abilities, personalities—against our own criteria (ideals) and against our physical and social surroundings. What we find leads us sometimes to change ourselves, sometimes to try to change the world. This is the process of adjustment.

These two attempts, at accommodation to the world and assimilation of the world, operate in the personal, physical, and social spheres. They entail such concepts as personal freedom and commitment, physical demands and comforts, and social relationships, responsibility, and love.

The articles in this section will consider the quest for personal adjustment in greater detail. As you study them, pay special attention to the role of the adaptive powers in this pursuit. The interplay is not only of personal, physical, and social factors, but of all aspects of the person—growth and development, motivation, sensation and perception, learning and thinking, and intelligence and abilities.

Toward a Concept of the Normal Personality

EDWARD JOSEPH SHOBEN, JR.

Personal responsibility in a social context forms a large part of the author's definition of the adjusted personality. This article is unusual not only for its positive orientation in a field in which the tendency is to overemphasize the pathological, but also for its incorporation of philosophical and theological wisdom into personality theory. Drawing on these varied sources, Shoben postulates a set of uniquely human potentialities, the fulfilment of which he defines as personal adjustment.

People are different from other animals in two important respects. First, they use symbols, not just in the sense of simple perception and reaction but in the more active sense of recalling the past, thinking about things absent, and considering the future. The second thing that is peculiar to people is a special social nature. Ants are social creatures, but only human beings are, throughout the course of their lives, *responsible* for one another.

From these two principles Shoben derives five characteristics of the well-adjusted person: self-control through consideration of consequences, personal responsibility, social responsibility, democratic social interest, and ideals. Note how this formulation, which depends on the fulfilment of these uniquely human potentialities, avoids the criticisms that apply to the usual definitions of normality.

Clinical practice and the behavioral sciences alike have typically focused on the pathological in their studies of personality and behavior dynamics. While much of crucial importance remains to be learned, there is an abundant empirical knowledge and an impressive body of theory concerning the deviant and the diseased, the anxious and the neurotic, the disturbed and the malad-

SOURCE: From Edward Joseph Shoben, Jr., "Toward a Concept of the Normal Personality," *American Psychologist* 12 (4) (1957):183–89. Copyright © 1957 by the American Psychological Association and reproduced by permission.

Note: This paper is revised from versions read on March 26, 1956, at the convention of the American Personnel and Guidance Association in Washington, D. C., and on November 16, 1956, at a conference on mental health research at Catholic University in Washington, D. C., under the joint sponsorship of Catholic University, the University of Maryland, and the U. S. Veterans Administration.

justed. In contrast, there is little information and even less conceptual clarity about the nature of psychological normality. Indeed, there are even those [5, 13] who argue that there is no such thing as a normal man; there are only those who manage their interpersonal relationships in such a way that others are strongly motivated to avoid them, even by committing them to a mental hospital or a prison, as opposed to those who do not incite such degrees of social ostracism.

This argument has two characteristics. First, it disposes of the issue by simply distributing people along a dimension of pathology. All men are a little queer, but some are much more so than others. Second, it has affinities with the two major ideas that have been brought to bear on the question of what constitutes normal or abnormal behavior: the statistical conception of the usual or the average and the notion of cultural relativism. If pathology is conceived as the extent to which one is tolerated by one's fellows, then any individual can theoretically be described in terms of some index number that reflects the degree of acceptability accorded him. The resulting distribution would effectively amount to an ordering of people from the least to the most pathological. Similarly, if the positions on such a continuum are thought of as functions of one's acceptance or avoidance by others, then they can only be defined by reference to some group. The implications here are twofold. First, the conception of pathology is necessarily relativistic, varying from group to group or culture to culture. Second, the degree of pathology is defined as the obverse of the degree of conformity to group norms. The more one's behavior conforms to the standards of the group, the less one is likely to be subject to social avoidance; whereas the more one's behavior deviates from the rules, the greater is the probability of ostracism to the point of institutional commitment.

Statistical and Relativistic Concepts of Normality

Yet it is doubtful that the issues are fully clarified by these statistical and culturally relativistic ideas. Is it most fruitful to regard normality or integrative behavior as merely reflecting a minimal degree of pathology, or may there be a certain merit in considering the asset side of personality, the positive aspects of human development? This question becomes particularly relevant when one is concerned with the socialization process or with the goals and outcomes of psychotherapy or various rehabilitative efforts.

It seems most improbable that the family, the church, and the school, the main agents of socialization, exist for the minimizing of inevitable pathological traits in the developing members of the community. Rather, parents, priests, and educators are likely to insist that their function is that of facilitating some sort of positive growth, the progressive acquisition of those characteristics, including skills, knowledge, and attitudes, which permit more productive, contributory, and satisfying ways of life. Similarly, while psychotherapists may sometimes accept the limited goals of simply trying to inhibit pathological processes, there are certainly those [11, 16] who take the position that therapy is to be judged more in terms of how much it contributes to a patient's ability to achieve adult gratifications rather than its sheer efficiency in reducing symptoms or shoring up pathological defenses.

A general concern for such a point of view seems to be emerging in the field of public mental health [26]. Beginning with an emphasis on treatment, the concept of community mental health swung to a preventive phase with the main interest focused on identifying the antecedents of mental disease and on reducing morbidity rates by attacking their determinants. The vogue of eugenics was one illustrative feature of this stage. More recently, there has been a considerable dissatisfaction with the whole notion of interpreting psychological states in terms of disease analogues [15, 23]. Maladjustive behavior patterns, the neuroses, and—perhaps to a lesser extent—the psychoses may possibly be better understood as disordered, ineffective, and defensive styles of life than as forms of sickness. In consequence, there seems to be a growing tendency to conceive of the public mental health enterprise as emphasizing positive development with the prevention and treatment of pathology regarded as vital but secondary.

But in what does positive development consist? The statistical concept of the average is not very helpful. Tiegs and Katz [27], for example, reported a study of college students who had been rated for fourteen different evidences of "nervousness." By and large, these traits were normally distributed, suggesting that those subjects rated low must be considered just as "abnormal" (unusual) as those rated high. This conception seems to provide a superficial quantitative model only at the expense of hopeless self-contradiction and violence to the ordinary categories of communication. Even in a case that at first blush seems to cause no difficulty, the problem remains. Criminal behavior, for example, is distributed in a J-shaped fashion with most cases concentrated at the point of zero offenses, ranging to a relatively few instances of many-time offenders. Few would argue that the usual behavior here is not also the most "positive." But one suspects that the sheer frequency of law-abiding behavior has little to do with its acknowledged integrative character. If conformity to social rules is generally considered more desirable than criminality, it is not because of its rate of occurrence but because of its consequences for both society and the individual.

Thus, a statistical emphasis on the usual as the criterion of positive adjustment or normality shades into a socially relativistic concept with an implied criterion of conformity. The terms *usual* or *most frequent* or *average* are meaningless without reference to some group, and this state of affairs poses two problems. First, conformity in itself, as history abundantly demonstrates, is a dubious guide to conduct. Innovation is as necessary to a culture's survival as are tradition and conservation, and conformity has frequently meant acquiescence in conditions undermining the maturity and positive development of human beings rather than their enhancement. On more personal levels, conformity sometimes seems related in some degree to personality processes that can quite properly be called pathological [2, 24]. Second, relativistic conceptions of normality pose serious questions as to the reference group against which any individual is to be assessed. Benedict [3], for example, has made it quite clear that behavior which is considered abnormal in one culture is quite acceptable in others, that certain forms of abnormalities which occur in some societies are absent in others, and that conduct which is thought completely normal in one group may be regarded as intensely pathological in another. Such observations, while descriptively sound, can lead readily to two troublesome inferences. One is that the storm trooper must be considered as the prototype of integrative adjustment in Nazi culture, the members of the Politburo as best representing human normality Soviet-style, and the cruelest adolescent in a delinquent gang as its most positively developed member. The other is that any evaluative judgment of cultures and societies must be regarded as inappropriate. Since normality is conceived only in terms of conformity to group standards, the group itself must be beyond appraisal. Thus, the suspicion and mistrust of Dobu [10], the sense of resigned futility that permeates Alor [6], and the regimentation that characterizes totalitarian nations can logically only be taken as norms in terms of which individual behavior may be interpreted, not as indications of abnormal tendencies in the cultures themselves.

Wegrocki [28], in criticizing such relativistic notions, argues that it is not the form of behavior, the actual acts themselves, that defines its normal or pathological character. Rather, it is its function. What he calls the "quintessence of abnormality" lies in reactions which represent an escape from conflicts and problems rather than a facing of them. This formulation, implying that integrative adjustments are those which most directly confront conflicts and problems, seems essentially free of the difficulties inherent in statistical conceptions and the idea of cultural relativism. But it presents troubles of its own. For instance, what does it mean to "face" a problem or conflict? On what ground, other than the most arbitrarily moralistic one, can such confrontations be defended as more positive than escape? Finally, does this facing of one's problems have any relationship to the matter of conformity in the sense of helping to clarify decisions regarding the acceptance or rejection of group standards?

To deal with such questions requires coming to grips with certain problems of value. It is at this point that the behavioral sciences and ethics meet and merge, and it seems unlikely that any conception of normality can be developed apart from some general considerations that are fundamentally moral. Once the purely relativistic ideas of normality are swept away, it becomes difficult to avoid some concern for the issues of happiness and right conduct (i.e., conduct leading to the greatest degree of human satisfaction) that are the traditional province of the literary interpreter of human experience, the theologian, and the moral philosopher. A primary challenge here is that of providing a rational and naturalistic basis for a concept of integrative adjustment that is at once consistent with the stance and contributions of empirical science and in harmony with whatever wisdom mankind has accumulated through its history.

Symbolic and Social Aspects of Human Nature

One way to meet this challenge is by frankly postulating a basic principle of value. The fundamental contention advanced here is that behavior is "positive" or "integrative" to the extent that it reflects the unique attributes of the human animal. There are undoubtedly other ways of approaching a fruitful concept of normality. Nevertheless, this assertion is consistent with the implications of organic evolution, escapes the fallacy of the survival-of-the-fittest doctrine in its various forms, and permits a derivation of more specific criteria of positive adjustment from the distinctive characteristics of man. No discontinuity within the phylogenetic scale need be assumed. It seems clear, however, that man, while certainly an animal, can hardly be described as "nothing but" an animal; and his normality or integration seems much more likely to consist in the fulfillment of his unique potentialities than in the development of those he shares with infrahuman organisms.

Foremost among these uniquely human potentialities, as Cassirer [4] and Langer [14] make clear, is the enormous capacity for symbolization. What is most characteristic of men is their pervasive employment of *propositional* language. While other organisms, especially dogs [22] and the higher apes [29], react to symbols, their faculty for doing so indicates only an ability to respond to mediate or representative as well as direct stimuli. Man, on the other hand, uses symbols designatively, as a vehicle for recollecting past events, for dealing with things which are not physically present, and for projecting experience into the future. Goldstein [12] makes the same point in his discussion of the "attitude toward the merely possible," the ability to deal with things that are only imagined or which are not part of an immediate, concrete situation. In patients whose speech has been impaired because of brain damage, this attitude toward the possible is disrupted. Thus, aphasics are typically unable to say such things as, "The snow is black" or "The moon shines in the daytime"; similarly, they are incapable of *pretending* to comb their hair or to take a drink of water, although they can actually *perform* these acts. Such patients appear to have lost the uniquely human capacity for thinking *about* things as well as directly "thinking things."

It is his symbolic ability, then, that makes man the only creature who can "look before and after and pine for what is not." Propositional speech makes it possible for him to learn from not only his own personal experience but from that of other men in other times and places, to forecast the consequences of his own behavior, and to have ideals. These three symbol-given attributes— the aptitude for capitalizing on experience, including the experience of others, over time; the capacity for foresight and the self-imposed control of behavior through the anticipation of its outcomes; and the ability to envision worlds closer than the present one to the heart's desire—constitute a basic set of distinctively human potentialities.

A second set of such potentialities seems related to the long period of helpless dependence that characterizes infancy and childhood. Made mandatory by the relative biological incompleteness of the human baby, this phase of development is likely to be lengthened as cultures become more complex. Thus, in such simpler societies as the Samoan [18], children can achieve a higher degree of independence at an earlier age than in the civilizations of the West, for example, where the necessity for learning complicated and specialized economic skills extends the period of dependence through adolescence and even into chronological young adulthood. The central point, however, is that unlike the young of any other species, human children in *all* cultural settings must spend a long time during which the gratification of their most basic needs is mediated by somebody else and is dependent on their relationship to somebody else.

This state of affairs exposes youngsters during their earliest and most formative stages of development to two fundamental conditions of human life. The first is that one's survival, contentment, and need fulfillment involve an inevitable element of reliance on other people. The second is that the relative autonomy, authority, and power that characterize the parent figures and others on whom one relies in childhood are always perceived to a greater or lesser extent in association with responsibility and a kind of altruism. That is, the enjoyment of adult privileges and status tends to occur in conjunction with the acceptance, in some degree, of responsibility for mediating, in some way, the need gratifications of others. Mowrer and Kluckhohn [20] seem to be speaking of a similar pattern when they describe the socialization process as progressing from childhood *dependency* through *independence* to adult *dependability*.

Moreover, this reciprocal relationship between reliance and responsibility seems to obtain on adult levels as well as between children and parents, with the degree of reciprocity a partial function of the complexity of the culture. In simpler societies, a relatively small number of persons may assume primary responsibility for virtually all of the needs of the group in excess of its bare subsistence demands. Under civilized conditions, however, the specialization made necessary by technology and the pattern of urban living means that each adult is dependent on some other adult in some way and that, conversely, he is responsible in some fashion for the welfare of some other adult. The difference between the simpler and the more complex cultures, however, is only one of degree. The crucial point is that, throughout human society, men are in one way or another dependent on each other both in the familiar situation of parents and children and in the course of adult living. This pattern of interdependency gives to human life a social character to be found nowhere else in the animal kingdom. Even among the remarkable social insects, the patterns of symbiosis found there seem to be a result of a genetically determined division of labor rather than the fulfillment of a potentiality for the mutual sharing of responsibilities for each other.

It is in this notion of the fulfillment of distinctively human potentialities that a fruitful conception of positive adjustment may have its roots. From the symbolic and peculiarly social character of human life, it may be possible to derive a set of potential attributes the cultivation of which results in something different from the mere absence of pathology and which form a standard against which to assess the degree of integration in individual persons. To accept this task is to attempt the construction of a normative or ideal model of a normal, positively developed, or integratively adjusted human being.

A Model of Integrative Adjustment

In the first place, it would seem that, as the symbolic capacity that endows man with foresight develops in an individual, there is a concomitant increase in his ability to control his own behavior by anticipating its probable long-range consequences. The normal person is, first of all, one who has learned that in many situations his greatest satisfaction is gained by foregoing the immediate opportunities for comfort and pleasure in the interest of more remote rewards. He lives according to what Paul Elmer More, the Anglican theologian, calls "the law of costingness":

> . . . the simple and tyrannical fact that, whether in the world physical, or in the world intellectual, or in the world spiritual, we can get nothing without paying an exacted price. The fool is he who ignores, and the villain is he who thinks he can outwit, the vigilance of the nemesis guarding this law of costingness . . . all [one's] progress is dependent on surrendering one interest or value for a higher interest or value [19, p. 158].

Mowrer and Ullman [21] have made the same point in arguing, from the results of an ingenious experiment, that normality results in large part from the acquired ability to subject impulses to control through the symbolic cues one presents to oneself in the course of estimating the consequences of one's own behavior. Through symbolization, the future outcomes of one's actions are drawn into the psychological present; the strength of more remote rewards or punishments is consequently increased; and a long-range inhibitory or facilitating effect on incipient conduct is thereby exercised.

This increase in self-control means a lessened need for control by external authority, and conformity consequently becomes a relatively unimportant issue. The integratively adjusted person either conforms to the standards of his group because their acceptance leads to the most rewarding long-range consequences for him, or he rebels against authority, whether of persons or of law or custom, on *considered* grounds. This considered form of revolt implies two things. The first is an honest conviction that rules or the ruler are somehow unjust and that the implementation of his own values is likely

to lead to a more broadly satisfying state of affairs. Such an attack on authority is very different from revolts that occur out of sheer needs for self-assertion
or desires for power or as expressions of displaced hostility. The main dimension of difference is that of honesty as opposed to deception. The normal
person is relatively well aware of his motives in either conforming or rebelling.
The pathological rebel, on the other hand, tends to deceive himself and
others about his goals. His reasons for nonconformity amount to rationalizations, and his justifications are typically projections. This kind of self-defeating
and socially disruptive deceptiveness is seen daily in clinical practice.

The second characteristic of nonconformity in the normal person is that
it is undertaken with an essential acceptance of the possible consequences.
Having considered the risks before hand, he is inclined neither to whine nor
to ask that his rebellious conduct be overlooked if he runs afoul of trouble.
In keeping with the "law of costingness," he is willing to pay the price for
behaving in accordance with his own idiosyncratic values. "We have the
right to lead our own lives," John Erskine [8] makes Helen of Troy say to her
daughter Hermione, "but that right implies another—to suffer the consequences. . . . Do your best, and if it's a mistake, hide nothing and be glad
to suffer for it. That's morality." A psychological paraphrase of this bit of
belletristic wisdom is not inappropriate: The assumption of responsibility [1]
for one's actions is one of the attributes of personal integration.

But if personal responsibility and self-control through foresight can be
derived as aspects of integrative adjustment from man's symbolic capacity, a
third characteristic of interpersonal responsibility can be deduced from his
social nature. If interdependency is an essential part of human social life,
then the normal person becomes one who can act dependably in relation to
others and at the same time acknowledge his need for others. The roots of
the former probably lie, as McClelland [17] has pointed out, in the role perceptions which developing children form of parent figures and other agents
of the socialization process. By conceiving of such people as at least in some
degree the nurturant guides of others and through identification with them,
the integratively adjusted individual "wants to be" himself trustworthy and
altruistic in the sense of being dependable and acting out a genuine concern
for the welfare of others as he can best conceive it. Altruism in this context,
therefore, means nothing sentimental. It certainly includes the making and
enforcement of disciplinary rules and the imposition of behavioral limits, but
only if these steps are motivated by an interest in helping others and express

[1] This conception of responsibility is by no means antideterministic. As Fingarette [8]
points out, one can *understand* his own or another's behavior, in the sense of accounting
for it or rationally explaining it, by the retrospective process of examining the past. Responsibility, on the other hand, is neither retrospective in orientation nor explanatory in function. It is future-oriented and refers to the *act* of proclaiming oneself as answerable for
one's own conduct and its consequences. Thus, "responsibility," in this context, is not a
logical term, implying causation, but a behavioral and attitudinal one, descriptive of a class
of human actions.

concern and affection rather than mere personal annoyance or the power conferred by a superior status.

Similarly, the acknowledgment of one's needs for others implies a learned capacity for forming and maintaining intimate interpersonal relationships. Erikson [7] refers to this aspect of the normal personality as the attitude of "basic trust," and it is not far from what can be meaningfully styled in plain language as the ability to love. One suspects that the origins of this ability lies in the long experience during childhood of having need gratifications frequently associated with the presence of another person, typically a parent figure. By this association and the process of generalization, one comes to attach a positive affect to others. But as the youngster develops, he gradually learns that the need-mediating behavior of others is maintained only by his reciprocating, by his entering into a relationship of mutuality with others. If this kind of mutuality is not required of him, he is likely to perpetuate his dependency beyond the period his biological level of development and the complexity of his culture define as appropriate; whereas if he is required to demonstrate this mutuality too soon, he is likely to form the schema that interpersonal relationships are essentially matters of traded favors, and that, instead of basic trust, the proper attitude is one of getting as much as possible while giving no more than necessary. The pursuit in research and thought of such hypotheses as these might shed a good deal of light on the determinants of friendship, marital happiness, and effective parenthood, the relational expressions of effective personal integration.

But there is still another interpersonal attitude relevant to a positive conception of adjustment that is somewhat different from that bound up with relationships of an intimate and personal kind. There is a sense in which each individual, even if he regards himself as unfortunate and unhappy, owes his essential humanity to the group which enabled him to survive his helpless infancy. As studies of feral children [25] have shown, even the humanly distinctive and enormously adaptive trait of propositional speech does not become usable without the stimulation and nurture of other people. A kind of obligation is therefore created for the person to be an asset rather than a burden to society. It is partly to the discharging of this obligation that Adler [1] referred in developing his concept of social interest as a mark of normality. While the notion certainly implies the learning of local loyalties and personal affections, it also transcends the provincial limits of group and era. Because man's symbolic capacity enables him to benefit from the record of human history and to anticipate the future, and because his pattern of social interdependency, especially in civilized societies, reaches across the boundaries of political units and parochial affiliations, it seems reasonable to expect the positively developed person to behave in such a fashion as to contribute, according to his own particular lights, to the general welfare of humanity, to take as his frame of reference mankind at large as best he understands it rather than his own group or clan.

Ideologies are at issue here, but there need be neither embarrassment nor a lack of room for debate regarding the specifics of policy and values in the hypothesis that democratic attitudes are closely bound up with personality integration. After all, democracy in psychological terms implies only a concern about others, a valuing of persons above things, and a willingness to participate in mutually gratifying relationships with many categories of persons, including those of which one has only vicarious knowledge. Departures from democratic attitudes in this psychological sense mean a restriction on the potentiality for friendship and imply both a fear of others and a valuation of such things as power over people, thus endangering the interpersonal rewards that come from acting on the attitude of basic trust. Democratic social interest, then, means simply the most direct route to the fulfillment of a distinctively human capacity derived from man's symbolic character and the inevitability of his social life.

Finally, man's ability to assume an attitude toward the "merely possible" suggests that the normal person has ideals and standards that he tries to live up to even though they often exceed his grasp. For an integrative adjustment does not consist in the atttainment of perfection but in a striving to act in accordance with the best principles of conduct that one can conceive. Operationally, this notion implies that there is an optimum discrepancy between one's self concept and one's ego ideal. Those for whom this discrepancy is too large (in favor, of course, of the ideal) are likely to condemn themselves to the frustration of never approximating their goals and to an almost perpetually low self-esteem. Those whose discrepancies are too low, on the other hand, are probably less than integratively adjusted either because they are failing to fulfill their human capacity to envision themselves as they could be or because they are self-deceptively overestimating themselves.

This model of integrative adjustment as characterized by self-control, personal responsibility, social responsibility, democratic social interest, and ideals must be regarded only in the most tentative fashion. Nevertheless, it does seem to take into account some realistic considerations. It avoids the impossible conception of the normal person as one who is always happy, free from conflict, and without problems. Rather, it suggests that he may often fall short of his ideals; and because of ignorance, the limitations under which an individual lives in a complex world, or the strength of immediate pressures, he may sometimes behave in ways that prove to be shortsighted or self-defeating. Consequently, he knows something of the experience of guilt at times, and because he tries to be fully aware of the risks he takes, he can hardly be entirely free from fear and worry. On the other hand, a person who is congruent to the model is likely to be one who enjoys a relatively consistent and high degree of self-respect and who elicits a predominantly positive and warm reaction from others. Moreover, it is such a person who seems to learn wisdom rather than hostile bitterness or pathologically frightened withdrawal from whatever disappointments or suffering may be his lot. Guilt, for example, becomes a challenge to his honesty, especially with himself but also with others; and it signalizes for him the desirability of modifying his behavior, of greater effort to live up to his ideals, rather than the need to defend himself by such mechanisms as rationalization or projection. Finally, the model permits a wide variation in the actual behaviors in which normal people may engage and even makes allowance for a wide range of disagreements among them. Integrative adjustment does not consist in the individual's fitting a preconceived behavioral mold. It may well consist in the degree to which his efforts fulfill the symbolic and social potentialities that are distinctively human.

References

1. ADLER, A. *Social Interest: A Challenge to Mankind.* London: Faber & Faber, 1938.
2. ADORNO, T. W.; FRENKEL-BRUNSWIK, ELSE; LEVINSON, D. J.; and SANFORD, R. N. *The Authoritarian Personality.* New York: Harper, 1950.
3. BENEDICT, RUTH. Anthropology and the abnormal. *J. Gen. Psychol.* 10 (1934):59–82.
4. CASSIRER, E. *An Essay on Man.* New Haven: Yale University Press, 1944.
5. DARRAH, L. W. The difficulty of being normal. *J. Nerv. Ment. Dis.* 90 (1939):730–39.
6. DuBois, CORA. *The People of Alor.* Minneapolis: University of Minnesota Press, 1944.
7. ERIKSON, E. H. *Childhood and Society.* New York: W. W. Norton, 1950.
8. ERSKINE, J. *The Private Life of Helen of Troy.* New York: Bobbs-Merrill Co., 1925.
9. FINGARETTE, H. Psychoanalytic perspectives on moral guilt and responsibility: A re-evaluation. *Phil. Phenomenal. Res.* 16 (1955):18–36.
10. FORTUNE, R. F. *Sorcerers of Dobu.* London: Routledge, 1932.
11. FROMM, E. *The Sane Society.* New York: Rinehart, 1955.
12. GOLDSTEIN, K. *Human Nature in the Light of Psychopathology.* Cambridge, Mass.: Harvard University Press, 1940.
13. HACKER, F. H. The concept of normality and its practical significance. *Amer. J. Orthopsychiat.* 15 (1945):47–64.
14. LANGER, SUSANNE K. *Philosophy in a New Key.* Cambridge, Mass.: Harvard University Press, 1942.
15. MARZOLF, S. S. The disease concept in psychology. *Psychol. Rev.* 54 (1947):211–21.
16. MAY, R. *Man's Search for Himself.* New York: W. W. Norton, 1953.
17. McCLELLAND, D. *Personality.* New York: William Sloane Associates, 1951.
18. MEAD, MARGARET. *Coming of Age in Samoa.* New York: William Morrow, 1928.
19. MORE, P. E. *The Catholic Faith.* Princeton: Princeton University Press, 1931.
20. MOWRER, O. H., and KLUCKHOHN, C. "A Dynamic Theory of Personality." In J. MvV. Hunt, ed. *Personality and the Behavior Disorders.* New York: Ronald Press, 1944, pp. 69–135.
21. MOWRER, O. H., and ULLMAN, A. D. Time as a determinant in integrative learning. *Psychol. Rev.* 52 (1945):61–90.
22. PAVLOV, I. P. *Conditioned Reflexes.* London: Oxford University Press, 1927.
23. RIESE, W. *The Conception of Disease.* New York: Philosophical Library, 1953.
24. RIESMAN, D. *The Lonely Crowd.* New Haven: Yale University Press, 1950.
25. SINGH, J. A. L., and ZINGG, R. M. *Wolf-Children and Feral Man.* New York: Harper, 1942.

The Sources of Student Dissent

KENNETH KENISTON

During the process of adjustment, we pass through a series of "crises" like those Marcia described with regard to occupation, religion, and politics. But certainly there are other crises, and among the most complex of these are crises of personal and social values. In this selection, Kenneth Keniston describes the way two distinctly different breeds of students react to traditional value systems. He distinguishes political activists from the culturally alienated. The former, he argues, are marked by their commitment to some activity concerning a general political, social, or ethical issue, while the latter are preoccupied with private, personal experience and divorce themselves from the social and political worlds. The activists operate in society; the alienated "drop out." Both of these groups, however, are dissenters. But what are the roots of their dissent? Personality factors, or institutional, cultural, historical conditions? Keniston maintains that there is no one source of student dissent, but rather that dissent follows on a certain interaction of all four sources. As he pursues this thesis, he draws an increasingly clear picture of the way these two different kinds of people, the activists and the alienated, respond to personal and social stimuli. Note especially the similarity between this portrayal and the psychosocial crises already described by Marcia.

The apparent upsurge of dissent among American college students is one of the more puzzling phenomena in recent American history. Less than a decade ago, commencement orators were decrying the "silence" of college students in the face of urgent national and international issues; but in the past two or three years, the same speakers have warned graduating classes across the country against the dangers of unreflective protest, irresponsible action and unselective dissent. Rarely in history has apparent apathy been replaced so rapidly by publicized activism, silence by strident dissent.

This "wave" of dissent among American college students has been much discussed. Especially in the mass media—popular magazines, newspapers

SOURCE: © 1967 by the Society for the Psychological Study of Social Issues. Reprinted from *Youth and Dissent* by Kenneth Keniston by permission of Harcourt Brace Jovanovich, Inc.

and television—articles of interpretation, explanation, deprecation and occasionally applause have appeared in enormous numbers. More important, from the first beginnings of the student civil rights movement, social scientists have been regular participant-observers and investigators of student dissent. There now exists a considerable body of reasearch that deals with the characteristics and settings of student dissent [see Lipset and Altbach, 1966; Block, Haan and Smith, forthcoming; Katz, 1967; Peterson, 1967 for summaries of this research]. To be sure, most of these studies are topical (centered around a particular protest or demonstration), and some of the more extensive studies are still in varying stages of incompletion. Yet enough evidence has already been gathered to permit tentative generalizations about the varieties, origins and future of student dissent in the nineteen sixties.

In the remarks to follow, I will attempt to gather together this evidence (along with my own research and informal observations) to provide tentative answers to three questions about student dissent today. First, what is the nature of student dissent in American colleges? Second, what are the sources of the recent "wave of protest" by college students? And third, what can we predict about the future of student dissent?

Two Varieties of Dissent

Dissent is by no means the dominant mood of American college students. Every responsible study or survey shows apathy and privatism far more dominant than dissent [see, for example, *Newsweek*, 1965; Katz, 1965; Reed, 1966; Peterson, 1966; Block, Haan and Smith, forthcoming]. On most of our twenty-two hundred campuses, student protest, student alienation and student unrest are something that happens elsewhere, or that characterizes a mere handful of "kooks" on the local campus. However we define "dissent," overt dissent is relatively infrequent and tends to be concentrated largely at the more selective, "progressive," and "academic" colleges and universities in America. Thus, Peterson's study of student protests [1966] finds political demonstrations concentrated in the larger universities and institutions of higher academic calibre, and almost totally absent at teachers colleges, technical institutes and non-academic denominational colleges. And even at the colleges that gather together the greatest number of dissenters, the vast majority of students—generally well over 95%—remain interested onlookers or opponents rather than active dissenters. Thus, whatever we say about student dissenters is said about a very small minority of America's six million college students. At most colleges, dissent is not visible at all.

Partly because the vast majority of American students remain largely uncritical of the wider society, fundamentally conformist in behavior and outlook, and basically "adjusted" to the prevailing collegiate, national and international order, the small minority of dissenting students is highly visible to the mass media. As I will argue later, such students are often distinctively talented; they "use" the mass media effectively; and they generally succeed in their goal of making themselves and their causes highly visible. Equally important, student dissenters of all types arouse deep and ambivalent feelings in non-dissenting students and adults—envy, resentment, admiration, repulsion, nostalgia and guilt. Such feelings contribute both to the selective over-attention dissenters receive and to the often distorted perceptions and interpretations of them and their activities. Thus, there has developed through the mass media and the imaginings of adults a more or less stereotyped—and generally incorrect—image of the student dissenter.

THE STEREOTYPED DISSENTER

The "stereotypical" dissenter as popularly portrayed is both a Bohemian and political activist. Bearded, be-Levi-ed, long-haired, dirty and unkempt, he is seen as profoundly disaffected from his society, often influenced by "radical" (Marxist, Communist, Maoist, or Castroite) ideas, an experimenter in sex and drugs, unconventional in his daily behavior. Frustrated and unhappy, often deeply maladjusted as a person, he is a "failure" (or as one U. S. senator put it, a "reject"). Certain academic communities like Berkeley are said to act as "magnets" for dissenters, who selectively attend colleges with a reputation as protest centers. Furthermore, dropouts or "nonstudents" who have failed in college cluster in large numbers around the fringes of such colleges, actively seeking pretexts for protests, refusing all compromise and impatient with ordinary democratic processes.

According to such popular analyses, the sources of dissent are to be found in the loss of certain traditional American virtues. The "breakdown" of American family life, high rates of divorce, the "softness" of American living, inadequate parents, and, above all, overindulgence and "spoiling" contribute to the prevalence of dissent. Brought up in undisciplined homes by parents unsure of their own values and standards, dissenters channel their frustration and anger against the older generation, against all authority, and against established institutions.

Similar themes are sometimes found in the interpretations of more scholarly commentators. "Generational conflict" is said to underlie the motivation to dissent, and a profound "alienation" from American society is seen as a factor of major importance in producing protests. Then, too, such factors as the poor quality and impersonality of American college education, the large size and lack of close student-faculty contact in the "multiversity" are sometimes seen as the latent or precipitating factors in student protests, regardless of the manifest issues around which students are organized. And still other scholarly analysts, usually men now disillusioned by the radicalism of the 1930's, have expressed fear of the dogmatism, rigidity and "authoritarianism of the left" of today's student activists.

ACTIVISM AND ALIENATION

These stereotyped views are, I believe, incorrect in a variety of ways. They. confuse two distinct varieties of student dissent; equally important, they fuse dissent with maladjustment. There are, of course, as many forms of dissent as there are individual dissenters; and any effort to counter the popular stereotype of the dissenter by pointing to the existence of distinct "types" of dissenters runs the risk of oversimplifying at a lower level of abstraction. Nonetheless, it seems to me useful to suggest that student dissenters generally fall somewhere along a continuum that runs between two ideal types—first, the political activist or protester, and second, the withdrawn, culturally alienated student.

THE ACTIVIST. The defining characteristic of the "new" activist is his participation in a student demonstration or group activity that concerns itself with some matter of general political, social or ethical principle. Characteristically, the activist feels that some injustice has been done, and attempts to "take a stand," "demonstrate" or in some fashion express his convictions. The specific issues in question range from protest against a paternalistic college administration's actions to disagreement with American Vietnam policies, from indignation at the exploitation of the poor to anger at the firing of a devoted teacher, from opposition to the Selective Service laws which exempt him but not the poor to—most important—outrage at the deprivation of the civil rights of other Americans.

The initial concern of the protester is almost always immediate, ad hoc and local. To be sure, the student who protests about one issue is likely to feel inclined or obliged to demonstrate his convictions on other issues as well [Heist, 1966]. But whatever the issue, the protester rarely demonstrates because his *own* interests are jeopardized, but rather because he perceives injustices being done to *others* less fortunate than himself. For example, one of the apparent paradoxes about protests against current draft policies is that the protesting students are selectively drawn from that subgroup *most* likely to receive student deferments for graduate work. The basis of protest is a general sense that the selective service rules and the war in Vietnam are unjust to others with whom the student is identified, but whose fate he does not share. If one runs down the list of "causes" taken up by student activists, in rare cases are demonstrations directed at improving the lot of the protesters themselves; identification with the oppressed is a more important motivating factor than an actual sense of immediate personal oppression.

The anti-ideological stance of today's activists has been noted by many commentators. This distrust of formal ideologies (and at times of articulate thought) makes it difficult to pinpoint the positive social and political values of student protesters. Clearly, many current American political institutions like de facto segregation are opposed; clearly, too, most students of the New Left reject careerism and familism as personal values. In this sense, we might think of the activist as (politically) "alienated." But this label seems to me more misleading than illuminating, for it overlooks the more basic *commitment* of most student activists to other ancient, traditional and credal American values like free speech, citizen's participation in decision-making, equal opportunity and justice. In so far as the activist rejects all or part of "the power structure," it is because current political realities fall so far short of the ideals he sees as central to the American creed. And in so far as he repudiates careerism and familism, it is because of his implicit allegiance to other human goals he sees, once again, as more crucial to American life. Thus, to emphasize the "alienation" of activists is to neglect their more basic allegiance to credal American ideals.

One of these ideals is, of course, a belief in the desirability of political and social action. Sustained in good measure by the successes of the student civil rights movement, the protester is usually convinced that demonstrations are effective in mobilizing public opinion, bringing moral or political pressure to bear, demonstrating the existence of his opinions, or, at times, in "bringing the machine to a halt." In this sense, then, despite his criticisms of existing political practices and social institutions, he is a political optimist. Moreover, the protester must believe in at least minimal organization and group activity; otherwise, he would find it impossible to take part, as he does, in any organized demonstrations or activities. Despite their search for more truly "democratic" forms of organization and action (e.g., participatory democracy), activists agree that group action is more effective than purely individual acts. To be sure, a belief in the value and efficacy of political action is not equivalent to endorsement of prevalent political institutions or forms of action. Thus, one characteristic of activists is their search for new forms of social action, protest and political organization (community organization, sit-ins, participatory democracy) that will be more effective and less oppressive than traditional political institutions.

THE CULTURALLY ALIENATED. In contrast to the politically optimistic, active, and socially concerned protester, the culturally alienated student is far too pessimistic and too firmly opposed to "the System" to wish to demonstrate his disapproval in any organized public way.[1] His demonstrations of dissent are private: through nonconformity of behavior, ideology and dress, through personal experimentation and above all through efforts to intensify his own subjective experience, he shows his distaste and disinterest in politics and society. The activist attempts to change the world around him, but the alienated student is convinced that meaningful change of the social and political world is impossible; instead, he considers "dropping out" the only real option.

Alienated students tend to be drawn from the same general social strata and colleges as protesters. But psychologically and ideologically, their backgrounds are often very different. Alienated students are more likely to be disturbed psychologically; and although they are often highly talented and

---

[1] The following paragraphs are based on the study of culturally aliented students described in *The Uncommitted* (1965). For a more extensive discussion of the overwhelmingly anti-political stance of these students, see Keniston [1966] and also Rigney and Smith [1961], Allen and Silverstein [1967], Watts and Whittaker [1967], and Whittaker and Watts [1967].

artistically gifted, they are less committed to academic values and intellectual achievement than are protesters. The alienated student's real campus is the school of the absurd, and he has more affinity for pessimistic existentialist ontology than for traditional American activism. Furthermore, such students usually find it psychologically and ideologically impossible to take part in organized group activities for any length of time, particularly when they are expected to assume responsibilities for leadership. Thus, on the rare occasions when they become involved in demonstrations, they usually prefer peripheral roles, avoid responsibilities and are considered a nuisance by serious activists [Draper, 1965].

Whereas the protesting student is likely to accept the basic political and social values of his parents, the alienated student almost always rejects his parents' values. In particular, he is likely to see his father as a man who has "sold out" to the pressures for success and status in American society: he is determined to avoid the fate that overtook his father. Toward their mothers, however, alienated students usually express a very special sympathy and identification. These mothers, far from encouraging their sons towards independence and achievement, generally seem to have been over-solicitous and and limiting. The most common family environment of the alienated-student-to-be consists of a parental schism supplemented by a special mother-son alliance of mutual understanding and maternal control and depreciation of the father [Keniston, 1965a].

In many colleges, alienated students often constitute a kind of hidden underground, disorganized and shifting in membership, in which students can temporarily or permanently withdraw from the ordinary pressures of college life. The alienated are especially attracted to the hallucinogenic drugs like marijuana, mescalin and LSD, precisely because these agents combine withdrawal from ordinary social life with the promise of greatly intensified subjectivity and perception. To the confirmed "acid head," what matters is intense, drug-assisted perception; the rest—including politics, social action, and student demonstrations—is usually seen as "role-playing." [2]

[2] The presence among student dissenters of a group of "nonstudents"—that is, drop-outs from college or graduate school, who congregate or remain near some academic center— has been much noted. In fact, however, student protesters seem somewhat *less* likely to drop out of college than do nonparticipants in demonstrations [Heist, 1966], and there is no evidence that dropping out of college is in any way related to dissent from American society [Keniston and Helmreich, 1965]. On the contrary, several studies suggest that the academically gifted and psychologically intact student who drops out of college voluntarily has few distinctive discontents about his college or about American society [Suezek and Alfort, 1966; Pervin et al., 1966; Wright, 1966]. If he is dissatisfied at all, it is with himself, usually for failing to take advantage of the "rich educational opportunities" he sees in his college. The motivations of students dropping out of college are complex and varied, but such motivations more often seem related to personal questions of self definition and parental identification or to a desire to escape relentless academic pressures, than to any explicit dissent from the Great Society. Thus, although a handful of students have chosen to drop out of college for a period in order to devote themselves to political and societal protest activities, there seems little reason in general to associate the drop-out with the dissenter, whether he be a protester or an alienated student. The opposite is nearer the truth.

The recent and much-publicized emergence of "hippie" subcultures in several major cities and increasingly on the campuses of many selective and progressive colleges illustrates the overwhelmingly apolitical stance of alienated youth. For although hippies oppose war and believe in inter-racial living, few have been willing or able to engage in anything beyond occasional peace marches or apolitical "human be-ins." Indeed, the hippies' emphasis on immediacy, "love" and "turning-on," together with his basic rejection of the traditional values of American life, inoculates him against involvement in long-range activist endeavors, like education or community organization, and even against the sustained effort needed to plan and execute demonstrations or marches. For the alienated hippie, American society is beyond redemption (or not worth trying to redeem); but the activist, no matter how intense his rejection of specific American policies and practices, retains a conviction that his society can and should be changed. Thus, despite occasional agreement in principle between the alienated and the activists, cooperation in practice has been rare, and usually ends with activists accusing the alienated of "irresponsibility," while the alienated are confirmed in their view of activists as moralistic, "up-tight," and "un-cool."

Obviously, no description of a type ever fits an individual perfectly. But by this rough typology, I mean to suggest that popular stereotypes which present a unified portrait of student dissent are gravely oversimplified. More specifically, they confuse the politically pessimistic and socially uncommitted alienated student with the politically hopeful and socially committed activist. To be sure, there are many students who fall between these two extremes, and some of them alternate between passionate search for intensified subjectivity and equally passionate efforts to remedy social and political injustices. And as I will later suggest, even within the student movement, one of the central tensions is between political activism and cultural alienation. Nonetheless, even to understand this tension we must first distinguish between the varieties of dissent apparent on American campuses.

Furthermore, the distinction between activist and alienated students as psychological types suggests the incompleteness of scholarly analyses that see social and historical factors as the only forces that "push" a student toward one or the other of these forms of dissent. To be sure, social and cultural factors are of immense importance in providing channels for the expression (or suppression) of dissent, and in determining *which* kinds of dissenters receive publicity, censure, support or ostracism in any historical period. But these factors cannot, in general, change a hippie into a committed activist, nor a SNCC field worker into a full-time "acid-head." Thus, the prototypical activist of 1966 is not the "same" student as the prototypical student bohemian of 1956, but is rather the politically aware but frustrated, academically oriented "privatist" of that era. Similarly, as I will argue below, the most compelling alternative to most activists is not the search for kicks or sentience but the quest for scholarly competence. And if culturally sanctioned opportunities for the expression of alienation were to disappear, most alienated students would turn to private psychopathology rather than to public activism.

Stated more generally, historical forces do not ordinarily transform radically the character, values and inclinations of an adult in later life. Rather, they thrust certain groups forward in some eras and discourage or suppress other groups. The recent alternation in styles of student dissent in America is therefore not to be explained so much by the malleability of individual character as by the power of society to bring activists into the limelight, providing them with the intellectual and moral instruments for action. Only a minority of potential dissenters fall close enough to the midpoint between alienation and activism so that they can constitute a "swing vote" acutely responsive to social and cultural pressures and styles. The rest, the majority, are characterologically committed to one or another style of dissent.

The Sources of Activism

What I have termed "alienated" students are by no means a new phenomenon in American life, or for that matter in industrialized societies. Bohemians, "beatniks" and artistically inclined undergraduates who rejected middle-class values have long been a part of the American student scene, especially at more selective colleges; they constituted the most visible form of dissent during the relative political "silence" of American students in the 1950's. What is distinctive about student dissent in recent years is the unexpected emergence of a vocal minority of politically and socially active students.[3] Much is now known about the characteristics of such students, and the circumstances under which protests are likely to be mounted. At the same time, many areas of ignorance remain. In the account to follow, I will attempt to formulate a series of general hypotheses concerning the sources of student activism.[4]

It is abundantly clear that no single factor will suffice to explain the increase of politically motivated activities and protests on American campuses. Even if we define an activist narrowly, as a student who (a) acts together with others in a group, (b) is concerned with some ethical, social, ideological or

---

[3] Student activism, albeit of a rather different nature, was also found in the nineteen thirties. For a discussion and contrast of student protest today and after the Depression, see Lipset [1966a].

[4] Throughout the following, I will use the terms "protester" and "activist" intercheangeably, although I am aware that some activists are not involved in protests. Furthermore, the category of "activist" is an embracing one, comprising at least three sub-classes. First, those who might be termed *reformers*, that is, students involved in community organization work, the Peace Corps, tutoring programs, Vista, etc., but not generally affiliated with any of the "New Left" organizations. Second, the group of *activists proper*, most of whom are or have been affiliated with organizations like the Free Speech Movement at Berkeley, Students for a Democratic Society, the Student Non-violent Coordinating Committee or the Congress on Racial Equality or the Vietnam Summer Project. Finally, there is a much publicized handful of students who might be considered *extremists*, who belong to doctrinaire Marxist and Trotskyite organizations like the now-defunct May Second Movement. No empirical study with which I am acquainted has investigated the differences between students in these three sub-groups. Most studies have concentrated on the "activist proper," and my remarks will be based on a reading of their data.

political issue, and (c) holds liberal or "radical" views, the sources of student activism and protest are complex and inter-related. At least four kinds of factors seem involved in any given protest. First, the individuals involved must be suitably predisposed by their personal backgrounds, values and motivations. Second, the likelihood of protest is far greater in certain kinds of educational and social settings. Third, socially directed protests require a special cultural climate, that is, certain distinctive values and views about the effectiveness and meaning of demonstrations, and about the wider society. And finally, some historical situations are especially conducive to protests.

The Protest-Prone Personality

A large and still-growing number of studies, conducted under different auspices, at different times and about different students, presents a remarkably consistent picture of the protest-prone individual [Aiken, Demerath and Marwell, 1966; Flacks, 1967; Gastwirth, 1965; Heist, 1965, 1966; Lyonns, 1965; Somers, 1965; Watts and Whittaker, 1966; Westby and Braungart, 1966; Katz, 1967; and Paulus, 1967]. For one, student protesters are generally outstanding students; the higher the student's grade average, the more outstanding his academic achievements, the more likely it is that he will become involved in any given political demonstration. Similarly, student activists come from families with liberal political values; a disproportionate number report that their parents hold views essentially similar to their own, and accept or support their activities. Thus, among the parents of protesters we find large numbers of liberal Democrats, plus an unusually large scattering of pacifists, socialists, etc. A disproportionate number of protesters come from Jewish families; and if the parents of activists are religious, they tend to be concentrated in the more liberal denominations—Reform Judaism, Unitarianism, the Society of Friends, etc. Such parents are reported to have high ethical and political standards, regardless of their actual religious convictions.

As might be expected of a group of politically liberal and academically talented students, a disproportionate number are drawn from professional and intellectual families of upper middle-class status. For example, compared with active student conservatives, members of protest groups tend to have higher parental incomes, more parental education, and less anxiety about social status [Westby and Braungart, 1966]. Another study finds that high levels of education distinguish the activist's family even in the grandparental generation [Flacks, 1967]. In brief, activists are not drawn from disadvantaged, status-anxious, underprivileged or uneducated groups; on the contrary, they are selectively recruited from among those young Americans who have had the most socially fortunate upbringings.

BASIC VALUE COMMITMENTS OF ACTIVISTS

The basic value commitments of the activist tend to be academic and non-vocational. Such students are rarely found among engineers, future teachers at teachers colleges, or students of business administration (see Trent and Craise's article in this issue [5]). Their over-all educational goals are those of a liberal education for its own sake, rather than specifically technical, vocational or professional preparation. Rejecting careerist and familist goals, activists espouse humanitarian, expressive and self-actualizing values. Perhaps because of these values, they delay career choice longer than their classmates [Flacks, 1967]. Nor are such students distinctively dogmatic, rigid or authoritarian. Quite the contrary, the substance and style of their beliefs and activities tends to be open, flexible and highly liberal. Their fields of academic specialization are nonvocational—the social sciences and the humanities. Once in college, they not only do well academically, but tend to persist in their academic commitments, dropping out *less* frequently than most of their classmates. As might be expected, a disproportionate number receive a B.A. within four years and continue on to graduate school, preparing themselves for academic careers.

Survey data also suggest that the activist is not distinctively dissatisfied with his college education. As will be noted below, activists generally attend colleges which provide the best, rather than the worst, undergraduate education available today. Objectively then, activists probably have less to complain about in their undergraduate educations than most other students. And subjectively as well, surveys show most activists, like most other American undergraduates, to be relatively well satisfied with their undergraduate educations [Somers, 1965; Kornhauser, 1967]. Thus, dissatisfaction with educational failings of the "impersonal multiversity," however important as a rallying cry, does not appear to be a distinctive cause of activism.

In contrast to their relative satisfaction with the quality of their educations, however, activists *are* distinctively dissatisfied with what might be termed the "civil-libertarian" defects of their college administrations. While no doubt a great many American undergraduates distrust "University Hall," this distrust is especially pronounced amongst student protesters [Kornhauser, 1967; Paulus, 1967]. Furthermore, activists tend to be more responsive than other students to deprivations of civil rights on campus as well as off campus, particularly when political pressures seem to motivate on campus policies they consider unjust. The same responsiveness increasingly extends to issues of "student power": i.e., student participation and decisions affecting campus life. Thus, bans on controversial speakers, censureship of student publications, and limitations on off-campus political or social action are likely to incense the activist, as is arbitrary "administration without the consent of the administered." But it is primarily perceived injustice or the denial of student rights by the administration—rather than poor educational quality, neglect by the faculty, or the impersonality of the multiversity—that agitates the activist.

Most studies of activists have concentrated on variables that are relatively

[5] *Journal of Social Issues* 23 (1967), no. 3, 34–51.

easy to measure: social class, academic achievements, explicit values and satisfaction with college. But these factors alone will not explain activism: more students possess the demographic and attitudinal characteristics of the protest-prone personality than are actually involved in protests and social action programs. Situational, institutional, cultural and historical factors (discussed below), obviously contribute to "catalyzing" a protest-prone personality into an actual activist. But it also seems that, within the broad demographic group so far defined, more specific psychodynamic factors contribute to activism.

ACTIVISTS . . . NOT IN REBELLION

In speculating about such factors, we leave the ground of established fact and enter the terrain of speculation, for only a few studies have explored the personality dynamics and family constellation of the activist, and most of these studies are impressionistic and clinical [e.g. Coles, 1967; Ehle, 1965; Draper, 1965; Fishman and Solomon n.d., 1964; Gastwirth, 1965; Newfield, 1966; Schneider, 1966; Solomon and Fishman, 1963, 1964; Zinn 1965]. But certain facts are clear. As noted, activists are *not*, on the whole, repudiating or rebelling against explicit parental values and ideologies. On the contrary, there is some evidence that such students are living out their parents' values in practice; and one study suggests that activists may be somewhat *closer* to their parents' values than non-activists [Flacks, 1967]. Thus, any simple concept of "generational conflict" or "rebellion against parental authority" is clearly oversimplified as applied to the motivations of most protesters.

ACTIVISTS . . . LIVING OUT PARENTAL VALUES

It does seem probable, however, that many activists are concerned with *living out expressed but unimplemented parental values*. Solomon and Fishman [1963], studying civil rights activists and peace marchers, argue that many demonstrators are "acting out" in their demonstrations the values which their parents explicitly believed, but did not have the courage or opportunity to practice or fight for. Similarly, when protesters criticize their fathers, it is usually over their fathers' failure to practice what they have preached to their children throughout their lives. Thus, in the personal background of the protester there is occasionally a suggestion that his father is less-than-"sincere" (and even at times "hypocritical") in his professions of political liberalism. In particular, both careerism and familism in parents are the objects of activist criticisms, the more so because these implicit goals often conflict with explicit parental values. And it may be that protesters receive both covert and overt support from their parents because the latter are secretly proud of their children's eagerness to implement the ideals they as parents have only given lip-service to. But whatever the ambivalences that bind parents with their activist children, it would be wrong to overemphasize them: what is most impressive is the solidarity of older and younger generations.

ACTIVISTS . . . FAMILY STRUCTURE

While no empirical study has tested this hypothesis, it seems probable that in many activist-producing families, the mother will have a dominant psychological influence on her son's development. I have already noted that the protester's cause is rarely himself, but rather alleviating the oppression of others. As a group, activists seem to possess an unusual *capacity for nurturant identification*—that is, for empathy and sympathy with the underdog, the oppressed and the needy. Such a capacity can have many origins, but its most likely source in upper-middle class professional families is identification with an active mother whose own work embodies nurturant concern for others. Flacks' finding that the mothers of activists are likely to be employed, often in professional or service roles like teaching and social work, is consistent with this hypothesis. In general in American society, middle-class women have greater social and financial freedom to work in jobs that are idealistically "fulfilling" as opposed to merely lucrative or prestigious. As a rule, then, in middle-class families, it is the mother who actively embodies in her life and work the humanitarian, social and political ideals that the father may share in principle but does not or cannot implement in his career.

Given what we know about the general charactristics of the families of protest-prone students, it also seems probable that the dominant ethos of their families is unusually egalitarian, permissive, "democratic," and highly individuated.* More specifically, we might expect that these will be families where children talk back to their parents at the dinner table, where free dialogue and discussion of feelings is encouraged, and where "rational" solutions are sought to everyday family problems and conflicts. We would also expect that such families would place a high premium on self-expression and intellectual independence, encouraging their children to make up their own minds to stand firm against group pressures. Once again, the mother seems the most likely carrier and epitome of these values, given her relative freedom from professional and financial pressures.

The contrast between such protest-prompting families and alienating families should be underlined. In both, the son's deepest emotional ties are often to his mother. But in the alienating family, the mother-son relationship is characterized by maternal control and intrusiveness, whereas in the protest-prompting family, the mother is a highly individuating force in her son's life, pushing him to independence and autonomy. Furthermore, the alienated student is determined to avoid the fate that befell his father, whereas the

* Editor's note: Note the consistency between Keniston's description and the analysis offered by Bronfenbrenner, above, and remember what the latter postulated about possible effects of the egalitarian family on the child.

protesting student wants merely to live out the values that his father has not always worked hard enough to practice. Finally, the egalitarian, permissive, democratic and individuating environment of the entire family of the protester contrasts with the overcontrolling, over-solicitous attitude of the mother in the alienating family, where the father is usually excluded from major emotional life within the family.

These hypotheses about the family background and psychodynamics of the protester are speculative, and future research may prove their invalidity. But regardless of whether *these* particular speculations are correct, it seems clear that in addition to the general social, demographic and attitudinal factors mentioned in most research, more specific familial and psychodynamic influences contribute to protest-proneness.

The Protest-Promoting Institution

However we define his characteristics, one activist alone cannot make a protest: the characteristics of the college or university he attends have much to do with whether his protest-proneness will ever be mobilized into actual activism. Politically, socially and ideologically motivated demonstrations and activities are most likely to occur at certain types of colleges; they are almost unknown at a majority of campuses. The effects of institutional characteristics on protests have been studied by Cowan [1966] and Peterson [1966], and by Sampson and by Brown in this issue.[6]

In order for an organized protest or related activities to occur, there must obviously be sufficient *numbers* of protest-prone students to form a group, these students must have an opportunity for *interaction* with each other, and there must be *leaders* to initiate and mount the protest. Thus, we might expect—and we indeed find—that protest is associated with institutional size, and particularly with the congregation of large numbers of protest-prone students in close proximity to each other. More important than sheer size alone, however, is the "image" of the institution: certain institutions selectively recruit students with protest-prone characteristics. Specifically, a reputation for academic excellence and freedom, coupled with highly selective admissions policies, will tend to congregate large numbers of potentially protesting students on one campus. Thus, certain institutions do act as "magnets" for potential activists, but not so much because of their reputations for political radicalism as because they are noted for their academic excellence. Among such institutions are some of the most selective and "progressive" private liberal arts colleges, major state universities (like Michigan, California at Berkeley and Wisconsin) which have long traditions of vivid undergraduate teaching and high admissions standards [Lipset and Altbach, 1966] and many of the more prestigious private universities.

[6] *Journal of Social Issues* 23 (1967), no. 3, 1–33, 92–107.

Once protest-prone students are on campus, they must have an opportunity to interact, to support one another, to develop common outlooks and shared policies—in short, to form an *activist subculture* with sufficient mass and potency to generate a demonstration or action program. Establishing "honors colleges" for talented and academically motivated students is one particularly effective way of creating a "critical mass" of protest-prone students. Similarly, inadequate on-campus housing indirectly results in the development of off-campus protest-prone subcultures (e.g., co-op houses) in residences where student activists can develop a high degree of ideological solidarity and organizational cohesion.

But even the presence of a critical mass of protest-prone undergraduates in an activist subculture is not enough to make a protest without leaders and issues. And in general, the most effective protest leaders have not been undergraduates, but teaching assistants. The presence of large numbers of exploited, underpaid, disgruntled and frustrated teacher assistants (or other equivalent graduate students and younger faculty members) is almost essential for organized and persistent protest. For one, advanced students tend to be more liberal politically and more sensitive to political issues than are most undergraduates—partly because education seems to have a liberalizing effect, and partly because students who persist into graduate school tend to be more liberal to start than those who drop out or go elsewhere. Furthermore, the frustrations of graduate students, especially at very large public universities, make them particularly sensitive to general problems of injustice, exploitation and oppression. Teaching assistants, graduate students and young faculty members also tend to be in daily and prolonged contact with students, are close enough to them in age to sense their mood, and are therefore in an excellent position to lead and organize student protests. Particularly at institutions which command little institutional allegiance from large numbers of highly capable graduate students [Lipset and Altbach, 1966] will such students be found among the leaders of the protest movement.

THE ISSUES OF PROTEST

Finally, issues are a necessity. In many cases, these issues are provided by historical developments on the national or international scene, a point to which I will return. But in some instances, as at Berkeley, "on-campus" issues are the focus of protest. And in other cases, off-campus and on-campus issues are fused, as in the recent protests at institutional cooperation with draft board policies considered unjust by demonstrating students. In providing such on-campus issues, the attitude of the university administration is central. Skillful handling of student complaints, the maintenance of open channels of communication between student leaders and faculty members, and administrative willingness to resist public and political pressures in order to protect the rights of students—all minimize the likelihood of organized protest. Conversely, a university administration that shows itself unduly sensitive to political, legislative or public pressures, that treats students arrogantly, ineptly, condescendingly, hypocritically or above all dishonestly, is asking for a demonstration.

Thus one reason for the relative absence of on-campus student protests and demonstrations on the campuses of private, nondenominational "academic" colleges and universities (which recruit many protest-prone students) probably lies in the liberal policies of the administrations. As Cowan [1966] notes, liberal students generally attend non-restrictive and "libertarian" colleges. Given an administration and faculty that supports or tolerates activism and student rights, student activists must generally find their issues off campus. The same students, confronting an administration unduly sensitive to political pressures from a conservative board of regents or State legislature, might engage in active on-campus protests. There is also some evidence that clever administrative manipulation of student complaints, even in the absence of genuine concern with student rights, can serve to dissipate the potentialities of protest [Keene, 1966].

Among the institutional factors often cited as motivating student protest is the largeness, impersonality, atomization, "multiversitification" etc., of the university. I have already noted that student protesters do not seem distinctively dissatisfied with their educations. Furthermore, the outstanding academic achievements and intellectual motivations of activists concentrate them, within any college, in the courses and programs that provide the most "personal" attention: honors programs, individual instruction, advanced seminars, and so on. Thus, they probably receive relatively *more* individual attention and a *higher* calibre of instruction than do non-protesters. Furthermore, protests generally tend to occur at the best, rather than the worst colleges, judged from the point of view of the quality of undergraduate instruction. Thus, despite the popularity of student slogans dealing with the impersonality and irrelevance of the multiversity, the absolute level of educational opportunities seems, if anything, positively related to the occurrence of protest: the better the institution, the more likely demonstrations are.

Nor can today's student activism be attributed in any direct way to mounting academic pressures. To be sure, activism is most manifest at those selective colleges where the "pressure to perform" [Keniston, 1965b] is greatest, where standards are highest, and where anxieties about being admitted to a "good" graduate or professional school are most pronounced. But, contrary to the argument of Lipset and Altbach [1966], the impact of academic pressure on activism seems negative rather than positive. Protest-prone students, with their superior academic attainments and strong intellectual commitments, seem especially vulnerable to a kind of academic professionalism that, because of the enormous demands it makes upon the student's energies, serves to cancel or preclude activism. Student demonstrations rarely take place during exam periods, and protests concerned with educational quality almost invariably seek an improvement of quality, rather than a lessening of pressure. Thus, though the pressure to perform doubtless affects *all* American students, it probably acts as a deterrent rather than a stimulus to student activism.

DEPRIVATION OF EXPECTATIONS

What probably does matter, however, is the *relative* deprivation of student expectations (see Brown, this issue [7]). A college that recruits large numbers of academically motivated and capable students into a less-than-first-rate education program, one that oversells entering freshmen on the virtues of the college, or one that reneges on implicit or explicit promises about the quality and freedom of education may well produce an "academic backlash" that will take the form of student protests over the quality of education. Even more important is the gap between expectations and actualities regarding freedom of student expression. Stern [1967] has demonstrated that most entering freshmen have extremely high hopes regarding the freedom of speech and action they will be able to exercise during college: most learn the real facts quickly, and graduate thoroughly disabused of their illusions. But since activists, as I have argued above, are particularly responsive to these issues, they are apt to tolerate disillusion less lightly, and to take up arms to concretize their dashed hopes. Compared to the frustration engendered by disillusionment regarding educational quality, the relative deprivation of civil libertarian hopes seems a more potent source of protests. And with regard to both issues, it must be recalled that protests have been *fewest* at institutions of low educational quality and little freedom for student expression. Thus, it is not the absolute level either of educational quality or of student freedom that matters, but the gap between student hopes and institutional facts.

The Protest-Prompting Cultural Climate

Even if a critical mass of interacting protest-prone students forms in an institution that provides leadership and issues, student protests are by no means inevitable, as the quiescence of American students during the nineteen fifties suggests. For protests to occur, other more broadly cultural factors, attitudes and values must be present. Protest activities must be seen as meaningful acts, either in an instrumental or an expressive sense; and activists must be convinced that the consequences of activism and protest will not be overwhelmingly damaging to them. During the 1950's, one much-discussed factor that may have militated against student activism was the conviction that the consequences of protest (blacklisting, F.B.I. investigations, problems in obtaining security clearance, difficulties in getting jobs) were both harmful to the individual and yet extremely likely. Even more important was the sense on the part of many politically conscious students that participation in left-

---

[7] *Journal of Social Issues* 23 (1967), no. 3, 92–107.

wing causes would merely show their naiveté, gullibility and political innocence without furthering any worthy cause. The prevailing climate was such
that protest was rarely seen as an act of any meaning or usefulness.

ACADEMIC SUPPORT

Today, in contrast, student protesters are not only criticized and excoriated
by a large segment of the general public, but—more crucial—actively defended, encouraged, lionized, praised, publicized, photographed, interviewed
and studied by a portion of the academic community. Since the primary
reference group of most activists is not the general public, but rather that
liberal segment of the academic world most sympathetic to protest, academic
support has a disproportionate impact on protest-prone students' perception
of their own activities. In addition, the active participation of admired faculty
members in protests, teach-ins and peace marches, acts as a further incentive
to students [Kelman, 1966]. Thus, in a minority of American colleges, subcultures have arisen where protest is felt to be both an important existential
act—a dignified way of "standing up to be counted"—and an effective way
of "bringing the machine to a halt," sometimes by 'disruptive acts (sit-ins,
strikes, etc.), more often by calling public attention to injustice.

UNIVERSALISM

An equally important, if less tangible "cultural" factor is the broad climate
of social criticism in American society. As Parsons [1951, 1960], White [1961],
and others have noted, one of the enduring themes of American society is
the pressure toward "universalism," that is, an increasing extension of principles like equality, equal opportunity, and fair protection of the law to all
groups within the society (and in recent years, to all groups in the world).
As affluence has increased in American society, impatience at the slow "progress" of non-affluent minority groups has also increased, not only among
students, but among other segments of the population. Even before the
advent of the student civil rights movement, support for racial segregation was
diminishing. Similarly, the current student concern for the "forgotten fifth"
was not so much initiated by student activists as it was taken up by them.
In this regard, student activists are both caught up in and in the vanguard
of a new wave of extension of universalism in American society. Although
the demands of student activists usually go far beyond the national consensus,
they nonetheless reflect (at the same time that they have helped advance)
one of the continuing trends in American social change.

A contrasting but equally enduring theme in American social criticism is
a more fundamental revulsion against the premises of industrial—and now
technological—society. Universalistic-liberal criticism blames our society because it has not extended its principles, privileges and benefits to all: the
complaint is injustice and the goal is to complete our unfinished business. But

alienated-romantic criticism questions the validity and importance of these same principles, privileges and benefits—the complaint is materialism and the goal is spiritual, aesthetic or expressive fulfillment. The tradition of revulsion against conformist, anti-aesthetic, materialistic, ugly, middle-class America runs through American writing from Melville through the "lost generation" to the "beat generation" and has been expressed concretely in the bohemian subcultures that have flourished in a few large American cities since the turn of the century. But today, the power of the romantic-alienated position has increased: one response to prosperity has been a more searching examination of the technological assumptions upon which prosperity has been based. Especially for the children of the upper middleclass, affluence is simply taken for granted, and the drive "to get ahead in the world" no longer makes sense for students to start out ahead. The meanings of life must be sought elsewhere, in art, sentience, philosophy, love, service to others, intensified experience, adventure—in short, in the broadly aesthetic or expressive realm.

DEVIANT VIEWS

Since neither the universalistic nor the romantic critique of modern society is new, these critiques affect the current student generation not only directly but indirectly, in that they have influenced the way many of today's college students were raised. Thus, a few of today's activists are children of the "radicals of the 1930's" [Lipset and Altbach, 1966]; and Flacks comments on the growing number of intellectual, professional upper middle-class families who have adopted "deviant" views of traditional American life and embodied these views in the practices by which they brought up their children. Thus, some of today's activists are the children of bohemians, college professors, etc. But in general, the explanation from parental "deviance" does not seem fully convincing. To be sure, the backgrounds of activists are "atypical" in a statistical sense, and thus might be termed empirically "deviant." It may indeed turn out that the parents of activists are distinguished by their emphasis on humanitarianism, intellectualism and romanticism, and by their lack of stress on moralism [Flacks, 1967]. But it is not obvious that such parental values can be termed "deviant" in any but a statistical sense. "Concern with the plight of others," "desire to realize intellectual capacities," and "lack of concern about the importance of strictly controlling personal impulses"—all these values might be thought of as more normative than deviant in upper middle-class suburban American society in 1966. Even "sensitivity to beauty and art" is becoming increasingly acceptable. Nor can the socio-economic facts of affluence, freedom from status anxiety, high educational levels, permissiveness with children, training for independence, etc. be considered normatively deviant in middle-class America. Thus, the sense in which activists are the deviant offspring of subculturally deviant parents remains to be clarified.

PSYCHOLOGICAL FLEXIBILITY

Another explanation seems equally plausible, at least as applied to some student activists—namely that their activism is closely related to the social and cultural conditions that promote high levels of psychological flexibility, complexity and integration. As Bay [1967] has argued, social scientists may be too reluctant to entertain the possibility that some political and social outlooks or activities are symptomatic of psychological "health," while others indicate "disturbance." In fact, many of the personal characteristics of activists—empathy, superior intellectual attainments, capacity for group involvement, strong humanitarian values, emphasis on self-realization, etc.—are consistent with the hypothesis that, as a group, they are unusually "healthy" psychologically. [See also Heist, 1966 and Trent and Craise in this issue [8]]. Similarly, the personal antecedents of activists—economic security, committed parents, humanitarian, liberal and permissive home environments, good education, etc.—are those that would seem to promote unusually high levels of psychological functioning. If this be correct, then former SDS president Tom Hayden's words [1966] may be a valid commentary on the cultural setting of activism:

> Most of the active student radicals today come from middle to upper middle-class professional homes. They were born with status and affluence as facts of life, not goals to be striven for. In their upbringing, their parents stressed the right of children to question and make judgments, producing perhaps the first generation of young people both affluent and independent of mind.

In agreeing with Bay [1967] that activists may be more psychologically "healthy" as a group than nonactivists, I am aware of the many difficulties entailed by this hypothesis. First, complexity, flexibility, integration, high levels of functioning, etc. are by no means easy to define, and the criteria for "positive mental health" remain vague and elusive. [See Jahoda, 1958.] Second, there are obviously many individuals with these same "healthy" characteristics who are not activists; and within the group of activists, there are many individuals with definite psychopathologies. In any social movement, a variety of individuals of highly diverse talents and motivations are bound to be involved, and global descriptions are certain to be oversimplified. Third, the explanation from "psychological health" and the explanation from "parental deviance" are not necessarily opposed. On the contrary, these two arguments become identical if we assume that the preconditions for high levels of psychological functioning are both statistically and normatively deviant in modern American society. This assumption seems quite plausible.

Whatever the most plausible explanation of the socio-cultural sources of

[8] *Journal of Social Issues* 23 (1967), no. 3, 34–51.

activism, the importance of prevailing attitudes toward student protest and of the climate of social criticism in America seems clear. In the past five years a conviction has arisen, at least among a minority of American college students, that protest and social action are effective and honorable. Furthermore, changes in American society, especially in middle-class child-rearing practices, mean that American students are increasingly responsive to both the universalistic and romantic critique of our society. Both strands of social criticism have been picked up by student activists in a rhetoric of protest that combines a major theme of impatience at the slow fulfillment of the credal ideals of American society with a more muted minor theme of aesthetic revulsion at technological society itself. By and large, activists respond most affirmatively to the first theme and alienated students to the second; but even within the student protest movement, these two themes coexist in uneasy tension.

The Protest-Producing Historical Situation

To separate what I have called the "cultural climate" from the "historical situation" is largely arbitrary. But by this latter term I hope to point to the special sensitivity of today's student activists to historical events and trends that do not immediately impinge upon their own lives. In other nations, and in the past, student protest movements seem to have been more closely related to immediate student frustrations than they are in America today. The "transformationist" (utopian, Marxist, universalistic or democratic) aspirations of activist youth in rapidly developing nations often seem closely related to their personal frustrations under oppressive regimes or at "feudal" practices in their societies; the "restorationist" (romantic, alienated) youth movements that have appeared in later stages of industrialization seem closely connected to a personal sense of the loss of a feudal, maternal, and "organic" past. [See Lifton, 1960, 1963, 1964.] Furthermore, both universalistic and romantic youth movements in other nations have traditionally been highly ideological, committed either to concepts of universal democracy and economic justice or to particularistic values of brotherhood, loyalty, feeling and nation.

ANTI-IDEOLOGICAL

Today's activists, in contrast, are rarely concerned with improving their own conditions and are highly motivated by identification with the oppressions of others. The anti-ideological bias of today's student activists has been underlined by virtually every commentator. Furthermore, as Flacks notes, the historical conditions that have produced protest elsewhere are largely absent in modern America; and the student "movement" in this country differs in important ways from student movements elsewhere. In many respects, then, today's American activists have no historical precedent, and only time will tell to what extent the appearance of organized student dissent in the 1960's is a product of locally American conditions, of the psychosocial effects of a technological affluence that will soon characterize other advanced nations, or of widespread changes in identity and style produced by psycho-historical factors that affect youth of all nations (thermonuclear warfare, increased culture contact, rapid communications, etc.).

SENSITIVITY TO WORLD EVENTS

But whatever the historical roots of protest, today's student protester seems uniquely sensitive to historical trends and events. In interviewing student activists I have been impressed with how often they mention some world-historical event as the catalyst for their activism—in some cases, witnessing via television of the Little Rock demonstrations over school integration, in another case, watching rioting Zengakuren students in Japan protesting the arrival of President Eisenhower, in other cases, particularly among Negro students, a strong identification with the rising black nationalism of recently independent African nations.

Several factors help explain this sensitivity to world events. For one, modern means of communication make the historical world more psychologically "available" to youth. Students today are exposed to world events and world trends with a speed and intensity that has no historical precedent. Revolutions, trends, fashions and fads are now worldwide; it takes but two or three years for fashions to spread from Carnaby Street to New York, New Delhi, Tokyo, Warsaw, Lagos and Lima. In particular, students who have been brought up in a tradition that makes them unusually empathic, humanitarian and universalistic in values may react more intensely to exposure via television to student demonstrations in Japan than to social pressures from their fellow seniors in Centerville High. Finally, this broadening of empathy is, I believe, part of a general modern trend toward the *internationalization of identity*. Hastened by modern communications and consolidated by the worldwide threat of nuclear warfare, this trend involves, in vanguard groups in many nations, a loosening of parochial and national allegiances in favor of a more inclusive sense of affinity with one's peers (and nonpeers) from all nations. In this respect, American student activists are both participants and leaders in the reorganization of psychosocial identity and ideology that is gradually emerging from the unique historical conditions of the twentieth century [Lifton, 1965].

A small but growing number of American students, then, exhibit a peculiar responsiveness to world-historical events—a responsiveness based partly on their own broad identification with others like them throughout the world, and partly on the availability of information about world events via the mass media. The impact of historical events, be they the worldwide revolution for human dignity and esteem, the rising aspirations of the developing nations, or the war in Vietnam, is greatly magnified upon such students; their primary identification is not their unreflective national identity, but their sense of affinity for Vietnamese peasants, Negro sharecroppers, demonstrating Zengakuren activists, exploited migrant workers, and the oppressed everywhere. One of the consequences of security, affluence and education is a growing sense of

personal involvement with those who are insecure, non-affluent and uneducated.

The Future of Student Activism

I have argued that no single factor can explain or help us predict the future of
the student protest movement in America: active expressions of dissent have
become more prevalent because of an *interaction* of individual, institutional,
cultural and historical factors. Affluence and education have changed the
environment within which middle-class children are raised, in turn producing
a minority of students with special sensitivity to the oppressed and the dissenting everywhere. At the same time, technological innovations like television have made available to these students abundant imagery of oppression
and dissent in America and in other nations. And each of these factors exerts
a potentiating influence on the others.

Given some understanding of the interaction of these factors, general
questions about the probable future of student activism in America can now
be broken down into four more specific questions: Are we likely to produce
(a) more protest-prone personalities? (b) more institutional settings in which
protests are likely? (c) a cultural climate that sanctions and encourages
activism? and (d) a historical situation that facilitates activism? To three of
the questions (a, b and d), I think the answer is a qualified yes; I would therefore expect that in the future, if the cultural climate remains the same, student
activism and protest would continue to be visible features on the American
social landscape.

Consider first the factors that promote protest-prone personalities. In the
coming generation there will be more and more students who come from the
upper middle-class, highly educated, politically liberal professional backgrounds from which protesters are selectively recruited [Michael, 1965]. Furthermore, we can expect that a significant and perhaps growing proportion of
these families will have the universalistic, humanitarian, egalitarian and
individualistic values found in the families of protesters. Finally, the expressive, permissive, democratic and autonomy-promoting atmosphere of these
families seems to be the emerging trend of middle-class America: older
patterns of "entrepreneurial-authoritarian" control are slowly giving way to
more "bureaucratic-democratic" techniques of socialization [Miller and Swanson, 1958]. Such secular changes in the American family would produce a
growing proportion of students with protest-prone personalities.

Institutional factors, I have argued, are of primary importance in so far as
they bring together a critical mass of suitably protest-predisposed students in
an atmosphere where they can interact, create their own subculture, develop
leadership and find issues. The growing size of major American universities,
their increasing academic and intellectual selectivity, and the emphasis on
"quality" education (honors programs, individual instruction, greater student
freedom)—all seem to promote the continuing development of activist sub-

cultures in a minority of American institutions. The increasing use of graduate student teaching assistants in major universities points to the growing availability of large numbers of potential "leaders" for student protests. Admittedly, a sudden increase in the administrative wisdom in college deans and presidents could reduce the number of available "on-campus" issues; but such a growth in wisdom does not seem imminent.

CULTURAL CLIMATE MAY CHANGE

In sharp contrast, a maintenance of the cultural climate required for continuation of activism during the coming years seems far more problematical. Much depends on the future course of the war in Vietnam. Continuing escalation of the war in Southeast Asia will convince many student activists that their efforts are doomed to ineffectuality. For as of mid-1967, anti-war activism has become the primary common cause of student protesters. The increasing militancy and exclusivity of the Negro student civil rights movement, its emphasis on "Black Power" and on grass-roots community organization work (to be done by Negroes) is rapidly pushing white activists out of civil rights work, thus depriving them of the issue upon which the current mood of student activism was built. This fact, coupled with the downgrading of the war on poverty, the decline of public enthusiasm for civil rights, and the increasing scarcity of public and private financing for work with the underprivileged sectors of American society, has already begun to turn activists away from domestic issues toward an increasingly single-minded focus on the war in Vietnam. Yet at the same time, increasing numbers of activists overtly or covertly despair of the efficacy of student attempts to mobilize public opinion against the war, much less to influence directly American foreign policies. Continuing escalation in Southeast Asia has also begun to create a more repressive atmosphere toward student (and other) protesters of the war, exemplified by the question, "Dissent or Treason"? Already the movement of activists back to full-time academic work is apparent.

Thus, the war in Vietnam, coupled by the "rejection" of white middle-class students by the vestigial black Civil Rights Movement is producing a crisis among activists, manifest by a "search for issues" and intense disagreement over strategy and tactics. At the same time, the diminution of support for student activism tends to exert a "radicalizing" effect upon those who remain committed activists—partly because frustration itself tends to radicalize the frustrated, and partly because many of the less dedicated and committed activists have dropped away from the movement. At the same time, most activists find it difficult to turn from civil rights or peace work toward "organizing the middle class" along lines suggested by alienated-romantic criticisms of technological society. On the whole, activists remain more responsive to universalistic issues like peace and civil rights than to primarily expressive or esthetic criticisms of American society. Furthermore, the practical and organizational problems of "organizing the middle class" are overwhelming. Were the student movement to be forced to turn away from universalistic issues like civil rights and peace to a romantic critique of the "quality of middle class life," my argument here implies that its following and efficacy would diminish considerably. Were this to happen, observations based on student activism of a more "universalistic" variety would have to be modified to take account of a more radical and yet more alienated membership. Thus, escalation or even continuation of the war in Vietnam, particularly over a long period, will reduce the likelihood of student activism.

Yet there are other, hopefully more permanent, trends in American culture that argue for a continuation of protests. The further extension of affluence in America will probably mean growing impatience over our society's failure to include the "forgotten fifth" in its prosperity: as the excluded and under-privileged become fewer in number, pressures to include them in American society will grow. Similarly, as more young Americans are brought up in affluent homes and subcultures, many will undoubtedly turn to question the value of monetary, familistic and careerist goals, looking instead toward expressive, romantic, experiential, humanitarian and self-actualizing pursuits to give their lives meaning. Thus, in the next decades, barring a major world conflagration, criticisms of American society will probably continue and intensify on two grounds: first, that it has excluded a significant minority from its prosperity, and second, that affluence alone is empty without humanitarian, aesthetic or expressive fulfillment. Both of these trends would strengthen the climate conducive to continuing activism.

WORLDWIDE PROTEST-PROMOTING PRESSURES . . .

Finally, protest-promoting pressures from the rest of the world will doubtless increase in the coming years. The esteem for revolution in developing nations, the rise of aspirations in the impoverished two-thirds of the world, and the spread of universalistic principles to other nations—all of these trends portend a growing international unrest, especially in the developing nations. If young Americans continue to be unusually responsive to the unfulfilled aspirations of those abroad, international trends will touch a minority of them deeply, inspiring them to overseas activities like the Peace Corps, to efforts to "internationalize" American foreign policies, and to an acute sensitivity to the frustrated aspirations of other Americans. Similarly, continuation of current American policies of supporting anti-communist but often repressive regimes in developing nations (particularly regimes anathema to student activists abroad) will tend to agitate American students as well. Thus, pressures from the probable world situation will support the continuance of student protests in American society.

In the next decades, then, I believe we can foresee the continuation, with short-range ebbs and falls, of activism in American society. Only if activists were to become convinced that protests were ineffectual or social action impossible is this trend likely to be fundamentally reversed. None of this will mean that protesters will become a majority among American students; but we can anticipate a slowly growing minority of the most talented, empathic, and intellectually independent of our students who will take up arms against injustice both here and abroad.

In Summary . . .

Throughout this discussion, I have emphasized the contrast between two types of students, two types of family backgrounds, and two sets of values that inspire dissent from the Great Society. On the one hand, I have discussed students I have termed alienated, whose values are apolitical, romantic, and aesthetic. These students are most responsive to "romantic" themes of social criticism; that is, they reject our society because of its dehumanizing effects, its lack of aesthetic quality and its failure to provide "spiritual" fulfillment to its members. And they are relatively impervious to appeals to social, economic or political justice. On the other hand, I have discussed activists, who are politically involved, humanitarian and universalistic in values. These students object to our society not because they oppose its basic principles, but because it fails to implement these principles fully at home and abroad.

In the future, the tension between the romantic-alienated and the universalistic-activist styles of dissent will probably increase. I would anticipate a growing polarization between those students and student groups who turn to highly personal and experiential pursuits like drugs, sex, art and intimacy, and those students who redouble their efforts to change American society. In the past five years, activists have been in the ascendant, and the alienated have been little involved in organized political protests. But a variety of possible events could reverse this ascendancy. A sense of ineffectuality, especially if coupled with repression of organized dissent, would obviously dishearten many activists. More important, the inability of the student protest movement to define its own long-range objectives, coupled with its intransigent hostility to ideology and efficient organization, means that *ad hoc* protests are too rarely linked to the explicit intellectual, political and social goals that alone can sustain prolonged efforts to change society. Without some shared sustaining vision of the society and world they are working to promote, and frustrated by the enormous obstacles that beset any social reformer, student activists would be likely to return to the library.

How and whether this tension between alienation and activism is resolved seems to me of the greatest importance. If a growing number of activists, frustrated by political ineffectuality or a mounting war in Southeast Asia, withdraw from active social concern into a narrowly academic quest for professional competence, then a considerable reservoir of the most talented young Americans will have been lost to our society and the world. The field of dissent would be left to the alienated, whose intense quest for *personal* salvation, meaning, creativity and revelation dulls their perception of the public world and inhibits attempts to better the lot of others. If, in contrast, tomorrow's potential activists can feel that their demonstrations and actions are effective in molding public opinion and, more important, in effecting needed social change, then the possibilities for constructive change in post-industrial American society are virtually without limit.

References

1. AIKEN, M., DEMERATH, N. J., and MARWELL, G. Conscience and confrontation: some preliminary findings on summer civil rights volunteers. University of Wisconsin, 1966. (Mimeographed paper.)

2. ALLEN, M., and SILVERSTEIN, H. Progress report: creative arts—alienated youth project. New York: March, 1967.

3. BAY, CHRISTIAN. Political and apolitical students: facts in search of theory. *Journal of Social Issues* 23, no. 3 (1967).

4. BERNREUTER, ROBERT G. The college student: He is thinking, talking, acting. *Penn State Alumni News*, July 1966.

5. BLOCK, J., HAAN, N., and SMITH, M. B. Activism and apathy in contemporary adolescents. In J. F. Adams, ed., *Contributions to the Understanding of Adolescence*. Boston: Allyn and Bacon, forthcoming.

6. COLES, ROBERT. Serpents and doves: Non-violent youth in the South. In Erik Erikson, ed., *The Challenge of Youth*. New York: Basic Books, 1963.

7. COLES, ROBERT. *Children of Crisis*. Boston: Little, Brown, 1967.

8. COWAN, JOHN LEWIS. Academic freedom, protest and university environments. Paper read at APA, New York, 1966.

9. DRAPER, HAL. *Berkeley, the New Student Revolt*. New York: Grove, 1965.

10. EHLE, JOHN. *The Free Men*. New York: Harper & Row, 1965.

11. ERIKSON, ERIK H., ed. *The Challenge of Youth*. New York: Basic Books, 1963.

12. FISHMAN, JACOB R., and SOLOMON, FREDERIC. Psychological observations on the student sit-in movement. *Proceedings of the Third World Congress of Psychiatry*. Toronto: University of Toronto/McGill, n.d.

13. FISHMAN, JACOB R., and SOLOMON, FREDERIC. Youth and social action. *The Journal of Social Issues* 20, no. 4 (1964):1–28.

14. FLACKS, RICHARD E. The liberated generation: An exploration of the roots of student protest. *Journal of Social Issues* 23, no. 3 (1967).

15. GASTWIRTH, D. Why students protest. Unpublished paper, Yale University, 1965.

16. HAYDEN, T. Quoted in *Comparative Education Review* 10 (1966):187.

17. HEIST, PAUL. Intellect and commitment: The faces of discontent. *Order and Freedom on the Campus*. Western Interstate Commission for Higher Education and the Center for the Study of Higher Education, 1965.

18. HEIST, PAUL. The dynamics of student discontent and protest. Paper read at APA, New York, 1966.

19. JAHODA, MARIE. *Current Concepts of Positive Mental Health*. New York: Basic Books, 1958.

20. KATZ, J. The learning environment: Social expectations and influences. Paper presented at American Council of Education, Washington, D. C., 1965.

21. KATZ, J. The student activists: Rights, needs and powers of undergraduates. Stanford: Institute for the Study of Human Problems, 1967.

22. KEENE, S. How one big university laid unrest to rest. *The American Student* 1 (1966):18–21.

23. KELMAN, H. D. Notes on faculty activism. *Letter to Michigan Alumni*, 1966.

24. KENISTON, KENNETH. American students and the "political revival." *The American Scholar* 32 (1962):40–64.

25. KENISTON, KENNETH. *The Uncommitted*. New York: Harcourt, Brace and World, 1965a.

26. KENISTON, KENNETH. The pressure to perform. *The Intercollegian*. September 1965b.

27. KENISTON, KENNETH. The faces in the lecture room. In R. S. Morison, ed., *The American University*. Boston: Houghton Mifflin, 1966a.

28. KENISTON, KENNETH. The psychology of alienated students. Paper read at APA, New York, 1966b.

29. KENISTON, KENNETH, and HELMREICH, R. An exploratory study of discontent and potential drop-outs at Yale. Yale University, 1965. (Mimeographed paper.)

30. KORNHAUSER, W. Alienation and participation in the mass university. Paper read at American Ortho-Psychiatric Association, Washington, D. C., 1967.

31. LIFTON, ROBERT JAY. Japanese youth: the search for the new and the pure. *The American Scholar* 30 (1960):332–44.

32. LIFTON, ROBERT JAY. Youth and history: Individual change in post-war Japan. In E. Erikson, ed., *The Challenge of Youth*. New York: Harper & Row, 1963.

33. LIFTON, ROBERT JAY. Individual patterns in historical change. *Comparative Studies in Society and History* 6 (1964):369–83.

34. LIFTON, ROBERT JAY. Protean man. Yale University, 1965. (Mimeographed paper.)

35. LIPSET, SEYMOUR M. Student opposition in the United States. *Government and Opposition* 1 (1966a):351–74.

36. LIPSET, SEYMOUR M. University students and politics in underdeveloped countries. *Comparative Education Review* 10 (1966b):132–62.

37. LIPSET, SEYMOUR M., and ALTBACH, P. G. Student politics and higher education in the United States. *Comparative Education Review* 10 (1966):320–49.

38. LIPSET, SEYMOUR M., and WOLIN, S. S., eds. *The Berkeley Student Revolt*. Garden City, N. Y.: Doubleday, 1965.

39. LYONNS, G. The police car demonstration: A survey of participants. In S. Lipset and S. Wolin, eds., *The Berkeley Student Revolt*. Garden City, N. Y.: Doubleday, 1965.

40. MICHAEL, DONALD NELSON. *The Next Generation. The Prospects Ahead for the Youth of Today and Tomorrow*. New York: Vintage, 1965.

41. MILLER, MICHAEL, and GILMORE, SUSAN, eds., *Revolution at Berkeley*. New York: Dell, 1965.

42. MILLER, DANIEL R., and SWANSON, GUY E. *The Changing American Parent*. New York: John Wiley & Sons, 1958.

43. NEWFIELD, JACK. *A Prophetic Minority*. New York: New American Library, 1966.

44. *Newsweek*. Campus, 1965. March 22, 1965.

45. PARSONS, TALCOTT. *The Social System*. Glencoe, Ill.: Free Press of Glencoe, 1951.

46. PARSONS, TALCOTT. *Structure and process in modern societies*. Glencoe, Ill.: Free Press of Glencoe, 1960.

47. PAULUS, G. A multivariate analysis study of student activist leaders, student government leaders, and non-activists. Cited in Richard E. Peterson, *The Student Left in American Higher Education*. Draft for Puerto Rico Conference on Students and Politics, 1967.

48. PERVIN, LAWRENCE A., REIK, L. E., and DALRYMPLE, W., eds., *The College Drop-Out and the Utilization of Talent*. Princeton: Princeton University Press, 1966.

49. PETERSON, RICHARD E. *The Scope of Organized Student Protest in 1964–65*. Princeton: Educational Testing Service, 1966.

50. PETERSON, RICHARD E. The student Left in American higher education. Draft for Puerto Rico Conference on Students and Politics, 1967.

51. REED, M. Student non-politics, or how to make irrelevancy a virtue. *American Student* 1, no. 3 (1966):7–10.

52. RIGNEY, FRANCIS J., and SMITH, L. D. *The Real Bohemia*. New York: Basic Books, 1961.

53. SCHNEIDER, PATRICIA. A study of members of SDS and YD at Harvard. Unpublished B.A. thesis, Wellesley College, 1966.

54. SOLOMON, FREDERIC, and FISHMAN, JACOB R. Perspectives on the student sit-in movement. *American Journal of Ortho-Psychiatry* 33 (1963):873–74.

55. SOLOMON, FREDERIC, and FISHMAN, JACOB R. Youth and peace: A psycho-social study of student peace demonstrators in Washington, D. C. *Journal of Social Issues* 20, no. 4 (1964):54–73.

56. SOMERS, R. H. The mainsprings of the rebellion: A survey of Berkeley students in November 1964. In S. Lipset and S. Wolin, eds., *The Berkeley Student Revolt*. Garden City, N. Y.: Doubleday, 1965.

57. STERN, G. Myth and reality in the American college. *AAUP Bulletin*. Winter 1966, pp. 408–14.

58. SUCZEK, ROBERT FRANCIS, and ALFERT, E. Personality characteristic of college drop-outs. University of California, 1966. (Mimeographed paper.)

59. TROW, MARTIN. Some lessons from Berkeley. Paper presented to American Council of Education, Washington, D. C., 1965.

60. WATTS, WILLIAM ARTHER, and WHITTAKER, D. Some socio-psychological differences between highly committed members of the Free Speech Movement and the student population at Berkeley. *Applied Behavioral Science* 2 (1966):41–62.

61. WATTS, WILLIAM ARTHER, and WHITTAKER, D. Socio-psychological characteristics of intellectually oriented, alienated youth: A study of the Berkeley nonstudent. University of California, Berkeley, 1967. (Mimeographed paper.)

62. WESTBY, D., and BRAUNGART, R. Class and politics in the family backgrounds of student political activists. *American Social Review* 31 (1966):690–92.

63. WHITE, WINSTON. *Beyond Conformity*. Glencoe, Ill.: Free Press of Glencoe, 1961.

64. WHITTAKER, D., and WATTS, W. A. Personality and value attitudes of intellectually disposed, alienated youth. Paper presented at APA, New York, 1966.

65. WRIGHT, E. O. Student leaves of absence from Harvard College: A personality and social system approach. Unpublished paper, Harvard University, 1966.

66. ZINN, HOWARD. *SNCC, the New Abolitionists*. Boston: Beacon Press, 1965.

Interpersonal Relationships—Crux of
the Sexual Renaissance

LESTER A. KIRKENDALL AND ROGER W. LIBBY

In this selection, Kirkendall and Libby argue that we are experiencing a wide-spread change with regard to sexual morality, a change in which preoccupation with intercourse is giving way to an emphasis on the quality of interpersonal relationships.

Consider three things: sexual activity (petting, intercourse, or whatever), your sex, and your relationship with another person. Physiological forces are clearly at work; no one doubts the body's role in sex. Personal factors are certainly involved, your needs, your sensitivities, your ambitions and ideals. But what tends to be overlooked is the basic social element, the relationship itself. Many questions proceed from consideration of the interplay of these three forces. To what extent is your personality (and the other person's) dependent on your (and his or her) sex? How does the interaction of two sex-governed personalities influence the quality of the relationship? How does sexual behavior affect the relationship? Conversely, how does the quality of the relationship affect sexual behavior, and how do your responses to the other person influence your personality and your physical state?

These questions are complex, and their answers lead to more questions. We can share the authors' disappointment as they note that answers are only beginning to come in, but we can second their appeal for a deeper commitment on the part of researchers to the kinds of issues implied by this sexual renaissance.

A debate over whether sexual morality is declining, or whether we are experiencing a sexual revolution, has broken into the open. The controversy, which has been brewing for over a decade, has been mulled by news media, magazines, books and professional conferences. Varying views have been expressed, but one thing is clear—the very foundations upon which sexual morality has

SOURCE: From *Journal of Social Issues* 22, no. 2 (1966): 45–59. Copyright © 1966 by the Society for the Psychological Study of Social Issues, a division of the American Psychological Association. Reprinted by permission.

rested, and which have governed the exercise of sexual behavior, are being challenged [16]. This, of course, is characteristic of a renaissance.

Many influential people are moving away from the view that sexual morality is defined by abstinence from nonmarital intercourse toward one in which morality is expressed through responsible sexual behavior and a sincere regard for the rights of others. While these people do not advocate nonmarital sexual relations, this possibility is clearly seen as more acceptable if entered in a responsible manner, and contained within a relationship characterized by integrity and mutual concern. In other words, the shift is from emphasis upon an act to emphasis upon the quality of interpersonal relationships.

Illustrations of the Shift

Liberal religious leaders probably provide the most striking illustration of this change. Selections from their writings and pronouncements could be extended considerably beyond the following quotations, but these three are indicative of the changing emphasis.

Douglas Rhymes, Canon Librarian of Southwalk Cathedral, writes:

> We are told that all sexual experience outside marriage is wrong, but we are given no particular rulings about sexual experience within marriage. Yet a person may just as easily be treated as a means to satisfy desire and be exploited for the gratification of another within marriage as outside it. It is strange that we concern ourselves so much with the morality of pre-marital and extra-marital sex, but seldom raise seriously the question of sexual morality within marriage. . . . [21, p. 25]

John A. T. Robinson, Bishop of Woolwich, in his controversial book asserts:

> . . . nothing can of itself always be labelled "wrong." One cannot, for instance, start from the position "sex relations before marriage" or "divorce" are wrong or sinful in themselves. They may be in 99 cases or even 100 cases out of 100, but they are not intrinsically so, for the only intrinsic evil is lack of love [22, p. 118].

Harvey Cox, who is a member of the Divinity School faculty at Harvard University comments:

> To refuse to deliver a prepared answer whenever the question of premarital intercourse pops up will have a healthy influence on the continuing conversation that is Christian ethics. . . . It gets us off dead-end arguments about virginity and chastity, forces us to think about fidelity to persons. It exposes the . . . subtle exploitation that poisons even the most immaculate Platonic relationships.
>
> By definition premarital refers to people who plan to marry someone some day. Premarital sexual conduct should therefore serve to strengthen the chances of sexual success and fidelity in marriage, and we must face the real question of whether avoidance of intercourse beforehand is always the best preparation [6, p. 215].

What is common to these quotes is readily seen. In each the focus is on what happens to persons within the context of the interpersonal relationship matrix in which they find themselves. Morality does not reside in complete sexual abstinence, nor immorality in having had nonmarital experience. Rather, sex derives its meaning from the extent to which it contributes to or detracts from the quality and meaning of the relationship in which it occurs, and relationships in general.

This changing emphasis is also reflected in marriage manuals—those books purporting to help couples toward an adequate sexual adjustment. One of the earliest to appear in the United States (1926) was *The Ideal Marriage* by Theodore Van de Velde. The physiological aspect predominates in this 320-page book. Thus 310 pages of the 320 are devoted to detailed descriptions of the genital organs and the reproductive system, their hygiene and care. The last 10 pages (one chapter) are devoted to the psychic, emotional, and mental hygiene of the ideal marriage.

To say that the psychological and emotional aspects are completely ignored except for this chapter is not wholly fair, but the book, written by a physician, carries the vivid imprint of the medical profession with its concentration on physiology. At the time of its publication it was a forward-looking book.

The rising concern for interpersonal relationships, however, can be seen in another book written by a physician, Dr. Mary Calderone, in 1960. Dr. Calderone tries to create for her readers a perception of sexuality which is embedded firmly in the total relationship. At one point she comments:

> Sex responsiveness comes to those who not only view sex as a sacred and cherished factor in living, but who also retain good perspective about it by being sensitive to the needs of their partners and by taking into account the warmth, graciousness and humor inherent in successful marital sex [5, p. 163].

The historical preoccupation with sex as an act has also been reflected in the character of sex research. Until recently it has concentrated on incidences and frequencies of various forms of sexual behavior. Some of the more pretentious studies broke incidences and frequencies of the total research population into smaller groups, e.g., Kinsey [12, 13]. He looked for possible differences in sex behavior in sub-groups distinguished by such factors as religious affiliations, socioeconomic levels, rural or urban residence, adequacy of sex education and similar factors. This analysis, of course, took into account situational factors which could and do influence interpersonal relationships. Strictly speaking, however, the research still remained outside the interpersonal relationships framework.

Implications of the Shift

If an increasing concern for sex as an interpersonal relationship is the trend of the sexual renaissance, and we think it is, then clearly we must know how sex and sexual functioning are affected by relationships and vice versa. An extensive psychological literature has been developed to explain individual functioning; individual differences, individual growth patterns, individual cognitive development have all been explored. But relatively little is known about *relationships* as such—their components, or what precisely causes them to flourish, or to wither and die. A psychology more concerned with interpersonal relationships is now much needed. This also suggests the need to develop a field of research devoted to understanding sex and interpersonal relationships.

Finally, as a psychology and a sociology of relationships is developed, and as research findings provide a tested body of content for teaching, parents and educators may find a new stance. They can become less concerned with interdicting sexual expression of any kind, and more concerned with building an understanding of those factors which facilitate or impede the development of interpersonal relationships.

Research Associating Sex and Interpersonal Relationships

It is only within the last few years that some research has come to focus on interpersonal aspects of sexual adjustment.

That this is a fruitful approach is already evident from the results of some of the recent studies. Such research is still meager in scope and its methods and procedures will undoubtedly be much improved with experience. Much still remains in the realm of speculation and conjecture. But a beginning has been made, and the findings are enlightening and exciting.

One generalization growing out of the studies can be advanced at this point. *A sexual relationship is an interpersonal relationship, and as such is subject to the same principles of interaction as are other relationships.* It too is affected by social, psychological, physiological and cultural forces. The effort, so characteristic of our culture, to pull sex out of the context of ordinary living, obscures this simple but important generalization. Yet research findings constantly remind us of it.

Ehrmann [7] examined the association of premarital sexual behavior and interpersonal relationships. He studied the progression of individuals through increasingly intense stages of intimacy as they moved toward or rejected premarital intercourse. He was interested in understanding the various stages of intimacy behavior in relation to a number of factors. The stages were related to the attitudes with which acquaintances, friends and lovers regarded sexual intimacy, the kinds of controls exercised, and other factors which helped build certain feelings and attitudes in interpersonal relationships.

Two conclusions will illustrate the character of his findings. In discussing the differences in male-female attitudes which are found as affectional ties deepen, Ehrmann writes:

> . . . males are more conservative and the females are more liberal in expressed personal codes of sex conduct and in actual behavior with lovers

than with nonlovers. In other words, the degree of physical intimacy actually experienced or considered permissible is among males *inversely* related and among females *directly* related to the intensity of familiarity and affection in the male-female relation. . . .

Female sexual expression is primarily and profoundly related to being in love and going steadily. . . . Male sexuality is more indirectly and less exclusively associated with romanticism and intimacy relationships [7, p. 269].

Ehrmann, then, has educed evidence that maleness and femaleness and affection influence the character of those interpersonal relationships expressed in sexual behavior.

Similarly, Schofield [24] in a study of 1,873 London boys and girls between the ages of 15 and 19 found that

Girls prefer a more permanent type of relationship in their sexual behaviour. Boys seem to want the opposite; they prefer diversity and so have more casual partners. . . . there is a direct association between the type of relationship a girl has achieved and the degree of intimacy she will permit . . . [24, p. 92].

Kirkendall [15] conducted a study which centered upon understanding the association which he believed to exist between interpersonal relationships and premarital intercourse. He posited three components of an interpersonal relationship—motivation, communication and attitudes toward the assumption of responsibility—and studied the impact of premarital intercourse on them. Two hundred college-level males reported sexual liaisons with 668 females. These liaisons were arrayed along a continuum of affectional involvement. The continuum was divided into six segments or levels which ranged from the prostitute level, where affection was rejected as a part of the relationship, to fiancees—a level involving deep affection.

The relationship components were then studied to determine their changing character as one moved along the continuum. Thus it was found that communication at the prostitute level had a distinct barter characteristic. At the second (pickup) level there was a testing and teasing type of communication. At the deep affectional and the fiancee level was much more concern for the development of the kind of communication which would result in understanding and insight.

Similarly, the apparent character of the motivation central to the sexual relationship changed from one end of the continuum to the other. As depth of emotional involvement increased, the motivation changed from a self-centered focus to a relationship-centered one. And, increasing emotional involvement resulted in an increasing readiness to assume the responsibilities involved in the sexual relationship.

The study thus provides clear evidence that considering premarital intercourse in blanket terms—as though intercourse with a prostitute could be equated with intercourse with a fiancee—submerged many nuances and shades of meaning. Until these interpersonal differentiations are taken into account, there is little chance of any realistic or meaningful understanding of the character of premarital intercourse.

Burgess and Wallin [4] explored the possibility that premarital intercourse might strengthen the relationship of fiancees who engaged in it. They asked those subjects (eighty-one men and seventy-four women) who reported experience in premarital intercourse if they felt the experience strengthened or weakened their relationship. Some 92.6% of the men and 90.6% of the women attributed a strengthening effect to intercourse, and only 1.2% of the men and 5.4% of the women considered intercourse to have a weakening effect. The remainder noted no change either way. Burgess and Wallin comment:

> . . . This finding could be construed as testimony for the beneficial consequences of premarital relations, but with some reservations. First, couples who refrained from having premarital intercourse were not asked whether not doing so strengthened or weakened their relationship. They might have reported unanimously that their relationship had been strengthened by their restraint.
>
> Such a finding could be interpreted as signifying one of two things: (a) that both groups are rationalizing or (b) that given the characteristics, expectations, and standards of those who have intercourse, the experience strengthens their relationships, and, similarly, that given the standards of the continent couples the cooperative effort of couple members to refrain from sex relations strengthens their union [4, p. 371–372].

Kirkendall [15], after an analysis of his data, reinterpreted the findings of Burgess and Wallin. He envisioned a more complex interplay than simply a reciprocating association between sexual experience and the strengthening or weakening of a relationship. He suggested this interpretation:

> Some deeply affectionate couples have, through the investment of time and mutual devotion, built a relationship which is significant to them, and in which they have developed a mutual respect. Some of these couples are relatively free from the customary inhibitions about sexual participation. Some couples with this kind of relationship and background can, and do, experience intercourse without damage to their total relationship. The expression "without damage" is used in preference to "strengthening," for it seems that in practically all instances "nondamaging" intercourse occurred in relationships which were already so strong in their own right that intercourse did not have much to offer toward strengthening them [15, p. 199–200].

Kirkendall's study raised a question which the data from his non–randomly selected population could not answer. What proportion of all premarital intercourse occurs at the various levels of his continuum? Of the 668 sexual associations in his survey, 25 (3.2%) involved fiancees and 95 (14.2%) couples with deep affection. Associations involving prostitutes, pickups or partners dated only for intercourse accounted for 432 (64.2%), and those with dating partners where there was little or no affection numbered 116 (17.4%). But would similar proportions be found if a random sampling were used? A study designed to answer this question is needed.

Several studies have linked sexual behavior at the adolescent or young adult level with presumed causal relationships which existed in childhood, particularly those involving some sort of deprivation, usually affectional. This view, of course, will be nothing new to those familiar with psychiatric literature.

An interesting study which demonstrates this linkage is reported by Harold Greenwald [11]. Greenwald studied twenty call girls, prostitutes who minister to a well-to-do clientele. He found that ". . . many of the tendencies which lead to the choice of the call girl profession appear early in youth. . . ." [11, p. 182] The childhood backgrounds of the call girls appeared to be lacking in genuine love or tenderness. "The fundamental preventive task, then, becomes strengthening the family as a source of love and growth" [11, p. 182].

Ellis and Sagarin [8], in their study of nymphomania, also suggest that its causation has its roots in inadequate childhood relationships.

In studies made at the San Francisco Psychiatric clinic, Lion [17] and Safir [23] found that promiscuity was related to personality deficiencies, and that these in turn were related to homes characterized by disorganization, weak or broken emotional ties, and lack of loyalties or identification with any person or group.

If a tie of this kind does exist, it would seem logical that changes in the capacity of experience improved personal relationships (arising, for example, through therapy) should result in some change in the sexual pattern. Support for this view comes from Berelson and Steiner [1]. In their inventory of scientific findings concerning human behavior, they say that

> Changes toward a more positive attitude regarding sexual activity and toward freer, more enjoyable sexual activity than the patient was previously capable of having, are reported as correlates of psychotherapy from several camps [1, p. 290].

Graham [10] obtained information on the frequency and degree of satisfaction in coitus from 65 married man and women before they began psychotherapy. The data from these couples was compared with similar information from 142 married men and women who had been in treatment for varying periods of time. The results indicated, with certain reservations, that psychotherapy did free individuals for "more frequent and more satisfactory coitus experience" [10, p. 95].

Let us explore this logic from another side. If disorganized and aberrant sexual patterns are more frequent in adolescents or young adults who have experienced some form of emotional deprivation in childhood, it seems reasonable to hypothesize that those who had experienced normal emotional satisfactions should display more of what is considered conventional in their sexual practices. Since studies are more commonly done with persons who are recognized as problems, this possibility is not so well documented. There is, however, some evidence to support this view.

Loeb [18] in a study involving junior and senior high school youth, attempted to differentiate between boys and girls who do and do not participate in premarital intercourse. He advanced these conclusions:

> First, teenagers who trust themselves and their ability to contribute to others and have learned to rely on others socially and emotionally are least likely to be involved in irresponsible sexual activity.
>
> Second, teen-agers who have learned to be comfortable in their appropriate sex roles (boys who like being boys and wish to be men, and girls who like being girls and wish to be women) are least likely to be involved in activities leading to indiscriminate sexuality [18].

Maslow [19] in his study of self-actualized people makes several comments about the character of sexual functioning and sexual satisfaction in people who are considerably above the average so far as emotional health is concerned. He says:

> . . . sex and love can be and most often are very perfectly fused with each other in (emotionally) healthy people . . . [19, p. 241].
>
> . . . self-actualizing men and women tend on the whole not to seek sex for its own sake, or to be satisfied with it alone when it comes . . . [19, p. 242].
>
> . . . sexual pleasures are found in their most intense and ecstatic perfection in self-actualizing people . . . [19, p. 242].
>
> These people do not *need* sensuality; they simply enjoy it when it occurs [19, p. 243].

Maslow feels that the "we don't need it, but we enjoy it when we have it" attitude can be regarded as mature; though the self-actualized person enjoys sex more intensely than the average person, he considers sex less central in his total frame of reference.

Loeb's and Maslow's findings, then, suggest that responsible sexual behavior and satisfying interpersonal relations and personal development are closely related.

Multifarious Associations Between Sex and Interpersonal Relationships

The data which have emerged from various studies also make it clear that a tremendous range of factors can influence the quality of relationships which contain sexual expression; that these factors can and do change from time to time in the course of the relationship; and that almost an unlimited range of consequences can result.

Thus, one of the very important factors influencing the meaning of sex in a relationship is the degree of fondness which a couple have for one another. As previously noted, Kirkendall [15] in his study utilized a continuum of affectional involvement. He found that the character of motivation and communication, and the readiness of men to assume responsibility for the consequences of intercourse changed with the degree of emotional involvement. For example, as the length of elapsed time in a dating relationship prior to intercourse increased, there was an increase in the amount of communication devoted to understanding and a decrease in the amount of argumentative-persuasive communication. This finding parallels the findings of Ehrmann [7].

Maturity and developmental level represent still other factors. Broderick [2, 3] has made some interesting studies on the appearance and progressive development of various sexual manifestations with age. In a study of children in a suburban community he found that for many children interest in the opposite sex begins in kindergarten or before. Kissing "which means something special" is found among boys and girls as early as the third and fourth grades. In some communities dating begins for a substantial number of children in the fifth and sixth grades, while "going steady" is common at the junior high school level.

Schofield [24] also found that "those who start dating, kissing and inceptive behavior at an early age are also more likely to have early sexual intercourse" [24, p. 73]. In an analysis of family backgrounds he also found that

> . . . girls who got on very well with their fathers were far less likely to be sexually experienced. . . .
> . . . boys who did not get on well with their mothers were more likely to be sexually experienced. . . .
> . . . girls who got on well with their mothers were less likely to be sexually experienced . . . . [24, p. 144].

Role concepts, which in turn may be influenced by other factors and conditions, influence the interplay between sexual behavior and interpersonal relationships. This association has already been noted in quoting some of Ehrmann's findings.

The interaction becomes extremely complex as role concepts, sexual standards, cultural changes, sheer biology, and still other factors all become involved in a single situation.

Reiss' work [20], especially his discussion of the interplay between role concepts and the double standard, makes this point most vividly. He shows clearly how adherence to the double standard conditions the individual's concept of his own role and the role of his sexual partners. Thus what the individual may conceive of as freely willed and consciously chosen behavior is actually controlled by concepts deeply rooted in a long-existing cultural pattern.

The complexity is further emphasized as the origins of the double standard are studied. Reiss sees the roots of the double standard as possibly existing in "man's muscular strength, muscular coordination and bone structure. . . ."

These "may have made him a better hunter than woman; it may have made him more adept at the use of weapons. Couple this hunting skill with the fact that women would often be incapacitated due to pregnancy and childrearing, and we have the beginning of male monopoly of power" [20, p. 92].

Reiss feels that "The core of the double standard seems to involve the notion of female inferiority" [20, p. 192].

Once the double standard became embedded in the mores, however, cultural concepts reinforced it and helped embed it still more deeply. Now, however, cultural developments have begun to weaken the power of the double standard. The declining importance of the physical strength of the male in the modern economy; the ability to make reproduction a voluntary matter; emphasis on freedom, equality, and rationality—these and other forces have been eroding the power of the double standard, and in the process have been altering the association between sexual behavior and interpersonal relationships.

Shuttleworth [25] made an incisive critique of Kinsey's views on masculine-feminine differences in interest in sex as a function and as a physical experience. In the process, he advanced a theoretical position of his own which suggests that much role behavior is inherent in the biological structures of the sexes. He argues that their respective biology disposes male and female to regard their sexual functioning differently. Males, for example, can experience the erotic pleasures of sex more easily and with less likelihood of negative repercussions than can females. This fact, then, has helped to formulate both male and female sex roles, the attitudes of men and women toward sex and themselves, and to condition their sexual behavior. If this theoretical view can be established, it definitely has implications for a better understanding of the kind of interpersonal behavior which can be expected to involve the sexes, and how it may develop.

Vincent's [29] study of unwed mothers helped demonstrate that a wide range of outcomes in interpersonal relationships can arise from the circumstances of premarital pregnancy. The attitudes of unwed mothers ranged from those who found the pregnancy a humiliating and terrifying experience to those who found it maturing and satisfying, from those who rejected their child to those who found great satisfaction in having it, from those who rejected and hated the father to those who accepted him fully. When considering the interpersonal reactions of unwed mothers, no stereotype is possible.

Sexual intercourse in our culture has been invested with so many meanings and such strong emotions have been tied to it that nonparticipation may have as many consequences for interpersonal relations as participation. Tebor [27] studied 100 virgin college males and found that a large proportion of them felt insecure about their virginity and pressured by their peers to obtain experience. At the same time significant adults—teachers and parents—were quite unaware of what sexual pattern these men were following, and provided them no support in their pattern of chastity.

Requirements for Research on the Renaissance

The theme of this article has been that a concern for interpersonal relationships as the central issue in the management of sexuality is displacing the traditional emphasis on the avoidance or renunciation of all non-marital sexual experience. Only as a shift of this sort occurs are we in any way justified in speaking of a sexual renaissance.

Some requirements, however, face social scientists who wish to understand this shift. We have four to suggest.

1. *It will be necessary to commit ourselves fully to the study of relationships rather than simply reflecting on them occasionally.* In the area of sex, concern has been over-focused on the physical acts of sex. Thus the senior author, while doing the research for his book, *Premarital Intercourse and Interpersonal Relationships,* became aware that he was giving undue attention to the act of premarital intercourse, even while trying to set it in an interpersonal relationship context. As a consequence, crucial data were ignored. For example, in selecting subjects, if one potential subject had engaged in much caressing and petting, but had renounced the opportunity for intercourse many times, while another possible subject had merely gone through the physical act of copulation a single time, the latter one was defined as a subject for the research and the first was by-passed as though he had engaged in no sexual nor any interpersonal behavior.

With this realization came a decision to do research on decisions made by individuals concerning sexual behavior, regardless of whether they had had intercourse. The result is a recently completed preliminary study in which 131 non-randomly selected males were interviewed [14]. Of this group 72 (55%) had not had intercourse, but apparently only 17 (13%) had not been in a situation which required a decision. Eleven of these had made a firm decision against intercourse, quite apart from any decision-requiring situation, thus leaving only six who had never faced the issue of decision-making. In other words, when one thought of sexual decision-making as an aspect of interpersonal relationships, rather than continuing to focus on whether or not an act had occurred, one greatly increased the number who were potential subjects, and vastly increased the range of interpersonal behavior available for study.

We offer one further illustration of the reorientation in thinking necessary as we come to accept a concern for relationships as the central issue. The view which emphasizes the quality of interpersonal relationships as of foremost concern is often labelled as "very permissive" when sex standards and behavior are under discussion. This conclusion is possible when concern is focused solely on whether the commission of a sexual act is or is not acceptable. Certainly the emphasis on interpersonal relationships diverts attention from the act to the consequences. But having moved into this position, one finds himself in a situation which is anything but permissive. Relationships and their outcome seem to be governed by principles which are unvarying and which cannot be repealed. The fiat of parents or the edicts of deans can be softened, but there is no tempering of the consequences of dishonesty, lack of self-discipline, and lack of respect for the rights of others upon interpersonal relationships. If one wishes warm, accepting interpersonal relationships with others he will be defeated by these practices and no one, regardless of his position of authority can change this fact. Proclamations and injunction will be of no avail. There is no permissiveness here!

2. *Conceptual definitions of relationships will have to be developed.* Several social scientists have initiated work on this. For example, Foote and Cottrell [9] have identified six components of interpersonal competence—health, intelligence, sympathy, judgment, creativity and autonomy. Schutz [26] has developed his FIRO test to measure interpersonal behavior around three interpersonal needs—the needs for inclusion, control and affection. As has been noted, Kirkendall [15] centered his study around three components—motivation, communication and readiness to assume responsibility. Communication and motivation have both been frequently recognized aspects of interpersonal relationships.

However, the conceptualization of relationships in a manner which will permit effective research is still at an embryonic level. The numerous (for there are undoubtedly many) components of relationships have still to be determined, and methods and instruments for their measurement must be developed and perfected. Interpersonal relationships as a field of psychological study should be developing concurrently, for only in this way can we gain the needed broadening of our horizons.

3. *Methods and procedures will have to be devised which will enable us to study relationships.* The perceptive reader will have noted that while studies have been cited because, in our estimation, they bore on interpersonal relationships, all of them with the exception of that by Burgess and Wallin [4] obtained their information on interpersonal relationships by using individuals rather than pairs or groups as subjects. This is quite limiting. Would we not get a different view of premarital intercourse if we could interview both partners to the experience rather than one?

Methods of dealing with couples and groups, and research procedures which can zero in on that subtle, intangible, yet real tie which binds two or more people in an association are needed. Some work has already been done in this direction, but it has not been applied to sex and interpersonal relationships.

4. *The isolation of the most important problems for research is a requirement for progress.* Opinions would naturally differ in regard to what these problems are. We would suggest, however, that since sex relationships *are* interpersonal relationships, the whole field of interpersonal relationships with sex as an integral part needs to be attacked.

Kirkendall [15] has suggestions for further research scattered throughout his book. He suggests such problems as an exploration of the importance of time spent and emotional involvement in a relationship as a factor in determining whether a relationship can sustain intercourse, the factors which produce "loss of respect" when sexual involvement occurs, the meaning of sexual non-involvement for a relationship, factors which impede or facilitate sexual communication, and the relation of knowledge of various kinds of success or failure in sexual relationships.

His study poses many questions which merit answering. How do the emotional involvements of male and female engaged in a sexual relationship differ, and how do they change as the relationship becomes more (or less) intense? How nearly alike, or how diverse, are the perceptions which male and female hold of the total relationship and of its sexual component at various stages in its development? How does the rejection of a proffered sexual relationship by either partner affect the one who extended the offer? And what are the reactions and what produced them in the person receiving it? If there are no sexual overtures, how does this affect relationships?

Which value systems make it most (and least) possible for a couple to communicate about sex? To adjust to tensions which may accompany intercourse or its cessation? Which enable a couple to cope most effectively to the possible traumas of having their relationship become public knowledge, or of pregnancy?

In what diverse ways do premarital sexual experiences affect marital adjustments? What enables some couples who have been premarital sexual partners to separate as friends? Why do others separate with bitterness and hostility? What relation has maturity in other aspects of life to maturity in assessing the meaning of and coping with sexual manifestations of various kinds in the premarital period?

The questions could go on endlessly, yet the isolation of important areas for research remains one of the important tasks before us.

References

1. BERELSON, BERNARD, and STEINER, GARY A. *Human Behavior*. New York: Harcourt, Brace & World, 1964.
2. BRODERICK, CARLFRED B. *Socio-Sexual Development in a Suburban Community*. University Park: Pennsylvania State University. Unpublished manuscript (mimeographed), 1963.
3. BRODERICK, CARLFRED B., and FOWLER, S. E. New patterns of relationships between the sexes among preadolescents. *Marriage and Family Living*, 23 (1961):27–30.
4. BURGESS, ERNEST W., and WALLIN, PAUL. *Engagement and Marriage*. Philadelphia: J. B. Lippincott, 1953.
5. CALDERONE, MARY. *Release from Sexual Tensions*. New York: Random House, 1960.
6. COX, HARVEY. *The Secular City*. New York: Macmillan, 1965.
7. EHRMANN, WINSTON. *Premarital Dating Behavior*. New York: Henry Holt, 1959.

8. ELLIS, ALBERT, and SAGARIN, EDWARD. *Nymphomania*. New York: Julian Messner, 1964.

9. FOOTE, NELSON, and COTTRELL, LEONARD S., JR. *Identity and Interpersonal Competence*. Chicago: University of Chicago Press, 1955.

10. GRAHAM, STANLEY R. The effects of psychoanalytically oriented psychotherapy on levels of frequency and satisfaction in sexual activity. *Journal of Clinical Psychology* 16 (1960):94–98.

11. GREENWALD, HAROLD. *The Call Girl*. New York: Ballantine Books, 1958.

12. KINSEY, ALFRED C., et al. *Sexual Behavior in the Human Female*. Philadelphia: W. B. Saunders, 1953.

13. KINSEY, ALFRED C., et al. *Sexual Behavior in the Human Male*. Philadelphia: Saunders, 1948.

14. KIRKENDALL, LESTER A. Characteristics of sexual decision-making. To be published in the *Journal of Sex Research*.

15. KIRKENDALL, LESTER A. *Premarital Intercourse and Interpersonal Relationships*. New York: Julian Press, 1961.

16. KIRKENDALL, LESTER A., and OGG, ELIZABETH. *Sex and Our Society*. New York: York: Public Affairs Committee, 1964, No. 366.

17. LION, ERNEST G., et al. *An Experiment in the Psychiatric Treatment of Promiscuous Girls*. San Francisco: City and County of San Francisco, Department of Public Health, 1945.

18. LOEB, MARTIN B. Social role and sexual identity in adolescent males. *Casework Papers*. New York: National Association of Social Workers, 1959.

19. MASLOW, ABRAHAM. *Motivation and Personality*. New York: Harpers, 1954.

20. REISS, IRA L. *Premarital Sexual Standards in America*. Glencoe, Ill.: Free Press of Glencoe, 1960.

21. RHYMES, DOUGLAS. *No New Morality*. Indianapolis: Bobbs-Merrill, 1964, p. 25.

22. ROBINSON, JOHN A. T. *Honest to God*. Philadelphia: Westminster Press, 1963, p. 118.

23. SAFIR, BENNO, M.D. *A Psychiatric Approach to the Treatment of Promiscuity*. New York: American Social Hygiene Association, 1949.

24. SCHOFIELD, MICHAEL. *The Sexual Behavior of Young People*. London: Longmans, Green, 1965.

25. SHUTTLEWORTH, FRANK. A biosocial and developmental theory of male and female sexuality. *Marriage and Family Living* 21 (1960):163–70.

26. SCHUTZ, WILLIAM C. *FIRO: A Three-Dimensional Theory of Interpersonal Behavior*. New York: Rinehart, 1958.

27. TEBOR, IRVING. "Selected Attributes, Interpersonal Relationships and Aspects of Psychosexual Behavior of One Hundred College Freshmen, Virgin Men." Unpublished Ph.D. Thesis, Oregon State College, 1957.

28. VAN DE VELDE, THEODORE H. *Ideal Marriage*. New York: Random House, 1926.

29. VINCENT, CLARK E. *Unmarried Mothers*. New York: Free Press, 1961.

Is Love an Art?

ERICH FROMM

Nothing more naturally follows Kirkendall and Libby's discussion of interpersonal relationships than this passage from *The Art of Loving*. Here Erich Fromm offers his suggestion that perhaps the most frequently encountered stumbling block in the process of human adjustment is the person's uncertainty about his or her role as loved one or lover, subject or object. The man or woman who chooses to try to be loved, to be a love object, is forced to try to attract lovers by striving to become rich, powerful, beautiful, sexy, or whatever the fashion of the time dictates. Similarly, the person who emphasizes seeking such an object must also seek the fashion of the time. Failure to find satisfaction in love is then attributed to concentration on the wrong object, and so another object search begins—if not for the rich, then for the beautiful or the powerful or the sexy. In this selection Fromm suggests a way out of this predicament.

Is love an art? Then it requires knowledge and effort. Or is love a pleasant sensation, which to experience is a matter of chance, something one "falls into" if one is lucky? This little book is based on the former premise, while undoubtedly the majority of people today believe in the latter.

Not that people think that love is not important. They are starved for it; they watch endless numbers of films about happy and unhappy love stories, they listen to hundreds of trashy songs about love—yet hardly anyone thinks that there is anything that needs to be learned about love.

This peculiar attitude is based on several premises which either singly or combined tend to uphold it. Most people see the problem of love primarily as that of *being loved*, rather than that of *loving*, of one's capacity to love. Hence the problem to them is how to be loved, how to be lovable. In pursuit of this aim they follow several paths. One, which is especially used by men, is to be successful, to be as powerful and rich as the social margin of one's position permits. Another, used especially by women, is to make oneself attractive,

SOURCE: From "Is Love an Art?" in *The Art of Loving* by Erich Fromm. Copyright © 1956 by Erich Fromm. Reprinted by permission of Harper & Row, Publishers, Inc.

by cultivating one's body, dress, etc. Other ways of making oneself attractive, used both by men and women, are to develop pleasant manners, interesting conversation, to be helpful, modest, inoffensive. Many of the ways to make oneself lovable are the same as those used to make oneself successful, "to win friends and influence people." As a matter of fact, what most people in our culture mean by being lovable is essentially a mixture between being popular and have sex appeal.

A second premise behind the attitude that there is nothing to be learned about love is the assumption that the problem of love is the problem of an *object*, not the problem of a *faculty*. People think that to *love* is simple, but that to find the right object to love—or to be loved by—is difficult. This attitude has several reasons rooted in the development of modern society. One reason is the great change which occurred in the twentieth century with respect to the choice of a "love object." In the Victorian age, as in many traditional cultures, love was mostly not a spontaneous personal experience which then might lead to marriage. On the contrary, marriage was contracted by convention—either by the respective families, or by a marriage broker, or without the help of such intermediaries; it was concluded on the basis of social considerations, and love was supposed to develop once the marriage had been concluded. In the last few generations the concept of romantic love has become almost universal in the Western world. In the United States, while considerations of a conventional nature are not entirely absent, to a vast extent people are in search of "romantic love," of the personal experience of love which then should lead to marriage. This new concept of freedom in love must have greatly enhanced the importance of the *object* as against the importance of the *function*.

Closely related to this factor is another feature characteristic of contemporary culture. Our whole culture is based on the appetite for buying, on the idea of a mutually favorable exchange. Modern man's happiness consists in the thrill of looking at the shop windows, and in buying all that he can afford to buy, either for cash or on installments. He (or she) looks at people in a similar way. For the man an attractive girl—and for the woman an attractive man—are the prizes they are after. "Attractive" usually means a nice package of qualities which are popular and sought after on the personality market. What specifically makes a person attractive depends on the fashion of the time, physically as well as mentally. During the twenties, a drinking and smoking girl, tough and sexy, was attractive; today the fashion demands more domesticity and coyness. At the end of the nineteenth and the beginning of this century, a man had to be aggressive and ambitious—today he has to be social and tolerant—in order to be an attractive "package." At any rate, the sense of falling in love develops usually only with regard to such human commodities as are within reach of one's own possibilities for exchange. I am out for a bargain; the object should be desirable from the standpoint of its social value, and at the same time should want me, considering my overt and hidden assets and potentialities. Two persons thus fall in love when they feel they have found the best object available on the market, considering the limitations of their own exchange values. Often, as in buying real estate, the hidden potentialities which can be developed play a considerable role in this bargain. In a culture in which the marketing orientation prevails, and in which material success is the outstanding value, there is little reason to be surprised that human love relations follow the same pattern of exchange which governs the commodity and the labor market.

The third error leading to the assumption that there is nothing to be learned about love lies in the confusion between the initial experience of *"falling"* in love, and the permanent state of *being* in love, or as we might better say, of "standing" in love. If two people who have been strangers, as all of us are, suddenly let the wall between them break down, and feel close, feel one, this moment of oneness is one of the most exhilarating, most exciting experiences in life. It is all the more wonderful and miraculous for persons who have been shut off, isolated, without love. This miracle of sudden intimacy is often facilitated if it is combined with, or initiated by, sexual attraction and consummation. However, this type of love is by its very nature not lasting. The two persons become well acquainted, their intimacy loses more and more its miraculous character, until their antagonism, their disappointments, their mutual boredom kill whatever is left of the initial excitement. Yet, in the beginning they do not know all this: in fact, they take the intensity of the infatuation, this being "crazy" about each other, for proof of the intensity of their love, while it may only prove the degree of their preceding loneliness.

This attitude—that nothing is easier than to love—has continued to be the prevalent idea about love in spite of the overwhelming evidence to the contrary. There is hardly any activity, any enterprise, which is started with such tremendous hopes and expectations, and yet, which fails so regularly, as love. If this were the case with any other activity, people would be eager to know the reasons for the failure, and to learn how one could do better— or they would give up the activity. Since the latter is impossible in the case of love, there seems to be only one adequate way to overcome the failure of love—to examine the reasons for this failure, and to proceed to study the meaning of love.

The first step to take is to become aware that *love is an art*, just as living is an art; if we want to learn how to love we must proceed in the same way we have to proceed if we want to learn any other art, say music, painting, carpentry, or the art of medicine or engineering.

What are the necessary steps in learning any art?

The process of learning an art can be divided conveniently into two parts: one, the mastery of the theory; the other, the mastery of the practice. If I want to learn the art of medicine, I must first know the facts about the human body, and about various diseases. When I have all this theoretical knowledge, I am by no means competent in the art of medicine. I shall become a master in this art only after a great deal of practice, until eventually the results of my theoretical knowledge and the results of my practice are blended into one—my intuition, the essence of the mastery of any art. But, aside from learning the theory and practice, there is a third factor necessary to becoming a master in any art—the mastery of the art must be a matter of ultimate concern; there must be nothing else in the world more important than the art. This holds true for music, for medicine, for carpentry—and for love. And, maybe, here lies the answer to the question of why people in our culture try so rarely to learn this art, in spite of their obvious failures: in spite of the deep-seated craving for love, almost everything else is considered to be more important than love: success, prestige, money, power—almost all our energy is used for the learning of how to achieve these aims, and almost none to learn the art of loving.

Could it be that only those things are considered worthy of being learned with which one can earn money or prestige, and that love, which "only" profits the soul, but is profitless in the modern sense, is a luxury we have no right to spend much energy on? However this may be, the following discussion will treat the art of loving in the sense of the foregoing divisions: first I shall discuss the theory of love—and this will comprise the greater part of the book; and secondly I shall discuss the practice of love—little as can be *said* about practice in this, as in any other field.

On Hanging Loose and Loving:
The Dilemma of Present Youth

HENRY MILLER

This portrait of present-day youth illustrates many of the points brought out by the other authors in this section. Here Henry Miller defines a dilemma involving freedom, authenticity, and intimacy. "Hanging loose" means the aspiration to a broader form of freedom than earlier generations ever felt, a freedom of both affect and sense, emotion and perception. Because the sensoria of modern youth have been overwhelmed by an avalanche of stimulation—glittering trinkets, flickering figures on television and in movies, myriad sights and sounds and smells—, these young people have become jaded to sensation, so buried in stimuli that they have become unable to make sense out of them, unable to perceive. This insentient state impels youth to seek new experiences, especially chemically created ones. Youth's affect has also been blunted. The Waspish, middle-class home, with its controlled and contrived emotion and expression, has formed a generation of people who crave emotion, who long for self-expression. This affective deficit drives them to sensitivity groups and other interpersonal encounters. Ethnicism, expressive politics, mystic philosophies, free sex, free love—all these are manifestations of these deadened senses and deprived affects. But the perceptions these youth find are void of passion, and their affection lacks duration. Hence the dilemma: They seek freedom without commitment when freedom *is* commitment.

Note the traces in this essay of the thoughts of other authors. Aren't these people Keniston's alienated young? Don't they focus on Fromm's object rather than the subject? Aren't they out of tune with the essence of the sexual renaissance? And, finally, don't they miss the whole point of adjustment as the development of their unique and personal potentials?

SOURCE: From *Journal of Social Issues* 27 (3):35–46. Copyright © 1971 by the Society for the Psychological Study of Social Issues, a division of the American Psychological Association. Reprinted by permission.

Note: The preparation of this manuscript was supported in part through NIMH Grant MH 1537 to Robert Wallerstein and Stephen Pittel, and in part through the Chapman Research Fund, Carmel, California for research on Psychosocial Factors in Drug Abuse. I would like also to acknowledge my indebtedness to the staff of the Haight Ashbury Research Project, whose data and discussions have contributed to my thinking.

A polemic in which it is argued that the use of drugs among contemporary American youth is but one of many different behaviors and mystiques pervading their life. Thus, a fascination with the encounter, with ethnicity, with expressive politics, with nomadism, with sexuality, as well as with drugs, suggests that youth are engaged in a frustrating dialectic between freedom and commitment. The search for freedom is not political but rather a groping for sensate and affectual liberation. The dilemma posed by the inevitable constraints of commitment generates an awesome paradox which accounts for the anguish of the generation.

To generalize about contemporary American youth is to deny the only thing we really know about them: they are, like all human beings, infinitely complex and diverse in their behaviors. It is an exercise in ignorance, then, to draw a portraiture of an entire generation. Nor is it a less grievous error to take a behavior thought to be pervasive among youth and characterize it through encapsulation. Drug usage, for example, cannot be isolated from other activities and mystiques; indeed, its meaning resides in a fabric of other behaviors.

But if we cannot talk of youth in general out of ignorance, and if we cannot talk of a specific behavior for fear of rendering the behavior meaningless, we can talk of things "in the air"—of ideas and speculations and ruminations and possibilities. Further, we can identify behaviors that some youths engage in at some times; we can observe that many youths concern themselves with certain things; and we can know that a small group of youths experiment with a cluster of behaviors and that these behaviors, as a totality, say something about the specific concerns of that group. Which is a tortured way of saying that this essay concerns itself with what is probably a small group of young people who are toying with an aggregate of concerns shared, in part, by a large number of youth. For convenience, we use the phrase "youth" or "contemporary youth," but the reader should not be misled by such shorthand language. In a very real sense, this is not a paper about any actual population of individuals; it is a paper about currents of concern.

HANGING LOOSE AND THE NEW FREEDOM

With this caution in mind, we argue that contemporary American youth hang loose—or at least they try to. It is an admirable state of being. And it bothers their parents.

To "hang loose" means to achieve a state of freedom far beyond the conventional political freedoms of enfranchisement and an equitable distribution of power; it means a liberation from the obligations presumed in conventional interpersonal involvement and internal moral pressures. To hang loose is to declare an independence from pernicious demands, especially those that have become stereotyped or ritualized. Hanging loose is the operational derivative of the cult of experience. Its antithesis is to be up-tight, a constraint on experience which has the quality of bondage.

The new freedom of contemporary youth is a freedom of experience in regard both to affect and to sensation. But like all freedoms in this paradoxical business of living, it carries a price. The wages of interpersonal liberty are in the currency of commitment or, if it is preferred, interpersonal meaning. Thus, the parameters of the generation gap become defined and the tragedy of contemporary youth is staged: commitment and freedom are juxtaposed as antagonistic goodies. It is all terribly unfair. Unfortunately, the injustice is denied by a repudiation of the antithetical element—a solution which allows for some cognitive comfort but which leaves a distress of the spirit which we call alienation in the young and neurosis in their parents.

However, the hang-loose state is more an aspiration than a condition, and this serves to make the dilemma of youth much more intense. One can have the new liberty only by not needing to have commitment. Unfortunately, the need for commitment seems to be a prerequisite of humanity; to hunger for that from which one wants to escape can be an unsettling state of affairs. To deny the existence of an antithesis does not mean that the antithesis does not exist. It may be gratuitous to add that to accept its existence does not insure a solution.

Youth, in their quest for the new freedom, turn to many things; dope is but one of several avenues toward the goal of experiential liberty. But we must remember that the use of drugs, like the other behaviors to be discussed, is in the nature of a search. Drug use does not proclaim liberty; rather, it announces an aspiration. More precisely, it is a means rather than an end, which accounts for the great reluctance of youth to treat the drug experience as an exercise in pure pleasure without any assumed beneficial carry-over.

The mystique of psychedelic drug use holds that the sensory apparatus of many has been thoroughly stultified by his inhibiting and one-track middle-class heritage. Man has eyes but cannot see, he has ears that do not hear, indeed he may have sense organs that have escaped altogether the notice of a despiritualized and empirical science. Psychedelia has the power to liberate the senses; perception becomes restored to its inherent, unfettered capability. There is no need to reiterate the now familiar apology of the acid head—"the blues are bluer, the sounds take shape" kind of argument. It is important to note, however, that the objective validity of these claims is of no account. It is the *experience* of sensory acuity that is crucial, not the fact. The subjective experience is real, the objective fact may be illusory.

Marijuana, that great democratizer of youth, is indeed a magic drug. The magic resides in what is most correctly thought of as its sacramental qualities, qualities that are reputed to liberate inherent sensation. That the drug may be essentially placebo is beside the point; the sacramental elements may exist in the expectations surrounding use as legitimately as in the molecular structure of the drug. The mystique of marijuana carries the message of sensory freedom to huge populations of youth, a message that reads "the banality of conventional sensation is not immutable." Beauty is perceivable;

whether it be in the object or the beholder is not an issue for youth. It is sufficient that, at long last, it can be declared to exist!

SENSATION AT THE EXPENSE OF PASSION

When the awareness of beauty is made possible by the sacrament of marijuana or of psychedelia there is a cost. The concomitant of exotic sensation is an aloof, if benign, detachment. Interpersonal relationships, while turned on, are characterized by their irrelevance. Young people are invariably kind to each other while stoned; they may be patient and tolerant, but they are fundamentally turned inward. It is with the benignity of Buddha that they relate—all well and good when contemplating the antics of mankind, but hardly the context within which to conduct a love affair. Marijuana allows for sensation at the expense of passion. When passion intrudes, as it sometimes does, we have a definition of a bad trip.

The mystique of psychedelic drugs, then, offers the promise of enriched sensate experience, and the promise in itself is sufficient to engender the experience. The psychological mechanism which allows sensation disallows commitment, hence the notable absence of affect which is commitment's offspring. One feels only about those things which are cared for.

How to account for this relentless press toward sensate experience? Surely, youth have had sensation—it is an inevitable concomitant of having lived—and so there must be something thought wrong with pre-drug sensation. Somehow it must be perceived as limited, unsatisfying, constrained—in a word, inauthentic. Authentic sensation is the sought-after experience, meaning in essence a sensation not preselected through conventional filters and not prejudged by a cultural lexicon of explanation. Psychedelia promises the sensation of the pristine, the experience of the untutored infant. Authenticity is an attribute of liberated perceptors.

DRUGS AND THE ENCOUNTER

The encounter, like the drug experience, is a search for freedom-authenticity. Whereas with drugs the authenticity sought is one of sensate experience, with the encounter authenticity of affect becomes the target of search. As with drugs, the authenticity—by the fiat of required expectation—must occur within a context of freedom. The first commandment of the encounter is the mandate immediately to discharge affect. Sin, within the dogma of the encounter, resides in a constraint of feeling. Cognitive control of passion, the tour de force of enlightened Western man, becomes the great antagonist in the encounter. Now, the encounter situation by virtue of the fact that it throws together an aggregate of strangers is not the most likely arena within which natural emotion is to be generated. Strangers in twentieth-century America are more apt to breed indifference than feeling. In most instances, then, the affect of the encounter is probably fabricated; the paradox of the encounter is that spontaneity is enforced. Again, experientially this is a moot point. What is sought is the experience of feeling rather than the legitimacy of feeling. As with drugs, authenticity comes with the dismissal of a priori controls and filters.

The encounter is an amazing device and its popularity among the young is as pervasive as is the use of drugs. The encounter presumes a poverty of affect within its participants—or, at least, a constraint of affect. Liberation from such poverty or constraint is the goal, and the mystique of the encounter is uniquely able to insure such a freedom. There is affect aplenty within the encounter; loving feelings and hateful feelings abound, all without conse-quence. The joyful tidings of the encounter are that "it is all right to have such feelings!" and there is no penalty for their expression. Needless to say, there is no objective reward either; the formulation of "feelings without ex-ternal consequence" is rather benign. It is tempting to suggest that such feelings, by definition, are trivial. At the very least they are inconsequential.

Again the question is raised: why the need for such a device as the en-counter? What was wrong with the history of affect which every participant must inevitably bring to the group?

"ETHNICS" AS EXPRESSIVE MODELS

Some clue might be obtained if we consider another preoccupation of youth: the ubiquitous affection for folk culture and ethnicity. The focus of interest in exotic culture is on the presumed freedom thought to exist within the ethnic personality. It is a kind of romanticization, but not a complete one; contemporary youth are much too hip politically to mistake poverty and oppression for nobility of spirit. Even though the presumption is false, it still exists: ethnics are expressive rather than repressed. They laugh, yell, feel, cry—indeed they behave in real life, it is thought, as American youth can behave only in the encounter. It is very difficult to determine how much of ethnic interest among American youth is a function of political conscious-ness and how much is a function of this need for expressive models. The black man, for example, is a target for sympathy as well as emulation—as is the Chicano, the Indian, the Vietnamese peasant, the Cuban *campesino*, the American hillbilly—the list is long. The sympathy derives from political motives; the emulation comes from personal need. That the latter exists, however, can be further inferred from the mystique of "soul," which along with dope and the encounter provides the texture of youthful ideology. Soul is not ambiguous; some people have it and some don't. Those who've got it are admirable; those who don't are hopeless. Thus Johnny Cash, Aretha Franklin, Janis Joplin, Zorba the Greek, Bobby Seale, and Jerry Rubin all have soul; Richard Nixon, Aristotle Onassis, Roy Wilkins, Guy Lombardo, and most college professors don't. To have soul is to have sensate experience and to feel deeply and openly. Ethnics, it is thought, are more apt to have soul than are the homogenized victims of suburban life. Youth may be imprecise but they are instinctively right; it is mind-boggling to visualize Richard Nixon in an encounter, or his cabinet passing a joint. Soulless individuals do not participate in soulful activities.

EXPRESSIVE POLITICS

It is by now quite trite to characterize the politics of youth as expressive politics, but it is still very accurate. In student politics we find the most blatant mixture of priorities: to change the world and to change one's self. Thus, rallies and demonstrations bearing on the most serious and catastrophic of events—war, racism, injustice, and oppression—take on festive forms. Music, dance, flowers, and joy intermingle with chilling analyses of imperialism, genocide, alienation, and atrocity. Policemen and national guardsmen may be greeted with a brick or a kiss. This is not, we should remind ourselves, hypocrisy or confusion or frivolity. It is a struggle between expression and calculation. We should also remind ourselves that the guerrilla—Che, Ho, or Mao—is a potent synthesis of these tensions wherein rational analysis and calculated program lead to an expressive form of action.

We have thus far been treating of the aspirations of youth—freedom and authenticity in terms of sensation and affect. Juxtaposed is the complicating spectre of commitment and community, concepts which have always put constraints on these aspirations. Freedom is sought in several arenas: dope promises a liberation of the senses, the encounter offers unrestrained affect, ethnicity and politics suggest that these freedoms are obtainable in real life. There are other behaviors in other arenas we could discuss to lend weight to the point.

NOMADISM AND THE NEW FREEDOM

One of the most dramatic characteristics of youth is their incredible mobility. They move with ease, with spontaneity, with what appears to their parents as a reckless and irresponsible lack of planning. They hitchhike across the land with what is now a ritualized costume of knapsack and Levis. They will sleep in parks or in doorways, or if the weather is ominous they will crash with friends or near-friends or strangers. The verb in this new nomadic language is magnificent in precise meaning; "crash" means that when one is tired and needs rest or sleep, one stops—wherever one happens to be. It resounds of emergency: there is nothing to be done when the motor runs down but to crash. Of course there will always be a place; it is not anything to worry about. The need to crash requires a solution. In a real sense, the site has no choice.

The fact of travel over Europe and the world, the fact of mobility within the country from town to town and from apartment to apartment, the fact that there are no possessions to impede movement, the fact that conceptions such as home town or root or base are becoming archaic, all this can hardly be explained by technology or instant communication or affluence. They may be necessary but are certainly not sufficient conditions for the nomadism of youth. Again, youth is more likely to be motivated by the cult of experience and the derivative thereof, the quest for freedom. The equation between physical mobility and freedom is an old formulation, albeit an erroneous one, especially if the freedom sought is existential. But as with drugs, the encounter, and the other arenas discussed, the issue has to do with the search and not the modality. Nomadism yields the illusion of liberty—indeed the experience if not the fact of liberty. And this is the decisive point.

FREEDOM AND SEX

The sexual behavior of today's youth encapsulates all of the difficulties with which they contend. If they strive to be liberated from the shackles which convention places on sensation and affect, then we would expect a rather energetic and experimental flavor to their sexual lives. And indeed youth participate in the sexual experience probably with a versatility and virtuosity that was once reserved for Don Juan. Technologically, their sex is impeccable; marriage manuals provide the camp for young America. For a young person to be "put together" sexually means that he or she is able to enjoy sex thoroughly; for him to "know where it's at" sexually means that he has the right to enjoy sex. Unless that right is to become farcical, it implies that such notions as fidelity and loyalty are out of place—they not only impede the accumulation of experience, they constrain freedom. The disrepute of the institution of marriage among youth is not a function of what is seen as its empirical failure. Marriage fails on ideological grounds: it is counter-liberating. The search for freedom and authenticity demands a new marriage vow: "I promise to love and honor you until I get tired of you," or "I promise to love and honor you until someone better comes along." Realistically, these vows have always been the only ones capable of fulfillment, but when they are placed in stark language they ring with a cynicism that jars even youth. What they fail to see is the subtlety of conventional marriage: its promise characterizes the actuality. Youth dismiss the promise as dishonest; they should see it as a statement of aspiration.

That the sexual liberty of youth has been callously exploitative is testified to by the recent popularity of Women's Liberation. Contrary to popular opinion, Women's Lib is sexually reactionary. Young women have been used by the new sexual ethic and they are beginning to realize it. Women's Lib advocates a liberation from their own liberation—that is to say, women wish now to be free to say "no" as well as "yes."

The sexual and love behavior of young people allows for the clash between freedom and commitment to occur in its most dramatic form. It is a simple truth that one can not have it both ways; yet, alas, youth construe this as an artifact of middle-class mentality. It is the anguished emptiness of the alienated that accompanies the search for existential liberty, and it is felt most deeply, where it must be felt, in their love lives. Sex there is in abundance but when love rears its ugly head there comes the moment of truth wherein something must give. All too often, pressed by the coercions of the new culture and by the *Zeitgeist*, it is love that goes. And so the search continues, the fore-doomed search for another lover who will fill the emptiness and make no demands.

The Search for Freedom, Authenticity, and Intimacy

We have with us a large population of unhappy young people. They search, with hunger, for the most noble of goals: freedom, authenticity, and intimacy. Freedom, by their definition, is a freedom of sensation and affect; their authenticity is one of unadulterated experience; their intimacy precludes the regulation which comes with reciprocity of need. But sensation without a context of a priori meaning is the privilege of the demented. Only madmen sense in the absence of structure—it is a definition of their disease. Affect without control is a characteristic of the animals. Authenticity means honesty, not manumission; and intimacy without durability denies the most human of qualities: memory and hope.

In the search for experiential freedom youth turn to many things:

DRUGS AND PSYCHEDELIA. They turn to drugs and the mystique of psychedelia in order to perceive truth and beauty. In a haze of sweet-smelling dope come sounds once lost in a network of noise and sights previously unseen in a cacophony of visual stimulation. The "vibes" are real enough with dope— and they are good. Banality and the boredom of jaded experience are banished. But the price of being stoned is to lose involvement; the acid head can sense but he cannot love.

THE ENCOUNTER. They turn to the encounter wherein affect is the godhead. But it is difficult to hate a stranger and to love a transient object. The encounter allows for love and hate only within the boundaries of superficiality. Passion without consequence is very much like the passion of suburban childhood—one feels only if feeling carries no price. But at least there is noise in the encounter; one can yell and coo and even cry. The accoutrements of passion exist even if the passion itself is rather thin.

ROMANTIC ETHNICITY. They turn to the promise of ethnicity and emulate the earthiness of the impoverished. Here the sterile comfort of technology and affluence can be dispensed with; stripped of plasticity and the hassle of material avarice one can feel the dirt and make things with one's hands. There is talk and laughter and song and dance and struggle—and it glitters alongside the memory of high school math and the hollowness of ease. But ethnicity cannot be manufactured on the spot and when it exists it always carries with it the encumbrance of regulation. The ethnic may have meaning, but he doesn't have existential freedom.

MYSTIC PHILOSOHY. They turn to the astrologers and numerologists, the I Ching and the Book of the Dead, the mystics and the demonologists to fill the void left by a dead God. But the configurations of the planets are as illusory as the Holy Trinity. The sweet comfort of an ordered and meaningful universe is not to be found in a supermarket of extra-natural offerings. The attainment of Eastern bliss requires an incredible discipline and denial; it is antagonistic to the pursuit of experience. It is too bad, but it is so.

EXPRESSIVE POLITICS. They turn to political cause, but when politics become a means rather than an end the platforms become bizarre and the strategies self-defeating. Napalm is an atrocity, but blowing grass in the face of Dow recruiters does not accommodate to the issue. It may be fun but it is not political. Youth know of the injustice of imperialism and racism; they know fraud and hypocrisy; they perceive the wickedness and egotism of conventional politics and institutions. They would like a change, they work for change, and yet personal change competes as a value. Self-sacrifice, the hallmark of the revolutionary, does not infect the generation. We can hardly fault them for that.

NOMADISM. They turn to the road, equating physical mobility with the longed-for freedom. Travel is not the right word—it connotes the tours and the hotels and the museums of their parents. The youth we are concerned with do not travel—they hitch and crash and split and rap their way across continents. They carry packs instead of cameras; they go for months, for years, rather than weeks; they live and work and bum in Europe and Africa and Asia. For them Katmandu is a commonplace; for their parents it was an exotic dream. But the nomadism of youth, their incredible mobility and self-imposed rootlessness, does not yield the freedom which is sought, a freedom of the spirit rather than of the body.

SEXUAL FREEDOM. And finally, youth turn to sex to fill the emptiness left by a search for freedom. If dope deprives as well as rewards, if the encounter is superficial, if ethnicity cannot be fabricated, if politics confuse, if mystery and wandering still yield a void, then one can enter into or be entered by another human body. But orgasms are a cheat; they are great fun but rather short-lived. They promise their own demise. It is not the spasm of human contact that is needed—it is the chronicity of it all. But that, of course, is the great enemy of freedom.

What Led to the Hopeless Search?

What accounts for this hopeless search and for the anguished ambivalence to interpersonal commitment? Any serious observer with any regard for the rules of evidence must equivocate at this point. The questions are too gross; the data which bear on the questions are ambiguous. It would, however, be a disservice to beg off at this decisive juncture and so we offer our speculations in the same spirit of exaggeration which has characterized this essay thus far.

THE QUESTIONABLE SUCCESS OF SCIENCE

Surprisingly, it is the success of science rather than its failure which provides the nutriment for search. Science killed God, but it is not only that. Gods are ubiquitous and appear as ideology as well as embodiments. Youth have gods aplenty, unrecognized and unacknowledged, perhaps, but good service-able gods nonetheless. Science did something more. It hit upon a secret and promoted that secret with enormous success and in the process the truth of it became distorted. The secret is that man and his institutions are extremely versatile and that structural variation is mankind's great talent. This secret—exposed, propagandized, and misunderstood—was transformed into the myth of cultural relativism and the myth has been swallowed whole by American youth: "All behaviors are relative and equally good" is the axiom of dis-affected search; "there is no right and no wrong"; "malevolence is a creation of man rather than Satan."

But this axiom is a corruption—it misses the point. What is lost is the knowledge that institutional arrangements are universal, rules exist every-where, and regulation is the common denominator of human interchange. What is relative is the detail, the surplusage; structure is absolute. Youth read Margaret Mead on the sexuality of Samoa and conclude that sexual freedom is a human possibility. They do not note that the Samoans have a multitude of sexual restrictions and constraints. The restrictions may be different from ours, but they are just as many and, in their own context, just as inhibiting. Youth know of many different gods and conclude that He does not exist. The opposite conclusion is more viable: He exists out of human necessity. They hear of magic mushrooms and peyote—the equipage of the shaman and curandero—but ignore the careful prescription surrounding these mysteries.

The myth of relativism—a relativism distorted beyond original recognition, a relativism fostered by misguided parents who spoke in the name of enlight-enment, by teachers in the name of liberalism, by intellectuals in the name of realism, and even by theologues in the name of reformism—this relativism run amok provides the cognitive climate for the search toward freedom.

DAMPENED AFFECT IN MIDDLE-CLASS SOCIETY

But the search needs more than a nutritious bed; it needs a propellant. And here the villain is the apotheosis made of self-control by the necessities of contemporary civilization. White, Waspish, middle-class youth were reared on a diet of too much cool; their parents had passions, but they kept them in tight rein. In its most dramatic form our youth grew up in homes that were strangers to the sounds and sights of emotion—no yelling, no screaming, no crying, no cackling delight. Rather, youth saw and heard a bland even modulation of affect. It was a surrealistic scene; benign flat faces which, at times, would half smile or half frown, voices consistent in decibel value, all concealing strong feelings which probably seeped out in convoluted and confusing form. Youth are right: it was the epitome of hypocrisy and inauthenticness and it choked and suffocated and deprived a generation. It must have frightened, too. Why else would stirring feelings be so assiduously controlled if not because they were so exquisitely dangerous? Our youth are impoverished. They were deprived of the most necessary of experiences, the experience of feeling deeply.

OVERLY STIMULATED SENSORIA

Whereas their affects were stultified, their sensoria were swamped in an avalanche of stimulation. In the beginning, perhaps throughout, it was toys. Crib gyms and multi-colored blocks and picture books and dozens of child guidance toys—toys built to stimulate and arouse and interest, all in color and smooth plastic, and all based on the false premise that curiosity is a function of the object and not the subject. Then television with its imbecilic yet provocative cartoons: animals that zoom and clank and soar and go squish, animated fictions that give certitude to the impossible. The searching generation is one reared on the TV cartoon, sucklings of Howdy-Doody and the Mickey Mouse Club. Later still, Dragnet, the Untouchables, and Marshall Dillon harassed the retina with images of dancing light. It was not the dramatized violence that was objectionable—children know reality from make-believe—it was the light itself and the rapidly shifting imagery. And there was the news and the movies and school; all throwing scene upon scene, image upon image, sound upon sound, on a weary and overloaded cerebral cortex which had no blueprint for organizing such a mountain of stimulation. Sensation is lost in a flood of sensation. It is no wonder that the blunting of sensation which comes with dope can appear as its sharpening.

Involvement and Commitment

Youth search, then, for the affect which was denied them, for the sensory experience which escaped them, and for the honesty and openness which they never saw. It is an admirable search, it is a necessary search, but alas it is a misguided one. Youth perpetuate the error of their parents; they emphasize the object and not the subject, they measure their freedom by a minima of external constraints rather than a maxima of internal possibilities. It is to the great lesson of mankind that they should attend: involvement brings liberation, commitment *is* freedom.

PART **7**

Psychotherapy and Intervention

When adaptive behaviors fail and adjustment falters, some form of intervention becomes necessary to redirect personal growth. Over the years a great number of different forms of therapy have evolved. These can be grouped into the physical approach, the psychological approach, and the social approach. The physical approach is characterized by its use of medical principles and techniques; included under this rubric are such interventions as chemotherapy (drug therapy), shock treatment, and psychosurgery. The psychological approach uses psychological principles and methods. This approach encompasses individual psychotherapy and its many variations (notably including Freudian psychoanalysis and Rogerian client-centered therapy) as well as behavior therapy. The third approach to therapeutic intervention is essentially a variant of the psychological approach. This variety, the social, uses psychological principles and techniques, but in a group setting. Alternatively called laboratory education, this kind of intervention includes T groups, encounter laboratories, and Tavistock Conferences.

The articles in this section will provide more detail about these different forms of intervention. Even more important, they will show that there is not just a one-to-one correspondence between the physical, psychological, and social therapies and the disorders in those specific spheres of human behavior, but that one therapeutic approach can be used to redirect growth in an apparently very different arena of behavior. Try to be especially alert for examples of this interplay.

The Nature of the Process:
General Factors

WILLIAM SCHOFIELD

By conservative count there are at least a dozen, perhaps as many as forty, different varieties of individual psychotherapy. A great deal of energy over the years has been committed to debating the merits of their various techniques, but these arguments have generally been inconclusive. Why? It stands to reason that, if skilled practitioners of each approach apparently meet with at least some success, and particularly if that success is with similar patients suffering similar complaints, then there might well be some elements *common* to all those approaches that account for their efficacy. If this is indeed the case, the differences among approaches become incidental; the potency lies in the common elements.

In this selection, William Schofield proposes such a set of common factors. He notes that all therapies rest on an articulated theoretical base. He contends that all methods share certain structural characteristics: a therapist who is an "expert conversationalist" (Schofield's definition of psychotherapy is "conversation with therapeutic intent") and who expects to help the patient; a patient who requests help and expects to be helped; and a relatively circumscribed relationship, in which the patient knows that he or she is accepted as a person and that the proceedings are entirely confidential. Looking more at the therapeutic process, Schofield points out that all systems of psychotherapy involve the patient's expression of previously hidden emotions and the therapist's assumption of a teacher's role, whether guide or tutor or model or source of reinforcement for appropriate behavior.

Whether or not research will bear out Schofield's hypothesis that these common factors account for the efficacy of psychotherapy, this selection stands as an exceptional introduction to individual psychotherapy.

. . . In a psychological analysis of potential common factors in various methods of psychotherapy it is well to start with a clear view of those dif-

SOURCE: William Schofield, *Psychotherapy: The Purchase of Friendship,* © 1964. Reprinted by permission of Prentice-Hall, Inc., Englewood Cliffs, New Jersey.

ferences which are explicit. A "school" of psychotherapy is identified by: (a) a theory of personality or of psychopathology, and (b) a set of techniques and rules for the conduct of therapy. Schools vary in the degree to which their prominence or uniqueness is related to the features of their *theory* or to the nature of their *tactics*. Freud wrote extensively on the theory of psychoanalysis but was relatively silent about treatment technique. The early appeal of Rogers's "nondirective" therapy was largely in the explicitness and simplicity of the methods he espoused rather than in his theory of personality. To the extent that each system of psychotherapy has an articulated theory it is easy to point out the differences among them at the level of *theory*. But, the theories do not have direct impact on the patient; patients do not "experience" the theories. Therapists of different theoretical persuasion may be of differing effectiveness because of the differences in their respective theories only in measure as those theoretical differences lead to differences in the way in which they conduct therapy—the actual process by which they interact with, learn about, and influence their patients.

Apparently extensive differences in two theories need not be paralleled by notable differences in therapeutic technique, especially as some theories of therapy specify very little about the tactics of treatment. Even where extensive differences are spelled out in the specific procedures of therapy associated with particular systems, it is not certain that these differences will be clearly manifested in the actual conduct of therapeutic interviews by representatives of the systems. In one survey of orthodox psychoanalysts who were "card-carrying" adherents to the Freudian school, it was found that there was striking lack of consistency with respect to a wide range of specific practices [3].

The differences among systems of psychotherapy either at the level of their personality theory or their prescribed modes of treatment will account for any potentially demonstrated difference in their effectiveness only to the extent that it is demonstrated that the clinicians practicing each system do in fact carry out significantly different processes in their patient contacts. But, as one factor common to all systems there is some theory, some more or less highly explicated theoretical formulation of psychopathology and the therapeutic process. It has been suggested that some sort of "systematic ideology" may be an essential element in successful therapy:

> Whether the therapist talks in terms of psychoanalysis or Christian Science is from this point of view relatively unimportant as compared with the *formal consistency* with which the doctrine employed is adhered to, for by virtue of this consistency the patient receives a schema for achieving some sort and degree of personality organization [6].

If we examine the broad outlines of psychotherapy as an interpersonal transaction, certain structural properties emerge which are unavoidably common to all forms of psychotherapy; these common factors do not contribute to differences in the conduct of the treatment and they cannot explain any differences in results which might be demonstrated for the "different" approaches. But these common factors may well be of considerable *potency* and may account for most of the positive results which each of the schools claim.

In essence, psychotherapy is conversation with therapeutic intent. As conversation it entails all of the modes of communication (some facilitant and some deterrent) that are active whenever two persons speak to one another. Language carries the major mediational load and is the primary transmitter of communication in conversation. We have long been aware of the distinctions between connotative and denotative language—words have "agreed upon" meanings as specified by the dictionary, but they also have more or less individualistic meanings for each person who uses them. Communication would be easier (simpler and more accurate) if it were humanly possible for persons to restrict their language to purely denotative words; it is not. While members of a culture may share the same official dictionary, they naturally do not share in identical personal experiences whereby words acquire the personal connotations that individuals unconsciously seek to use in their conversations. Some words make for better communication because they have a scientifically precise definition, or in the nature of things to which they refer there is a limited range of possible connotations; other words tend to contribute a lot of "static" to communication because they do not permit of objective definition but rather represent certain personal meanings of high frequency in a particular group of persons. The following lists will suggest this aspect of the communication problem:

More Denotative Words	*More Connotative Words*
Inch	Good
Minute	Strong
Black	Liberal
Round	Pretty
North	Smart

This is only one of the problem areas receiving intensive investigation in the rapidly evolving technical fields known as psycholinguistics and communication theory.

Man has long been aware that his oral communications are neither given nor received purely in terms of the words spoken (and their explicit or implicit meanings) but that additional and particular meanings are communicated by the general context of their utterance. The most important part of this contextual communication is undoubtedly the facial expression of the conversants. The particular meaning of a word is frequently signaled by a frown or a smile or a grimace. And responses to questions or assertions may be wordlessly communicated by a nod, by a smile, by "silence freighted with meaning." When communication is emotionally charged, when the topic of conversation is loaded with emotional "meanings" as is frequently the case in psychotherapy, it is imperative that the therapist be skilled in receiving (and sending?) wordless messages or words whose meaning has been silently labeled by the emotional attitude of the sender. In accepting candidates for advanced training in the specialty of psychotherapy, it is generally true that considerable emphasis is given to intellectual ability, with applicants of very superior general intelligence being preferred. There is little in the nature of substantive information or treatment technique to be learned that justifies such emphasis. However, sensitivity to the subtle aspects of the wordless communications in psychotherapy is a most important dimension of therapeutic skill. This skill is not too readily learned but rather reflects native or very early acquired aptitudes that are highly correlated with general intelligence. And a high level of general intelligence is required to meet the scholastic requirements (many of them irrelevant to psychotherapy) that loom large in the formal education of the physician, psychologist, and social worker.

This nonlinguistic aspect of oral communication is a difficult area for research but it is part of the total domain of psycholinguistics. Any general theory of communication must and will encompass the conversations of psychotherapy and, as a general theory, the researches generated by it must inevitably show those particulars of the communication process which are common to all such conversations. Thus, the essentials of the communication process are identical regardless of the school of psychotherapy under whose aegis a particular therapeutic conversation is being conducted. The participants do not have access to special communication media beyond those of any other conversation—they are limited to words and sentences, to assertions and questions, to the silent "labels" of smiles and frowns, tics and tears, and to silences. Within the frame of the communality of the communication process which is shared by all approaches to psychotherapy is a particular common factor—the therapist. Regardless of his theoretical allegiance, the therapist is an expert conversationalist whose specialized equipment includes sensitivity to the emotional nuances of the patients' communication, an ability to listen selectively, facility in encouraging the patient to start and continue conversation, deftness in leading the patient to particular topics, capacity both to tolerate the patient's silences and to use his own silence in communicating. These are basic common skills of all expert psychotherapists, contributing to their capacity to establish and maintain communication. The presence of these skills in high degree is, unfortunately, not necessarily correlated with the achievement of a valid understanding of the patient (a common goal of most schools) nor with achievement of successful treatment (the ultimate goal of all schools).

Although this section is concerned with the factors common to all psychotherapies, it is well to point out those areas in which explicit differences are clearly possible and even likely. The essential elements and processes of communication are shared alike by all schools, but the selection and emphasis of *topics* for conversation may well differ systematically. In accordance with one theory, the theorist may emphasize certain topics for exploration (and explanation) to the exclusion of others, and in a variety of ways restrict the therapeutic conversation to these topics. Another school will emphasize that the topics for discussion should be arrived at spontaneously and determined primarily by the patient. One theory may emphasize the self-concept as the topic of therapeutic conversation while another may focus on specific symptomatology. A theory which was more "correct" about the topics to be conversed about might achieve some potentially demonstrable margin of success beyond that of other approaches by virtue of this "correctness."

Indirect research evidence suggests that there may be less actual consistent variation in the favored topics of different therapists than their theories would suggest. For example, one would expect psychoanalytically oriented therapists to encourage their patients to reveal their sex attitudes and histories. When a group of such therapists was asked for extended, structured descriptions of patients whom they had been treating for at least 25 hours, it was found that they frequently did not have information about such matters as attitudes toward masturbation, extra-marital relations, and other topics [4].

There are additional structural aspects of the therapeutic conversation which set it apart from other classes of person-to-person communication but which are common to all forms of psychotherapy. One of these is the status relationships of therapy. The therapist has a certain status of ascendancy, authority, or power. This status is expressed through certain symbols: he has a title (most frequently that of "doctor"), he has certificates and diplomas which imply that he has received special, technical training, he is a member of (or closely affiliated with members of) an established profession from which he derives his visible identification as a "socially sanctioned healer" [2]. He may derive additional symbolic identification from his place of business (clinic or hospital), from his professional dress (the white coat), or from his "tools" (e.g., Rorschach cards, tape recorder).

Part of the ascendant status of the therapist is reflective of the fact that his client is supplicant. The patient, suffering and wanting to be helped, seeks out the therapist and comes to him. "Almost all psychotherapy is to some degree disturbing to the patient because it is deflating to the ego to be so maladjusted that it becomes necessary to place oneself in the embarrassing position of having to admit failure and seek help from others" [7]. This subjectively experienced lowered status of the client has potential for affecting the therapeutic process positively at the beginning of treatment and negatively in later stages. In the beginning he may be more ready to accept the suggestions of the ascendant therapist while later on, when less acutely distressed, his persisting sensitivity to the status differential can motivate obstinacies that are too luxuriously interpreted as "transference" phenomena [1].

This status relationship which is common, at least initially, to all psychotherapies generates or supports certain psychological qualities that are universal. In brief, both the therapist and the patient from their respective positions have certain expectancies. The therapist honestly expects to be able to help his client; he knows the dimensions of his status and from these dimensions (training, experience, membership) he expects to be helpful. From this underlying expectation his basic attitude is one of confidence and in a variety of ways his positive expectation and confidence are communicated to the patient.

The patient expects to be helped because in seeking out the therapist he is following the general recommendation of his society as to where he is to expect to be helped. Some patients go reluctantly, even resentfully, to the therapist and without any preformed faith in the process. But even these, since they are never literally forced, cannot be thoroughly convinced that nothing will happen. Increasingly in our society because of the improved education of the public the patient brings to his therapist a readiness to be helped and some faith in the process. Together these initial expectancies of the therapist and the patient provide a positive psychological atmosphere for the powerful healing effects of implicit suggestion. These implicit forces of suggestion are augmented by the social structuring of the on-going therapy as a series of controlled conversations in which, according to some theory that yields "formal consistency," the therapist seeks to persuade the patient (and the patient to be persuaded?) toward new views of himself, and of his problems. These status-derived forces of general suggestion and persuasion are common to all forms of psychotherapy.

Apart from the status roles of the two participants, still another structural factor is common to all approaches. The relationship between the therapist and his patient is not a spontaneous one but rather a controlled, circumscribed, or limited one [1, 2]. The frequency of visits, generally regular (and most commonly weekly), their timing and duration, are explicitly determined. What is permissible and desirable for the patient to do during the treatment hour is controlled and what demands he may make of his therapist are very definitely limited. In light of the prolonged nature of the relationship, the intimacy of the material shared, and the qualities of rapport and mutual respect that are engendered, this fact of definite controls on what the patient may do or fail to do, and what he can require of the therapist, constitutes what may be the most distinctive feature of the therapeutic relationship. This feature of controlled relationship is espoused in nearly all methods of psychotherapy.

The quality of the relationship is given specific attention in all formulations of psychotherapy and certain aspects of the relationship are given universal emphasis. There is general agreement that it is the responsibility of the therapist to be accepting of the patient and to communicate his acceptance to the patient. This acceptance of the patient is a complex of therapist attitudes that includes respect for the patient as an individual, positive regard for his personality and his potential, warmth, kindness, and continuing willingness to help no matter what the symptoms or defects of the patient. Most crucially, this attitude of acceptance requires that the therapist relate to his patient in a nonjudgmental, noncritical, nonpunitive way. Of course, failures of conformity, socially inimical attitudes, or even antisocial behavior may not be at the heart of the problem for which the patient seeks help and the therapist may learn of them only incidentally, but he must avoid value assessments which cause him inadvertently to communicate a rejection of the patient. This is a difficult quality of relationship both to describe and to establish effectively. The therapist may share many of his society's values and mores and will not think that it is good for them to be violated or neglected, but it is not his function to condemn or to try to re-create an individual in his own image. This quality of "acceptance" *in our culture at this time* is peculiarly restricted to the psychotherapeutic contract, but it is common to all such contracts. In this sense, psychotherapy provides a very special, perhaps ideal, form of friendship.

It is reasonable to presume that a further reflection of the communality of the quality of acceptance is found in the expectation of the average patient who seeks a therapeutic relationship. The hopeful expectation of "unconditional positive regard" from somebody may well be one of the common factors leading to an increasing demand for psychotherapy and contributing to a positive response when it is available [5].

Whether or not the impact of the mental health movement and its attendant educational programs has created a general expectation of the therapeutically prescribed acceptance, it seems that a majority of patients have an expectation that their revelation of self and others will be treated with complete confidentiality. Again, in the principle that the patient's communications are "privileged" and protected in principle and by law from release in any form or medium which would cause him or others embarrassment or hurt, we have a structural factor shared by all schools of psychotherapy. As a common factor of the therapy contract, it may significantly contribute to the total therapeutic impact of the relationship. It is, by contrast, a notable characteristic of our general culture that we are gossipy and notoriously indifferent to the ethics of personal confidences!

We have reviewed aspects of psychotherapeutic relationship that are basically of a structural nature, that stem from the universal status factors of supplicant and benefactor and from the general provisions of the psychotherapeutic contract. Are there any aspects of the *process* of psychotherapy that permit of the possibility of being general and not restricted to those therapeutic conversations which eventuate under the aegis of a particular theory? Over fifty years ago, when psychotherapy was aborning, Josef Breuer discovered the principle of catharsis. He observed that patients who were able to recall the origins of a symptom and to give uninhibited expression to the emotions attendant upon the situation in which it evolved were subsequently relieved symptomatically and generally improved in their over-all adjustment. This function of emotional purging or catharsis came gradually to be perceived as but one phase of a more general process in which the patient, under the accepting, encouraging, and supportive friendship of the therapist, was enabled to give expression to his conflicts, his anxiety, his guilts, his resentments, to relieve his previously bottled up feelings without fear of rejection or misunderstanding. To this basic process whereby the suffering supplicant is helped to achieve release from the tormenting burden of his previously suppressed (or repressed) emotions, from the personal isolation stemming from his previously unshared feelings, is given the name ventilation. Catharsis and ventilation are the naturally inevitable first steps in any truly intimate personal relationship, requiring nothing more than an *accepting* (and probably understanding) auditor. It is difficult to imagine any formal psychotherapy which could either in theory or *expert* practice deliberately prevent the occurrence of such ventilation.* And ventilation and catharsis as general factors may prove to account for a sizable portion of the total therapeutic impact of all psychotherapies.

In the prolonged relationships of intensive psychotherapy, it must be recognized that the patient has opportunity for repeated expression of "punishable" ideas and feelings which do not lead in therapy to punishment or rejection. The anxiety originally accompanying the thoughts is gradually extinguished or reduced through repeated expression without pain. Then it is possible for the patient to see his *bêtes noires* differently, to think differently about them, and to plan imaginatively to react differently to their real life representations. Eventually, with the support and positive suggestion of the therapist, he is able to experiment with new modes of response to those persons and situations which are anxiety symbols and, eventually, to extend the process of learning (and extinction of inappropriate, anxious responses) to the "real" world outside of his therapist's office.

Although there are differences in interpretation as to the elements of the process, differences in emphasis as to whether it is mostly an extinction of old, inappropriate responses or an acquisition of new more appropriate responses, differences as to whether there are basic generalities or necessary specifics in the content of neurosis, nearly all psychotherapists agree that psychotherapy is a learning process. In this learning, the therapist serves as guide, tutor, model, and primary source of reward. To the extent that all therapists partake of the role of teacher, self-acknowledged or not, we have yet another common dimension.

Considering the range and basic nature of these dimensions and processes which are common to all forms of conversation with therapeutic intent, it is remarkable that so many have found so much to say about such a variety of apparent diversities in theory and practice. But in our culture it is far more acceptable to present oneself as an expert in some moderately occult and complex professionalized technique than to suggest the more modest (grandiose?) claim to being generally perceptive and intelligent about personal problems. Certainly the average counselor can much sooner be confident that he is technically proficient than he can be assured that he is wise.

---

* It is possible that full ventilation may be prevented or delayed by the inexperienced, insensitive, or inept therapist who is overly active and insufficiently appreciative of the self-curative forces in nature.

In view of the extensive variety and possibly sizable therapeutic power of those factors which do appear to be shared by all schools of psychotherapy, it is suggested that we might do well to concentrate our researches on these potential mechanisms of the psychotherapeutic effect, and to emphasize carefully the methods of optimizing their influence when selecting and training psychotherapists, rather than to pursue almost exclusively the search for differences in therapeutic practice that *theoretically* should be there and *theoretically* should make a difference.

References

1. BLACK, JOHN D. Common factors of the patient-therapist relationships in diverse psychotherapies. *J. Clin. Psychol.* 8 (1952):304, 302–6.

2. FRANK, JEROME D. *Persuasion and Healing: A Comparative Study of Psychotherapy.* Baltimore: Johns Hopkins Press, 1961, p. 2.

3. GLOVER, EDWARD. *The Technique of Psycho-Analysis.* New York: International Universities Press, 1955.

4. GLUECK, BERNARD C., MEEHL, PAUL E., and SCHOFIELD, WILLIAM. "The Skilled Clinician's Assessment of Personality." Research Project, University of Minnesota, Department of Psychiatry, and Institute of Living, Hartford, Connecticut. Supported by grants from the Ford Foundation and the National Institute for Mental Health.

5. ROGERS, CARL R. The necessary and sufficient conditions of therapeutic personality change. *J. Consult. Psychol.* 21 (1957):95–103.

6. ROSENZWEIG, SAUL. Some implicit common factors in diverse methods of psychotherapy. *Amer. J. Orthopsychiat.* 6 (1936):412–15.

7. THORNE, FREDERICK C. A critique of non-directive methods of psychotherapy. *J. Abn. Soc. Psychol.* 39 (1944): 459–70.

Perspectives on Drug Use

HELEN H. NOWLIS

Psychologists cannot prescribe drugs. But, by virtue of the "team" approach to therapy, in which psychiatrists and other physicians (who can prescribe drugs) cooperate with psychologists and other professionals, the use of drugs is a common adjunct to psychotherapy. Unfortunately, the choice of which drug to prescribe is not at all a simple matter. We cannot always say that this particular drug is the "right" one for this particular disorder; we cannot even say for certain what effect a certain drug will have on the particular person. Too many other factors enter in. The therapist who prescribes drugs needs to consider not only the chemistry of the drugs themselves, but how this chemistry interacts with the living organism. The therapist needs to be aware of the dosage, the usage patterns, the frequency according to which and the setting in which the drugs are taken. Finally, he needs to be alert to the meaning of drugs to the patient and to the patient's society.

Although this article was not really intended to be a primer on chemotherapy, it points out very clearly the complex considerations that must be attended to in any drug therapy program.

Man has always used chemical substances to change mood, feeling, and perception; he probably always will. The substances used will depend upon the changes he desires or values and his perception of the effects of available substances in relation to those changes. Substances now widely used fall into three general categories: (a) Ups, (b) Downs, and (c) those which change the way one perceives one's self or one's physical and social environment. All drug use, legal or illegal, involves risk at some dosage level for some individuals under some circumstances; determination of what risks are to be tolerated for what benefits is clearly a value judgment. The important issue then becomes who shall make these value judgments and according to what system of values.

SOURCE: From *Journal of Social Issues* 27 (3):7–21. Copyright © 1971 by the Society for the Psychological Study of Social Issues, a division of the American Psychological Association. Reprinted by permission.

Drug use sounds like a fairly unitary phenomenon which ought to be, and unfortunately often is, rather simply described. It is in fact an extremely complex set of phenomena. This complexity is a function of drugs themselves and how they interact with the organism, the amounts and patterns and frequency and setting of use of different drugs, and of the meaning and function of drug use to the individual and to society. Lack of recognition of these complexities is one of the main reasons for current confusion and controversy and for ineffective individual and social action.

Society at large has fallen into an either-or trap and has failed to make the discriminations so necessary for understanding and for intelligent action. Most people believe that drugs are either good or bad, safe or dangerous, that individuals are drug users or non-users. Any meaningful discussion of drug use must be based on careful discriminations among drugs and types of drug use, among people who use and how and why they use.

There are some inescapable facts about drugs and drug action and about people and the things they do. They are not the "facts" most people seek. For a variety of historical and psychological reasons most people find it difficult to think of drug effects in terms of probabilities and uncertainties, of dose-response curves, of multiple effects (some desirable and some undesirable), of reactions which vary from individual to individual and from time to time in the same individual. None of these are consistent with the widely held view of drugs as magic potions having within them great power over man and beast for good or evil. Drugs have no effects until they interact with an organism—biologically, psychologically, and socially defined. Organisms, especially when they are human, are large or small, old or young, healthy or sick, happy or depressed, cautious or adventuresome, anxious or secure. Human organisms have language. They live in cultures and subcultures. All of these variations and many more influence the drug-person interaction. Drugs do not have the ability to level these variations. In fact, they often enhance them.

Whether the goal is to describe why, how, and with what effect man uses chemicals, to control certain types of drug use, or to predict or influence drug use in the future, we must try to discriminate clearly between what chemicals do and what people do. Both are important but they must not be confused.

A DRUG IS A DRUG

The title of this special issue * carefully avoids the word "drug." One can speculate that this was in order to include among man's chemical comforts a number of chemicals which many resist labeling as drugs and which are called beverages or cigarettes. Or perhaps it was to single out those chemicals which, among other things, alter man's mood, feeling, or perception. In either case it avoids a word that currently arouses so much feeling and emo-

* Editor's note: "Chemical Comforts of Man: The Future."

tion that it has a drug-like effect in many. It may, however, be the better part of wisdom to try to rehabilitate the term, difficult as that will be. As long as chemical comforts include substances which are called drugs, whether they be medicines and "good" or socially disapproved substances and "bad," along with substances called beverages and cigarettes, there is a great temptation to believe that they are indeed different and act according to different principles.

From a strictly scientific point of view, *drug* is defined as any substance which by its chemical nature affects the structure or function of the living organism. This definition is objective. It is not based on value judgments about proper and improper, legal and illegal reasons for use. It includes medicines, both prescription and over-the-counter, socially disapproved substances which are increasingly and indiscriminately labeled "narcotics," beverage alcohol, caffeine, cigarettes, and even foods. It also includes many agricultural and industrial chemicals and pollutants. It provides a basis from which to consider any special class of substance no matter how it is classified or for what purpose it is used and assumes that all chemicals act according to the same basic principles.

BIOCHEMICAL CHANGES AND BEHAVIORAL CHANGES

All drugs are chemicals or contain chemicals which interact with the complex biochemical system that is the living organism. Changes in that biochemical system are related to changes in the perceptions, feelings, and behavior of the organism in ways we as yet see only in a mirror darkly.

Changes in perceptions, feelings, and behavior are a function of complex interactions among the nature of the substance, the amount present in the body at any one time, the route and speed of administration of the substance, the physiological characteristics and current physiological state of the individual, the psychological characteristics and current psychological state of the individual, the physical and social setting of the individual when he takes the substance, the reasons why he takes the substance, and what he expects the changes will be.

For every substance there is a dose response curve. This is simply a way of describing the modal response of a given population to increasing amounts of that substance. It is a statistical abstraction with all that that implies. There are three critical points on such a curve. The first is the "effective" dose (ED_{50}), which depends on what effect one is seeking or is ready to observe or measure. ED_{50} is the dosage level required to produce the desired effect in 50 percent of a given population; by definition this also means that 50 percent did not show the particular effect at ED_{50}. It does not mean that there were not other effects at dosages smaller than ED_{50}. The second critical point is the "toxic" dose (TD_{50}), which—again—depends on what effects one defines as toxic. The third is the lethal dose (LD_{50}). Although defining the response in this instance presents no problems, the actual dose is, as in the other two instances, a statistical abstraction. LD_{50} is that dosage by which, not at which, 50 percent of a given group of animals die. To complicate matters further, even this determination may change by a wide margin if the animals are tested under stress, i.e., crowded into a small cage rather than housed normally. Even in medicine the safety of a drug is a function of the distance on the dose response curve between the effective dose and the toxic dose, and this will vary from individual to individual.

All drugs have multiple effects, most of which are termed "side effects." Some of these side effects are harmful, some simply annoying; many of them occur in some people at dosage levels below those effective for the desired effect. Some are ignored or tolerated because the desired effect is valued; some are not tolerated because the sought-for effect is not considered of sufficient value. A widely used minor tranquilizer, at dosage levels considered effective in relieving psychic tension and resultant somatic symptoms, may in some individuals also produce such side effects as drowsiness, confusion, double vision, nausea, fatigue, depression, jaundice, skin rash, ataxia, slurred speech, tremor, dizziness, and such paradoxical reactions as acute hyperexcited states, anxiety, insomnia, hallucinations, rage. Reducing the dosage level may reduce or eliminate many of these side effects, but at the same time the desired effect may be eliminated.

The principal reason why drugs do not have predictable and reliable effects is because the other term in the drug-organism interaction is so complex and so variable. Except in high dosages, the effect of many drugs is more a function of non-drug factors than of the drug itself. So important are these factors that in many instances a placebo, or sugar pill, can produce "drug effects."

Individuals vary in weight, age, sex, sickness and health, in the way in which they react to their perception of physiological and psychological changes in themselves and their physical and social environment, and in the meaning and significance of these perceptions to their personal and social adjustment. These are all influential factors in determining the response to any drug. Few have any difficulty recognizing and accepting this with regard to alcohol. Having ingested the same amount of alcohol, some individuals will be gay and talkative, some relaxed and drowsy, some loud and boisterous, some aggressive, some abusive, some destructive. The difference is not the drug or the amount of the drug but the individual and the situation. But we call alcohol a beverage.

All of these principles apply to all drugs but they are especially influential when drugs act primarily on the central nervous system and modify mood, feeling, and perception. How they act and where they act within this system is in most cases still a matter of hypothesis. How biochemical changes in the central nervous system are related to changes in behavior is still in the realm of conjecture. From the point of view of man's voluntary use of chemicals, the key factor is that they produce changes, at least some of which are valued.

The effects of psychoactive drugs, like those of all drugs, are dose-related. At low or moderate doses they are, even more than other drugs, a result of non-drug factors such as the psychological characteristics of the individual, the reasons why he uses the drug, what he expects the effects will be, the physical and social setting in which he uses it, how he perceives its use or non-use as instrumental in contributing to or interfering with his important goals, how his friends, his sub-culture, and his society define and respond to his drug use. These psychological and social factors not only influence the reaction to a specific drug but they are key factors in determining use or non-use, choice of substance, and pattern and circumstances of use.

DRUGS USED FOR MEDICAL REASONS

The major drugs currently used, both legally and illegally, are chemical comforters. The largest single class of prescriptions is for mood-changing drugs—for pain relievers, tranquilizers, anti-depressants, anti-anxiety drugs, stimulants, and sedatives. Alcohol and caffeine are almost universally used, and cigarette consumption remains high despite vigorous efforts to halt it. A high proportion of over-the-counter drugs falls in the same category as their names attest.

All of these substances are increasingly used on a daily basis for varying periods of time, regularly enough and for long enough to be described validly as resulting in psychological dependence and, with prolonged use of increasing amounts of some, physiological dependence.

In the majority of instances these drugs are used by adults. Except for alcohol, caffeine, and nicotine, which are not considered drugs, they are deemed to be appropriate treatment for legitimate complaints and to contribute to the effective functioning of the individual in society—as long as they have the approval of the medical profession.

In the case of alcohol and caffeine, both have been institutionalized socially rather than through medicine even though both drugs are or have been used medically. Both are used by most people as contributing to personal and social functioning. Excessive use of either may interfere, in a given individual, with his personal and social functioning.

It is important to reiterate that all of these drugs act according to the principles discussed above. Their effects are a function of dose. For each there is an effective dose, a toxic dose, and, for most, a lethal dose. All of them have multiple effects. Their side effects are often critical, including such common effects as drowsiness, distractibility, irritability, temporary lapse of memory, and, more rarely, hallucinations, intoxication, hyperexcitability, and similar phenomena. The effects of all of them at moderate dose levels are highly dependent on non-drug factors. At high dose levels, and for some individuals at much lower levels, all may be dangerous. Some have been demonstrated to produce a statistically significant increase in chromosome breakage in white blood cells. Some, when taken during certain critical periods of pregnancy, produce a statistically significant increase in fetal deformities.

DRUGS USED FOR NON-MEDICAL REASONS

Many of these same drugs and a host of others are used by the young and the not-so-young without benefit of prescription and for non-medical reasons. The reasons for use are still primarily to change mood or feeling but often not changes which society considers appropriate. Under such circumstances the drugs are declared illegal and dangerous and their use criminal. Once this happens, their use is viewed from a totally different perspective. There is preoccupation with toxic reactions, with the effects of high dosages, and with psychological dependence. There is a great interest in and concern for who uses them, how often, and why. Many are persuaded that these drugs, or even the same drugs they use for approved reasons, are a completely different kind which act according to different principles.

All of these drugs have dose-response curves—effective, toxic, and lethal. The effects of all are influenced by the non-drug factors discussed above; all have multiple effects; all have side effects, some of which may be harmful and some of which can be ignored; at high dose levels and for some individuals at much lower dose levels, all may be dangerous. Some probably increase the probability of chromosome breakage in white blood cells; it is likely that some increase the probability of fetal deformities during critical periods of pregnancy.

ALL DRUGS INVOLVE RISK

All of this would suggest that there should be relatively more concern than is currently held for drugs used for medically approved reasons, and relatively less concern than the current level of panic for drugs used for non-medically approved reasons. *But there should be great concern for both.* All drugs involve risks, some more than others. The real questions are: how much risk for what benefit? and who should decide and on what basis? These are "people problems," not drug problems.

RISK-BENEFIT DECISIONS ARE VALUE JUDGMENTS

The discomforts of man are myriad. Throughout history he has sought relief from cold, hunger, deprivation, anxiety, pain, and boredom, primarily through whatever substances were available to him in his environment. In most instances these were plants which contained a variety of chemical substances which were identified only long after their use was established. Their effects were originally discovered by trial and error, and their virtues and dangers, whether real or imagined, became part of the lore of a group. Their continued use and spread was a function of the prevalence of the particular need that they were believed to fulfill and its relationship to the needs and values of the group or the society in which they were used.

Since as drugs they had effects other than those which were sought and their effects varied with amount, frequency of use, the characteristics of the user, the set and the setting in which they were used, different individuals and groups of individuals made different value judgments as to the appropriateness of the benefits and the seriousness of the risks.

Through much the same basic processes, modern man has used a wide variety of chemical substances and the use of each substance or class of substances has been institutionalized. Societies have decided what needs are legitimate, what effects are valuable, what risks are tolerable. These decisions are usually made on the basis of the general attitudes, values, and beliefs which characterize the society or powerful groups within it. They are based on value judgments about specific drugs, about drug effects, about the reasons for using drugs, and about the people who use or do not use them. These judgments lie in the eye of the beholder, not in the drug.

It is a basic psychological principle that man does not ordinarily continue to do something that does not fulfill some need, real or imagined. To persist, behavior must be reinforced. To the extent that it does fulfill a need he will continue to do it, often at risk, unless it interferes with some more important need. If drug use does not fulfill some need it will be abandoned. The need may be closely related to real or imagined effects of the drug or may be social rather than chemical. Society's (or a sub-culture's) definition of and response to use of a given substance, rather than any pharmacological or psychological effects of that substance, may give it meaning which determines the decision either to try, to stop, or to continue use. Use of specific substances may determine group membership or status within a group or among groups. It may function as either sign or symptom of rebellion, alienation, independence, sophistication. Persistence in or abandonment of a variety of behaviors is an important, though indirect, statement about individual and social values.

Drugs Currently Used

Presently man seeks comfort with a wide variety of chemicals. Merely to describe the incidence or prevalence of the use or nonuse of specific substances is not very useful even if it could be done reliably and validly. It may, in fact, lead to false conclusions. In order to describe use, it is essential to define use and to make distinctions among drugs and among patterns of use of specific drugs. Using LSD daily is a very different phenomenon than using marijuana daily. Smoking three joints in one evening once a week has a different meaning than one joint three times a week.

Until recently, and even now except for some conducted scientifically, surveys have tended to distinguish only between any use and non-use, and between legal or illegal drugs or drug use. Legal is defined as for medically approved reasons and with medical supervision, however indirect. Illegal is defined as for non–medically approved reasons or having no medically accepted uses. The criteria of use vs. non-use and legal vs. illegal substances make for very strange bedfellows and serve primarily as an imperfect measure of the prevalence of one particular category of deviant behavior.

Useful and meaningful assessments which can provide a basis for understanding and influencing drug use or abuse must, at a minimum, distinguish among drugs, or at least functionally meaningful groups of drugs, and among patterns of use of specific drugs or meaningful groups of drugs. Additionally it is helpful if the various uses of any specific drug are considered in the context of all similar drugs and use by any particular groups in context of use by all groups.

ALCOHOL

Any survey of drugs which does not begin with alcohol can lead only to a distorted picture of drug use. Alcohol is the most commonly used comforter. It is usually the first non-medical drug to be used. Acute and chronic effects of various patterns of use are well documented. The British Medical Council on Alcoholism (*New York Times*, 1970) has estimated that there are 300,000 teenage alcoholics (without defining "alcoholic"). The Council is reported to consider that youthful alcoholism is a medical and social problem that surpasses narcotic addiction and that the potential teenage drinking problem should give far more cause for alarm than does drug addiction.

But alcohol is a drug! It is the fact that a psychoactive drug is being used in amounts and with a frequency which can result in all of the things implied in the designation as alcoholic which is significant, not simply that it is alcohol.

Virtually every survey of adolescent drug use which has included alcohol use and has inquired into outcomes indicates that some use of alcohol is almost universal, and that adolescents report more bad outcomes from both single and repeated use of alcohol than of any other drug.

MARIJUANA

The next most frequently and widely used non-medical drug is marijuana. Estimates as to the number of Americans who have utilized marijuana at least once range from 12 to 20 million. All surveys indicate tremendous variations from region to region, community to community. The National Institute of Mental Health has estimated (February, 1970), on the basis of all of the information available to it, that between 20 to 40 percent of all high school and college students have tried marijuana. Of this number, 65 percent had used marijuana less than ten times, 25 percent occasionally when it was available, and 10 percent as often as once a week. The most that this indicates is that between 7 and 14 percent of students find marijuana *use* (not to be necessarily equated with the effects of marijuana as a drug) rewarding enough to use it occasionally, and 2 to 4 percent gain satisfaction sufficient to use it as often as once a week—at considerable legal risk. The more challenging figure, given current societal beliefs and reactions, is the 50 to 60 percent who never try or who try and do not continue to use it.

Since marijuana is a drug, or more accurately a plant which contains a number of drugs, it is not surprising that, as is true of all drugs, excessive amounts may produce toxic reactions. Side effects may be annoying to some, harmful to others, and lead to panic reactions in the unwary.

UPS

"Ups" are primarily those drugs which are classified as stimulants. Caffeine, now institutionalized through the American breakfast, coffee break, and coffee shop, has at times in its history been illegal and painted as a villain. In amounts usually ingested, it is for most people a mild stimulant. For some, even small amounts cause sleeplessness, jitteriness, irritability, or an upset stomach. It is sold over-the-counter in concentrated form and is used in combination drugs to counteract the drowsiness which is often a side effect of a number of commonly used medications.

Various forms of amphetamines (e.g., Benzedrine, Dexedrine, Methedrine) are used both legally and illegally. They are classified as stimulants because of their action on the central nervous system. They also produce constriction of peripheral blood vessels, increase blood pressure and heart rate, relax smooth muscles of the stomach, intestines, and bladder, and suppress appetite. Which is effect and which is side effect depends on why they are taken. Because of their appetite suppressing effect they are widely used in weight reduction programs. Though perhaps helpful in temporarily suppressing appetite, they also produce feelings of energy and alertness, reduction in distractibility, relief of depression, and talkativeness in many individuals. Many who start using amphetamines for appetite reduction continue using them for these stimulant effects.

Prolonged use of amphetamines in excessively high dosages may result, in some individuals, in development of psychotic symptoms with predominance of paranoid or persecutory ideas. When injected in high doses frequently over a period of several days ("speeding"), the result is long periods of activity and wakefulness during which little food is eaten. At the end of such an episode there is a "crash." This may be accompanied in some individuals by severe depression. When the response to that depression is more speed, as is often the case, a difficult and dangerous cycle may begin.

Although legally classified as a narcotic, cocaine is a stimulant. Derived from the coca leaf, it has long been used to mask hunger and fatigue and to produce feelings of energy and power. Use of cocaine has recently increased in some areas.

DOWNS

"Downs" are usually equated with sedatives such as the barbiturates. If classified on the basis of how those who use them feel, rather than on the basis of chemical structure or medical use, they include alcohol, barbiturates, minor tranquilizers, and the opiates. Medical and pharmacological arguments as to whether a substance is a sedative, a hypnotic, a hypnotic sedative, a depressant, or a narcotic (defined as producing sleep and stupor and relieving pain) are of little interest to the growing number of amateur pharmacologists. To them they are all Downs. The important fact is that they bring you down when you are up too high. Like alcohol, in sufficient amounts they all produce intoxication in some individuals.

It is significant that at least part of the increase in use of heroin is a result of its use to "come down" from a speed trip. It is possible that the "street pharmacology" may result in classifications of drugs which will prove more useful in terms of understanding and influencing non-medical drug use.

Contrary to popular belief, alcohol is a "downer" and, it should be noted, illegal for those under a certain age (18 or 21, depending on state laws).

LSD-LIKE DRUGS

An increasing group of substances, almost all of which were originally of plant origin, have at least one thing in common. Their major effect is to change perceptions and to dissolve, at least temporarily, habitual ways of looking at the world and at one's self. There are more scientific ways of describing them, but, again reverting to the pragmatic street pharmacology, they are good for "tripping," for exploring, for getting outside of one's self, for getting new insights, for "getting off the natural." For years prisoners have sought any means to "get off the natural," including raiding the kitchen for nutmeg.

To call these substances psychotomimetics, psychodysleptics, hallucinogens, or psychedelics, is to invite argument. In some individuals under some circumstances, they result in reactions which resemble psychoses. In many individuals at some dosage levels, there are most certainly deviations from "normal" in perception and functioning which are exactly what is sought. They, like many other drugs, may produce hallucinations or pseudohallucinations in some individuals at some dosage level, but this does not help in understanding their use or their appeal. Many insist that their effects are mind-manifesting (psychedelic). To use any one of these terms involves a value judgment based, in most instances, on overgeneralization without regard for dose and for individual differences in response.

Included in this group of substances are LSD, mescaline, psilocybin, THC^9 (Δ^9-Trans-tetrahydracannabinol derived from cannabis), to mention only a few. Street pharmacologists have discovered or produced others which are primarily combinations of these with a variety of other drugs—STP, LBJ, FDA, PCP, HOG, PEACE, the list is endless. They appear, cause a flurry in establishment circles while they are analyzed, result in some sick young people, and generally go away, or, what is most alarming, go down the age scale.

SOLVENTS

Among younger adolescents in some areas, airplane glue and a number of solvents are inhaled, primarily for their intoxicating effect. Getting drunk or feeling dizzy has always appealed to some youngsters. Alcohol has been and still is the drug of choice. Perhaps because they are easier for a youngster to obtain, perhaps because they are defined as more daring, solvents of all kinds are used for this purpose.

It is becoming increasingly academic to engage in scientific discussions of the properties and actions of any of these substances. They are available only on the black market and the only assurance that they are what they are thought to be and contain any approximation of the dose reported is what someone told someone who says so. Except for amphetamines, barbiturates, and other drugs produced legally but diverted into the illegal market there is virtually no quality control. Although mescaline would seem to be replacing LSD as a drug of choice, there is very little if any pure mescaline on the market.

Beyond Drugs to People

In order to understand current non-medical drug use it is necessary to go far beyond the cataloguing of substances (pharmacologically defined where possible), the listing of effects, and the counting of users and non-users of each. The focus must shift from drugs to people, go beyond pharmacological effects to the meaning and function of drug use. The response of society and of various social groups is crucial in determining that meaning.

Just as there is a dose response curve for drugs, there is a use response curve for drug use. This curve is also a statistical abstraction hiding tremendous individual variability, and it too has at least three critical points: initial use, continued use, and compulsive use.

Initial use has less to do with a drug and its pharmacological action than with the significance of drug use and expectations of effect. It involves an individual and his beliefs about a drug and its effects, and it involves society and how it defines that drug and its users. Reasons for experimenting include curiosity, a desire for some physical, psychological, or social change, social pressure, and communicating to friends, family, or society something about one's identity. Of significance are social definitions of drug use as adult, daring, deviant, "cool." Choice of substance is a function of availability, of beliefs about the effects, and of the status of use of the substance as socially defined.

The majority of experimenters do not become users. Curiosity is satisfied;

status is gained; it did not do what it was supposed to do; it was unpleasant or frightening; it is not worth the risk.

Whether an individual continues to use a substance is determined by the degree to which it serves some personal or socially meaningful function, the degree to which its use brings about some physical, psychological, or social change, real or imagined, which is perceived as more pleasant than unpleasant, more desirable or functional than undesirable or dysfunctional. Desirable and functional need not correspond to stated social norms.

The reasons for continuing may or may not be related to reasons for trying. In the process of use, new functions of use may develop. These may lead to continued use, to intensified use, or to abandoning use. What started from curiosity may be continued because it was fun, because it provided acceptance into a group, or because it made one feel better.

The majority of users remain at the moderate level, using moderately and on "appropriate" occasions, as in the case of alcohol. They are able to enjoy whatever benefits they find and avoid the hazards of excessive amounts and frequency of use. For them their drug use does not become a central factor in their lives.

When use goes beyond moderate in amount and frequency and appropriate in occasion, two factors become crucial. The first is the centrality of the function served by the drug use and the second involves characteristics of the particular substance used. Drug use which serves an important function for a given individual usually requires repeated use since its effects are necessarily temporary and in most instances do nothing more than produce a temporary change. Relief of persisting pain, anxiety, or depression, escape from unpleasant realities, avoidance of painful experiences, support of a social role or identity, or any of the central personal and social functions drug use can appear to serve, require continued drug use.

Some drugs, notably opiates, alcohol, barbiturates, amphetamines, and nicotine, produce tolerance. With repeated frequent use, increasing amounts are required to produce the same effect. Not only do these drugs produce tolerance but, if used in sufficient amounts with sufficient frequency over a long enough period of time, they produce physiological dependence. The drug must be used to feel normal and to avoid being physically ill. The amount, frequency, and length of use necessary to produce physiological dependence varies with the drug and with the individual.

Physical and psychological dependence on a drug which at best provides temporary relief of symptoms or escape from reality, especially if that drug is illegal and expensive, is good for neither the individual nor society. But relatively few who use become dependent in this sense.

The Real Drug Problem

Historically, the use of drugs outside of medicine has served to explain all manner of social deviance. In the process it has become a symbol and a means of communicating deviance. As such it can also serve as a badge and a rallying point for groups that wish to proclaim their deviance. A number of different groups have adopted drug use both as a rationale for particular subcultures and as a response to the problems encountered in being deviant.

LSD was not what Timothy Leary and the League for Spiritual Discovery were all about. The League was a direct attack on majority values which were considered to be hypocritical. Marijuana was not what the hippies were all about. The original hippie movement was a rebellion against and a retreat from a dominant society which, in their eyes, was not living according to the values it proclaimed.

Man has always sought chemical comforts. Which chemical for which discomfort has varied from time to time and from place to place. Until recently, on balance, man has mostly used the chemical comforts with reasonable intelligence, in moderate amounts, and on appropriate occasions, in order to make life more pleasant, to feel better, to relieve temporary malaise, to facilitate social activity, and to solidify groups. He probably always will. But something new has been added. Technology has produced a bewildering array of new and complex drugs specifically fashioned to do particular things. When these drugs are used to prevent or to cure states agreed upon as disease we hail them. When they produce side effects which for some become main effects, i.e., sought in their own right, we become uneasy. When they are used to change mood or modify behavior, to get high, to improve memory, to reduce aggression, to make the unruly manageable, serious questions are raised.

According to what criteria are effects to be judged acceptable or unacceptable? Is it desirable to improve memory or intelligence, to reduce aggression? Who shall decide, the individual or society? Who within society? Who shall decide which drugs shall be developed for which purposes? These questions are already with us and are at the heart of the current "drug problem."

In order to approach an intelligent consideration of these issues there must be an understanding of what drugs are and how they act, what drugs do and what people do, the complex personal factors which influence the outcomes of drug use, the role of society's definition of and response to any particular drug use by any particular group in determining the nature and extent of the outcomes of that use. As the nature of the biochemical organism is better understood, and it will be, and as the relationship of biochemical changes to changes in behavior is pursued, and it is being pursued, the nature and range of possible behavior modification will be expanded and the challenges increased.

Summary

Some of man's chemical comforts are called drugs, some are not; some are illegal and some are legal. Regardless of label or of legal status, all are drugs and all act according to the same basic principles. The effects of all are a function of complex interactions between an amount and pattern of use of the substance and the individual, physiologically, psychologically, and socially defined. The meaning and function, real or imagined, that effect and use of a drug serve for a given individual or group of individuals determine to a major degree the substance used, the pattern and frequency of use, and the outcomes of use. Meaning and function may be determined by either personal or social factors.

Drugs currently in use, both legally and illegally, are primarily Ups, Downs, or any of a variety of substances which change perceptions of the self or of the social or physical environment. Choice of substance is a function of the individual's reasons for use and his beliefs about the effectiveness of a given substance in relation to those reasons. Amount and pattern of use are more important than the mere fact of use. Distinctions must be made at least among experimenters, regular users, and compulsive users. The definition of each will vary from substance to substance.

All drugs involve risks at some dosage level, in some people, under some circumstances. The real question is: How much risk should be tolerated for what benefit and who should decide? This is a question of values, not of drugs.

References

1. *New York Times*, July 31, 1970.
2. NIMH Report, February 1970.

Behavorial Approaches to Family and Couple Therapy

ROBERT LIBERMAN

Behavior therapy derives from principles of learning like those recounted in Holland's article in Part 4. Behavior therapists look on disorders as patterns of inappropriate responses that can be modified by the application of positive and negative reinforcement, shaping, fading, modeling, punishment, and so forth. Although some therapists have tried to apply these principles to patients with severe and complex personality disorders, behavior techniques seem most effective for the modification of more specific maladies like smoking, overeating, and tics.

The following article outlines the diagnostic and treatment procedures followed by most behavior therapists and describes a number of cases in which these procedures were successful. Liberman's work, however, differs from the work of many other behavior therapists in that he deals in especially complex social milieus; he needs to be alert not only to the behavior of his patient but also to the behavior of all other people in the situation. Of particular interest in this respect is his behavioral analysis of interpersonal relationships. Note how the different family members reinforce each other, and watch how Liberman attempts to change those relationships by controlling the behavior of the different people involved. The so-called primary reinforcers (food, drink, and sex) are not appropriate here, so Liberman makes use of social reinforcers like attention and recognition.

Although behavior therapy is not included under the heading of individual psychotherapy, it does, at least as Liberman defines it, share some of the common factors Schofield listed: an articulated theory, therapist-patient status relationships, and the acceptance of the patient as a person. It does not, however, make any explicit provision for catharsis or ventilation, nor does it really require any conversation between therapist and patient nor any expectation, on the part of the patient, to be helped. The usual application of behavior therapy would be considered one of the "psychological approaches" (based on psychological prin-

SOURCE: From Robert Liberman, "Behavioral Approaches to Family and Couple Therapy," *American Journal of Orthopsychiatry* 40 (1) (January 1970):106–18. Copyright ©, the American Orthopsychiatry Association, Inc. Reproduced by permission.

ciples and techniques), but Liberman's version of it, because of the social setting, makes his work a social form of intervention.

The current splurge of couple and family therapies is not simply an accident or passing fad. These increasingly used modes of treatment for psychiatric problems are anchored in a sound foundation and are not likely to blow away. The foundation of these newer therapies lies in the opportunity they offer to induce significant behavioral change in the participants by a major restructuring of their interpersonal environments.

Couple and family therapy can be particularly potent means of behavior modification because the interpersonal milieu that undergoes change is that of the day-to-day, face-to-face encounter and individual experiences with the most important people in his life—his spouse or members of his immediate family. When these therapies are successful it is because the therapist is able to guide the members of the couple or family into changing their modes of dealing with each other. In behavioral or learning terms, we can translate "ways of dealing with each other" into consequences of behavior or *contingencies of reinforcement*. Instead of rewarding maladaptive behavior with attention and concern, the family members learn to give each other recognition and approval for desired behavior.

Since the family is a system of interlocking, reciprocal behaviors (including affective behavior), family therapy proceeds best when each of the members learns how to change his or her responsiveness to the others. Family therapy should be a learning experience for all the members involved. For simplification, however, this paper will analyze family pathology and therapy from the point of view of the family responding to a single member.

Typically, families that come for treatment have coped with the maladaptive or deviant behavior of one member by responding to it over the years with anger, nagging, babying, conciliation, irritation, or sympathy. These responses, however punishing they might seem on the surface, have the effect of reinforcing the deviance, that is, increasing the frequency or intensity of the deviant behavior in the future. Reinforcement occurs because the attention offered is viewed and felt by the deviant member as positive concern and interest. In many families with a deviant member, there is little social interaction and the individuals tend to lead lives relatively isolated from each other. Because of this overall lack of interaction, when interaction does occur in response to a member's "abnormal" behavior, such behavior is powerfully reinforced [14].

Verbal and nonverbal means of giving attention and recognition can be termed *social reinforcement* (as contrasted with food or sex, which are termed *primary reinforcement*). Social reinforcement represents the most important source of motivation for human behavior [6, 19]. Often massive amounts of such "concern" or social reinforcement are communicated to the deviant members, focused and contingent upon the member's maladaptive behavior.

The deviant member gets the message: "So long as you continue to produce this undesirable behavior (symptoms), we will be interested and concerned in you." Learning the lesson of such messages leads to the development and maintenance of symptomatic or deviant behavior and to characterological patterns of activity and identity. Sometimes, the message of concern and interest is within the awareness of the "sick" member. Individuals with a conscious awareness of these contingencies are frequently termed "manipulative" by mental health professionals since they are adept at generating social reinforcement for their maladaptive behavior. But learning can occur without an individual's awareness or insight, in which case we view the maladaptive behavior as being unconsciously motivated.

Massive amounts of contingent social reinforcement are not necessary to maintain deviant behavior. Especially after the behavior has developed, occasional or *intermittent reinforcement* will promote very durable continuation of the behavior. Laboratory studies have shown that intermittent reinforcement produces behavior that is most resistant to extinction [6].

Many family therapists [7, 8, 21] have demonstrated that the interest and concern family members show in the deviance of one member can be in the service of their own psychological economy. Maintaining a "sick" person in the family can be gratifying (reinforcing) to others, albeit at some cost in comfort and equanimity. Patterson [15] describes how this reciprocal reinforcement can maintain deviant behavior by using the example of a child who demands an ice cream cone while shopping with his mother in a supermarket. The reinforcer for this "demand behavior" is compliance by the mother, but if she ignores the demand, the effect is to increase the rate or loudness of the demand. Loud demands or shrieks by a child in a supermarket are aversive to the mother; that is, her noncompliance is punished. When the mother finally buys the ice cream cone, the aversive tantrum ends. The reinforcer for the child's tantrum is the ice cream cone. The reinforcing contingency for the mother was the termination of the "scene" in the supermarket. In this reciprocal fashion, the tantrum behavior is maintained. I shall return to this important aspect of family psychopathology—the mutually reinforcing or symbiotic nature of deviance—in the case studies below. Indeed, the balance between the aversive and gratifying consequences of maladaptive behavior in a member on the other family members is the crucial determinant of motivation for and response to treatment.

Changing the contingencies by which the patient gets acknowledgment and concern from other members of his family is the basic principle of learning that underlies the potency of family or couple therapy. Social reinforcement is made contingent on desired, adaptive behavior instead of maladaptive and symptomatic behavior. It is the task of the therapist in collaboration with the family or couple to (1) specify the maladaptive behavior, (2) choose reasonable goals which are alternative, adaptive behaviors, (3) direct and guide the family to change the contingencies of their social reinforcement patterns from maladaptive to adaptive target behaviors.

Another principle of learning involved in the process of successful family therapy is modeling, also called imitation or identification. The model, sometimes the therapist but also other members of the family, exhibits desired, adaptive behavior which then is imitated by the patient. Imitation or identification occurs when the model is an esteemed person (therapist, admired family member) and when the model receives positive reinforcement (approval) for his behavior from others [3]. The amount of observational learning will be governed by the degree to which a family member pays attention to the modeling cues, has the capacity to process and rehearse the cues, and possesses the necessary components in his behavioral experience which can be combined to reproduce the more complex, currently modeled behavior.

Imitative learning enables an individual to short-circuit the tedious and lengthy process of trial-and-error (or reward) learning while incorporating complex chains of behavior into his repertoire. Much of the behaviors which reflect the enduring part of our culture are to a large extent transmitted by repeated observation of behavior displayed by social models, particularly familial models. If performed frequently enough and rewarded in turn with approval by others, the imitated behavior will become incorporated into the patient's behavioral repertoire. The principles of imitative learning have been exploited with clinical success by researchers working with autistic children [12], phobic youngsters [4], and mute, chronic psychotics [18]. How modeling can be used in family therapy will be illustrated in the cases cited below.

I will limit the scope of the case examples to couples and families; however, the same principles of learning apply to group therapy [11, 17] and with some modification to individual psychotherapy [9]. Although learning theory has been associated in clinical psychiatry with its systematic and explicit application in the new behavior therapies, it should be emphasized that learning theory offers a generic and unitary explanation of the processes mediating change in all psychotherapies, including psychoanalytic ones [1, 13].

Technique

Before getting to the case material, I would like to outline the main features of an application of behavior theory to family therapy. The three major areas of technical concern for the therapist are:

1. *creating and maintaining a positive therapeutic alliance;*
2. *making a behavioral analysis of the problem(s); and*
3. *implementing the behavioral principles of reinforcement and modeling in the context of ongoing interpersonal interactions.*

Without the positive therapeutic alliance between the therapist and those he is helping, there can be little or no successful intervention. The working alliance is the lever which stimulates change. In learning terms, the positive relationship between therapist and patient(s) permits the therapist to serve as a social reinforcer and model; in other words, to build up adaptive behaviors and allow maladaptive behaviors to extinguish. The therapist is an effective reinforcer and model for the patients to the extent that the patients value him and hold him in high regard and warm esteem.

Clinicians have described the ingredients that go into this positive therapist-patient relationship in many different ways. Terminology varies with the "school" of psychotherapy to which the clinician adheres. Psychoanalysts have contributed notions such as "positive transference" and an alliance between the therapist and the patient's "observing ego." Reality therapists call for a trusting involvement with the patient. Some clinicians have termed it a "supportive relationship" implying sympathy, respect, and concern on the part of the therapist. Recent research has labeled the critical aspects of the therapist-client relationship: nonpossessive warmth, accurate empathy, and genuine concern [20]. Truax and his colleagues [20] have been able to successfully operationalize these concepts and to teach them to selected individuals. They have further shown that therapists high on these attributes are more successful in psychotherapy than those who are not. Whatever the labels, a necessary if not sufficient condition for therapeutic change in patients is a doctor-patient relationship that is infused with mutual respect, warmth, trust, and affection.

In my experience, these qualities of the therapeutic alliance can be developed through a period of initial evaluation of the patient or family. The early therapist-family contacts, proceeding during the first few interviews, offer an opportunity to the therapist to show unconditional warmth, acceptance, and concern for the clients and their problems.

Also during the first few sessions, while the therapeutic relationship is being established, the therapist must do his "diagnostic." In a learning approach to family therapy, the diagnostic consists of a *behavioral* or *functional analysis* of the problems. In making his behavioral analysis, the therapist, in collaboration with the family, asks two major questions:

1. What behavior is maladaptive or problematic—what behavior in the designated patient should be increased or decreased? Each person, in turn, is asked, (1) what changes would you like to see in others in the family, and (2) how would you like to be different from the way you are now? Answering these questions forces the therapist to choose carefully *specific behavioral goals*.

2. What environmental and interpersonal contingencies currently support the problematic behavior—that is, what is maintaining undesirable behavior or reducing the likelihood of more adaptive responses? This is called a "functional analysis of behavior," and also can include an analysis of the development of symptomatic or maladaptive behavior, the "conditioning history" of the patient. The mutual patterns of social reinforcement in the family deserve special scrunity in this analysis since their deciphering and clarification

become central to an understanding of the case and to the formulation of therapeutic strategy.

It should be noted that the behavioral analysis of the problem doesn't end after the initial sessions, but by necessity continues throughout the course of therapy. As the problem behaviors change during treatment, so must the analysis of what maintains these behaviors. New sources of reinforcement for the patient and family members must be assessed. In this sense, the behavioral approach to family therapy is dynamic.

The third aspect of behavioral technique is the actual choice and implementation of therapeutic strategy and tactics. Which interpersonal transactions between the therapist and family members and among the family members can serve to alter the problem behavior in a more adaptive direction? The therapist acts as an educator, using his value as a social reinforcer to instruct the family or couple in changing their ways of dealing with each other. Some of the possible tactics are described in the case studies below.

A helpful way to conceptualize these tactics is to view them as "behavioral change experiments" where the therapist and family together re-program the contingencies of reinforcement operating in the family system. The behavioral change experiments consist of family members responding to each other in various ways, with the responses contingent on more desired reciprocal ways of relating. Ballentine [2] views the behavioral change experiments, starting with small but well-defined successes, as leading to (1) a shift toward more optimistic and hopeful expectations; (2) an emphasis on doing things differently while giving the responsibility for change to each family member; (3) "encouragement of an observational outlook which forces family members to look closely at themselves and their relationships with one another, rather than looking 'inside' themselves with incessant why's and wherefores"; and (4) "the generation of empirical data which can be instrumental to further change, since they often expose sequences of family action and reaction in particularly graphic and unambiguous fashion."

The therapist also uses his importance as a model to illustrate desired modes of responding differentially to behavior that at times is maladaptive and at other times approaches more desirable form. The operant conditioning principle of "shaping" is used, whereby gradual approximations to the desired end behavior are reinforced with approval and spontaneous and genuine interest by the therapist. Through his instructions and example, the therapist teaches shaping to the members of the couple or family. Role playing or behavioral rehearsal are among the useful tactics employed in generating improved patterns of interaction among the family members.

The therapist using a behavioral model does not act like a teaching machine, devoid of emotional expression. Just as therapists using other theoretical schemas, he is most effective in his role as an educator when he expresses himself with affect in a comfortable, human style developed during his clinical training and in his life as a whole. Since intermittent reinforcement produces more durable behavior, the therapist may employ trial terminations, tapering off the frequency of sessions prior to termination and "booster" sessions [1]. The strategy and tactics of this behavioral approach to couples and families will be more clearly delineated in the case studies that follow. A more systematic and detailed outline of the behavior modification approach is presented in Table 1. The specification and implications of the items in this outline can be found in the manual by Reese [16].

TABLE 1. *A Behavioral Model for Learning (adapted from E. P. Reese* [16])

---

1. Specify the final performance (therapeutic goals):
   Identify the behavior.
   Determine how it is to be measured.
2. Determine the current baseline rate of the desired behavior.
3. Structure a favorable situation for eliciting the desired behavior by providing cues for the appropriate behavior and removing cues for incompatible, inappropriate behavior.
4. Establish motivation by locating reinforcers, depriving the individual of reinforcers (if necessary), and withholding reinforcers for inappropriate behavior.
5. Enable the individual to become comfortable in the therapeutic setting and to become familiar with the reinforcers.
6. Shape the desired behavior:
   Reinforce successive approximations of the therapeutic goals.
   Raise the criterion for reinforcement gradually.
   Present reinforcement immediately, contingent upon the behavior.
7. Fade out the specific cues in the therapeutic setting to promote generalization of acquired behavior.
8. Reinforce intermittently to facilitate durability of the gains.
9. Keep continuous, objective records.

Case #1

Mrs. D is a 35-year-old housewife and mother of three children who had a 15-year history of severe, migranous headaches. She had had frequent medical hospitalizations for her headaches (without any organic problems being found), and also a 1½-year period of intensive, psychodynamically oriented, individual psychotherapy. She found relief from her headaches only after retreating to her bed for periods of days to a week with the use of narcotics.

After a brief period of evaluation by me, she again developed intractable headaches and was hospitalized. A full neurological workup revealed no neuropathology. At this time I recommended that I continue with the patient and her husband in couple therapy. It had previously become clear to me that the patient's headaches were serving an important purpose in the economy of her marital relationship: headaches and the resultant debilitation were the sure way the patient could elicit and maintain her husband's concern and interest in her. On his part, her husband was an active, action-oriented man who found it difficult to sit down and engage in conversation. He came home from work, read the newspaper, tinkered with his car, made repairs on the house, or watched TV. Mrs. D got her husband's clear-cut attention only when she developed headaches, stopped functioning as mother and wife, and took to her bed. At these times Mr. D was very solicitous and caring. He gave her medication, stayed home to take care of the children, and called the doctor.

My analysis of the situation led me to the strategy of redirecting Mr. D's attention to the adaptive strivings and the maternal and wifely behavior of his wife. During ten 45-minute sessions, I shared my analysis of the problem with Mr. and Mrs. D and encouraged them to reciprocally restructure their marital relationship. Once involved in a trusting and confident relationship with me, Mr. D worked hard to give his wife attention and approval for her day-to-day efforts as a mother and housewife. When he came home from work, instead of burying himself in the newspaper he inquired about the day at home and discussed with his wife problems concerning the children. He occasionally rewarded his wife's homemaking efforts by taking her out to a movie or to dinner (something they had not done for years). While watching TV he had his wife sit close to him or on his lap. In return, Mrs. D was taught to reward her husband's new efforts at intimacy with affection and appreciation. She let him know how much she liked to talk with him about the day's events. She prepared special dishes for him and kissed him warmly when he took initiative in expressing affection toward her. On the other hand, Mr. D was instructed to pay minimal attention to his wife's headaches. He was reassured that in so doing, he would be helping her decrease their frequency and severity. He was no longer to give her medication, cater to her when she was ill, or call the doctor for her. If she got a headache, she was to help herself and he was to carry on with his regular routine insofar as possible. I emphasized that *he should not, overall, decrease his attentiveness to his wife, but rather change the timing and direction of his attentiveness.* Thus the behavioral contingencies of Mr. D's attention changed from headaches to housework, from invalidism to active coping and functioning as mother and wife.

Within ten sessions, both were seriously immersed in this new approach toward each other. Their marriage was different and more satisfying to both. Their sex life improved. Their children were better behaved, as they quickly learned to apply the same reinforcement principles in reacting to the children and to reach a consensus in responding to their children's limit-testing. Mrs. D got a job as a department store clerk (a job she enjoyed and which provided her with further reinforcement—money and attention from people for "healthy" behavior). She was given recognition by her husband for her efforts to collaborate in improving the family's financial condition. She still had headaches, but they were mild and short-lived and she took care of them herself. Everyone was happier including Mrs. D's internist who no longer was receiving emergency calls from her husband.

A followup call to Mr. and Mrs. D one year later found them maintaining their progress. She has occasional headaches but has not had to retreat to bed or enter a hospital.

Case #2

Mrs. S is a 34-year-old mother of five who herself came from a family of ten siblings. She wanted very badly to equal her mother's output of children and also wanted to prove to her husband that he was potent and fertile. He had a congenital hypospadius and had been told by a physician prior to their marriage that he probably could not have children. Unfortunately Mrs. S was Rh negative and her husband Rh positive. After their fifth child she had a series of spontaneous abortions because of the Rh incompatibility. Each was followed by a severe depression. Soon the depressions ran into each other and she was given a course of 150 EST's.* The EST's had the effect of making her confused and unable to function at home while not significantly lifting the depressions. She had some successful short-term supportive psychotherapy but again plunged into a depression after a hysterectomy.

Her husband, like Mr. D in the previous case, found it hard to tolerate his wife's conversation, especially since it was taken up mostly by complaints and tearfulness. He escaped from the unhappy home situation by plunging himself into his work, holding two jobs simultaneously. When he was home, he was too tired for any conversation or meaningful interaction with his wife. Their sexual interaction was nil. Although Mrs. S tried hard to maintain her household and raise her children and even hold a part-time job, she received little acknowledgment for her efforts from her husband who became more distant and peripheral as the years went by.

My behavioral analysis pointed to a lack of reinforcement from Mrs. S's husband for her adaptive strivings. Consequently her depressions, with their large hypochondriacal components, represented her desperate attempt to elicit her husband's attention and concern. Although her somatic complaints and self-depreciating accusations were aversive for her husband, the only way he knew how to "turn them off" was to offer sympathy, reassure her of his devotion to her, and occasionally stay home from work. Naturally, his nurturing her in this manner had the effect of reinforcing the very behavior he was trying to terminate.

During five half-hour couple sessions I focused primarily on Mr. S, who was the mediating agent of reinforcement for his wife and hence the person who could potentially modify her behavior. I actively redirected his attention from his wife "the unhappy, depressed woman" to his wife "the coping woman." I forthrightly recommended to him that he drop his extra job, at least for the time being, in order to be at home in the evening to converse with his wife about the day's events, especially her approximations at successful homemaking. I showed by my own example

---

* Editor's note: EST, electroshock or electroconvulsive therapy, is a procedure that involves passing electrical current through the head of an anesthetized and chemically relaxed patient. EST is generally considered the "treatment of choice" for severe depression. Some degree of confusion and memory loss, usually short-lived, typically accompanies EST, especially when many treatments are administered.

(modeling) how to support his wife in her efforts to assert herself reasonably with her intrusive mother-in-law and an obnoxious neighbor.

A turning point came after the second session, when I received a desperate phone call from Mr. S one evening. He told me that his wife had called from her job and tearfully complained that she could not go on and that he must come and bring her home. He asked me what he should do. I indicated that this was a crucial moment, that he should call her back and briefly acknowledge her distress but at the same time emphasize the importance of her finishing the evening's work. I further suggested that he meet her as usual after work and take her out for an ice cream soda. This would get across to her his abiding interest and recognition for her positive efforts in a genuine and spontaneous way. With this support from me, he followed my suggestions and within two weeks Mrs. S's depression had completely lifted.

She was shortly thereafter given a job promotion, which served as an extrinsic reinforcement for her improved work performance and was the occasion for additional reinforcement from me and her husband during the next therapy session. We terminated after the fifth session, a time limit we had initially agreed on.

Eight months later at followup they reported being "happier together than ever before."

Case #3

Edward is a 23-year-old young man who had received much psychotherapy, special schooling, and occupational counseling and training during the past 17 years. He was diagnosed at different times as a childhood schizophrenic and as mentally subnormal. At age 6 he was evaluated by a child psychiatry clinic and given three years of psychodynamic therapy by a psychoanalyst. He had started many remedial programs and finished almost none of them. He, in fact, was a chronic failure—in schools as well as in jobs. His parents viewed him as slightly retarded despite his low normal intelligence on IQ tests. He was infantilized by his mother and largely ignored or criticized by his father. He was used by his mother, who was domineering and aggressive, as an ally against the weak and passive father. When I began seeing them in a family evaluation, Edward was in the process of failing in the most recent rehabilitation effort—an evening, adult high school.

The initial goals of the family treatment, then, were (1) to disengage Edward from the clasp of his protective mother, (2) to get his father to offer himself as a model and as a source of encouragement (reinforcement) for Edward's desires and efforts towards independence, (3) to structure Edward's life with occupational and social opportunities that he could not initiate on his own. Fortunately the Jewish Vocational Service in Boston offers an excellent rehabilitation program based on the same basic principles of learning that have been elucidated in this article. I referred Edward to it and at the same time introduced him to a social club for ex-mental patients which has a constant whirl of activities daily and on weekends.

During our weekly family sessions, I used modeling and role-playing to help Edward's parents positively reinforce his beginning efforts at the J.V.S. and the social club. After three months at the J.V.S., Edward secured a job and now after another seven months has a job tenure and membership in the union. He has been an active member of the social club and has gone on weekend trips with groups there—something he had never done before. He is now "graduating" to another social club, a singles' group in a church, and has started action on getting his driver's license.

The family sessions were not easy or without occasional storms, usually generated by Edward's mother as she from time to time felt "left out." She needed my support and interest (reinforcement) in her problems as a hard-working and unappreciated mother at these times. Because of the positive therapeutic relationship cemented over a period of nine months, Edward's parents slowly began to be able to substitute positive reinforcement for his gradually improving efforts at work and play instead of the previous blanket criticism (also, paradoxically, a kind of social reinforcement) he had received from them for his failures. I encouraged the father to share openly with Edward his own experiences as a young man reaching for independence, thereby serving as a model for his son.

The parents needed constant reinforcement (approval) from me for trying out new ways of responding to Edward's behavior; for example, to eliminate the usual nagging of him to do his chores around the house (which only served to increase the lethargic slothful behavior which accrues from the attention) and to indicate instead pleasure when he mows the lawn even if he forgets to rake the grass and trim the hedge. They learned to give Edward approval when he takes the garbage out even if he doesn't do it "their" way. And they learned how to spend time listening to Edward pour out his enthusiasm for his job even if they feel he is a bit too exuberant.

Our family sessions were tapered to twice monthly and then to once a month. Termination went smoothly after one year of treatment.

Case #4

Mr. and Mrs. F have a long history of marital strife. There was a year-long separation early in their marriage and several attempts at marriage counseling lasting three years. Mr. F has paranoid trends which are reflected in his extreme sensitivity to any lack of affection or commitment toward him by his wife. He is very jealous of her close-knit relationship with her parents. Mrs. F is a disheveled and unorganized woman who has been unable to meet her husband's expectations for an orderly and accomplished homemaker or competent manager of their five children. Their marriage has been marked by frequent mutual accusations and depreciation, angry withdrawal and sullenness.

My strategy with this couple, whom I saw for 15 sessions, was to teach them to stop reinforcing each other with attention and emotionality for undesired behavior and to begin eliciting desired behavior in each other using the principle of *shaping*. Tactically, I structured the therapy sessions with an important "ground-rule": No criticism or harping were allowed and they were to spend the time telling each other what the other had done during the past week that approached the desired behaviors. As they gave positive feedback to each other for approximations to the behaviors each valued in the other, I served as an auxiliary source of positive acknowledgment, reinforcing the reinforcer.

We began by clearly delineating what specific behaviors were desired by each of them in the other and by my giving them homework assignments in making gradual efforts to approximate the behavioral goals. For instance, Mr. F incessantly complained about his wife's lack of care in handling the evening meal—the disarray of the table setting, lack of tablecloth, disorderly clearing of the dishes. Mrs. F grudgingly agreed that there was room for improvement and I instructed her to make a start by using a tablecloth nightly. Mr. F in turn was told the importance of his giving her positive and consistent attention for her effort, since this was important to him. After one week they reported that they had been able to fulfill the assignment and that the evening meal was more enjoyable. Mrs. F had increased her performance to the complete satisfaction of her husband, who meanwhile had continued to give her positive support for her progress.

A similar process occurred in another problem area. Mr. F felt that his wife should do more sewing (mending clothes, putting on missing buttons) and should iron his shirts (which he had always done himself). Mrs. F was fed up with the home they lived in, which was much too small for their expanded family. Mr. F resolutely refused to consider moving to larger quarters because he felt it would not affect the quality of his wife's homemaking performance. I instructed Mrs. F to begin to do more sewing and ironing and Mr. F to reinforce this by starting to consider moving to a new home. He was to concretize this by spending part of each Sunday reviewing the real estate section of the newspaper with his wife and to make visits to homes that were advertised for sale. He was to make clear to her that his interest in a new home was *contingent* upon her improvements as a homemaker.

Between the third and sixth sessions, Mrs. F's father—who was ill with terminal lung cancer—was admitted to the hospital and died. During this period, we emphasized the importance of Mr. F giving his wife solace and support. I positively reinforced Mr. F's efforts in this direction. He was able to help his wife over her period of sadness and mourning despite his long-standing antagonism toward her father. Mrs. F in turn, with my encouragement, responded to her husband's sympathetic behavior with affection and appreciation. Although far from having an idyllic marriage, Mr. and Mrs. F have made tangible gains in moving closer toward each other.

Discussion

There is too much confusion in the rationales and techniques underlying current practices in family therapy. Although attempts to convey the method of family therapy always suffer when done through the written word, I do not share the belief that "the vital communications in all forms of psychotherapy are intuitive, felt, unspoken, and unconscious [7]. Although this article is not meant as a "how to do it" treatise for family therapists, I do intend it as a preliminary attempt to apply a few of the basic principles of imitative learning and operant conditioning to couple and family therapy.

Although the rationalized conceptualization of family therapy practiced by psychoanalytically oriented therapists differs from the learning and behavioral approach described here, closer examination of the actual techniques used reveals marked similarity. For example Framo [7], in explaining the theory behind his family therapy, writes:

> The overriding goal of the intensive middle phases consists in understanding and working through, often through transference to each other and to the therapists, the introjects of the parents so that the parents can see and experience how those difficulties manifested in the present family system have emerged from their unconscious attempts to perpetuate or master old conflicts arising from their families of origin. . . . The essence of the true work of family therapy is in the tracing of the vicissitudes of early object-relationships, and . . . the exceedingly intricate transformations which occur as a function of the intrapsychic and transactional blending of the old and new family systems of the parents. . . .

Despite the use of psychoanalytic constructs, Framo describes the actual process of family therapy in ways that are very compatible within a learning framework. He writes:

> Those techniques which prompt family interaction are the most productive in the long run. . . . It is especially useful to concentrate on here-and-now feelings; this method usually penetrated much deeper than dealing with feelings described in retrospect. . . . As we gained experience in working with families we became less hesitant about taking more forceful, active positions in order to help the family become unshackled from their rigid patterns.

Framo goes on to give illustrations of his work with families in which differential reinforcement for behavior considered more desirable and appropriate is given by the therapists. In dealing with angry and aggressive mothers, "we learned to avoid noticing what they did (e.g. emotional infighting) and pay attention to what they missed in life." Trying to activate passive fathers, "the therapists make every conscious effort to build him up during the sessions. . . . A number of techniques have been tried: forcing more interaction between the husband and wife; assigning tasks; having a female therapist give encouragement in a flattering way; occasional individual sessions with the father." Zuk [23] describes his technique of family therapy in ways that fit into a reinforcement framework. He views the cornerstone of the technique the exploration and attempt "to shift the balance of pathogenic relating among family members so that new forms of relating become possible." Zuk further delineates the therapist's tactics as a "go-between" in which he uses his leverage to "constantly structure and direct the treatment situation."

It should be emphasized that the behavioral approach does not simplistically reduce the family system and family interaction to individualistic or dyadic mechanisms of reinforcement. The richness and complexity of family interaction is appreciated by the family therapist working within a behavioral framework. For instance, Ballentine [2] states:

> Behavior within a system cannot be so easily modified by focusing on the behavioral contingencies existing within any two-person subsystem, since one person's behavior in relation to a second's is often determined by behaviors of others within the system . . . the behavioral contingencies within a family system are manifold and constitute a matrix of multiple behavioral contingencies.

The complexity of family contingencies is exemplified by a transient problem which arose in Case #3. As Edward developed more independence from his parents and spent less and less time at home, his parents began to argue more angrily. Edward had served as a buffer between them—taking sides, being used as a scapegoat for their hostility, and serving as a "problem child" who required joint parental action and solidarity. With their buffer gone, the husband-wife relationship intensified and friction developed. Since the therapeutic goals were limited to Edward's emancipation from his parents and since it seemed that the parents were sufficiently symbiotic to contain a temporary eruption of hostility, the therapist's major efforts at this point were aimed at protecting Edward from backsliding in response to guilt or family pressure. The strategy worked, and within a few weeks the parents had reached a new modus vivendi with each other while Edward continued to consolidate and extend his gains.

A behavioral and learning approach to family therapy differs from a more psychoanalytic one. The therapist defines his role as an educator in collaboration with the family; therefore, the assigning of "sickness" labels to members, with its potential for moral blame, does not occur as it does under the medical model embodied in the psychoanalytic concept of underlying conflict or disease. There is no need for family members to acknowledge publicly their "weaknesses" or irrationality since insight per se is not considered vital.

The behavioral approach, with its more systematic and specific guidelines, makes it less likely that a therapist will adventitiously reinforce or model contradictory behavior patterns. The behavioral approach, consistently applied, is potentially more effective and faster. When patients do not respond to behavioral techniques, the therapist can use his more empirical attitude to ask why and perhaps to try another technique. The orientation is more experimental and "the patient is always right," with the burden on the therapist to devise effective interventions. In the psychoanalytic approach, the tendency has been for the therapist to decide that their failures are caused by patients who were inappropriate for the technique rather than viewing the technique as needing modification for the particular patient.

The work of behaviorally oriented family therapists is not restricted to the here-and-now of the therapy sessions. As the cases described reveal, much of the effort involves collaboration and involvement with adjunctive agencies such as schools, rehabilitation services, medication, and work settings. Family therapists are moving toward this total systems approach.

The advantages of behavioral approaches to family therapy sketched in this paper remain to be proven by systematic research. Such research is now proceeding [5, 10, 15, 22]. Much work will go into demonstrating that family processes are "essentially behavioral sequences which can be sorted out, specified and measured with a fair degree of accuracy and precision [2]. Hopefully, further clinical and research progress made by behaviorally oriented therapists will challenge all family therapists, regardless of theoretical leanings, to specify more clearly their interventions, their goals, and their empirical results. If these challenges are accepted seriously, the field of family therapy will likely improve and gain stature as a scientifically grounded modality.

References

1. ALEXANDER, F. The dynamics of psychotherapy in the light of learning theory. *Internat. J. Psychiat.* 1 (1965):189–207.
2. BALLENTINE, R. The family therapist as a behavioral systems engineer . . . and a responsible one. Paper read at Georgetown Univ. Symp. on Fam. Psychother. Washington, 1968.
3. BANDURA, A., and WALTERS, R. *Social Learning and Personality Development.* New York: Holt, Rinehart and Winston, 1963.
4. BANDURA, A., GRUSEC, J., and MENLOVE, F. Vicarious extinction of avoidance behavior. *Personality and Soc. Psychol.* 5 (1967):16–23.
5. DUNHAM, R. Ex post facto reconstruction of conditioning schedules in family interaction. In Irvin M. Cohen, ed. *Family Structure, Dynamics and Therapy.* Psychiatric Research No. 20, Amer. Psychiat. Assn., Washington, 1966, pp. 107–14.
6. FERSTER, C. Essentials of a science of behavior. In J. I. Nurnberger, C. B. Ferster, and J. P. Brady, eds. *An Introduction to the Science of Human Behavior.* New York: Appleton-Century-Crofts, 1963.
7. FRAMO, J. Rationale and techniques of intensive family therapy. In I. Boszormenyi-Nagy and J. L. Framo, eds. *Intensive Family Therapy.* New York: Hoeber Medical Division, 1965.
8. HANDEL, G., ed. *The Psychosocial Interior of the Family.* Chicago: Aldine, 1967.
9. KRASNER, L. The therapist as a social reinforcement machine. In H. Strupp and L. Luborsky, eds. *Research in Psychotherapy.* Washington: Amer. Psychol. Assn., 1962.
10. LEWINSOHN, P., WEINSTEIN, M., and SHAW, D. Depression: a clinical research approach. In Proceedings, 1968 Conference, Assn. Advan. Behav. Ther., San Francisco, 1969.
11. LIBERMAN, R. A behavioral approach to group dynamics. *Behav. Ther.*, 1970.

12. Lovaas, O., et al. Acquisition of imitative speech by schizophrenic children. *Science* 151 (1966):705–7.
13. Marmor, J. Theories of learning and psychotherapeutic process. *Brit. J. Psychiat.* 112 (1966):363–66.
14. Patterson, G., et al. Reprogramming the social environment. *Child Psychol. and Psychiat.* 8 (1967):181–95.
15. Patterson, G., and Reid, J. Reciprocity and coercion: Two facets of social systems. Paper read at 9th Ann. Inst. for Res. in Clin. Psychol. Univ. of Kansas, 1967.
16. Reese, E. *The Analysis of Human Operant Behavior.* Dubuque, Iowa: Wm. C. Brown, 1966.
17. Shapiro, D., and Birk, L. Group therapy in experimental perspectives. *Internat. J. Group Psychother.* 17 (1967):211–24.
18. Sherman, J. Use of reinforcement and imitation to reinstate verbal behavior in mute psychotics. *J. Abnorm. Psychol.* 70 (1965):155–64.
19. Skinner, B. *Science and Human Behavior.* New York: Macmillan, 1953.
20. Truax, C., and Carkhuff, R. *Toward Effective Counseling and Psychotherapy: Training and Practice.* Chicago: Aldine, 1967.
21. Vogel, E., and Bell, N. The emotionally disturbed child as the family scapegoat. In N. W. Bell and E. F. Vogel, eds., *A Modern Introduction to the Family.* New York: Free Press, 1960.
22. Zeilberger, J., Sampen, S., and Sloane, H. Modification of a child's problem behaviors in the home with the mother as therapist. *J. Appl. Behav. Anal.* 1 (1968): 47–53.
23. Zuk, G. Family therapy. *Arch. Gen. Psychiat.* 16 (1967):71–79.

Understanding Laboratory Education: An Overview

CLAYTON P. ALDERFER

Probably no form of intervention has gained so much public attention in so short a time as the group approach. Sensational descriptions of nude marathons and "touchie-feelies" pollute the literature. Department stores advertise group games designed to probe—and perhaps to ravage—the depths of our personalities. Fliers urge us to find "joy and freedom" through communal massage—at $100 a day!

These are not what we mean when we talk about group therapy. In stark contrast to this commercial quackery, Clayton Alderfer offers a responsible description of the varieties of laboratory education. He distinguishes encounter laboratories (which stress learning about the individual), T groups (which try to enhance human relations skills), and Tavistock conferences (psychoanalytically oriented self-study groups). In much the manner of Schofield, he seeks elements common to all three types. He notes that each involves relatively small numbers of participants and tends to isolate itself from the distractions of the rest of the world; he points out that all three proceed in a rather unstructured fashion and that they all include at least one trained staff member. The rest of his paper is quite evenly divided between descriptions of the three kinds of groups and comparisons among them. He outlines the claims and discusses the criticisms of the group movement and raises (but does not really answer) some probing questions about the ethics and effectiveness of group sessions. This article should encourage us to be cautious about group therapy but to suspend judgment until more answers to the questions formulated by Alderfer are available.

Laboratory education—learning about human behavior through experiences in group activities—is simultaneously an evolving educational technology, a loosely defined philosophy, and a social movement. Most of its practitioners

SOURCE: From *Monthly Labor Review*, December 1970, pp. 18–28, published by the Bureau of Labor Statistics, U.S. Department of Labor, Washington D.C. Reprinted by permission.

believe that human interactions can be better understood and more effectively carried out, and, as a consequence, more gratifying to the participants. Thus, laboratory education offers the promise of radically changing the way we understand and act in human relationships. Much of this promise has been realized.

But not all of the aspirations have been fully achieved. The failures, the incompleteness, and the sense of even greater possibilities have led many persons to be critical of laboratory education. Some of these criticisms are based on carefully collected data which has been subjected to thorough analysis. Other evaluations have been severely biased and often sensationalistic, whether the conclusions were positive or negative. This article reviews the current status of laboratory education, with an emphasis on identifying major areas of conflict and explaining why the disagreements take the form that they do.

Common Processes of Learning

The term *laboratory education* refers to a set of assumptions and practices. The various forms of laboratory education include a number of common elements such as acceptance of experience-based learning technology, recognition of the role of emotions in human relationships, and utilization of the small group (10 to 12 persons) as a central component in training designs.

The learning laboratory usually takes place on a "cultural island." Participants are taken away from their normal day-to-day activities to a setting where the learning experiences occur. Frequently this new setting is naturally beautiful, but at the very least it is different and thereby provides the participant with both safety from former distractions and a setting that does not necessarily reinforce his usual ways of behaving. A second component of the laboratory involves the use of unstructured or semistructured learning tools. The staff usually attempts to design a set of experiences that serve to heighten certain aspects of human behavior and emotions. Participants learn by becoming actively involved in these activities and by developing skills which allow them to observe both themselves and others during these experiences. A person is asked to engage himself in the unfolding events and later to step back and try to see the patterns in his own and others' behavior. Much of the sense of excitement and high level of emotionality comes from the participant's becoming involved. Experiential learning is based on the assumption that experience precedes intellectual understanding. A continuing challenge in designing laboratories is to achieve that optimal degree of involvement which allows a person to flavor the richness of human interaction but is not so compelling that he loses all sense of what is happening.

A key element in almost all laboratory designs is the small group, typically quite unstructured and serving as a primary group for most participants during the varied laboratory program. One or two staff members meet regularly with the small group to aid participants' learning.

VARIATIONS IN LABORATORY METHODS

Differences among various laboratory methods tend to emerge around the nature of the small group activities. Three frequently used names for the small groups are encounter groups, T groups, and self study groups. The professional organizations most closely identified with these group labels are, respectively, Esalen Institute, National Training Laboratories Institute for Applied Behavioral Science, and Tavistock Institute of Human Relations. The varied names for the group provide clues about the different nature of the learning experiences offered and of the whole laboratories which utilize the particular type of group. Differences (which tend to be of degree only) include relative focus on intrapsychic, interpersonal, intragroup, or intergroup phenomena; emphasize the personal in comparison to the professional qualities of the staff; and explicitly include the place of thinking in laboratory activities.

Reliable data on the extent of laboratory training are difficult to come by Table 1 gives estimates, provided by leaders in the three areas, on the number of participants. In actual practice there are many more laboratories than those covered by these estimates. Warner Burke, Director, Center for Organization Studies, NTL, estimates that the 1970 NTL figure represented about 5 percent of the laboratories conducted in the United States. The overwhelming majority are being conducted independently of the NTL by business firms, educational institutions, church groups, and so on. But though the table understates the actual number of participants it does illustrate the rapid growth in laboratory education.

ENCOUNTER LABORATORIES

The encounter group, the Esalen Institute, and personal growth laboratories in general tend to focus primarily on learning about the individual. Encounter groups tend to produce experiences where a person examines himself in new and different ways, aided by others. A participant in this kind of experience is encouraged to look inward to himself, to become more in touch with his fantasy life, and to become more aware of his physical activities. Part of the emphasis on body movement includes attention to nonverbal communications. A person may learn to attend more fully to his own nonverbal communications, to read others' signs more adequately, and to practice being more effective in his body language. Psychodramatic techniques are often used in laboratories of this kind. Frequently the focus in these exercises is on interpersonal relationships that have been troublesome for people in the past. Other group members are asked to volunteer to be "stand-ins" for or representatives of a key person in a participant's life history. Staff members help set the stage for these encounters, sometimes actively taking

TABLE. 1 *Participants in Experiential Laboratories Sponsored by Three Organizations in the United States*

Sponsoring Group	Approximate Number of Participants [1]		
	1962	1965	1970
Esalen	. . .	600	11,000
National Training Laboratories	900	. . .	2,400
Tavistock	. . .	100	250

[1] These estimates were provided by Richard Price and Stuart Miller of Esalen; Warner Burke and Patricia Walton of National Training Laboratories; and Edward Klein of Tavistock.

part themselves, and almost always leading the discussion and working through of the events after they happen.

Personal growth laboratories contain more components than the encounter group, however. Various exercises in body movement and artistic expression are frequently employed. It is not uncommon for the staff to include members of the performing arts such as modern dance or theater. Some of the key writings which give greater detail, flavor, and rationale for these methods include Schutz [1967], Murphy [1967], Perls [1969], and Rogers [1969]. John Weir is another key figure in the development of encounter laboratories, but to this writer's knowledge he has not written of his ideas or developments.

There can be little doubt that many persons who attend encounter-oriented laboratories have joyful, freeing experiences. The ever increasing popularity of the Esalen Institute and personal growth laboratories testifies to this [Murphy, 1967; Shepard, 1970]. Yet these experiences have also been validly criticized. With the focus of the laboratories on freeing people and making them more expressive, little of their learning experience is directed toward examining the consequences of excessive self-expression. Because the laboratories produce potent effects so rapidly, they also tend to spawn disciples very readily [Lakin, 1969]. It is not uncommon for participants to start their own groups and "turn on" their friends after as few as one or two group experiences. Within the laboratory itself, participants may be tempted to engage in personality analyses of each other for which they are ill-equipped [Argyris, 1967].

Staff members tend to be central in the learning processes and often are charismatic figures. They frequently seem magical in the techniques they employ and in the effects they can have on some people [Haigh, 1968]. As a consequence some participants tend to copy the manifest qualities of staff members' behavior without careful or thoughtful examination of what or how they are learning.

Another factor which is likely to work against a more critical examination of the learning processes by participants is the tendency for an anti-intellectual bias to develop. While the laboratories are a potent counterforce to our culture's excessive reliance on rational intellective activities, they seem to forget that thinking is also part of the human potential. Encounter laboratories give relatively little attention to how thinking and talking can be reincorporated into a person's behavioral repertoire after he has become more emotionally and physically free.

Although all laboratories find the boundary between education and therapy to be a fine one, perhaps the line is thinnest in the encounter laboratories [Jenkins, 1962]. Many staff members for encounter laboratories are also practicing psychotherapists. The new techniques which have developed through encounter laboratories have also had an impact on the practice of psychotherapy, and the latter has affected the laboratories [Burton, 1969].

Both the beauty and the limitations of the encounter approach are captured in the frequently quoted works of Frederick S. Perls:

> I do my thing, and you do your thing.
> I am not in this world to live up to your expectations.
> And you are not in this world to live up to mine.
> You are you and I am I,
> And if by chance we find each other, it's beautiful.

The sense of individuality and freedom in these words is unmistakable. But missing is the recognition that commitments can be reached by mutuality and that a superordinate goal may sometimes require the suppression of certain individual needs in order for others to be expressed.

T GROUP LABORATORIES

The T group (for human relations training) and the National Training Laboratories Institute at its outset were developed to increase the human relations skills which people brought to their leadership, group, and organizational relationships. Bradford, Benne, and Lippitt, the men whose original conversations led to the founding of NTL, were social psychologists who were interested in both research and action [Bradford, 1967]. The initial focus of learning was on interpersonal and intragroup phenomena. National Training Laboratories has grown considerably over the years, however, and today it conducts laboratories focused on individual growth and intergroup relations. Nevertheless, the initial focus on interpersonal and intragroup phenomena still conditions much of what T groups and NTL are about.

T group laboratories often tend to be focused on the interpersonal impact that members make on each other. In the unstructured T groups, members examine their leadership, membership, and other roles. They see the consequences of different kinds of leadership styles and attempt to learn about the complex interrelationships between group processes and group effectiveness.

A T group leader acts as a person who is also a professional. He does not deny that he is more experienced and knowledgeable than most group members, but he does not act in such a way as to increase the natural distance between himself and group members. He is likely to discuss his own feelings when he sees that as useful to himself and others. He attempts to establish relationships of mutuality between himself and group members. Recognizing that some members of a group will assume that he is like other key figures in their lives, he is willing to examine the impact of his own behavior on others, but he is also likely to ask group members to concentrate on his group behavior when giving feedback. He is likely to assume that people learn not only from what he says but also from how he behaves.

The T group tradition has produced a considerable amount of empirical research (for example, *The Journal of Applied Behavioral Science*) and theorizing [Bradford, Gibb, and Benne, 1964; Argyris, 1962, 1969]. The quality of this work has sometimes been questioned by thoughtful critics [Dunnette and Campbell, 1968; House, 1967], with good reason. Frequently laboratory education research has consisted of poorly designed studies from which the investigators have drawn unjustified conclusions. Control groups have often been missing. Measuring instruments have been poorly designed. More recently, investigators have addressed directly the special problems of research on laboratory education and are now utilizing research designs which offer greater promise in terms of the kinds of conclusions one might draw [Rubin, 1967; Harrison, 1971; Alderfer and Lodahl, 1971].

Democratic values have played an important part in much of the thinking that has influenced T group theory and practice [Whyte, 1953]. The impact of democratic practices has undoubtedly been a strong factor in accounting for the wide diversity of practice, the high degree of innovation, and the strong sense of collaboration and commitment experienced by many members of the NTL system. Nevertheless, the profusion of democratic values has also served as a means for avoiding some more difficult issues.

In a long overdue action, National Training Laboratories has recently begun to develop the organizational machinery for accrediting group leaders. For a long time NTL had been unofficially granting credentials to practitioners by publishing lists of those persons who were elected to positions of Professional Member, Associate, or Fellow [Schein and Bennis, 1965]. In order not to emphasize its exclusiveness, however, NTL consistently maintained the public position that it was not an accrediting agency. Now the focusing of public attention on the quality of group leadership and NTL's eminence in the field has led the organization to change its course.

National Training Laboratories' initial focus was toward interpersonal and intragroup phenomena. For some time there was a tendency for the key learnings from this level of analysis to be transferred uncritically to larger units, such as intergroup relations and larger social systems. A key paper in this line of thought was by Slater and Bennis [1964], who proclaimed "Democracy Is Inevitable." More recently, Bennis [1970] has revised his original thinking, and NTL has become increasingly involved with intergroup concerns, especially those surrounding racism in our society.

TAVISTOCK CONFERENCES

The self-study group has evolved from a tradition which traces its roots to modern psychoanalytic theory of object relations [Klein, 1959]. During World War II, British psychoanalyst W. R. Bion discovered that groups were a useful way to treat psychiatric casualties from the war. His group work led to his writing of *Experiences in Groups* [1959], a book that has become a classic in the field and a key theoretical work for leaders of Tavistock study groups. Although Tavistock theories have evolved from the psychoanalytic tradition, the conferences are directed to learning, not therapeutic goals [Rice, 1965].

Authority relationships form a key element in the learning process of self-study groups. Tavistock staff members, who are called consultants, remain distant and remote in their relationships with group members. They think about their behavior in terms of "staying in role," with the intent of contributing to the group's exploration of relations within the group. In carrying out their roles, the consultants are very punctual in entering and leaving group meetings, dress in relatively formal attire, and intervene in group activity only when they believe it will promote learning. Their statements tend to be metaphorical and they consistently point out how members seem to be relating to them, often as surrogates for other key figures such as parents, siblings, lovers, and the like [Astrachan and Klein, 1971; Redlich and Astrachan, 1969].

Tavistock laboratories also focus on intergroup relations through the use of exercises which ask participants to negotiate among groups in order to make a decision or carry out a task. These activities serve to underline the impact of individual, subgroup, and group boundaries. The analysis of boundaries plays a key role in Tavistock theory and methods. One of the key learnings is the types of fantasy and mythmaking that groups indulge in with respect to each other across group boundaries. A. K. Rice's work [1965, 1969] on laboratory design and on individual, group, and intergroup transactions as boundary crossings is the major conceptual work in this area.

Staff members direct their interventions to the group rather than to any individual. The latter's behavior or statements, however, are assumed to express group concerns unless contradicted by others. Thus, whenever a person speaks in the group he is viewed as speaking for the group and his statement is viewed as representing some element of the group opinion.

Little in the staff behavior allows one to determine the degree to which the interventions cause the study group behavior or merely reflect it. Consultants rarely discuss their own feelings with the group, although they do use their feelings as an important source of data for understanding group events [Rice, 1965]. It might be expected that group members would focus much of their attention on the consultant when he intervenes in the group activity yet behaves in a relatively inaccessible manner. Important questions can be raised about the generality of the learning about leadership that participants achieve in study groups. It is one thing to learn that persons develop vivid and hostile fantasies about persons who appear to be leaders yet deny the role, who behave in distant ways and speak metaphorically about their perceptions of the group. It may be a mistake, however, to assume that reactions of this sort are representative of typical reaction to authority figures regardless of how they behave.

Tavistock consultants do not suggest that their behavior is a model for group members to follow. Yet a question can be raised as to whether modeling occurs nonetheless. There is research to support the notion that modeling or imitation is a general human learning process [Bandura and Walters, 1963]. If modeling does occur in study groups, then it would appear that the Tavistock style of study group would teach participants to be leaders who do not share their feelings, remain personally distant from the group, talk in metaphors, focus attention on themselves by their mode of intervention, and hold quite strictly to the prescribed definition of their roles.

This writer has serious questions about whether these types of learning are very useful for small group effectiveness. However, there are times when learning of this kind is realistic. Leaders of large social systems cannot be seen regularly by more than a few members. They frequently serve as spokesmen for the group. To come to terms with leaders in this kind of role, group members have little choice but to rely on their fantasies and therefore to project and transfer their reactions from prior relationships. Learnings from study group and intergroup activities in a Tavistock laboratory can be very enlightening with regard to multiple group functioning in large scale social systems.

Comparison of Laboratory Approaches

The primary learning and dangers differ among the three approaches to laboratory education. For encounter group laboratories, the primary target is individual expression and artistic creativity. A danger in this approach is that participants may learn to act out their impulses without realistically considering the consequences of their behavior for themselves and for others. T group laboratories primarily aid learning about mutuality, trust, and collaboration. There is a danger that democratic values and behavior may be applied in situations where they are not realistic or appropriate. Moreover, differences among individuals with regard to task or professional competence may be ignored because they tamper with the norm that everyone is equal. Tavistock laboratories promote learning about authority relationships and the functions of group boundaries. It is possible that consultant behavior in the study group may become a model for nonmutuality when this kind of behavior is neither necessary nor effective.

The common theme in the criticisms of each of these approaches to learning by experience is that the particular approach may lead to unwarranted generalization. Learning which evolves from a particular approach does not apply to all situations. At first glance it would appear that this caution is clear to understand and easy to apply. But the learning processes of laboratory education do not lend themselves readily to a norm of moderation. Over-attention to concerns about being too self-expressive can prevent a person from taking the risks which would enable him to become more free and spontaneous. Fear of being overwhelmed by a pseudodemocratic horde may prevent a person from exposing enough of himself to really find out what can be gained by sharing more of himself with the group. The need to feel competent or free of tension may inhibit a person from exposing himself to his fantasies about distant leaders or to engage in the turbulent processes of intergroup negotiations. It is difficult to write critically about the different approaches to laboratory education without unintentionally colluding with the very human processes—fear, hostility, fantasy, and so on—that prevent persons from learning about themselves and their complex relations with others.

The kinds of laboratory education described in this article represent efforts to apply behavioral science concepts to increase learning about human rela-tionships. Each of the laboratories exists as an educational setting. However, although all approaches aim to transfer learning to nonlaboratory settings, an active role for the staff in promoting transfer typically ends with the con-clusion of the laboratory. Additional developments in the direct utilization of behavioral science knowledge for organizational change through the use of experiential methods will be the subject of a future article.

Public and Professional Criticism

During the past several years, a number of articles have been devoted to laboratory education, both in widely circulated newspapers and magazines and in professional journals. Not all of this coverage has been comprehensive or unbiased. Some has been blatantly slanted and inaccurate. The purpose of this section is to alert the reader to some of the forms that public and profes-sional criticism has taken and to caution him against putting too much credence in sensationalistic accounts.

NEWSPAPERS AND MAGAZINES

The front page of the *Wall Street Journal* on July 14, 1969, carried a story with the headline, "Some Companies See More Harm Than Good in Sensitivity Training—Frank Exchanges Sometimes Hamper Work; Sessions Can Produce Breakdowns—A Tough Boss Turns Meek." The lead paragraph was, "Last year a big New York consumer products company sent Mrs. D, a product manager, to a week-long sensitivity training program. She got so sensitive she quit the company." In this article, a number of key academic authorities were cited to support the author's slant, but the full range of professional opinion was not presented. In a number of instances the writer obtained opinions from persons who had participated in symposia or debates on laboratory education but chose to present only the critical side of the controversy. He cited Marvin Dunnette and John Campbell [1969] on the subject of research findings but did not include Chris Argyris [1968] who had raised questions with them about research procedures. Warren Bennis [1966] has written extensively about the conditions under which laboratory methods are likely to result in constructive organizational change but nowhere was his work included.

In contrast to the above article, *Today's Health* featured a discussion of laboratory education from a more balanced perspective. The title of this article was "Sensitivity Training: Fad, Fraud, or New Frontier." The lead paragraph in the piece was, "Here's a comprehensive, up-to-the-minute look at a new dimension in human relations—its problems (misguided do-gooders), its bizarre aspects (T group bums looking for thrills), and its outlook (potential for good)." This article, too, had a bit of sensationalism, for it only included pictures of encounter labs where the participants were engaged in active nonverbal behaviors. But for one who was willing to read the text, author Ted J. Rakstis provided a sampling of informed opinion, both inside and outside the medical profession as well as inside and outside the laboratory education profession. Cautions, criticisms, and potentials all received attention and discussion. The reader looking for a final definitive opinion would not be satisfied by Rakstis' piece, but one looking for a delineation of the issues so he could make more informed choices would be aided by it.

PSYCHIATRISTS

An issue on which one might expect psychiatrists to agree concerns the impact of laboratory education on mental health. They do not, and the December 1969 issue of the *American Journal of Psychiatry* shows a broad range of differences. At one extreme, there is the paper by Ralph Cranshaw who asked, "How Sensitive Is Sensitivity Training?" He reported three cases of psychiatric problems which arose in conjunction with persons attending laboratory programs, and he noted that his colleagues had encountered similar cases. He argued that the responsibilities of laboratory trainers had not been fully defined and implied that the practitioners of sensitivity training could be justly accused of irresponsible experimentation with human beings. He charged that education in the form of sensitivity does not include the concepts of freedom, truth, and empathy in its operation. In his conclusion he stated, "The medical profession can say, to those who will listen, that sensitivity training is insensitive to the individual, for he is not seen as a whole person."

There were some very questionable qualities about the Cranshaw paper. With an $n = 3$ sample the writer seemed willing to generalize to the entire operation of sensitivity training. One of the three cases was under treatment with Cranshaw prior to attending the laboratory which preceded his hospitalization for emotional difficulties. Cranshaw did not raise such questions as whether the hospitalization might have occurred regardless of the laboratory experience, whether his own efforts at treatment might have hastened the need for hospitalization, or whether the hospitalization was a constructive or destructive experience for the client. When arguing that freedom, empathy, and truth are not part of the code of operations for sensitivity training, Cranshaw was simply not fully informed. Key writings in the field by Argyris [1962], Bennis [1966], and Bradford et al. [1964] have consistently emphasized these values.

The way Cranshaw approached his critique was unfortunate because the issues he raised with regard to possible harm to participants, areas of responsibility among trainers, and the necessity for free choice for participants are important. They can be handled adequately only by continually confronting them. The errors in logic and fact in his presentation, however, probably reduce the kind of positive effect which his points could have.

At the other extreme of psychiatric reaction is the paper by Cadden and others [1969], who reported their experiences with a voluntary program of laboratory education for incoming medical students. They found no evidence that the group experiences precipitated emotional illnesses. In contrast, they noted that the laboratory experiences aided several students in becoming aware of their need for psychiatric consultation. The overall need for psychiatric consultation among first-year students, however, was reduced in comparison to preceding years because the groups made it possible to handle certain situational crises more effectively. They also noted that the laboratory program seemed to improve student-faculty communication. The contrast with Cranshaw's reactions could hardly be more marked.

There is no reason to assume that only one of the two critiques is accurate, however. Both refer to rather specific cases. One underlines the dangers; the other shows realized potential. It would be a serious error to assume that because some laboratories are poorly conducted or some individuals poorly handled, all similar activities share these outcomes. It would be equally unfortunate to assume that because one system found benefits for individuals and groups, all systems will also benefit without careful planning and competent execution.

T GROUP TRAINERS

The inhouse controversies which were featured in the Landmarks issue of *The Journal of Applied Behavioral Science* [1967, 3(2)] focused on the differences in approach to laboratory education. In the one case, Argyris [1967], who has consistently contributed to T group practice, theory, and research, raised issues with the encounter group wing of NTL. He found many of the trends in personal growth laboratories to be running counter to the initial goals and concepts of the National Training Laboratories. Several NTL trainers responded to Argyris' issues, but there was little consensus among their responses. Some, such as Kingsbury [1967] and Shepard [1967], sharply disagreed with him. Others such as Coffey [1967] and Work [1967] essentially agreed with him. Those who disagreed were more active in conducting personal growth laboratories than those who agreed.

In the same edition, Bass questioned whether the T group with its focus on openness and collaboration provided a full enough range of learnings to permit transfer to organization level issues. He was particularly concerned with learnings about competing interest groups, distant leaders, and organizational demands which sometimes require suppressing individual and small group interests. Few of the commentators on the Bass paper agreed with all of the premises of his arguments, but most agreed in whole or in part with his general conclusions.

Major areas of disagreement emerged within the NTL tradition when the interpersonal and intragroup focus became more oriented to the individual and when the inadequacies of using only collaborative models in large social systems became apparent. The inhouse controversies closely paralleled the various emphases featured among the different types of laboratory education programs. The potential payoff from constructive dialogue among practitioners from the various orientations is high, because the strengths and limitations of the approaches are often complementary.

Empirical Research and Ethical Questions

Most thoughtful discussions of laboratory education pay some attention to what has been or can be offered by empirical research. Many of the controversial issues could be clarified, differentiated, and possibly even resolved if the appropriate empirical studies were carried out. Ideally, research produces unambiguous answers to precisely defined questions. Practically, this rarely happens. During the past several years there have been two independent efforts to review the research literature on laboratory education [House, 1967; Campbell and Dunnette, 1968]. These reviews reached some, though not identical, agreement in their conclusions. However, several of the commentators on laboratory education have written as if there was no research or that one could not draw conclusions from it [Gottschalk and Pattison, 1969; Rakstis, 1970].

House [1967] stated his major conclusions as follows:

> It has been shown that T group training is not only capable of inducing anxiety, but the anxiety is an intended part of the training. Such induced anxiety may have the very unrewarding effect of unsettling, upsetting, and frustrating those subjected to it. The method may also have the intended effect of inducing more consideration for subordinates, less dependence on others, less demand for subservience from others, and better communication through more adequate and objective listening.

Campbell and Dunnette [1968] concluded:

> The evidence, though limited, is reasonably convincing that T-group training does induce behavioral changes in the "back home" setting. . . . It still cannot be said with any certainty whether T groups lead to greater or lesser changes in self-perceptions than other types of group experience, the simple passage of time, or the mere act of filling out a self-description questionnaire. . . .

House [1967] laid greater emphasis on the role of anxiety and tension in the learning process of laboratory education than Campbell and Dunnette [1968] did. Meanwhile, Campbell and Dunnette [1968] gave more attention to the inadequacies of current research designs than House did. They also differentiated more precisely than House between behavioral and attitudinal changes as a result of laboratory education. Reading House, one would probably feel relatively sure that important changes came from laboratory education, but the reader would also be encouraged to examine whether the costs of the changes were worth the payoff. Reading Campbell and Dunnette, one would probably be less certain about the type of changes, especially with regard to attitudes, that could be credited to laboratory education. One would also be alerted to many of the methodological errors that have been made in laboratory education research.

Elsewhere, this writer has commented on the House and Campbell-Dunnette reviews [Alderfer, 1970]. House tends to underemphasize the fact that most important or significant change processes include anxiety. The key question concerns whether the participants and staff are equipped to deal with the tensions effectively, not with whether they should exist. Poor instruments and inadequate controls do contaminate many laboratory education research studies. It is also true, however, that studies frequently had different sources of invalidity and yet reached the same conclusions. Studies with better designs had ways of checking sources of error even though they could not completely control them. My conclusion, therefore, was that the two reviews were conservative both with respect to the potential dangers in the methods and with respect to the kind of payoffs that could be expected.

Most of the research reviewed to date has been directed toward seeing whether T group laboratories result in behavior and attitude changes for participants when they return to work settings. There has been far less research, if any, on similar or related questions for encounter and Tavistock laboratories. Much of the public concern over laboratory education has been tied directly or indirectly to personal growth laboratories. The lack of empirical research on these very potent learning settings should be changed. A similar point applies to the Tavistock laboratories, and there are indications that research of this kind is being carried out [Astrachan and Klein, 1971].

Lakin's [1969] delineation of ethical issues in laboratory education offers a paradigm for thinking through many of the needed researches. We need to study more about the processes that lead persons to attend laboratories, including questions of how to identify persons who might be harmed and who are most likely to benefit. The work of Steele [1968] and Rubin [1967] offer promise in this direction, but it is only a bare beginning. We need to know more about the effect of various design components, staff behavior, and laboratory processes, such as that offered by the research of Argyris [1962], Culbert [1968], Harrison and Lubin [1965], Bolman [1970; 1971], Schmuck et al. [1969], Lubin and Zuckerman [1969], and Alderfer and Lodahl [1971]. But the number of questions that could be addressed is much greater than the answers so far provided. Quite a few studies have been addressed to assessing the outcomes of laboratory education, but still more with better designs and instrumentation are needed. Especially important are questions with regard to changes in interpersonal and intergroup behavior as a result of laboratory programs. What we know about laboratory-induced changes in behavior exists almost entirely at the individual level.

Both the critics and the advocates of laboratory education are people. They have their own unique combinations of needs, values, abilities, and personal styles. They participate in interpersonal relationships with each other. They belong to overlapping and competing groups. Their reactions (including this author's) to laboratory education are bound to be influenced by these factors.

Questions of knowledge, professional competence, and ethical behavior are closely intertwined. When it is well known that a particular behavioral pattern is harmful, a professional who consciously or unconsciously undertakes such a pattern should be questioned on ethical grounds. So often the issues are not clear, however. Sometimes conservative members of a profession or of a competing profession raise ethical questions about innovations because they fear that they will soon have to revise or change some of their own well established ideas or behavior if the new concepts are proven valid. The value of innovation for its own sake should never be a reason for infringing on the freedom or individuality of human beings. Nor should the inertia of tradition serve to block the responsible experimentation that is so necessary if we are to become more effective in coping with the many social problems that we face in today's world.

These issues define some very fine lines to draw. Reasonable and competent professionals have disagreed and will continue to disagree on specific cases. The important conditions for public welfare and for professional growth are that issues of professional practice be subject to continual examination by those who are equipped to do so, that theory development and empirical research go along with new developments in professional practice, and that the outcomes of these dialogues be shared among the professions and with the public.

References

1. ALDERFER, C., and LODAHL, T. M. A quasi-experiment on the use of experiential methods in the classroom. *Journal of Applied Behavioral Science*, 1971, in press.

2. ALDERFER, C. Subcultures in behavioral science and the interpretation of research on experiential methods. *Proceedings of the Twenty-second Annual Winter Meeting, IRRA,* 1969, pp. 98–108.

3. ARGYRIS, C. Conditions for competence acquisition and therapy. *Journal of Applied Behavioral Science* 4 (1968):147–78.

4. ARGYRIS, C. *Interpersonal Competence and Organizational Effectiveness.* Homewood, Ill.: Dorsey, 1962.

5. ARGYRIS, C. Issues in evaluating laboratory education. *Industrial Relations* 8 (1968): 28–40.

6. ARGYRIS, C. On the future of laboratory education. *Journal of Applied Behavioral Science* 3 (1967):153–83.

7. ASTRACHAN, B. M., and KLEIN, E. B. Learning in groups. *Journal of Applied Behavioral Science,* 1971, in press.

8. BANDURA, A., and WALTERS, R. H. *Social Learning and Personality Development.* New York: Holt, Rinehart, and Winston, 1963.

9. BASS, B. M. The anarchist movement and the T-group: Some possible lessons for organizational development. *Journal of Applied Behavioral Science* 3 (1967):211–27.

10. BENNIS, W. G. *Changing Organizations.* New York: McGraw-Hill, 1966.

11. BENNIS, W. G. A funny thing happened on the way to the future. *American Psychologist* 25 (1970):595–608.

12. BOLMAN, L. Some effects of trainers on their T groups. *Journal of Applied Behavioral Science,* 1971, in press.

13. BRADFORD, L. P. Biography of an institution. *Journal of Applied Behavioral Science* 3 (1967):127–43.

14. BURTON, A., ed. *Encounter.* San Francisco: Jossey-Bass, 1969.

15. CADDEN, J. J.; FLACH, F. F.; BLAKESLEE, S.; and CHARLTON, R. Growth in medical students through group process. *American Journal of Psychiatry* 126 (1969):862–73.

16. CALAME, B. E. The truth hurts. *Wall Street Journal,* July 14, 1969, p. 1.

17. CAMPBELL, J. P., and DUNETTE, M. D. Effectiveness of T-group experiences in managerial training and development. *Psychological Bulletin* 70 (1968):73–104.

18. COFFEY, H. S. Some fundamental issues raised. *Journal of Applied Behavioral Science* 3 (1967):184–85.

19. CRANSHAW, R. How sensitive is sensitivity training? *American Journal of Psychiatry* 126 (1969):868–73.

20. CULBERT, S. A. Trainer self-disclosure and member growth in two T-groups. *Journal of Applied Behavioral Science* 4 (1968):25–46.

21. DUNNETTE, M. D., and CAMPBELL, J. P. Laboratory Education: Impact on people and organizations. *Industrial Relations* 8 (1969):1–27.

22. GOTTSCHALK, L. A., and PATTISON, E. M. Psychiatric perspectives on T-groups and the laboratory movement: An overview. *American Journal of Psychiatry* 126 (1969): 823–39.

23. HAIGH, G. V. A personal growth crisis in laboratory training. *Journal of Applied Behavioral Science* 4 (1968):437–52.

24. HARRISON, R. Problems in the design and interpretation of research on human relations training. *Journal of Applied Behavioral Science,* 1971, in press.

25. HARRISON, R., and LUBIN, B. Personal style, group composition, and learning. *Journal of Applied Behavioral Science* 1 (1965):286–301.

26. HOUSE, R. J. T-group education and leadership effectiveness: a review of the empiric literature and a critical evaluation. *Personnel Psychology* 20 (1967):1–32.

27. JENKINS, D. H. Ethics and responsibility in human relations training. In Weschler, I. R., and Schein, E. H., *Issues in Human Relations Training*. Washington, NTL–NEA, 1962, pp. 108–13.

28. KINGSBURY, S. An open letter to Chris Argyris. *Journal of Applied Behavioral Science* 3 (1967):186–99.

29. KLEIN, M. *Our adult world and its roots in infancy*. Tavistock Pamphlet No. 2.

30. LAKIN, M. Some ethical issues in sensitivity training. *American Psychologist* 24 (1969):923–28.

31. LUBIN, B., and ZUCKERMAN, M. Level of arousal in laboratory training. *Journal of Applied Behavioral Science* 5 (1969):483–90.

32. MURPHY, M. Esalen: Where it's at. *Readings in Psychology Today*. Delmar, Cal.: C.R.M., 1967, pp. 410–15.

33. PERLS, F. S. *Ego, Hunger, and Aggression*. New York: Random House, 1969.

34. RAKSTIS, T. Sensitivity training: Fad, fraud, or new frontier. *Today's Health* 48(1) (1970):20–25, 86.

35. REDLICH, F. C., and ASTRACHAN, B. Group dynamics training. *American Journal of Psychiatry* 125 (1969):1501–7.

36. RICE, A. K. Individual, group, and intergroup processes. *Human Relations* 22 (1969): 565–84.

37. RICE, A. K. *Learning for Leadership*. London: Tavistock, 1965.

38. ROGERS, C. R. The group comes of age. *Psychology Today* 3 (1969):27–31; 58–61.

39. RUBIN, I. The reduction of prejudice through laboratory training. *Journal of Applied Behavioral Science* 3 (1967): 29–50.

40. SCHEIN, E. H., and BENNIS, W. G. *Personal and Organizational Change through Group Methods*. New York: John Wiley & Sons, 1965.

41. SHEPARD, H. A. In defense of clumsiness. *Journal of Applied Behavioral Science* 3 (1967):204–5.

42. SHEPARD, H. A. Personal growth laboratories: Toward an alternative culture. *Journal of Applied Behavioral Science* 6 (1970):259–68.

43. SCHMUCK, R. A., RUNKEL, P. J., and LONGMEYER, D. Improving organizational problem solving in a school faculty. *Journal of Applied Behavioral Science* 5 (1969):455–82.

44. SCHUTZ, W. C. *Joy: Expanding Human Awareness*. New York: Grove Press, 1967.

45. SLATER, P. E., and BENNIS, W. G. Democracy is inevitable. *Harvard Business Review* 42(2) (1964):51–59.

46. STEELE, F. I. Personality and the laboratory style. *Journal of Applied Behavioral Science* 4 (1968):25–46.

47. WHYTE, W. F. *Leadership and group participation*. New York State School of Industrial and Labor Relations, May 1953.

48. WORK, H. H. To Chris Argyris. *Journal of Applied Behavioral Science* 3 (1967): 208–9.

Yoga and Psychoanalysis

J. S. NEKI

This selection justaposes yoga and psychoanalysis. These two orthodox and historic systems are remarkably similar in their theories of the structure of the mind, their principles of motivation, and even in their inadequacies. At the same time, they differ sharply in some critical respects, most notably in their views regarding the mechanism of repression. In spite of this and other doctrinal conflicts, Neki finds the two systems essentially complementary.

Psychoanalysis is a form of individual psychotherapy based on psychological principles and techniques advanced by Sigmund Freud. In Freud's view, the personality is tripartite, consisting of the id, the superego, and the ego. The id, that "reservoir of untamed passion," is characterized by its complete orientation to immediate wish fulfilment (the pleasure principle). Unconscious sexual and aggressive impulses originate in the id and continually seek expression. At the other extreme is the superego, the strict moral "conscience" that is the source of prohibitions and guilt feelings as well as goals and aspirations. The ego is the "executive" part of the personality. It is constantly in touch with the outside world and strives to tame the libidinal impulses of the id (under guidance from the superego) and to control the moral promptings of the superego (under impetus from the id). The ego's function is to make decisions about what the person should do by keeping both id and superego out of conflict with the world (reality principle). Freud considered ignorance of these unconscious conflicts as the essential element of neurosis. Consequently, the techniques of psychoanalysis—free association, dream analysis, and so forth—are designed to explode those conflicts into full consciousness.

Yoga is a means to personal growth that developed out of thousands of years of Eastern tradition. It distinguishes conscious and superconscious mental states. Between the person's present state and superconsciousness are all manner of impediments—anger, impurity, violence, cravings—that come under the general heading of "ignorance." The goal of yoga is the elimination of these impediments, and its principal technique is disciplined concentration, or meditation. Therein lies the greatest conflict between yoga and psychoanalysis: While psychoanalysis

SOURCE: From J. S. Neki, "Yoga and Psychoanalysis," *Comprehensive Psychiatry* 8 (3) (1967):160–67. Copyright © 1967 by Grune and Stratton, Publishers, New York. Reprinted by permission of Grune & Stratton, Publishers.

tries to dispel ignorance by bringing psychic conflicts into full consciousness, yoga tries more to still those conflicts, to repress them. To psychoanalysis, suppression of memories, thoughts, and desires is anathema; to yoga, it is essential.

It is at this same point that yoga differs most dramatically from the general values of Western psychology. Psychology urges the individual to a form of personal growth that is outward-directed, that emphasizes interaction with the world, particularly with the social world. Yoga directs the person inward, away from association with the world and with other people. That, to the Western psychologist, is yoga's greatest deficiency.

A confusing blend of popular interest and suspicion surrounds both Yoga and psychoanalysis—two great systems concerned with mental health. Yoga, to the common man, is either an esoteric, exotic philosophy, an introspective psychology, mystical mumbo jumbo, or glorified jujitsu. Likewise, psychoanalysis is believed by many to be a way of getting rid of complexes, the old "confession" idea in a modern guise, a philosophy of psychic determinism, or an imaginative psychomythology.

There are similarities as well as differences between the basic ideas, methods, and aims of analytical psychology and the psychological system of Yoga. Before a consideration of these can be made, however, it is important to rectify the popular misconceptions about both systems and approach them with the spirit of scientific enquiry.

Yoga is of immense age. It is one of the oldest techniques and formal systems of the psychological discipline of self-actualization; it is at least as old as the Aryan invasion of India. Perhaps, as indicated by the more recent archeological findings, it existed even in the pre-Aryan age. The indigenous people of India were possessed with the knowledge of Yoga and taught it to their conquerors. A formal shape was given to this system by Patanjali, whose Yogic aphorisms are believed to have been written in the third century before Christ. That Yoga has been perennially popular for the last two and a half millennia speaks much for its vitality.

The word *Yoga*, having two recognized Sanskrit roots, has two possible meanings: "to mediate" and "to join." It does not merely have an association with the English word *yoke*; in fact, Yoga means the yoking or joining of the unenlightened nature of man to the superhuman in him. It signifies disciplining of the mind by mental concentration—"the restricting of the fluctuations of the mind-stuff," in the words of Patanjali [9]. When the mind is so controlled, "the seer abideth in himself." When such a control is lacking, the self identifies the interminable flux of the mind, which is the source of obscuration and ignorance. Yoga aims at dispelling this ignorance and making direct contact with "Right Knowledge." Since, for the Yogi, truth is not merely a fact but also a value, he does not rest content with discovering the truth but goes on further to practice it in his living, and that is the personal discipline of Yoga to which the Yogi willingly submits. This discipline consists of eight constituents (*angās*): *Yama* or self-restraint, *Niyam* or observance, *Āsana* or postures, *Prānāyam* or control of the vital breath, *Pratyāhār* or withdrawal of the senses, *Dhārnā* or steadying of the mind, *Dhyān* or meditation, and *Samādhi* or comtemplation. The aim of all these is to assist man to ascend from the restricted and narrow levels of consciousness to a true enlightenment.

Whereas Yoga has its roots in antiquity, psychoanalysis is not even one century old. It was only in 1895 that Freud, the founder of psychoanalysis, formulated his psychotherapeutic system for the first time.

Psychoanalysis means two things. The first is the technique devised by Freud for investigating the human mind on the subjective aspect of one's life. The second is the body of theory which has emerged from it. We are here concerned with its first connotation, according to which psychoanalysis is a system of psychology and a method of treatment of mental and nervous disorders characterized by a dynamic view of all aspects of mental life, conscious and unconscious, with special emphasis upon the phenomena of the unconscious; and by an elaborate technique of investigation and treatment, based on the employment of continuous free association. Besides free association, it also employs such techniques as dream analysis to recover forgotten memories, repressed desires, and unconscious complexes which exert a disturbing influence on the conscious life of an individual.

According to Freud, ideas or desires of sexual origin are the major constituents of the great repository of repressed elements—the unconscious. The cure of psychic disturbances is affected by bringing the repressed items into the full consciousness of the individual [3].

On a first look, Eastern Yoga and Western Psychoanalysis do not seem to have much in common except that they both, somehow, talk about "mind." However, they merit a closer inspection so that we may understand the similarities of, and the differences between, these two great psychological systems.

A stumbling block to such an attempt is the fact that both have many subsystems and offshoots. The many brands of Yoga—*Hatha Yoga, Rāja Yoga, Karma Yoga, Bhakti Yoga, Jnāna Yoga,* etc.—almost match in number the varieties of psychoanalysis: the Jungian analytical psychology, the Adlerian individual psychology, and the Neo-Freudian schools of Alexander, Rank, Sullivan, Horney, etc.—all deviations from Freud's original hypotheses. However, we may circumvent this difficulty by choosing to concern ourselves with the main theme in Yoga as well as in Psychoanalysis and not with their variations.

As a starting point, one notices that both systems are concerned with inner psychic reality. Both recognize mind as being many-layered. While psychoanalysis delves downward and distinguishes preconscious and unconscious (the last may further be subdivided, with Jung, into a personal and a collective unconscious) from the conscious mental life, Yoga seems to explore upward. It leaves behind the conscious mental activity and its unconscious springs and strives for a state of superconsciousness or pure consciousness. Here, "upward" and "downward" do not denote a spatial direction, for in the sphere of mind, such a direction would not be tenable. They only denote an opposing or, at least, a nonidentical approach. However, what is common between the two approaches is that they do not consider empirical consciousness as the only dimension of human mind.

Another point of vital similarity between the two systems is that both recognise the hierarchy of superego and id. According to the psychoanalytical concept, *id* represents the chief impersonal dynamic and the source of mental energy. It is "the source of instinctive energy for the individual" and is chiefly unconscious. The *ego*, which is in certain ways the antithesis of the *id*, and in certain other ways of the *superego*, is derived from the *id* passing through the preconscious in infancy and childhood—differentiation being brought about by the activities of "perceptual consciousness." The *superego* is, roughly, the earliest moral code of the child and approximates what is popularly known as the conscience (although it is much more moral than the conscience with which we are familiar). It is the moral critic that maintains in the *ego* an unconscious guilt sense. The Yogic conception, however, is somewhat different, though more comprehensive. In a poetical metaphor, *Katha Upanishad* says: "Know that the *Self* is the lord of the chariot, the *body*, verily is the chariot; know that the *soul* is the charioteer, and emotion the reins. They say that the *bodily powers* are the horses and the *external world* is their field. When the self, the bodily powers and emotions are joined together, this is the *right enjoyer*. But for the unwise, with emotion ever unrestrained, his bodily powers run away with him, like the unruly horses of the charioteer" [6].

One of the great common merits of the two systems is the conception of energy or a "vital force" at work through the whole psychic system. In psychoanalytic parlance it is called the *libido*, while in Yogic terminology it is called the *Prāna*. The two, however, are not identical with one another. The *libido* is defined by Freud as the energy of those instincts which have to do with all that may be comprised under the word "love" [3]. The concept is obviously something much wider than is familiarly known as the sex urge. The frequent modern usage which keeps the two close together emanates from Freud's claim that we cannot separate self-love from sexual love on the one hand, and on the other, love for parents and children, friendship and love for humanity in general, and also devotion to concrete objects and abstract ideas. Our justification lies in the fact that these tendencies are expression of the same instinctive activities [3]. It may be useful to note here that the analytical system of Jung makes use of the term *libido* in a much broader sense—something that represents the total striving of the individual. As such it is analogous to Bergson's "elan vital" or to McDougall's "horme" [2].

Prāna of Yoga literally means breath. But this word figures in early Indian philosophy as "vital air" and "life" itself. . . . "So, *prāna* is not the breath, but the breath of life," says Ernest Wood, a Western authority on Yoga, "and as breathing is the primary and fundamental function of the body, so is this 'electricity' required for the vitality of all the organs, and although the old teachers of Yoga were not able to describe it in terms of something else already known, something other than itself (which is the basis of describing), they came as near as they could to describing it by calling it vital air or vitality. In our day, we have the idea of electricity to draw upon; we can say that the body, like a battery, is well or ill charged with vitality" [12].

In psychoanalysis, as also in Yoga, ignorance is considered to be the root cause of misery. The psychoanalyst ascribes the production of neurotic symptoms to unconscious mental processes—such as repression, regression, projection, etc.—about which the sufferer is ignorant. The analyst—through the weapons of abreaction, free association, dream analysis, transference, etc.— helps the patient to understand these mechanisms and the genesis of his symptoms. The therapeutic goal, therefore, is providing the patient with an insight into the true nature of his ailment. Yoga also considers ignorance or *avidyā* as the basis of all misery. However, this ignorance is of a different magnitude. Yoga divides mental states (*Vrittis*) into *Klista* (afflicted or hindered) and *aklista* (unafflicted or unhindered). The former can all be reduced to one category—states of ignorance (*avidyā*)—while the latter can all be called states of knowledge (*prajnā*). Now ignorance takes the forms of mistaking the nonself for the self (*asmita*), the unpure for the pure (*rāga*), the painful for the pleasurable (*dvesa*), inasmuch as in anger and hatred there is a peculiar pleasure attached though the experience is really painful, and the evanescent for the eternal (*abhinivesa*) [12]. Because of all these forms of ignorance, the pleasures of the body are mistaken for delights of the soul, and the changing scenes of the mental and physical worlds are considered constant and abiding. The aim of Yoga is to dispel this *avidyā* and to bring about enlightenment or true knowledge through certain forms of meditation and other practices aimed at the control of the roving mind. Both Yoga and psychoanalytic therapy are thus "rooted in the doctrine of the liberation of the individual and are, therefore, opposed to 'escape' whether it assumes the form of archaism, or futurism or asceticism" [5].

Both Yoga and psychoanalysis enjoin that life should not be governed by the *pleasure principle*. According to psychoanalysis it is the reality principle that, in a mature personality, modifies the pleasure principle appreciably. According to Yoga, however, it is the *nirvāna-principle* that supplants the pleasure principle. Freud maintains that, "the Nirvāna-principle expresses the tendency of the death instincts, the pleasure-principle represents the claims of the Libido and that modification of it, the reality-principle, that influences the outer world" [3]. However, in the Indian systems of philosophy, *Nirvāna* (although literally it means "to blow out," as a candle) does not place emphasis on annihilation, but specifically aims at the removal of ignorance and craving [12].

Self-dissatisfaction is common to the students of both Yoga and psychoanalysis. It is this that leads to an inner searching-out. Both systems insist upon a personal mentor. In Yoga, it is the *guru*, and in psychoanalysis it is the psychoanalyst. The *guru* in Yoga can be one who is himself adept in Yogic practices and has attainments in the spiritual field; a psychoanalyst can be one who has himself been psychoanalyzed. Both systems stress utter truthfulness. One who plays self-deception benefits neither from psychoanalysis nor from Yoga. According to Mahāvāgg, "When confessed the sin becomes less, since it becomes the truth." [8] According to psychoanalysis, catharsis, or the "talking-out therapy" requires utter truthfulness.

The law of psychic determinism, which does not take human behavior for granted but considers it to be due to some underlying unconscious causes, constitutes the philosophic substratum of both systems. In Yoga, it is the doctrine of *Karma* which supplies this psychic determinism. In the words of Sarvepalli Radhakrishnan, "The law of Karma is assured as valid and our life, its character and length, are all determined by it. Though we do not remember our past lives, we can infer particulars about them from tendencies of the present and other tendencies will cease to exist on the disappearance of the cause (*hetu*), motive (*phala*), substratum (*āsraya*), and object (*ālambanā*). The root cause is *avidyā*, though we may have other proximate causes; the motive refers to the purpose with reference to which any conation becomes operative in the present; *citta* is the substratum of the residual potencies and the object is that which excites the potencies [10]. In psychoanalysis also, determinism is provided by an inflexible conception of causality.

The aim of psychoanalytic psychotherapy is, according to Freud, "to increase the area of rational consciousness." Our intellect may not be able to conquer the instinctive tendencies straightaway, but persistence is sure to yield fruit. This is called *bhāvanā* in Yoga. *Bhāvanā* means "bringing back to mind, consciously, again and again." Freud himself seems to agree with this when he says, "We may insist as much as we like that human intellect is weak in comparison with human instincts, and be right in doing so. Nevertheless, there is something peculiar about this weakness. The voice of the intellect is a soft one, but it does not rest until it has gained a hearing. Ultimately, after endlessly repeated rebuffs, it succeeds. This is one of the few points in which one may be optimistic about the future of mankind. The primacy of the intellect lies in the far, but still probably not infinite, distance" [3].

The tussle between the id and the superego (in Freudian language) is called *Vichhinnatā* in Yoga—literally, intercepted activity, intercepted as a result of conflict between two strong emotional urges.

In his struggle for existence, man is generally torn between two conflicting tendencies: one, to transcend his animal nature (the progressive tendency), and another, to return to it (the regressive tendency). In the words of Erich Fromm, "Man's life is determined by the inescapable alternative between regression and progression, between return to animal existence and arrival at human existence. Any attempt to return is painful; it inevitably leads to suffering and mental sickness, to death either psychologically or mentally (insanity). Every step forward is frightening and painful too until a certain point is reached where fear and doubt have only minor proportions" [11]. Yoga also stresses this freedom from fear, or *abhaya*, as a characteristic of man's true development.

While the two systems resemble each other in many ways, they have also been criticized on similar lines. Foremost among such criticisms is that directed against their psychic determinism. The thoroughgoing determinism in both systems leaves little freedom of will and thus raises important ethical issues. In fact, Freud attributed the earlier unpopularity of his doctrines to "its most fundamental feature, determinism," whereby he had robbed man of "his cherished illusion," free will.*

Another charge to which both systems are jointly exposed is that they concern themselves merely with the relation of the individual human organism to his inner psychic reality while taking no interest in the social organism and therefore giving no place to social thought.

A third criticism that both share is that they have a scanty core of established facts but a huge system of theoretical concepts superimposed on these facts. When, therefore, even a part of a system becomes questionable, some people tend to reject the entire system. As more and more of the theoretical concepts of these systems come to be discarded, the systems come to stand more and more exposed to the danger of an outright rejection. Notwithstanding a vast amount of theory, however, there seems to be in them an abundant quantum of enduring truth at the core which seems to have vouched for their popularity.

In spite of the fundamental similarities outlined above, the two systems are significantly different from each other in their inception, aims and application.

While Yoga is rooted in philosophic doctrines and mystic practices of ancient India, psychoanalysis sprouted as a medical technique and still claims to be a clinical discipline. Although much philosophic development has taken place as a superstructure upon basic psychoanalytical ideas, and although Yoga has developed techniques which have what may be called a clinical bearing, also being concerned with physical and mental health, the two systems have not been able to come near each other in any way. Sprung up from the clinical soil, despite its philosophical offshoots, psychoanalysis mainly exists and exerts its force as a clinical technique. Starting as an enquiry into the meaning and purpose of human existence, Yoga has paid no attention to any therapeutic techniques. In the field of mental health, psychoanalysis is a curative technique. It has the possibilities of being extended as a preventive measure also, but Yoga purports neither to cure nor to prevent mental ailments directly; it stands for positive physical and mental health and is thus also preventive incidentally. In fact, where the possibilities of psychoanalysis end, those of Yoga seem to begin.

This holds true not only of their respective aims, but also of their territories. While the essential soil of psychoanalysis is the unconscious, it does not re-

---

* Editor's note: Recall Matson's remarks about determinism in psychoanalysis (p. 120).

ceive any accent from Yoga. Yoga concerns itself neither with the empirical consciousness nor with the psychoanalytical unconscious, but with pure primordial consciousness, with its manifold possibilities of manifesting in a hundred limited consciousnesses. So, while psychoanalysis only purports to light up the unconscious recesses of the mind inaccessible to the empirical consciousness, Yoga strives to quell the empirical consciousness so that the blinding light of the superconsciousness shines through.

That is the reason why their techniques run counter to each other. While psychoanalysis starts with free association and encourages associative ramblings, it is these that Yoga strives to quell. That coveted state of mental void (*shunya*) that Yoga tries to achieve—in which a spaceless, timeless state of eternal bliss reigns—is attainable by practicing withdrawal from the sense impressions and controlling the roving of the mind in random associative thought. That is why it strives to shut out images, dreams, reveries, and the like, while dream and phantasy are the stuff psychoanalysis thrives upon.

Yogic practices employ suppression—a willful banishing of memories, thoughts and desires from the consciousness—as their primary technique, while psychoanalysis abhors suppression. In fact, this is exactly what it strives to remove—inhibitions, suppressions, repressions, etc. That is why Yoga may be styled a system of self-control, while psychoanalysis may be styled a system of self-expression. Whereas in Yoga the sole emphasis is upon the harnessing of desires, in psychoanalysis it is upon living them out, even though in a symbolized or "sublimated" form. This basic antithesis has, perhaps, been the reason why psychoanalysis has not been able to take roots in India, because in the land of Yoga the Yogic doctrine of self-control, with its great emphasis on suppression and inhibition, has for millenniums soaked into the cultural soil.

Yoga and psychoanalysis have different attitudes toward moral and religious issues. Whereas one form of Yoga, *Bhakti-Yoga,* is entirely based on a religious sentiment, and belief in God is a welcome aid in the practices of all types of Yoga, Freud [4] considers religion a mere universal illusion and predicts a bleak future for it.

However, notwithstanding even these sharp doctrinal antitheses between Yoga and psychoanalysis, it is possible to visualize the possibility of their being brought together; they do not supplant, but supplement, each other. As pointed out previously, where the scope and jurisdiction of one ends, that of the other begins; and whatever overlap exists can vouch for the necessary bond for their mutual synthesis. The large number of similarities between the two systems outlined in the foregoing discussion tend to ensure further the possibilities of success in such an endeavor. While psychoanalysis has shed tremendous light on endopsychic dynamisms, Yoga provides useful insights in the field of psychosomatic and somatopsychic interrelationships. While psychoanalysis remains a therapeutic weapon, Yoga stands out as a discipline of promoting positive mental health. Their mutual exclusiveness thus does not preclude the possibility of their synthesis.

It would be useful to conclude with Eilhard von Domarus' summation of the situation:

"It is impossible to do justice here to the metaphysical achievement of Hinduism and its bearing upon the psycho-therapy. Psychologically, the West with its empirical historical approach to all problems, including those of the mind, has added to our knowledge of the mind, and psychoanalysis is the most formidable method yet discovered for the penetration of the mind's working. . . . Modern psychotherapy and Hinduism are not mutually exclusive alternatives, but properly understood supplement each other [11].

References

1. BHATTACHARYA, HARIDAS. *Yoga Psychology.* In *The Cultural Heritage of India.* Vol. III. Calcutta, The Ramkrishna Mission Inst. of Culture, 1953.
2. CRICHTON-MILLER, H. *Psychoanalysis and its Derivatives.* London: Home University Library, 1948.
3. FREUD, S. Collected Papers. Translated by J. Riviere and V. Woolf. London: Institute of Psychoanalysis, 1924–25.
4. FREUD, S. *The Future of an Illusion.* New York: Liveright, 1949.
5. GAITONDE, M. R. Hindu philosophy and analytic psychotherapy. *Compr. Psychiat.* 2 (1961):299–303.
6. *Kathopanishad.* 3:1–3, 4–5.
7. KUVALYANANDA, SWAMI, and VINEKAR, S. L. *Yoga Therapy.* New Delhi, Central Health Education Bureau, 1963.
8. MAHAVAGG. Quoted by J. C. Malhotra in *Yoga and Mental Hygiene,* Proceedings of the Third World Congress of Psychiatry, 1960.
9. PATANJALI. Yoga Sutras.
10. RADHAKRISHNAN, SARVEPALLI. *Indian Philosophy,* Vol. 2. London: George Allen & Unwin, 1958.
11. VON DOMARUS, EILHARD. *American Handbook of Psychiatry,* Vol. 2. New York: Basic Books, Inc., 1959.
12. WOOD, ERNST. *Yoga.* Harmondsworth: Pelican Books, 1961.

PART 8

Social Issues

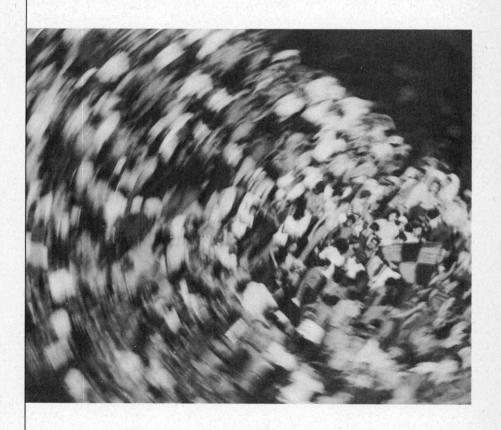

Just as the understanding and application of psychological principles and techniques can help relieve the suffering of the individual, so they can be applied to the problems of people collectively, that is, to society. The preceding section showed some of the ways in which the physical approach, the psychological approach, and the social approach can help to direct or redirect individual growth. The present section offers some suggestions about how these three approaches can benefit society as a whole.

There are two discernible clusters of articles here. The first three articles illustrate psychological analyses of certain social problems—prejudice, poverty, and violence. In spite of their diversity of content and approach, they are bound by a common thread. Their argument is that if we can understand the specific aspects of a problem, we are in a far better position to combat that problem than if we merely face it on a global level. It does us little good just to take the position that we must eliminate prejudice, poverty, and violence; rather we have to resolve these problems into their elements, and understand them, if we are to remedy them. Thus Raab and Lipset analyze prejudice. As they tease out its components, some rather startling facts appear that offer hope for the eventual control of prejudiced behavior. Similarly Beiser examines poverty in terms of its specific effects on the person. From his examination, he deduces some tactics for a more efficient and ultimately more humane "war on poverty." And Wolfgang discusses some of the sources of human violence. As his argument takes shape, it becomes clear how we might achieve at least a partial resolution of the problem.

The remaining articles are somewhat more speculative. They too share a common core: what our society could be like if we were to bring available tools to bear on our mutual concerns. Schwitzgebel suggests a variety of applications for psychotechnology, from parking problems to international relations. Kline speculates about probable psychopharmaceutical advances that could affect many areas of our lives, from controlling unwanted aggression to producing rehabilitative guilt. And, finally, Rogers outlines choices that we have to make with regard to interpersonal relationships. Because we now have—or soon will have—the technical capacity to control much of our destiny, we need to make careful decisions now about what that destiny should be.

Each of these articles is rare for its combination of provocative content and responsible perspective.

The Prejudiced Society

EARL RAAB AND SEYMOUR MARTIN LIPSET

It is not enough simply to say that people should not be prejudiced. It does little good just to pass laws against prejudice. In order to reduce or eliminate prejudice in interpersonal or intergroup relations, we need to undertake a detailed analysis of the problem of prejudice.

Common sense tells us that prejudice starts with a stereotype, a generalized attitude toward some group of people that does not allow for individual differences among members of the group. Because of some personal experience with members of that group, hostility builds on the stereotype and our attitude toward the entire group turns negative. The negative attitude then causes us to behave negatively toward the people in the group.

Very little of that common-sense analysis is correct, according to the authors of the following article. Their scientific analysis of the problem of prejudice suggests that the opposite of common sense is more nearly the truth. Stereotypes are involved in prejudice, but there seems to be very little correspondence between stereotyping a group and bearing hostility toward that group. Negative attitudes are certainly operating, but they seem to have little relationship to personal experience with members of the group; on the contrary, the less the personal experience with the people, apparently the more intense the negative attitude. Finally, and perhaps the most dramatic difference between what common sense and science tells us, prejudiced attitudes do not cause prejudiced behavior, but prejudiced behavior creates prejudiced attitudes. This last phenomenon holds true not only in the evident case in which parents' behavior shapes children's attitudes (see Bronfenbrenner's article), but in the more general process of socialization, in which society's behavior influences the attitudes of all members of society.

This article serves as another example of the influence of social behavior on personal behavior. But more important, because it provides us with a more detailed understanding of the phenomenon of prejudice, it suggests some ways in which psychological principles can be applied to alleviate an important social problem.

SOURCE: From *The Prejudiced Society* by Earl Raab and Seymour Martin Lipset, copyright © 1962 by Earl Raab. Reprinted by permission of Doubleday & Company, Inc.

The problem of prejudice, as it presents itself to society, consists of overt acts which deny equal status or opportunity to people because of their racial, religious or ethnic identity. However, "prejudice" is often used in a specialized sense to describe an individual's state of mind or attitude. There has long been a popular tendency to reify "prejudiced attitude"; to conceive of it as a little mental package tucked away in a corner of the brain, waiting for the proper stimulus to bring it to life. According to this view, if a person has "a prejudiced attitude" against Filipinos, then when a Filipino brushes up against him, or enters the same room he's in, or applies to him for a job, or tries to move next door, this attitude would be triggered and the "prejudiced person" would act accordingly.

The evidence clearly indicates, however, that prejudiced attitudes are very far from being neat little mental packages; and that, at the very least, they do not predetermine prejudiced behavior.

Gordon Allport has partly defined an attitude as a "mental and neural state of readiness" [1]. The meaningful reference here is to the fact that an attitude is a "mental and neural" state and not just to the fact that it is a state of readiness. A mechanical jack-in-the-box, crouched on its springs, might be said to have an attitude of readiness. Its attitude is such that it will jump up when the cover is removed. But a human attitude describes an internal state that has an independent existence, apart from any resultant behavior. If a child were simulating a jack-in-the-box in a school play, his attitude towards jumping out of the box in which he was crouched might consist of a combination of elements, e.g. he may be displeased about the physical prospect of jumping out; on the other hand, he may have a strong fear of the derision he will face if he fails to jump. Both of these elements comprise his "attitude about jumping" at a given point. The attitude exists as a real fact even if the show is cancelled and he never does have the opportunity of jumping or not jumping.

HOSTILITY AND STEREOTYPE

It is common to think of the prejudiced attitude as consisting of both hostility and an over-generalization or stereotype. It is even common to think of the hostility as flowing from the stereotype. But, in fact, it is possible for an individual to have the stereotype without the hostility, or the hostility without the stereotype. It is possible to cloak two groups with the same stereotype, and have different feelings about them. Saenger and Flowerman questioned some 450 college students as to their feelings of dislike for a number of human groups. They also asked these students to indicate the characteristics which they believed marked these groups. Presumably their likes or dislikes would be based on the kinds of characteristics which they attributed to these groups. This was not the case. Students who expressed a dislike for Jews ascribed to them characteristics which they also ascribed to other groups for whom they did *not* express a dislike. For example, 31 per cent of the students complained that the Jews were mercenary; but 24 per cent of them complained that Americans were mercenary and 38 per cent that businessmen were mercenary. However, Jews were more often disliked for this quality than were Americans or businessmen.

In a study made by B. M. Kramer, he marked off five "distance zones" from an area in which Negroes were moving and interviewed white residents in each of the zones. Zone 1 was the closest to this area of expanding Negro movement. Zone 5 was the most remote, three miles away. There was a general desire among white residents in all five zones to exclude Negroes from their neighborhoods. Kramer checked the stereotypes held by these white residents about Negroes, e.g., that Negroes were personally unclean or diseased. In Zone 1, where the white residents had the closest contact with the Negroes, only 5 per cent offered such stereotypes as reasons for exclusion; as against 25 per cent of the residents in Zone 5. However, the intensity of hostility in Zone 1 was higher than in Zone 5; in Zone 1, 64 percent of the residents made spontaneous expressions of hostility, as against only 4 per cent in Zone 5. Whatever else may have been involved in the situation, it was clear that hostility and stereotype were not tied to each other.

A negative stereotype may exist without hostility; hostility without a negative stereotype; a combination of both cognitive and emotional elements may exist with varying degrees of intensity and with varying targets. A prejudiced attitude is indeed not a homogeneous mental package. Prejudiced attitude #1 is different from prejudiced attitude #2, and there is almost an endless variety of possibilities.

FRAME OF REFERENCE—THE SITUATIONAL FACTOR

Not only do prejudiced attitudes differ widely from one individual to another, but they tend to differ from one situation to another for any given individual. For an attitude is not a thing, it is a process; it is an interaction. It is an interaction involving not only the person and the object, but all other factors that are present in any situation. A crude illustration: In his own home town, Jones may have the deepest contempt for Smith, who lives up the block. He considers Smith a rough character with bad manners and worse taste, socially unacceptable and intellectually barren. Jones has a *feeling* of distaste when he thinks of Smith, and avoids him conscientiously. It happens that Jones, alone on an unguided world tour, has a transportation breakdown in a primitive village in a backward country. The villagers are unfriendly, unlettered and unsanitary. Into this unhappy and improbable scene, after a couple of days, rides Smith. Jones may well greet him with a joyful embrace, rather than with distaste. His image of Smith as a boor may be replaced by the image of a man who at least has the good sense to speak English and to wash his hands before eating. Whether or not this feeling and image will carry over in any way when the two men return to their home town is another matter—but the fact remains that a different external situation has evoked a different attitude.

Sherif and Cantril have called this situational factor "frame of reference." They write:

> The term "frame of reference" is simply used to denote the function-ally related factors (present and past) which operate at the moment to determine the particular properties of a psychological phenomenon (such as perception, judgment, affectivity).

In psychological literature, the critical importance of the situational factor is supported by experiments on many levels. Wever and Zener had subjects judge the weight of a series of objects as "light" or "heavy." When the series of objects was changed from a light series to a heavy series, the same object that was formerly judged heavy was now perceived as light. McGarvey had her subjects rate the "social prestige" of various occupations and found that the desirability of any given occupation was dependent on the kind of occu-pational series with which it appeared.

Many research roads lead to the understanding that prejudiced attitudes can be highly situational in character. One evening at a summer camp, 30 young men were tested as to their attitudes towards Japanese-Americans. Following this, they were scheduled to attend a show at a local theatre. In-stead, their show-going was cancelled, and they were forced to accomplish a series of complicated tasks. The same night, following the tasks, their atti-tudes towards Japanese-Americans were retested, and were found to be less favorable than they had been earlier in the evening. Nothing had changed in the interim with respect to the young men vis-a-vis Japanese-Americans, but some other factors in the situation had changed.

Deitrich Reitzes examined a situation, in which a group of white people had favorable attitudes towards Negroes at work and in shopping centers, but had unfavorable attitudes towards them living in their residential neigh-borhood. He traced these inconsistencies to different attitudinal "fields"; that is, each of these situations had different external forces operating to form the interaction of attitude. The unions to which the white people belonged were actively committed to intergroup equality at work. The Chamber of Com-merce and business groups in the area involved were actively seeking Negro trade. The neighborhood civic club, however, was actively exclusionist. There were different "collective interests" involved in the different situa-tions. In short, an individual does not typically have "an attitude" towards Negroes; he has many different attitudes depending on the circum-stances.

There are a number of different ways in which this "situational" character of prejudice may be described:

A general attitude, about Negroes, for example, does not predetermine specific attitudes about Negroes. In other words, if a person has a general stereotype of Negroes, and a general hostility towards Negroes, this does not automatically mean that he will have an unfavorable attitude towards working in the same factory with Negroes.

One specific attitude towards Negroes, e.g., working with them, may have a quite different texture from another specific attitude, e.g., living next to them.

The same person may have one attitude about working next to Negroes in one situation, and a different attitude about working next to them in another situation.

In sum, a prejudiced attitude may shift from one moment and situation to another.

DISPARITY BETWEEN THE ATTITUDE AND THE ACT

The situational nature of prejudice is evident, too, in the mass of evidence concerning the disparity between *expressed* attitudes and behavior.

A Chinese couple traveled twice across the United States, and up and down the Pacific Coast. During the course of this trip, they asked for service in hundreds of hotels, auto camps, tourist homes and restaurants. They were refused accommodations in only one sleeping place, and in none of the eating places. Six months after their trip, R. T. LaPiere sent a mail questionnaire to each of these places asking if Chinese could be accommodated. Over 90 per cent of the 47 sleeping places and of the 81 eating places that replied said that Chinese would *not* be accommodated.

In a Northeastern suburban community, three young women, two white and one Negro, entered 11 restaurants. They encountered no problems, and received nothing less than exemplary service. Two weeks later a letter was sent to the same restaurants asking for reservations for a similar group. There was no answer to the letters, and great resistance to the follow-up phone calls.

Saenger and Gilbert studied customer reactions to the employment of Negro sales personnel in New York City department stores. One group they interrogated had been observed as customers in stores where there were both Negro and white clerks. Twenty per cent of those who had bought from Negro clerks said they would disapprove of the policy of employing Negro clerks in the department stores; 21 per cent of those who had bought from white clerks expressed the same attitude. In other words, prejudice towards Negro clerks did not cause customers to avoid them in the stores. Over 40 per cent of those who said they would not buy in a store with Negro clerks had actually been observed not only in such a store but at a counter where there was a Negro clerk. One-third of those who said they would never buy from a Negro clerk had been observed buying from a Negro clerk less than an hour before they were interviewed.

THE BEHAVIOR—NOT THE ATTITUDE

It is true, of course, that the *expression* of an attitude may be different from, or at least only a surface part of an attitude. A person who is asked whether he would have any objection to rooming with someone of another racial extraction may honestly say, and honestly believe, that he is free of such prejudiced attitudes. But he may find, to his own shock, that when it comes down to it, he does have internal resistance to such a relationship; or indeed, without realizing it himself, he may find reasons and devices for avoiding such a relationship. Likewise, he may say that he *does* have objections, and when it comes down to it, he may not have these objections, or may not find them operative. His initial response may depend on the circumstances: who asks him and where. His ultimate reaction may also depend on the circumstances. This disparity between attitude as expressed and as it ultimately affects behavior merely re-emphasizes the *situational* character of the whole complex of prejudice. And it is the act of prejudice, not the attitude itself, which is the social problem of prejudice as earlier defined.

Andrew Kapos surveyed the attitudes of 30 segregated white gentile fraternities at the University of Michigan in 1953. He found a more intensive feeling of general prejudice against Jews than against Negroes. But he also found more willingness to admit Jews than Negroes to the fraternities, possibly because of the group standards which the fraternity members felt existed in the world around them. The attitudes of almost a thousand Texas manufacturers towards Negroes were tested; and the results were compared with the actual hiring practices of these manufacturers. It was found that the general atttiude of a man towards Negroes had little to do with whether or not he employed them. An employer's willingness to hire Negroes was not significantly related to the degree of general hostility he felt or expressed towards Negroes.

In Panama there are places where one side of a street falls in the American Canal Zone, and the other side of the same street falls in Panamanian territory. Biesanz and Smith found that Panamanian Negroes tend to conform to discriminatory practices when they go to the Zone side of the street; while white Americans tend to adjust to nondiscriminatory practices when they go to the Panamanian side.

Whether in the fraternities of Ann Arbor, the factories of Texas, or the streets of Panama, it is not the prejudiced attitude which is itself important to the social problem of prejudice. It is the act of excluding Negroes from the fraternities and from the factories that makes prejudice a problem for society. The attitudes are important to that problem only insofar as they *cause* these acts. It is clear, however, that a prejudiced attitude is not a kind of pushbutton, nor a constant psychic bundle; it is, more accurately, an interaction in any given situation. It is clear that general attitudes of prejudice do not necessarily predetermine prejudiced behavior; it is clear that a specific attitude at one moment does not predetermine the act that will eventuate at another moment. What, then, *is* the relationship between attitudes and behavior?

Learning Prejudice

Prejudiced behavior typically shapes and alters prejudiced attitudes. The learning of prejudice is affected primarily by the kinds of social situations in which people live.

The fact that attitudes do not necessarily predetermine behavior, does not mean that attitudes and behavior do not typically accompany each other. The human being is not a mechanical jack-in-the-box. We do normally have feelings and conceptions that accompany our behavior. But our feelings and conceptions—our attitudes—do not necessarily *precede* our behavior. The attitude of the boy who is going to jump out of the box in the school play may be altered by the very fact that he is going to jump out of the box; just as his attitude immediately after his act may be shaped by the bare fact that he did jump out.

In brief, behavior typically shapes and alters attitudes. Cantril examined attitude polls on the subject of "lend-lease" assistance to the Allies before the United States was involved in World War II. He found that immediately after Congress actually passed lend-lease legislation, attitudes toward such legislation became more favorable by about 10 per cent. The point, according to Cantril is that public opinion tends to follow accomplished fact.

Stouffer and his associates asked white soldiers: How would you like it if your division had companies which included both Negro and white platoons? Seven per cent of those who already were in a company with Negro platoons replied that they disliked the situation; 20 per cent of those questioned who were in the same regiment but not in the same company as Negro platoons replied that they would dislike it; 24 per cent of those who were in the same division but not the same regiment as Negro platoons replied that they would dislike it; 62 per cent of those questioned who were not even in the same division as Negro platoons replied that they would dislike it. The further they were from the accomplished fact, the more they disliked it.

Deutsch and Collins surveyed attitudes of white residents in four different public housing projects in New York. In two, Negro and white families were assigned indiscriminately to the same apartment buildings. In the other two, Negroes were assigned to different buildings within the same project.

In all cases, the assignments were made under an automatic procedure that did not take into account the preference of those assigned. Asked if they would dislike living in the same buildings with Negroes, about three-quarters of the white respondents in the segregated projects said they would, as against only about one-quarter of those already living in the fully integrated units. About 50 per cent of those in the integrated projects said they desired to be friendly with their Negro neighbors, as against only about 10 per cent in the segregated projects. General attitudes towards Negroes seemed to be affected as well: about 75 per cent of those in the integrated units said they respected Negroes in general, as against well below 50 per cent of those in the segregated projects.

ATTITUDES AFTER THE FACT

Many research studies show that specific attitudes change after the fact, e.g.: attitudes towards living in the same neighborhood, serving in the same Army company. These studies are evidence that specific attitudes do shape themselves to specific behavior. However these studies do *not* indicate that a shift in one specific attitude towards a minority group will necessarily affect other specific attitudes towards the same group; or that a shift in a specific attitude will always affect the expression of a general attitude as it apparently did in the Deutsch and Collins study.

Harding and Hogrefe studied the attitudes of white employees towards Negro co-workers in department stores. The white employees were divided into three groups according to the nature and extent of their contact with Negroes. Group I included those who had worked in departments where there had been at least one Negro whose job was on an equal or superior plane. Group II included those who had worked in departments where Negroes had been of lower working status than themselves. Those in Group III had never worked in a department with Negroes.

They were all asked: "How would you feel about taking a new job in which there were both Negroes and white people doing the same kind of work as you?" Seventy-three per cent of Group I, 61 per cent of Group II, and 48 per cent of Group III said they would be favorable. But there was no significant difference between the three groups when they were asked, for example, whether they would want to sit next to Negroes on the bus or train. The experience of working with Negroes apparently only produced a more favorable attitude towards Negroes in that specific "fellow-employee" frame of reference.

A further clue may be found in the study of Daniel Wilner and his associates of attitudes of white residents in public housing projects. This three-year study compared two kinds of white tenants: those who lived close to Negroes and those who lived at a relative distance. In neither case was the distance a matter of choice for the white residents who had been assigned to their quarters in these public projects. As in the Deutsch-Collins study, it was discovered that attitudes changed favorably as the distance to the Negroes decreased. Not only was there a significant difference in the specific attitude (i.e., living near Negroes), but again an apparent shift in general attitudes. In one project, for example, where Negroes and whites lived in the same buildings, 53 per cent of the respondents said that they generally liked and respected Negroes; in another project where the buildings were all-white and all-Negro, only 36 per cent of the respondents said that they generally liked and respected Negroes.

However, the Wilner study went further. Among one group of women who lived close to Negroes, 32 per cent who had no personal contact with their Negro neighbors beyond casual greetings, had a high degree of general esteem for Negroes; 45 per cent who, in addition, had extended street conversation with their Negro neighbors had a high degree of general esteem for Negroes; and 74 per cent who had neighborly associations with Negroes, i.e., behaved like neighbors, had a high degree of esteem generally for Negroes.

Proximity was not a matter of choice but of automatic assignment. The greater the proximity, the more likely was there to be neighbor-like activity. A point made by the Wilner study is that the shift in general attitudes came not so much from mere contact or proximity, but from a changed pattern of behavior. The white residents who *acted* like neighbors came most often to *feel* like neighbors on many levels.

I. N. Brophy found a very marked reduction in general anti-Negro prejudice among white merchant seamen who, without the benefit of choice, had worked with Negro sailors. Thirty-three per cent of those who had never shipped with Negroes were rated as unprejudiced; 46 per cent of those who had shipped with Negroes once; 62 per cent who had shipped with Negroes twice; and 82 per cent of those who had shipped with Negroes five or more times were rated as unprejudiced. This was in sharp contrast to the Harding and Hogrefe study of the limited shifts in general attitudes for whites who had worked with Negroes in department stores. But these seamen not only worked together very closely, but also lived together 24 hours a day. And neighborly relationships are, of course, more general and encompassing than working relationships.

BEHAVIOR SHAPES ATTITUDE

In other words, evidence indicates that specific attitudes shape themselves to behavior. People who actually work with Negroes, especially as equals, develop attitudes favorable towards working with Negroes. People who actually are neighbors of Negroes develop attitudes favorable towards being neighbors of Negroes. Evidence also indicates that general attitudes shape themselves to behavior only if that behavior is itself general in nature. People who behave towards Negroes as full equals on every level tend to develop attitudes toward them as full equals on every level.

Thus, the mass of modern evidence runs counter to the "attitudes-first" fallacy, which holds that prejudice is a lurking state of mind that spills over into overt behavior. It might be more accurate to say that the prejudiced state of mind is typically a function of behavior; except for the danger that *this* formula might be over-simplified into a kind of reverse fallacy. Actually, there emerges an understanding that the key to prejudice must be found *out-side* the realm of attitude-behavior relationships. The evidence has demonstrated how both attitudes and behavior are affected by the social frame of reference to which they occur.

In an integrated housing situation, attitudes and behavior are different than in a segregated housing situation. In an integrated army situation, attitudes and behavior are different than in a segregated army situation. In a shopping center situation attitudes and behavior towards Negroes are different than in a neighborhood situation. On one side of a Panamanian street, a white man's behavior towards Negroes may be different than on the other side of the street. It is this *situational* factor which is central to both attitude and behavior; which can stand outside any behavior-attitude spiral and avoid the fruitless question: "Which comes first?"

The effect of the situational factor on the social problem of prejudice can be found in the dramatic story of post-war integration in the armed forces. A military installation comprises a kind of community in itself, with its own community practices and patterns. Soldiers, sailors, marines and airmen for the most part live as well as work within the military setting. Traditionally, the armed forces community had followed the racial patterns of the nation's lowest common denominator: the deep South. The assumption was made that only in this way could the armed forces accommodate the young men from the South as well as from other parts of the country who entered the services with deep-set attitudes of prejudice. Segregation was the rule on almost every level. Most military leaders expected it to stay that way indefinitely. In 1948, however, an edict was handed down by administrative order from President Truman's office: the armed forces were to be thoroughly and effectively integrated.

In its own inimitable way, the armed forces implemented this edict by a series of direct military orders. Today, there is effective integration throughout all the branches of service. In 1953, in an extensive survey of the effects of the desegregation edict five years after it was issued, Lee Nichols was able to report that Negroes and whites, from all parts of the country were not just training and fighting together, but were also eating at the same tables, sleeping in the same quarters, drinking beer together, going to church and the movies together.

BEYOND THE CALL OF DUTY

A typical illustration of the process has been provided by Brigadier General Frank McConnell who had been assigned, shortly after the integregation edict, to command a major training base in South Carolina. Customarily, as the recruits poured in, the Negroes were separated from the whites and established in separate organizations. General McConnell issued an order that the next 55 draftees who arrived would comprise a platoon, regardless of their color, and that this procedure would be followed with all subsequent arrivals.

The order was issued verbally and "that," he said "was the end of segregation in Fort Jackson." There were no interracial incidents then or thereafter.

"I would see recruits, Negro and white, walking down the street, all buddying together," said the General. "The attitude of the Southern soldiers was that this was the Army way; they accepted it the same way they accepted getting booted out of bed at 5:30 in the morning."

This was the Army way. This was the new social situation, the new set of practices which surrrounded the white soldier who had been accustomed to quite another way of life. His new community accepted it, he accepted it. There were no incidents of any consequence. Scattered grumbling that was heard when the policy was announced, but before it was implemented, disappeared when integration actually took place. Apprehension had been unwarranted. A Congressional committee reported that "the almost total absence of opposition that had been anticipated in the enlisted men is a contributing factor in the success of this policy. The men were more ready for equality of treatment than the officer corps had realized." Commanders reported that interracial incidents had *lessened* under the policy of integration, as a result of the lessening of tensions.

The servicemen did not necessarily retain these specific attitudes or behavior patterns when they returned to their home towns: The situational factors had shifted back again. In many cases, their *general* attitudes may have altered somewhat, at least temporarily, because of their total-living experiences in integration; and the aspiration levels of the Negro servicemen may also have been raised as a result. But they settled back without difficulty in the segregated patterns of their home communities. More definitively, the practices of the armed forces had a direct impact on certain practices in the non-military community. Negro and white soldiers sat side by side on a city bus in Columbia, South Carolina, where such mingling was actually prohibited by law. Restaurants near military posts decided to admit Negroes along with white soldiers, partly because white and Negro soldiers began to accompany each other in town. In Amarillo, Texas, the USO club was opened to Negro airmen for the first time. Amarillo University began to admit Negroes to its extension classes, George L. P. Weaver, formerly of the CIO, told Lee Nichols that the elimination of segregation in the armed forces opened new job opportunities for Negroes with government contractors; indeed in the integrated military, Negro servicemen were often able to learn vocational skills which they otherwise could have had no opportunity to learn.

At the very least, within the relatively uncomplicated society bounded by the armed forces, the *social problem* of prejudice had been virtually eliminated by the outlawing of prejudiced practices. Equality of opportunity is in effect. The aspirations of the non-whites within the military setting are being met. Interracial "incidents" and tensions have been reduced. This is not really being enforced at bayonet point, but has come to be accepted by servicemen. In terms of attitudes, they have, by and large, responded "beyond the call of duty," in their fraternization with fellow-servicemen of another race. Not only has behavior changed, which is the crux of the social problem, but behavior has patently shaped attitudes.

THE SITUATION OR THE PERSONALITY

Perhaps then the most effective and workable approach to understanding the phenomenon of prejudice is through an investigation of the kinds of *social situations* which give rise to and sustain prejudiced behavior and attitudes. This is a sharply different approach from that which would investigate what kinds of *people* are prone to prejudice.

This is not to underestimate the special validity of an approach to prejudice from the vantage point of personality and personality differences. There are good reasons for making such a psychological approach. Prejudice serves an emotional function for many people. It helps them to shift blame from themselves to others, to rationalize their aggressions, or otherwise provides an outlet for their special emotional needs. Some people with special emotional needs have a special susceptibility to prejudice. In attempting to understand or remedy the particular virulence or persistence of a given individual's prejudice, it is often necessary to understand his psychological history.

One white factory worker got along very well with his co-worker who happened to be Negro. They were friendly, ate their lunches together, worked together harmoniously. Suddenly the white worker began to have severe marital troubles and seemed headed towards a divorce. He began to make slurring references to the Negro's race and they finally had to be separated. Another man, bitter because he was making no progress in his business firm, blamed the "Jews" in top management and became vocally anti-Semitic, although it turned out that there weren't any Jews in the management of the firm. One study of veterans found that those who were generally frustrated and felt that they had been subject to "bad breaks" in the service were more often prejudiced than those who felt they had experienced "good breaks" in the service. There is evidence that many of those who stigmatize the Negro as hypersexual are indeed guilt-ridden by their own sexuality, and are attempting to rid themselves of that guilt by projecting it onto the Negro.

The body of psychological knowledge which throws light on these reactions is extremely helpful in explaining individual differences and in helping to treat individual problems. Since certain emotional needs are universal, in one degree or another, this knowledge even helps to explain the special "attractiveness" that prejudice seems to have for human beings in general.

But it does not explain the specific *social problem* of prejudice with which our society is currently burdened. Presumably the factory worker who was having trouble with his wife would have found *some* scapegoat, even if there were no Negro available. It might have been the thinnest man in the factory, or the fattest, or the one with red hair, or perhaps just the one with whom he was most incompatible. The need to blame other people instead of oneself; irrelevantly to work out on other people one's guilt or aggressiveness or fear is an unhealthy condition in itself. It is a problem in mental health. Those who have this problem are undoubtedly more susceptible to prejudice and to other social aberrations than those who do not have such a problem. But this condition itself does not create the specific social evils attending prejudice as described earlier. It is only when these problems are displaced on groups and help establish a deep-going pattern of denying equal opportunity to specific groups that the social problem of prejudice emerges. In short, the factory worker's psychological reaction does not create the social problem of prejudice, it merely operates within the social framework of a pattern of prejudice which already exists.

Furthermore, the psychological approach, as valuable as it is, does not explain the preponderance of people who engage in prejudiced behavior, but do *not* have special emotional problems. It does not explain the widespread pattern of prejudice. It does not explain why prejudice is more intense in one place and time than in another.

THE LESSONS OF SOCIAL SITUATIONS

These aspects of the social problem of prejudice are explainable only in terms of our *learning* prejudice much as we learn our other basic patterns of social behavior. But people do not typically learn their social values and social behavior in the same way that they learn the arithmetic table. It is not a matter of formal training or mere intellectual acceptance. A child may "learn" the social precept that it is wrong to steal, but may steal nonetheless. He has effectively learned the social value of honesty only to the extent that he has "internalized" that value; i.e., to the extent that this social value has become a natural and unthinking part of his behavior. It is not that he weighs consequences, but that it would "go against his grain" to steal.

This is not the kind of learning which basically is effected in the classroom, or even at the mother's knee. It is shaped fundamentally not by lecture or exhortation, but, in a kind of "creeping socialization," by the kinds of social situations in which people live, and, especially, in which they grow up.

It then becomes necessary to define more precisely the nature of "social situation" as it applies to prejudice; and to discover the kinds of social situations which give rise to and sustain prejudice.

The Prejudiced Community

The pattern of community practices is the fountainhead of prejudice: of prejudiced behavior and of prejudiced attitudes.

The growing child learns his social behavior primarily by following the modes and models of behavior around him. Indeed, he has little choice. He learns how to behave towards people of other racial and religious groups by seeing how other people behave, and by automatically participating in the behavior patterns which already exist.

Consider the extreme but not atypical case of a community where the Negro population has been traditionally subordinate on every level. The Negro with whom the young child comes into contact is a domestic in his home; or an elevator operator or janitor or a worker in some other menial capacity. The Negroes he knows are not as well educated as the white people he knows, nor as well dressed, nor as well housed. The white people in his community do not socialize with Negroes, nor share the same public accommodations with them. No Negroes sit down at the same dinner table with him or with the people he knows; Negroes are not customers in the restaurants or hotels to which he is taken. Negroes are addressed by their first name, but always address the white people as "Mr." or "Mrs." They do not go to the same school as white children. They sit in separate sections of the bus. They use different rest rooms in the bus stations. If there is a tight fit on the sidewalk, it is the Negro pedestrian who gives way.

These are the social situations, i.e., the overt sets of relationships with which the child is surrounded. He does not have to be *told* that Negroes are "inferior," or what his relationships to them are supposed to be. These are apparent. Even more important, he is part of the white community and necessarily he *behaves* within the framework of these existing relationships. It is not just that his parents use a different rest room than do the Negroes. *He* uses a different rest room than the Negroes. *He* sits in the white section of the bus. *He* behaves towards them as social inferiors, and naturally comes to accept them as social inferiors. It isn't necessary to inculcate in him explicit attitudes about the social inferiority of Negroes. More likely, it is necessary for him to develop attitudes that do not conflict with his behavior.

Negroes conform to the prevailing patterns in such a community not only because they must, but also in part because they have accepted the values of the dominant community, and for the same reasons. They have been part of the same behavior patterns.

This process takes place at an early age. In one nursery school study, when pre-school Negro children were given a white and Negro doll to play with, they almost uniformly preferred the white doll.

SCHOOLS FOR PREJUDICE

There is a tendency to believe that these kinds of prejudicial behavior patterns are to be found preponderantly in the deep South. It is often startling to those in the northern and western parts of the country to find, by the most casual self-survey, the extent to which their own communities are "schools for prejudice" by dint of similar ongoing situations.

In the North and West, Negroes and whites typically live in different neighborhoods. That these Negro neighborhoods are usually inferior to the white is a fact readily apparent to the young observer. The proportion of substandard housing occupied by Negroes in 1952, according to U. S. Census standards, was six times as great as that occupied by whites. This was a uniform condition around the country. Nor is residential separatism restricted to the racial level. The Anti-Defamation League found, in a 1959 survey, that housing segregation on a religious basis was becoming more prevalent than was thought to be the case. For example, it found that a number of residential communities in the Chicago area were almost completely closed to Jews, and others had "large areas where Jews are barred."

Negroes typically work in lower-status jobs in communities throughout the nation. An index of this comparative status is the fact that the average earnings of the Negro worker is little more than half that of the white worker. This is partly the result of the history of educational and economic disadvantage which is the heritage of the Negro. But it is to a large extent the result of current prejudice. Where surveys have been made of job orders by employers in the North and West, in communities as widely separated as Los Angeles and Chicago, it has been found that at least 75 per cent of the job orders for white collar workers specify "white only." At least 25 per cent of these job orders specify "Christian only." (In 1959, the State of California took steps to remedy this situation with the passage of a ·Fair Employment Practices Act.)

It has been estimated that about one-quarter of the Negro school children *outside* the South go to schools that are in fact substantially all-Negro, and about half go to schools where there is only token mixing. This is largely a result of segregated housing patterns.

John P. Dean supervised a study of 248 cities, ranging in population from 10 thousand to 500 thousand, to determine the extent to which American Jews were thoroughly integrated. Three tests were used: admission to Junior League; admission to country clubs and city clubs; admission to exclusive residential areas. In one-third of the cities, Jews are denied admission to all three. In only 20 out of the 248 cities are some Jews accepted in all three, and these 20 are smaller cities. In more than half of the 50 largest cities in the study, Jews are denied admission to all three categories; and in only one are they admitted to all three.

These behavior patterns are not only the substance of prejudice as a social problem; they are also the breeding conditions of prejudice. In a very real sense, prejudiced behavior reproduces itself; carries within it its own seeds of continuity. In the same sense, prejudice is a dramatic example of the "self-fulfilling prophecy." The prejudiced image of a Negro as a constitutionally menial worker is sustained by the prejudiced behavior which in fact freezes him as a menial worker.

THE PROJECTION OF PREJUDICE

The learning of prejudice is a natural result of actual participation in patterns of prejudiced behavior; or of first-hand observation of the patterns of prejudiced behavior in the community; but it may also result from *vicarious* participation, or *second-hand* observation of the patterns of prejudice behavior. A society provides many "cues" for social behavior, e.g.: "white" and "colored" signs above public drinking fountains; or classified ads in the newspapers which read "gentile only"; or house-for-sale signs which read "white only" or "restricted."

In these several ways, then, it is on the level of actual behavior situations that the normal reproduction of prejudice is effected. It is within the framework of these behavior situations that individual differences, except perhaps the most pathological, operate. It is on the base of these behavior situations that the behavior-attitude spiral of prejudice builds. Attitudes and explicit ideologies are most firmly constructed on the foundation of these existing social situations.

Indeed, the attitudes which must develop to accompany human behavior are *implied* in this behavior and it is in this way that such attitudes are primarily learned rather than by direct instruction. By the time a child is told for the first time that "Negroes are inferior," he is already convinced of it. On the other hand, by the time he is told for the first time that "Negroes are *not* inferior" it is already often too late. He will resist the idea. Or, if he is finally intellectually convinced of the fact that Negroes are not inferior, he may evade the consequences. He may find some other reason for behaving towards the Negroes *as though* they were inferior. It is axiomatic in all learning situations that rhetorical exhortations have little chance of success when they are in battle against actual behavior patterns. For example, a child will not tend to be honest because his father tells him to be, if the same father is constantly engaged in dishonest practice himself.

Studies of the development of prejudice in children show that young children who have not yet been involved in prejudiced behavior patterns, may pick up prejudiced talk, but this doesn't affect their unprejudiced behavior. Later, after having become involved in prejudiced behavior patterns, they may pick up democratic language in the schools or elsewhere, but this doesn't affect their prejudiced behavior. By the age of 15, Gordon Allport points out, "considerable skill is shown in imitating the adult pattern" [2].

They are now able to rationalize their prejudiced behavior whenever necessary and resort to the prejudiced ideologies which do not precede but follow prejudiced behavior patterns.

In brief, the pattern of *community practices* serves as the primary source of prejudice in behavior and attitude. This does not mean that we are merely back on the causative merry-go-round, where behavior chases attitude and attitude chases behavior in a dismally unending circle. "Community practices" connotes more than just the sum total of individual behavior at any given time. It means customary collective behavior. It means collective habits which tend to perpetuate themselves with their own momentum, such as the collective habit of smoking tobacco or drinking coffee.

Similarly, prejudiced community practices typically reproduce themselves by force of *custom*. All other things being equal, these practices are passed automatically from one generation to the next. John Dollard, after studying traditional patterns of prejudice in a Southern town, wrote:

> The master defense against accurate social perception . . . is always . . . the tremendous conviction of rightness about any behavior form which exists. What is done is de facto right and is justified by the consideration that it has not been invented by current culture bearers but comes to them through sacred tradition.

THE PERSISTENCE OF PREJUDICE

The sheer power of custom re-creates prejudiced community practices— which in turn, typically, breeds individual practices of prejudice, and, then, individual attitudes of prejudice. As a matter of fact, it is possible for prejudiced custom to persist without building up *any* corresponding attitudes.

For example, it has become commonplace for investigators of prejudiced employment practices to find the following kind of situation:

A personnel officer in a large firm tells a Jewish applicant, in effect, that he is sorry but the firm does not hire Jews as salesmen. A complaint is brought to the head of the firm, who expresses genuine astonishment. "What difference does it make?" he asks. "A good salesman is a good salesman." A visit is then made to the personnel officer who himself expresses genuine astonishment. No Jews had ever been hired by that firm, and he had just assumed that it was policy.

The department stores of a city with a fairly large Negro population had never hired a Negro clerk. As the store owners were approached on this situation, one by one, they indicated that they really had no objection to employing Negroes, and really hadn't given the matter much thought. It just "hasn't been done." One department store departed from the custom and hired Negro clerks; the others followed cheerfully and without incident.

These customary community practices, with or without corresponding attitudes, are the "frame of reference," the *situational* key to the prevention of and altering of the widespread phenomenon of prejudiced behavior and prejudiced attitudes. This pattern of community practices is the basic remedial target, rather than emotional maladjustment, or any given set of prejudiced attitudes. When this pattern of community practice changes—whether by law, direct action or otherwise; whether willingly or reluctantly—the prevailing pattern of community attitudes will be likely to change accordingly. Laws prohibiting the sale of liquor in the United States have dramatically failed to change attitudes about liquor; but these laws have failed to change community practices in the first place. There is impressive indication however, that in the area of social relationships, and specifically in the area of intergroup relationships, community practices *can* be changed prior to corresponding attitudinal changes, and will then serve to effect such attitudinal changes.

References

1. ALLPORT, GORDON W. "Attitudes." In O. Murchison, ed., *A Handbook of Social Psychology*. Worcester: Clark University Press, 1935, p. 798.
2. ALLPORT, GORDON W. *The Nature of Prejudice*. Cambridge: Addison-Wesley, 1954, p. 310.

Poverty, Social Disintegration and Personality

MORTON BEISER

The most commonly advocated way of combating poverty is to pour more and more money into "depressed areas." But such haphazard spending, this author argues, is doomed to failure. Again, the problem has to be understood.

In the first part of this article, Morton Beiser draws from traditional vocational psychology and from the newer ego-analytic writings of Erik Erikson (see Marcia's article) in an attempt to understand what being poor really does to the person and to discover how this knowledge can be used to help resolve the problem. He is interested not just in the raw facts but in molding the facts into a conceptual framework to guide and organize thinking, research, and action. According to Beiser's model, personality functioning is divided into three areas: personality traits, skills (adaptive behaviors), and psychological well-being. He draws together the results of different studies as they apply to all three areas, but pays special attention to the poor person's psychological well-being as defined by Erikson's eight stages. In the second part of the article, Beiser discusses the experience of a group of poor people who progressed from a state of social disintegration into a cohesive social unit. In this particular community, the key element of intervention was a program designed to facilitate group activity. From this small start the people learned practical problem-solving skills previously foreign to them, and apparently from the exercise of those skills, seemed to shed some undesirable

SOURCE: From *Journal of Social Issues* 21 (1):56–78. Copyright © 1965 by the Society for the Psychological Study of Social Issues, a division of the American Psychological Association. Reprinted by permission.

Note: The work upon which this article is based has been conducted as part of the Cornell Program in Social Psychiatry, directed by Alexander H. Leighton, M.D., and has been supported through funds provided by the National Institute of Mental Health, the Milbank Memorial Fund, the Carnegie Corporation of New York, and the Dominion Provincial Mental Health Grants of Canada. The foundations are not, of course, the authors, owners, publishers or proprietors of this report and are not to be understood as approving, by virtue of their grants, any of the statements made or views expressed therein.

The author is grateful to A. H. Leighton, D. C. Leighton and I. T. Stone, members of the Cornell Program in Social Psychiatry who provided access to much of the field material and original research data upon which this article is based. A. H. Leighton's theoretical contributions and suggestions have been particularly helpful.

personality traits and to make progress in terms of their own psychological well-being. Thus social behavior influenced personal state of mind, and understanding the specifics of a community's problem led to an efficient and effective resolution of that problem.

Introduction: Issues and Definitions

In recent years, poverty has become a subject of central concern in many fields of scientific inquiry. The consideration of this problem comes at a time when there is much enthusiasm for "multidisciplinary approaches" in the behavioral sciences.

As a reflection of this particular combination of interest and approach, we have had research teams exploring the relationship between poverty and such individual matters as psychopathology [18, 20, 23, 26, 29, 33], life style [9, 12], and patterns of family life [5, 22]. There have also been workers who focus upon the relationship between individual functioning and perpetuation of the social condition [19].

While much of value has been accomplished, one must confess to a nagging feeling of dissatisfaction. The information remains at many different levels of abstraction and is couched in many different guises. Correlations have been demonstrated but there have been relatively few attempts to go beyond correlation, to a demonstration of the process through which social factors on the one hand and personality variables on the other are related.

A clinical psychiatrist or psychologist confronted with the information available must feel a certain dismay. Clearly his chances of helping to alleviate human misery among the poor with the techniques he knows are severely limited [18, 29]. The rallying cry for the development of new techniques has been heard. However, where in this confusing welter of information are the action implications to be found and how are implications to be translated into procedures?

Some of the confusion results from difficulties with language. A more fundamental problem, however, has been the failure to experiment with new conceptual models. Allied with the need for this is the need to adapt old conceptual models to the new material available, and to the needs of investigators from different scientific disciplines who are attempting to communicate with one another.

In this paper, an attempt will be made to discuss the impact of poverty on the individual, using some concepts about personality development and functioning as organizing frames of reference.

This will be done in order to help pull together, in a meaningful way, reports in the literature, originating from different areas of scientific discourse. Additional material will be presented which has arisen as a result of the research efforts of a multidisciplinary team of behavioral scientists who belong to the Cornell Program in Social Psychiatry. Implications for programs which attempt to provide therapeutic services will then be discussed.

Poverty and Social Disintegration form a part of the title of this paper and together they help to define the major *social* variable with which we are concerned. Clearly, there are different ways of being poor; the poverty of a university student is not the same as the poverty of an inhabitant of a rural slum. The concern in this paper is with the individual who lives with those conditions which Leighton has called "poverty in the context of social disintegration" [20, 23, 24, 26]. The characteristics and life style which Leighton describes resemble those which Oscar Lewis has collected under the rubric of "the culture of poverty," and encompasses that group whom S. M. Miller has called "the unstable poor." Subsequent references to this group of the poor will be to "the disintegrated poor" and, for variety, to the culture of poverty.

Both terms highlight the concept of a pervasive set of life conditions which include, besides material deprivations, unstable social conditions, lack of patterns of leadership and followership, a weak and fragmented network of communication, lack of a sense of community and a superabundance of hostility both directed at those outside the culture and expressed among the members of the culture themselves.

The other major variable to be considered is the individual.

The description of a "Modal type" is in many respects antithetical to the ethos of psychology and psychological medicine, which stress the uniqueness of the individual. However, certain aspects of personality functioning among the disintegrated poor emerge with sufficient clarity and frequency that they demand attention. For the purpose of discussion, these may be classed as (1) personality traits; (2) level of skills; and (3) the state of psychological well-being.

TRAITS

Several different authors, studying different groups of the disintegrated poor have described characteristic personality traits. These descriptions are remarkable in that they are so similar. The trait described include a lack of future orientation, an inability to defer gratification, apathy and suspiciousness [24, 27, 33]. These characteristics probably serve to perpetuate the culture. The poor individual suffers because there are relatively few resources available to him. In addition, however, he frequently fails to make use of those resources which are available to him because of his attitudes.

SKILLS

During the process of socialization, an individual must acquire an armamentarium of skills, the use of which will enable him to function within the larger culture's technology. Depending upon circumstances, these necessary skills may embrace anything from canoe-building to literacy. If he fails to acquire such skills, he will probably be unable to partake in the consumption of goods and services available to those who are better endowed. Individuals living in conditions of social disintegration characteristically fail to develop these abilities.

The definition of skills can be expanded to include even more basic aspects of personality functioning such as perception, cognition and the use of language. Accumulating evidence suggests that the poor suffer deficits in these areas as well [29].

Between these two levels of skills, there exists an intermediate body which might be collectively termed "social skills." Their importance has largely been neglected. The ability to know where to go for appropriate help in a situation seems mundane enough, but its lack may be paralyzing for the individual.

A rather broad repertoire of skills is called for in complex social situations. These include the recognition of nuances in behavior, the ability to assess another's motivations accurately and the discrimination of affects both in one's self and in other people. There is some evidence that the disintegrated poor tend to see others in block terms and lack such discriminatory facilities [33, 34].

PSYCHOLOGICAL WELL-BEING

The disintegrated poor suffer from a deficit in skills, and recent studies indicate that their difficulties are further complicated by a plethora of symptoms— peptic ulcer, eczema and other psychophysiological reactions; palpitations, sleeplessness, apprehensivness and depression, the hallmarks of psychoneurosis; alcoholism and other conditions generally labelled sociopathic [32, 33].

This is, of course, a partial listing of what falls under the general heading of psychopathology, the traditional concern of psychiatry.

Within the field of psychiatry, there is no unified body of theory accounting for the genesis of psychopathology which has found universal acceptance. However, most of the "dynamic" interpretations are reducible to some common elements.

The maintenance of a relative psychological equilibrium is felt to depend in part on the control of intrapsychic conflict, for which purpose a system of defenses is operative. There is also a constant, dynamic interaction between the intrapsychic state and adaption to external reality.

Psychopathology is posited to occur when there is a breakdown in this system, either as a result of changes within the individual or in the reality he faces. The technique of psychotherapy is grounded in such a model.

The disintegrated poor harbor the majority of the community's psychopathology. The attempts of community care-givers, including psychiatrists, psychologists, and social workers, to relieve this situation have been discouraging [18, 29].

It is evident that a revision in thinking about psychopathology is called for. The helping professions cannot continue to turn their attention only to the neurotic whose conflicts and symptoms interfere with the ability to learn new tasks, to function in a family setting or to work satisfactorily. Experience with disadvantaged groups highlights the importance of recognizing the possibility of a reverse order of cause and effect as well.[1] A deficit in skills may have direct implications for the development of mental illness [6, 7], and may in itself constitute the point of attack in attempting to alleviate such distress. This point will be discussed in greater detail later.

The demonstration of correlations between the condition of poverty in the context of social disintegration and poor psychological health has been an important advance in our knowledge.

If the findings are left at this stage, however, little of benefit can result. With a knowledge merely that poverty is bad for people the way is open only for breast-beating and pious platitudes about doing *something* to alleviate the condition.

Without a model of *how* poverty and social disintegration can be harmful, it would seem virtually impossible to plan effective programs to reverse such effects. The disadvantaged poor do not seem to need more clinics and more therapists. There is, however, a need for the development of new techniques with a firm basis in knowledge about how the difficulties of individual personalities may in part be a product of the social conditions with which we are concerned.

Part of this paper will be concerned with the study of individual development within the culture of poverty. This provides an avenue by which the patterning of relationships between poverty, social disintegration and the individual can be studied. For such a task, the model of personality development chosen must be sufficiently broad that it encompasses biological determinants while at the same time providing the opportunity to assess the modifying impact of social forces.

Erik Erikson has discussed personality development in a manner which fulfills these criteria and which is adaptable for our specific purpose.

Briefly, a well integrated personality (in Erikson's terms Ego Integrity) is one which contains the following components acquired as the result of a more or less orderly unfolding of developmental sequences: (1) the sense of *basic trust* (others have called it the sense of security [8]) which develops from early experiences of being loved and results in a basic conviction of self-worth; (2) the sense of autonomy which results from satisfying early experiences with self mastery; (3) the capacity for initiative. This is a pervasive and rewarding sense of being able to initiate and carry through actions, even competitive ones, without guilt and fear; (4) the feeling of *industry* and the inner feeling

1 Readers familiar with the psychiatric literature will recognize that this line of thinking is based upon the body of theory loosely called "ego psychology." What has been described as the traditional concern of psychiatry roughly parallels the concepts of "defensive" and "synthetic" ego functions. The "skills" described parallel the "autonomous" ego functions described by Hartman. Readers who may be interested in pursuing this topic in greater depth are referred to the works of Beres, the Cummings, Hartman, and Numberg cited in the bibliography. D. Rapoport has also made significant theoretical contributions.

of reward which comes from partaking successfully in the economy and technology of the larger society; (5) the sense of *identity* or consistency which results from a harmonious blending of roles and value systems acquired through membership in various groups, such as the family and the peer group; (6) the ability to form a genuine love relationship, to experience intimacy; (7) the sense of *generativity*, or satisfaction which arises from guiding the next generation and, allied with this, from having pursued one's special interests during adulthood; and (8) the feeling of *integrity*, the satisfaction with one's life as it has been lived.

These are the constituents of a well-integrated personality. According to Erikson, they arise in part from emerging biological and in part from socio-cultural demands. The developing personality passes through a series of "epigenetic crises" and the resolution of each of these is essential for continuing development and integration. Erikson gives these epigenetic crises the rather poetic title "The Eight Ages of Man."

Within the culture of poverty, the chances of such satisfactory resolution of the epigenetic crises are limited. The following discussion will illustrate this point, which is not only of theoretical interest but also suggests certain action implications.[2, 3]

BASIC TRUST VERSUS BASIC MISTRUST

Erikson does not mean to suggest by this title that the infant forms sophisticated notions about trust, but rather that he develops some rudimentary sense that his environment is dependable and relatively consistent.

The achievement of a sense of belongingness, of familiarity and inner goodness depends heavily upon early human relationships, particularly with the mother. A certain continuity and sameness of experience must be provided in order to enhance a primitive sense of identity.

Life in disintegrated communities is characterized by evanescent human relationships. This finds poignant illustration in the life stories of Lewis' *Children of Sanchez* and is reflected in some available "hard data" as well. For instance, in Stirling County, disintegrated and well-integrated communities were studied. In the disintegrated communities, 30 per cent of the homes were psychologically broken and an additional 18 per cent physically broken. Figures from two well-integrated communities, one English-Protestant and the other French-Catholic were obtained. In the former, 16 per cent were

2 Many of the illustrations in this discussion are drawn from the work of the Cornell group in Stirling County. This is a rural county in a Canadian maritime province which has been under study for many years. A great deal of the work has consisted of comparisons between "integrated" and "disintegrated" communities in the county. Findings and hypotheses with relevance for psychiatry as well as the social sciences have emerged, and have been more extensively reported elsewhere [5, 20, 23, 24, 26].

3 The following presentation owes a debt to the work and influence of Bingham Dai as well as to Erikson.

psychologically broken and 22 per cent physically broken; in the latter only 5 per cent and 11 per cent respectively.

The infant born into a disintegrated community is faced with circumstances which militate against the successful resolution of his first developmental task. In place of continuity and sameness, he experiences instability and disruption of the environment. Frequently, this is caused by physical illness or death. A high proportion of consensual and common law marital arrangements as well as other unsuitable arrangements, such as children being raised by their grand-parents while their parents live elsewhere, contribute to the generally unre-liable atmosphere.

A former patient who was raised in a rural slum has given the author per-mission to reprint these moving excerpts from her autobiography.

> My mother died when I was six months of age and my aunt took me and kept me. My aunt died when I was six years of age, and my uncle died when I was seven years of age.
>
> . . . .
>
> I was just shifted around from place to place. After no one in the family wanted me, I was put in the county home at the age of nine years old.
>
> . . . .
>
> After a cousin here in —— found out that I could do housework and take care of myself, she came and got me.
>
> . . . .
>
> Before I came to —— I had one week trial to be adopted by a minister and his wife and it did not work. The minister and his wife were caught feeding me on the back porch in a pan in the winter time. I had to sleep behind a table in a back room. Now I have not one in the world except the Lord, my friends and myself. (Anon)

In reality, this unfortunate woman had no true "friends." Whenever there was a chance of forming an intimate relationship with someone, she would sabotage this by going on drinking sprees, making excessive demands, or initiating other such distancing maneuvers. The interest of a fellow human being aroused suspiciousness and the fear that she would be exploited.

The apathy, the suspiciousness and the self-disparagement of the disinte-grated poor have often been described. With such histories as this patient's in hand, it does not seem difficult to trace the genesis of such characteristics.

Other authors have commented on a lack of future orientation and an inability to defer gratification. These characteristics probably result, at least in part, from a lack of positive opportunities at a critical time. The developing personality has no chance to establish a sense of continuity between past and present, a sense which is so dependent upon the presence of enduring human relationships.

Another characteristic of the adult personalities is intolerance for ambiguity and for change. A striking example of this comes from a field worker in the Stirling County Study, who interviewed respondents to determine their reactions to an agricultural development project. Interviews with the community members made it clear that no one really understood the nature of the project and all had refused to attend the meetings organized to discuss this. Instead, they had indulged in speculation and rumor, most of it with a paranoid flavor and based on the premise that the "haves" were attempting to take away something from the "have nots."

Recent experimental work has demonstrated that certain animals, deprived of significant positive experiences at a crucial time, find it difficult to assimilate new experience and show responses which look like apathetic withdrawal or fearful aggressiveness if forcibly exposed [11]. Other such ethological studies substantiate a relationship between social ineptness and early deprivations [15, 16]. The parallel tendency of the people in Stirling County to lapse into apathy or sullenness in a novel situation is striking. It suggests that there is perhaps a precursor to those skills we have already considered. It is unclear what this may be, but certainly one of the components seems to be the ability to discriminate cues, and this may be dependent on critical experience.

One is always tempted to account for characteristics such as those described, by the simplest explanation. It seems to be "common sense" that a group of low-paid and irregularly employed people would think of the world as being completely unpredictable. However, it has been reported that people who have had a stable past are more apt to manage during unexpected situations such as economic depression on unemployment than those who have experienced considerable prior deprivation. There is a difference in attitudes and coping abilities, dependent in part upon the early environment [28].

The utility of Erikson's developmental scheme becomes apparent in helping to explain such observations. It is not a situation alone but a combination of past experience, the perception of a situation and the situation itself which determines the outcome.

AUTONOMY VERSUS SHAME AND DOUBT

The development of the infant's locomotor apparatus ushers in a stage of obstinacy and rebelliousness. A battle is waged between the child, who senses new capacities in his body and in his social dealings, and the frustrating forces in his environment.

During this period, the attitude of the extra-familial culture impinges forcibly upon the child. The form in which his parents choose to discipline and the issues over which they discipline him, reflect the attitude of the larger culture towards the matter of self-control versus the motoric expression of impulses. The child's experiences during this stage are a powerful determinant of his "self-control" or lack of it, as an adult.

Patterns of control by others seem to vary predictably with other social variables. In Stirling County, parental disciplinary techniques in integrated and disintegrated communities were compared. It was found that parents in the disintegrated areas were more inconsistent, used less reasoning and verbalization, relied less on examples of good behavior, and were less apt to praise good behavior. On the other hand, ridicule was used extensively by the disintegrated poor.

Of the use of ridicule, or shaming, Erikson has this to say:

> . . . shaming exploits an increasing sense of being small, which can develop only as the child stands up and as his awareness permits him to note the relative measures of size and power.

The sense of powerlessness among the poor often reflects an only too realistic appraisal of their condition. However, there are indications that this is also a "set" which may have its antecedents in early development. The attitude which we might label the "what good will it do?" stance, no matter what the "it" happens to be, is familiar to those who attempt to work with groups of the disintegrated poor. This stance indicates a deep-rooted feeling of helplessness and smallness in the face of an omnipotent "they." Because of such attitudes, organizers found it virtually impossible to form a union of mill workers in one of Stirling's disintegrated areas, in spite of the fact that the men worked under truly deplorable conditions.

Duvall has added to our knowledge of differences in the patterns of punishment according to social factors. In describing the working class parent (a broader group than the one under consideration, but inclusive of it), she points out the tendency to make his child conform to externally imposed standards. The middle class parent on the other hand stresses internal dynamics, motivation and self control [22]. Perhaps conscience by and large is a middle class notion.

Many reasons for the relative failure of psychotherapy with patients from economically deprived groups have been advanced. Perhaps an additional one lies in the inappropriateness of the model. Traditional psychotherapy stresses a relationship based on the parent-child model, with the "parent" in this case once again stressing motivation and self control, primarily by verbal means. This relationship is consistent with the experience of a middle class patient but strange to the patient who has grown up in the culture of poverty.

INITIATIVE VERSUS GUILT

This stage is ushered in at about age three and includes the "oedipal period" of classical psychoanalysis. The child, during this time, "grows together" and adds new dimensions to his personality.

> Initiative adds to autonomy the quality of undertaking, planning and "attacking" a task for the sake of being active and on the move, where before self-will, more often than not, inspired acts of defiance or, at any rate, protested independence. [Erikson, p. 255.]

Haggstrom, in a significant paper, points up the *powerlessness* of the poor. In his sense, this powerlessness goes beyond our consideration of lack of autonomy under Stage II. Haggstrom is describing a situation of enforced dependency with little scope to initiate or carry through action. Not only is there a failure to instill the confidence, hope and skills for future action during childhood socialization but there are no social positions provided within which the adult disintegrated poor may act.

There are differential consequences of this. Because of the greater expectation for males to be sources of power in our culture, the consequences of powerlessness for lower class men is usually greater than that for women.

There are many homes which are broken and in which the father is physically absent. Even when present, however, burdened as he is with a *sense* of impotence and faced daily with his *real* powerlessness in the society at large, he fails to provide an adequate role model.

The following incident, involving youths from a disintegrated neighborhood, illustrates some important features. An anthropologist was with them acting as a participant observer.

After many days of monotonous, aimless driving from small town to small town and back again, the young men banded together to attend a dance.

> En route to the dance, the boys noticed a police officer behind us, and it was discussed who should take the rap for the liquor if we got caught— the consensus being that J. and Z. should claim it as theirs. As we continued on our way, with the policeman still behind us, the boys became quite nervous, and it was decided we ought to pull in at a filling station and let him pass. We pulled in and the policeman followed us. This further heightened the anxiety. As we sat wondering what would happen next, he spoke briefly to the attendant and then left.

The group then proceeded to the dance.

> . . . as soon as we got to the dance all the liquor was going to be taken out of the car and consumed; there would be none carried back with us in any case. At the hall, the liquor was unloaded and taken to the woods, after the distressful discovery that nobody had brought a bottle opener. Z. went over to a group standing near the hall and came back with an individual whom I had not seen before but whom the others seemed well acquainted with, who opened all the bottles for them.
>
> . . . .
>
> The beer was consumed first, the bottles being frequently passed around and chugged hurriedly, then it was time to try the "hard stuff," (the wine). There were two bottles of this, and after everyone had sampled a little of it, the pop bottles were produced and about half the contents of each was either thrown out or hurriedly drunk, then re-filled with wine. Ginger ale was held to be the best because it was "strong" and killed the taste of the wine altogether. At length this was consumed, and at Z's suggestion, it was decided that everyone was "feeling good enough to go in and have some fun" now. The remaining wine was hidden in the bushes, and we walked on up to the hall. The conversation during the brief drinking bout was concerned primarily with how the liquor and the various mixtures tasted, and frequent arguing about who had how much

of their share of the supply. As we walked to the dance, the talk was about fighting, C. saying he didn't like to fight because he wasn't good but if anyone started anything he would, and J. saying if he started anything he would knock him, but otherwise he would take his part.

Several themes are strikingly evident as we follow the progress of the group towards their destination—difficulty with authority (the police), the ritual preparation for an unchanneled release of aggression (the ceremony of beer and wine) and confusion of feeling, with aggression and hostility appearing in a situation ordinarily considered social and sexual (a dance). It is of interest that this continued throughout the evening. None of the boys actually danced with a girl; instead the emphasis was on the "fight" against a vague, generalized "other," who "might want to make trouble."

This behavior, although unintelligible and apparently meaningless at first, clearly is explicable. It represents a fusion of problems inherited from crucial phases of development, notably II and III. The inconsistent disciplinary practices previously mentioned lead to difficulty in interpersonal relationship, particularly with authority figures. When an act may bring violent retribution on one occasion and not on another, authority comes to be seen as capricious and punitive. The life style frequently becomes one of sudden, violent discharge of emotions (cf. Gans' "Action seekers"), a tendency augmented by the sense of powerlessness and frustration.

INDUSTRY VERSUS INFERIORITY

All cultures recognize the appearance of this stage and provide some systematic instruction for children in the fundamentals of technology. The child becomes progressively able to handle the utensils, tools and weapons used by adults. At the same time, he becomes involved in doing things with others, that is, what Erikson calls "a sense of the *technological ethos*" of a culture develops at this time.

If, however, a child experiences a sense of inadequacy in his own tools and skills or of his status among his tool partners, he may be discouraged from identification with them and from entering into the technology of the larger culture.

In our culture, the school system is the main agency of socialization during this period. As many authors have pointed out, the school system as it now exists, tends to emphasize the lack of skills with which the child of poverty comes and further widen the gap between him, the system within which he is expected to function and his fellows.

Deutsch has emphasized the dangers that accrue. Not only is there often too great a gap between the child's origin and the expectations of the school system but he is also allowed to see more of the products of a consumer society in school than he is accustomed to. He soon learns that these are available to everyone but him. The idea of being an outsider is thus reinforced.

Due to lack of experience, the child from such a background is deficient in verbal skills, has an inadequate concept of time and is relatively lacking in the ability to organize and discriminate the nuances of his environment.

However, the lack of achievement in the school system may be grounded upon more than these deficiencies in skills. Cleveland and Longaker have called attention to the "disparagement syndrome" which is so prevalent in the disintegrated areas in Stirling County. In order to avoid the disparagement and ridicule of his fellows, the individual may be led to an *active renunciation of his capabilities*. For example, a girl in one of these communities attempted to dress more attractively; the opinion voiced about her was, ". . . she thinks the sun rises and sets on her ass." The girl reverted to the more slovenly mode of the neighborhood.

Children also bring with them the heritage of chronic hostility and distrust with which they have grown up. They have grown up among adults who avoid each other, indulge in vituperative gossip and petty thievery and who make continued reports to the police of actual or rumored illegal activities of neighbors [33]. It is difficult to see how these children could enter easily into cooperative enterprises with peers, activities which are essential to the development of a sense of the "technological ethos" of the larger adult society.

Failure to achieve skills in school results in more than social problems, such as getting and holding jobs. It also has definite mental health implications. The individual with these deficits feels that he is different. His sense of alienation from the larger society is increased as is his sense inferiority and despair.

IDENTITY VERSUS ROLE CONFUSION

The youth at puberty experiences two great pressures, both of which seem to arise almost overnight. One of these is primarily of internal origin and results from hormonal changes; the other is primarily external and comes from a change in societal attitudes.

This phase is often marked by confusion and turmoil. There is a questioning of values, and an attempt at self-reaffirmation. By the latter phrase we mean first that the individual is engaged in reaffirming the meaning of an adopted role such as the sexual one. He is also attempting to establish some sense of continuity between his past and his future, which includes the obligation to choose an occupation.

The adolescent has been compared to an immigrant newly arrived in a strange land. He is forced at this point to question his basic assumptions about himself in relationship to his world. In doing this, he relies heavily upon a fundamental system of beliefs.

Hallowell has described the manner in which a belief system may lend stability to an individual undergoing the process of acculturation. The analogy of the adolescent and the immigrant then highlights one of the functions of puberty rites. They often serve to confirm the values inculcated during the period of childhood socialization, while at the same time adding the dimension of meaningfulness for adult life. Thus, a core system of values provides a source of stability during the potentially disruptive transformation from childhood to adulthood.

In the disintegrated areas of Stirling County, preparation for this transition is largely negative. There is no system of beliefs which proves stable in the face of the testing and scrutinizing which is characteristic of this period. Instead, a value system which reflects that of the larger society is preached by adults, but, upon examination, is found to be lacking in the sense of commitment necessary to make it useful.

The people are nominally religious but church attendance is sparse. Honesty is held to be a virtue but children are often exposed to discussions about their parents' adventures involving petty thievery. Sexual promiscuity is openly discussed and initiation to it comes at an early age, although a show of puritanism is also attempted.

Identification with adults who act as models either because of real or idealized traits is important during this period, but difficult in the disintegrated communities. Within the net of general disparagement, it would be difficult indeed to find a model to emulate who had escaped the pejoratives and gossip of the neighborhood.

It is of interest that the youths in these communities do follow the common pattern of forming age groups. These groups probably do not represent an adolescent subculture with norms and regulating functions such as has been found elsewhere. The groups in the disintegrated areas lack definite patterns of leadership and followership and there seems to be little commitment to them. According to the respondents interviewed, such groups form "just for fun" and are apt to be shortlived. If there are any norms and values, these seem to center about a general conviction of worthlessness. When asked to identify themselves, one such group said, ". . . we're the no-goods from M." Another adolescent group, discussing community services said, "Any doctor who'd come here to work, couldn't be any good."

Knowledge about these peer groups and their importance remains largely impressionistic but it is a phenomenon which merits further study. When these adolescents become adults, they enter into the patterns of mutual avoidance described among their parents, and groups cease to exist. If one feels that groups have the potential to exert a beneficial effect upon malfunctioning personalities, it would seem that more attention should be paid to these spontaneously formed groups and the possibility of mobilizing them with such a goal in mind.

INTIMACY VERSUS ISOLATION

Having established his identity, the individual must now move to the next phase of development, in which he is willing to fuse this identity with another. This is a necessary ingredient for the development of mature heterosexual intimacy, or love.

The following is the way one of the residents of a disintegrated community in Stirling County described his "love affair" with the woman who became his wife:

> I met V. a year before I married her. I was peddling fish while working on the farm and I sold some fish to her people. One time there was a dance going on and V. asked me to take her there. Instead of going back home I took her to my house that night and she stayed with us for a week. After that she went back home for a day—but didn't want to stay with her folks so she came back with us and lived there for one year till I married her. She was twenty years old then. (The Interviewer asked why she didn't want to stay at home.) She didn't think they could give her what she wanted because they had a big family—lots of children.

This rather pathetic story illustrates a pervasive theme—two people who look in their marriages for the security denied them during their early years. Disappointment is almost inevitable.

The husband in our story was always a reticent individual. Since his marriage, he has become even more so. He often seems depressed and ashamed of his wife and family, but says he never communicates his feelings to his wife because she would laugh at him. His wife continues her search for love and security through a series of extra-marital affairs. The openness of her promiscuity serves to make her husband the butt of community jokes and in this way she punishes him for his failure to fulfill her needs.[4]

There is always the possibility that marriage will prove fortuitous for handicapped individuals. For the disintegrated poor, however, the choice of a mate is limited and marriages are often contracted not through a sense of intimacy and a wish for fusion, but on the basis of unrealistic hopes and expectations.

GENERATIVITY VERSUS STAGNATION

The requirements of this stage are:

1. The ability to make an adequate living.
2. The ability to assume the responsibilities of parenthood.
3. The ability to contribute to the welfare of society at large.[5]

For our purposes, consideration of this stage can be conveniently included with that of the following and final one, what Erikson has called:

EGO INTEGRITY VERSUS DESPAIR

While he confesses an inability to define this stage satisfactorily, Erikson dis-

---

[4] This case history is fictional but based upon several typical life histories.

[5] This is a paraphrase of what Dai has to say about this developmental stage. Dai has contributed a model of personality development, which at times overlaps Erikson's and is at times complementary to it. Dai's contribution evolved independently of Erikson, which makes the similarities even more striking.

cusses the characteristics of it. Important among these are a sense of emotional integration, a sense of order and meaning, and a feeling of satisfaction with life. Despair is signified by the thought that time is now too short to attempt to start another life and hence there is a pervasive fear of death.

A fictitious "life story" of a man living in a disintegrated neighborhood will illustrate some important points.[6]

Mr. X. is a fifty-five-year-old man living in a rather notorious rural slum.

He lives in a shabby shack with his second wife and four children. With little discomfiture, Mr. X. reports he has not worked for the past ten years because he suffers from an ulcer, his heart pounds when he exerts himself and he has shortness of breath. To relieve these symptoms, as well as his sleeplessness and "unsteady nerves," the family has run up a huge bill for patent medicines, which they can never hope to repay. Mr. X. is phobic of crowds and so does not attend church. Because of his phobia, he and his wife rely on their young children to do the family shopping and find themselves ever deeper in debt.

Mr. X. described his early life as fairly happy. His father was sick for twenty years from his stomach. In spite of this, he sired eight children with several different women with whom he lived in common law arrangements.

Schooling held little attraction for Mr. X., who began working on and off in the woods at age seven. "It was nice in the woods because no one bothered you there." He finally left school when he was fourteen. About ten years ago, employment began to be irregular and it was about that time he noticed pains in his stomach which were later diagnosed as a peptic ulcer.

There was a short period when he worked at "winching" but then the boats stopped coming. The once-bustling harbor in town is now largely deserted.

This history, not an unusual one for the region, illustrates how "Despair" may come about as a result of multiple interactions between psychopathology, personality traits and a lack of skills with which to participate in a changing society.

Mr. X.'s symptoms began when the limited skills he had were no longer marketable. This forced him into a dependent stance, one which is difficult for him to tolerate because of early life experiences. His resultant psychopathology intensifies his social inadequacies, so that he runs up bills he cannot pay. This, in turn, contributes to his reputation as a "bum" so that individuals and agencies who might be interested in involving him in job retraining, etc. look elsewhere for cases with "better motivation." The hypochondriacal concern with, and elaboration of, his symptoms is doubtless the attempt of a man in despair to legitimize his present status. "I can't work and I am a no-good father," he says but the reason quickly follows, ". . . it's because I've been sick all these years."

---

[6] This is, in reality, a condensation of several "typical" histories. It is "typical" without being true of any one individual known to us in Stirling County.

Discussion

The discussion to this point, as in most psychiatric presentations, has stressed the negative and the pathological. Indeed, it might seem that the noxious influences and resultant patterns described are so "deep" as to be ineradicable. It might seem that there is nothing for us to do but join the poor in "despair" over this condition. There are indications, however, that this need not be so.

SUMMARY OF THE CORNELL EXPERIENCE WITH A DISINTEGRATED COMMUNITY IN STIRLING COUNTY

In 1949, the Cornell group in Social Psychiatry selected a disintegrated community for intensive investigation. The 118 people living here suffered the effects of low and very undependable incomes. They had an unenviable reputation as workers and were "the last to be hired and the first to be fired." The educational level was nominally 4th and 5th grade but there were 8 adults who actually could neither read nor write. There was a high prevalence of broken marriages, inter-parental strife and child neglect. It did not really represent a community but a neighborhood in which there was a great deal of indifference and hostility. There were no formal organizations or groups, and church attendance, although espoused as good, was not frequent.

> The disintegrated character of the social organization was paralleled by prevailing values and sentiments . . . there were strong sentiments of self-disparagement, mistrust of each other and mistrust of outsiders, especially those in positions of authority. Work was regarded as virtueless, a necessary evil to be avoided when possible; and the people were little permeated with ideas of foresight and planning. The future was thought to be uncontrollable and most people felt that the best thing to do with a dollar was to spend it at once, for only in that way could one be assured of getting full use of it [24].

A mental health survey in 1952 revealed that, together with their lack of skills and these damaging attitudes, the people suffered a high prevalence of psychiatric symptoms such as depression, anxiety and psychosomatic complaints. The prevalence of these symptoms was much higher than in the "integrated" communities studied.[7]

The result was a vicious spiral in which the lack of skills, the sentiments and the psychopathology militated against satisfactory interactions with each other and against effective interdigitation with the larger society. Their poor performance at schools, jobs, etc. reinforced the impression of surrounding communities that this was a collection of inferior people. Rejection by the larger

[7] Prevalence figures were obtained by means of a probability sample survey of a whole county, with greater intensity of sampling in representative integrated and distintegrated communities.

society in turn reinforced the focus community members' feelings of apathy and suspiciousness and thus the self-perpetuating spiral continued in its downward direction.

It should be added that the history of the region does not lend support to a "misery seeking each other out" hypothesis nor to an explanation of this community's existence as a result of genetic inferiority. Rather, it seems that cultural isolation and a precipitous loss in the community's economic base initiated the trend towards disintegration [24, 33].

In 1962, a resurvey revealed that a change had taken place. The integration of the community, as measured by social science techniques, had changed significantly, and in an upward direction. Parallel with this change at a sociocultural level, there were changes at the level of the individual. The prevalence rate of impairing psychiatric disorders was now considerably lower. Other communities which were disintegrated at the time of original survey (1952) and remained so in 1962 showed no comparable shift in the prevalence of psychiatric disorder.

THE PROCESS OF COMMUNITY CHANGE

A more detailed survey of the process of community change has been reported [24, 33]. Some salient features should be repeated here, however.

The man in charge of adult education for the region, became interested in community development. His focus for intervention made use of real knowledge about the area and was happily selected. His program recognized the principal type of existing organization that there was, namely a loose pattern of visiting among the women in the community. Entertainment was offered (movies in the schoolhouse) which, at first, were attended in the main by the women. This proved to be sufficiently attractive that other community members began to come. Then, gradually, the development process was placed in the hands of the community. Their first task was to raise money to wire the schoolhouse in order that the movies would continue and develop into an educational program. The effort was successful. The result was an immediate and tangible reward plus the beginning of community cooperation for a public purpose.

With the same objective, namely the promotion of group activity, the local school teacher generated the consolidation of the loose organization of women around the central issue of schooling for the children. The most important outcome of this was the development of interest in having the district admitted to the consolidated school of the region. This meant transportation by daily bus for all children above sixth grade to the consolidated school in a town some miles away where the educational opportunities were considerably richer and the way clear for going on through high school. It also meant an increase in taxes for people from other communities in the school district. The taxpayers of course opposed such a move. Rarely, if ever, had the people from the disintegrated focus community appeared at district meetings where school questions were decided and therefore they had never used their potential power as voters. Now, despite continuing apathy and resistance, those in favor of admission stimulated enough of an attendance from the neighborhood to vote the measure through.

The emphasis of this development program was, and is, on the development of skills (employable skills, skills in organization, etc.). The alleviation of impairing psychiatric symptoms was a fortuitous by-product.

COMMUNITY DEVELOPMENT: MENTAL HEALTH IMPLICATIONS

Further analysis is of course necessary to determine, for example, the direct comparability of the 1952 and 1962 samples. However, based on this experience, some preliminary hypotheses and their possible implications for community mental health programs seem in order.

In recent years, there has been a developing interest in "community mental health." Under this banner, many programs have been devised and instituted.

The less imaginative of such programs have stressed the need to provide more therapists and more brick and mortar facilities. The difficulty with such approaches is that the services they seek to develop cater to those who are at least in need of help. Among poor patients, it is those who are closest to being middle class in their values and outlook who find their way to patient rosters in mental health clinics. However, there is always a large residue whom psychiatry cannot reach. For these people, we have developed a balm to assuage our hurt pride; it consists of such labels as "hard core problems" and "inadequate motivation."

Caplan's "crisis theory" approach is an example of a more imaginative approach to this problem. This calls for the delineation of crises for a population at risk and the mobilization of community care-givers around these crises. Psychiatrists act as consultants to the care-givers, who in turn impart help when it is needed and at a time when people are particularly open to outside aid. For people in disintegrated communities, crises may occur with bewildering frequency, hence the need for such services.

Caplan's approach is an ingenious variation of traditional psychiatric techniques. There is a fundamental difficulty in trying to apply it in disintegrated communities, without some further considerations.

In these areas, the people have never learned to utilize the resources of the community and the group. Even worse, they usually avoid and are suspicious of community agencies, particularly when these are introduced de novo.

A necessary preliminary to the effective use of environmental resources, and this includes mental health facilities, is community social organization. If patterns of leadership, followership and acting together in concert are not developed, individuals will remain in the confines of a cycle which includes increased risk of crisis, a lack of agencies to deal with crisis and an inability to effectively utilize even those resources which are available.

This would suggest that, before introducing mental health facilities, the level of community development should be assessed. In some instances, it may be necessary to attack the latter problem before the former can be considered.

In addition to this, the experience of the Cornell program suggests that community social organization may in itself exert a therapeutic effect.

This requires further study, but some considerations seem reasonable.

Community development fosters interaction. Interaction creates sentiments among people and these are usually solidary sentiments [6]. In view of the discussion of difficulties inherited from Stage I, it is important to point out that the type of interaction is characterized, at least in the beginning phases, by sociability without intense obligation. These types of peer relationships are often therapeutic, in a broad sense and may, indeed, be easier to tolerate than the kind of relationship implied in traditional psychotherapy which rests on a parent-child model. For the person with problems in the area of trust, peer relationships may be less threatening and more supportive than a patient-therapist one, with its subtleties of superordinate-subordinate positions and implied dependence [6]. This also suggests that peer relationships are less complex and therefore may be easier to deal with.

In addition to a new ability to receive support from group relationships, one can imagine the tremendous boost in self-esteem these people must have experienced in being able to exert some control over their own and their children's destinies, with regard to the school question. Group action made success possible in spite of opposition from the surrounding areas. There have been other reports in the literature which indicate that, when aggression can find an outlet in a socially constructive form, there is a corresponding drop in antisocial activities [31]. Thus, the problems left over from Stages II and III may find a partial solution in the fostering of group activities which promote a sense of power and initiative, and which can be harnessed in a constructive manner.

Stage IV, the age of Industry, suggests another chapter in the story of our disintegrated community. After their admission to the consolidated school system, the children from the disintegrated area were easily picked out by their manners, habits of dress, etc. Some months later, at a general assembly, the principal of the school noticed that these children seemed to be absent. Assuming that they had dropped out, he asked an assistant about them. He learned that they were still present, but now had blended so successfully with the other children that they were no longer conspicuous.

It should be noted that this was a consolidated school in a rural area and therefore the gap between the "top" and "bottom" of the social echelon was not too great. There was really a continuum represented, with the children from the focus area falling at the low end of this. Leighton points out that change is therefore possible, but it must be gradual and it must seem attainable. The children in this instance were presented with an adequate range of transitional models whom they could emulate [24].

It has become a truism that education is necessary for effective participation in a changing economy. In addition to the practical benefits of education, one should not overlook the impact which a lack of it may have on feelings of isolation and inferiority.

Programs of community development are generally aimed at improving the skills of the people involved. In our example, there was an improvement in social, political, and technological skills in the broadest sense. However, in addition there are indications of changes in attitudes and general mental health.

This demonstrates the principle that change may be beneficial for individuals, which should not surprise us—for change, if it can be assimilated, provides the individual with a new range of coping abilities and responses. An ideal is that the individual should develop a wide enough repertoire that he can cope with most situations. Once the individual has learned a wide variety of things such as reading, manipulating objects, writing and doing arithmetic, he has an armamentarium of practical, problem-solving skills that will provide him with a variety of possible solutions to conflicts.

If Mr. X. in our example had had a wider range of skills and coping responses, the economic change in the community might not have had the effect it did upon him. To the person armed with enough alternatives, such a situation would have presented a "problem," but might not have assumed the proportions of a major crisis.

MENTAL HEALTH: IMPLICATIONS FOR COMMUNITY DEVELOPMENT

Programs which promote the development of skills may in themselves be therapeutic under propitious circumstances. This, of course, has been the traditional approach of programs aimed at social development, which have stressed job retraining, school enrichment programs and so forth. A note of caution should be sounded, however. These programs have by and large neglected the crippling effects of psychiatric disorder.

Change brings with it increased stress to people who are already in distress. Experiments with groups demonstrate that people in distress turn to others in the same situation for support [30]. For a population exposed to a program of economic change for example, this would mean that the individuals should be able to use each other for support. In disintegrated communities individuals do not use each other in this manner because of long-standing attitudes towards and conflicts over trust and intimacy.

This serves to re-emphasize a point made earlier. The promotion of community social organization is important not only because it facilitates the introduction of services but because it also probably has mental health implications. If people can be helped to overcome some of their reluctance to act in concert, by the gradual promotion of nonthreatening group activities, a powerful therapeutic agent has been mobilized.

Another approach to this problem has been proposed by Leighton. He suggests that the provision of medication to people faced with the prospect of change might make it easier for the individual to explore new resources provided. Once the process of exploration has begun to take hold and the individual begins to use resources that exist both within and without, better functioning in all areas of his personality can be expected [25].

If people can be helped over the "hump" so to speak, with this form of support, they may learn a new range of practical, problem-solving skills that will provide a variety of possible solutions to conflicts.

In summary, it is important to point out that the introduction of services for individuals cannot be dictated by cliches like "more mental health facilities and more therapists" or "educational opportunities unlimited." Instead, the development of programs requires a knowledge of the community, its level of development and a firm grasp of realizable goals. It is necessary to have a knowledge of the attitudes, lack of skills and possible psychopathology which characterize the disintegrated poor and a working model for the genesis of these characteristics.

It is only against such a background that effective programs for intervention can emerge and the effects of such programs upon the individual be assessed.

References

1. BAKER, A. A.; JONES, MAXWELL; MERRY, JULIUS; and POMRYN, B. A. A community method of psychotherapy. *British Journal of Medical Psychology* 26 (1953):222–44.
2. BERES, DAVID. *Ego Deviation and the Problem of Schizophrenia*. Psychoanalytic Study of the Child, Vol. 12. New York: International Universities Press, 1956. Pp. 164–235.
3. BERNSTEIN, BASIL. Social Class, Speech Systems and Psychotherapy. In Riessman, Frank, et al., eds. *Mental Health of the Poor*. Glencoe, Ill.: Free Press of Glencoe, 1964. Pp. 194–204.
4. CAPLAN, GERALD. *Principles of Preventive Psychiatry*. New York: Basic Books, 1964.
5. CLEVELAND, E. J., and LONGAKER, W. D. Neurotic Patterns in the Family. In Leighton, Alexander H., Clausen, John A., and Wilson, Robert N. *Explorations in Social Psychiatry*. New York: Basic Books, 1957. Pp. 167–200.
6. CUMMING, JOHN, and CUMMING, ELAINE. *Ego and Milieu*. New York: Atherton Press, 1963.
7. CUMMING, JOHN. The inadequacy syndrome. *Psychiatric Quarterly*, October 1963, pp. 1–11.
8. DAI, BINGHAM, in MAVCKA, J., and VALIEN, P., eds. *Race Relations: Problems and Theory*. Chapel Hill: University of North Carolina Press, 1961.
9. DEUTSCH, MARTIN P. The Disadvantaged Child and the Learning Process. In Riessman, Frank, et al., eds. *Mental Health*, pp. 172–87.
10. ERIKSON, ERIK H. *Childhood and Society*. New York: W. W. Norton and Company, 1963.
11. FULLER, JOHN. "The K-Puppies." *Discovery*, February 1964.
12. GANS, HERBERT. Routine Seekers and Action Seekers. In Riessman, Frank, et al., eds. *Mental Health*, pp. 155–58.
13. HAGGSTROM, WARREN C. The Power of the Poor. In Riessman, Frank, et al., eds. *Mental Health*, pp. 205–26.

14. HALLOWELL, A. IRVING. Values, acculturation and mental health. *American Journal of Orthopsychiatry*, October 1950, pp. 732–43.

15. HARLOW, HARRY, and HARLOW, MARGARET K. The effect of rearing conditions on behavior. *Bull. Menninger Clinic*, September 1962, pp. 213–24.

16. HARLOW, HARRY F., and HARLOW, MARGARET K. Social deprivation in monkeys. *Scientific American*, November 1962, pp. 3–10.

17. HARTMANN, HEINZ. *Ego Psychology and the Problem of Adaptation.* New York: International Universities Press, 1958.

18. HOLLINGSHEAD, AUGUST B., and REDLICH, FREDERICK C. *Social Class and Mental Illness.* New York: John Wiley & Sons, 1958.

19. HOWELLS, JOHN G. The Psychopathogenesis of Hard Core Families. Paper read at APA, New York, May 6, 1965.

20. HUGHES, CHARLES C.; TREMBLAY, M. A.; RAPOPORT, ROBERT N.; and LEIGHTON, ALEXANDER H. *People of Cove and Woodlot.* New York: Basic Books, 1960.

21. JONES, MAXWELL. *Social Psychiatry.* London: Tavistock Publications, 1952.

22. KOHN, MELVIN C. Social Class and Parent-Child Relationships: An Interpretation. In Riessman, Frank, et al., eds. *Mental Health.*

23. LEIGHTON, ALEXANDER H. *My Name Is Legion.* New York: Basic Books, 1959.

24. LEIGHTON, ALEXANDER H. Poverty and social change. *Scientific American*, May 1965.

25. LEIGHTON, ALEXANDER H. "Cultural Change." In press.

26. LEIGHTON, DOROTHEA C.; HARDING, JOHN S.; MACKLIN, DAVID B.; MACMILLAN, ALLISTER M.; and LEIGHTON, ALEXANDER H. *The Character of Danger.* New York: Basic Books, 1963.

27. LEWIS, OSCAR. *The Children of Sanchez.* New York: Random House, 1961.

28. MILLER, S. M. The American Lower Classes: A Typological Approach. In Riessman, Frank, et al., eds. *Mental Health*, pp. 139–54.

29. RIESSMAN, FRANK, COHEN, JEROME, and PEARL, ARTHUR, eds. *Mental Health of the Poor.* Glencoe, Ill.: Free Press of Glencoe, 1964.

30. SCHACHTER, SIDNEY. *The Psychology of Affiliation.* Stanford: Stanford University Press, 1959.

31. SOLOMON, FREDERIC; WALKER, WALTER L.; O'CONNOR, GARRETT, J.; and FISHMAN, JACOB, R. Civil rights activity and reduction in crime among Negroes. *Arch. Gen. Psychiatry* 12 (March 1965):227–36.

32. SROLE, LEO, et al. *Mental Health in the Metropolis*, Vol. 1. Thomas A. C. Rennie Series in Social Psychiatry. New York: McGraw-Hill, 1961.

33. STONE, I. T., LEIGHTON, DOROTHEA C., and LEIGHTON, ALEXANDER H. *Poverty and the Individual.* Paper presented at Conference on Poverty amidst Affluence, University of West Virginia, May 1965. To be published.

34. WITTENBERG, RUDOLPH M. Personality Adjustment through Social Action. In Riessman, Frank, et al., eds. *Mental Health*, pp. 378–92.

Violence and Human Behavior

MARVIN E. WOLFGANG

Although this article briefly reminds us that human violence is influenced by physiological, psychological, and sociocultural conditions, the author's principal focus is the social determination of violence. Wolfgang looks on violence as essentially a learned response, a form of adaptive behavior undertaken in lieu of other adaptive behaviors. He treats violence in much the same way as Raab and Lipset and Beiser treated prejudice and poverty. He emphasizes "socialization into violence."

This perspective of violence as a learned response helps us to uncover some of the sources of violence. If violent behavior is to be learned, there may be a model and there must be some kind of reinforcement. Not only are models of violence present in our culture, but they are hard to avoid. We see parents and teachers, guards and riot police, and even governmental officials all of whom use force or threat of force to control other people. We see the paraphernalia of control all around us: guns, clubs, and other implements of war. The media offer us models of violent behavior. We are taught that it is "masculine" to be physically assertive; advertisements for guns and even for cars make it clear what society says we have to do to be masculine. Together, all these contribute to the process of socialization into violence.

But more important than the model is the reinforcer. Parents win. Teachers win. The stronger party—whether person or nation—imposes its will on the weaker. At least vicariously then, the person is reinforced for being violent.

What of the control of violence? Elimination of some models may be feasible; we can legislate against weaponry, we can teach against machismo. But what can change the power base of social relationships, of parent and teacher over child, of The Man over Everyman, of strong nation over weak? How can we remove or counter the model? More important, how can we eliminate the reinforcer, extinguish violent behavior? If observing the dominance of strong over weak is reinforcing, how can we change this apparent fact of life? These are the dilemmas of human violence. These are the questions to which Wolfgang addresses himself.

SOURCE: Address delivered at the Annual Meeting of the American Psychological Association, Washington, D. C., August 30, 1969. Reprinted by permission.

I am honored to share some reflections on violence with my distinguished colleagues in psychology. As a sociologist-criminologist and Research Director of the National Commission on the Causes and Prevention of Violence during most of this past year, I have been writing, reading, and thinking about violence in a variety of forms, so that what I can say now is but a résumé of many previous thoughts of my own and of others.[1] I take no credit for original thinking, only the responsibility for the peculiar twists of the language to express some ideas.

I have been torn in my preparation for this address between wanting to cover material from the laboratory on aggression, the psychological studies of reactions to films, electronic impulses imposed on critical centers of the brain, the influence of the XYY gene syndrome, to interesting analyses of assassinations, firearms, crimes, and student violence. So extensive in scope and intensive in detail is our present national inquiry of violence that I can but hope that some of the dozen or so volumes that we expect to publish will have some interest to scholars and the public in general. My own remarks here are highly selective, more sociological than psychological, and generally devoid of the statistics needed to buttress argument. I shall concentrate on only a few general areas of concern.

When the dictatorial Duke of Athens was compelled by an angry mob to flee Florence in 1343, some of his political assistants were grabbed on the street, tortured, and murdered. The apex of the mob fury was reached in the scene described as follows by Machiavelli:

> Those who could not wound them while alive, wounded them after they were dead; and not satisfied with tearing them to pieces, they hewed their bodies with swords, tore them with their hands, and even with their teeth. And that every sense might be satiated with vengeance, having first heard their moans, seen their wounds, and touched their lacerated bodies, they wished even the stomach to be satisfied, that having glutted the external sense, the one within might also have its share [3].

This mob action helped to sustain Machiavelli's insistence that "the rage of men is certainly always found greater, and their revenge more furious upon the recovery of liberty, than when it has only been defended." [3]

My reason for referring to this scene is patent: to draw upon an example of riot and violence from a beautiful city at the most glorious time in its history, to show the brutal side of man's behavior in the midst of another period's affluence, political enlightenment, and highly humanistic culture.

Man is not innately criminal, violent, or aggressive. He responds to people, events, or other kinds of stimuli that precipitate violative, violent, or aggressive behavior. But he learns what is fearful or frustrating so that the things

[1] I am drawing upon materials from the National Commission on the Causes and Prevention of Violence, especially from the Task Forces on Individual Acts, codirected by Melvin Tumin and Donald Mulvihill, and on Group Violence, directed by Jerome Skolnick. I am also using some ideas that appear in my previous writings (such as Wolfgang, 1968, 1969).

to which he reacts are interpreted by him as such, and the resolution of events which he defines as problems is also learned. Cats, dogs, monkeys do not shoot their adversaries because they cannot or have not learned to use guns. Only man has the capacity to make and to use such artificial weapons designed to destroy himself and others.

This general introduction leads to my first major topic, which is the socialization into violence, with an emphasis on the fact that our culture provides a variety of learning processes that develop an acceptance of the use of violence, often labelled legitimate. Much of my concern is with America because I know it best and because I am involved in a national scrutiny of my own society. If I sound a bit critical of the United States at times it is because we are critically analyzing our posture relative to violence.

I shall also speak much about youth because youth is a time of movement and physical activity, and acts of physical aggression, whether performed by monkeys or homo sapiens, whether or not injurious to others, are most likely to be performed by the young.

Socialization into Violence

LEGITIMIZED VIOLENCE

Violence can be viewed as physical injury to persons and damage or destruction of property and abstractly is neither legitimate nor illegitimate. Judgment of legitimacy is based on the agent, the target, the ends sought and the context in which violence occurs. Whether physical force is good or bad is always decided in a culture value setting. The positive or negative eufunctional or dysfunctional aspects of violence depend on the observer's perspective.

There is, however, no society that does not contain in its normative system elements of acceptable limits to violence. Thus, the use of physical force by parents to restrain and punish children is permitted, tolerated, encouraged, and is thereby part of the normative process by which every society regulates its child rearing. There are, of course, varying degrees of parental force expected and used in different cultures and times, and there are upper limits vaguely defined as excessive and brutal. The battered child syndrome is an increasingly recorded phenomenon in several Western societies.

The point is, however, that our norms approve or permit parents to apply force largely for their own ends against the child. The application of force is a form of violence and may be used consciously to discipline the child to the limits of permitted behavior, to reduce the domestic noise level, to express parental disapproval, and even unconsciously as a displacement for aggression actually meant for other targets. This model of parent-child interaction is a universal feature of all human societies. The model is one that the child himself comes to ingest, i.e., that superior force is power permitting manipulation of others and can be a functional tool for securing a superordinate position over others, for obtaining desires and ends.

The violence in which the child himself engages is but an expressed extension of this basic model. The use of physical restraint and force is not a feature only in lower-class families, although studies have shown that its persistent use, and use in greater frequency over a longer span of childhood, is more common in that social class. The substitutions, by middle-class parents, of withdrawal of rights and affection, of deprivation of liberty, and of other techniques, are designed to replace the need for force. They are also ways of masking the supreme means of control, namely, physical force.

Violence and the threat of violence form the ultimate weapons of any society for maintaining itself against external and internal attacks. All societies finally resort to violence to solve problems that arise from such attacks. War is aggressive force between nations and is legitimized within each. Relativity of moral judgments about violence is quite clear in the case of war. When the American colonies collected themselves together in the eighteenth century to sever metropolitan ties, we called the action revolution and good despite the violence it engendered. When some states in the nineteenth century sought to bifurcate the nation, we called the action civil war and bad and lamented the bloodshed. The Nazis gave justice to our bombs and enlisted the world's generation of youth to react violently to violence. Violence becomes viewed as a rapid collective problem solver, from the three and twenty stabs in Caesar, according to Suetonius, to riots in city streets or college grounds.

There are international conflicts in which our countries have been involved and for which the label of legitimacy has been seriously questioned by substantial numbers within our own territory. Vietnam is such an episode. And when this happens, a society becomes more conscious of the process of socializing its own youth to accept violence as a mode of response. When war is glorified in a nation's history and included as part of the child's educational materials, a moral judgment about the legitimacy of violence is surely and firmly made.

Socialization means changing the individual into a personality; it is the process of cultural transmission, of relaying through the social funnel of family and friends a set of beliefs, attitudes, values, speech, and habits. When the front-line instruments of war become part of the physical features of a child's life space, when cannons, rifles, grenades, and soldiers are moved from real battlefields to the mind of the child and the plastic world of his playroom and are among the objects touched and manipulated by the child in the process of becoming, then some set of values associated with the legitimacy and recognition of the superiority of violent activity is also transmitted.

It is our youth who man the weapons of war. But they must be trained to have reduced fear and increased anger, to rationalize their being mobilized into a phalanx of force. Youth must be socialized into acceptance of the collective will that drives and flies them into battle against their individual desires. From Roman troops who marched through Britain to United States soldiers who struggle in Vietnam, the still-forming limbs of youth have been used to push political philosophies through history.

It is always an older generation that thrusts its younger ones into battle. Decisions made with maps and oval tables in the conference halls of power are made by men whose own youth has passed. Not privy to the policies that formed their own fate, the young are used to play the games of violence imposed on them by their elders. I am not here questioning, but only describing, the process which creates its own cultural justification. But I am implying that the process and the justifications that envelop it are part of the socialization of generations into violence. We might question whether the generation that designs, or the generation that fights war is the truly violent one.

There are many other areas of social life which witness the protection of order by representatives of control. In their roles and persons, they corporealize the actual or potential use of legitimized violence. The police and national guard are the most obvious of these agents, but there are also the less visible and more silent cadres of guards in prisons, mental institutions, banks, parks, and museums. Even less seen but subjectively self-legitimized, are unofficial groups like the lynching mobs of yesteryear, the Minutemen and vigilantes of the rural South and urban North, and certain black militants who have armed their members for assault. The presence of all these groups, ranging from the culturally prescribed to the barely tolerated, has diffusive effects that are part of the socializing experience of youth into the acceptance of violence as a means of control. The more these agents of real or potential aggression are used, the more impact such use has in socializing others to the functional utility of violence. If the official legitimacy of violence is stressed, many of the young generation exposed to such values will have heightened acceptance of its use. On the other hand, many who are identified with the targets of officially legitimized violence will respond in like manner, thereby confirming their need to use violence to combat violence. And this message is passed on to yet another group of the younger generation who learn to attack the guardian executors of the larger society with their own contrived version of legitimate violence.

MASCULINITY

Social scientists, psychologists, and psychiatrists have often stressed the importance of the theme of masculinity in American culture and the effect this image of the strong masculine role has had on child rearing and the general socialization process. The middle-class child today has some difficulty if he seeks to match himself to the old masculine model and he may sometimes become neurotic and insecure. Among the lower classes, says Walter Miller, the continuity of the physically assertive male is still one of the "focal concerns." The desire to prove one's masculinity, added to the desire to become a successful male adult member of the lower-class culture, requires adolescent "rehearsal" of the toughness, heavy drinking, and quick, aggressive response to certain stimuli that are characteristic of the lower-class adult male. Such rehearsal involves activities not necessarily delinquent but often participation in conduct that is defined as delinquent by the middle class. *Machismo* is still a viable term in various cultures, and especially among the young in the lower class, that equates maleness with overt physical aggression. The genesis reaches far into the biological evolution of the species, into the history of civilization; it was found on the peripheries of expanding colonial powers, on the frontiers of America, and it has been at the core of the less verbally articulate classes. Efforts to explain its persistence include rejection by the male child of female dominance at home and school and rejection of the association of morality with femininity; the result is the antithesis, that of being physically aggressive, which in turn often leads to delinquency and crime.

Males commonly carry the role of committing the required deeds of assault, of investigating homicides and suicides, being mortician assistants, handling the injuries of highways; in short, men are required to assume responsibility for the physical public injuries and tragedies of humanity. Women are protected, faces are turned, from such displays. It is also the male who is expected to use violence in prescribed ways and at prescribed times, during which he must be sufficiently desensitized to the pain he inflicts, whether in the street or playground, on a battlefield or in a bomber. It should not be unexpected, therefore, that most delinquent acts of physical injury are also commited by males.

THE MASS MEDIA

Other features of our culture in general, such as the mass media, may promote acceptability of male violence or make violence so banal that large segments of the population are no longer sensitive to expressions of violence. At least these features fail to encourage nonviolence. Whether television viewing or otherwise vicariously experiencing violence functions as a catharsis is not a scientifically resolved issue. The weight of most research seems counter-indicated. The sheer frequency of screened violence, its intensity as well as context, and the myriad forms it takes, cannot be claimed to instill firm notions of nonviolence in the children who are witnesses. Unless the logic of the assertion that violence in mass media encourages violent behavior is destroyed by scientifically acceptable evidence, we play dangerous games with the socialization process and its adult products.

AUTOMOBILE ADVERTISING

Even automobile advertising in America evokes many of the attributes of aggression, particularly male aggression, and seeks to affect purchasing habits by drawing upon the existing pool of socializing forces. Despite pamphlets distributed to young drivers by car manufacturers to encourage courteous driving habits, these same manufacturers advertise aggression behind the wheel by linking their cars and the drivers to masculine might. In a short time I can only give the tenor of their appeal [13, 4].

Glamour and thrill in the cars are meant to be associated with speed and power through such verbs as "roars," "growls"; adjectives like "dynamic," "powerful," "exciting," "wild," "ferocious," "swinging"; nouns like "missile," "rocket," "tiger," "stinger." Phrases of advertising include: "just pull the trigger," "start billing yourself as the human cannon ball," "want action?", "fire the second stage," "aim it at the road." Longer excerpts make clear the intended associations: (a) "For stab-and-steer men, there is a new 3-speed automatic you can lock in any gear . . . make small noises in your throat. Atta boy tiger." (b) "Bring on the Mustangs, Wildcats, Impalas . . . We'll even squash a few Spyders while we're at it. Dodge has made it a little harder to survive in the asphalt jungle. They just uncaged the Coronet." (c) "This year let yourself go for power." (d) "All new! All muscle! . . . with Advanced Thrust engineering . . . and an almost neurotic urge to get going. Drive it like you hate it—it's cheaper than psychiatry." (e) "Nobody said a nice car can't play mean now and then."

There are appeals to virility and masculinity: "Get with the man-sized Dart"; "Sleek, lean, muscled new style . . . improved cat-quick handling"; "Burly and businesslike"; "Go ahead, be rebellious. Demand more 'big.' More 'hot' "; "Come rid yourself of prematurely gray driving"; "The 300 has muscle"; "Bold Plymouth Fury"; "A man's kind of action! Bold! . . . It's the man's car for men who like their action big . . . gives a man that 'in charge' feeling."

It is difficult to factor out the contribution this kind of advertising makes to the traffic accidents of the young, both as victims and agents. That the association is present is clear. Traffic accidents are the leading cause of death among children and youth. Of all youth 13 to 25 years of age who died in a recent ten-year span, 42 per cent died as the result of traffic accidents. The young are our worst drivers, as reflected in part through insurance rates. Persons under 25 are 19 per cent of all licensed drivers but cause over 30 per cent of the accidents. Two-fifths of all teen-age drivers are involved in traffic accidents each year [4].

Such advertising through car magazines, read by thousands of youth, reaches into the later adolescent socializing process and can be faulted for adding to the violence in our culture if not on the road.

GUNS

Much the same can be said about guns in American society but I shall not burden this gentle audience long with this problem. The Firearms Task Force Report of the National Commission on Violence has now been published and calls for more control over handguns. The appeal to masculinity is again present, and the general awareness of young males about guns forms yet another part of the socialization into violence. The best current estimate is that there are at least 100 million guns in the United States. If evenly distributed there would be one for every male in the country. But they are not evenly distributed. The South East and South Central regions have highest gun possession, as do males under 25. These are also the regions and the age group of highest rates of homicide.

Nearly 3,000 persons in the United States are fatal victims of firearms accidents each year, and at least another 20,000 are injured by firearms accidents. About 65 per cent of our criminal homicides involve firearms.

The ease with which guns can be purchased is well documented. During the past decade about 30 million new guns have been added by domestic production and importation. Weak or unenforced control statutes on possession or use make guns available to almost anyone who wants one. And to this availability is added the stimulus of advertising not unlike that which I have read about automobiles.

Mail-order advertisement in America, the highest gun-to-population ratio in the world, the virtual glorification of guns in our history, and the daily displays on television of guns in the hands of heroes can surely play no role in minimizing violence in the socialization process.

I have spoken of guns, automobile advertising, and legitimized violence because they are features given scanty attention among the socializing forces that mold the personalities, shape the values, and form the mentality of many youth in our society. As we unpack the mixed bag of culture inputs presented to youth, we become increasingly aware that a high proportion are violence-laden, and that they are often offered for absorption with the palliative of legitimacy and social acceptability. They can now be seen more clearly as further extensions of the basic model of physical force found in parent-child interaction. Violence, thus viewed, is a continuous variable, measured in degrees of severity and intensity, legitimacy and illegitimacy.

Illegitimate violence is not qualitatively different from but is continuous with and dynamically similar to legitimate violence. It is to the clearly illegitimate forms of violence—the delinquencies and crimes—and the more blatant criminogenic forces of our society that I should now like briefly to turn to understand another dimension of the relation between culture and violence.

Urban Violence

THE SUBCULTURE OF VIOLENCE

The forces that generate conditions conducive to crime and riots are strongest in our urban communities. Urban areas with mass populations, greater wealth, more commercial establishments, and more products of our technology also provide more frequent opportunities for theft and greater chance of violence.

Victims are impersonalized, property is insured, consumer goods in more abundance are vividly displayed and are more portable.

Urban life is commonly characterized by population density, spatial mobility, ethnic and class heterogeneity, reduced family functions, and greater anonymity. When, on a scale, these traits are found in high degree, and when they are combined with poverty, physical deterioration, low education, residence in industrial and commercial centers, unemployment or unskilled labor, economic dependency, marital instability or breaks, poor or absent male models for young boys, overcrowding, lack of legitimate opportunities to make a better life, the absence of positive anticriminal behavior patterns, higher frequency of organic diseases, and a cultural minority status of inferiority, it is generally assumed that social-psychological mechanisms leading to deviance, crime, and violence are more likely to emerge.

It is abundantly clear even to the most casual observer that Negroes in American society are the current carriers of a ghetto tradition in our cities. More than any other socially defined group, they are the recipients of urban deterioration and the social-psychological forces leading to legal deviance. And for this reason, concern with crime in the American city is commonly a concern with Negro crime.

Although there are good reasons for raising serious questions about criminal statistics that report race of the offender and the fact that official crime rates for Negroes are in general three or four times higher than white rates, and although Negroes probably suffer more injustices than whites in the law enforcement process from arrest to imprisonment, it is no surprise that the most valid efforts to measure crime still find Negro crime rates high. When the untoward aspects of urban life are found among Italians, Germans, Poles, or almost any other group, their crime rates are similarly high. Relative deprivation and social disqualification are thus dramatically chained to despair and delinquency.

All of this is not meant to obscure the fact that poverty also exists in small towns and rural areas. But when multiplied by congested thousands and transmitted over generations, poverty, as Oscar Lewis has claimed, becomes a culture. The expectations of social intercourse change, and irritable, frustrated parents often become neglectful and aggressive. The children inherit *a subculture of violence* [2] where physically aggressive responses are either expected or required by all members sharing not only the tenement's plumbing but also its system of values. Ready access and resort to weapons in this milieu may be essential to protection against others who respond in similarly violent ways. Carrying a knife or some other protective device becomes a common symbol of willingness to participate in violence, to expect violence, and to be ready for its retaliation.

A subculture of violence is not the product of cities alone. The Thugs of India, the *vendetta barbaricina* in Sardinia, the *mafioso* in Sicily have

[2] For a fuller description of this thesis, see Wolfgang and Ferracuti, 1967.

existed for a long time. But the contemporary American city has the major accoutrements not only for the genesis but also for the highly accelerated development of this subculture, and it is from this subculture that most violent crimes come.

The use of violence in such a subculture is not viewed as illicit conduct, and the users do not have to deal with feelings of guilt about their aggression. Violence can become a part of the life style, the theme for solving difficult problems, and is used primarily between persons and groups who themselves rely upon the same supportive values and norms. A carrier and user of violence will not be burdened by conscious guilt, then, mainly because the recipient of his violence shares in the same subculture and has similar class, occupation, residence, age, and other attributes which characterize the subuniverse of persons sharing in the subculture of violence.

DELINQUENCY IN A BIRTH COHORT

Now there is a relatively small cadre of young citizens who are born into and grow up in a subculture pocket of residential propinquity, poverty and psychological depression, ungoverned households and wedless mothers, where the subculture of violence is nurtured and transmitted across generations as well as city streets. Yet, this relatively small group, fostered by inadequate urban renewal, occupational, educational, and housing programs, and unchecked by community service agencies or correctional strategies, can and does inflict most of the serious, violent social harm on a community.

Relative to this assertion are some new kinds of evidence about juvenile crime and particularly violence that are being analyzed by the Center for Studies in Criminology and Criminal Law at the University of Pennsylvania under support from the National Institute of Mental Health. The data constitute a unique collection of information in the United States about a birth cohort of boys born in 1945. Approximately 10,000 males, born in that year and resident in Philadelphia at least from ages 10 to 18, have been analyzed in a variety of ways. Using school records, offense reports from the police, and some military information, the Center has, among other things, followed the delinquency careers of those boys in the cohort who *ever* had any contact with the police. The cohort is probably typical of other urban cohorts in the United States.

Some of the findings from this Philadelphia study are particularly pertinent for more understanding about youth and crimes of violence. Of the total birth cohort of 9,946 boys born in 1945, about 85 per cent were born in Philadelphia and about 95 per cent went through the Philadelphia school system from first grade. From the entire cohort, 3,475, or 35 per cent, were delinquent, meaning that they had at least one contact with the police before reaching age 18. Of the 7,043 white subjects, 2,017, or 29.64 per cent were delinquent. Of the 2,902 nonwhites, 1,458, or 50.24 per cent were delinquent.

It is a dramatic and disturbing fact that slightly more than half of all Negro boys born in the same year were delinquent—more than were nondelinquent.

Of special significance is the fact that only 627 boys were classified as chronic offenders, or heavy repeaters, meaning that they committed five or more offenses during their juvenile court ages. These chronic offenders represent only 6.3 per cent of the entire birth cohort. Yet, these 627 boys were responsible for 5,305 delinquencies, which is 52 per cent of all the delinquencies committed by the entire birth cohort.

Chronic offenders are heavily represented among those who commit violent offenses. Of the 815 personal attacks (homicide, rape, aggravated and simple assaults), 450, or 53 per cent, were committed by chronic offenders; of the 2,257 property offenses, 1,397, or 62 per cent, were from chronic offenders; and of 193 robberies, 135, or 71 per cent, were from chronic offenders. Of all violent offenses committed by nonwhites, 70 per cent were committed by chronic boys; of all violent acts of committed by whites, 45 per cent were performed by chronic boys.

Clearly, these chronic offenders represent what is often referred to as the "hard core" delinquents. That such a high proportion of offenses—particuarly serious acts of violence—are funnelled through a relatively small number of offenders, is a fact that loudly claims attention for a social action policy of intervention. Under the assumption that these offenses are the most serious and the ones to reduce in any deterrence or prevention program, and that most of the other forms of delinquency are relatively trivial, the pivotal point of social cost reduction appears to be when juveniles have committed their first offenses. To produce delinquency desisting at this stage in the biography of the child might thus be considered the most efficient procedure. More nonwhites go on after the first offense, and perhaps the major concern should be with this racial group. Nearly 30 per cent of the nonwhite boys compared to only 10 per cent of the white boys, fall into the chronic offender category of having committed five or more offenses.

URBAN RIOTS

There is a still more serious form of violence today—that of group violence. The United States has recently experienced race riots that offer fundamental threats to the entire social system. To deny the political utility of such violence would be neither easy nor valid. Not until violence erupted did the United States Congress move to enact the first major civil rights legislation since the Civil War.

Nearly every major city in the land has experienced riots and civil disorder during the past few years. There were 239 violent outbursts by Negroes that involved at least 200,000 people and resulted in more than 8,000 casualties, including 191 deaths, most of them Negroes. More than 30,000 white Americans have taken part in violent clashes with civil rights demonstrators, causing more than 150 injuries. Some 200 major acts of white terrorism against blacks and civil rights workers have resulted in some 20 deaths and more than 100 serious casualties.[3]

When men perceive oppression as their lot and know of others not oppressed, when ordered avenues of change are blocked by kings or legislators or some vague variety of any social system, the oppressed will either resign themselves to fate or rise up to taste the fruit of freedom, and having tasted will want the feast.

Like whites, Negroes are men who have learned of their oppression. By forced migration they became slaves. The politics of war redefined their citizenry but little their status. Slaves became servants in the economics of change. The quiet process of elevation has been too slow for all but a trickle of black humanity to enjoy white privilege, and today color is a description not of the skin but of one's status. That status is a depressed, deprived, and now frustrating one.

But group violence is not a new phenomenon in American society. Our history suggests violence as severe as or worse than now. We might discount the Revolution and the War between the States, the latter of which took approximately a half million lives. But we cannot neglect the Shay and Whiskey Rebellions over debts and taxes; the slaughter and subjugation of American Indians; the Know-Nothings who fought rising Irish political power, who had a 48-hour orgy of mob violence in St. Louis in 1854 in which a dozen persons were killed and 50 homes of Irish Catholics wrecked and looted, who killed 20 persons in a two-day riot in Louisville the next year and burned two churches and two parochial schools in Philadelphia; and the Irish antidraft riot in New York in 1863 that killed nearly 2,000 and injured 8,000 in four days.

There were the bloody railroad strikes in 1877 that killed 150; the Rocky Mountain mining wars that took the lives of 198, including a governor, at the turn of the century; the brutal Molly Maguires, a secret band of Irish miners in Pennsylvania; the Wobblies, or Industrial Workers of the World; the industrial and railroad police who brutally beat laborers from Pennsylvania to California; the garment workers' strike in Chicago in 1910 that resulted in 7 deaths, an unknown number of seriously injured, and 874 arrests; the 20 lives lost in the Illinois Central Railroad strike in 1911; the 1919 steel strike in which 20 persons perished; the national cotton textile labor dispute of 1934 that spread from Georgia and South Carolina to Alabama, even to Rhode Island and Connecticut, with 21 deaths and 10,000 soldiers on strike duty.[4]

By 1871 the invisible empire of the Ku Klux Klan "had a membership of over half a million, and a Congressional investigation that year uncovered

---

[3] These compilations have been made by the staff of the National Commission on the Causes and Prevention of Violence and appear in the *Progress Report.*
[4] Most of this history of labor violence has been abstracted from Taft, 1966.

hangings, shootings, whippings, and mutilations in the thousands. In Louisiana alone, 2000 persons had been killed, wounded, or injured in a short few weeks before the election of 1868. The commanding general of federal forces in Texas reported: 'Murders of Negroes are so common as to render it impossible to keep accurate accounts of them' " [1].

That violence is not unique to the United States is an assertion that needs no more than a few illustrations. The aftermath of the French Revolution had a kind of terror and bloodshed never witnessed in this country; the 1843 student riots in France spread throughout Europe; assassinations occurred from Austrian Archduke Francis Ferdinand in 1914 to Prime Minister Verwoerd in South Africa. The Nazis need not even be mentioned. There is still fresh in history the tortures in French Algeria; the Stalinist terrors of a generation; the mob violence and riots off and on for another generation involving Pakistanis and Indians; the current Nigerian civil war; the student and union violence in France; the *violencia* of Colombia for nearly twenty years that resulted in the assassination of Dr. Jorge Gaitan in 1948 and an estimated 200,000 deaths up to 1967; the confused "cultural revolution" in mainland China; and the horrendous, little-publicized massacre of 400,000 persons in recent years in Indonesia.

Violence in America's past, in the past and present of other nations, does not diminish it in our current scene. But its present dimensions and our instant explanations should be viewed within these perspectives.

While not having a firm political ideology any more than students who riot on campus, the "young militant" Negroes responsible for the fire-bombing and the sniping—the bitter and alienated activists—surely perceive the bureaucrats and the broader social order as distant impersonal targets for distaste and disruption. Having seen that it is possible to get attention and dethrone the complacency of the white establishment, and having gained hope that their lot can be improved, they regard their present deprivation as unendurable. In referring to the French Revolution, De Tocqueville said:

> A people which has supported without complaint, as if they were not felt, the most oppressive laws, violently throws them off as soon as their weight is lightened. The social order destroyed by a revolution is always better than that which immediately preceded it. . . . The end which was suffered patiently as inevitable seems unendurable as soon as the idea of escaping from it is conceived [9].

To riot is a crime in any state penal code definition. To incite to riot, to loot, burglarize, set on fire, destroy property, rob, assault, shoot, carry deadly weapons—each of these is a crime. Surely the unrecorded number of crimes and of unapprehended offenders in riots is enormous.

But in another sense, not compatible with a legalistic proximate cause notion, the white society, as the Kerner Commission noted, is responsible for inciting to riot. While displaying before the Negro poor the democratic idealism of opportunity, it has inflicted on them the prejudice, the economic blockage of opportunities, the subjugation, and the alienation from power and participation in democracy that have produced among Negroes the power to respond, exploding now in attacks to express their feelings. The urban riots thus far are a mixed bag of some confusing revolutionary ideology among a few, anomic acts expressive of social malaise among many, and almost adventuresome play among still others. Should there be another round of riot, it will be either moderate skirmishes in more muted tones, reflecting a skewness toward dissipation of the ghetto thrust, or more violent guerrilla warfare that can result only in more stringent repressive force by the state. If riots this summer are few or more moderate, we might conclude that the massively diffused efforts for better police-community relations, coalitions of white businessmen with the Negro community, and all our other strategies of solution that reject tokenism and gradualism are beginning to pay off.

I am inclined to link the causes of urban riots and those of urban crime. Where riots have begun, crime rates have been highest, especially crimes of violence. The social forces that have generated crime overlay the forces that erupt into riot. The players in both dramas are the same or similar. The parallelism is too strong to ignore or deny. Correct the conditions causing the one phenomenon and we change the other concomitantly.

Student Violence

Student violence is yet another and slightly different form of group violence experienced in most societies today. England may have a much lower homicide rate than the United States, but she is sharing the pains of student protest in not dissimilar ways.

I can only touch lightly on this topic but I would like to underscore the element of cultural contagion and the fact that many protests are peaceful demonstrations. But some escalate into violence, often as a result of excessive reaction by the police.

During 1967–68 in the United States, about 70,000 antiwar and antidraft protestors staged more than 170 demonstrations in cities and universities across the country. Of these, only 36 involved violence, including 15 in which counterdemonstrators initiated violence. Only 8 resulted in reported injuries, a total of 800. During last year, student demonstrations of war and campus issues involving more than 100,000 participants, occurred on more than 100 campuses. About 220 demonstrations took place. A few resulted in seizure of university facilities, police intervention, riot, property damage, injury, and even death; and several institutions were brought to a halt.[5]

Here are a few descriptions commonly reported in news accounts:

   a) Over 4,500 police with shields rushed into [the] University early this morning and, using tear gas, tried to force out 300 students barricaded in . . . the main building.

[5] See note 3.

b) Hundreds of students today ransacked the office of [the] University Rector and tried to throw him out a window. . . . After a wild meeting of 2,000 students in the central university building, about 500 rushed toward the rector's office, painting slogans on the walls as they went.

c) . . . a month old student strike was complicated by a partial walk-out by teachers. Mounted police charged groups of students along off-campus streets; rocks flew and the toll of arrests and injuries climbed steadily.

d) The Dean . . . was imprisoned for eight days in an occupied university building and subjected to "mass collective bargaining" until he was finally allowed to leave, exhausted, on a stretcher.

e) A hard core of about 150 radical students caused havoc at the . . . University . . . today. They smashed doors and windows, broke into cupboards, flung files around, piled up furniture as barricades, and manned hoses ready to fight the police.

These are a few typical reports of student violence during the early part of this year. There is at least a score of specific criminal offenses lodged in these activities. The locale in each report has been deleted in order to demonstrate clearly how widespread and similar is the violence. The difficulty one has in distinguishing the universities attests to the extent and similarity of the conditions.[6] In some cases it is instrumental violence to obtain clarified parochial goals; in other cases it is a generalized effort at sheer confrontation for the sake of disruption. Often, in either case, "The commitment to violence is clear-cut. Said an anarchist leader of the . . . students who first began the dispute . . .: 'Simply, the situation is a battle against the entrenched and direct power of the State. This power equals violence. To fight back we must employ direct violence. There is no other choice.' " [7] This is a quotation from a student at Tokyo University, but the comment is heard in similar tones from San Francisco State to the Sorbonne.

It is important to keep in mind that most student protest has not been violent, that it has captured the sentiments of many who are no longer young, and that the social effects of youthful protest are systemic. Most students are not radically, wholly, or injuriously involved in the activism on campuses. Reports rather consistently indicate that only about one or two per cent of all students in America and in England are actively involved in protests. This figure may be most misleading, however, for some students weave in and out of periods of activity, but the ardor and forcefulness which the active members bring to their tasks have indeed created political, economic, international attention. Events seem to move more swiftly than the pen. The analysis made last month, however sophisticated at the time, may seem outmoded this month. The liberal who gained his stance ten years

---

[6] The following list identifies the source of information and the universities where the student violence occurred: (a) *The Times* (London), 18 January 1969—Tokyo University; (b) *International Herald Tribune*, 18 January 1969—Barcelona University; (c) *Time*, 17 January 1969—San Francisco State College, California; (d) *The Times*, 8 January 1969 —Tokyo University; (e) *The Times*, 24 January 1969—Free University of Berlin.

ago for integration of the races is today fighting a new style segregation suggested by the militant blacks who want not only separate Afro-American departments, faculty, and budget for black students at San Francisco State College but separate black dormitories there, at Yale, and elsewhere. Black power is a term that takes on more meanings as time goes on, adding money and guns to the former meaning of dignity and identity. The desire to participate in decision-making episodes affecting one's own life shifts partly to a wish for confrontation. Dialogue changes into duologue, a term Abraham Kaplan uses to refer to two parties who talk *at*, rather than *to*, one another without listening. Responses to student demands range from repression to reasoned arguments that student leaders often do not heed.

Whether student protest becomes violent depends on the intensity of the protestors' feelings, the response of the forces who try to control the protest, the leaders' rhetoric, and many other things. But escalation into violence is not the usual pattern of demonstrative protest.

Nor should student activists necessarily be viewed as rebelling against the values of their parents. On the contrary, our current studies in the United States (and apparently in England as well) indicate that the students appear to be trying to implement those very values through their action. Student activists are recruited from the better students, they were raised in families that have valued esthetic and intellectual interests over money and material success, and have transmitted to the children notions of humanitarianism and free expression that sometimes question authority, convention, and tradition. It is not "permissiveness" so much as parental interests in political and socially conscious activity that are commonly related to this group of active youth.

The growth and complexity of university structure have combined with increasing involvement in issues of national policy and inadequate channels for expression of disagreement and participation of student and faculty in the decisions that affect their lives on campus. At the same time, radical student activists concerned with these issues have been attracted to such movements as The Students for a Democratic Society (SDS), which claims 7,000 dues-paying national members and about 35,000 members in its several hundred local chapters.

Scores of other single-issue groups on campuses across the United States and in England range from civil rights support groups to leagues for sexual freedom. They are generally not involved in violence around these issues, but their numbers reflect increased student participation in public affairs and the volatile potential of campus politics. They are showing, instead, their desire for more personal autonomy, greater latitude for self-expression.

Until recently, Negro university students were smaller in number, politically impotent if not indifferent, and considerably individualistic. Black power groups on campus have offered direction and organizational vehicles for young educated Negro students to find collective expression of grievance and identification with the black community as well as with fellow black students. Black Student Unions and Afro-American Associations have recently emerged on many campuses with increasing numbers of black students. The black student leaders are as militant and violent or more so than the white radicals, especially in terms of tactics used. The principal difference appears to be that black student groups wish to negotiate specific reforms and concessions while the white student radicals often seek only confronting authority with their protests and serve no guiding ideology or specific target. Militancy and violent tactics of black students seem to augment the militant stance of white students. Moreover, internecine battles for power are beginning to occur among the black organizations and may occur eventually between white and black radicals. The white radical commitment to justice and equality is often answered with derision and skepticism by blacks.

Much of the white student movement and whatever violence it engenders is without many ideological supports. There are, nonetheless, values expressed but not always followed: compassion instead of coercion, people above property, total involvement (to the point of holding administrators hostage or running risks of urban guerrilla fighting), distrust of constituted authority (white or black), sexual freedom, privacy of one's own organism (to ingest what one wants, including drugs), rejection of bureaucratic hierachicalism and hypocrisy. From an earlier external interest in poor blacks in Mississippi, students from relatively affluent middle-class families shifted to more militancy as they became interested in the Vietnamese. Then, almost suddenly, they were fighting less for others and more for themselves. Abstract principles of justice and equality through student power, and the problems of the war in Vietnam, were concretized by specific objections to university-military contracts, and were personalized by threat of the draft. And in the process of these shifts, increasing use of violence was the accompaniment. Ironically, a kind of romantic element has mixed with the personal as attention is also focused on the sterility of the power structure and an emphasis on human values. Dissent finds targets in mass production, creature comforts, and industrial technocracy. But these features of the New Left have little thrust toward politicization that could resemble an earlier era's underpinning of labor unrest with Marxism.

Some observers have noted that violence most often erupts, or occurs in most intense fashion, when the university authorities and police overreact. Perhaps this is a lesson learned from the Columbia and recent Harvard riots. Daniel Bell, my colleague in Sociology at Columbia, views the behavior of the police as the major cause that "radicalized" the Columbia student body.

Confrontation is a militant and violent means of arousing moderates to join in the movement and the action. It is used to alert the public to the issues. And it may dislodge the qualities of patience and quietude from young middle-class radicals whose traditional ethics of nonviolence have been politically inhibiting. Confrontation can cause many of the otherwise docile students who have been living only the quiet revolution of thought to commit themselves seriously to the revolution of action, however violent it may become. These are a few of the tenets of the tactics used by the SDS and other radical students. They are the kinds of tactics that elicit, if not encourage, violence.

Because many students are still committed to pacifist or liberal democratic ideals and are as much concerned with university courses as with causes, they are becoming disturbed by the new waves of violence, uncomfortable with the rude, uncouth attacks and the increasingly anti-intellectual stance of the radical student movement. As this movement becomes more militant with its strategy of confrontation, it may grow more isolated and loose, and fail to attract the large cadre of moderate students whose sense of social justice is being offended by a violence more "nasty and brutal" in its Hegelian pre-politicality than the power structure they at first rejected.

The response to student protest places the major burden on the universities themselves. University administrators are the front-line forces who must cope with the challenges of most of the protest of middle-class youth when it becomes violent.

The university today appears to have accepted the assertion that it is a microcosm of society. The university is also a step beyond this minimirror of its context. It is a community of young citizens and of scholars who not only harbor and enrich the knowledge so tediously acquired in the past, but who should engage constantly in questioning and reassessing that knowledge, which includes ideas about the functions and values of the present society. The capacity to inquire and to analyze the results of inquiry is the most fundamental feature of a university. To which I might add Sir Eric Ashby's (1969) cogent comment that the university should provide an "environment for the continuous polishing of one mind by another" [8]. To maintain and strengthen this capacity is the purpose of every university administration.

But the concept of stern authority by the university over the *civil* life of its students is now nearly anachronistic. The traditional intradisciplinary measures used by the university to regulate, in assumed parental role, the personal lives of its younger citizens can little longer be of adequate utility for most universities in the United States. Few, if any, universities enjoy the collegiate loyalty of Cambridge and Oxford. The judicial structure of the contemporary university does not reproduce the rules of evidence, qualified judges, accredited legal counsel, and the other features of legal authority to handle major civil and criminal violations. Many of the violent violations on campus today are far beyond the internal differences of a family affair.

The distinction between academic and civil roles must therefore somehow be made both for the university administration and the students. If students are violent and disruptive they must be judged by the proper role they are taking and by the proper agency of response. If they question what is *academic* in character, the university cannot resort to a claim for allegiance to campus spirit and loyalty to an old-fashioned authority. Their questioning should be honored with respect and engaged by the administration in full debate if courses, curriculum, and other academic affairs are at issue. Where the right of the university to assert authority over certain matters is questioned, it must be earned by argument, if necessary.

Conclusion

When violence occurs in crime or protest, youth is often its vehicle. But most crimes and most protests are not violent, even when youth are involved.

There are many different kinds of violence; some of it is legitimized by the norms of the society and ranges from the force used in parent-child interaction to the conduct of national war. The older generations of most societies are not entirely free from the use of violence, either in the earlier version of their own youth or in the context of their later years. The conduct of a war is but one of the more obvious examples. Moreover, an older generation may be but slightly removed from the posture of most proximate cause for various kinds of violence that a society comes to tolerate. Not yet arrived at positions of power where responsibilities are shared, youth cannot be blamed for a society that yields violence because it fails to make automobiles and highways safer, fails to reduce high rates of infant mortality, to move more vigorously to reform cities of blight and organized crime, or to control the manufacture and sale of guns.

Violence is largely a learned response. If in the everyday of life man witnesses the display of violence in an abundance of styles, it takes on a banality and he may come to accept its use in encounters with his own environment.

It might be said that for all their protest against their established elders, youth in a sense rely on the patience, understanding, tolerance, and responsibility of the older generation to check their escalating demands at the crunch point of the utterly impossible. One of the privileges of youth is having the ability to afford to complain and question [2]. The older generation becomes immersed in running the system and must rely upon the younger to provide the pressure needed to question and reform it. Even when they show displeasure at the tactics of student protest and riot, the older generation may have sneaking suspicions that youth could be right about many things. Like the ordinary German who a generation ago slowly became aware that something terrible was going on at the edge of town, so those in middle age are having their conscience aroused by youth and feel that more than a few things around them may not be well. There is merit in some of the disturbance from the student youth who are often idealistic, if not well-clothed with an ideology. "You'd never believe," said one professor in the midst of student protests at the London School of Economics, "that a group could be so dedicated and saintly and such a terrible nuisance" [6].

If the response to youthful violence is exclusive repression, the response may well assume the violence it seeks to halt. Perhaps, instead, a growing flexibility to change and an understanding of youth's requests will be the older generation's final weapon. The thrust of youth's protests may be dissipated in the soft belly of the establishment. And violence will be dethroned. Whatever the outcome of current crises, the annual layer of each newly arriving cohort folds into the fabric of society and continues to enrich the cloth.

Violence is a means of seeking power and may be defined as an act of despair committed when the door is closed to alternative resolutions. It comes from the failure to have a more abundant repertoire of means to gain a goal.

The lessons to be learned from current collective violence seem clear: as Columbia University officials remarked recently, acts wherein muscles usurp the role of minds are alien to a university. I suggest the same dictum for the larger society. Where reason is ruined and collective violence is viable, the social system has failed to provide the kind of participatory democracy we basically extol.

In the abstract there can be no side of violence with virtue. The course of the dominant society built on law and intrinsically the inheritor of the value of nonviolence must be to maintain itself. The black militant who would burn cities or the student who would destroy an administration building harbors no better way of life than the Ku Klux Klaner who would burn crosses or bomb Sunday schools. But the responsibility of that dominant society is to offer alternatives for expression, provide reasonable access to the thrones of power, permit grievances to be known, and execute the provisions of our Constitution with dispatch.

Change occurs in all societies, albeit the change in some may be slow or unplanned. It is when persons opposed to change become intransigent and those who wish to promote change are willing to resort to violence that order becomes disorder. When protest moves to riot and riot to rebellion, dissent is transformed into disruption. The right to exercise dissent peaceably is our basic political guarantee. But when physical harm occurs, another guarantee is called into focus and is used to force assaulters to retreat. This kind of balance is a fundamental which the police and the courts were designed to protect and maintain.

Perhaps Abraham Lincoln asked the basic question about violence most succinctly: "Must a government of necessity be too strong for the liberties of its own people, or too weak to maintain its own existence?" I trust that both our countries are sufficiently sensitive to the liberties of all to listen and strong enough to maintain them with justice under the rule of law.

References

1. FORSTER, ARNOLD. Violence in the Fanatical Left and Right, *Annals of the American Academy of Political and Social Science* (March 1966), p. 143.
2. LORBER, RICHARD, and FLADELL, ERNEST. The Generation Gap, *Life*, no. 17, May 1968.

3. MACHIAVELLI, NIECOLO. *History of Florence and of the Affairs of Italy.* London: M. Walter Dunne, 1901, book 2, p. 100.

4. O'CONNELL, JEFFREY. Lambs to Slaughter, *Columbia Journalism Review* (Fall 1967), pp. 21–28.
   A careful comparison between the automobile industry's safe-driving publications and magazine advertisements.

5. TAFT, PHILIP. Violence in American Labor Disputes, *Annals of the American Academy of Political and Social Science* (March 1966), pp. 127–40.

6. *The Sunday Times* (London), January 26, 1969.

7. *The Times*, January 19, 1969.

8. *Time* magazine, international ed., April 18, 1969, p. 40.

9. TOCQUEVILLE, ALEXIS DE. *L'Ancien Régime*, M. W. Patterson, trans. Oxford: Basil Blackwell, 1949, p. 186. Cited and brought to my attention by Judd Marmor in "Some Psychological Aspects of Contemporary Urban Violence," n.d. (mimeographed paper).

10. WOLFGANG, MARVIN E. Violence, U.S.A., *Crime and Delinquency* (October 1968), pp. 289–305.

11. WOLFGANG, MARVIN E. Youth and Violence. Washington, D. C.: Dept. of Health, Education and Welfare, Office of Juvenile Delinquency and Youth Development, April 1969.

12. WOLFGANG, MARVIN E., and FERRACUTI, FRANCO. *The Subculture of Violence.* London: Tavistock, 1967.

13. YARLEY, C. B., and SWEENEY, C. A. Automobile Safety; Speed and Racing Advertising. U. S. Federal Trade Commission, November 15, 1966.

Behavior Instrumentation and Social Technology

ROBERT L. SCHWITZGEBEL

The three closing articles speculate about some of the dramatic changes that might be effected in our society if certain psychological principles and techniques were put to use. In the first of these selections, Schwitzgebel combines learning principles (see Holland's and Liberman's articles) with technology and emerges with ideas for devices that might facilitate the general operation of society and reduce the suffering of some of its people.

Besides suggesting a number of unusual applications of laboratory principles to extra-laboratory behavior control, Schwitzgebel's discussion of the emerging field of "psychotechnology" provides the opportunity for some reflection on the issues and ethics of behavior manipulation. Many scholars have offered many thoughts about behavior manipulation, but perhaps no one has put the matter more sharply than Herbert C. Kelman (*Journal of Social Issues*, April 1965, pp. 31–46). He offers two arguments. First, manipulation of behavior is bad because it deprives the person of the exercise of free will, an essential component of humanity. He proposes this argument regardless of the form of manipulation (threats or promises, rewards or punishments, devices of any sort) and regardless of the reason for the manipulation (for good end or bad). Kelman's second argument is that effective behavior change inevitably involves some degree of manipulation, whether in education, psychotherapy, or politics. Thus he sets us on the horns of a dilemma; no matter which argument we choose, we are in an unsatisfactory position because we are forced to relinquish some good and advocate some evil. To produce effective educational, therapeutic, or political change requires us to violate the essence of the person; to preserve the essence of the person requires us to forgo effective change.

If this is truly a dilemma, if we must accept both arguments without qualification, then the problem is insoluble. We are put in an "ethically ambiguous" situation and the most we can do is try to maximize the good and minimize the evil. Some steps we might take toward these ends include making all of society,

SOURCE: From Robert L. Schwitzgebel, "Behavior Instrumentation and Social Technology," *American Psychologist* 25 (6) (1970):491–99. Copyright © 1970 by the American Psychological Association and reproduced by permission.

including ourselves, aware of the manipulative aspects of interpersonal behavior, building some sort of protection into the system (for example, teaching principles of resistance to control as well as principles of control), and emphasizing in our work the enhancement of freedom of choice (for example, stressing this freedom in our teachings and writings, and spelling out in our work the options open to the people we affect). These are by no means a solution to the problem; at best they constitute a framework for further discussion. In this respect, a review of the articles by Liberman, Delgado, Matson, and Nowlis, and also a careful study of that of Schwitzgebel, all in terms of the dilemma and Kelman's proposals, could be a highly productive enterprise.

What would have happened if the East coast power failure and the Cuban missile crises had occurred by accident on the same day?

Psychologists seldom ask such questions seriously—not because a possible Orson Welles' "War-of-the-Worlds" answer is so unpredictable or insignificant, but because, as behavioral scientists, we have greater professional regard for rigorous irrelevancy than relevant vagary. The historical origins of this preference (e.g., philosophical operationalism, prestige of physical science models, etc.) are neither obscure nor without merit. At issue is whether conceptual "tools" and strategies can now be developed that will permit psychology to be both socially relevant *and* methodologically rigorous.

It does not appear that this task can be wisely postponed. What makes our present social conflicts particularly dangerous is that they increasingly tend to come at the same time [Platt, 1969]. On a one-at-a-time basis, administrators may get some enjoyment and sense of importance from such challenges, but multiple crises (such as happened in New York City in 1968 with the sequence of teacher, police, garbage, and longshoremen's strikes) may exhaust rational processes. In the next few years, we are likely to see accelerated and critical stress on our already overburdened decision-making structures. A massive mobilization of scientific and technical resources may be required to deal successfully with social problems of the magnitude of nuclear confrontations, overpopulation, racial conflict, pollution, crime, etc. As an initial step, it seems to me, psychologists might legitimately attempt to define subissues into scientifically or, more appropriately, technologically tractable terms.

Administrative "Machinery"

It is a rather common assumption, indeed complaint, that technical innovations force alterations in the established social order of a culture. For example, the style of government, as well as the physical configuration of towns, was substantially altered when systems for transporting water were mechanized so that people no longer visited the communal well. Today, transportation devices and mass media are recognized as major influences in our social life. In this "indirect" way, the engineer and the technician are revolutionaries: they rearrange materials in a manner that necessarily elicits changes in social structure. (Somewhat ironically, the technician tends to go unnoticed in his revolutionary role because, as an individual, he is most typically a quiet, middle-class, politically conservative family man.) Several contemporary devices purposefully designed to control group behavior may illustrate some potentialities of this form of technological intervention.

Traffic signals are widely and successfully employed to regulate certain types of interaction involving vehicular and pedestrian movement. This discriminative stimulus display apparatus periodically inhibits individual movement in a manner designed to maximize overall speed. The cost/effectiveness of such a device compares quite favorably to that of a human (i.e., traffic policeman) assigned the same task. Similarly, parking meters regulate vehicular flow and collect revenue more accurately and probably more honestly than might otherwise be the case. Turnstiles, air raid sirens, burglar alarms, and recorded rumor-control telephone messages are also designed to regulate group behavior.

Clocks, usually used in conjunction with auditory signals, are more-or-less standard equipment in every school and factory. A particularly clever use of the clock should be credited to the English shipbuilder William Willett, who "invented" daylight savings time. The inefficient way of getting large numbers of employees to arrive at work earlier would be to pass a law specifying that as of a certain date, all business hours will be changed. Despite rational arguments and perhaps general agreement regarding the benefits of an extra hour of daylight, resistance would probably be widespread. Only a very courageous public official might risk his office for this beneficial and unselfish social reform. Yet the simple procedure of setting our clocks forward by one hour keeps the discriminative stimulus intact—that is, the alarm still rings at "7:30 A.M."—but the behavior is effectively changed. It might be worth considering whether we could bring other cooperative or gregarious behavior under stimulus control of the clock (we do so now on New Year's Eve!) which might be activated in times of crisis.

The use of instrumentation per se does not constitute a novel approach to social or community problems. What may be novel is the *type* of hardware and, even more fundamentally, *the principles of behavior control that the hardware uses.* The typical pattern of converting psychological information and theory into social action attempts to disseminate data by verbal and printed means to legislators and institutional administrators who are expected, in turn, to modify laws or regulations to conform to the new data. This procedure has not, however, proven noticeably successful. A survey by Blum and Funkhouser [1967] indicated that most legislators had not sought and would not seek the advice of psychologists or psychiatrists on changes in sex and drug laws. Lagey [1962] reported that of 143 demonstration programs presumably erecting models suitable for community treatment of multiproblem families, only 3 or 4 were converted into day-to-day working arrangements by existing community agencies. Passing psychological knowledge through legislative and administrative channels is inefficient and obsolete; data should go directly into hardware. It might be said that technology is the scientific tail that wags the social dog. Once we recognize the potency of such relationship, we will not rely so heavily on our traditional and less responsive management procedures.

One principle that might be built into administrative hardware would be regulated "trigger" actions or positive feedback, by which a relatively small stimulus is capable of inducing a predictable chain reaction. In our physical technologies, this principle is often employed. For example, we seed clouds with a small amount of silver iodide to increase rainfall for agricultural purposes. Similarly, an electrical or mechanical device may be viewed as a "social enzyme" or what Weinberg [1967] calls a "technological fix." The traumatic alternation in the course of political affairs caused by assassinations is facilitated, in part, by our manufacture of guns.

In discussing feedback functions of simple sociotechnical inventions such as the credit card, Platt [1966] has commented:

> The alternation of group behavior in such chain reactions can be so dramatic and extensive that one is almost tempted to think that every social problem might be solvable by one of those socio-technical inventions, especially if it is endowed with a pleasurable feedback character, and so with a self-amplifying character at every step for the individual user. The kind of thing I have in mind is the elimination of barter and the creation of commerce by the invention of the coin. . . . To educate billions rapidly, invent programmed teaching by books or machines with instant individual feedback. To feed the world on algae—that "nasty little green vegetable"—turn it into a cocktail snack; that is, find a way to make it delicious and desirable. . . . The laborious frontal attacks of uplift groups and mass meetings and legislation—laborious because they are attacks at the stabilizing level of self-stabilizing systems—become unnecessary. Perhaps organizations and groups should offer rewards to stimulate socio-technical inventions that could lead in desired directions [pp. 44–47].

A particularly dramatic contemporary illustration of the pressure that technical innovation can bring to bear on established social structures is the development of birth-control methods. The Roman Catholic Church has survived centuries of ideological onslaughts, but the nonverbal and sensual motivations facilitated by medical technology are a different type of challenge. It is entirely possible that historians may someday record how the Church—having had benefit of some of the greatest scholastics, but not technicians—survived the Reformation, but not the contraceptive!

At the risk of seeming very naïve about practical limitations, I would like to propose several devices or automated arrangements for social administration. Even if these are not feasible, they may at least serve some heuristic purpose.

UNITED NATIONS' COOPERATIVE INDEX

A substantial proportion of our federal government budget in international affairs is devoted to the designing and production of social control hardware. Unfortunately, since we rely heavily on a policy of "deterrence" involving punishment or the threat of aversive sanctions, the product is purposefully not very appealing. Shifting just a small portion of the $71 billion defense budget from the development of weaponry to devices for measuring and positively reinforcing desirable behaviors of large groups might alter the entire hazardous course of foreign diplomacy and domestic urban affairs.

In a very simplified way, Azrin and Lindsley's [1956] study of the reinforcement of cooperation between children, without overt instruction, is suggestive of what might be done. For example, a cooperation/conflict index might be established at the United Nations to indicate the degree of conflict among member states. Selected sampling might be based on variables, such as exchange or withdrawal of diplomats, which have already been established as political indicators [cf. Feierabend and Feierabend, 1966; Tanter, 1966] and processed by an on-line computer. The index level could be reported daily in a manner similar to stock market indexes. Monetary or other considerations administered through the United Nations, World Bank, or even private philanthropic institutions could be made contingent upon a predetermined performance. The importance of the index rests on the fact that it could serve as an empirically based cue for positive action, in contrast to the attention and publicity presently attendant upon conflict. Some type of continuous and sensitive monitoring is absolutely essential in order to obtain relevant base rates prior to attempted shaping and reinforcement of cooperative acts.

BONUS PARKING METERS

In locations of only moderate traffic congestion, parking meters with a green flag in addition to the usual red one could be installed to encourage drivers to park in such areas. The green flag appearing at irregular intervals would signal that the driver was eligible for a "bonus" such as a partial rebate on automobile registration fees, tickets to a civic event, etc. These positive consequences would be delivered by patrolmen in a manner similar to the traditional aversive consequences. This counterconditioning procedure would very likely be more effective, and probably not much more expensive, than present public relation programs initiated by police departments to improve their "image." During a special campaign a few years ago, policemen in Rochester, New York, gave flowers to proficient women drivers.

FARE-ADJUSTED TOLL ROADS

The fare presently charged on toll roads is the same, or even reduced, during hours of peak traffic. To encourage use during nonpeak hours, toll rates should be positively correlated with increased traffic flow. One might have special toll-free hours, relieving a certain number of toll agents and offsetting potential revenue loss.

ELECTRONIC REHABILITATION SYSTEM

A remote radio communication system using belt transceivers is presently undergoing prototype testing [Schwitzgebel, 1969]. Systems of this type can monitor geographical location and psychophysiological variables, as well as permit two-way coded communication with persons in their natural social environment. Probable subject populations include individuals susceptible to emergency medical conditions that occasionally preclude calling for help (e.g., epilepsy, diabetes, myocardial infarctions), geriatric or psychiatric outpatients, and parolees. It is conceivable, for example, that convicts might be given the option of incarceration or parole with mandatory electronic surveillance. In terms of prison costs (about $3,200 per year per inmate), treatment effectiveness, and invasion of privacy (few situations are *less* private than prison), an electronic parole system is a potentially feasible alternative. These systems can also be used for positive secondary reinforcement of prosocial behavior.

AUTOMATED PUBLIC OPINION SAMPLING

Voting machines are an obvious first step in the direction of automated polling. This arrangement, however, is still rather cumbersome and probably too infrequent. Response terminals using telephone lines might be placed in a selected sample of homes for the purpose of obtaining a prompt estimate of public opinion, similar to present television show ranking procedures. Such sampling would probably be subject to less bias than responses to mailed questionnaires or counting unsolicited letters. An educational function might also be served by involving citizens in simulated policy making. For example, an educational television station in Boston televised a war game and invited the viewers to phone in their judgments to members of the teams representing various nations ["The Most Dangerous Game," 1968].

TWO-WAY PUBLIC TELEVISION

Two-way closed-circuit television might be installed between certain public institutions and locations easily accessible to the general public. The television terminals could be placed, for example, at fairgrounds, college campuses, bus terminals, or airports where people tend to have leisure time. For 25 cents, say, a person could then converse a specified brief period of time with someone confined to an institution for reasons of health or social deviancy (e.g., patients in a veterans' hospital, inmates at reformatories or prisons, elderly persons confined to sanitariums). Individuals in the institution could work for the privilege of receiving these "calls." This arrangement might facilitate socialization at *both* terminals—or it might have an opposite, polarizing effect. Since these conversations could be easily video taped, the system might prove to be a useful tool in social research.

Behavioral Prosthetics

The pioneering work of Francis Galton and of Alexander Graham Bell might serve as models for smaller initial efforts on an *individual* basis. Galton's tireless ingenuity and empiricism led him among many other things, to become interested in designing apparatus that would physically measure a person's emotion or attitude. He took as an illustration the "inclination of one person toward another" and suggested that this might be quantified for two people sitting next to each other at a dinner table by attaching strain gauges to the legs of the chairs and then measuring shifts in weight [Galton, 1884]. The telephone was a direct outgrowth of Bell's work as a speech therapist and his interest in reducing the social isolation of handicapped persons.

Recently a number of devices have been designed by psychologists to correct functional deficits or to otherwise alter individual behavior. The "Mowrer sheet" [Mowrer and Mowrer, 1938] for the treatment of enuresis is probably the most widely known device of this type. This pad electrode arrangement has been redesigned to include warning and aversive auditory stimuli [Lovibond, 1963] or electric shock [Crosby, 1950]. Other instrumentation in clinical practice includes auditory or vibrotactile rhythm devices to inhibit stutterting [Azrin, Jones, and Flye, 1968; Brady, 1968], a time-delay cigarette pack [Azrin and Powell, 1968], a mechanically augmented toilet-training chair [Cheney, 1968]. Clark [1968], Lang [1969], and Migler and Wolpe [1967] have automated certain aspects of desensitization procedures. A general survey of behavior-modification devices has been presented elsewhere [Schwitzgebel, 1968].

Future clinical instrumentation might profitably focus on the designing of apparatus ("behavioral prostheses") appropriately used in the everyday pursuits of patients. Simple communication tools, miniaturized behavior recording devices, partially automated prompting or reinforcing apparatus, and portable multisensory teaching aids are likely candidates. The establishment of interdisciplinary teams of clinical psychologists and engineers is likely to become increasingly common, perhaps eventually paralleling current efforts in biomedical engineering.*

Professional Issues

A psychologist who undertakes the design and testing of behavior instrument systems is not likely to fit comfortably into traditional professional roles. He

---

* Editor's note: A brief history of the evolution of man has been deleted.

is neither (1) a theoretician nor (2) an applied scientist. But this should not be too disturbing. The ultimate criteria of professional competency of the practitioner are not the degree of theoretical sophistication or quantity of scientific findings utilized. His sine qua non is an ethically produced "cure rate" or other empirically verifiable evidence of behavior change.[1]

The "behavior instrumentician" should be easily distinguishable from the theoretician or the theoretically oriented clinician. His day-to-day activities are much more similar to the experimentalist or artist than to the verbal scholar. He manipulates material (organic or inorganic), not words. He deals with tangible, physical, sensual stimuli—the "stuff of" rather than "thoughts about" behavior. If one characterizes psychotherapy in the traditional Freudian sense of a "word cure," then the behavior technologist or instrumentician is *not* a psychotherapist. Of course, he uses words and theoretical constructs, but these are not his product any more than nonverbal tools such as a pencil and paper define the product of the verbal scholar. In this respect, the psychoanalyst, novelist, or lawyer have modes of dealing with human behavior clearly distinguishable from those of the physician, architect, or jailer.

Psychology has yet to develop a physical technology for behavior modification. There is a hint of this, however, when writers refer to practitioners as "behavioral engineers" [Ayllon and Michael, 1959], "social reinforcement machines" [Krasner, 1962], or "transducers" [Barker, 1965]. Although a technological model of the practitioner's task seems obviously more compatible with the mechanistic orientations of certain mathematical, cybernetic, and learning theory interpretations of behavior, there is no intention here to preclude the use of organismic or growth-oriented analogues. For example, a landscape architect is a technician-artist who plans certain organic environments.

The second point made earlier was that the psychological practitioner is not appropriately, or at least necessarily, characterized as an applied scientist. The technologist's goal—in contrast to the specification of abstract principles in scientific endeavors—is to create a practical product or system. Kranzberg [1968] and others have argued that historical evidence does not sustain the usual metaphorical assumption that technology "grows out of" or "flows from" science. The existence of a certain scientific work prior to its technological exploitation (e.g., the caloric theory of heat, which preceded but was probably not used in Watt's development of the steam engine) does not constitute proof that technologists drew upon it. Price [1965], analyzing the frequency of author citations in scientific periodicals, concluded that, "In general, new technology will flow from old technology rather than from any interaction there might be between the analogous but separate cumulating structures of science and technology [p. 561]."

[1] David McClelland suggested during a colloquium, facetiously, I believe, that a Ph.D. in clinical psychology should be awarded to anyone who could demonstrate, using acceptable scientific procedure, that he had "cured" six people.

Breger and McGaugh's [1965] allegation that contemporary behavior therapies have in fact very little basis in learning theory apparently hit a professionally sensitive spot. In view of the complex and often temporally loose relationship between scientific and technical advances, their critique may not have been too inaccurate. This is, however, by no means fatal to the development of a behavior technology. A series of empirically demonstrated principles of behavior modification might well be developed prior to, or independent of, their scientific explanation. Franks [1966] has claimed that "much of the practice of behavior therapy is at present an application not so much of learning theory as of learning technology [p. 46]." And this obviously squares with the previously cited analysis of scientific literature by Price [1965].

Uncritical or premature adherence to scientific findings or models may inhibit the development of a pragmatic and socially relevant behavior technology. Such technology would not be antiscientific; it might or might not be prescientific. The centaurlike model of the practitioner as clinician-scientist, while somewhat appealing in the abstract, has been difficult to implement (cf. Levy, 1962), because such creatures could only exist en masse if somehow the disparate historical origins and functions of technologists and scientists could be eluded.

Toward a Metatechnology

The most frequently voiced fears regarding technology include potentially excessive or malicious control of individual behavior, a threat of uniformity, and (if nothing worse) just plain boredom. The fear of control is, in part, I believe, a nightmarish and unrealistic combination of historical fact (e.g., technical proficiency of the Nazis in World War II), science fiction (e.g., 1984; Brave New World), and generalization of traditional research strategy (i.e., emphasis on controlled laboratory experiments rather than ecological field studies).

A common illustration of potential or actual misuse of technology is wire-tapping or other electronic surveillance procedures. At the present time, some law enforcement agencies trace the movement of a suspect by surreptitiously placing a miniaturized transmitter on his car; and the use of wire-tapping is now well documented. One of the first issues to be considered in evaluating the social threat of this or similar developments is technical feasibility. On the basis of a fairly thorough survey by our laboratory engineer [Bird, 1969], it was estimated that a computer-based radio system capable of locating individuals in a city approximately 24×24 kilometers would require two hundred and twenty-five 100-watt base station transceivers at 5-kilometer intervals at a total system cost of about $9 million, including 10,000 personally attached transponder units at $500 each. Systems of this magnitude are barely feasible and could hardly be installed without public knowledge. Brainwashing, hypnosis, and subliminal advertising have in the past elicited seemingly similar unwarranted public alarm.

The greatest threat to civil liberty occurs prior to public exposure when no democratic determination has been made regarding legitimate applications of a technical innovation. Secret technique or information is, however, time limited. Two decades ago, Norbert Wiener [1950] pointed out that information, by its very nature, precludes ultimate secrecy. Repressive measures tend to augment breakdown of social order because weapons used *against* police soon become as effective as those used *by* police, a situation parallel to the international weapons race. In increasingly communication-rich, high-energy cultures, regulatory agencies will be able to "buy" less and less time by strategies relying on secret information. The only organizations that will be able to survive—or that will in fact constitute—any foreseeable social technocracy will necessarily exercise control by means of individually rewarding, nonrepressive, nonsecretive procedures. This is an optimistic and tentative, but, I think, essentially tenable proposition.

A more realistic and immediate threat from technological advance than excessive social control is the possibility of sudden disorganization and chaos. Complexly balanced organizations are vulnerable to manipulation by adroitly placed pressure. The accidental east coast electrical blackout in November 1965 previously mentioned is a notable example of technical vulnerability. Basic institutional stability of governments, universities, and unions appears increasingly threatened by uncompromising group action of even a relatively few individuals. Guerrilla actions against public water supplies, communication networks, and transportation could temporarily paralyze, if not seriously injure, "Big Brother."

In international affairs, one would be even more hard-pressed to make a convincing case that technology has thus far brought much control, uniformity, or boredom—except perhaps at the level of ubiquitous Coca Cola franchises (and, even then, tourists often complain that it doesn't taste the same). It is possible that sometime in the future we will develop a cruel and excessively subtle psychotechnology, but this is not a problem of highest priority. Most commentators seem to agree that *Homo sapiens* faces long-term success and short-term disaster.

Much of our present hostile technology—this includes devices that indiscriminately cause pollution or destroy natural resources—will most likely "fade away" if effective and economically feasible alternatives become apparent. Philosophical discussion, restrictive legislation, or the singing of protest songs on electric guitars is more accurately viewed as a symptom than a solution. A practical metatechnology must concern itself with relatively nonaversive means of regulating "spontaneous" innovations and of encouraging others. The most elegant and efficient control is exercised in the equipment design phase or earlier. Because approximately 80% of the manufacturing assets in the United States is controlled by about 2,000 of the largest corporations [Ray, 1968], a natural pressure point exists for shaping the direction and products of our cumulative technical knowledge. Systematic research fund allocation, tax rebates, predistribution screening procedures, similar to those now used by the Food and Drug Administration for drugs, are the kind of procedures that could be used to direct technological developments [Schwitzgebel, 1967].

Scattered efforts are now under way to study the reciprocal influences of technology, social impact, and public policy. The boundaries of this problem, though still rather vaguely defined, are beginning to delineate a field of study. Some emerging signs include interdisciplinary programs such as Columbia University's Institute for the Study of Science in Human Affairs; Cornell University's Program on Science, Technology and Society; Harvard University's Program in Technology and Society; the work of the Committee on Science and Public Policy of the National Academy of Sciences; publication of a bibliography on science, technology, and public policy [Caldwell, 1968]; and the formation of a Congressional subcommittee on science, research, and development. These efforts can be distinguished from traditional academic concerns since they do not, at least directly, deal with the substance, history, or philosophy of science or technology.

It has been suggested [Platt, 1962] that the dominant fact in the long run in shaping the kind of inventions we generate is likely to be the steady pressure of elementary human desires:

> To be warm and full and free, these are our first needs, . . . but what dissolves and remolds societies unaware is that we also want, like children, to have sweet smells, music, pictures, entertainment, bright lights, and powerful servants. We want to make magic, to run like the wind and to fly like the birds and to talk across miles and to be as beautiful as gods and to know how everything works [p. 62].

Our inventiveness should be able to capture, in tangible form, something of ancient dream and myth. By making our physical environment and our physical selves increasingly responsive to human intention, the distinction between matter and fantasy will gradually diminish. Thus, if we can meet our short-term social crises, the human odyssey will inevitably move toward new dimensions of being. In this, it seems to me, psychologists should find a certain measure of challenge and excitement.

References

1. AYLLON, J., and MICHAEL, J. The psychiatric nurse as a behavioral engineer. *Journal of the Experimental Analysis of Behavior* 2 (1959):323–34.
2. AZRIN, N., JONES, R., and FLYE, B. Behavioral engineering: Control of a motor and verbal (stuttering) response by rhythmic stimuli. *Journal of Applied Behavior Analysis* 1 (1968):283–96.
3. AZRIN, N. H., and LINDSLEY, O. R. The reinforcement of cooperation between children. *Journal of Abnormal and Social Psychology* 52 (1956):100–2.
4. AZRIN, N., and POWELL, J. Behavioral engineering: The reduction of smoking behavior by a conditioning apparatus and procedure. *Journal of Applied Behavior Analysis* 3 (1968):193–200.

5. BARKER, R. G. Explorations in ecological psychology. *American Psychologist* 20 (1965):1–14.

6. BERNAL, P. D. *The World, the Flesh and the Devil.* [No publisher] 1929. [Cited in A. C. Clarke, ed. *Profiles of the Future.* New York: Harper & Row, 1958.]

7. BIRD, R. M. Theory and Application of Remote Instrumentation Systems for Behavioral Research. Unpublished doctoral dissertation, School of Engineering, University of California, Los Angeles, 1969.

8. BLUM, R. H., and FUNKHOUSER, M. L. A lobby for people? *American Psychologist* 22 (1967):208–10.

9. BRADY, J. P. A behavioral approach to stuttering. *American Journal of Psychiatry* 125 (1968):843–48.

10. BREGER, L., and McGAUGH, J. L. Critique and reformulation of "learning-theory" approaches to psychotherapy and neurosis. *Psychological Bulletin* 63 (1965):338–58.

11. CALDWELL, L. K., ed. *Science, Technology, and Public Policy: A Selected and Annotated Bibliography.* Vol. 1. Bloomington: Indiana University, Department of Government, 1968.

12. CALHOUN, J. B. Space and the strategy of life. *Ekistics* 29 (175) (1970).

13. CHENEY, C. D. Mechanically augmented human toilet training. Available from Psychology Department, Eastern Washington State College, 1968. (Mimeographed paper.)

14. CLARK, J. H. Hypnotizing with a teaching machine. *Science Journal* (London) 4 (1968):19.

15. CROSBY, N. D. Essential enuresis: Successful treatment based on physiological concepts. *Medical Journal of Australia* 2 (1950):533–43.

16. DELGADO, J. M. R. *Physical Control of the Mind: Toward a Psychocivilized Society.* New York: Harper & Row, 1969.

17. DEWAN, E. M. Communication by voluntary control of the electroencephalogram. *Proceedings of the Symposium of Biomedical Engineering* 1 (1966):349–51.

18. FEIERABEND, I., and FEIERABEND, R. Aggressive behaviors within politics, 1948–1962: A cross-national study. *Journal of Conflict Resolution* 10 (1966):249–71.

19. FRANKS, C. M. Clinical application of conditioning and other behavioral techniques: Conceptual and professional considerations. *Conditional Reflex* 1 (1966):36–50.

20. FÜLÖP-MILLER, R. *Leaders, Dreamers, and Rebels.* New York: Viking Press, 1935.

21. GALTON, F. Measurement of character. *Fortnightly Review* 36 (1884):179–85.

22. GORDON, T. J., and HELMER, O. *Report on a Long-Range Forecasting Study.* Santa Monica, Calif.: Rand Corporation, 1964.

23. KRANZBERG, M. The disunity of science-technology. *American Scientist* 56 (1968): 21–34.

24. KRASNER, L. The therapist as a social reinforcement machine. In H. H. Strupp, and L. Luborsky, eds. *Research in Psychotherapy,* Vol. 2. Washington, D. C.: American Psychological Association, 1962.

25. LAGEY, J. Community treatment programs for multi-problem families. Available from Research Department, Community Chest, Vancouver, B.C., Canada, 1962. Cited in E. L. Phillips, and D. M. Wiener, eds. *Short-term Psychotherapy and Structured Behavior Change.* New York: McGraw-Hill, 1966.

26. LANG, P. J. The on-line computer in behavior therapy research. *American Psychologist* 24 (1969):236–39.

27. LEVY, L. H. The skew in clinical psychology. *American Psychologist* 17 (1962):244–49.

28. LOVIBOND, S. H. The mechanism of conditioning treatment of enuresis. *Behaviour Research and Therapy* 1 (1963):17–21.

29. MIGLER, B., and WOLPE, J. Automated self-desensitization: A case report. *Behaviour Research and Therapy* 5 (1967):133–35.

30. The most dangerous game: An experiment in interviewer-responsive television. *Audiovisual Instruction* 12 (1968):473–76.

31. MOWRER, O. H., and MOWRER, W. M. Enuresis: A method for its study and treatment. *American Journal of Orthopsychiatry* 8 (1938):436–59.

32. ORWELL, G. *1984*. New York: Harcourt, Brace & World, 1949.

33. PLATT, J. R. *The Excitement of Science*. Boston: Houghton Mifflin, 1962.

34. PLATT, J. R. *The Step to Man*. New York: John Wiley & Sons, 1966.

35. PLATT, J. R. What we must do. *Science* 166 (1969):1115–21.

36. PRICE, D. J. DeS. Is technology historically independent of science?: A study in statistical historiography. *Technology and Culture* 6 (1965):533–67.

37. RAY, P. H. Human ecology, technology, and the need for social planning. *American Behavioral Scientist* 2 (1968):16–19.

38. SCHWITZGEBEL, R. L. Electronic innovation in the behavioral sciences. *American Psychologist* 22 (1967):364–70.

39. SCHWITZGEBEL, R. L. Survey of electromechanical devices for behavior modification. *Psychological Bulletin* 70 (1968):444–59.

40. SCHWITZGEBEL, R. L. A remote instrumentation system for behavior modification: A preliminary report. In R. Rubin and C. M. Franks, eds. *Advances in Behavior Therapy, 1968*. New York: Academic Press, 1969.

41. TANTER, R. Dimensions of conflict behavior within and between nations. *Journal of Conflict Resolution* 10 (1966):41–61.

42. WEINBERG, A. M. Social problems and national socio-technical institutes. In National Academy of Sciences, *Applied science and technological progress*. Washington, D. C.: United States Government Printing Office, 1967.

43. WHITE, R. J. Experimental transplantation of the brain. In F. T. Rapoport and J. Dausset, eds. *Human Transplantation*. New York: Grune & Stratton, 1968.

44. WIENER, N. *The Human Use of Human Beings*. Boston: Houghton Mifflin, 1950.

The Future of Drugs and
Drug of the Future

NATHAN S. KLINE

Kline, like Schwitzgebel, looks to the future. But instead of concentrating on technology, he speculates about possibilities for amelioration of the human condition by the application of drugs.

In this respect, it is important to remember that drugs do not always behave as we might like them to. Many factors influence their effects. Nowlis has already emphasized that drug effect is a function of complex interactions between the substance (the chemistry of the drug; the amount and pattern of ingestion) and the person (physiologically, psychologically, and socioculturally defined). She stressed the indeterminacies and uncertainties of drug application in terms of dosage response curves, multiple effects, and variability of reaction from person to person and from time to time in the same person. Kline, too, notes some of these influences. He points out that heredity, environment, psychological makeup, expectation, physiology, and timing all make a difference in the effects that drugs will have.

The point of all these cautions is that even though we may speculate about the many and exciting uses to which drugs might eventually be put, there are still a great number of questions that need to be answered. As usual in psychology, things are not so neat as we should like them to be.

Drugs have played an important role in man's experience for thousands of years, first in relation to religious and ritualistic functions, later for a variety of secular reasons as well. Social, psychological, and technological factors set the stage for today's drug problem. It is becoming increasingly clear that the problem is not drugs, but the manner and purpose of their use. Life styles can be altered by drugs, positively as well as negatively. Pharmacological treatment can provide relief for abnormal psychological states and correct potential pathology. New knowledge is also opening

SOURCE: From *Journal of Social Issues* 27 (3):73–87. Copyright © 1971 by the Society for the Psychological Study of Social Issues, a division of the American Psychological Association. Reprinted by permission.

vistas for enlarging man's creative and productive capacities. Man himself remains the key determinant.

From times immemorial man has been plunged in a pharmacological environment and even today all but the most primitive tribes make quite extensive use of drugs. The growing concern about such drug use is usually misplaced onto the drugs themselves whereas it is clear that the problem is the manner and purpose of their use. Drugs, like art, music, and the dance, originally served primarily religious and ritual functions. Among the surviving peyote cults of Mexico [Furst, undated] and the Ayuasqua users of Northern Peru,[1] in the back country of Nepal [Sharma, undated], as well as in numerous other places, it is the spirit of the plant or of some deity summoned through the drug-taking which is the purpose of its use. The circumstances are almost always ceremonial and the expectations of response quite explicit. As traditions deteriorate (as when a tribe dweller migrates to a cosmopolitan city or a foreign worker violates, and encourages others to violate, "outworn" restrictions) the drugs are utilized for other purposes. In fact, some of the drugs never make the transition because of violent and disagreeable side effects which are accepted within the ritual context but not otherwise.

Setting aside the ritualistic purpose of inducing the spirits to favor us, what are the secular motives that lead us to use drugs which alter thinking, feeling, and behaving? Some of the reasons, obviously not all mutually exclusive, would be relief of psychological discomfort (guilt, insecurity, anxiousness, regret, etc.); escape *from* emotional anaesthesia (lack of any or sufficient feeling, pleasant or unpleasant, of which boredom is one variant); escape *into* emotional anaesthesia; curiosity; rebellion or non-conformity; group pressure (belongingness, daring, etc.); pleasure seeking; search for "meaning"; providing a rationalization for economic, social, and other forms of failure.

In viewing the users it is helpful to distinguish between those who are unaware that they are using drugs (e.g., the nice old ladies who take "tonics" containing alcohol and opiates); the deliberate individual user who takes the drug for its own sake when the drug is legally and legitimately obtained (e.g., alcohol, caffeine) and when it is illicitly obtained; the group user for whom it serves some secondary purpose such as enhanced conviviality or more intimate feeling of relatedness; those who are prone to drug dependence, i.e., the continuing, periodic, or sporadic need to experience sensations produced by the drug or to relieve discomforts which might otherwise occur.

Other considerations which involve both initial and continued use are properties of the drug (dependency development, duration of action, tolerance, sensitization, potentiation, sequelae, chromosome alterations, etc.); availability of the drug (cost, enforcement if illegal, medical channels, ease of manufacturing, etc.); environmental inducements or restraints (warnings or "temptations" via media of mass communication, prestige of use, etc.).

Difficulties arise because of the vague border between disease and discom-

[1] C. A. Seguin. Personal communication, 1971.

fort in the psychological universe. There are substantial areas of physical discomfort which are not regarded as disease, but the distinction is unclear in the mental and emotional field. The situation is further complicated because drugs have been used to ease such psychological discomfort under *non*medical sanction.

> Life as we find it is too hard for us; it entails too much pain, too many disappointments, impossible tasks. We cannot dispense with auxiliary constructions. . . . There are perhaps three of these means: powerful diversions of interest which lead us to care little about our misery; substitutive gratifications which lessen it; and intoxicating substances which make us insensitive to it [Freud, 1951, p. 25].
>
> The services rendered by intoxicating substances in the struggle for happiness and in warding off misery rank so highly as a benefit that both individuals and races have given them an established position within their libido-economy. It is not merely the immediate gain in pleasure which one owes to them but also a measure of that independence of the outer world which is so sorely craved [Freud, 1951, p. 31].

The medical use derives from religious-spiritual beginnings. As late as the Middle Ages in our own Western medicine the generally accepted belief was that the zodiac sign under which an individual was born determined his individual response to particular drugs—as did the time of gathering and preparing them. Paracelsus, Newton, and others in the vanguard of secularism were generally accepting of this approach. In the refugee settlement established by the Dalai Lama of Tibet, the medical and astrological activities are combined [Office of His Holiness, 1969]. We are inclined to regard the invocations for spiritual assistance in early medical texts (e.g., the Ebers papyrus of 1500 B.C.) as irrelevant concessions to current prejudice. The evidence, however, is that the medical practitioners were quite serious: Without the spiritual influences how could one account for the success of an identical treatment in one case and its failure in another?

Although the conditions favoring its application had been present for a considerable time, it was the introduction of the synthetic products of chemistry (and the refinement of natural products) that set the stage for today's problem. Within the past century the conviction has become almost universal that through chemistry we will eventually succeed in finding treatment for all medical disorders. The insistence that emotional and mental disorders are medical has naturally led to their inclusion as amenable to pharmacological management—and in fact there have been some brilliant successes.

Even Freud is most moralistic about the use of drugs for such purposes since he adds to the quotation above: "In certain circumstances they are to blame when valuable energies which could have been used to improve the lot of humanity are uselessly wasted" [Freud, 1951, p. 31].

Anxiety and depression are part of the human condition and without them we would be other than we are—for better or for worse. Most would argue that the very extremes of anxiety and depression should be treated, but where is the border to be drawn? Shall it differ from one individual to another depending on his or her tolerance? Shall different groups (based on age, sex, or occupation, for instance) be handled differently? The proposals which follow are in general not strictly medical since they do not deal with the rectification of pathology. Perhaps we should not "tinker with the levers which control eternity." But since we do know that we are being influenced in our decisions and feelings and behavior it is really not a question of avoiding influence but deciding whether we wish to leave the pressures to special interest groups or to random events, or whether we wish to attempt control of our own destinies—a more responsible but probably no less dangerous venture.

Ways in Which Drugs Can Alter Life Patterns

CORRECTION OF EXISTING SYMPTOMS

There are a surprisingly large number of persons who suffer from diseases which affect their life style. High on such a list would be chronic depression which may manifest itself in such forms as fatigue, underachievement, hypochondriasis, etc., as well as in its more obvious manifestations. Appropriate treatment can alter the total life pattern. As one patient put it, "Now for the first time I feel like I always knew I should feel."

Not only relief of abnormal psychological states (anxiety, phobias, obsessions, etc.) but also pharmacological treatment of physical pathology (hypothyroidism, diabetes, chronic prostatitis, colitis, etc.) can entail a radical alteration of life pattern.

CORRECTION OF POTENTIAL PATHOLOGY

The administration of drugs may prevent the development of conditions which would be severaly disabling by supplying some missing ingredient as in pellagra, cretinism, and other endocrine deficiency disorders. A curious reversal is phenylketonuria where the treatment is to subtract from the diet, as far as possible, the foods with phenylalanine since it cannot be appropriately metabolized. There are several similar amino-acid and other inborn errors of metabolism whose correction radically alters the way the life pattern will develop.

PREVENTION OF ACUTE SYMPTOMS

Excruciating pain, uncontrolled euphoria, dementia, and deliria can abruptly precipitate irreversible changes. Thus prevention of such acute symptoms by anesthetics, tranquilizers, etc., may similarly alter a life pattern by preventing its disruption.

PREVENTION OR RELIEF OF CHRONIC SYMPTOMS

Recurrent or continuing pathology such as angina, mucous colitis, hiccoughs, or depression can lead to profound alterations in how one feels, thinks, and acts. Thus drugs which prevent or relieve such states are profoundly life-altering. Current interest in lithium (for recurrent affective disorders) is one example of the importance of this approach.

ACUTE DRUG-INDUCED PATHOLOGY

At times alterations in life patterns can be produced by deliberate or accidental use of drugs on a single occasion. One of my most notable failures in treatment was a PhD studying in London who attempted suicide with cyanide. The resultant impairment was an immovable and inseparable mixture of physical and psychological trauma which in no way damaged his intelligence but nevertheless made him hopelessly and retrogressively dependent.

In susceptible individuals, LSD and similarly acting drugs may produce permanent dissociation after a single administration.

PATHOLOGY INDUCED BY CHRONIC DRUG USE

The character of the Mad Hatter in *Alice in Wonderland* was drawn from life. In the preparation of felt for hats, mercury was commonly used and the fumes plus the quantity accidentally ingested produced a type of organic deterioration resulting eventually in dementia. Thus sizeable number of hatters did become "mad" as a result of chronic mercury poisoning.

It may well be that chronic air pollution, chemical sprays of food, or radioactive fall-out may someday be found to have had a similar effect on our own life patterns.

MINOR REALITY-RELIEVERS

Drugs are widely used to alter life patterns in ways other than the correction or production of gross pathology. In our own culture there are tens of millions of persons whose lives are markedly more happy because of the use of caffeine, alcohol, nicotine, and even amphetamines and barbiturates. Unfortunately with some of these drugs (e.g., alcohol, amphetamines, barbiturates) a percentage of users become ab-users; in other instances (e.g., nicotine) there may be unfortunate side effects such as heart disease and cancer; in others (e.g., coffee and tea) there are only very rarely undesirable consequences. There is some reason to be hopeful that methods of preventing addiction can be developed.

In different cultures other drugs have been used for similar purposes, e.g., cannabis sativa (whether as hashish, bhang, marijuana or some other form), qat (kat), coca leaves.

Controlled use in one culture by no means guarantees that a drug can be imported "safely" into another culture. The introduction of alcohol to the American Indian and of opium to India and China had disastrous consequences. It is too early to tell what results cannabis use by the middle and upper classes will have here in the U.S.A.

INDUCTION OF TRANSCENDENTAL STATES

The recorded use of drugs in conjunction with religious or mystical ecstasy dates back at least as far as the Eleusinian mysteries and probably even earlier, to the time of the Egyptian Middle Kingdom. The actual beginnings are lost in proto-history. From hashish use by the *hashashin* (assassins) under Hasan Sabah, to the hallucinogenic candles burned at the witches' Sabbaths, to current use of LSD to induce psychedelic states, there has always been a great value placed on drugs to effect major conversions of life patterns. Drugs may produce dissociation and perceptual pathology (including hallucinations), but obviously a great deal more is involved in determining what will result.

Factors Determining How Drugs Induce Alterations of Life Patterns

Aside from the chemical structure of the drug itself and its expected action on the organism, there are other influences which determine what actually does happen.

HEREDITARY POTENTIALS

There was until fairly recent years a great neglect of pharmacogenetic influence. The impetus to a good deal of this work was a demonstration in 1938 that atropine esterase occurred in some rabbits but not others, which explained the puzzling observation made in 1852 by Schroff, a Viennese physician, that some strains of rabbits enjoyed eating belladonna leaves that were fatal to other rabbits. McClearn and Rodgers [1961] demonstrated clear and pronounced strain differences in alcohol preference of highly inbred groups. The possibility of the preference being due to learned behavior was ruled out since "pups cross-fostered on mothers of other strains showed preference patterns consistent with the genetic rather than the foster line."

> Certain strains of mice will even drink to their own detriment. We thus conclude that we have demonstrated a close analogue to the condition of human alcoholism: specifically identifiable physiological changes of an undesirable sort, resulting from prolonged voluntary ingestion of alcohol by animals with alternating access to adequate diet, continued their level

of ingestion following the physiological changes [McClearn and Rodgers, 1961, p. 119].

The capacity of drugs to alter life patterns in one individual but not in another in many cases may be related to hereditary potentials.

ENVIRONMENTAL CONDITIONS

Physical environment has long been known to influence drug response. The amount of oxygen available (high or low altitude), season, and the temperature of the environment are obvious factors.

Certain drugs such as barbiturates and alcohol are disinhibitors and resultant behavior depends strongly on the social environment. If given to an individual in a quiet room, they induce sleep, but to the individual who is attending a noisy party there is usually overstimulation.

At times hereditary factors interplay with environmental circumstances. Stimulants such as the amphetamines are about eight times as toxic to mice crowded into one large cage as to litter mates caged singly. However, for certain strains of mice (DBA/2 or BDF mice) this susceptibility does not hold. Thus social environmental conditions as well as physical ones can be shown to influence drug response in animals as well as in humans.

PSYCHOLOGICAL STRUCTURE

Anxiety-prone individuals respond in a different way to medication than do those not so inclined [DiMascio and Rinkel, 1964; Heninger, DiMascio, and Klerman, 1965; Janke, 1960, 1966; Klerman, 1961; Liernert and Traxel, 1959; Luoto, 1964; McPeake and DiMascio, 1964; Munkelt and Othmer, 1965; Nowlis and Nowlis, 1956; Shagass, 1960]. Introversion and extroversion tendencies are also important factors, as is intellectual capability [Rickels, 1965].

EXPECTATIONS

To a surprising degree we derive from experience that which we anticipate and we live out our expectations of ourselves. The diversity of response to drugs is at least partially accounted for by the fact that many of the drugs cause dissociation. Once the always tenuous restraints of reality are further released, it is not difficult to see why events follow closely after the heart of desire or apprehension. The "revealed" state, once experienced, can produce a permanent conversion.

PHYSIOLOGICAL STATE

Hunger, sleep deprivation, and reduced oxygen supply brought on by hyperventilation or by retarded breathing (as in Yoga) usually accentuate the speed and depth of drug action. Reportedly, elevated blood sugar provides an extra depth of response with certain drugs (e.g., marijuana). The general state of nutrition, recent diet, the presence or absence of other drugs—even at times those used months before [Esser and Kline, 1967]—may alter responses. There are curious combinations. The use of Calabar beans in ritual trials is based on the fact that in the presence of high adrenalin the drug is poisonous, but otherwise it is relatively harmless.

Thus alterations in physiological states can determine the extent of a drug response and whether it will have any long-term or even short-term effects.

TIMING

One of the most basic of biological phenomena is the constant waxings and wanings in addition to diurnal rhythms. Lack of appropriate techniques for measuring, storing, and analyzing data of this type led in the past to serious neglect of this problem. High speed data collection techniques and computers with large enough memory cores have brought us within sight of dealing with this area, although the soft-ware (i.e., the programs) for analysis are still generally lacking.

Timing is crucial in at least three ways. First, it is important to know when in the life cycle the drug is given; there are often specific periods, prenatal as well as post-partum, when, and only when, the fetus or neonate is susceptible. Second, the effect of a drug on a specific parameter or even the total organism may differ depending on whether that specific parameter is ebbing or flowing; this in turn may determine whether there is or is not a permanent alteration in the life pattern. And finally, for some, but not all drugs, the time of day has been shown to strongly affect the response.

Probable Future Alterations of Life Patterns by Drugs

Implication of the future directions in which drug usage is likely to go already exist in a substantial number of the pharmaceuticals presently available. Some of these are currently regarded as side effects, but it is almost an aphorism that today's side effects are tomorrow's therapy. The shortened sleep need with monoamine oxidase inhibitors, the reduced sexual sensitivity, or even the shortened memory span have, each of them, possible therapeutic applications. The real problems in the field of psychopharmaceuticals are not so much the creation of any of the following classes of drugs, but determining who should make the decisions as to when they should be used, on whom, and by whom.

Unquestionably, additional and probably even more startling drug actions will occur as fall-out from other research in the field. As newer possibilities occur, and as we gain experience with those already available or possible, there is also likely to be a shift in attitude in respect to this most important question of who shall exercise control.

PROLONG CHILDHOOD AND (SHORTEN?) ADOLESCENCE

The average human life span has been greatly prolonged in the past century, but this occurred primarily by the reduction in infant mortality and the reduction of deaths from pneumonia in the older age groups. Unfortunately there is little we can do to reverse or prevent the depredations of aging. Even in the best of health the years beyond "three score years and ten" are not usually one's best.

One of the features which has made human civilization possible is the prolonged childhood of man, since it is then that he is most susceptible to education. It has been this vastly extended period as compared with other animals that has been a unique feature of the human venture. Hence it would appear sensible to try to prolong life another few decades by extending the period during which the acquisition of knowledge and skills comes most easily. We are already doing this in a social sense, since the time at which one finishes college is already half a dozen years beyond physical maturity.

Conceivably, if childhood were adequate, the turbulence of adolescence could be short-circuited, with avoidance of many of the problems which thereafter continue to plague people in later life. It would seem sensible to arrange adolescence so that it lasted no more than two hours of some Sunday afternoon.

REDUCE NEED FOR SLEEP

As previously indicated, this has already occurred as a side effect of some of the antidepressant drugs. Based on the rigorous training of the Mogul Emperors, as well as current physiological evidence, it appears entirely possible that three to three and a half hours sleep is all that is really required. The habit of sleeping longer quite possibly developed as a survival trait, since it was not safe for a creature such as man with his poor night vision (along with his other inadequacies) to go wandering about at a time of day when he was so little protected.

With the increasing knowledge of the functions of Rapid Eye Movement (REM) time and the various stages of sleep, it now looks as though we may be able to simulate or induce the bioelectric-biochemical activity required and conceivably be able totally to circumvent the need for sleep. Constructive use of these additional billions of man hours every day is indeed a challenge.

PROVIDE SAFE SHORT-ACTING INTOXICANTS

At least under the present rituals and routines in which we live, it seems almost essential that periods of relief be provided. Safe, rapidly-acting intoxicants that produce satisfactory dissociation and euphoria would be most valuable. The appeals of alcohol, of marijuana, of opiates, amphetamines, etc., are at least in part because they do possess some degree of such activity. However, none of them serves ideally for the purpose. It is quite likely that if acknowldgment were given of the desirability of such a pharmaceutical, it could be produced within a matter of a few years at most.

REGULATE SEXUAL RESPONSES

Man is one of the few creatures in whom sexual activity is not seasonal. His constant restlessness on this score provides him with both more pleasures and more problems than any other bodily function. Pharmacological regulation of some aspects of this behavior is already available and others will probably be achieved in the next few years. Banking the fires or stoking them biochemically so that temperature and activity could match more closely the appropriate environmental circumstances would increase the sum total of pleasure and, at the same time, allow man to devote more of his time, intelligence, and energy to more exclusively human activities.

CONTROL AFFECT AND AGGRESSION

There is some evidence that electrolyte balance is related to control of excessive excursions of affect and aggression. Perhaps the skeptical attitudes of Americans toward balneology and mineral water has been mistaken. Chlorination and fluoridation of water have been generally accepted as health measures. Why not lithium in the water supply as well—if it is capable of preventing pathology without circumscribing normal human feelings?

MEDIATE NUTRITION, METABOLISM, AND PHYSICAL GROWTH

At least as great and possibly greater than psychosomatic effects are the somatopsychic ones. Adequate control of the genetic code or of the messenger functions should enable us, within a few decades, to eliminate most gross physical pathology so that deviations so extreme as to be regarded as ugly will no longer occur. A great deal of the psychopathology which arises because one human regards himself as physically or aesthetically inferior to another could be eliminated. This type of investigation is already under way.

INCREASE OR DECREASE REACTIVITY (ALERTNESS, RELAXATION)

Some of the pharmaceuticals available permit us to extend to a small degree the period of reactivity by deferring fatigue. There are others which partially work to permit relaxation when hyper-alertness would only be a nuisance. It is quite possible that appropriate "natural" products (plants, etc.) already exist that would provide the lead towards synthesizing virtually ideal substances for these purposes. Recognition of the need and conscious search would perhaps provide these agents almost at once.

PROLONG OR SHORTEN MEMORY

How much remarkably more rich life would be if we were able to remember whatever we wished. On the other hand, how terribly cruel if we could not forget those things we had seen or done which were unbearable. We are close enough to understanding how memory works to expect that within another decade such agents could become a reality.

INDUCE OR PREVENT LEARNING

EXPERIENCE WITHOUT REINFORCEMENT.   There are certain experiences through which one must unavoidably pass that may well scar the organism for an indefinite period. To some degree we do protect ourselves by not incorporating these events into our total psychic organization. In other cases unfortunately we do not have such control. Somewhat improved analyses of the biochemical changes which occur during such states should allow us, within the foreseeable future, to have available drugs which would prevent fatal flawing.

VICARIOUSLY WITH REINFORCEMENT.   On the other hand, there are both positive and negative experiences which would greatly enhance performance if the lesson they had to provide could be learned. Tentative beginnings have already been made in the use of drugs which would enhance the learning capacity of the individual so that the "experience" could be achieved vicariously via movies, reading, or being told.

The availability of such inducements to learning would likely alter the total educational process so that the time consumed to acquire any one segment would be greatly reduced and the scope greatly broadened to include character education as well.

PRODUCE OR DISCONTINUE TRANSFERENCE

The great desire to establish or discontinue transference relationships is overtly evident in primitive societies where the demand for love philters is a high priority item. In only slightly disguised form the use of chemicals as deodorants, mouth washes, and perfumes is essentially for the same purpose.

It would undoubtedly be construed as an invasion of privacy to give someone a pharmaceutical without his knowledge or permission. On the other hand, if one could turn off, it would no longer be really necessary in most cases to involve the party of the second part. In theory at least there is no reason why the deconditioning experience should not be greatly augmented through the use of appropriate drugs.

The potential uses in terms of psychotherapy with involved oedipal situations present an almost limitless potential.

PROVOKE OR RELIEVE GUILT

The biochemical correlates of many of the affective states are being subjected to investigation at the present time. Use of a technique such as that of Delgado [1969] should make it possible directly to evaluate not only what such correlates are, but whether the introduction of them will in turn produce the emotional state itself. According to one theory, the whole penal system is directed toward this end. How much simpler life would be if sufficient sense of guilt could be produced relevant to a particular type of situation to prevent its repetition. Punishment would then be truly rehabilitative and practically instantaneous.

At other times an undeserved and unwarranted feeling of guilt can ruin an entire life and even those of others touching it. A substantial part of what a psychiatrist does is to attempt to relieve such unwarranted and destructive guilt feelings. There is already evidence that this can be done pharmacologically in respect to anxiety which may well be an important component of guilt. Some interesting ethical and legal problems arise so that if such a drug is perfected, it may be that a board consisting of a judge and a clergyman as well as a psychiatrist would have to agree that such relief of guilt was justifiable before appropriate medication could be given.

FOSTER OR TERMINATE MOTHERING BEHAVIOR

With mothering behavior so typical of certain animals it appears highly probable that there are "juices" which mediate in the production of this behavior. By enhancing or interfering with their production, it is possible that the extent of such behavior could be controlled. There are cases where an increase of this function would be in order, but undoubtedly the greatest use would be in terminating such behavior once it had outlived its usefulness. The human female gets involved in more difficulties—and in turn involves others in problems—more because of excess inappropiate mothering behavior than because of untoward sexual passion or, for that matter, any other emotion.

SHORTEN OR EXTEND EXPERIENCED TIME

Drugs capable of altering our sense of time to some degree at least are already in existence. Jazz musicians credit both marijuana and the opiates with a capacity to extend the experience of time so that both the appreciation and production of music is greatly enhanced. There are various other occupations where this capacity would be quite important, e.g., magicians, ball players, etc. On the other hand, there are certain experiences which one wishes to have done with as rapidly as possible and any agent which speeded up the passage of experienced time would be useful.

CREATE CONDITIONS OF JAMAIS VU (NOVELTY) OR DÉJÀ VU (FAMILIARITY)

Married life would be considerably altered if one could bring to one's mate the feeling of fresh wonder that often characterizes the initial or early experiences. The same would hold true in many business partnerships and other working relationships. On occasion some of the dissociating drugs do produce reactions of this sort, but they are as yet too crude and unpredictable to be used specifically for this purpose.

It would not do to have all situations or even the majority of them of the "novelty" type. Indeed, it is also important to have available a compound which would create a feeling of familiarity, in order to deal more competently with problems that are made more difficult simply because they are new. Some of the euphoriant drugs tend in this direction.

DEEPEN OUR AWARENESS OF BEAUTY AND OUR SENSE OF AWE

By deepening our appreciation of the beauty which surrounds us and allowing us to experience afresh the awe of human existence, we can perhaps better discover—both emotionally and intellectually—the nature of the human venture It is this type of appeal that has made drugs so familiar an adjunct to religious ecstasies. This usage should be developed with enough improvement in the drugs themselves to insure that the experiences be expansions of reality rather than deceptions into para-universes.

Drugs and Destiny

All of these—and many more to come—are probes into the extension and control of our destinies. There is no more suitable ending than this quotation from Alexander Pope:

> Know then thyself, presume not God to scan,
> The proper study of mankind is Man.
> Placed on this isthmus of a middle state,
> A being darkly wise, and rudely great;
> With too much knowledge for the sceptic side,
> With too much weakness for the stoic's pride,
> He hangs between; in doubt to act or rest;
> In doubt to deem himself a god, or beast;
> In doubt his mind or body to prefer;
> Born but to die, and reasoning but to err;
> Sole judge of truth, in endless error hurl'd:
> The glory, jest and riddle of the world!

[*Essay on Man*, 1733]

References

1. DELGADO, J. Salmon Lecture. Presented to the New York Academy of Medicine, 1969.
2. DiMASCIO, A., and RINKEL, M. In M. Rinkel, ed. *Specific and Non-Specific Factors in Psychopharmacology.* New York: Philosophical Library, 1964.
3. ESSER, A. H., and KLINE, N. S. Routine blood pressure measurement in psychiatric research. *Journal of Clinical Pharmacology* 3 (1967):162–67.
4. FREUD, S. *Civilization and Its Discontents.* London: Hogarth Press, 1951.
5. FURST, P. (Film) *To Find Our Life.* Los Angeles: Latin American Center, University of California, undated.
6. HENINGER, G., DiMASCIO, A., and KLERMAN, G. L. Personality factors in variability of response to phenothiazines. *American Journal of Psychiatry* 121 (1965):1091–94.
7. JANKE, W. On the dependence of the effect of psychotropic substances on the affective stability. *Medicina Experimentals* 2 (1960):217–23.
8. JANKE, W. Über psychische Wirkungen verschiedener Tranquilizer bei gesunden, emotional labilen Personen. *Psychopharmacologia* 8 (1966):340–74.
9. KLERMAN, G. L. *Transactions of the Sixth Research Conference on Cooperative Chemotherapy Studies in Psychiatry* 6 (1961):339.
10. LIENERT, G. A., and TRAXEL, W. The effects of meprobamate and alcohol on galvanic skin response. *Journal of Psychology* 48 (1959):329–34.
11. LUOTO, K. Personality and placebo effects upon timing behavior. *Journal of Abnormal and Social Psychology* 68 (1964):54–61.
12. McCLEARN, G. E., and RODGERS, D. A. Genetic factors in alcohol preference of laboratory mice. *Journal of Comparative and Physiological Psychology* 54 (1961): 116–19.
13. McPEAKE, J. D., and DiMASCIO, A. Drug-personality interaction in the learning of a nonsense syllabic task. *Psychological Reports* 15 (1964):405–6.
14. MUNKELT, P., and OTHMER, E. Der Einfluss der psychischen Stabilität resp. Labilität und der Körpe-konstitution der Versuchspersonen auf die Wirkung des Psychotonicums 7- [2′ (1″-Methyl-2″-phenylaethylamino) -aethyl] -theophyllin HCl. *Arzneimittelforschung* 15 (1965):843–49.
15. NOWLIS, V., and NOWLIS, H. H. The description and analysis of mood. *Annals of the New York Academy of Sciences* 65 (1956):345–55.
16. OFFICE OF HIS HOLINESS THE DALAI LAMA. *Tibetans in Exile.* New Delhi: Gutenberg Press, 1969.
17. POPE, A. *Essay on Man.* M. Mack, ed. London: Methuen, 1950.
18. RICKELS, K. Some comments on non-drug factors in psychiatric drug therapy. *Psychosomatics* 8 (1965):303–9.
19. SHAGASS, C. In L. Uhr and J. G. Miller, eds. *Drugs and Behavior.* New York: John Wiley & Sons, 1960.
20. SHARMA, B. P. *Native Healers of Nepal.* Unpublished manuscript, undated.

Interpersonal Relationships: U.S.A. 2000

CARL R. ROGERS

As Matson has already pointed out, there are two crucial components to human-istic psychology: commitment to the exercise of free choice, and commitment to human becoming. This final selection clearly reflects those commitments. Rogers's article is filled with despair and hope—despair mostly at the current state of human affairs, and hope that because of humankind's "magnetic attraction to the experience of change, growth, fulfillment" we shall choose to follow routes that will lead us to personal and interpersonal enrichment. He outlines some of the alternatives we face with respect to important social issues: urban crowding, close-ness and intimacy, man-woman and parent-child relationships, education, industry, religion, and poverty.

Recall at this point Kelman's dilemma (page 544): behavior manipulation is bad because it deprives the person of the exercise of free will, but effective social change inevitably requires some form of behavior manipulation. Clearly Kelman and Rogers are in agreement in their emphasis on freedom of choice; certainly Rogers favors the former of the two arguments. But (as Kelman himself points out) Rogers tends to sidestep the second argument. Rogers implies that dedi-cation to free choice and the use of techniques that promote free choice free the influencer from the taint of manipulation. But his position fails to take note of the complexities of interpersonal influence, the social processes described through-out this book. Even the article that follows is manipulative—how many of us can reject Rogers's persuasive arguments? Thus Rogers too is caught in the di-lemma. At best he is in the "ethically ambiguous" situation in which he must maximize the good (free choice) and minimize the evil (manipulation). As you study this final article, watch for reflections of Kelman's arguments and consider the ways in which Rogers faces those ethical ambiguities.

I want to make it very clear at the outset that I am not making predictions

SOURCE: Reproduced by special permission from the *Journal of Applied Behavioral Science*, "Interpersonal Relationships: USA 2000," Carl R. Rogers, pages 265–80. Copyright © 1968 by the NTL Institute for Applied Behavioral Science.
Note: This paper was part of a symposium entitled "USA 2000," sponsored by the Esalen Institute and held in San Francisco, California, January 10, 1968.

about the year 2000. I am going to sketch possibilities, alternative routes which we may travel.

One important reason for refusing to make predictions is that for the first time in history man is not only taking his future seriously, but he also has adequate technology and power to shape and form that future. He is endeavoring to *choose* his future rather than simply living out some inevitable trend. And we do not know what he will choose. So we do not know what man's relation to man will be in this country 32 years from now. But we can see certain possibilities.

Man's Greatest Problem

Before I try to sketch some of those possibilities I should like to point to the greatest problem which man faces in the years to come. It is not the hydrogen bomb, fearful as that may be. It is not the population explosion, though the consequences of that are awful to contemplate. It is instead a problem which is rarely mentioned or discussed. It is the question of how much change the human being can accept, absorb, and assimilate, and the rate at which he can take it. Can he keep up with the ever-increasing rate of technological change, or is there some point at which the human organism goes to pieces? Can he leave the static ways and static guidelines which have dominated all of his history and adopt the process ways, the continual changingness which must be his if he is to survive?

There is much to make us pessimistic about this. If we consider the incredible difficulties in bringing about change in our great bureaucracies of government, education, and religion, we become hopeless. When we see how frequently the people take action which is clearly against their long-range welfare—such as the resolute refusal to face up to the problem of the urban ghettos—we become discouraged.

But I see two elements on the other side of the balance. The first is the ability of the Western democratic cultures to respond appropriately—at the very last cliff-hanging moment—to those trends which challenge their survival.

The second element I have observed in individuals in therapy, in intensive encounter groups, and in organizations. It is the magnetic attraction of the experience of change, growth, fulfillment. Even though growth may involve intense pain and suffering, once the individual or group has tasted the excitement of this changingness, persons are drawn to it as to a magnet. Once a degree of actualization has been savored, the individual or the group is willing to take the frightening risk of launching out into a world of process, with few fixed landmarks, where the direction is guided from within. So, in this field of interpersonal relations, though there is much reason for despair, I believe that if our citizens experience something of the pain and risk of a growth toward personal enrichment they will grasp for more.

With this context of uncertainty about our ability or willingness to assimilate change, let us look at some specific areas of interpersonal relationships as they may be.

Urban Crowding and Its Possible Effects

The world population will more than double in the next 32 years, a ghastly trend which will affect us in unknown ways. The population of the United States, which was comfortably remembered in my grammar school days in 1915 as 100 million, 52 years later reached 200 million, 22 years from now is predicted to reach 300 million, and in the year 2000 will be between 320 and 340 million, though hopefully it will be starting to stabilize itself at about that time. The great bulk of these millions will reside in a great megalopolis, of which there will probably be three. One trend which we may follow is to crowd more and more closely together, as we are now crowded in our ghettos. I understand that Philip Hauser, the noted demographer, has stated that if all of us were crowded together as closely as the residents of Harlem all of the people in the entire United States could be contained in the five boroughs of New York City. The future may resemble this, if we choose to push in more and more closely together.

Such crowding has consequences. Even in rats, as Calhoun [1] has so vividly shown, overcrowding results in poor mothering, poor nest building, bizarre sexual behavior, cannibalism, and complete alienation, with some rats behaving like zombies, paying no attention to others, coming out of their solitary burrows only for food. The resemblance to human behavior in crowded rooming-house areas, the complete lack of involvement which permits people to watch a long-drawn-out murder without so much as calling the police, the poor family relationships—this could be a trend which will be carried even further by the year 2000.

On the other hand, we could learn to decentralize our great urban areas, to make them manageable, to provide not only for more efficiency but for warmer and more human interpersonal relationships. We could use more space, build smaller cities with great park and garden areas, devise plans for neighborhood building which would promote *humanization*, not dehumanization. What will the choice be?

Closeness and Intimacy in the Year 2000

In my estimation, one of the most rapidly growing social phenomena in the United States is the spread of the intensive group experience—sensitivity training, basic encounter groups, T groups (the labels are unimportant). The growth of this phenomenon is rendered more striking when one realizes that it is a "grass roots" movement. There is not a university nor a foundation nor a government agency which has given it any significant approval or support until the last five or six years. Yet it has permeated industry, is coming into education, is reaching families, professionals in the helping fields, and many other individuals. Why? I believe it is because people—ordinary people— have discovered that it alleviates their loneliness and permits them to grow, to risk, to change. It brings persons into real relationships with persons.

In our affluent society the individual's survival needs are satisfied. For the first time, he is freed to become aware of his isolation, aware of his alienation, aware of the fact that he is, during most of his life, a role interacting with other roles, a mask meeting other masks. And for the first time he is aware that this is not a *necessary* tragedy of life; that he does not have to live out his days in this fashion. So he is seeking, with great determination and inventive-ness, ways of modifying this existential loneliness. The intensive group experi-ence, perhaps the most significant social invention of this century, is an important one of these ways.

What will grow out of the current use of basic encounter groups, marathons, "labs," and the like? I have no idea what *forms* will proliferate out of these roots during the coming decades, but I believe men will discover new bases of intimacy which will be highly fulfilling. I believe there will be possibilities for the *rapid* development of closeness between and among persons, a closeness which is not artificial, but is real and deep, and which will be well suited to our increasing mobility of living. Temporary relationships will be able to achieve the richness and meaning which heretofore have been associated only with lifelong attachments.

There will be more awareness of what is going on within the person, an openness to all of one's experience—the sensory input of sound and taste and hearing and sight and smell, the richness of kaleidoscopically changing ideas and concepts, the wealth of feelings—positive, negative, and ambivalent, intense and moderate—toward oneself and toward others.

There will be the development of a whole new style of communication in which the person can, in effect, say, "I'm telling you the way it *is*, in me—my ideas, my desires, my feelings, my hopes, my angers, my fears, my despairs," and where the response will be equally open. We shall be experimenting with ways in which a whole person can communicate himself to another whole person. We shall discover that security resides not in hiding oneself but in being more fully known, and consequently in coming to know the other more fully. Aloneness will be something one chooses out of a desire for privacy, not an isolation into which one is forced.

In all of this I believe we shall be experimenting with a new ideal of what man may become, a model very *sharply* different from the historical view of man as a creature playing various appropriate roles. We seem to be aiming for a new *reality* in relationships, a new openness in communication, a love for one another which grows not out of a romantic blindness but out of the profound respect which is nearly always engendered by reality in relation-ships.

I recognize that many individuals in our culture are frightened in the depths of their being by this new picture of man—this flowing, changing, open, expressive, creative person. They may be able to stop the trend or even to reverse it. It is conceivable that we shall go in for the manufactured "image," as on TV, or may insist more strongly than ever that teachers are *teachers*, parents are *parents*, bosses are *manipulators*—that we may rigidify every role and stereotype in new and more armorplated ways. We may insist with new force that the only significant aspect of man is his rational and intellectual being and that nothing else matters. We may assert that he is a machine and no more. Yet I do not believe this will happen. The magnetism of the new man, toward which we are groping, is too great. Much of what I say in the remainder of this paper is based on the conviction that we are, for better or for worse, in labor pains and growth pains—turning toward this new view of man as becoming and being—a continuing, growing *process*.

Man-Woman Relationships

What do the coming decades hold for us in the realm of intimacy between boy and girl, man and woman? Here too enormous forces are at work, and choices are being made which will not, I believe, be reversed by the year 2000.

In the first place the trend toward greater freedom in sexual relationships, in adolescents and adults, is likely to continue, whether this direction frightens us or not. Many elements have conspired together to bring about a change in such behavior, and the advent of "the Pill" is only one of these. It seems probable that sexual intimacy will be a part of "going steady" or of any continuing special interest in a member of the opposite sex. The attitude of prurience is fast dying out, and sexual activity is seen as a potentially joyful and enriching part of a relationship. The attitude of possessiveness—of owning another person, which historically has dominated sexual unions—is likely to be greatly diminished. It is certain that there will be enormous variations in the quality of these sexual relationships—from those where sex is a purely physical contact which has almost the same solitary quality as masturbation to those in which the sexual aspect is an expression of an increasing sharing of feelings, of experiences, of interests, of each other.

By the year 2000 it will be quite feasible to ensure that there will be no children in a union. By one of the several means currently under study, each individual will be assured of lasting infertility in early adolescence. It will take positive action, permissible only after a thoughtful decision, to reestablish fertility. This will reverse the present situation where only by positive action can one *prevent* conception. Also, by that time, computerized matching of prospective partners will be far more sophisticated than it is today and will be of great help to an individual in finding a congenial companion of the opposite sex.

Some of the temporary unions thus formed may be legalized as a type of marriage—with no permanent commitment, with no children (by mutual agreement), and, if the union breaks up, no legal accusations, no necessity for showing legal cause, and no alimony.

It is becoming increasingly clear that a man-woman relationship will have *permanence* only in the degree in which it satisfies the emotional, psychological, intellectual, and physical needs of the partners. This means that the *permanent* marriage of the future will be even better than marriage in the present, because the ideals and goals for that marriage will be of a higher order. The partners will be demanding more of the relationship than they do today.

If a couple feel deeply committed to each other and mutually wish to remain together to raise a family, then this will be a new and more binding type of marriage. Each will accept the obligations involved in having and rearing children. There may be a mutual agreement as to whether or not the marriage includes sexual faithfulness to one's mate. Perhaps by the year 2000 we shall have reached the point where, through education and social pressure, a couple will decide to have children only when they have shown evidence of a mature commitment to each other, of a sort which is likely to have permanence.

What I am describing is a whole continuum of man-woman relationships, from the most casual dating and casual sex relationship to a rich and fulfilling partnership in which communication is open and real, where each is concerned with promoting the personal growth of the partner, and where there is a long-range commitment to each other which will form a sound basis for having and rearing children in an environment of love. Some parts of this continuum will exist within a legal framework; some will not.

One may say, with a large measure of truth, that much of this continuum already exists. But an awareness of, and an open acceptance of, this continuum by society will change its whole quality. Suppose it were openly accepted that some "marriages" are no more than ill-mated and transitory unions and that they will be broken. If children are not permitted in such marriages, then one divorce in every two marriages (the current rate in California) is no longer seen as a tragedy. The dissolving of the union may be painful, but it is not a *social* catastrophe, and the experience may be a necessary step in the personal growth of the two individuals toward greater maturity.

Parents and Children

What of the relationships between parents and their children? Here it is terribly difficult to foresee the future. If parents in general hold to the static views which have served reasonably well through the centuries of little change—"I know the values that are important in life," "I am wiser than my child in knowing the direction his life should take"—then the generation gap will grow so large that our culture will literally be split wide open. This may be the course of future events.

But there are straws in the wind which point in another way. Some parents wish to be *persons*—growing, changing persons—living in person-to-person relationships with the youngsters in their families. So we see the development of family encounter groups (still in their infancy) in which parents learn about themselves from their own and others' children, and children learn about themselves from their own and others' parents. Here the self-insights, the awareness of how one comes across to the other generation, bring changes in behavior and new ways of relating based on an open respect for oneself, out of which can grow a genuine respect for the other.

A new type of parent education is also developing in which there is respect for the parent as a person with feelings and rights as well as for the child and his feelings and rights. We find family groups where parent and child each *listen* to the other, where honest, open expression is also mutual. Parental authority and childhood submission give way before a realness which confronts realness. Such family relationships are not necessarily smooth, and the problems of process living are as perplexing as the problems brought on by static views; but there is communication and there is respect, and the generation gap becomes simply the communication gap which in some degree separates all individuals.

It may be hard for us to realize that some help for this new type of family relationship may come from industry. Some corporations, realizing that to start to educate a child at six is much too late, are beginning to dream up learning activities, learning "packages," which will not only be fun for the children but which will involve the whole family in mutually pleasurable and communicative activities. Everyone will have a good time learning—together.

Let me turn to quite a different facet of the relations of parents and children. What will the future hold for children from broken homes—who will continue to exist even if my most optimistic speculations come true? I trust there will be widespread experimentation in dealing with these youngsters. Perhaps we should take a lesson from the *kibbutzim*, where the child is cared for and gains his security from workers who love children and are trained to care for them, and where the contacts with parents, though relatively brief, tend to be full of love and fun. Perhaps some the "hippie" groups are showing the way in their small, close communities where the child is, ideally at least, cared for by all. We are in desperate need of creative approaches to this problem. Almost anything would be better than the present situation. Now the child is often fought over in court. He learns that one parent is bad, the other good. He is often exposed to the attempts of each parent to win him away, emotionally, from the other. He is often experienced as a burden by the mother, who is attempting to reestablish herself in a job and a new life. Or he is the sole focus of the mother's affections, which may be even worse. *He* is the one who suffers from divorce, and we have been most unimaginative in trying to promote his welfare. Hence my hope is that there will be many types of experimentation three decades from now, in helping the child of divorced parents to grow in the most favorable possible environment.

Learning in Interpersonal Relationships

What of education in the year 2000, especially as it involves interpersonal relationships?

It is possible that education will continue much as it is—concerned only with words, symbols, rational concepts based on the authoritative role of the teacher, further dehumanized by teaching machines, computerized knowledge, and increased use of tests and examinations. This is possible, because educators are showing greater resistance to change than any other institutional group. Yet I regard it as unlikely, because a revolution in education is long overdue, and the unrest of students is only one sign of this. So that I am going to speculate on some of the other possibilities.

It seems likely that schools will be greatly deemphasized in favor of a much broader, thoughtfully devised *environment for learning*, where the experiences of the student will be challenging, rewarding, affirmative, and pleasurable.

The teacher or professor will have largely disappeared. His place will be taken by a facilitator of learning, chosen for his facilitative attitudes as much as for his knowledge. He will be skilled in stimulating individual and group initiative in learning, skilled in facilitating discussions-in-depth of the *meaning* to the student of what is being learned, skilled in fostering creativity, skilled in providing the resources for learning. Among these resources will be much in the way of programmed learning, to be used as the student finds these learnings appropriate; much in the way of audio-visual aids such as filmed lectures and demonstrations by experts in each field; much in the way of computerized knowledge on which the student can draw. But these "hardware" possibilities are not my main concern.

We shall, I believe, see the facilitator focusing his major attention on the prime period for learning—from infancy to age six or eight. Among the most important learnings will be the personal and interpersonal. Every child will develop confidence in his own ability to learn, since he will be rewarded for learning at his own pace. Each child will learn that he is a person of worth, because he has unique and worthwhile capacities. He will learn how to be himself in a group—to listen, but also to speak, to learn about himself, but also to confront and give feedback to others. He will learn to be an individual, not a faceless conformist. He will learn, through simulations and computerized games, to meet many of the life problems he will face. He will find it permissible to engage in fantasy and daydreams, to think creative thoughts, to capture these in words or paints or constructions. He will find that learning, even difficult learning, is fun, both as an individual activity and in cooperation with others. His discipline will be self-discipline.

His learning will not be confined to the ancient intellectual concepts and specializations. It will not be a *preparation* for living. It will be, in itself, an *experience* in living. Feelings of inadequacy, hatred, a desire for power, feelings of love and awe and respect, feelings of fear and dread, unhappiness with parents or with other children—all these will be an open part of his curriculum, as worthy of exploration as history or mathematics. In fact this openness to feelings will enable him to learn content material more readily. His will be an education in becoming a whole human being, and the learnings will involve him deeply, openly, exploringly, in an awareness of his relationship to himself, an awareness of his relationships to the world of others, as well as in an awareness of the world of abstract knowledge.

Because learning has been exciting, because he has participated heavily and responsibly in choosing the directions of his learning, because he has discovered the world to be a fantastically changing place, he will wish to continue his learning into adult life. Thus communities will set up centers which are rich environments for learning, and the student will *never be graduated*. He will always be a part of a "commencement."

Persons in Industry

In view of my past prejudices I find it somewhat difficult but necessary to say that of all of the institutions of present-day American life, industry is perhaps best prepared to meet the year 2000. I am not speaking of its technical ability. I am speaking of the vision it is acquiring in regard to the importance of persons, of interpersonal relationships, and of open communication. That vision, to be sure, is often unrealized but it does exist.

Let me speculate briefly on the interpersonal aspect of industrial functioning. It is becoming increasingly clear to the leaders of any complex modern industry that the old hierarchical system of boss and employees is obsolete. If a factory is turning out one simple product, such a system may still work. But if it is in the business of producing vehicles for space or elaborate electronic devices, it is definitely inadequate. What takes its place? The only road to true efficiency seems to be that of persons communicating freely with persons—from below to above, from peer to peer, from above to below, from a member of one division to a member of another division. It is only through this elaborate, individually initiated network of open human communication that the essential information and know-how can pervade the organization. No one individual can possibly "direct" such complexity.

Thus if I were to hazard a guess in regard to industry in the year 2000 it would be something different from the predictions about increasing technical skill, increasing automation, increasing management by computers, and the like. All of those predictions will doubtless come true but the interpersonal aspect is less often discussed. I see many industries, by the year 2000, giving as much attention to the quality of interpersonal relationships and the quality of communication as they currently do to the technological aspects of their business. They will come to value persons as persons, and to recognize that only out of the *communicated* knowledge of all members of the organization can innovation and progress come. They will pay more attention to breakdowns in personal communication than to breakdowns of the circuitry in their computers. They will be forced to recognize that only as they are promoting the growth and fulfillment of the individuals on the payroll will they be promoting the growth and development of the organization.

What I have said will apply, I believe, not only to persons in management but to persons classed as "labor." The distinction grows less with every technological advance. It also applies, obviously, to the increasingly direct and personal communication between persons in management and persons in the labor force, if an industry is to become and remain healthily productive.

Religion as Interpersonal Living

Historically, much of man's life has revolved around his relationship to his God or gods and around his relationship to others who share his religious views. What will be the situation three decades from now?

It is definitely conceivable that out of a deep fear of the rapidly changing world he is creating, man may seek refuge in a sure dogma, a simplistic answer to life's complexities, a religion which will serve him as a security blanket. This seems unlikely, but I can image the circumstances under which it might occur.

The more likely possibility—or so it appears to me—is that by the year 2000, *institutionalized* religion, already on the wane as a significant factor in everyday life, will have faded to a point where it is of only slight importance in the community. Theology may still exist as a scholastic exercise, but in reality the God of authoritative answers will be not only dead but buried.

This does not mean at all that the concerns which have been the basis of religion will have vanished. The mysterious process of life, the mystery of the universe and how it came to be, the tragedy of man's alienation from himself and from others, the puzzle of the meaning of individual life—these mysteries will all be very much present. There may, indeed, be a *greater appreciation* of mystery as our knowledge increases (just as theoretical physicists now marvel at the true *mystery* of what they have discovered).

But religion, to the extent that the term is used, will consist of tentatively held hypotheses which are lived out and corrected in the interpersonal world. Groups, probably much smaller than present-day congregations, will wrestle with the ethical and moral and philosophical questions which are posed by the rapidly changing world. The individual will forge, with the support of the group, the stance he will take in the universe—a stance which he cannot regard as final because more data will continually be coming in.

In the open questioning and honest struggle to face reality which exist in such a group, it is likely that a sense of true community will develop—a community based not on a common creed nor an unchanging ritual but on the personal ties of individuals who have become deeply related to one another as they attempt to comprehend and to face, as living men, the mysteries of existence. The religion of the future will be man's existential choice of his way of living in an unknown tomorrow, a choice made more bearable because formed in a community of individuals who are like-minded, but like-minded only in their searching.

In line with the thread which runs through all of my remarks, it may well be that out of these many searching groups there may emerge a more unitary view of man, a view which might bind us together. Man as a creature with ability to remember the past and foresee the future, a creature with the capacity for choosing among alternatives, a creature whose deepest urges are for harmonious and loving relationships with his fellows, a creature with the capacity to understand the reasons for his destructive behavior, man as a person who has at least limited powers to form himself and to shape his future in the way he desires—this might be a crude sketch of the unifying view which could give us hope in a universe we cannot understand.

The Relationship with the Slum Dweller

I have left until the last the most difficult area: the relationship between the persons in the urban ghettos (Negroes and other minority groups) and the persons outside the ghetto.

Our inability to accept the changing nature of this anguished struggle is one of the deepest reasons for pessimism regarding the future. The more favored community seems, thus far, unwilling and unable to understand the effects upon individuals of a lifetime of defeat, frustration, and rejection. It seems, thus far, unable to comprehend that rebellion is *most* likely, not least likely, to occur in the very cities and situations in which there is, at last, some hope. We seem reluctant to give the ghetto dweller responsibility, the one thing which might restore his human dignity—because he will make mistakes. We seem to have no recognition that learning from mistakes is the only true way to independence. And, most tragically of all, we appear—on both sides—to have lost the belief that communication is possible. Thus I cannot deny the possibility that the next decades will see a growing rebellion, a bloody guerrilla warfare in our cities, with concentration camps, with military govern-ment, with fear and hatred in the heart of every citizen. It took a century for the hatreds between the North and the South to diminish to manageable proportions. How many centuries will it take for the hatreds of this new war to die down, a war which it may be too late to prevent?

What makes it, from my point of view, incredibly tragic is that the deepest, most basic issues revolve around communication. Distrust, suspicion, disillu-sionment have grown to such mammoth proportions on both sides—though perhaps especially on the part of the ghetto dweller—that it is taken for granted that communication is no longer possible. Yet funds, however great, and vocational retraining and housing projects and all the rest can do little with free, direct, honest communication between persons.

Is it impossible? It is my contention that if we mounted a massive effort to reestablish communication, in groups ranging from militant blacks through liberals of both colors to conservative whites; if we drew into this effort dedicated individuals, from the ghetto and outside, who were desirous of improving relationships; if we drew on the expert knowledge available in the social and behavioral sciences; if we backed this effort with a sum at least equivalent to the cost of all our B-52 bombers—then there might be a chance of preventing the bloody tragedy which faces us.

I should not want to be understood as saying that improved communication, improved interpersonal relationships, would *resolve* the situation. What I am saying is that if, in small groups or large, the hatreds and the disillusionments could be accepted and *understood*; if suspicion and despair could be fully voiced and met with respect; then out of such groups might slowly grow a mutual respect in which responsible decisions could be taken and realistic solutions worked out. In these decisions the ghetto dweller would be a fully involved participant, as would the person from outside. Leadership in the ghetto would meet on a fully equal basis with leadership in the "establishment." Both would bear responsibility, through black power and white power, for seeing that the decisions were *carried out*. Idealistic, you say? But we have the knowledge and the wealth which would make such a massive effort possible. And if we choose to follow the present trend, we have in South Vietnam a full color picture of how guerrilla warfare not only sacrifices lives but brutalizes the minds and hearts of the living. Shall we permit it to happen here? Or shall we choose to make a great and concerted effort to behave as persons with persons? On this issue I dare not even speculate.

Conclusion

Perhaps it is just as well that I conclude on this somberly precarious note. I hope I have made it clear that the potentialities for change and enrichment in the interpersonal world of the year 2000 most assuredly exist. There can be more of intimacy, less of loneliness, an infusion of emotional and intellectual learning in our relationships, better ways of resolving conflicts openly, man-woman relationships which are enriching, family relationships which are real, a sense of community which enables us to face the unknown. All of this is possible if as a people we choose to move into the new mode of living openly as a continually changing process.

Reference

1. CALHOUN, J. B. Population density and social pathology. *Sci. American* 206 (2) (1962):139–50.

Index

Abilities, specific, 262
Abstract thought, sex differences in, 284
  See also Sex differences
Abstraction, 240-41
  See also Learning
Activism, 357-84
  future of, 378-82
  sources of, 364-65
  See Protest; *See also* Activist students
Activist students, 357-84, esp. 360-61
  and family structure, 368-69
  and parental values, 367-68
  and rebellion, 367
  values of, 365-67
Adaptation and culture, 138, 140
Adaptation effects, long-term, 161-62
Adaptation level, 154, 159-62
Adjustment, integrative, 351-55
Admixture studies, 318
Adolescence, sexual behavior in, 20-26
  boys, 21-23
  and educational level, 25
  and emotional relations, 22-23
  and fantasy, 22
  girls, 23-26
  and guilt, 21
  masturbation, 20-21, 23
  non-sexual purposes, 24
  romantic vs. erotic, 24
  and social class, 25
Adolescence, shortening of through drugs, 565
Adulthood, sexual behavior in, 26-27
Advertising
  and subliminal stimulation (q.v.), 177-78
  use of sex in, 172-75
  and violence, 528-29
Affect, control of through drugs, 566
Affection
  effects of parental expression of, 10
  expression of, and freedom, 405-407, 410-13
  See also Expressiveness
Aggression, control of through drugs, 566
Alcohol, 433
Alienated students, 357-84, esp. 361-64
Analysis of behavior, 231-45, 433-55
  See also Behavior modification
Analysis of variance, 316n., 317n.
Analytic thought, sex differences in, 285
  See also Sex differences
Anonymity, 107-109
Anxiety evoked by ESB, 75-77
  See Brain, electrical stimulation of

Apathy
  as reaction pattern to stress (q.v.), 223
  as reason for inaction, 91-92
"Armchair theorizing," 268-69
"As-if" emotions, 165
Associative learning and mnemonic devices, 205
  See Mnemonic devices
Attitudes, 484
  See also Prejudice
Attractiveness and love, 400
Authenticity, 406-407, 410-13
Autonomy and ego integrity, 508-509
Awe, experience of, 569

Barrier between learning and thinking, 247-54
Base rate of behavior, 446t.
Beauty, appreciation of, 569
Behavior control, principles of, 546
  See Behavior modification
Behavior engineering, 231-45
  See Behavior modification
  See also Teaching machines; Learning
Behavior instrumentation, 544-56
  See also Behavior modification
Behavior modification, 440-55
  base rates, 446t.
  ethics, 571
  goal setting, 444-46
  and group therapy, 443
  and individual psychotherapy, 443
  modeling, 443
  and psychoanalysis, 443, 454-56
  reinforcement, 441-55
  shaping, 445
  and therapist-patient relationships, 443-44
Behavior therapy, 440-55
  See Behavior modification
Behavior without awareness, 178-81
  See also Subliminal stimulation
Behavioral effects of drug use, 428-30
Behaviorism, 122-23
Binet Intelligence Scales, 259
Biochemical effects of drug use, 428-30
Biographical information, 277-79
Bodily functioning, cognitive effects on, 164-70
Brain
  and external stimuli, 132-33
  and internal stimuli, 133
  and motivation, 135
  and stress, 135, 137, 142
  See Brain, electrical stimulation of

Brain, electrical stimulation of, 73-90
    anxiety, fear, and violence, 74-79
    friendliness and conversation, 84-85
    hallucinations, recollections, and illusions,
        85-88
    perception of suffering, 74-75
    pleasure, 79-84
Brainwashing, 221-30
Bystander intervention in emergencies,
        90-100, 104-105
    See also Helping in emergencies

California Psychological Inventory, 270-76,
    334
Catharsis, 424
Chemical base of memory, 219
Chemical comforts of man, 426-39
    See Drug use
Childhood
    prolonging of through drugs, 565
    sexual behavior in, 17-20
Child-rearing practices, 3-14
    discipline, 5-6
    expression of affection, 10
    permissiveness, 6, 10
    and personality development, 9
    relationships between parents, 9-12
    and sex of child, 6-11
    and social class, 6-9
    and socialization, 6-9
Cities
    "atmosphere" of, 111-14
    and civilities, 107
    cognitive maps of, 116-19
    experience of living in, 101-19
    and "overload," 101-19
    sources of differences between, 116-19
    and strangers, 105-107
    tempo and pace of, 115
    visual components of, 115
    vs. towns, role behavior in, 109
Civilities, 107
Coding schemata, 201, 204-205
    See Mnemonic devices
Cognitive effects of bodily functioning,
    164-70
Cognitive maps of cities, 116-19
"Cold" emotions, 165
Collative variables, 157-58
    See also Stimulation, dimensions of
Commitment, 405-13
    See also Freedom
Common factors in psychotherapy, 417-25
    See Psychotherapy, common factors in
Communication in psychotherapy, 419-21
Community change
    example of, 516-21
    mental health implications, 518-21
Community practices as a source of prejudice,
    495-98

Complex processes, measurement of, 259
Complexity of stimulation, 157
Conditioning
    See Reinforcement
Conditions of behavior, 138
"Content," measurement of intellectual, 265
Contingencies of reinforcement, 441
Controlled observation, 238-39
    See also Learning
Conversation evoked by ESB, 84-85
    See Brain, electrical stimulation of
"Conversation with therapeutic intent," 447,
    419-21
Correlation, 319n.
Couple therapy, 440-55
CPI (California Psychological Inventory),
    270-76, 334
Creativity, 324-41
Critical periods, 141
Crowding, effects of, 45-46, 573
Cultural determinants of behavior, 137-43
    See also Culture
Culture
    and adaptation, 138-40
    diversity of, 139
    functional interdependence, 140
    and stress, 137
    and taboo, 139
Curriculum, episodic, 250-51

Déjà vu and drugs, 569
Delinquency and violence, 532-33
Despair and ego integrity, 514-15
Determinism, 120, 352n., 477
Differences, measurement of human, 258
Discipline, "direct" vs. "psychological," 5-6
Discrimination training, 240-41
    See also Learning
Dissent, varieties of, 358-64
    See Protest
    See also Activist students
Diversity of culture, 139
"Dope," 405
Dose response curves, 427-29, 436
"Double standard" in sexual activity, 393-94
Doubt and ego integrity, 508-509
"Downs" (drug classification), 435
Dreaming, 52-70
    creative aspects, 60-64
    evolutionary and developmental aspects,
        53-56
    as a growth phenomenon, 67-68
    hypnagogic and hypnopompic states, 60
    paranormal aspects, 64-66
    and problem solving, 62-64
    psychological and sociological aspects,
        56-60
    and REM (rapid eye movements), 53-60
    and telepathy, 64-66
"Drop-outs," 357-84

Drug effects, factors influencing, 428-32, 562-64
 See also Drug use
Drug-organism interaction, 428-30
 See also Drug use
Drug use
 alteration of life patterns, 560-62
 biochemical and behavioral effects, 428-30
 criteria for "appropriate," 438
 dose-response curves, 427-29
 and drug-organism interaction, 428-30
 and freedom, 405, 410
 and the future, 557-70
 history of, 559
 meaning and function of, 436-39
 multiple effects, 427, 429-30
 reactions to, 426-39
 reasons for, 430-31, 558-59
 risk-benefit decisions, 431-32
 symbol of deviance, 437-38
Drugs, classifications of, 432-36, 560-69

Echoic behavior, 238
Education, end-product of, 253-54
Ego, 472-75
Ego identity, 28-38
 See Ego identity status
Ego identity status, 31-38
 definition, measurement, validation of, 28-38
 "foreclosure," 31, 34-35
 "identity achievement," 31-33
 "identity diffusion," 30-31, 35-36
 "moratorium," 31, 33-34
 and occupation, 32-36
 and politics, 32-36
 and religion, 32-36
 See also Ego integrity
Ego integrity, 505-15
 and autonomy, 508-509
 and despair, 514-15
 and generativity, 514
 and identity, 512-13
 and industry, 511-12
 and initiative, 509
 and intimacy, 513-14
 and role confusion, 512-13
 and trust, 506-507
 See also Ego identity status
Ego-psychoanalytic theory, 29
Electroshock therapy, 448
Emitted behavior, 236
 See also Learning
Emotional relations and sexual behavior, 22-23
Emotional states, labeling of, 167-70
Encounter, 406-407
Encounter laboratories, 458-60
 See also Laboratory education

Environmental components of intelligence, 293-307
 See also Intelligence
Environmental determinants of human life, 39-51
 and adaptation, 40, 43-46, 49-50
 and development, 40, 42-45
 and need for wide range of stimulation, 40, 47-48, 50-51
 physical environment, 40-48
 social environment, 49-51
Environmental psychology, 154-63
Episodic (atomized) curriculum, 250-51
Esalen Institute, 458-60
ESB (electrical stimulation of the brain), 73-90
 See Brain, electrical stimulation of
EST (electroshock therapy), 448
Esthetics, environmental, 155-63
Ethics
 and adjustment, 348
 and behavior instrumentation, 544-45
 and behavior manipulation, 571
 and subliminal stimulation, 190-93
Ethnicity and expressiveness, 407, 410
Eugenics, 319-20
Euthenics, 319
Evoked potentials, 312n.
Excellence in education vs. self-expression, 252
Expression of affection, effects of parental, 10
Expressiveness, 407-13
 and folk culture (ethnicity), 10, 407
 and politics, 408, 411

Factor analysis, 262, 269
Fading, 237-38
 See also Learning
"Falling" vs. "being" in love, 401
 See Love
Family structure and personality development, 9-12
Family therapy, 440-55
Fantasy, sexual, 21-22
Fear evoked by ESB, 77-78
Field dependence vs. field independence, 286
Folk culture and expressiveness, 407, 410
"Foreclosure" (ego identity status), 31, 34-35
Frame of reference, 485-87, 499
Freedom
 of affect and sensation, 405-407, 410-13
 and commitment, 405, 413
 and drugs, 405-406, 410
 and mobility, 409, 411
 and nomadism, 408-409, 411
 and sensory experience, 405-406, 410-13
 and sex, 409-11
Friendliness evoked by ESB, 84-85
Functional interdependence of culture, 140

Generativity and ego integrity, 514
Genes as determinants of response potential, 39, 50
Genetic-differences hypothesis, 309-10
Genetic-environmental interactionism, 310
Genotype, 311, 316-17
Goals, behavioral, 444-46
Gradual progression, 236
    See also Learning
Group composition, effects on helping, 97
Group factors of intelligence, 262
Group size, effects on helping, 95
Group therapy, 456-71
    See Laboratory education
Growth
    environmental influences on, 42-44
    human attraction to, 572
Guilt
    controlled by drugs, 568
    and sexual behavior, 18, 21
Guns and violence, 529-30

h^2 (heritability), 309, 316n., 319, 321-22
Hallucinations evoked by ESB, 85-88
"Hanging loose" and loving, 403-13
Helping in emergencies, 90-100, 104-105
    group composition, effects of, 97
    group size, effects of, 95
    and overload, 104-105
Heriditary Genius (Galton), 258
Heritability of IQ, 308-23
Hostility and stereotype, 484-85
    See also Prejudice
Human life, environmental determinants of, 39-51
    See Environmental determinants of human life
Humanistic psychology, 120-29, 571
    and Behaviorism, 122-23, 125
    and intersubjectivity, 126
    and I-thou, 126
    and Psychoanalysis, 123-25
    and respect for human beings, 121, 125-29
Hypnagogic state, 60
Hypnopompic state, 60

Id, 472-75
Ideals, 345
"Identity achievement" (ego identity status), 31-33
Identity crisis, 28-38
"Identity diffusion" (ego identity status), 30-31, 35-36
Identity and ego integrity, 512-13
Ignorance and yoga, 472
Illusions evoked by ESB, 85-88
Immediate reinforcement, 233
    See Learning
Imprinting, 141, 156

Incongruity of stimulation, 157-58
"Independence of Mind," 289
Individual differences, 257-79
    See also Sex differences
Inductive reasoning, measurement of, 263
Industry and ego integrity, 511-12
Industry, interpersonal relationships in, 579-80
Inferiority and ego integrity, 511-12
Initiative and ego integrity, 509
Innate behavior, 131-32
    critical periods, 141-42
    imprinting, 141-42
Intellect, woman's vs. man's, 280-92
    See also Sex differences
Intellectual functioning, measurement of, 304-305
    See also Intelligence
Intelligence
    environmental components, 293-307
    general, 262
    general vs. specific abilities, 293
    inborn capacity vs. observable functioning, 293-94
    and maternal care, 295-98
    measurement of, 261-66
    paranatal influences, 294-95
    and personality characteristics, 301-304
    prenatal influences, 294-95
    sex differences in, 280-92
    and sociocultural influences, 298-301
Intelligence quotient
    changes in, 304-305
    and genetic-differences hypothesis, 309-10
    and genetic-environmental interactionism, 310
    heritability of, 308-23
    and meritocracy, 313-15
    and racial-differences hypothesis, 310-13
    unknowns, 308-23
Intelligence tests, 305
Intensity of stimulation, 157
International relations in the future, 578-79
Interpersonal relationships
    and crowding, 573
    in the future, 571-82
    in industry, 579-80
    and intimacy, 573-74
    man-woman, 575-76
    and minorities, 581-82
    need for definitions of, 396
    need to isolate problems of, 396-97
    need for research methodology, 396
    need for research on, 395-96
    parent-child, 576-77
    and religion, 580-81
Intersubjectivity, 126
Interview, use of in personnel selection, 278

Intimacy, 409-10, 513-14, 573-74
Intoxicants, 565-66
IQ *See* Intelligence quotient
Isolation and ego integrity, 513-14
Item analysis, 260
I-thou, 126

Jamais vu and drugs, 569
James-Lange view of motivation, 165

Karma, 477
Knowledge, manipulation and organization of, 246-47

Labeling of emotional states, 167-70
Laboratory education, 456-71
  common factors in, 457
  comparison of different forms, 463-64
  criticisms of, 464-67
  empirical research on, 465, 467-68
  ethical issues in, 468-69
  forms of, 458
Language skills
  sex differences in, 283
  sociocultural influences, 300-301
Learning
  controlled by drugs, 567
  in education vs. in psychology, 231-45
  and fading, 237-38
  generic, 246-54
  and gradual progression, 236
  passivity vs. activity in, 249-50
  of prejudice, 489-500
    See Prejudice
  and psychotherapy, 440-55
    See Behavior modification
  and reinforcement, 236
  and thinking, 248-54
  See also Reinforcement
Levels of consciousness
  id, ego, superego, 472, 475
  and subliminal stimulation, 185-86
Libido, 15, 475
Limen (threshold), 176
  See also Subliminal stimulation
Love
  as art, 399-402
  and attractiveness, 400
  "being in" vs. "falling in," 401
  loving vs. being loved, 399
  object vs. subject, 400
  practice and theory of, 401-402
Loving, 403-13
  vs. being loved, 399
  and "hanging loose," 403-13
  See Love
LSD-like drugs, 435-36

Malnutrition, effects of, 44

Maps, cognitive, of cities, 116-19
Marijuana, 405-406, 433
Market research, example of, 172-75
"Masculinity" and violence, 527-28
Masturbation, 20-21, 23
Maternal care, influences on intelligence of, 295-98
  See also Intelligence
Mathematical skills, differences in, 283
Maximum performance measures, 257-66
Measurement
  of human differences, 257-79
  maximum performance measures, 257-66
  typical behavior measures, 257, 268-79
Memory
  controlled by drugs, 567
  measurement of, 263
  transfer, 211-20
Mental age, 262
  See also Intelligence quotient
Meritocracy and IQ, 313-15
Metabolism mediated by drugs, 566
Metatechnology, 552-54
Metrical scale of intelligence (Binet), 261
Minnesota Multiphasic Personality Inventory (MMPI), 270, 330-31
Minnesota Vocational Interest Inventory (MVII), 270
Minorities, future relations with, 581-82
MMPI, 270, 330-31
Mnemonic devices, 201-10
  appropriate materials for, 203-204
  and associative learning, 205
  coding schemata for, 20, 204-205
  educational applications of, 207-10
  multiple methods, 207
  narrative chaining method, 207
  pegwords, 201, 206-207
  and role learning, 201, 203-204
Mobility of youth, 409, 411
Modeling, 443
"Moratorium" (ego identity status), 31, 33-34
Mothering behavior controlled by drugs, 568
Motivation, James-Lange view of, 165
Motor skills, measurement of, 266-68
Multiple effects of drug use, 427, 429-30

Narrative chaining methods, 207
  See Mnemonic devices
National Training Laboratories (NTL), 459-61, 466-67
Nature-nurture controversy, 39-51
Newly seeing, 149-53
Nirvana principle, 476
Nomadism of youth, 408-409, 411
Normality, 346-49
Novelty of stimulation, 157
Numbers aptitude, measurement of, 263
Nutrition mediated by drugs, 566

Object vs. subject in love, 400
Observing behavior, need for control of, 238
Occupation and ego identity status, 32-36
Operations, measurement of intellectual, 265
Overlaod, 101-19
Overstimulation, 156

Pace of cities, 115
Paranatal influences on intelligence, 294-95
Parental behavior, changes in, 5
Parking meters, 548
    See Behavior instrumentation
Passion and thinking, 248, 251-52
Pegwords
    See Mnemonic devices
Perceiver characteristics and subliminal
        stimulation, 188-90
Perception
    conditions of, 149-53
    influence of irrelevant variables, 172-75
    subliminal, 176-98
        See Subliminal stimulation
    of suffering via ESB, 74-75
    vs. seeing, 149-53
Perceptual skills
    measurement of, 264
    sex differences in, 284
Permissiveness, effects of parental, 6, 10
Personal growth laboratories, 458-60
    See also Laboratory education
Personal responsibility, 345
Personality characteristics and intelligence,
        301-304
Personality development
    and child-rearing practices, 9
    and family structure, 9-12
Personnel selection, 276-79
Phenotype, 311, 316-17, 319
Physical environment, 154-63
Physical growth mediated by drugs, 566
Physiological determinants of behavior,
        130-38
    See also Brain
Planarians (flatworms) and memory transfer,
        211-20
Pleasure evoked by ESB, 79-84
Pleasure principle, 472, 476
Politics and ego identity status, 32-36
Population increase, effect of, 40-41
Poverty
    and personality, 501-22
    and psychological well being, 504-506
    and skills, 503-504
Prejudice, 483-500
    attitudes vs. acts, 487-89
    behavior shapes attitudes, 489-95
    and community practices, 495-98
    and frame of reference, 485-87
    hostility and stereotype, 484-85

learning of, 489-500
    psychological component, 494-95
    situational character, 485-87
Premarital intercourse
    effects of, 390-92
    and interpersonal attitudes, 388-92
    and quality of relationship, 389-91
    See also Sexual activity
Prenatal influences on intelligence, 294-95
Principles of behavior, 138
Principles of learning, 231-45
    See Learning; Reinforcement
Prisoners of war (Korean War), 221-30
    See Stress, reaction patterns to
Problem solving and dreaming, 62-64
Products, measurement of intellectual, 266
Propositional language, 349
Prosthetics, behavioral, 550
Protest
    and academic support, 373
    anti-ideological, 376-77
    and changing cultural climate, 379-80
    and deprivation of expectations, 372
    and deviant views, 374
    issues of, 370-72
    - producing historical situation, 376-78
    - promoting institutions, 369-72
    - prompting cultural climate, 372-76
    - prone personality, 365-69
    and psychological flexibility, 375-76
    and sensitivity to world events, 377-78
    and universalism, 373-74
    and world-wide pressures, 380-81
Psychedelia, 405-406, 410
Psychoanalysis
    and behavior modification, 443, 454-56
    criticisms of, 123-25, 478
    differentiated from humanism, 123-25
    essentials of, 472, 474
    techniques of, 472
    and yoga, 472-80
Psychosexual development, 15-27
Psychosexual stages, 29
Psychosocial crises, 29
Psychotechnology, 544-56
Psychotherapy, common factors in, 417-25
Psychotherapy, individual, 417-25
Public opinion sampling, automated, 549

Race as caste, 317
Racial differences hypothesis (IQ), 310-13
Reactions to drugs, 427
Reactivity controlled by drugs, 566-67
Recollections evoked by ESB, 85-88
Regression effect, 318n.
Rehabilitation systems, electronic, 549
Reinforcement
    immediate, 233
    intermittent, 442, 446

Reinforcement (Cont.)
  and learning, 236
  primary, 441
  reciprocal, 442
  social, 441-55
  See also Learning
Relationships
  See Interpersonal relationships
Relativistic definition of normality, 346-49
Religion
  and ego identity status, 32-36
  and interpersonal relationships, 580-81
REM (rapid eye movements), 53-60
  See Dreaming
Respect for human beings, 121, 125-29
Responsibility
  diffusion of, 90-100, 104-107
    See also Helping in emergencies
  personal, 345
  social, 345, 350-51
Rhythms of nature, adaptation to, 47
Riots and violence, 533-36
Risk-benefit decisions and drug use, 431-43
RNA (ribonucleic acid), 211, 216, 219
Role confusion and ego identity, 512-13
Rote learning, 201, 203-204
  See also Mnemonic devices

Scripted behavior, sexual behavior as an
  example of, 16
Seeing vs. perceiving, 149-53
Self-actualization and sexual activity, 392
Self-control, 345
Self-expression
  See also Expressiveness
Self-expression vs. excellence in education,
  252
Sensate freedom, 405-407, 410-13
Set, psychological, 285
Sex
  and advertising, 172-75
  of child and child-rearing practices, 6-11
  of child and sex role, 19
  and freedom, 409-11
  See also Sex differences; Sex roles; Sexual
    activity
Sex differences
  in abstract thought, 284
  in analytic thought, 285
  in field dependency, 286
  in "independence of mind," 289
  intellectual, 280-92
  in intelligence, 282
  in language skills, 283
  in mathematical skills, 283
  in perceptual skills, 284
  and psychological set, 285
Sex roles
  learned in childhood, 17-20

  and sex of child, 19
  and social class, 19
Sexual activity
  and developmental level, 393
  and "double standard," 393-94
  and interpersonal relationships, 395-98
    See Interpersonal relationships
  male vs. female interest in, 388-89, 394
  and pathology, 391-93
  and self-actualization, 392
    See also Premarital intercourse
Sexual development, 15-27
  See Adolescence, sexual behavior in; Child-
    hood, sexual behavior in; Adulthood,
    sexual behavior in
Sexual morality
  changing, 385-88
    implications of, 387-88
  See also Sexual activity; Premarital inter-
    course
Sexual responses, regulation of through drugs,
  566
Shame and ego integrity, 508-509
Shaping, 445, 450
Significance, statistical, 173n.
Situational character of prejudice, 485-87,
  499
Sleep, reduction of need for through drugs,
  565
Slum-dwellers, future relations with, 581-82
Social class and sex role, 19
Social interest, 345
Social responsibility, 345, 350-51
Social structure
  and personality, 501-22
  undermining of, 225-30
  See Stress, reaction patterns to
Socialization
  of children, 6-9, 3-13
  into violence, 523-30
  See Violence
Solvents, 436
Spatial aptitude, measurement of, 263
Specific abilities vs. general intelligence,
  293
See Intelligence
Stagnation and ego integrity, 514
Stanford-Binet intelligence test, 262n., 282
Statistical definition of normality, 346-49
Stereotype and hostility, 484-85
  See Prejudice
Stimulation
  adaptation level, 154
  and brain, 132-33
  dimensions of, 157-59
  effects of environmental, 154-63
  need for wide range of, 40, 47-48, 50-51
  optimal level, 154, 159
  psychology of, 154-63

Stimulation (Cont.)
  subliminal, 176-98
    See Subliminal stimulation
Stimulus factors and human behavior, 155
Strangers, willingness to trust and assist,
    105-107
Stress
  and apathy, 223
  and brain, 135, 137, 142
  and brainwashing, 221-30
  and culture, 137
  reaction patterns to, 221-30
  and withdrawal, 229
Strong Vocational Interest Blank, 270, 273,
    276
Students and violence, 536-41
Subliminal perception, 176-98
    See Subliminal stimulation
Subliminal stimulation
  in advertising, 177-78
  ethics of, 190-93
  and levels of consciousness, 185-86
  and perceiver characteristics, 188-90
  technological problems in, 186-88
  types of behavior influenced by, 183-85
Superconsciousness, 472
Superego, 472, 475
Suppression, 472-73, 479
Surprisingness of stimulation, 157-58
Symbolic ability, 349-51

T group laboratories, 460-61
    See Laboratory education
Taboo and culture, 139
Tavistock conferences, 462-63
    See Laboratory education
Teachers, quality of, 252-53
Teaching machines and principles of
    learning, 231-45
    See also Learning
Technique vs. technology in education, 232
    See also Teaching machines; Learning
Technological change, ability to endure, 572
Technology
  of education, 232
    See also Teaching machines; Learning
  social, 544-56
  vs. technique in education, 232
    See also Teaching machines; Learning
Telepathy and dreaming, 64-66
Television, two-way, 549-50
Tempo and pace of cities, 115
Test, statistical, 174n.
Test development, empirical method of, 261,
    269-76
Testing, history of, 256-66
Thanatos, 124
Theory, need for, 101-102

Thinking
  and learning, 248-54
  and passion, 248, 251-52
Third revolution in psychology, 120-29
    See Humanistic psychology
Three Faces of Intellect (Guilford), 265-66
Thresholds, 176, 181-82
    See Subliminal stimulation
Time perception controlled by drugs, 568-69
Toll roads, fare-adjusted, 548
Towns vs. cities, role behavior in, 109
    See also Cities
Transference controlled by drugs, 567
Tripartite personality, 472
Trust and ego integrity, 506-507
Typical behavior measures, 257, 268-79

Unconscious, 472
Understimulation, 156
United Nations' Cooperative Index, 548
"Up tight" vs. "hanging loose," 404
"Ups" (drug classification), 434
    See Drug use
Urban environment, effects of, 40-41, 48
    See Cities
Urban experiences, 111-15
    See Cities

Variance
  analysis of, 316n., 317n.
  defined, 316n.
Variation of stimulation, 157
Ventilation, 424
Verbal comprehension, measurement of, 262
Victim's likelihood of being helped, 96
    See also Helping in emergencies
Violence
  and automobile advertising, 528-29
  and delinquency, 532-33
  evoked by ESB, 78-79
  and guns, 529-30
  as learned response, 523-30
  legitimized, 525-27
  and "masculinity," 527-28
  and mass media, 528
  and students, 536-41
  subculture of, 530-32
  urban, 530-36
  and urban riots, 533-36
Vision, mechanics of, 149-53

Withdrawal as reaction to stress, 229
Woman's intellect vs. man's, 280-92
Women intellectuals, problems of, 290-91
Word fluency, measurement of, 263

Yoga
  criticisms of, 472-73, 478

Yoga (Cont.)
 essentials of, 472-73
 and psychoanalysis, 472-80

subsystems of, 474
Youth, 403-13
 See Adolescence; Student activists

1 2 3 4 5 6 7 8 9 0